FROM THE MOST TRUSTED NA

JOHNSON COUNTY PUBLIC LIBRARY
W9-CCC-746

Frommer

EASYGUIDE TO SEATTLE, PORTLAND AND THE OREGON COAST

Quick to Read • Easy to Carry • For Expert Advice In All Price Ranges

By Donald Olson

WITHDRAWN
MAR 22 2018
Johnson County Public Library
401 State Street
Franklin, IN 46131

FROMMER'S STAR RATINGS SYSTEM

Every hotel, restaurant, and attraction listed in this guide has been ranked for quality and value. Here's what the stars mean:

★ Recommended
★★ Highly Recommended
★★★ A must! Don't miss!

AN IMPORTANT NOTE

The world is a dynamic place. Hotels change ownership, restaurants hike their prices, museums alter their opening hours, and buses and trains change their routings. And all of this can occur in the several months after our authors have visited, inspected, and written about these hotels, restaurants, museums, and transportation services. Though we have made valiant efforts to keep all our information fresh and up-to-date, some few changes can inevitably occur in the periods before a revised edition of this guidebook is published. So please bear with us if a tiny number of the details in this book have changed. Please also note that we have no responsibility or liability for any inaccuracy or errors or omissions, or for inconvenience, loss, damage, or expenses suffered by anyone as a result of assertions in this guide.

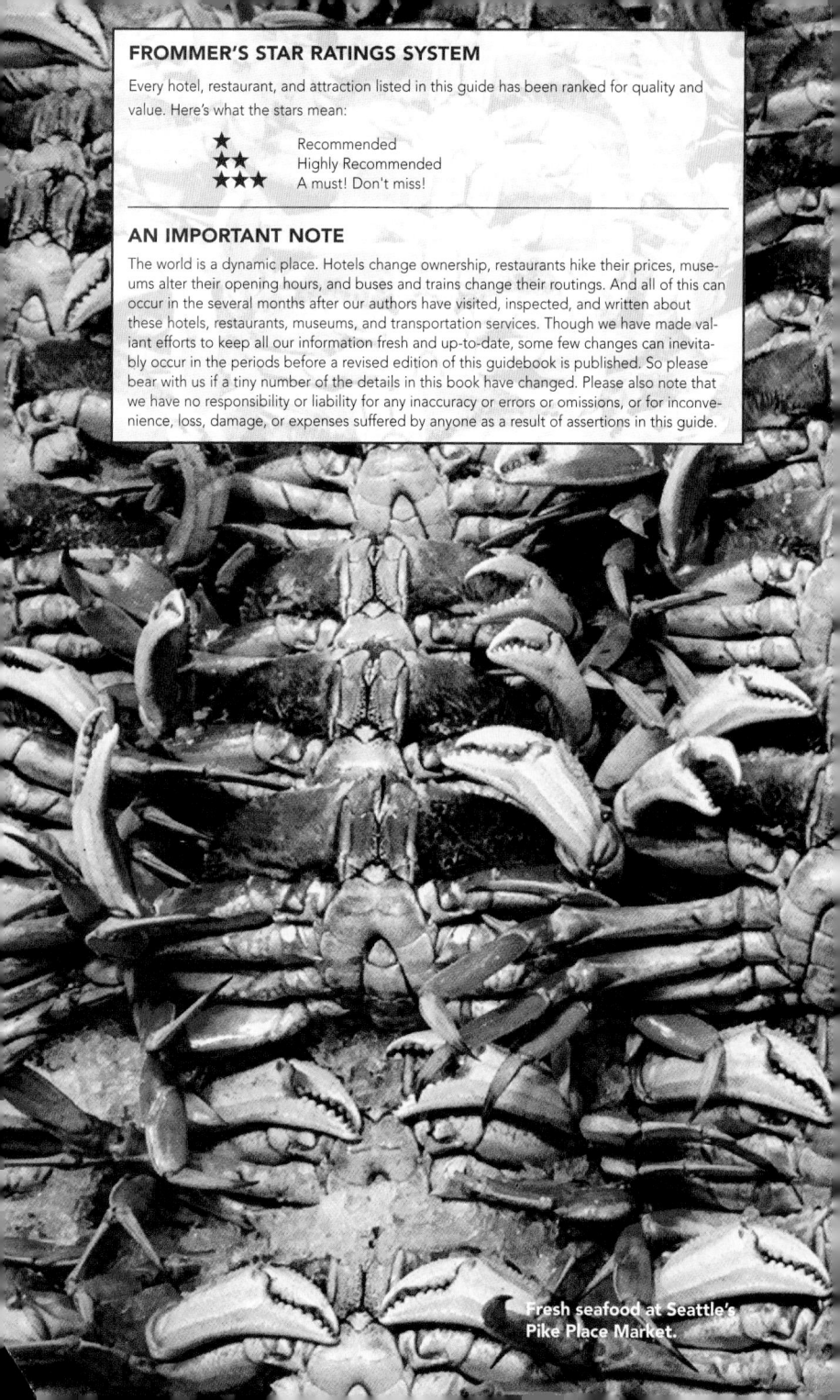

Fresh seafood at Seattle's Pike Place Market.

1 THE BEST OF SEATTLE, PORTLAND & THE OREGON COAST 1

2 SUGGESTED ITINERARIES 17

3 SEATTLE, PORTLAND & THE OREGON COAST IN CONTEXT 43

Seattle Today 44
Portland Today 46
The Oregon Coast Today 48
A Brief History of the Pacific Northwest 50
When to Go 58

4 SEATTLE 61

Essentials 62
Getting Around 67
When to Go 69
Exploring Seattle 71
Organized Tours 86
Where to Stay 88
Where to Eat 102
Shopping 118
Outdoor Pursuits 122
Spectator Sports 123
The Performing Arts & Nightlife 124
Day Trips from Seattle 129

5 PORTLAND 137

Essentials 140
Getting Around 146
When to Go 149
Exploring Portland 150
Organized Tours 164
Outdoor Pursuits 166
Where to Stay 167
Where to Eat 180
Shopping 194
The Performing Arts & Nightlife 199
Spectator Sports 207
Day Trips from Portland 207
The Wine Country 208
Mount Hood 214
The Columbia Gorge 218

6 THE OREGON COAST 225

The North Coast 230
The Central Coast 262
The South Coast 285

7 FAST FACTS 302

Seattle, Portland & Oregon Coast 302

INDEX 307

MAP LIST 317

ABOUT THE AUTHOR 319

A man runs with his dogs on Cannon Beach in Oregon.

A LOOK AT SEATTLE, PORTLAND AND THE COAST OF OREGON

National fixations, fads and trends are often born in the Pacific Northwest. This is, after all, is the place where fancy coffees first became an American obsession. And it was in Portland and Seattle that the fashion of wearing hiking clothes to restaurants and nightspots became acceptable, grunge rock was born, and environmentalism became mainstream. If it's cutting edge, chances are that it first came from here.

That's not to say that visitors from elsewhere are made to feel out-of-sync. "Nice" is considered "cool" in these parts. And while this is an increasingly techy area, it's also a region infatuated with nature. Here you are surrounded by awe-inspiring mountains, jagged coastline, vineyards and handsome farms.

In the pages that follow, you'll discover a few of the reasons why so many visitors become residents--or at least decide to visit again. Seattle, Portland and the Oregon Coast are destinations that are nothing less than addictive.

Seattle is the only major U.S. city where one can fish for salmon within city limits. Here, a group of anglers gather on a pier in Elliott Bay.

SEATTLE

Pikes Market is a treasure trove of artisinal food, fresh produce and other goods. Its first major expansion in 40 years occurred in June of 2017, when a new hall opened on the site where a market building burned to the ground in 1974.

Pier 66 in downtown Seattle.

A view of downtown Seattle from the ferry.

A Calder sculpture frames the Seattle Space Needle at Olympic Sculpture Park (p. 74).

On Bill Spiedel's Underground Tour (p. 79), visitors step down into the past, exploring the layers of history left by the city's great fire in 1889.

The Seattle skyline after dark.

The Seattle Great Wheel is the tallest Ferris Wheel on the West Coast. More on p. 76.

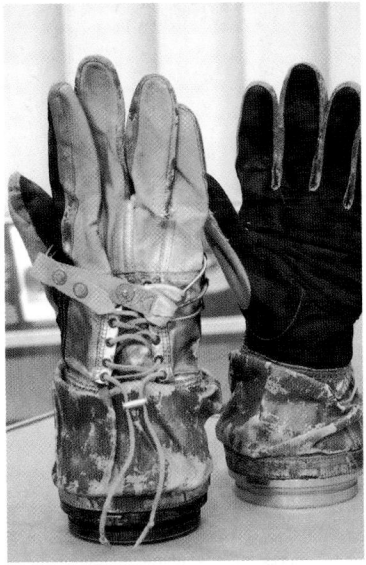

Gemini space suit gloves from the Apollo Exhibit at the Museum of Flight (p. 83).

An otherworldly landscape at Chihuly Garden and Glass Museum (see p. 77).

Portland has the most breweries in the United States, but Seattle's beer scene is "hopping", too. Pictured here is the Pike Pub at Pike Brewing (see p. 125).

The Pacific Northwest Ballet company (p. 126) performs an original work called *Emergence*.

A concert at McMenamins Kennedy School (p. 203).

PORTLAND

Sunrise View of Portland, Oregon from the Pittock Mansion (p. 126).

Bikes zip along the Eastbank Esplanade, a pontoon bridge.

Kayakers on the Willamette River.

The beloved white stag sign became a City of Portland historic landmark in 1977.

Joggers in Forest Park (p. 161).

Riding the Portland Aerial Tram (p. 144).

Buskers play a set in Pioneer Courthouse Square (p. 151).

At the massive Powell's City of Books (p. 196) every book you've ever wanted to read is available. No, really.

The Portland Art Museum (p. 155) is best known for Native American Art, and contemporary pieces, like this Kenny Scharf installation.

The colors and scents will make you gasp, and the flower names will make you giggle, at the famed International Rose Test Garden (p. 158).

World class wineries are just an hour outside Portland in the Willamette Valley (p. 210).

Another excellent day trip: the mighty Multnomah Falls (p. 221).

Portland's exquisite Japanese Garden (p. 160).

A barista works her magic at one of the city's top coffee bars.

THE OREGON COAST

A kayaker battling strong rapids on the Rogue River (p. 289).

Buyoys in Astoria, Oregon (p. 230).

Triplets explore the dunes along the Oregon Coast.

A Black Oystercatcher.

A diving suit from the 1940's at the Columbia River Maritime Museum in Astoria (p. 234).

Yaquina Head Lighthouse (p. 274).

Vacationers stroll along Indian Beach in Ecola State Park (p. 252).

The largest sea lion cave in the world is on the Oregon Coast. See p. 279 for how to visit it without disturbing its tenants.

Historic Fort Clatstop (p. 240), founded by explorers Lewis and Clark, is a worthy "time machine" attraction.

Tourists watch swimming sharks from below at the Oregon Coast Aquarium in Newport (p. 273).

Sand boarding at Oregon Dunes National Recreation Area (p. 285).

Slope soaring on the Oregon Coast.

THE BEST OF SEATTLE, PORTLAND & THE OREGON COAST

1

The rest of Washington and Oregon are worth exploring too, of course, and you could spend days, weeks, or months doing just that. But Seattle and Portland are the best places to begin any exploration of this fascinating and fast-growing region; on easy day trips from both cities you can get to an amazingly diverse array of scenic and historic highlights, including giant peaks in the Cascade Range, the Columbia River Gorge, and the Oregon Wine Country.

As for the Oregon coast—well, it may leave you speechless, and not just because the wind on one of its towering headlands has sucked your breath away. These 364 miles (586 km) of coastline have a wild and dramatic splendor that is exciting, invigorating, and unforgettable. In the categories below, I've listed some of the highlights—the bests of the bests—to get you revved up and ready for your trip to the Pacific Northwest.

THE best AUTHENTIC EXPERIENCES

Seattle

- **Exploring Pike Place Market:** It's the oldest covered market in the country, and it's certainly one of the busiest, used by Seattle residents and restaurateurs looking for the freshest fish and produce. But the retail range of this world-unto-itself extends way beyond seafood, fruit, and vegetables and includes dozens of restaurants, intriguing shops, and stalls selling artisan products of all kinds. See p. 71.
- **Riding a ferry:** Seattle is one of the few cities where people live on islands and commute to work by ferry. An easy ferry ride to

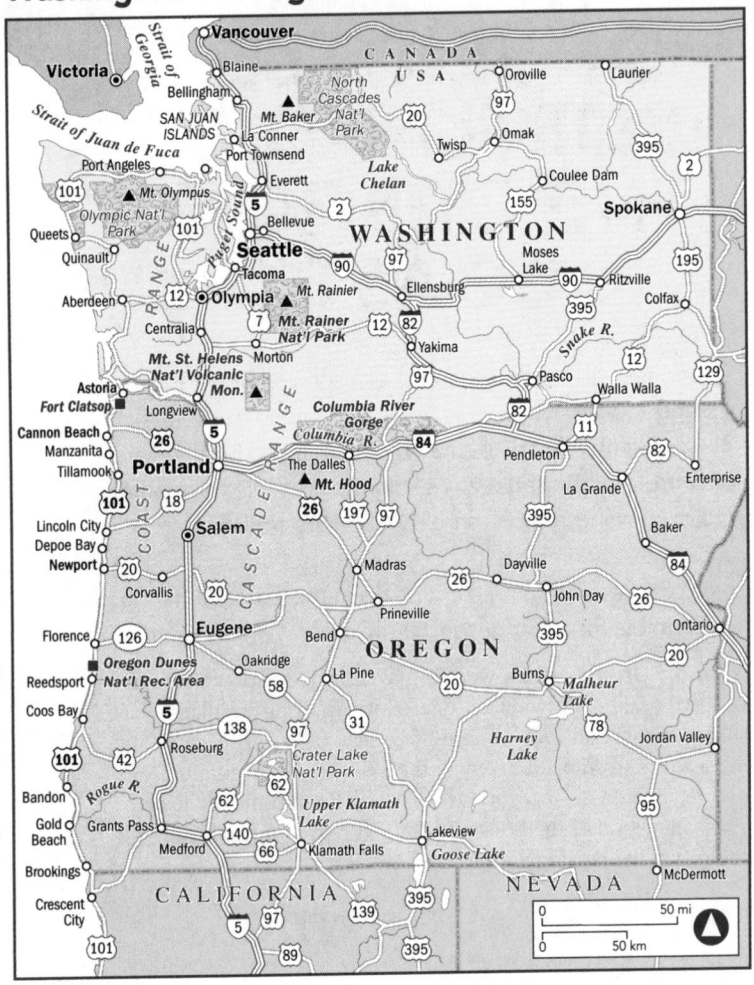

Bainbridge Island or Bremerton gets you out on Puget Sound and gives you a water's-eye view of the city's topography and skyline. See "Getting Around" in chapter 4, p. 67.

- **Strolling the waterfront:** Of course it's touristy—that's part of the fun. Presided over by the Seattle Great Wheel, a giant Ferris wheel, the waterfront is a wonderfully strollable area with fish and chips and fresh oysters along the way; bayside plazas with views of the Olympic Mountains; the Seattle Aquarium; piers for excursion boats and cruise ships; and lots of shops and restaurants. The area around the waterfront is being completely transformed now that the hideous elevated highway beside it is being demolished. See "The Waterfront" under "Neighborhoods in Brief" in chapter 4, p. 65.

- **Taking the Underground Tour:** For one of the most entertaining and authentic city tours you'll ever take, head underground with your witty guide to learn about Seattle's early days before and after the Great Fire and the Yukon Gold Rush, the two events that helped define the city as it is today. The commentary is frank and funny, and the warren of underground tunnels that were once streets is fascinating. See p. 79.
- **Fooling around in Fremont:** Downtown Seattle is exciting and full of attractions, but a stroll through the Fremont neighborhood will give you an up-close-and-personal glimpse of life in one of the funkiest and most interesting neighborhoods in the city, where a giant troll crouches beneath a bridge and the streets are lined with ethnic restaurants and eclectic shops. See "Fremont" under "Neighborhoods in Brief" in chapter 4, p. 66.
- **Viewing the City from Smith Tower:** I used to think the Space Needle had the best view (okay, probably it does), but my real fave when it comes to panoramas is the Observatory on the 35th floor of the Smith Tower. Opened in 1914, this gorgeously restored building was for decades the tallest building west of the Mississippi. Hop into one of the original, manually operated cage elevators and be whisked to the observatory for an eye-popping view, and then enjoy a drink in the Prohibition-era Chinese Room. See p. 80.

Portland

- **Walking around downtown:** Portland's downtown is compact and complex, with an attractive mixture of buildings, bridges, architectural styles, parks, and plazas that makes it wonderful for walking. From Tom McCall Waterfront Park right along the Willamette to Pioneer Square and the South Park Blocks, this is one of the most attractive, human-scale downtowns you'll ever see.
- **Sipping a latte at Caffe Umbria in the Pearl District.** It's the best latte in Portland, and the most attractive and congenial cafe in the upscale Pearl District. Order your java, take a seat, and people watch. See p. 192.
- **Browsing through Powell's City of Books:** Even if you're totally committed to reading on your tablet, you shouldn't miss Powell's. One of the world's largest bookstores, Powell's is as much a tourist attraction as it is a store. Readers know they will be able to find a new or used copy of just about anything in one of Powell's color-coded rooms. But beware: Once you're inside and start browsing, it's difficult to tear yourself away. See p. 196.
- **Enjoying a microbrew in a brewpub:** As you've probably heard, there are more microbreweries in Portland that any other city in the world. Portland's numerous brewpubs are typically casual, super-friendly spots with good food (often but not always on the order of pizza and burgers) where Portlanders of all stripes congregate. See "Brewpubs" in chapter 5, p. 202.
- **Hiking in Forest Park:** Few cities can claim, as Portland can, to have one of the largest urban forests in the world within its city limits. Giant Forest

Park covers thousands of acres in Northwest and Southwest Portland and forms part of a wildlife corridor that stretches all the way to the Coast Range. Put on a pair of comfortable walking shoes and hook up to one of the many trails that crisscross this vast urban green space. See p. 161.

- **Sniffing the roses at the International Rose Test Garden:** The City of Roses loves its roses, and nowhere else in Portland is a rose more of a rose more of a rose than at the International Rose Test Garden. Visitors are wowed by the fragrant spectacle of tens of thousands of roses in all shapes and colors growing on terraces in beautiful Washington Park. See p. 158.
- **Strolling in the Portland Japanese Garden:** It's considered the most authentic Japanese garden outside of Japan, and in 2017 it expanded to include a new building and plazas by famed Japanese architect Kengo Kuma. So slow your pace and see the world around you with new eyes. See p. 160.
- **Riding the rails:** Take your pick: MAX, the light-rail train, or the Portland Streetcar. Buy a ticket, hop on, and go for a ride—it hardly matters where. Portland is way ahead of the curve when it comes to providing public transportation, and if you are coming from a place where you are a prisoner of your car, what could be more enjoyable than to let someone else do the driving? See "Getting Around" in chapter 5, p. 146.
- **Nosing around North Portland:** The transformation of North Portland over the last decade has been truly astonishing. North Mississippi, North Russell, and North Alberta have all become destination neighborhoods loaded with shops, galleries, and restaurants in neighborhoods (now branded as "districts") that were once off the grid. See "Northeast Portland" under "Neighborhoods" in chapter 5, p. 145.

The Oregon Coast

- **Whale-watching:** Every year, about 18,000 giant gray whales migrate from the Bering Sea to Baja and back again. From beaches, viewpoints, and headlands all up and down the coast you can often catch sight of a whale herd spouting its way north or south, and at Depoe Bay you can arrange for a whale-watching excursion to get even closer. See p. 234.
- **Assessing Astoria:** In the past few years, Astoria has undergone a dramatic transformation. Founded in 1811 at the mouth of the Columbia River, this former fur, lumber and salmon cannery town is now dressed up and ready for visitors with new hotels, restaurants, and heritage museums and houses that make exploring its old streets, downtown and waterfront a real voyage of discovery. See chapter 6, p. 230.
- **Walking on Cannon Beach:** On a clear sunny day, it's probably the busiest beach on the coast, but on a weekday or if the weather is gray and wet, you might have it all to yourself. Cannon Beach is one of the great beaches of Oregon, and the town of Cannon Beach, though touristy, is also the most charming. See p. 249.
- **Looping the Three Capes Scenic Loop:** For an eye-opening look at Oregon's dramatic North Coast, take this loop drive between Tillamook and Pacific

City. Three spectacular headlands, a lighthouse, hiking trails, and eye-popping views of the thundering surf will wake up your senses. See p. 259.

- **Discovering Newport:** Though it relies on tourism and draws thousands of visitors to the acclaimed Oregon Coast Aquarium, Newport is also one of the most authentic and "real" working towns on the Oregon coast. Walk down the Bayfront and you'll have seafood restaurants on one side and the commercial fish warehouses on the other. And the old Nye Beach neighborhood is a charming throwback to a century ago when Newport became one of Oregon's first beach resort towns. See p. 270.
- **Alighting at Yaquina Bay Lighthouse:** You can (seasonally) visit seven of the nine historic lighthouses along the Oregon coast, but this lighthouse near Newport is perhaps the most easily accessible, and it happens to preside over Yaquina Head, designated an "Outstanding Natural Area." Before heading into the lighthouse, check out the visitor center to learn more about what life was like for the lighthouse keepers who manned these lonely lights and kept them burning through gales and ferocious storms. See p. 275.
- **Exploring the tide pools:** All up and down the Oregon coast, beautiful and amazing creatures cling to rocks near the shore and are nourished by the surging waters of the Pacific. Tentacled sea anemones, sea urchins, and starfish inhabit rocky tide pools that you can visit, including some at Cannon Beach. Whenever there is a good tide pool area, I mention it in the Oregon coast chapter. See chapter 6.

THE best HOTELS

Seattle

- **The Arctic Club Hotel:** A former men's club founded by guys who struck it rich either in or because of the Yukon Gold Rush, the Arctic Club celebrates its history by giving its large, big-windowed rooms and public spaces the Art Deco look of the club's heyday. See p. 88.
- **The Edgewater:** Built atop a pier on the Seattle waterfront, this boutique hotel is the only hotel in Seattle to have rooms directly on the water. In fact, guests, including the Beatles, used to fish from their windows. It has a very good restaurant with views to the Olympic Mountains. See p. 96.
- **Executive Hotel Pacific:** Built in the 1920s, the hotel has the compact rooms of that era to prove it. But they've all been upgraded to boutique hotel standards but happily, NOT boutique hotel prices. A great value. See p. 95.
- **Hotel Ändra:** Its design and furnishings are coolly Scandinavian, and its comfort level is Seattle all the way. Vibrant colors, natural fabrics, and beautiful materials and detailing make this boutique hotel in Belltown a real treat. See p. 97.
- **Sorrento Hotel:** It may be one of Seattle's great historic hotels, but there's nothing fusty or outdated at the Sorrento. Period charm and character shine through in the guestrooms and public spaces that are loaded with original

detailing but also full of color and cool comfort—and more amenities than you'd find at hotels costing twice as much. See p. 100.

- **Inn at the Market:** For sheer romantic appeal, this cozy boutique hotel can't be beat. Its secretive little courtyard entrance makes it feel hidden from the world, and yet it's directly beside Pike Street Market, one of the busiest spots in Seattle. Some of the rooms have big views out over Elliott Bay to the Olympics. See p. 96.
- **Inn at Virginia Mason & The Baroness Hotel:** Up on First Hill, within easy walking distance of downtown and not far from the Frye Art Museum, the two buildings operated as hotels by Virginia Mason Hospital are heritage gems built as apartment buildings in the 1920s and 1930s. There's a wealth of authentic, unchanged period detail in both of these meticulously cared-for buildings, where you will stay in a former apartment for a fraction of the cost of a downtown hotel. See p. 100.

Portland

- **Ace Hotel:** It was the second Ace Hotel after Seattle and, like that Ace, it is a creative and quirky re-use of a century-old building, emulating "European-style" hotels—which means that some of the rooms share a bathroom. With a good restaurant on one side and a good coffee bar on the other (and more-than-reasonable prices), the Ace captures Portland's creative spirit. See p. 173.
- **The Benson:** With its crystal chandeliers, walnut paneling, and ornate plasterwork ceiling in the lobby, this 1912 vintage hotel is Portland's most elegant lodging. The rooms are quiet and traditional, and the service is first-rate. See p. 167.
- **Embassy Suites:** Unlike other Embassy Suites, this is a historic hotel, dating from 1912 with an unbelievably ornate lobby, but it still has those spacious suites that are great for families. Plus, there's a pool, complimentary cocktails at night, and a full hot breakfast in the morning. See p. 173.
- **Hotel deLuxe:** The deLuxe takes its theme from the Golden Age of Hollywood. It offers rooms with a pastel color scheme that makes them glow like southern California—even when the weather is gray. The fabulous, '50s-era Driftwood Room has craft cocktails and small plates that keep everyone happy. See p. 174.
- **Hotel Lućia:** This downtown Portland hotel is sleek and stylish and loaded with original art and a fascinating collection of photographs by White House photographer David Hume Kennerly. The rooms are simple without being simplistic, and on-site Imperial restaurant is a Portland haute spot. See p. 174.
- **Hotel Modera:** Whoever thought a 1950s-era downtown motor lodge could be turned into such a cool hotel? The makeover made Hotel Modera downtown's most sophisticated place to stay, with an outdoor lounge that draws guests and locals. See p. 175.
- **Inn @ Northrup Station:** This fun-loving and comfortably cheerful hotel in Northwest Portland sets the tone with bright colors and retro-styling. The rooms are like little self-contained apartments with kitchens (or kitchenettes) and balconies. See p. 177.

- **McMenamins Kennedy School:** Only in Portland, and only because of the historical preservationists and brewmeister McMenamins, would a former elementary school be turned into a destination hotel where you can stay in former classrooms and walk halls that are now alive with restaurants, bars, and even a movie theater in the gym. See p. 178.
- **Portland Mayor's Mansion:** One of Portland's pre-eminent early-20th-century architects designed this brick mansion that sits right on gorgeous Laurelhurst Park. Now operated as a B&B, the house has most of its original fixtures and is a luxurious and comfortable place to stay with a park right in the backyard. See p. 179.
- **Hotel Vintage:** A complete remake has transformed this formerly sedate wine-themed hotel in the heart of downtown into a hyper-wine-themed hipster haven with a lobby bar called Bacchus and restyled rooms that are wonderfully comfortable and convenient as well as classily cool and up-to-the-minute. See p. 171.

The Oregon Coast

This list runs from north to south along the coast.

- **Cannery Pier Hotel** (Astoria): This luxurious hotel, built on the site of a former salmon cannery on the Columbia River has big, glass-walled rooms directly on the river and a host of upscale amenities. Cannery Pier is the best catch in Astoria. See p. 236.
- **The Ocean Lodge** (Cannon Beach): The views are panoramic and the rooms are cozy and designed for contemporary comfort at this mid-sized inn. Step out on your balcony for a breath of fresh sea air, or step outside and you'll be right on one of the most famous beaches in Oregon. See p. 254.
- **Stephanie Inn** (Cannon Beach): The most traditional and upscale hotel in artsy, affluent Cannon Beach enjoys a beachfront setting, a fine-dining restaurant, and luxurious rooms with private balconies and oceanfront views. The Stephanie is a romantic, pampering retreat. See p. 254.
- **Channel House** (Depoe Bay): The in-your-face views from the rooms in this small inn—situated on a cliff directly above the ocean and to one side of the narrow channel into tiny Depoe Bay—are probably the most dramatic on the entire coast. You can soak in your outdoor hot tub and enjoy the spectacle. See p. 269.
- **Sylvia Beach Hotel** (Newport): One of the coast's earliest resort hotels, going way back to the early 1900s, this literary-minded hotel has a unique charm and character. Each room is dedicated to a writer with appropriate accoutrements, and there is a marvelous library upstairs. No phones or TVs, but you do get Wi-Fi. See p. 276.
- **Heceta Head Lightstation** (near Yachats): A former lighthouse keeper's home, with the Heceta Head Lighthouse just down the path, this Victorian-era B&B is set high on a cliff with a truly spectacular outlook. You get breakfast, and maybe you'll even meet the ghost. See p. 279.
- **Overleaf Lodge** (Yachats): This friendly resort hotel offers some pretty amazing views to go along with the comforts of its freshly refurbed

oceanfront rooms. The coastal path right outside lets you enjoy a wonderful walk along a scenic section of the coast. See p. 281.

- **Tu Tu' Tun Lodge** (Gold Beach): A secluded setting on the lower Rogue River guarantees tranquility at this gorgeous-inside-and-out lodge. All the materials are real, and so are the people who greet you. It's the best around, and only 15 minutes from Gold Beach. See p. 299.

THE best RESTAURANTS

Seattle

- **Poppy:** The fabulous food at this always-fun and always-surprising Capitol Hill restaurant is locally sourced and served Indian style, in multi-plate thalis. The assortment of tastes and textures in one of the daily thalis is exciting and delicious. Once you taste the sweet potato fries, you'll never be the same. See p. 113.
- **Lola:** The rich smells and savory tastes of Greece and the Mediterranean add up to memorable meals at this casually sophisticated restaurant in Belltown. Lamb is the specialty and what you should have—and maybe a big, fresh Greek salad to go with it. See p. 111.
- **Tilth:** There's a tasting menu for every taste at this award-winning restaurant in Wallingford. Chef and owner Maria Hines whips up a mouthwatering and ever-changing menu of organic seasonal delicacies in one of the few restaurants in the U.S. to receive an organic certification. Vegetarian, vegan, gluten-free—creative delights are available for every taste and dietary preference. See p. 116.
- **Canlis:** Many a Seattleite will tell you that this venerable restaurant in the Fremont neighborhood is where the "fresh, local" Pacific Northwest style of cooking began in 1950. There are dishes on the menu that are as delicious today as they were 60-some years ago, but there are also artful new preparations for changing tastes and palettes. If you want a dress-up dining experience, this is it. See p. 114.
- **Shiro's Sushi Restaurant:** Ask any Seattleite where to find the best sushi in town and they'll tell you Shiro's. The sushi and sashimi are so fresh you can taste the sea. See p. 111.
- **Café Campagne:** It isn't fancy, it isn't overpriced, and it's anything but pretentious—but if you're looking for classic French bistro food, this restaurant on Post Alley, right next to Pike Place Market, is just the place. Mussels, of course, and steak and frites, that's the sort of meal you'll enjoy at this little hideaway. See p. 108.
- **Shuckers:** What's a meal in Seattle without fresh oysters? Visit Shucker's, attached to the gorgeous old Fairmont Olympic Hotel, for the very best selection prepared any way you like. Come early for happy hour and you can get them on the half-shell for two bucks a pop. But you can also enjoy them pan-fried or baked. The daily selection of fresh fish is also outstanding, and the crab cakes are wonderful. See p. 103.

Portland

- **Andina:** Who knew Peruvian food could be so multifaceted and so loaded with flavor? Peruvians did, of course, and now Portland knows, too. This is a perennially popular scene restaurant at dinnertime, so reserve a table and join the happy crowd. See p. 187.
- **Ava Gene's:** If you want to see what's cooking over on SE Division, one of Portland's hottest new dining destinations pay a visit to this attractive trattoria, and order some food to share family-style with the whole table. Super-fresh local ingredients and sophisticatedly simple Italian cooking techniques make for a memorable meal on all fronts. See p. 190.
- **Le Pigeon:** Some people aren't entirely comfortable with the shared-table scheme, but most people find it part of the congenial and mouth-watering culinary experience found at this top-ranked Portland bistro. See p. 189.
- **Pok Pok:** This Thai restaurant on what is now SE Division's restaurant row helped jump-start the Portland food scene. Forget glamor: you'll be eating at a picnic table. Forget reservations: they don't take 'em. But don't forget to bring your appetite, because the sizzling, spicy delicacies are wonderful, and great for sharing. See p. 191.
- **St. Jack:** They left their cozy old digs and moved across the river to a sleek new spot on NW 23rd, and thank goodness they brought their kitchen and cooking techniques with them, because St. Jack offers some of the best French food in Portland. See p. 188.
- **Tasty n Alder:** It's a kind of casual steakhouse, albeit on the nontraditional side, where in addition to grilled meats you can get fresh grilled seafood and dishes that can be shared. See p. 185.
- **Toro Bravo:** Portland has many restaurants that serve small plates, but few that serve Spanish tapas of this superb quality. Every taste is revelatory, which may account for the long lines. Any wait, however, is worth it. See p. 189.

The Oregon Coast

This list goes from north to south.

- **BRIDGEwater Bistro** (Astoria): It's dressy if you want it to be, but since this is the Oregon coast, it's casual, too. It's also one of the top restaurants in Astoria. Bridgewater's sits on a pier right on the river so you'll have great view of the mighty Columbia as you dine on ciopinno, fresh halibut in season, or one of the daily fish cakes. See p. 238.
- **Clemente's** (Astoria): At lunchtime, stop in at this waterside restaurant and enjoy a halibut or oyster sandwich, or fish and chips made from freshly caught halibut, salmon, cod, or oysters. Everything served here is locally sourced and you'll never go wrong with the seafood. See p. 239.
- **Roseanna's Cafe** (Oceanside): You can expect a long wait to get a table here on a summer weekend, but the view of the haystack rocks just offshore makes this place a must-stop stop on the scenic Three Capes Scenic Loop. See p. 261.
- **The Irish Table** (Canon Beach): It's a small restaurant with a small menu, and it sits on the main road through Cannon Beach so it doesn't have a view,

but diners flock to The Irish Table for filling delights like shepherd's pie, lamb chops, and a selection of fresh fish, simply prepared. See p. 256.

- **Newman's at 988** (Cannon Beach): The menu is French- and Italian-inspired but relies exclusively on the freshest ingredients of the Pacific Northwest. The cooking is inventive, the dishes are beautifully presented, and there's a good wine list. See p. 256.
- **Stephanie Inn** (Cannon Beach): The fine-dining restaurant at the Stephanie Inn is a lot more formal than most restaurants on the Oregon coast, but the seasonally changing menu presents diners with the freshest local products, and the cooking is creative without being overbearing. See p. 256.
- **Restaurant Beck** (Depoe Bay): With windows that look out to Whale Cove, one of the prettiest little coves on the Oregon coast, this stylish, modern restaurant is a foodie's dream come true—highly creative cuisine and a view to match. Sunset dinners are unforgettable. See p. 270.
- **Tidal Raves** (Depoe Bay): When the surf's up, you can practically forget about getting a table at this oceanfront restaurant. The windows overlook a rugged shoreline known for putting on some of the coast's best displays of crashing waves. See p. 270.
- **Local Ocean** (Newport): The fish couldn't be any fresher—it comes from boats that unload their fresh-caught fish right across the street from this airy Bayfront restaurant. Get whatever is in season and maybe share a small plate or two. See p. 276.
- **Alloro Wine Bar** (Bandon): The ingredients are local, the cooking style is Italian, and the result is an unusually tasty and satisfying meal. Serving both locals and international visitors who've come to Bandon to play at the world-class Bandon Dunes Golf Resort, this little restaurant is surprisingly sophisticated and yet deliciously simple. Come for a glass of vino if not for dinner, and check out the crowd. See p. 294.
- **The Gallery** (Bandon Dunes Golf Resort): You don't have to be a golfer or even a guest to enjoy dining on the 18th hole at Bandon Dunes Golf Resort. The resort's fine-dining restaurant is just that—fine dining, with great service, great wine, and great food, all of it sourced locally and prepared with creative simplicity to bring out all the flavors. See p. 295.

THE best NATURAL WONDERS

Seattle

- **Alki Beach:** The closest Seattle comes to a L.A.-style "hang-out" beach, Alki Beach in West Seattle is where the first white settlers set up camp—and packed it up after one wet, miserable winter to move across the bay. Today's Seattleites don't let the weather keep them away from this stretch of rocky, sandy beach with its photo-op views of the Seattle skyline, the ever-popular (but overpriced) Salty's on Alki Beach restaurant, and the paved walkway that lets you enjoy it all. You can reach Alki Beach by water taxi from Pier 55. See p. 116.

- **Elliott Bay:** If you're in Seattle, you're going to see Elliott Bay no matter what, because it forms the scenic backdrop to the entire downtown and west side of the city. Part of Puget Sound, a huge island-studded inlet of the Pacific Ocean, Elliott Bay provides a waterway from Seattle to the ocean and is one of the busiest ports in the U.S. You'll see ferries, sailboats, fishing trawlers, cruise ships, excursion boats, and pleasure craft of all kinds plying its waters. Taking a ferry over to Bainbridge Island is one of the easiest ways to get out on the bay yourself. See p. 68.
- **Lake Washington:** The main part of central Seattle is wedged between saltwater Elliott Bay to the west and freshwater Lake Washington to the east. The two are connected by the Lake Washington Ship Canal and the Hiram M. Chittenden Locks, a series of historic locks that provide a passing parade of boat traffic. Lake Washington is a major recreational area for Seattle, and its shoreline is dotted with lovely old parks and beaches. See p. 82.
- **Mount Rainier National Park:** With its glaciers and easily accessible alpine meadows, Mount Rainier is Washington's favorite mountain. Sunrise and Paradise are the two best vantage points for viewing the massive bulk of Mount Rainier, and in these two areas of the park, you'll also find some of the best hiking trails. See p. 131.

Portland

- **Columbia Gorge National Scenic Area:** Carved by ice-age floodwaters, the Columbia Gorge is a unique feature of the Oregon landscape and begins just a few miles east of Portland. The Historic Columbia Gorge Highway winds past waterfalls cascading down the basalt cliffs of the gorge, passes memorable viewpoints, and ends near Multnomah Falls, one of the tallest waterfalls in the country. See p. 218.
- **Mount Hood:** As Oregon's tallest mountain and the closest Cascade peak to Portland, Mount Hood is a recreational paradise 12 months a year. Hiking trails, alpine lakes, free-flowing rivers, and year-round skiing make this one of the most appealing natural attractions in the state. See p. 214.

The Oregon Coast

- **The Columbia River at Astoria:** The mighty Columbia is the second-longest river in the U.S. and the one most associated with Pacific Northwest history, since Lewis and Clark rafted down it to reach the Pacific in 1805. The river's mouth, near present-day Astoria, is some 14 miles wide, and its treacherous bar has been dubbed the "Graveyard of the Pacific." At Astoria, it's the Columbia that rules the waves. Take the Riverwalk along the old waterfront to get a feel for this legendary river, spanned by the giant Astoria-Megler Bridge. See "Astoria" in chapter 6, p. 230.
- **Three Capes Scenic Loop:** Really, the entire Oregon coast counts as a "best natural attraction," but for a dramatic introduction to the scenic splendors of the North Coast, this drive between Tillamook and Pacific City can't be beat. Giant headlands, sandy beaches, windswept vistas, dense forest, even a lighthouse—you'll see it all on this memorable drive. See p. 259.

- **Oregon Dunes National Recreation Area:** Towering sand dunes stretch for some 50 miles along the coast between Florence and Coos Bay, forming the Oregon Dunes National Recreation Area. This sand-seared area contains lakes where you can boat and swim and trails for hiking, horseback riding, and off-road vehicles. See p. 285.
- **Rogue River at Gold Beach:** Oregon's South Coast is called the Wild Rivers Coast because six free-flowing rivers hurtle down from the coastal mountain ranges to empty into the Pacific. None is more fabled than the Rogue River, which pours into the ocean at Gold Beach. Zane Grey was one of the earliest to write about the salmon fishing on this river, and it has since become a mecca for white-water rafting. See p. 295.

THE best MUSEUMS & HISTORIC SITES

Seattle

- **Chihuly Garden and Glass:** Tacoma-born Dale Chihuly is the best-known glass artist in the world, and this exciting museum, beside the Space Needle, presents an outstanding retrospective of his work, from early pieces inspired by Indian baskets and pottery to the writhing, fluorescent colors of his famous chandeliers and marine environments. The virtuosity and vibrancy of the work will amaze. See p. 77.
- **Seattle Art Museum (SAM):** Considered the best art museum north of San Francisco, SAM is particularly noteworthy for its outstanding collection of Northwest Native American art and artifacts. Another fascinating gallery is devoted to the history of Pacific Northwest painting, crafts, and sculpture. In addition, the museum has some intriguing contemporary pieces and often hosts major traveling exhibits. See p. 72.
- **Museum of History and Industry (MOHAI):** Set in the former Naval Reserve building on Lake Union, MOHAI is a must for anyone interested in the story of Seattle and how it grew. The exhibits here are fun and fascinating, and they span the city's history from the Great Fire and Yukon Gold Rush to the founding of Microsoft, plus everything in between. Historic photographs and artifacts provide vivid glimpses into the city's boom-or-bust past. See p. 82.
- **Museum of Flight:** Seattle's aircraft industry began in 1916 and has grown over the years to become one of the largest in the world. The Museum of Flight at Boeing Field is dedicated to airplanes and spacecraft, from early biplanes to satellites and space stations launched by Russia and NASA. Out on the field you can walk through a Concorde (remember sonic booms?) and the first Air Force One. Along the way, there are lots of hands-on exhibits and info about the of the aircraft industry in Seattle. See p. 83.
- **Olympic Sculpture Park:** An outstanding collection of outdoor sculpture has been assembled in this park at the north end of the waterfront overlooking Elliott Bay. Monumental pieces by Richard Serra, Alexander Calder,

and Claes Oldenburg are interspersed with sculptures by lesser-known artists. Admission is free to this offshoot of the Seattle Art Museum, and there's a pavilion where you can sit with a coffee or a glass of wine and enjoy the view. See p. 74.

Portland

- **Pittock Mansion:** Completed in 1914, this enormous French Renaissance Revival chateau, built for the owner of *The Oregonian* newspaper, occupies the highest point in Northwest Portland. Wander through rooms paneled with rare woods and sheathed in rare marbles, and enjoy the panoramic view of Portland from the gardens. See p. 162.
- **Portland Art Museum:** The collection of Native American art and artifacts is reason enough to visit Portland's art museum. It has a small collection of French Impressionists and galleries of contemporary Northwest art, and it hosts interesting but smaller-scale traveling shows. See p. 155.

The Oregon Coast

- **Columbia River Maritime Museum** (Astoria): The mighty Columbia River empties into the Pacific at Astoria, site of the oldest settlement west of the Mississippi. The collection of heritage boats, from Coast Guard rescue ships to fishing trawlers, and a docked light station that you can visit, highlight the many ways that the Columbia has been integral to Astoria's history. Nautical artifacts and memorabilia are scattered throughout this compact, well-designed museum, including rare maps, cannons washed up from shipwrecks, and exhibits explaining Astoria's once-thriving salmon canning industry. See p. 234.
- **Flavel House** (Astoria): Built in the 1880s for a wealthy sea captain, Flavel House is the grandest and most historic house in Astoria. On a self-guided tour, you can wander through the enormous rooms, furnished with original and period furniture, and see how the other half lived back when. See p. 235.
- **Fort Clatsop–Lewis & Clark National Historic Park** (near Astoria): Of all the early explorers, Meriwether Lewis and William Clark are most ingrained in the consciousness of Pacific Northwesterners. On orders from President Thomas Jefferson, these two intrepid adventurers assembled the Corps of Discovery and traveled from St. Louis to the Pacific Ocean, traversing half the continent and going where no whites had ever gone before. When they reached the Pacific in 1805, they built a fort like the replica seen at this national historic park and spent a cold, wet winter there before heading back to civilization. See p. 240.
- **Yaquina Bay Lighthouse** (Newport): The oldest lighthouse on the Oregon coast, dating from 1871, is an unusual structure, built of wood and looks more like a house than a lighthouse. Now part of Yaquina Bay State Recreation Site, the lighthouse is open as a museum so you can go inside to visit the lighthouse keepers' quarters and gaze out over the same coast they kept watch over some 140 years ago. See p. 275.

THE best GARDENS

Seattle

- **Washington Park Arboretum:** One of the Northwest's great arboretums, it was established in the 1930s and is planted with an extraordinary variety of specimen trees from the Pacific Northwest and around the world. In the springtime, Azalea Way—planted with thousands of azaleas and other flowering trees, plants, and shrubs—is an unforgettable sight. See p. 84.
- **Seattle Japanese Garden:** A traditional "strolling pond garden" designed around a lake in the Washington Park Arboretum, the Seattle Japanese Garden was one of the first Japanese gardens to be created in the U.S., and with its meticulous plantings, rocks, and stone lanterns, it is a highlight for any garden lover visiting Seattle. See p. 84.

Portland

- **International Rose Test Gardens:** You can't help but stop to sniff the roses at this enormous and enormously popular rose garden in Portland's Washington Park. Thousands of roses romance the eye and nose, blooming in fragrant profusion from late May into September. See p. 158.
- **Lan Su Chinese Garden:** The newest and most unusual (to Western eyes) of Portland's three major gardens, Lan Su was designed and constructed in Portland's Chinatown by a team from Suzhou, China, who created a classical Chinese scholar's garden of a type that was popular during the Ming dynasty. Winding paths with intricate stonework lead to ornate pavilions and colonnades around a lake, with sculpted rocks and carefully chosen plants to add even more interest along the way. See p. 154.
- **Portland Japanese Garden:** Situated in the hills above the rose gardens in Washington Park, the Portland Japanese Garden is considered the most authentic Japanese garden outside of Japan. With five different garden types based on Buddhist, Shinto, Taoist, and Zen principles, this exquisitely designed and maintained garden should be high on the list of anyone who loves gardens, no matter what time of year. See p. 160.

The Oregon Coast

- **Shore Acres State Park** (Charleston): It's rare to find roses blooming along the Oregon coast, but they are the summer stars at this formal garden, created decades ago on a bluff overlooking the Pacific. See p. 288.

THE best FAMILY ATTRACTIONS

Seattle

- **Argosy Cruises:** Head down to Pier 55 on the waterfront to catch one of the excursion cruises offered by this long-established tour-boat company.

You can choose from a tour of Elliott Bay, a locks cruise over to lake Washington, or a trip to Tillicum Village, where Native American hosts put on a salmon bake and perform tradition dances. See p. 77.

- **Museum of Flight:** A fascinating collection of airplanes and spacecraft are on display in this enormous museum at Boeing Field, and hey, you can steer a spaceship in one of the many interactive kid-friendly exhibits. See p. 83.
- **Seattle Aquarium:** This aquarium on the waterfront is a top place to familiarize yourself with the sea life of the region. Get up close to giant Pacific octopuses, touch a sea anemone, watch the fish of Puget Sound in giant tanks, and enjoy sea otters and harbor seals out on the pier. See p. 74.
- **Seattle Center:** Take the vintage monorail from downtown to the site of the 1962 World's Fair, where you can zoom up to the top of the Space Needle for an outstanding view of the entire city, then explore the interactive Pacific Science Center with its animatronic dinosaurs. See chapter 4.
- **Seattle Great Wheel:** Up, up, and around. The Seattle Great Wheel is the largest Ferris wheel on the West Coast and takes you up in enclosed, non-shaky compartments for breathtaking views of Elliott Bay, the Olympic Mountains, and the Seattle skyline. See p. 76.
- **Smith Tower:** It's not as tall as the Space Needle, but Smith Tower is a lot more fun. This wonderful old building, completed in 1914, was for years the tallest skyscraper in the city. It has all of its original features, including some of the last manually operated cage elevators in the country. These will whisk you up to the 35th floor for an outstanding view. See p. 80.

Portland

- **Oregon Museum of Science and Industry (OMSI):** With an OMNIMAX theater, a planetarium, a submarine, and loads of hands-on exhibits, this Portland museum is fun for kids and adults alike. See p. 163.
- **Oregon Zoo:** The state's top tourist attraction has elephants, apes, naked mole rats, bats, wolves, and hundreds of other animals in natural-looking habitats and enclosures. The zoo is a large one, and it can easily take up to 3 or 4 hours to see it all. See p. 158.
- **Washington Park:** Along with two world-class gardens there's also a big kids' playground, a miniature train that runs to the Oregon Zoo, and the World Forestry Discovery Museum—plus lots of walks and trails through this beautiful park near downtown Portland. See p. 157.

The Oregon Coast

- **Oregon Coast Aquarium** (Newport): This is the biggest attraction on the Oregon coast, and justly so. Tufted puffins and sea otters are always entertaining, while tide pools, jellyfish tanks, sharks, and a giant octopus contribute to the appeal of this well-designed public aquarium. See p. 273.
- **Sea Lion Caves** (north of Florence): This massive cave, the largest sea cave in the country, is home to hundreds of Steller sea lions that lounge on the rocks beneath busy U.S. 101. An elevator takes you to a viewing window

where you can see the sea lions in their protected natural habitat. See p. 279.

- **Walking on an ocean beach:** All the beaches along the Oregon coast are free and open to the public (though you may have to pay a day-use fee at state parks), and most of them are flat and sandy. Explore tide pools, collect sand dollars, watch the sea birds and maybe the sea lions, and feel the giant power of the Pacific as it comes crashing onto the shore and offshore rocks. The coast's best beaches are described throughout chapter 6.
- **Whale-watching excursion** (Depoe Bay): There is nothing more exciting than catching sight of one of the giant gray whales that migrate up and down the Oregon coast. There are whale-watching viewpoints all up and down the coast, but Tradewinds Charters in Depoe Bay offers excursions out into the open waters to get a closer look. Have your sea legs about you, because the waters can be choppy and the swells can, well, get to you. See "Whale-Watching" in the "Depoe Bay" section of chapter 6, p. 268.

SUGGESTED ITINERARIES

2

Are you going just to Seattle, or just to Portland, or just to the Oregon coast—or are you going to a combination or all of them?

Those are some of the questions I'll try and tackle in this chapter. The answers are made even more complex by the fact that, on day trips from both Seattle and Portland, you can visit mountain peaks, volcanoes, river gorges, wine country, and the coast, too. The variety and richness of this region is mind-boggling.

The truth is: there's no wrong or right way to plan a vacation in the Pacific Northwest. What I will attempt to do is suggest some logical, and logistically sound, ways to schedule your time, so you're not sitting in traffic, or rushing from attraction to attraction. Sound good? Let's get started.

THE BEST OF SEATTLE IN 3 DAYS

This 3-day itinerary is perfect for long weekends. If you have more time, use the 5 days itinerary below it, which will allow you to enjoy a couple of day trips and see the region in more depth.

Day 1

Spend your first day in Seattle getting a feel for the lay of the land, the spread of the sea, the riches of the country's greatest market and its renowned outdoor art museum. You'll be outside more than inside, and along the way you'll enjoy fantastic views that capture the personality of Seattle.

You'll start at the iconic **Pike Place Market** ★★★ (p. 71). There, in the oldest covered market in the country you'll feel the pulse of downtown Seattle. The market is a "follow your nose" sort of place, and you can easily lose track of time as you browse the fish and produce stalls and explore the shops in the Down Under section. Plan on spending at a good 2 hours poking around this lively, colorful and endlessly fascinating hive of Seattle shopping. Then, **stop for lunch** at one of the market's eateries; our suggestions on p. 74. The nation's first Starbucks is right at the entrance of the market, and you can stop for coffee there—or better yet, just a selfie (the coffee is no better here than it is at the nation's other Starbucks).

The Best of Seattle in 3 Days

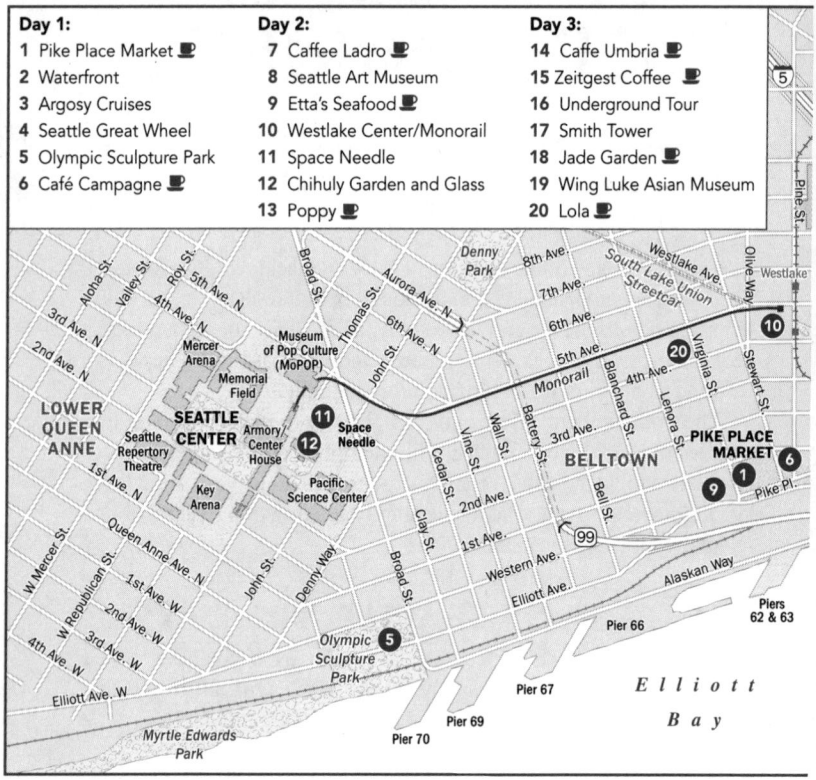

Next it's time to experience Seattle from the water, because water is a defining characteristic of the city's personality. From the market, head down to the Seattle **Waterfront** ★★★ (p. 74) to take the 1:25pm Harbor Cruise on an excursion boat operated by **Argosy Cruises** (p. 77) at Pier 55. The boat does sometimes sell out, so reserve your ticket in advance (but if you forget to do so, try your luck at the pier ticket office). On this 1-hour narrated tour you'll cruise around Elliott Bay, the watery heart and soul of Seattle, learning more about the city's maritime history. The trip is enhanced by unobstructed views of the city's photogenic skyline with its towers, hills, and iconic Space Needle.

After your harbor tour, stroll north from the ferry terminal along the busy Waterfront. You've had a view of the skyline from the water, now get a view west, out over the water to the Olympic Mountains, by taking a ride on the **Seattle Great Wheel** ★★ (p. 76). (Do this only if the sky is relatively clear or you won't get much of a view.)

After the 15-minute ride on the Great Wheel, continue walking north along the busy waterfront—it's a flat, easy path and great for

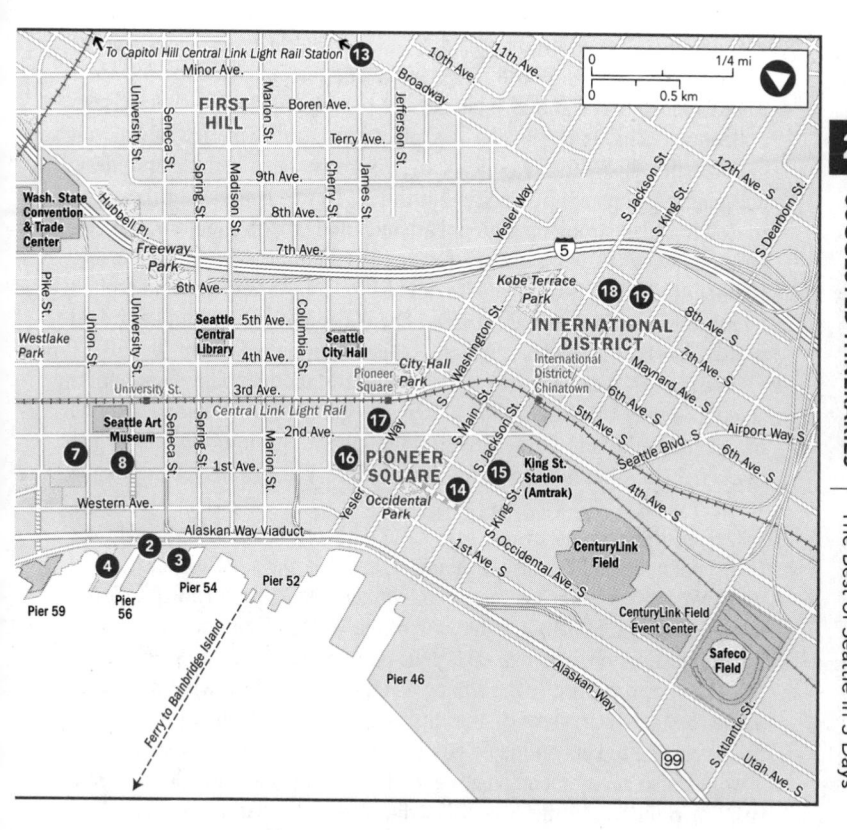

people-watching. You'll pass piers where you can sit, shops where you can browse, the aquarium, and some terminal buildings before you arrive, in just over a mile at the famed **Olympic Sculpture Park** ★★★ (p. 74). This is the Northwest's greatest display of outdoor sculpture created by an A-list roster of renowned artists. Take the self-guided path that leads up past giant works by the likes of Alexander Calder and Louise Bourgeois and provides still more far-reaching views of Elliott Bay and the Olympics.

From the sculpture park, make your way back to your starting point, the Pike Street Market, by following 1st Avenue south. (If you don't want to make the 25-minute trek, hop on the Route 99 bus that heads south along 1st Avenue back to the market.) Choose a restaurant in the market or on the Waterfront for dinner. **Café Campagne** ★★ (p. 108) is an excellent, reasonably priced pick. The water view is better but the prices more elevated at **Aqua** ★★ (p. 109).

Day 2 is your downtown and Seattle Center day, focusing on the city's cultural riches. Start your morning with coffee and a baked treat at **Caffe**

Ladro Espresso Bar & Bakery ★★ (p. 117). When you're fueled, head over to the **Seattle Art Museum** ★★★ (p. 72), or SAM. You can't miss it—literally—because right outside is one of Seattle's most iconic pieces of public art: Jonathan Borofsky's giant kinetic sculpture *Hammering Man.* There's much to see at SAM, but be sure to seek out the Native American collections. This is one of the few places in North America where you can see the distinctive woodcarving, basketry, beadwork, embroidery, and paintings created by Pacific Northwest Native American tribes. The museum is also strong on regional art and another stop should be the galleries showing the work of the so-called Big Four artists (Guy Anderson, Kenneth Callahan, Morris Graves, and Mark Tobey) active in and around Seattle and La Conner in the 1950s. There's an entire museum dedicated to their work in La Conner, which you can visit on a day trip (p. 130).

From SAM, dart back over to Pike Place Market (by now you understand its endless allure) for lunch, maybe a quick bowl of chowder at one of the market's hole-in-the-wall restaurants, or, at the north end of the market, **Etta's Seafood** ★★ (p. 109), where you can sit outside if the weather is nice.

One of the seminal events in Seattle's history was the 1962 World's Fair, which shaped the city in many significant ways. After lunch, head up to Westlake Center and catch the vintage 1962 **monorail** (p. 67) for the quick ride to **Seattle Center,** site of the World's Fair and still a major Seattle destination. You can take your pick of attractions at Seattle Center. The star, however, is the **Space Needle** ★★ (p. 79), which provides a spectacular 360° view of the city. *Important:* be sure to book your Space Needle tickets online or you may be in line for more than 2 hours. I would also recommend visiting **Chihuly Garden and Glass** ★★★ (p. 77), right below the Space Needle, for a fascinating chronological tour of Dale Chihuly's glass art; you can see it all in under an hour.

Your time so far has been spent in and around downtown Seattle and at Seattle Center, but at least one of Seattle's distinctive neighborhoods should be on your agenda. For a change of Seattle scene, and a good place for dinner, head up to **Capitol Hill** (p. 66), just east of downtown, and dine at **Poppy** ★★★ (p. 113), noted for its unique thali-style meals that include a main course with several delicious side dishes. Stroll south along Broadway after dinner and you'll get a sense of the Capitol Hill neighborhood, one of the oldest in the city and once the capitol of counter-culture. It's becoming gentrified, like the rest of the city, but it still has a youthful buzz and energy.

Day 3

Now it's time to head back in time to have a look at the oldest part of Seattle, in and around the Pioneer Square neighborhood. And since you're in coffee-centric Seattle, you have to start the day with java at **Caffe Umbria** ★★★ (p. 117)—it offers delicious blends and creamy lattes.

After your coffee (those pastries look pretty tempting, too), take the wonderfully entertaining **Bill Speidel's Underground Tour** ★★★ (p. 79), where you'll wander through tunnels that were once streets and hear anecdotes about life in early Seattle. Afterward, head up to the observation deck on the 35th floor of **Smith Tower** ★★★ (p. 80), a 1914 skyscraper that retains its historic character and gorgeous period details. You're no doubt hungry now, so head over to the nearby **Chinatown/International District** for dim sum at **Jade Garden** ★ (p. 111) and a look around the neighborhood. A visit to the **Wing Luke Asian Museum** ★★ (p. 82) is a great way to round out your day. The museum tells the story of the Asians and Pacific Islanders who have played a significant role in Seattle's diverse cultural mix since the coming of the railroad.

On your last evening in Seattle, have dinner at one of Seattle's many fine restaurants.

SEATTLE IN 5 DAYS

Day 4

Follow the itinerary above for your first 3 days. On day 4, head down to Pier 52 and take a ferry over to Winslow on **Bainbridge Island.** There is regular ferry service throughout the day, and the ferry ride will give you more photo-op views of the Seattle skyline. You can take your car on the ferry, which will help you explore a bit of the island, with its residential areas tucked in amongst forests and along the shoreline. A much cheaper option is to walk on as a passenger (and bring a bike to get around). Either way, spend a little time exploring Winslow, the small harbor town where the ferry docks—it's a sweet place to stroll and browse in small shops—then drive, bike or take the bus to **Bloedel Reserve** ★★★ (p. 86), one of the great gardens of the Pacific Northwest. Give yourself an hour-and-a-half to explore this 150-acre garden with its native plants and naturalistic landscaping. You can have a meal in Winslow before heading back to Seattle, but you will be back in plenty of time to arrange for dinner at a Seattle restaurant of your choice.

Day 5

You've seen the Waterfront, downtown, Pioneer Square, taken a ferry to Bainbridge Island—now it's time to visit a mountain. Mount Rainier, to be exact. This is a full-day day trip, so you'll need to get an early start and either rent a car or arrange an escorted tour. There are many ways to explore **Mount Rainier National Park** ★★★ (p. 131), but not to be missed is the short, easy hike along **Patriarchs Trail** ★★★ to see a majestic stand of enormous old-growth cedars. Have a casual lunch or afternoon refreshments at the **National Park Inn** ★ or **Paradise Inn** ★★, atmospheric alpine lodges, before heading back to Seattle.

The Best of Seattle in 5 Days

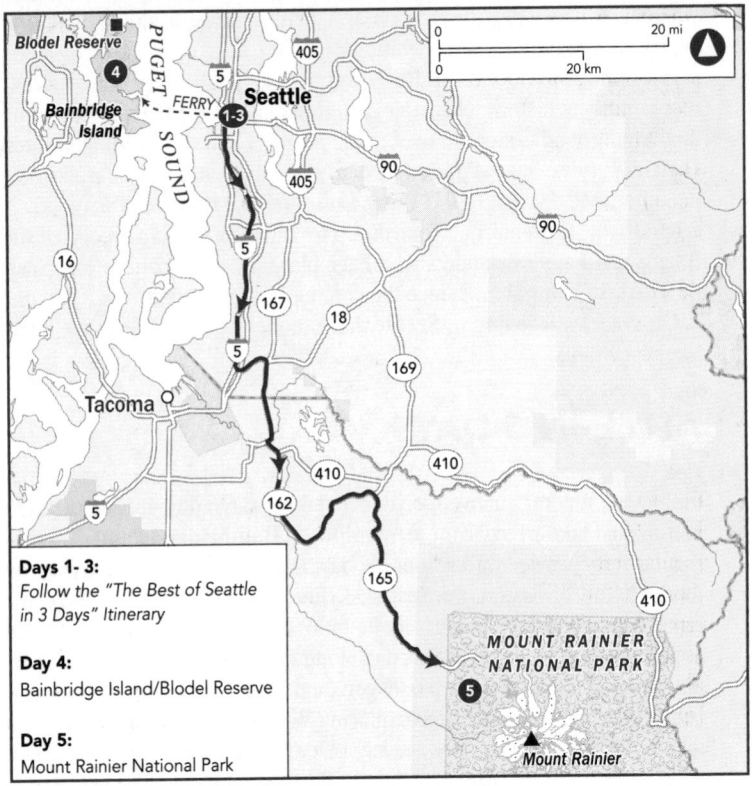

PORTLAND IN 3 DAYS

All the major city attractions are covered in this 3-day itinerary. If you have more time to spend in Portland, I've expanded the itinerary to 5 days so you can get out and see more of this wonderfully scenic region.

Day 1

Spend your first day in Portland seeing the downtown area. With its compact blocks and interesting mix of buildings, architectural styles, and parks, downtown Portland is easy to walk (or bike) and a pleasure to explore.

Start right in the heart of downtown at **Pioneer Courthouse Square** ★★★ (p. 142), referred to as "Portland's living room." Here you'll get a feel for the city's face and fashions as commuters get off the buses, streetcars and MAX light-rail lines that flank this transportation hub. A big Starbucks on the southwest corner of the square has outdoor tables where you can sit in nice weather watching the passing parade and looking out over the waterfall fountain and zany weather machine. Pioneer Square is downtown shopping central, with a flagship Nordstrom right across from the square and most of downtown's major stores within a four-block radius. Grab lunch in midtown.

Head up to the **South Park Blocks** (p. 143), just a couple of minutes' walk, and have a look around the **Portland Art Museum** ★★ (p. 155), especially its Native American collection. This should take about 2 hours. From the museum, walk south to a few blocks to have a look at the waterfall-like **Ira Keller Fountain** ★ (p. 154), a splashing evocation of Oregon's cliffs and rivers. From there, head down Salmon Street four blocks to **Tom McCall Waterfront Park** ★★★ (p. 156), where you can stroll along the esplanade with Portland's skyline on one side and the river with its historic bridges on the other. **Jake's Famous Crawfish** ★★ (p. 184), Portland's oldest restaurant, is an atmospheric choice for happy hour or dinner. The easiest way to get there from waterfront park is to take Stark St. west through downtown for 12 blocks. It won't take more than 15 minutes.

Day 2

Head first to the **Oregon Historical Society Museum** ★★ (p. 155) on the South Park Blocks, across from the Portland Art Museum, for a compelling look at Oregon's and Portland's pioneer and more recent history, as well as its Native American roots. You'll likely want to linger for about 2 hours at the museum, as there are many short videos, audio posts and artifacts to examine.

Then its lunch at one of Portland's famous **food carts** (p. 186). They are found at various locales around downtown, though we recommend both the "pods" of carts at SW 9th and SW10th avenues (see p. 182), as they have some stellar options. To see the offerings at other carts visit **www.foodcartsportland.com**.

For over a 100 years Portland has been called the City of Roses. So now it's time to smell these blossoms at the 100-year-old **International Rose Test Garden** ★★★ (p. 158) in **Washington Park** ★★★ (p. 157) in the southwest hills. Take MAX (the light-rail), drive, bike or walk (it's about a half-hour steady walk from downtown) to marvel at this dazzling display of tens of thousands of roses on a hillside overlooking downtown and Mount Hood.

After you've sniffed and snapped (with a camera) your fill of roses, head up to the **Portland Japanese Garden** ★★★ (p. 160), on the hillside directly above the rose gardens. This superlative garden will introduce you to an ancient and entirely different gardening style. There's never been a better time to visit. In 2017 the Portland Japanese Garden opened a $30.5-million expansion by famed Japanese architect Kengo Kuma that transformed the central plaza and added striking new buildings that house the gift shop, performance spaces and a glass-walled teahouse.

There really aren't any places to eat right in the park, so make your way back downtown to enjoy happy hour at any one of Portland's restaurants, or a dinner at someplace special, like **Tasty n Alder** ★★ (p. 185).

The Best of Portland in 3 Days or 5 Days

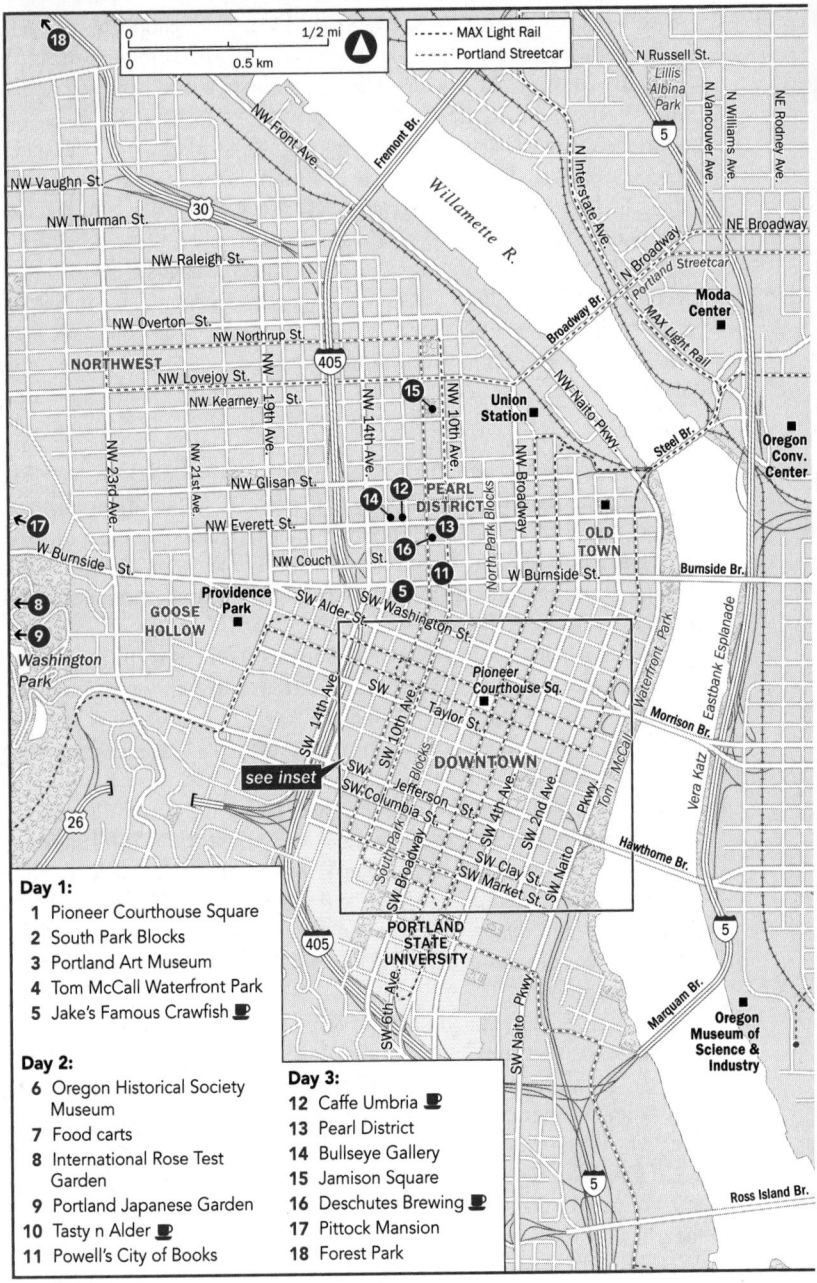

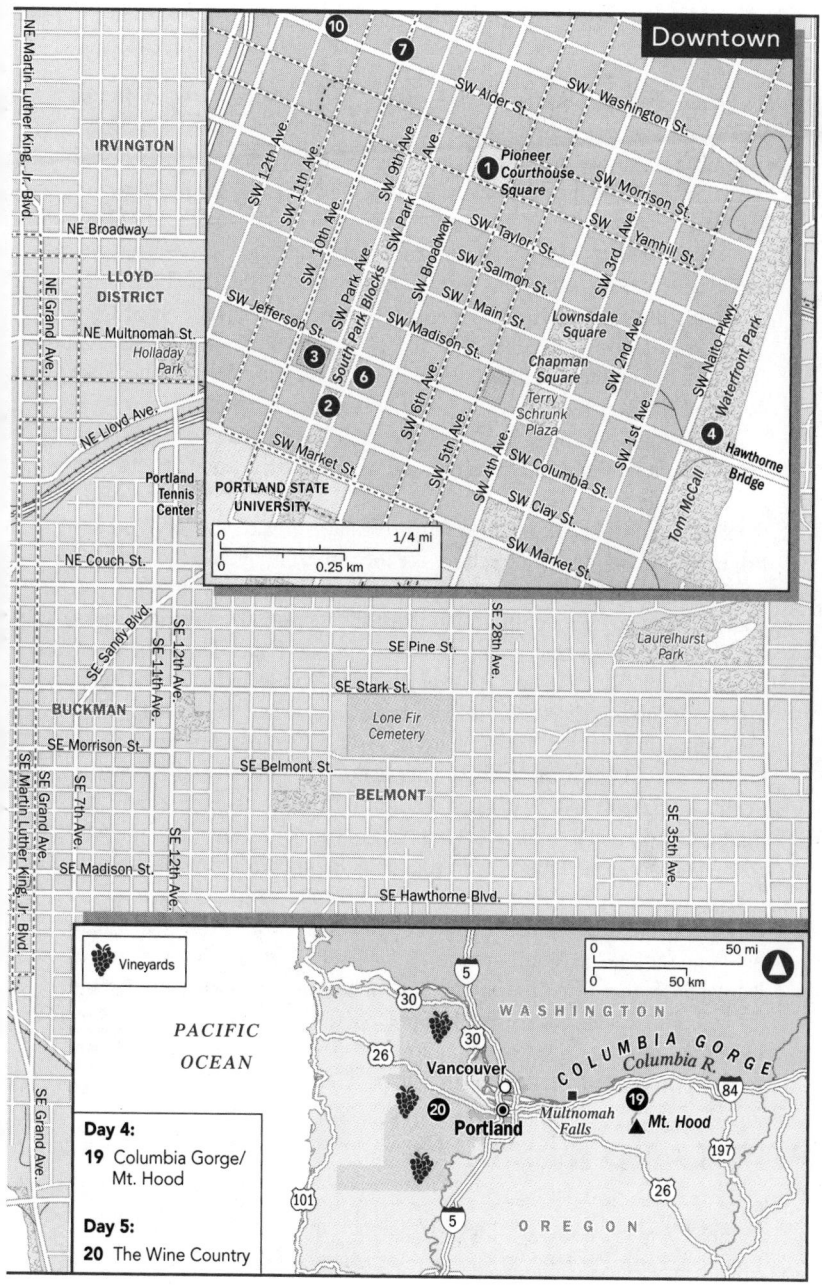
Downtown
SW Alder St.
SW Washington St.
SW Morrison St.
SW Taylor St.
SW Salmon St.
SW Main St.
SW Madison St.
SW Market St.
SW Columbia St.
SW Clay St.
SW Jefferson St.
SW 12th Ave.
SW 11th Ave.
SW 10th Ave.
SW Park Ave.
South Park Blocks
SW 9th Ave.
SW Broadway
SW 6th Ave.
SW 5th Ave.
SW 4th Ave.
SW 3rd Ave.
SW 2nd Ave.
SW 1st Ave.
SW Yamhill St.
SW Naito Pkwy.
Pioneer Courthouse Square
Lownsdale Square
Chapman Square
Terry Schrunk Plaza
Waterfront Park
Hawthorne Bridge
Tom McCall
PORTLAND STATE UNIVERSITY
0 1/4 mi
0 0.25 km
IRVINGTON
NE Broadway
LLOYD DISTRICT
NE Multnomah St.
Holladay Park
NE Lloyd Ave.
NE Grand Ave.
NE Martin Luther King, Jr. Blvd.
Portland Tennis Center
NE Couch St.
SE Sandy Blvd.
SE 12th Ave.
SE 11th Ave.
SE Pine St.
SE 28th Ave.
Laurelhurst Park
SE Stark St.
Lone Fir Cemetery
BUCKMAN
SE Morrison St.
SE Belmont St.
BELMONT
SE 7th Ave.
SE Grand Ave.
SE Martin Luther King, Jr. Blvd.
SE Madison St.
SE 35th Ave.
SE Hawthorne Blvd.
Vineyards
PACIFIC OCEAN
0 50 mi
0 50 km
WASHINGTON
OREGON
COLUMBIA GORGE
Columbia R.
Vancouver
Portland
Multnomah Falls
Mt. Hood
Day 4:
19 Columbia Gorge/ Mt. Hood
Day 5:
20 The Wine Country

After dinner, head over to mega-store, and literary powerhouse, **Powell's City of Books** ★★★ (p. 196), which is open late every night of the week and often hosts terrific book signings and other events.

Day 3

It's time to explore a Portland neighborhood and the largest urban forest in North America, with a stop at one of Portland's largest and most scenically-sited historic homes. Start the day at **Caffe Umbria** ★★★ (p. 192), the nicest coffee bar in the Pearl District. Afterward, explore the Pearl, which has been transformed over the past 20 years from an industrial area of low-rise warehouses to a dynamic mix of art galleries, new residences and parks, with an ever-expanding restaurant and shopping scene. I'd recommend stopping in at the **Bullseye Gallery** ★★★, p. 195), just a block away from Caffe Umbria, because they always show impressive works that break the boundaries of glass (but don't break the glass itself). The Pearl is a good spot to have lunch, too. See our suggestions, starting on p. 187.

After strolling through the urban Pearl, a leafy change of pace is in order. Catch the **Portland Streetcar** going south to Burnside St. and then the 20 bus heading west up Burnside. Ask the driver to drop you off at the stop for **Pittock Mansion** ★★ (p. 162) at Burnside and NW Barnes Rd. If you're driving, the directions are the same, only you'll turn into the curving drive that leads up to the mansion's parking lot. If you're on foot, you'll follow an easy uphill trail to reach the mansion's entrance, or take the free shuttle bus that runs from June through Labor Day. The enormous French Renaissance Revival chateau, completed in 1914 on a 1,000-foot-high crest in Forest Park, is the largest and most opulent historic house in Portland. Take one of the 40-minute tours offered throughout the day to learn more about this historic landmark and its role in Portland's history. After touring the house, filled with rare woods and marbles, walk down to the viewpoint at the end of the lawn to enjoy one of the best all-around views of Portland, including three mountain peaks.

If you're in the mood for a hike, the **Wildwood Trail** at the end of the parking lot will take you downhill through Forest Park to Thurman Street, but that's at least an hour's walk. Alternatively, make your way back to Burnside on foot or on the shuttle bus for a return trip downtown on the 20 bus. For dinner, head over to SE Division, one of the city's newer restaurant rows, to dine on authentic Thai street food at **Pok Pok** ★★★ (p. 191) or fabulous Italian cuisine at **Ava Gene's** ★★★ (p. 190).

PORTLAND IN 5 DAYS

Day 4

Follow the suggestions for days 1 to 3 above, and then rent a car for your final 2 days in Portland so you can see some of the state's magnificent scenery. On day 4, head east out of town on I-84. The spectacular **Columbia Gorge** ★★★ (p. 218) begins just a few miles east of downtown. For the most scenic drive, take the **Columbia Gorge Historic Highway**—we just call it "the Old Gorge Highway"—the first scenic road to be built in Oregon back in the 1920s, with bridges and walls constructed by Italian stonemasons. The old highway takes you up to **Crown Point** ★★★ (p. 220), where the breathtaking view extends for over 30 miles.

Continue on the old highway and you will pass a handful of sparkling, rushing waterfalls until you come finally to the tallest and most dramatic waterfall of all—**Multnomah Falls** ★★★ (p. 221), one of the highest waterfalls in North America. Have lunch at historic **Multnomah Falls Lodge** ★★ (p. 223).

At this point you can jog back to I-84, the faster and newer highway that runs closer to the river. (Please note, however, that a wildfire in September 2017 charred part of the forest in the Gorge.) From here, you can head south and continue your expedition by driving up and over **Mount Hood** ★★★ (p. 214). **Timberline Lodge** ★★★ (p. 215) is one of the greatest alpine lodges ever built; inside and out it is a rugged yet sophisticated creation of the Works Progress Administration under Franklin D. Roosevelt in the 1930s. You can have a coffee or dinner at the lodge, or return to Portland, about 2 hours away.

Day 5

Oregon is famous for the quality of its wines, particularly pinot noirs. Vineyards are scattered throughout the western part of the state—west of the Cascades, that is—but the ones closest to Portland are in the North Willamette Valley. Have a look in chapter 5 at the day trip called **"The Wine Country"** (p. 208), and head into the rolling hills of the valley to visit and taste wine at some of the outstanding vineyards there. And you can reach the Valley in about an hour, if the traffic gods are with you.

SEATTLE & PORTLAND IN 1 WEEK

This itinerary is intended for travelers who plan to spend the majority of their time in Seattle and Portland, the two largest and most exciting cities in the Pacific Northwest. You can make the 178-mile (286 km) trip between the two cities by **car** in about 3 hours, depending on traffic (with an accident on the highway or slow-moving traffic, the trip can take up to 5 hr.). **Amtrak** has regular service between Portland and Seattle throughout the day, and **Bolt Bus** offers inexpensive bus service between the two cities; expect to spend about 3½ hours on either train or bus. There are also flights from **Sea-Tac International Airport** (p. 62) to **Portland International Airport** (p. 140) throughout the day, generally on smaller commuter aircraft; by air, the trip takes about 40 minutes. You will find information on all of these transportation options discussed in the "Getting There" sections in chapter 5 and chapter 6. If you don't want to backtrack to Seattle at the end of your Portland visit, see if you can fly into Seattle and out of Portland. There is often no great price difference in booking your flight itinerary this way.

Days 1–2: Seattle

To get a good dose of Seattle, follow the suggestions for days 1 and 2 in "The Best of Seattle in 3 Days," p. 17.

Day 3: Seattle/Day trip to LaConner & Skagit Valley

If it's tulip season, you definitely don't want to miss seeing the **tulip fields** in and around the town of **LaConner ★★★,** 70 miles (113 km) north of Seattle in the **Skagit Valley**. The Skagit Valley is the prime tulip-growing area in the U.S., and the vast, colorful tulip fields rival and perhaps surpass those in Holland. Have lunch in LaConner and stroll its lovely old streets. And if it's not tulip time, you'll enjoy exploring the charming town of LaConner and visiting its surprisingly good art museum devoted to the "Big Four" Northwest artists of the 1950s and '60s. You'll need a car for this trip, but it's an easy shot up I-5. You can easily be back in Seattle in time for a farewell dinner. For full details, see LaConner & the Skagit Valley under "Day Trips" in Chapter 4 (p. 129).

Days 4–5: Portland

For suggestions on how to spend your first 2 days in Portland, see "Day 1" and "Day 2" under "Portland in 3 Days," above.

Day 6: Portland/Columbia Gorge

Spend your last day in Portland by taking a day trip down the **Columbia Gorge** (p. 218), as outlined in "Day 4" under "Portland in 5 Days," above. I would suggest that you make this a full-day trip by going on from Multnomah Falls to Timberline Lodge on Mt. Hood. Doing this, you will be getting a grand look at the grandest scenery near Portland.

SEATTLE, PORTLAND & THE OREGON COAST IN 1 WEEK

Here's a suggested itinerary that gives you a couple of exciting days in Seattle and Portland and then continues on from Portland to take in some of the scenic grandeur of Oregon's North Coast. As with the "Seattle & Portland in 1 Week" itinerary above, you will need to plan out how you want to get from Seattle to Portland—by car, train, bus, or airplane—but once in Portland you will need to rent or use your own car for the Oregon coast part of this 1-week itinerary.

Days 1–2: Seattle

To get a good dose of Seattle, follow the suggestions in days 1 and 2 in "The Best of Seattle in 3 Days," p. 17.

Days 3–4: Portland

On day 3, if you're driving the 178 miles (286 km) down to Portland, head out of Seattle as early as you can to escape the morning rush hour. However you travel, you won't be settled in Portland until late morning

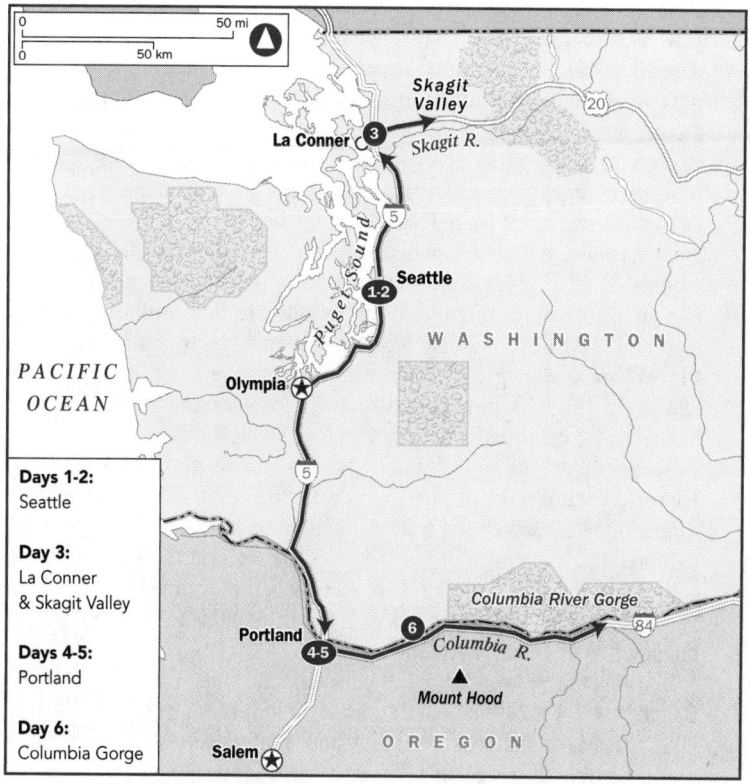

or early afternoon. Spend your first afternoon in the City of Roses at the two magnificent gardens in **Washington Park** (p. 157), the **International Rose Test Garden** ★★★ (p. 158) and the **Portland Japanese Garden** ★★★ (p. 160).

Afterward, depending on what you are in the mood for, you might want to have dinner at **St. Jack** ★★ (French; p. 188), or **Bamboo Sushi** ★★ (Japanese, sushi/sashimi; p. 185) on NW 23rd Avenue, or at **Caffe Mingo** ★★ (Italian; p. 188) on NW 21st Avenue. All three restaurants are just minutes from Washington Park. From any of them you can easily get back downtown via the Portland streetcar.

On day 4, explore downtown Portland, visiting **Pioneer Courthouse Square** ★★★ (p. 151), the **South Park Blocks** (p. 143), and the **Oregon Historical Society Museum** ★★ (p. 155). Have lunch at one of Portland's trend-setting food carts (p. 186) and then continue your downtown urban adventuring by strolling through **Chapman and Lownsdale squares** ★★ (p. 151) and **Tom McCall Waterfront Park** ★★★ (p. 156). Have dinner and a craft beer at one of Portland's many microbreweries (p. 140)—this is the microbrewery capital of the country, after all.

Day 5: Astoria/Cannon Beach

As mentioned above, you will need a car for the final 3 days of your whirlwind Pacific Northwest tour. Today you'll head west to the Pacific Ocean, but first you'll be able to marvel at the huge size of the Columbia River where it empties into the ocean at **Astoria** ★★★ (p. 230). The trip to Astoria, depending on your route, will take 1½ to 2 hours. Here, at the site of the oldest settlement west of the Mississippi, you can spend an enjoyable and enlightening hour visiting the compact and well-done **Columbia River Maritime Museum** ★★ (p. 234), which outlines the human history of the mighty Columbia with exhibits, artifacts, and heritage boats. Nearby, and also worth a few minutes of your time, is the **Flavel House** ★★ (p. 235), an ornate brick mansion built for a sea captain in the 1880s. Astoria is undergoing a long-overdue renaissance and has several good restaurants where you can have lunch.

Save another hour to visit **Fort Clatsop—Lewis and Clark National Historic Park** ★★★ (p. 240), 5 miles (8 km) south of Astoria. Here, in a clearing in the woods, on a site thought to be just yards from the original fort, stands a replica of Fort Clatsop, the wooden fort built by Lewis and Clark and the Corps of Discovery when they finally reached the Pacific Ocean in 1805 after trekking for 18 months across a wilderness unknown to non-Native Americans.

You'll get some wonderful ocean/beach time when you reach **Cannon Beach** ★★★ (p. 249), about 22 miles (35 km) south of Fort Clatsop on U.S. 101. Make this your overnight stop. With towering Haystack Rock jutting up from the shore, this flat, sandy beach is one of the best along the entire coast for long walks (no matter what the weather). The town is the most charming and affluent on the Oregon coast and offers lots of shopping and a handful of restaurants that are among the top dining spots anywhere along the coast. If you have time before the light fades, pay a visit to gorgeous **Ecola State Park** ★★★ (p. 252) at the north end of town, with miles of beach and forested hiking trails with panoramic ocean views.

Day 6: Three Capes Scenic Loop/Depoe Bay/Newport

Continuing south from Cannon Beach on U.S. 101, in about 40 miles (64 km) you'll come to Tillamook. Just south of Tillamook, watch for the turnoff for the **Three Capes Scenic Loop** ★★★ (p. 259), a scene-stealing byway on Oregon's North Coast. The 35-mile loop drive leaves U.S. 101 and winds past three wind-swept capes (one with a lighthouse) with viewpoints, beaches, picnic areas, and hiking trails. At Pacific City, the scenic byway rejoins U.S. 101, the main coast highway. It's another 22 miles (35 km) to **Lincoln City** ★ (p. 263), a good spot for lunch or a

Seattle, Portland & the Oregon Coast in 1 Week

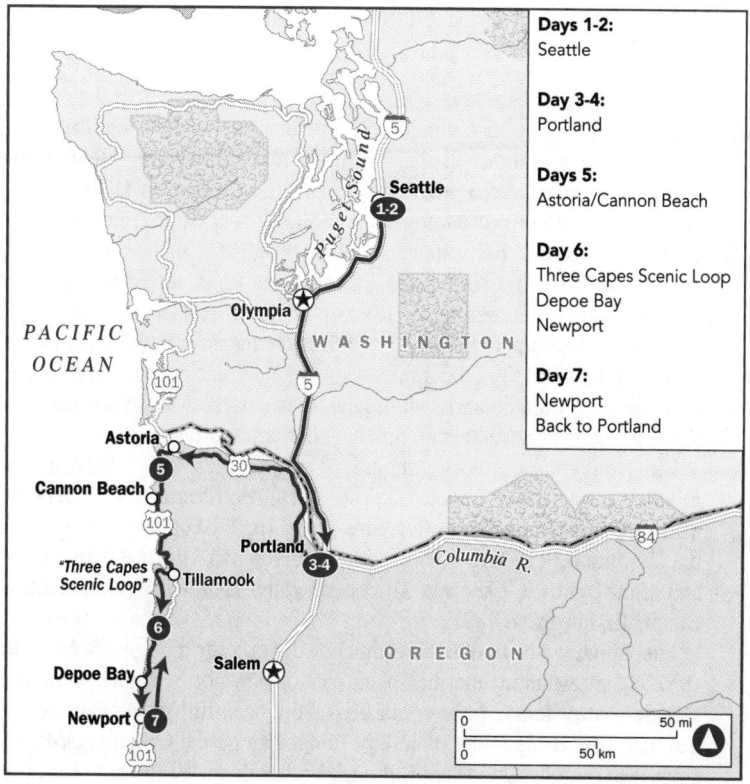

coffee. For a casual, fish-and-chips lunch with an ocean view, try **Kyllo's Seafood & Grill** ★★ (p. 267) at the south end of Lincoln City.

At Lincoln City, the Central Coast region begins. Continue on U.S. 101 to tiny **Depoe Bay** ★★ (p. 267) with the world's smallest harbor. If you don't suffer from seasickness, sign up for a whale-watching expedition that will take you out onto the open waters of the bay, where a herd of giant gray whales spends part of every summer, and other gray whales pass back and forth on their annual migration. The tours are offered daily year-round but before booking ask if any whales have been sighted that day, or your only sight will be the surging sea.

In about 13 miles you'll reach **Newport** ★★★ (p. 270), the most intriguing town on the Oregon coast (you are now on the Central Coast). If you took a whale-watching cruise, you'll likely be arriving in the late afternoon. Spend what remains of the day strolling along Newport's busy **Bayfront** ★★ (p. 272), and exploring the charming, artsy neighborhood of **Nye Beach** ★★★ (p. 273), the town's oldest residential area. Here you can enjoy an invigorating stroll on long, sandy Nye Beach. Now it's time to decide on a restaurant for dinner—**Local Ocean** ★★★ (p. 276) offers the freshest seafood, but **Saffron Salmon** ★★ (p. 277) will give you the best view of Newport Bay.

Day 7: Newport/Portland

There's a lot more to enjoy in Newport before you head back to Portland. Start your explorations at the not-to-be-missed **Yaquina Head Outstanding Natural Area** ★★★ (p. 274), site of **Yaquina Head Lighthouse,** one of the most photogenic and easily accessible lighthouses on the Oregon coast. With its unusual cobble beach and offshore rocks serving as resting and roosting spots for seals, sea lions, tufted puffins, and other sea birds, the area really lives up to its official designation as an "outstanding natural area." Have a look at the displays in the visitor center that tell about life in the lighthouses (a lonely occupation if ever there was one), and then go and visit the lighthouse itself. A stairway gets you down to the beach—not sand, this one, but cobblestones.

But Newport has two lighthouses, and your next stop is the oldest lighthouse on the Oregon coast, a two-story wood-frame house found at **Yaquina Bay State Recreation Site** ★★★ (p. 275) on the north side of the Yaquina Bay Bridge in Newport. Here you can visit the living quarters of the lighthouse keepers who operated the light when the lighthouse cast its first beam in 1871.

Fuel up with a bowl of thick clam chowder or a shrimp salad at **Mo's** ★ (p. 276), a restaurant that has been part of Newport's dining scene for decades. After lunch, head south across the beautiful green span of the Yaquina Bay Bridge, one of several bridges along the Oregon coast that were designed by Conde McCullough and built as WPA projects in the 1930s. On the south side of the bridge, make your way down to Newport's star attraction, the **Oregon Coast Aquarium** ★★★ (p. 273). It's one of the great aquariums of the West Coast and a place you don't want to rush through—give yourself at least a couple of hours. The facility concentrates on local and West Coast marine life and has giant aquariums, a walk-through aquarium with sharks, and outdoor exhibits with tufted puffins, sea otters, and sea lions. It's both educational and fun, and a memorable way to end your Oregon coast experience.

Now it's time to head back up to U.S. 101 and start the drive back to Portland. It's about a 2½-hour drive via U.S. 20 and I-5.

THE OREGON COAST IN 1 WEEK

The Oregon coast stretches from Astoria in the north to Brookings in the south, a distance of about 364 miles (586 km). U.S. 101, the main artery, winds, climbs, twists, and curves along the entire coast, often but not always with the ocean in view. Staying on this (usually) two-lane highway, you could easily cover the entire coast in 2 or certainly 3 days. But why do that when there is so much to see? Spending a week exploring the Oregon coast will reinvigorate your senses, especially if you are an active traveler who likes to get out and go for a walk on the beach—even if it's rainy—or hike along a forest trail with stunning views of the Pacific below.

Bear in mind that the Oregon coast is not a bikini-and-surfboard playground. No, no, no. The water's too cold for swimming, and if you crashed your surfboard into one of the offshore rocks, you'd be a goner. The Oregon coast is wild, windy, rocky, forested, with a lot of towns and villages that almost look like afterthoughts. But this rugged seascape offers exciting sights and experiences like whale watching, surf-pounded white-sand beaches, giant headlands, lonely lighthouses, and scenic byways that leave the highway and take you to places of spectacular natural grandeur.

So here's a weeklong itinerary just for the Oregon coast. Of course, you will need a car. Bring a fleece, a hoodie, a hat, and some kind of rain gear, no matter what time of year you visit. If you travel with a tent or RV, there are excellent campgrounds in state parks all along the coast; I list all of them along the way. For a quick overview of campgrounds, visit **http://visittheoregoncoast.com/activities/camping**. Remember, too, that you will need a Forest Service–issued **Oregon Pacific Coast Passport** day-use pass to park or camp at the many state parks along the way. A 5-day pass costs $10; information on passes can be obtained at **www.fs.fed.us**.

Day 1: Astoria/Cannon Beach

Today, you'll head west from Portland to the Pacific Ocean, but before you actually meet up with the sea, you'll encounter the 14-mile-wide mouth of the Columbia River at **Astoria** ★★★ (p. 230). The trip to Astoria, depending on your route, will take 1½ to 2 hours. This historic river city, home to a good maritime museum, historic house, and other sights, is worth a couple of hours, longer if you want to have lunch or stroll along the **Riverwalk** ★★★ (p. 232). For ideas on how to spend your time in Astoria, see "Day 5" under "Seattle, Portland & the Oregon Coast in 1 Week," above.

From Astoria, head south about 5 miles (8 km) to visit **Fort Clatsop—Lewis and Clark National Historic Park** ★★★ (p. 240), site of the 1805 winter headquarters of the trailblazing explorers Meriwether Lewis and William Clark and their Corps of Discovery.

Continue on to **Cannon Beach** ★★★ (p. 249), about 22 miles (36 km) south of Astoria, for your first overnight stay along the Oregon coast. This is your first big Oregon beach experience, and it's a doozy, with scenic Haystack Rock rising out of the sea and miles of flat, sandy, surf-pounded beach to stroll on and enjoy. Cannon Beach is perhaps the most charming and affluent town along the coast, and it has any number of fine ocean-view hotels and restaurants that are definitely a cut above the average.

Try also to pay a visit to gorgeous **Ecola State Park** ★★★ (p. 252) at the north end of town, with miles of beach and forested hiking trails with panoramic ocean views.

The Oregon Coast in 1 Week

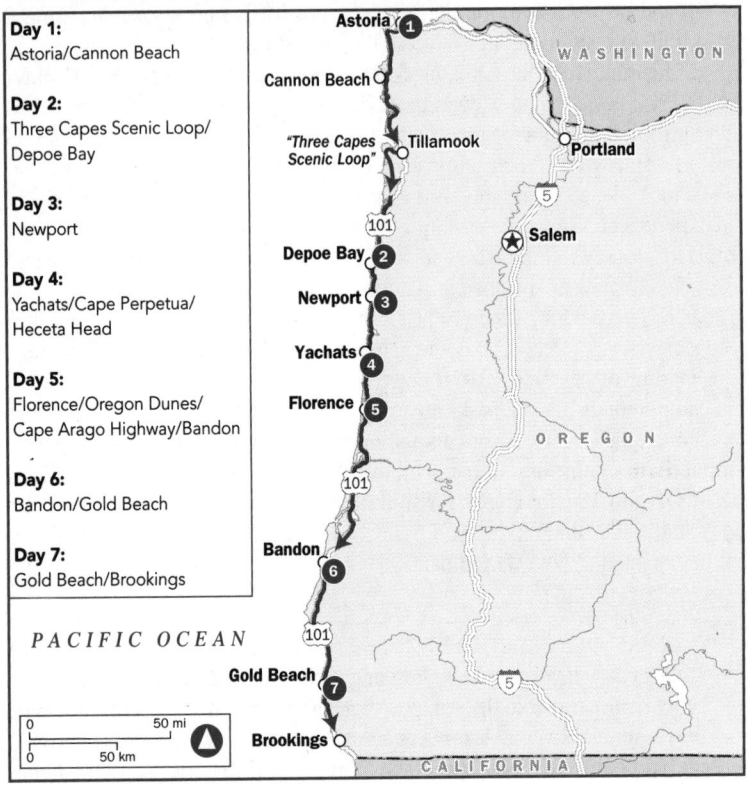

Day 2: Three Capes Scenic Loop/Depoe Bay

Continuing south from Cannon Beach on U.S. 101, in about 40 miles (64 km) you'll come to Tillamook, situated in an important dairy region of lush green fields. If you're a cheese-lover, stop at the **Tillamook Cheese Factory** ★ (p. 258) to sample Oregon's most famous dairy product (you can also get an ice cream). Just south of Tillamook, watch for the turnoff for the **Three Capes Scenic Loop** ★★★ (p. 259), a 35-mile loop drive that leaves U.S. 101 and takes you to three giant headlands where you can hike, camp, or just enjoy the spectacular scenery from viewpoints along the way. **Roseanna's Cafe** ★ (p. 261) in Oceanside is one possible lunch-with-an-ocean-view stop along the route, or you can continue on through Pacific City, where the scenic loop rejoins U.S. 101.

Continue on U.S. 101 to **Depoe Bay** ★★ (p. 263). Here, whale-watching excursion boats chug out from the nation's smallest harbor and into the open sea for possible sightings of the 20-ton gray whales that pass along the Oregon coast during their annual migration. If you get seasick, skip it; otherwise, this is one of your best opportunities to view gray whales from the water rather than shore. See p. 286 for info on how to pre-book a cruise. There's also a Whale Watching Center (p. 269) in Depoe Bay where you can learn more about these remarkable mammals. If you take a whale-watching trip, plan on spending at least 3 hours in Depoe Bay and on the water. You can push on to Newport, but I would recommend that you spend the night in Depoe Bay.

Day 3: Newport

The busy coast town of **Newport** ★★★ (p. 270), with the largest commercial fishing fleet on the coast, is about 13 miles (21 km) south of Depoe Bay. There's a lot to see in Newport, so make it your day 3 overnight stop.

About 5 miles (8 km) north of Newport, follow the signs for **Yaquina Head Outstanding Natural Area** ★★★ (p. 274), site of **Yaquina Head Lighthouse,** built in 1873 and open to visitors. The basalt headland here extends a mile out into the sea, with a series of dramatic offshore rocks that serve as wildlife sanctuaries for seabirds and seals. A staircase leads down to an unusual beach covered with cobbles, not sand, worn smooth by the sea. It's a remarkable and remarkably scenic area. Plan to spend at least an hour here, in the visitor center, the lighthouse, and exploring the beach.

From Yaquina Head, head south into Newport and get yourself checked into your hotel. Around lunch time, stop and find a place to eat along Newport's **Bayfront** ★★ (p. 272), where tourists and fishermen from the city's fishing fleets share the street, and you can find seafood restaurants where your fish was caught just hours before.

After lunch, make your way to **Yaquina Bay State Recreation Site** ★★★ (p. 275) on the north side of the Yaquina Bay Bridge. Here you'll find a very unusual lighthouse, the oldest one on the Oregon coast, dating from 1871. It is really a two-story wooden house with a light atop the roof. This lighthouse, one of the nine lighthouses on the Oregon coast, was decommissioned in 1873, when the Yaquina Head Lighthouse went into operation. You can tour the living quarters of the lighthouse keepers and enjoy a magnificent view over Yaquina Bay.

Newport has one of the most famous bridges on the Oregon coast, a long, graceful span designed by Conde McCullough in the 1930s. Cross the Yaquina Bay Bridge and follow the signs to the **Oregon Coast Aquarium** ★★★ (p. 273), the top tourist attraction on the Oregon coast and one of the finest aquariums on the West Coast. You'll pass through an outdoor aviary with tufted puffins, and outdoor pools with sea otters, before reaching the fascinating tanks within. Give yourself a minimum of 2 hours here.

It's been a full day, but what about a walk on a beach before dinner? Head to the **Nye Beach** ★★★ (p. 273) neighborhood, where you'll find access to a long, wonderfully strollable beach. Newport was one of the first resort towns on the Oregon coast, and many of the homes in Nye Beach date from the early 1900s.

Day 4: Yachats/Cape Perpetua/Heceta Head

Let's be frank: from here to the California border, it's mostly about the scenery. There won't be any more big indoor tourist attractions such as the Oregon Coast Aquarium. But there will be areas of exceptional beauty, another lighthouse or two, and some interesting and at times charming coastal communities along the way. Like **Yachats** ★★★ (p. 277), 24 miles (39 km) south of Newport on—what else?—U.S. 101. This artsy and affluent village—it's pronounced *Yah*-hots, by the way—has no commercial development of any kind. But with an oceanfront like this, who wants commerce? If the magic of the place strikes your fancy, make it your overnight stop for day 4. Then all you need to do is enjoy the sea and the scenery. The beach here is marked by lots of rocky coves and tide pools, and you can beachcomb to your heart's content, because along this part of the Central Oregon coast, agates frequently wash ashore after storms. At its southern end, the town of 700 people is lorded over by the towering bulk of Cape Perpetua, a 600-foot-high headland that juts out into the Pacific and is the highest point on the Oregon coast.

At some point during the day, drive south another 2½ miles to the **Cape Perpetua Scenic Area** ★★★ (p. 278). There is enough variety and natural splendor here to keep you occupied for hours. Recreational possibilities here include breathtaking, headland-top vistas, hiking trails through old-growth forest areas, shoreline tide pools, and a natural formation called the Devil's Churn, where the force of incoming waves into a narrow fissure sends geysers of seawater high into the air.

Back in Yachats, you'll be pleased to find that there are several top-quality restaurants, including **Ona** ★ (p. 282), **Heidi's Italian Dinners** ★★ (p. 282), and **Luna Sea Fish House** ★★ (p. 282).

Day 5: Florence/Oregon Dunes/Cape Arago Highway/Bandon

On the morning of day 5, head south again, up and over Cape Perpetua, and keep your eyes peeled for **Heceta Head Lighthouse State Scenic Viewpoint** ★★★ (p. 279). And have your camera ready. Heceta Head Lighthouse sits at the edge of a rocky promontory above the crashing waves of the Pacific. You can also, seasonally, park and head in for a closer look at the lighthouse and the Victorian-era lighthouse-keeper's house that is run as a B&B. and where yours truly had a possible run-in with the resident ghost. (The **Heceta Head Lightstation** ★★, p. 279, would be a good alternative to staying in Yachats.)

Just 1 mile south is one of the Oregon coast's most long-lived natural attractions, **Sea Lion Caves** ★★ (p. 279). It's a wildlife-viewing area, but it's set up as a tourist attraction. An elevator takes you down to a viewing window that lets you peer into a giant sea cave that happens to be the largest sea lion rookery on the West Coast.

In another 6 miles (10 km) look for a highway sign marked **Darlingtonia State Natural Site** ★ (p. 279). Although it's very small, this little marshy area beside U.S. 101 is eerily beautiful. It's the home of the rare and endangered *Darlingtonia californica*, or cobra lily, a carnivorous (just insects, don't worry) plant that is found only in boggy coastal areas in southern Oregon and northern California. The mass of emerald-green plants rise up from the marshy ground like thousands of eyeless cobras. I hope this gorgeous little patch of ancient nature is not going to disappear because of a changing climate.

Your lunch stop is the old river town of **Florence** ★★ (p. 283), which got its start during the days of the California Gold Rush, when timber and provisions were floated down the Siuslaw River to be transported to San Francisco. The Siuslaw flows right through the heart of town, and the wooden storefront buildings along its riverside promenade give this small coastal community some real historical character. The most prominent building on Bay Street, a white false-fronted former general store, is now the **Bridgewater Fish House and Zebra Bar** ★ (p. 284), a good lunch spot. After lunch, spend a few minutes strolling along Bay Street before heading south.

Although there's no official boundary line, the South Coast begins just south of Florence, and so does the **Oregon Dunes National Recreation Area** ★★ (p. 285). If you like sand dunes, this 50-mile (80 kmz) swath of towering dunes between the shoreline and U.S. 101 is an area you will want to explore. Otherwise, continue south past Coos Bay, the largest town on the coast, and look for the turn-off for the **Cape Arago Highway** ★★★ south of town.

You may not want to stop at all of the three state parks on the Cape Arago Highway, but they are all worth visiting. The first is **Sunset Bay State Park** ★ (p. 288), a sheltered cove beneath high sandstone cliffs with such (relatively) placid waters that you can actually take a dip there—it's really the only place along the entire coast where swimming is possible. The second is **Shore Acres State Park** ★★★ (p. 288), an extremely rare formal garden created almost a century ago by a shipping tycoon who lost his house and fortune but left behind his rose gardens and sunken pond garden to be rediscovered decades later and restored to their former glory. This is probably the only rose garden you'll ever visit where you'll hear seals barking in the distance. A trail leads down from the garden to a gorgeous little cove with a white-sand beach. The third spot is **Cape Arago State Park** ★★ (p. 289), where offshore rocks, part of the Oregon Islands National Wildlife Refuge, harbor hundreds of seals and seabirds.

Another natural treasure in the area, little visited but absolutely sublime, is the **South Slough National Estuarine Research Reserve** ★★★ (p. 289), the first federally protected estuary in the U.S. (1971) with thousands of acres of unspoiled coastal habitat along the Coos river.

After you've visited one, or all, of the state parks, continue south on U.S. 101 to **Bandon** ★★★ (p. 289), where you'll overnight. A stop is all the nicer because Bandon has some very good restaurants: **Alloro Wine Bar** ★★★ (p. 294), **The Loft Restaurant & Bar** ★★ (p. 295), **Lord**

Bennett's Restaurant and Lounge ★ (p. 295), and **The Gallery** ★★★ (p. 295), the fine-dining restaurant at Bandon Dunes Golf Resort.

Day 6: Bandon/Gold Beach

If you're a golfer, Bandon may have been your destination all along. Golfers from all over the world descend on this small community to play at the five world-class links courses at **Bandon Dunes Golf Resort** ★★★ (p. 292). But this coastal community, located where the Coquille River spills into the Pacific, was popular with visitors long before the duffers took over. At one point Bandon was called the "Playground of the Pacific" because, in the days before roads, passenger steamers would stop here on their trips between San Francisco and Seattle. The attractions of those days are gone, mostly wiped out in a 1936 fire. What remains is what was always here—a magnificent beach with a whole gallery of giant offshore rocks and monoliths that have been given fanciful names like Face Rock (it resembles a face staring up), Table Rock, the Sisters, and Cat and Kittens. You can see Bandon's famous rock formations—they are all part of the Oregon Islands National Wildlife Refuge—and walk on the beach, by taking Beach Loop Drive to **Bullards Beach State Park** ★★★ (p. 294). You'll also be able to visit the **Coquille River Lighthouse** ★★★ (p. 291), a sturdy, octagonal building with a light that cast its first beam in 1896.

As you head south from Bandon on U.S. 101 you will pass—surprise?—cranberry fields. This area is also known as the Cranberry Capital of Oregon. Many of the cranberries are now part of huge corporate farming operations, but during the harvest season, from mid-October to early December, some local farmers offer tours of their family-owned cranberry growing operations; check the website **www.thebandonguide.com** for dates, times and locations. If you visit Bandon the second weekend in September you can enjoy the annual Cranberry Festival. Otherwise, you can find homemade cranberry products at **Misty Meadows** (p. 291), a store on the east side of the highway a few miles south of Bandon that sells jams and jellies made with local cranberries and fruits.

Then it's another 59 miles (95 km) to **Gold Beach** ★★★, where the fabled Rogue River empties into the sea. You have a few good choices for dinner: **Spinner's** ★★ (p. 301), **Nor'wester Seafood** ★ (p. 301), or the quirkier **Anna's by the Sea** ★★ (p. 300).

Day 7: Gold Beach/Brookings

Make a jet-boat trip up the Rogue your special experience of the day. Three different excursions cover three different lengths of the Rogue, but the best is the 104-mile (167 km) wilderness whitewater trip that takes you up to the wild and scenic part of the river. Along the way you will stop for lunch at one of the rustic fishing lodges along the river. It's an exciting and memorable 7-hour trip, and it's suitable for all ages. See p. 300 for more about booking with **Jerry's Rogue Jets** (p. 297); the two other jet-boat trips last 4½ and 5 hours. If ripping along in a jet boat is not your style, there are several fabulous hiking options in the Gold Beach area. The easily walkable **Frances Schrader Old Growth Trail** ★★★ (p. 297) takes you to a rare stand of giant trees; the **Rogue River Walk** ★★★ (p. 297) traverses a scenic area above the famous river.

The 28 miles (45 km) between Gold Beach and Brookings is a scenic corridor with several pull-outs and state parks where you can stop to enjoy the view. Approaching Brookings, U.S. 101 moves down to skirt the ocean on a flat coastal plain. This area of the South Coast is referred to as the Banana Belt of Oregon because the climate and somewhat sheltered topography fosters the growth of semi-tropical plants. Most of the nation's Easter lilies are grown here.

To reach inland I-5 from Brookings, take U.S. 199 east to Grant's Pass. From there, it's a straight shot back up to Portland, a 246-mile (396-km) trip that takes about 5 hours.

SEATTLE, PORTLAND & THE OREGON COAST FOR FAMILIES

The Pacific Northwest is often cited for its family-friendliness. If you are traveling with children, you will indeed find that there are many child-oriented things to see and do in Seattle, Portland, and along the Oregon coast. This is a great opportunity to introduce your kids to nature—perhaps as you learn more about it yourself. You can, without too much difficulty, go carless in Seattle and Portland, and you can get from one city to the other via train or bus if you don't want to drive. For the last 2 days, however, you will need a car

---

Days 1–2: Seattle

A stroll on the Seattle **waterfront** ★★★ (p. 74) is a lovely way to start your visit. Here you'll find the **Seattle Aquarium** ★★ (p. 74), a great place to spend the morning getting your kids acquainted with the animals that live in and around Puget Sound. Have a seafood-themed lunch at Ivar's Fish Bar ★★ (p. 110) right on the waterfront. In the afternoon, enjoy one of the boat tours offered by **Argosy Cruises** (p. 77). There's a 1-hour harbor cruise, and longer cruises to Lake Washington and the Hiram M. Chittenden Locks.

Instead of or in addition to a boat tour with Argosy, you can take a passenger ferry over to **Bainbridge Island** or a shorter ride on the King County Water Taxi to **Alki Beach** in West Seattle for a fun and easy excursion that gives kids the excitement of being on the water. A lot will depend on the age of your children and their patience levels. While you're on the waterfront, the kids will certainly spot its newest attraction, the **Seattle Great Wheel** ★★ (p. 76). This is the tallest Ferris wheel on the West Coast; the ride takes about 15 minutes

On **day 2**, get on the vintage **monorail** downtown at Westlake Center and whiz north to **Seattle Center,** built for the 1962 World's Fair. At Seattle Center, you can zoom up to the observation deck of the **Space Needle** ★★ (p. 79). Younger kids will find plenty of play activities at the **Pacific Science Center** ★ (p. 78), which has some great animatronic dinosaurs and a lovely butterfly house, in addition to many other hands-on science-related exhibits. I personally find the **Museum of Pop Culture** (p. 78) to be vastly over-rated and overpriced, but if your kids are avid, and I mean avid, Trekkies or lovers of sci-fi, they will probably enjoy it. More fun, and educational, would be to head over to Pioneer Square and take the **Underground Tour** ★★★ (p. 79) through the tunnels of Seattle's past.

Days 3–4: Portland

On day 4, head down to Portland. If you're not driving the 178 miles (286 km), there are other transportation options including Amtrak, which makes the Seattle-Portland run several times a day and takes about 3½ to 4 hours. By car, without traffic snags, the trip takes about 3 hours.

Explore the City of Roses via MAX, the light-rail train, and/or the Portland Streetcar—kids love both of them (so do I, and I'm not a kid). Start your first day at **Washington Park** ★★★ (p. 157). Your kids may not flip for the roses in the **International Rose Test Garden** ★★★ (p. 158), but they will enjoy the little train that runs from the garden to the **Oregon Zoo** ★★★ (p. 158). It's a large zoo and you can easily spend 3 hours there.

On your second day, head over to the east side via MAX or Portland Streetcar to visit the **Oregon Museum of Science and Industry (OMSI)** ★★ (p. 163), a hands on museum, with an actual submarine to tour. After exploring the museum, if it's summer and the weather is nice, take an excursion to **Oaks Amusement Park** ★★ (p. 163), about 5 miles south on the Willamette River. One of the last remaining "old-style" amusement parks in the U.S., Oaks Park was built in 1905 for the Lewis and Clark Exposition. The rides are pretty gentle and there is a famous roller rink where you can all rent skates and spin around to music. If you're not driving, I'd suggest you take an Uber or taxi over to Oaks Park. This is a lovely way to end the day, and you can even walk from the park right down to a beach on the Willamette River.

Day 5: Portland/Columbia Gorge National Scenic Area/Mount Hood

On day 5, head east out of Portland on I-84. The spectacular **Columbia Gorge National Scenic Area** ★★★ (p. 218) begins just a few miles east of downtown. For maximum excitement, take the **Columbia Gorge Historic Highway,** the first scenic road to be built in Oregon back in the 1920s. The old highway takes you up to **Crown Point** ★★ (p. 220), where the breathtaking view up and down the gorge extends for over 30

Seattle, Portland & the Oregon Coast for Families

miles. Continue on the old highway and you will pass a handful of gorgeous waterfalls until you come finally to the tallest and most dramatic waterfall of all—**Multnomah Falls** ★★★ (p. 221). You can walk up an easy paved path to view the thundering falls from fairly close up. Just after Multnomah Falls, the old highway ends and returns you to I-84. Continue your expedition up and over **Mount Hood** ★★★ (p. 214) to **Timberline Lodge** ★★★ (p. 216), where you can hike or have lunch or dinner. Returning to Portland will take you about 2 hours. (But please note: a September 2017 wildfire in the Gorge scorched the area around Eagle Creek, and the full extent of damage was not known as of press time.)

Day 6: Cannon Beach

Today, it's time to introduce the family to the Pacific Ocean. From Portland it takes about 2 hours to get to **Cannon Beach** ★★★ (p. 249) by car. Make this an overnight trip, and be sure to book your hotel or campsite well in advance if you are traveling in the summer. With towering

Haystack Rock jutting up from the shore, this flat, sandy beach is one of the best along the entire coast for long beach walks. And I have never yet met a kid who didn't love running, walking, skipping, and digging on Cannon Beach.

In addition to getting all revved up on the beach, try to pay a visit to **Ecola State Park** ★★★ (p. 252) at the north end of town, where you'll find miles of beach and forested hiking trails with stunning ocean views.

Day 7: Three Capes Scenic Loop/Depoe Bay/Newport

Continuing south from Cannon Beach on U.S. 101, in about 40 miles (64 km) you'll come to Tillamook. Just south of Tillamook, watch for the turnoff for the **Three Capes Scenic Loop** ★★★ (p. 259), a 35-mile loop drive that winds past three giant headlands (one with a lighthouse) with viewpoints, beaches, picnic areas, and hiking trails. From Pacific City, where the loop drive ends, continue south on U.S. 101 for 34 miles (55 km) to tiny **Depoe Bay** ★★ (p. 267), where you can take a whale-watching expedition out onto the open waters of the bay to view (hopefully) giant gray whales on their annual migration. Again, it's best to reserve a whale-watching trip in advance of your arrival. What could be more thrilling than to spot a spouting whale!

From Depoe Bay, continue on U.S. 101 for 13 miles (21 km) to **Newport** ★★★ (p. 270). If you've taken the Three Capes Loop and done a whale-watching excursion in Depoe Bay, you won't be arriving in Newport until later in the afternoon. Spend the rest of the day strolling along the busy **Bayfront** ★★ (p. 272) and the charming, artsy neighborhood of **Nye Beach** ★★★ (p. 273) with its long, sandy beach.

There's a lot more to enjoy in Newport before you head back to Portland. Start your explorations at the not-to-be-missed **Yaquina Head Outstanding Natural Area** ★★★ (p. 274), site of Yaquina Head Lighthouse, one of the most photogenic and easily accessible lighthouses on the Oregon coast. The offshore monoliths here are wildlife refuges where you'll see seals and hundreds of sea birds. You'll need to allot about an hour-and-a-half to explore the beach and the lighthouse.

Finally, if you haven't taken the whale-watching trip, and if you're up for another aquarium head south, back into Newport and across the Yaquina Bay Bridge. On the south side of the bridge, you'll find Newport's star attraction, the **Oregon Coast Aquarium** ★★★ (p. 273). It's one of the great aquariums of the West Coast—yes, it's better than Seattle's—and a place you don't want to rush through. Give yourself at least a couple of hours. The facility concentrates on local and West Coast marine life and has a walk-through aquarium with sharks and outdoor exhibits with tufted puffins, sea otters and sea lions. It will be a fun and memorable way to wind up your Pacific Northwest adventures.

SEATTLE, PORTLAND & THE OREGON COAST IN CONTEXT

3

Here's the question I am most frequently asked by people who haven't been to the Pacific Northwest: "I've heard it's wonderful out there, and that the people are so nice, but what's it really like?"

The simple answer, of course, is that it's pretty wonderful and that the people are, in fact, so nice that strangers will smile and say hello to you on the street. That's more likely to happen in Portland than Seattle, I must point out. The pace in both cities is fairly relaxed—but more relaxed in Portland than Seattle.

What it all boils down to is that most of the people who live in Seattle and Portland *want* to live there. More and more of them have moved there from somewhere else, and despite the urban travails that plague all of us, those transplants tend to remain. It's called "livability," a nebulous but seductive word if there ever was one. Nature plays a big role, and mobility (Seattle and Portland traffic notwithstanding), safe neighborhoods, an arts-and-culture scene, good food, good beer, and good wine all play a part. Perhaps marijuana does, too, though I'd hate to think that it's the cannabis that is drawing record numbers of visitors and newbies to the Northwest. What I can say, unequivocally, is that both Seattle and Portland are absolutely booming.

The Oregon coast is an entirely different kettle of fish, as it were, and people gravitate toward it not so much as a potential place to live (unless it's a second home) but as a place where the ocean is in charge and Nature calls the shots.

You'll learn more about Seattle, Portland, and the Oregon coast in the chapters that follow. Here I want to give you, first of all, a general snapshot of Portland, Seattle, and the Oregon coast as they are today. After that, I've provided a short, general history of the region, followed by historic timelines for both Seattle and Portland. All this material is meant to give you a deeper understanding of the past and present of the Pacific Northwest.

SEATTLE TODAY

If you distilled Seattle's history into five points, it would read something like this: a great fire (1889), a frenzied gold rush (1897), a World's Fair (1962), the formation of an airplane company called Boeing (1917), and the emergence of a game-changing computer company named Microsoft (1975). Wait, we'd better add a sixth point: the arrival of Amazon's massive corporate headquarters in 2017.

Of course, the city's location on Puget Sound didn't hurt, either, because that gave Seattle access to the Pacific Ocean. For much of its relatively brief existence, Seattle was the wettest, wildest city in the Pacific Northwest, a gritty maritime depot that became the jumping-off point for tens of thousands of Alaska-bound gold-seekers.

Puget Sound was Seattle's gateway to the rest of the world until the railroad arrived, at which point it became a major freight terminus by land and a port by sea. Then Boeing and the aerospace industry came along, and Seattle took to the air, too. A wartime boom in shipbuilding and plane manufacturing bumped the city's fortunes up another notch. The Seattle World's Fair of 1962 was another turning point, an event that introduced this unique and atmospheric city on Elliott Bay to a new generation of visitors. Then came computers and software, personified by Bill Gates and Paul Allen of Microsoft, and Seattle was again "discovered" by the rest of the world. Now it's the hub of worldwide retail and communications giant Amazon. That's some track record. The city experienced phenomenal growth in the 1980s, and turned into a Big City where people raced around with a Starbucks cup in one hand and a cellphone in the other. And during the real-estate bubble it did more than bubble—it frothed, and it continues to froth today.

SEATTLE DATELINE

1792 British Capt. George Vancouver explores and names Puget Sound.

1851 The Denny party makes land at Alki Point (now West Seattle) and endures a harsh first winter with the help of local Indian tribes.

1852 Denny and gang move their town to the more temperate east side of the Puget Sound; "Doc" Maynard names the town Seattle after Chief Sealth of the local Duwamish tribe.

1853 Henry Yesler opens the first of many sawmills to be built in the Puget Sound area.

1861 The University of Washington (then called Territorial University) opens its doors to students.

1863 *The Gazette*, later to become the *Seattle Post-Intelligencer*, publishes its first newspaper.

1878 Seattle gets its first telephones.

1885 Chinese immigrants are forced out of Seattle.

1889 Twenty-five blocks of Seattle burn to the ground in the Great Fire, prompting a frenzy of building—several feet higher than the original shops had been.

So it's safe to say that when Seattle sees an opportunity, it takes it and runs, flies, jumps and builds. This opportunistic nature is what makes for its highs and lows, its booms and busts, and gives it the big city edge and push that Portland looks at half-longingly yet doesn't quite covet. The collapse of the over-inflated real estate market was like a temporary blip in Seattle's now-reheated economy, which has sent property values soaring even higher. Microsoft co-founder Paul Allen's Vulcan company continues with its ambitious redevelopment of Seattle's South Lake Union neighborhood, now home to the world headquarters of Amazon and attracting new biotech companies. With the economy currently booming, Seattle building and development is back in full swing. Cranes rise up all over the South Lake Union area, which is quickly integrating with the rest of urban Seattle, and other building and rebuilding projects are advancing in downtown. Down on the waterfront, the new Seattle Great Wheel started spinning in 2013 and instantly became a new landmark.

The biggest building project in Seattle right now is not about construction but deconstruction. The horrible Alaskan Way Viaduct, put up in the 1950s directly next to the waterfront, effectively cutting off downtown from the harbor, is *finally* being dismantled. A giant tunnel will make the endless and noisy traffic along the waterfront disappear and the site of the viaduct will become a giant waterside park. This is a huge operation and will completely transform the city by bringing it back to the waterfront where it began. But what is actually happening with this highly anticipated project remains rather mysterious and the opening date is never fixed. Bertha, the huge boring machine used to create the tunnel, was damaged in 2014, and that delayed the project for months, perhaps years. In the meantime, lots of work has been done along the waterfront, including a new pavement with glass windows to let in light and help baby salmon find their way to the sea and back again.

1889 Washington becomes the nation's 42nd state.

1893 Transcontinental Great Northern Railway reaches Seattle.

1897–1899 Seattle booms as a stopping-off point for Klondike gold-seekers.

1907 Pike Place Market brings farmers and customers directly together.

1914 Smith Tower is completed in Seattle, becoming the tallest building west of Ohio.

1917 Construction is complete on the Lake Washington Ship Canal (Hiram M. Chittenden Locks).

1917 Boeing Airplane Co. is launched.

1919 Eddie Bauer's first store opens.

1921 The Alien Land Law is passed in Washington, restricting Asian immigrants' rights to own or lease property.

1924 Native Americans are made U.S. citizens.

1926 Seattle elects the first woman mayor of any major U.S. city.

1940 Lake Washington Floating Bridge becomes the first of its kind in the world.

continues

Despite its reputation for foot dragging when it comes to public transit, Seattle finally got a light-rail system up and running (maybe taking a hint of transportation-savvy Portland) and has continued to expand it. The Link light-rail that runs between Seattle Tacoma International Airport and downtown Seattle opened a new extension north to Capitol Hill and the University of Washington in 2016. Seattle also has two new streetcar lines, one that runs from downtown to South Lake Union and another that runs north-south along Broadway on Capitol Hill. But Seattle also continues to have some of the worst traffic congestion outside of L.A. (or, now, Portland). If you visit with a car, avoid driving at rush hour or, better yet, avoid driving altogether.

Aerospace giant Boeing, once the region's biggest employer and the engine that drove Seattle's economy, is still in the running but technology (Microsoft) and order-fulfillment (Amazon) are now key players in Seattle's future.

Like any big city in a global economy, Seattle has seen its share of boom and bust. That, in fact, is what Seattle is all about. Economy aside, however, Seattleites continue to share a common interest in the outdoors, and it is this interest that tends to dominate the character of the Puget Sound region. If winters are long, gray, and rainy, well, you just put on a colorful rain jacket, fill the travel mug with a double tall latte, and head for the hills anyway.

PORTLAND TODAY

Given its popularity today, you'd never know that up until about 20 years ago, Portland remained the undiscovered city of the West Coast. Frankly, many Portlanders liked it that way. If you lived in Portland, you knew how special it was and you didn't want to see it spoiled.

The slogan "Don't Californicate Oregon" applied to Portland as much as to the rest of the state. Portland wasn't a wealthy city, like San Francisco to the

1942 FDR signs order sending Japanese Americans from the West Coast to internment camps; thousands in the Seattle area are forced to abandon their homes and businesses.

1942 Seattle native Jimi Hendrix is born.

1949 Sea-Tac International Airport is opened.

1951 Washington State Ferries begin service on Puget Sound.

1954 First successful passenger jet, Boeing 707, takes off.

1962 Seattle builds Space Needle and monorail for the Seattle World's Fair.

1966 Boeing builds 747 assembly plant.

1970s Boeing layoffs devastate the local economy.

1971 Starbucks opens its first shop.

1975 Microsoft is founded by Bill Gates and Paul Allen in Albuquerque; three years later it moves to Seattle area.

1979 The Seattle SuperSonics win the NBA Championship.

south, and it didn't have the boom-or-bust bravura of Seattle to the north. Although it was the largest inland port on the West Coast, Portland didn't feel connected to the larger world, the way the ocean seaports of San Francisco and Seattle did. It was a quiet, lovely, liberal, and somewhat insular mid-sized metropolis that people loved for its family-friendly neighborhoods and proximity to the ocean, mountains, and high desert. It was a place where residents were aware of their environment and proud of their gardens. The city was progressive enough to install a light rail system back in the 1970s and turn a six-lane highway into downtown's Tom McCall Waterfront Park. There was a large countercultural scene to keep things quirky, and a homegrown arts scene that produced some fine work.

As you might have guessed, it was all of these elements that eventually attracted a new wave of residents and visitors to Portland. The city has gone from hippie to hipster, and from provincial to pop-culture icon, in a very short time. Watching its evolution has been nothing short of astonishing.

This change has led to a kind of inner-city density and sometimes stress the likes of which house-with-big-yard Portland has never known. It has also led to clogged streets and traffic jams that may be the norm in other cities but are frustrating and bewildering to Portlanders accustomed to getting from one side of town to the other in 10 minutes instead of 90. I suppose micro-apartments and crowded streets are inevitable when you surround yourself with a green belt to help fight sprawl, as Portland did decades ago. It's worked beautifully, and saved the endlessly gorgeous countryside around the city from turning into an endlessly depressing suburban parking lot. But in the process it has squeezed more people and cars into Portland.

I'm just being honest here. Portlanders used to pride themselves on being low-key and off-the-radar. You never went into a bar, coffee shop, or restaurant and had to listen to an actor talking about their agent, or a developer

1999 A World Trade Organization conference in downtown Seattle prompts riots, property damage, and accusations of police misconduct.

2001 The Nisqually Earthquake causes extensive damage to many older Seattle buildings.

2004 Washington elects Christine Gregoire in tightest governor's race in U.S. history, giving Washington state three women in its powerful political positions—two U.S. senators and the governor.

2009 The Link light rail station opens at SeaTac Airport, providing rapid mass transportation from downtown Seattle to the airport.

2010 A new law makes it a primary offense to text message or hold a cellphone to your ear while driving.

2012 Washington State legalizes same-sex marriage and possession of small amounts of marijuana for recreational use; the two events are in no way related.

continues

talking about real-estate prices. That just wasn't Portland. But now it is. Some folks love the endless construction that is transforming the main thoroughfares, and the buzzy food and coffee scene. Others wonder if all this growth might end up diminishing the very qualities that draw people to Portland. It's quite a balancing act to keep the charm that was here while building for what's to come: more people.

You don't come to Portland for its cultural benefits so much as to just hang out. It is the cultural capital of the state, of course, and has long had a lively arts and literature scene. **Powell's City of Books** is one of the finest bookstores in the world and is justifiably a tourist attraction by itself. The **Oregon Symphony** can hold its own with any orchestra in the country. Portland was one of the originators (after Seattle) of the phenomenally popular First Thursday gallery-hopping idea. The garage-band and grunge music scene is not as feverish as it was a decade ago, but it's still out and about.

THE OREGON COAST TODAY

Well, one thing that will never change is the relatively unspoiled beauty of the Oregon coast. Or will it? In the recent past, the biggest environmental controversies had to do with turning ports on the Oregon coast into shipping depots for the export of natural gas and coal to Asia. There is real reason for concern, and battle lines have been drawn between environmentalists and concerned citizens on one side, and eager developers and business interests on the other. That issue has quieted down but threatens to re-erupt at any moment.

The two ports in question are Astoria and Coos Bay. Both cities came into prominence as processing centers (lumber and salmon) and shipping depots, and both have suffered economic hardship since the decline of the timber and fishing industries.

2013 After two terms as state senator and 11 years as state representative, Ed Murray becomes the first openly gay mayor of Seattle. Work begins on the demolition of Alaskan Way, a 1950s-era viaduct that blights the downtown waterfront; a new tunnel will carry traffic, and streets adjacent to Seattle's waterfront will eventually be transformed into a park.

2014 Seattle Seahawks beat the Denver Broncos and win the Super Bowl. An estimated 700,000 people celebrate the event at a downtown parade.

2014 Massive mudslide in Oso, 60 miles northeast of Seattle, kills 41 people, destroys dozens of homes, a highway, and a river.

2017 Online sales giant Amazon opens three high-rise office towers as part of its world headquarters in South Lake Union area of Seattle. By 2018, this huge development project will include three biospheres enclosing gardens and amenities.

Astoria is undergoing a renaissance right now, thanks in part to its proximity to Portland, the arrival of seasonal cruise ships (which means thousands of passengers disembark to spend a few hours in Astoria), and to the stock of fine old houses and buildings that are being rediscovered and restored. The ball got rolling with the restoration of the Liberty Theater—now a downtown performing arts center—and the Union Hotel, and the establishment of a number of new restaurants and cafes.

Some of us remember the Oregon coast as it used to be, a place of simple, unpretentious, damp-smelling beach cottages, indifferent or nonexistent restaurants (even with all that seafood), and nothing but the roar of the surf and the crackle of a fire to keep you company. Those were the Days Before Casinos (DBC), when you went to the coast to dig for razor clams, look for Japanese glass floats, and walk on deserted beaches. You can still do all three, but you can also go to casinos in Lincoln City and Coos Bay, have meals of a caliber previously unknown, and watch the crashing waves from the warm, bubbling safety of a Jacuzzi.

Everything really started to change along the coast in the late 1980s and early 1990s, when people from elsewhere (read: with money) started to realize how incredibly magnificent this coastline is—a place where you could watch herds of 50-ton gray whales passing by on their annual migration from the Bering Sea to Baja Mexico. The amount of new building and development along the North Coast, the coast closest to Portland, has been enormous. But if you haven't been to the Oregon coast before, you probably won't notice it the way some of us do.

And let's shout hooray for the People's Coast. That's what the Oregon coast is called. Why? Because not an inch of it is privately owned. By which I mean *the entire shoreline*—with its clean, beautiful, white-sand beaches, towering

PORTLAND DATELINE

1805 Lewis and Clark camp along the Columbia Slough in what is now North Portland.

1830s The site of present-day Portland is a small clearing in the woods on the west side of the Willamette River, used by Chinookan Indian tribes, including the Multnomah and the Clackamas, and French-Canadian fur traders traveling between Oregon City and Fort Vancouver, the Hudson's Bay trading headquarters on the Columbia River.

1842 Opening of the Oregon Trail.

1843 Asa Lovejoy and William Overton file a joint land claim for the riverside clearing. Overton, who lacked the 25¢ filing fee, later sells his portion to Francis W. Pettygrove.

1845 Pettygrove wants the new townsite to be called Portland, after his hometown in Maine. Lovejoy wants it to be called Boston. The two New Englanders flip a coin and the site—today's downtown—becomes Portland.

continues

headlands, dramatic offshore monoliths, secretive little coves, crashing waves, seals and seabirds. It's all there for you to enjoy.

The towns and communities on the coast are small and can no longer rely on commercial fishing and logging to keep them afloat. So tourism plays a major role in the coast economy. There's been an uptick in the number of upscale places to stay and the number of good restaurants to eat. When inlanders hear that a huge storm is due to hit the Oregon coast, with 100mph winds, they don't anticipate disaster—they get on the horn and make a reservation at their favorite oceanfront hotel.

The arrival of Bandon Dunes Golf Resort in 1999 put the small Central Coast town of Bandon on the map—for golfers, anyway. People arrive from all over the world to play at these 5 links courses that are modeled after the heritage courses in Scotland and Ireland. "Golf as it was meant to be played" is the resort's tag line. That means you walk the course and play in natural surroundings. It's really pretty great.

But playing in natural surroundings is, ultimately, what the Oregon coast is all about. A trip to the coast (or "the beach" as Oregonians say) is partly about being cozy despite the elements, and partly about reconnecting with those very elements. It's a powerful, unpredictable place, the Oregon coast, and if you give yourself up to it, and don't complain about the wind and the weather, you will enjoy a wonderful world of natural wonders.

A BRIEF HISTORY OF THE PACIFIC NORTHWEST

PREHISTORY Native American habitation in the Pacific Northwest dates back at least 10,000 years, perhaps 12,000 years. Before the arrival of

1848 Congress establishes the Territorial Government of Oregon, and nearby Oregon City becomes its capital the following year.

1850 Under the Donation Land Act, males arriving in the Oregon Territory by Dec. 1, 1850 can claim 320 acres (twice that amount for married couples) if they agree to cultivate the land. As a result, land-hungry pioneers—about a quarter of them from New England and New York—pour into the Willamette Valley. In 1848, when Lovejoy and Pettygrove platted the first streets, Portland had a population of about 80. Two years later, an 1850 census counted just over 800 people. Stumps of fir trees cut down for the newly laid-out streets gave rise to the city's first nickname: Stumptown. Puddletown, another nickname, referred to the rain-filled tracks and ruts.

1851 The city officially incorporates, and the first plank road (part of today's Canyon Rd.) is laid, providing a trade route between Portland and the farmlands of the Tualatin Valley.

Euro-Americans in the region that is today's Washington and Oregon, there were hundreds of distinct Northwest tribes speaking over 50 languages. Between the 1780s, when white explorers and traders first began frequenting the Northwest coast, and the 1830s, when the first settlers began arriving, the Native American population of the Northwest was reduced to perhaps one-tenth of its historic numbers, wiped out by diseases such as smallpox, measles, malaria, and influenza. Native Americans had no resistance to these European diseases and entire tribes were decimated by fast-spreading epidemics.

Throughout the Puget Sound region, numerous small tribes subsisted primarily on salmon, halibut, shellfish, and whales. Seafood was a mainstay of the native diet. Cedar trees were the most important building material. Rot-resistant cedar wood and bark was used to build longhouses, large canoes, even clothing. The natural abundance of the region allowed many of tribes to develop complex cultures. The Columbia River tribes became the richest of the Oregon tribes through their control of Celilo Falls, the richest salmon-fishing area in the Northwest. Today, Celilo Falls are gone, inundated by the water impounded behind The Dalles Dam, completed in 1957, and the enormous fish runs that were a mainstay of Native American life have been reduced to a trickle of what they once were.

THE AGE OF EXPLORATION Though a Spanish ship reached what is now southern Oregon in 1542, the Spanish had no interest in the gray and rainy Northwest coast. Nor did famed British buccaneer Sir Francis Drake, who in 1579 sailed his ship the *Golden Hind* as far north as the mouth of Oregon's Rogue River. Drake called off his explorations in the face of what he described as "thicke and stinking fogges."

In 1775, Spanish explorers Bruno de Heceta and Juan Francisco de la Bodega y Quadra charted much of the Northwest coast, and though they found

1850s–'80s Situated at the head of navigation on the Willamette, Portland quickly emerges as the region's best site for the development of a shipping port and trade center. Passengers and cargo from the East Coast come in ships sailing around Cape Horn; trade extends across the Pacific to China. The California Gold Rush and the rapid growth of San Francisco fuel the city's river-trade economy. The region's vast conifer forests provide lumber for ships and the new towns springing up throughout the West.

1860s A second wave of immigrants, this time from Ireland, Germany, China, Japan, England, Scandinavia, and Canada, starts to arrive in 1860. East Portland, where most of the city's newly arrived foreigners and transient workers live, is laid out in 1850–51 and incorporated in 1870; it remains a separate town until it being annexed by the City of Portland in 1891.

1872–1873 Disastrous fires destroy all of Portland's early wood-framed waterfront buildings and lead to

continues

the mouth of the Columbia River, they did not enter it. Four of the Oregon coast's most scenic headlands—Cape Perpetua, Heceta Head, Cape Arago, and Cape Blanco—bear names from these early Spanish explorations.

Within a few years, Spanish claims to the region were challenged by English and Russian traders who found the native people eager to trade furs. The Chinese would pay astronomical prices for Northwest furs, especially sea otter pelts. By 1785, the fur trade between the Northwest and China was well underway, with the British asserting a claim to the Pacific Northwest. The Spanish and English teetered on the brink of war, but a settlement was reached in 1792 with Captain George Vancouver serving as English envoy. Vancouver (Vancouver, Washington; Vancouver, British Columbia; and Vancouver Island were all named for him) spent time exploring and mapping much of the Northwest. Though he passed off the Columbia River as unimportant, he sailed up the Strait of Juan de Fuca and discovered a large inland sea that he named Puget Sound, after one of his lieutenants.

A new player entered the Northwest arena of trade and exploration in the person of American trader Robert Gray. Risking a passage through treacherous sandbars, Gray sailed his ship, *Columbia Rediviva,* into the mouth of the long-speculated-upon Great River of the West, which he named the Columbia River after his ship. Gray's discovery established the first American claim to the region.

Thomas Jefferson decided that the United States needed to find a better route overland to the Northwest and commissioned Meriwether Lewis and William Clark to lead an expedition up the Missouri River in hopes of finding a single easy portage that would lead to the Columbia River. Beginning in 1804, the members of the Lewis and Clark expedition (the Corps of Discovery) paddled up the Missouri, crossed the Rocky Mountains, and paddled

the construction of brick buildings with cast-iron facades and structural supports. A significant number of late-19th-century cast-iron commercial buildings—more, in fact, than in any other city west of the Rockies—still remain in the Yamhill and Skidmore/Old Town districts along 1st, 2nd, and 3rd avenues.

1880–1900 Major expansion continues as immigrants from around the world arrive, hoping to make their fortunes in shipping, farming, lumber, and gold.

1883 Arrival of the first transcontinental railroad.

1887 With the completion of the Portland-San Francisco rail line, the city's reliance on the river begins to diminish. East and West Portland are joined by the Morrison Bridge, the first span across the Willamette.

1889 Downtown streets are illuminated by electric street lamps fueled by hydropower from Willamette Falls in Oregon City.

1890s The business center gradually shifts to the west, away from the waterfront, as fashionable new buildings and public institutions begin to rise on downtown's Morrison Street in the 1890s.

down the Columbia River to its mouth. After spending the very dismal, wet winter of 1805 to 1806 at Fort Clatsop (p. 240), near today's Astoria, Oregon, the expedition headed back east. Discoveries made by the expedition added greatly to the scientific and geographical knowledge of the continent.

In 1819, the Spanish relinquished all claims north of the present California-Oregon state line, and the Russians gave up their claims to all lands south of Alaska. This left only the British and Americans dickering for control of the Northwest.

SETTLEMENT Only 6 years after Lewis and Clark spent the winter at the mouth of the Columbia, employees of John Jacob Astor's Pacific Fur Company managed to establish themselves at the mouth of the Columbia River on the Oregon side at a site they called Fort Astoria. With the decline of the sea otter population, British fur traders turned to beaver and headed inland up the Columbia River. In 1824, the Hudson Bay Company (HBC) established its Northwest headquarters at Fort Vancouver, 100 miles up the Columbia near the mouth of the Willamette River (today's Vancouver, Washington). Between 1824 and 1846, when the 49th parallel was established as the boundary between British and American northwestern lands, Fort Vancouver was the most important settlement in the region. (Today, a replica of the fort has been built and is part of the Vancouver National Historic Reserve.)

By the 1830s, the future of the Northwest had arrived in the form of American missionaries, and in 1840, a slow trickle of American settlers began making the 2,500-mile journey across the continent. Their destination was the Oregon Country, which was promoted as a veritable Eden with wide expanses of land just waiting to be claimed. The small population of retired trappers, missionaries, and HBC employees living at Fort Vancouver and nearby Oregon City formed a provisional government in anticipation of the land-claim

1900–1910 Portland's population doubles.

1905 Lewis and Clark Exposition is held in northwest Portland. The city's growth is due, in large part, to this well-planned exercise in city boosterism that introduced tens of thousands of visitors to the city. In 1903, to help prepare for the event, noted Boston landscape architect John Olmsted (stepson of Frederick Law Olmsted, who designed New York's Central Park) is hired to design a site plan for the exposition and to develop a citywide park plan.

1905–1929 Early land claims are subdivided as the city experiences two major real-estate booms, one from 1905 to 1913 and another from 1922 to 1928. Electric trolleys carry people throughout the downtown area and to new east-side flatland neighborhoods such as Sellwood, Ladd's Addition, and Irvington, Portland's first "streetcar suburbs." More affluent Portlanders built homes in the "highlands" of southwest and northwest Portland on streets that curve around and rise in sharp switchbacks up the hills.

continues

problems that would arise with the influx of settlers to the region. The losers in the land grab that ensued were, of course, the Native Americans who had lived, fished, and hunted the land for untold generations.

In 1844, Oregon City became the first incorporated town west of the Rocky Mountains. This outpost in the wilderness, a gateway to the fertile lands of the Willamette Valley, was the destination of the wagon trains that began traveling the Oregon Trail, and which each year brought more and more settlers to the region. When all the land in the Willamette Valley was claimed, settlers began fanning out to different regions of the Northwest, and during the late 1840s and early 1850s many new towns, including Seattle and Portland, were founded.

Subsequent demand for territorial status and U.S. military protection brought about the establishment of the first U.S. territory west of the Rockies. Although the line between American and British land in the Northwest had been established in 1846 at the 49th parallel (the current U.S.-Canada border), it was not until 1848 that Oregon was finally given U.S. territorial status. Washington had to wait until 1853 to officially become a territory. Oregon became a state in 1859, Washington in 1889.

In 1881, the first transcontinental railroad reached Spokane, in eastern Washington, and finally linked the Northwest with the eastern United States. In 1893, trains reached Seattle. The arrival of the railroads (and, earlier, steam ships) led to a great leap forward for the development of Washington and Oregon No longer a remote wilderness, the Pacific Northwest began to attract industry.

INDUSTRIALIZATION & THE 20TH CENTURY From the very beginning of Euro-American settlement in the Northwest, the region based its growth on a short-sighted, resource-extractive economy. The early fur traders

Tall commercial buildings with steel frames and distinctive white terra-cotta facades with classical detailing were constructed along the major downtown streetcar lines.

1929 Construction of the seawall on the Willamette River ends the floods that were a regular occurrence in downtown Portland since the city's founding.

1930s Construction in Portland comes to a virtual standstill.

1941–1945 The demand for workers in Portland's shipyards creates a phenomenal wartime boom. Men and women are brought in by chartered trains from the East Coast and employed by the Kaiser shipbuilding yards in Vancouver, Washington and Portland. At the peak of wartime production in 1943–1944, metropolitan Portland counted some 140,000 defense workers. The city's population leapt from 501,000 to 661,000. A significant number of these workers were African-Americans who settled in North and Northeast Portland.

1942 FDR signs order sending Japanese Americans from the West Coast to internment camps;

completely wiped out Washington's and Oregon's sea otter population (which has since been reestablished, with otters from Alaska, off the Olympic Peninsula) and the beaver population after that. Lumber and salmon, the two natural resources that Washington and Oregon had in the greatest abundance, were both exploited relentlessly, and the history of the timber and salmon-fishing industries ran parallel to one another for more than a century. At the close of the 20th century, both industries had arrived at similar situations—severely depleted wild resources that required government intervention to preserve the remaining old-growth forests and wild salmon populations.

The 1897 gold rush in Alaska and the Klondike brought great prosperity to Seattle. However, trees were still the foundation of the state's economy. Nurtured on steady rains, Douglas fir, Sitka spruce, western red cedar, and hemlock grew as much as 300 feet tall. Washington's first sawmill began operation near present-day Vancouver, Washington in 1828, and between the 1850s and 1870s, Washington sawmills supplied the growing California market as well as a limited foreign market. When the transcontinental railroads arrived in the 1880s, mills began shipping to the eastern states. Oregon, too, cut down its trees and overfished its rivers, exporting both by ship to San Francisco during the gold rush years and to worldwide markets for more than 100 years.

At the outbreak of World War I, more than 20% of the forestlands in the Northwest were owned and being clear-cut by three companies—Weyerhaeuser, the Northern Pacific Railroad, and the Southern Pacific Railroad—and more than 50% of the workforce labored in the timber industry.

The timber industry has always been extremely susceptible to fluctuations in the economy and experienced a roller-coaster ride of boom and bust throughout the 20th century. Boom times in the 1970s brought on record-breaking production that came to a screeching halt in the 1980s and 1990s,

thousands in the Portland area are forced to abandon their homes and businesses.

1948 A catastrophic flood completely destroys Vanport, a suburban Portland city built to house 17,500 wartime workers.

1950s–1960s As streetcars vanish and a car culture takes over, many of Portland's oldest buildings and west-side neighborhoods are demolished to make way for highways and parking lots. The city's first high-rise towers appear on the downtown skyline in the late 1960s.

1970s Portland's reputation as one of the country's best-planned cities dates back to 1972 when the Downtown Plan was approved by the city council. This detailed agenda, which set forth new strategies for land use, commercial development, architecture, and public transportation, resulted in a series of urban renewal projects that effectively reclaimed the downtown area for pedestrians. In the following years, a new light-rail system was built; a transit mall was constructed; a parking lot in

continues

first with a nationwide recession, and then with the listing of the northern spotted owl as a threatened species. By the 1980s, environmentalists, shocked by vast clear-cuts on public lands, began trying to save the last old-growth trees. Today the battle between the timber industry and environmentalists continues.

Just as trees in the Northwest were huge and plentiful, so too were the salmon. These fish, which spend their adult lives in the ocean before returning to fresh water to spawn, were the dietary mainstay of Northwest Native Americans for thousands of years before the first whites arrived in the region. However, within 10 years of the opening of the first salmon cannery in the Northwest, the fish population was severely depleted. In 1877, the first fish hatchery was developed to replenish dwindling runs of salmon. Salmon canning reached a peak on the Columbia River in Astoria in 1895 and on Puget Sound in 1913. Later in the 20th century, salmon runs would be further reduced by the construction of numerous dams on the Columbia and Snake rivers. Although fish ladders help adult salmon make their journeys upstream, the young salmon heading downstream have no such help, and a large percentage are killed by the turbines of hydroelectric dams. One solution to this problem has been the barging and trucking of young salmon downriver. Today the salmon populations of the Northwest are so diminished that entire runs of salmon have been listed as threatened or endangered.

For over 150 years, agriculture has played a major role in Oregon's economy. Tree-cutting in the Willamette Valley south of Portland began in the 1850s and turned what had been a vast oak savannah into some of the richest farmland in the world. The subsequent damming of Northwest rivers for hydropower and irrigation also made it possible to farm high-desert lands east of the Cascades in both Oregon and Washington. Crops in the Willamette

the center of the downtown was refashioned into a public piazza; and the highway that ran along the downtown waterfront was replaced by Tom McCall Waterfront Park. Historic structures were preserved, and ordinances limited the height of new buildings, protecting views of the mountains.

1971 Nike founded. Oregon becomes the first state to pass a bottle bill mandating a refundable deposit on beer and soft-drink cans and bottles.

1980 Mt. St. Helens erupts, coating the city with volcanic ash but otherwise doing no damage.

1980s Portland's Urban Growth Boundary is designed to preserve neighboring farmlands and open spaces from unchecked commercial development.

1980s–1990s The city is roiled by several virulent and costly anti-gay rights battles fomented by a homophobic right-wing "Christian" group called the Oregon Citizens Alliance (OCA).

Valley now include vegetables, hazelnuts and grass seed. Orchards in the Hood Valley continue to produce rich harvests of cherries, peaches, apples, apricots and pears. Giant agribusiness is taking over much of the farming, but smaller, independent, artisanal farms are also flourishing: you'll find their products and produce at farmer's markets throughout the summer. In recent decades, Willamette Valley plant nurseries have become a multi-billion-dollar industry, supplying trees, shrubs, bulbs and innumerable garden plants to gardeners throughout the world.

In 1916, William Boeing launched a small seaplane from the waters of Seattle's Lake Union and laid down the foundation for what would become the Seattle area's single largest employer: Boeing. The company became a major employer in Seattle when it began manufacturing B-17s and B-29s during World War II and today continues to be one of the largest employers in Washington state. However, this has had its drawbacks for Seattle. The city's fortunes were for many years so closely linked to the aircraft manufacturer that any cutback in production at Boeing had a devastating ripple effect on the local economy. And Boeing, because of its power, holds Seattle hostage in terms of tax breaks, threatening to move elsewhere if their demands are not met. However, with the global ascendancy of Bill Gates's software giant Microsoft (based just outside Seattle), and the arrival of online shipping giant Amazon, which now has its world headquarters in the South Lake Union area of Seattle, the Seattle economy has become more tech-driven.

In Portland, Kaiser Steel played a major role in the shipbuilding boom of World War II. The war brought over 100,000 workers to the Portland shipyards—including the city's first African-Americans—and many of the new arrivals stayed after the war was over. Today, the Portland economy is a mixture of high-tech, advertising, health care, and sports apparel and equipment.

1993 Soon after a geologic study verifies the existence of two earthquake faults under the city, a quake measuring 5.6 on the Richter scale rocks the entire region. Its epicenter is located about 30 miles south of Portland. Since that time, city seismic codes have been updated to make buildings more earthquake-resistant.

1996 A flood causes considerable damage in low-lying areas north and south of downtown. The same year, rapid snowmelt and above-average rainfall combined with tree-cutting and erosion results in mudslides and property damage in residential sections of the West Hills.

1998 Oregon is the first state to legalize euthanasia with the Death with Dignity Act.

2004 With no advance warning, Multnomah County (Portland) issues marriage licenses for same-sex couples. Over 3,000 couples rush to get married.

continues

International swimwear giant Jantzen started in Portland in 1916 and for decades its name and logo were emblazoned on a famous sign at the west end of the Burnside Bridge (today Jantzen is owned by Perry Ellis International). Portland-based Columbia Sportswear began in 1938 and became a nationally recognized brand in the 1990s. Nike was founded in Portland in 1971. Underarmour is now building a headquarters in Portland, too.

WHEN TO GO

Seattle & Portland

In Portland and Seattle we like to say that summer begins on July 5th. It's mostly true—or as true as anything can be in an age of rapid climate change. So if you are planning to spend your holidays in either city, and want to maximize your chances for sunshine and warm weather, July through mid-September are the best months to visit.

The summers truly are splendid and life in both cities moves outdoors as much as possible. The parks are verdant, the gardens are glorious, there are outdoor festivals galore, and you can sit outside comfortably all evening, until it gets chilly enough for a sweater. That's the beauty of summer in Seattle and Portland—no matter how hot the day, the nights cool down (sometimes by 30 degrees) so that you need a blanket. And when it's hot, it's dry, not humid, because the hot air comes from the deserts east of the Cascades and flows down the Columbia Gorge and through the valleys to Portland and Seattle. The downside when it gets very warm and the winds stop blowing is inversion and air pollution. Ick. One can only hope the record-setting 100-plus temps combined with smoke from forest fires in summer, 2017, were an anomaly. Over 33,000 acres in the scenic Columbia River Gorge were destroyed when

2005 After a court challenge and public referendum, Multnomah County rescinds same-sex marriage ruling and sends all married same-sex couples refund checks for their license fees.

2008 Oregon Legislature passes the Oregon Family Fairness Act, which makes it possible for same-sex couples to legally establish a domestic partnership.

2008–2013 Nationwide recession results in unemployment figures in Portland that are among the highest in the nation. It doesn't matter. People keep moving to Portland anyway.

2014 Voters pass Measure 91 allowing for the non-medical cultivation, use and sale of marijuana.

2014-2017 Portland grows at a phenomenal rate, resulting in a citywide building boom and traffic problems.

2017-2018 Summer forest fires in the Columbia Gorge and southern Oregon burn over 150,000 acres and blanket the region with smoke that makes the air quality in Portland the worst in the country. Sixth and final season of the TV series Portlandia airs. People continue to pour into Portland.

a 15-year-old boy threw illegal firecrackers into a beautiful but tinder-dry canyon, and the Chetco Bar fire in the Siskiyou Mountains in southwestern Oregon burned over 150,000 acres, turning the air in Brookings, near the California border, into an unhealthy haze. Those of us who live out here know that the climate is changing because we've seen it change in our lifetimes. What we don't know is the long-term effect of that change on Oregon.

Nobody but gardeners believe me when I tell them that Portland and Seattle actually have what is considered a Mediterranean climate. What this means is that it generally rains almost constantly in one form or another from mid-October through June, with plenty of clear days and periods of truly great weather along the way. From November through March, the temperature remains temperate, rarely dipping below freezing and usually hovering in the 40s. (Again, honesty compels me to report that there were several days of snow and freezing temps in 2017.) By April it starts warming up, though the precipitation persists, and by May and June temperatures rise to the mid-70s with (of late) sudden spikes into the 80s and even low 90s (all temperatures in Fahrenheit). Plants love this climate, and so do gardeners.

June is when Portland holds its famous Rose Festival, but I've often thought it should be called the Rain Festival because it always seems to rain during the two big parades. Why not celebrate what makes life out here so green?

But can I convince you to come earlier in the year? If you are a gardener, in love with the egregious excesses of spring, come to Seattle or Portland in late April through May. You will be dazzled by the exuberance of spring in the Northwest, as cherry trees burst into pink bloom; camellias open; rhododendrons, azaleas, magnolias, and dogwoods flower; and the tulip fields near Portland and Seattle rival—maybe surpass—those in Holland. Yes, the springtime weather is very changeable, and you will have rain, but you also won't miss the floral fecundity of these two cities when spring is at its freshest and richest.

The heavenly summer weather often stretches out through September, sometimes into early October. This, too, is a fabulous time to visit because of the bounty you'll find at the farmers markets and the cultural pleasures you'll enjoy as the performing arts venues swing into performance mode.

As for winter—well, if you're a skier or snowboarder, you know why winter would be a good time to come. The mountains (Mount Rainier and Mount Hood) are generally ready to chairlift skiers up their slopes by mid-November—though I hasten to add that in recent years the snow has been arriving later and staying longer.

Oregon Coast

The Oregon coast is entirely different. Expect rain and wind year-round, though less of it from June through September. Many visitors come to the Oregon coast in July and August expecting clear skies and windless days only to find the beaches enveloped in thick fog. That's because hot inland air draws a wet blanket of moisture from the Pacific eastward and hangs it up on the coastal mountain ranges. The summer fogs, more common along the South Coast, don't dissipate until late afternoon, and then come back the next day. But you may be lucky, and certainly if you visit in the summer it will be warmer—but not warm enough to go without a fleece or sweatshirt. That's because of the winds blowing in off the Pacific.

My advice, weather-wise, is to visit from early- to mid-September. But, as you will hear me pointing out throughout this guide, you don't visit the Oregon coast because of the weather, you visit it because of the nature. The best months for spotting migrating gray whales are mid-December to mid-January and March through June (some whales hang around all summer long). There are headlands where winter winds are clocked at 140mph, and storms so fierce that they reconfigure entire beaches. We love it. It's the Oregon coast.

SEATTLE

A quick 360-degree scan of the horizon on a sunny day in Seattle will present a mesmerizing view, over the shimmering waters of Puget Sound to the snow-covered peaks of the Olympic Mountains to the west and the massive mound of Mount Rainier to the east. In between, there's the iconic Space Needle and all the towers of downtown Seattle and, more recently, the South Lake Union area where Amazon is building its corporate world headquarters.

With sights like these, it's easy to see why people would want to live and visit here. The 1993 movie *Sleepless in Seattle* helped to romanticize a city that nobody saw as particularly romantic—until the tech boom brought Seattle into the national consciousness and gave the city and its residents a new edge of sophistication. It's now Tech Central and, inevitably, is losing some of its old, gritty flavor.

Although the weather in Seattle is notoriously drizzly, the residents for the most part don't let precipitation stand between them and the outdoors. The temptation is too great to head for the hills, the river, the beach, the Sound, or the San Juan Islands. Consequently, life in Seattle tends to revolve as much around parks, gardens, waterfronts, and other outdoor spaces and activities as it does around such traditional urban pastimes as shopping, the performing arts, and dining. And when the city's green spaces aren't wild enough to satisfy, there is something wilder close at hand. If you live in Seattle, you can be in a national park, national forest, or state park within an hour or two.

The region's outdoors aesthetic does not, however, preclude a strong support of the arts. The **Seattle Opera** is one of the finest companies in the country (well known for its stagings of Wagner's *Ring* cycle), as is the **Seattle Symphony**, which performs in downtown's **Benaroya Hall.** Seattle also has the best theater scene on the West Coast. (It's where playwright August Wilson got his start and made his mark before Broadway.)

The visual arts aren't overlooked either. The **Seattle Art Museum** had to add new galleries to accommodate its ever-growing collections, which provide an overview of regional art from the carved, woven, and painted objects created by native tribes of the Pacific Northwest to the shimmering Modernist canvases of the 1950s Northwest School and on to major works by world-renowned artists today. **Chihuly Garden and Glass,** a flamboyant museum dedicated exclusively to the work of Tacoma-born glass-master Dale Chihuly opened next to the Space Needle in 2012. The **Olympic Sculpture Park,** a free, open-air sculpture museum at the north end of the waterfront, features works by an international roster of sculptors.

The city supports other museums, too, and two old ones are being given new homes. The **Burke Museum of Natural History and Culture** at the University of Washington and the **Nordic Heritage Center** in Ballard are both scheduled to move into brand new museums in 2019 and 2018, respectively.

Seattle's location amid great natural splendor and its up-to-the-nanosecond trendoid consciousness adds to the pleasures and excitement of a visit. Yes, it does rain a lot, but it's *supposed* to. That's what this northerly Pacific Northwest maritime climate west of the Cascades does: It precipitates. Without those gray, misty days with the smell of saltwater in the air, it wouldn't be Seattle—and you might not appreciate the clear days, when the Olympic Mountains glow far across the water to the west and Mount Rainier appears majestically to the east. Nor, without the precip, would you see as much green. If you look around at the green coniferous forests that are another characteristic of this moist, temperate climate, you'll understand why Seattle's nickname is The Emerald City. The name has nothing to do with Oz, but there is a natural and self-made magic to the place. It's casual and caffeinated, definitely into good food, arts, and recreation, and offers visitors plenty to see and do, along with a great big dose of fresh sea air.

ESSENTIALS

ARRIVING

BY PLANE **Seattle-Tacoma International Airport (Sea-Tac),** 17801 International Blvd. (www.portseattle.org/sea-tac; ✆ **206/787-5388**), is located about 14 miles south of downtown Seattle.

By far the most convenient way to get to downtown Seattle from the airport is by taking Sound Transit's (www.soundtransit.org) **Link Light Rail** service, which runs from the airport to the University of Washington with several stops along the way. Trains operate from 5am to 1am Monday through Saturday and 6am to midnight on Sundays, arriving and departing every 7½ to 15 minutes, depending on the time of day. The SeaTac Airport Station, reached by a covered walkway, is located on the fourth floor of the airport garage (follow signs from the terminals). The adult fare from the airport to one of the downtown stops is $2.25 to $3.25 (fare is based on distance traveled); seniors pay $1 to $1.75, depending on zones traveled. Buy your ticket from a vending machine on the platform before you board. The trip takes approximately 35 minutes.

It's slower and far less convenient, but you can also take a bus operated by **King County Metro Transit** (http://metro.kingcounty.gov) into the city. Sound Transit Metro bus stops are located on International Boulevard (State Hwy. 99) and South 176th Street by the Link Light Rail Station. To reach them, take the walkway through the north end of the fourth floor of the Airport Parking Garage to the Sound Transit Link Light Rail Station and exit to

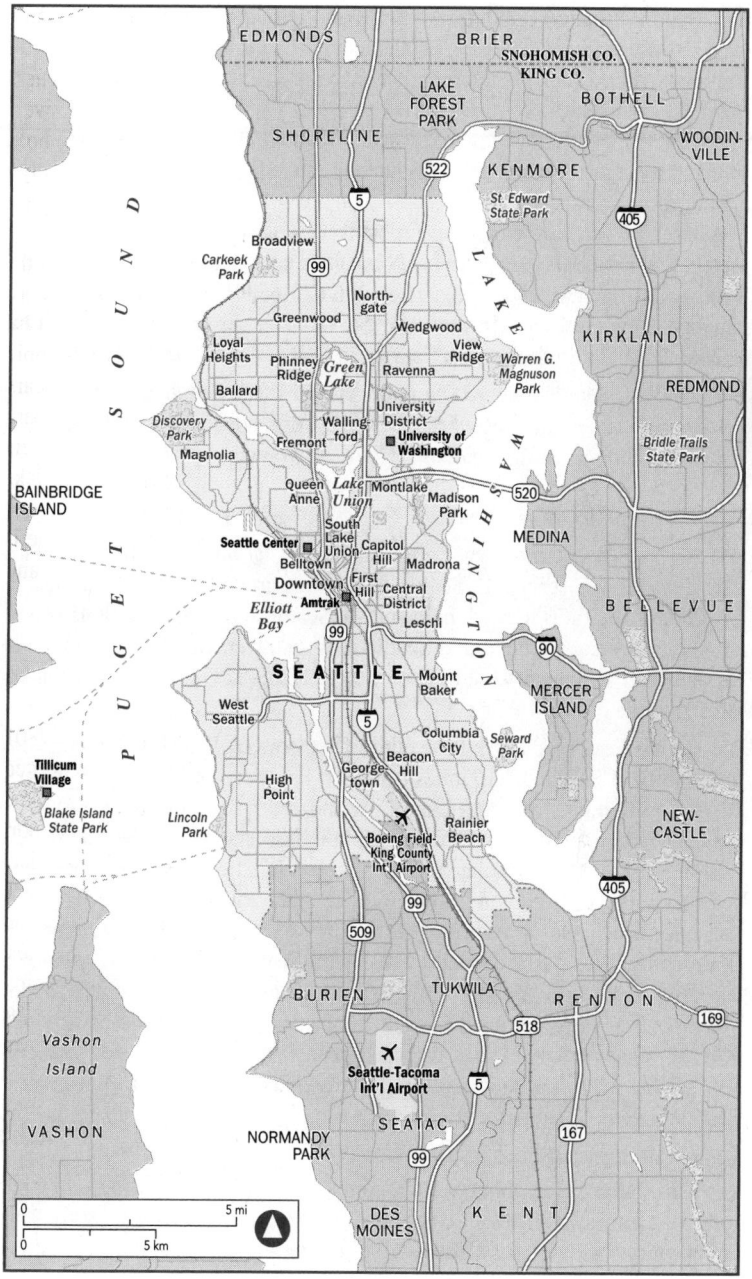
EDMONDS
BRIER
SNOHOMISH CO.
KING CO.
LAKE FOREST PARK
BOTHELL
SHORELINE
WOODINVILLE
522
KENMORE
St. Edward State Park
405
5
Broadview
Carkeek Park
99
North-gate
Greenwood
Wedgwood
View Ridge
KIRKLAND
Loyal Heights
Phinney Ridge
Green Lake
Ravenna
Warren G. Magnuson Park
REDMOND
Ballard
University District
Discovery Park
Walling-ford
University of Washington
Fremont
Magnolia
Bridle Trails State Park
BAINBRIDGE ISLAND
Queen Anne
Lake Union
Montlake
Madison Park
520
South Lake Union
Seattle Center
Capitol Hill
MEDINA
Belltown
Madrona
Downtown
First Hill
Central District
Amtrak
Elliott Bay
Leschi
BELLEVUE
99
90
SEATTLE
Mount Baker
MERCER ISLAND
West Seattle
5
Columbia City
Seward Park
Beacon Hill
Tillicum Village
George-town
High Point
Blake Island State Park
Lincoln Park
Rainier Beach
NEW-CASTLE
Boeing Field-King County Int'l Airport
405
99
509
BURIEN
TUKWILA
RENTON
518
169
Vashon Island
Seattle-Tacoma Int'l Airport
5
VASHON
SEATAC
NORMANDY PARK
167
99
0
5 mi
0
5 km
DES MOINES
KENT
PUGET SOUND
LAKE WASHINGTON

International Boulevard. Departure times are shown on information signs at the bus stop, or you can pick up printed bus timetables at the Ground Transportation Information Booth on the Baggage Claim level near door number 16 (across from baggage carousel 12). Fares are the same as for the Link Light Rail; pay with cash upon boarding, but have the exact fare because driver's do not make change.

By car, the trip to downtown Seattle takes about 30 minutes, depending on traffic. All major rental car agencies have counters in the lower, baggage claim area of the airport.

A metered taxi ride from the airport to downtown Seattle costs approximately $50 to $60. However, many companies now charge a lower fixed rate. **Yellow Cab** (www.yellowtaxi.net; ✆ **206/622-6500**), available outside the baggage claim area, and **Horizon Car Service** (www.seattleairport-taxi.com; ✆ **206/306-2000**) both charge a flat rate of $40 to downtown Seattle.

BY TRAIN Seattle is served by **Amtrak** trains (www.amtrak.com) running north from Los Angeles, San Francisco and Portland, south from Vancouver, British Columbia, and points east. Trains arrive and depart from the newly revamped **King Street Station,** 303 South Jackson St., near the Pioneer Square area of downtown Seattle.

BY BUS **Greyhound** (www.greyhound.com; ✆ **800/345-3109**) provides long-distance bus service to Seattle from cities around the U.S. The Seattle Greyhound Station is located in downtown Seattle at 811 Stewart St. If you're traveling between Portland and Seattle or Vancouver, British Columbia and Seattle, **Bolt Bus** (www.boltbus.com; ✆ **877/265-8287**) offers super-cheap rates and free onboard Wi-Fi.

BY CAR Seattle is 110 miles south of Vancouver, British Columbia, 175 miles north of Portland, 810 miles from San Francisco, 1,190 miles from Los Angeles, 835 miles from Salt Lake City, and 285 miles from Spokane. I-5 is the main north–south artery, running south to Portland and all the way to San Diego, north to the Canadian border. I-405 is Seattle's eastside bypass and accesses Bellevue, Redmond, and Kirkland on the east side of Lake Washington. I-90, which ends at I-5, connects Seattle to Spokane in the eastern part of Washington. Wash. 520 connects I-405 with Seattle just north of downtown and also ends at I-5. Wash. 99, the Alaskan Way Viaduct, is another major north–south highway through downtown Seattle, but it's slated to be removed (when, no one seems to know; work has been delayed) and replaced by a tunnel. All the major car-rental agencies have offices in Seattle and at or near Sea-Tac International Airport.

VISITOR INFORMATION

For more information about Seattle, contact **Seattle's Convention and Visitors Bureau** (www.visitseattle.org; ✆ **866/732-2695** or 206/461-5800). This organization operates the **Seattle Visitor Center** in the Upper Pike Street Lobby of the Washington State Convention and Trade Center, Seventh Avenue and Pike Street (✆ **206/461-5840;** open Mon–Fri and summer weekends

9am–5pm); and the **Market Information Center,** Southwest Corner of 1st Avenue and Pike Street in the Pike Place Market (✆ **206/461-5840;** open daily 10am–6pm). For additional information on other parts of Washington, contact **Washington State Tourism** (www.experiencewa.com; ✆ **800/544-1800**).

Neighborhoods in Brief

Seattle is a maritime city wedged between Elliott Bay in Puget Sound to the west, and giant, freshwater Lake Washington to the east. The freshwater lake is connected to the saltwater Sound by the Chittenden Locks and Lake Union at the north end of downtown. Puget Sound is dotted with islands that are not part of Seattle proper but are bedroom communities served by commuter ferries; the most prominent and populous are Bainbridge Island, Vashon Island, and Whidbey Island.

Downtown This is Seattle's main business district and can be defined roughly as the area from Pioneer Square in the south to around Pike Place Market in the north, and from First Avenue to Eighth Avenue. It's characterized by steep streets, high-rise office buildings, luxury and boutique hotels, and a high density of shops and shopping malls. This is also where you'll find the Seattle Art Museum and Benaroya Hall, home to the Seattle Symphony and the city's major downtown concert venue. Hotels in this area are convenient to Pioneer Square, Pike Place Market, and the Convention Center.

The Waterfront The Seattle waterfront stretches along Alaskan Way from roughly Washington Street in the south to Broad Street and Myrtle Edwards Park in the north. This is the most touristy neighborhood in Seattle, presided over by the Seattle Great Wheel. In addition to the many tacky gift shops, fish-and-chips windows, and tour-boat docks, you'll also find the city's only waterfront hotel (The Edgewater), the Seattle Aquarium, and, at its northern end, the must-see Olympic Sculpture Park.

Belltown This neighborhood, stretching north from Pike Place Market to Seattle Center, is home to the city's liveliest restaurant and club scene and is constantly expanding and redefining itself. There are some good, out-of-downtown shops and a couple of good hotels, including the Warwick and The Ace.

Seattle Center One of the city's tourist magnets, Seattle Center occupies the site of the famous 1962 World's Fair and is still served by a vintage monorail from downtown. Towering above it all is the iconic Space Needle, and here you'll find the Pacific Science Center and Chihuly Garden and Glass. Seattle Center wasn't really a "neighborhood" but in the last couple of years new apartment buildings have gone up on the surrounding streets.

Pioneer Square The Pioneer Square Historic District, known for its restored 1890s buildings, is centered on the corner of First Avenue and Yesler Way. This is the oldest settled part of Seattle, and its tree-lined streets and cobblestone plazas make it the most atmospheric neighborhood downtown. Pioneer Square (which refers to the neighborhood, not a specific square) is full of antiques shops, art galleries, restaurants, bars, and nightclubs; it's also where you'll find the wonderfully entertaining Underground Tour.

South Lake Union At the north end of downtown, extending east of Seattle Center to the southern and western shores of Lake Union, this is Seattle's newest and still developing neighborhood. Most of it is owned and has been developed by Microsoft gazillionaire Paul Allen—but the main corporate presence here is now Amazon, with three new towers and biospheres forming the company's world headquarters. Formerly a low-rise warehouse and industrial area, South Lake Union has been transformed over the last decade into a residential and business neighborhood for high-tech and biotech companies. A streetcar line connects the area to downtown. The Pan Pacific Hotel serves the high-end business side of the neighborhood. The fascinating Museum of History and Industry (MOHAI) is housed in the former Naval Reserve building on Lake Union.

Chinatown/International District Known to locals as the I.D., this small but distinctive neighborhood is home to a large Asian population. Here you'll find the Wing Luke Asian Museum, Hing Hay Park (a small park with an ornate pagoda), Uwajimaya (an Asian supermarket), and many small shops and restaurants. The Chinatown/International District begins around Fifth Avenue South and South Jackson Street.

First Hill Because it is home to several large hospitals, this hilly neighborhood just east of downtown and across I-5 is called "Pill Hill" by Seattleites. First Hill is home to the Frye Art Museum and a couple of good hotels. It is an old Seattle residential neighborhood, too; once grand, now not so but with some nice strollable streets.

Capitol Hill To the northeast of downtown, centered along Broadway near Volunteer Park, Capitol Hill is Seattle's main gay neighborhood and has long been a popular youth-culture shopping and entertainment district. Broadway sidewalks are often crowded, and it is nearly impossible to find a parking space. In recent years, the area has been undergoing a big spruce-up. New condominiums have been built on Broadway, and along 12th Avenue, near the intersection with Pike Street and there are now some good restaurants. Outside its commercial area, parts of Capitol Hill are undeniably attractive, with fine old homes and mansions; Volunteer Park is one of Seattle's great parks and contains a wonderful plant conservatory and the Seattle Asian Museum.

University District This neighborhood in the northeast section of the city surrounding the University of Washington is called the U District for short. Because it's a college neighborhood, it's a good place to find inexpensive ethnic restaurants, pubs, clubs, espresso bars, and music stores. Visitors come to this area to visit the great Washington Park Arboretum and the gorgeous Seattle Japanese Garden.

Queen Anne Hill With its great city and water views, affluent Queen Anne, just northwest of Seattle Center, has long been one of the most prestigious residential areas in Seattle and features some of Seattle's oldest homes. The neighborhood is divided into the Upper Queen Anne and Lower Queen Anne. Upper Queen Anne is very peaceful and abounds in moderately priced restaurants. Lower Queen Anne, adjacent to theaters and Marion Oliver McCaw Hall at Seattle Center, is something of a theater district and has a more urban character.

Fremont If you have time to visit only one neighborhood outside of downtown, make it Fremont. North of the Lake Washington Ship Canal between Wallingford and Ballard, Fremont is home to Seattle's best-loved piece of public art—*Waiting for the Interurban*—as well as the famous *Fremont Troll* sculpture. This is Seattle's most independent neighborhood, filled with eclectic shops and ethnic restaurants. During the summer, there's a Sunday flea market. The neighborhood celebrates its left-leaning vitality with a yearly street fair—watch for the nude bicyclists!

Ballard In northwest Seattle, bordering the Lake Washington Ship Canal and Puget Sound, Ballard is a former (hard-)working-class Scandinavian community that prides itself in its past (the Nordic History Museum is here) and is rediscovering its old urban charms and character. One of Seattle's most enjoyable neighborhoods, Ballard is a great place to discover off-the-beaten-path shops and restaurants. Art galleries and interesting boutiques and shops are set along the tree-shaded streets of the neighborhood's old commercial center, also the site of Ballard's famous Sunday Farmers Market. Ray's Boathouse is probably the best-known of Ballard's restaurants.

The Eastside Home to Bill Gates, Microsoft, countless high-tech spinoff companies, and seemingly endless suburbs, the Eastside lies across Lake Washington from Seattle proper and comprises the cities of Kirkland, Bellevue, Redmond, and a few other smaller communities. As the presence of Bill Gates's mansion attests, there are some pretty wealthy neighborhoods here; but except for Bellevue this isn't an area that draws tourists.

West Seattle West Seattle, across from the downtown port facility, is not just the site of the terminal for ferries to Vashon Island and the Kitsap Peninsula. It's also the site of Seattle's favorite beach, Alki, which is as close to a Southern California beach experience as you'll find in the Northwest. Here, too, is the waterfront restaurant with the best view of Seattle: Salty's on Alki Beach. Seattle's very first white settlers landed on Alki Point, but after a miserably wet winter moved east to the area that would become Pioneer Square.

GETTING AROUND

Seattle is a sprawling city with lots of neighborhoods to explore, a lively downtown core, and a half-carny waterfront that attracts the sea-lion's share of tourist attention. Seattle is notorious for its traffic jams, so avoid them: most visitors find they do just fine here on foot, or using public transportation. Unless you're planning on taking a lot of day trips out of the city, you don't need your own car to enjoy a vacation in Seattle.

BY PUBLIC TRANSPORTATION

BY BUS Seattle's **Metro** (http://metro.kingcounty.gov; ✆ **800/542-7876** in Washington or 206/553-3000) bus and electric trolley system covers all of greater Seattle. Fares are based on zones and travel time. Off-peak fares for all zones are $2.25 for adults, 75¢ for seniors, and $1.25 for ages 6–18. During peak commuter hours, adult fares go up to $2.50 for 1 zone, $3.00 for 2 zones; senior and children fares remain the same. Use exact change and pay on the bus.

BY STREETCAR One line of the **Seattle Streetcar** (www.seattlestreetcar.org) runs from downtown to Lake Union. A newer line Capitol Hill line runs north-south along Broadway to Pioneer Square. The Lake Union line will take you to the Museum of History and Industry on lake Union; the Pioneer Square line will deposit you in the heart of Seattle's historic district, where you'll find the Underground Tour, Smith Tower Observation Deck, and lots of architectural and artistic character. Fares are $2.50 for adults, $1 for seniors, $1.50 for ages 6 to 17.

BY LIGHT RAIL The **Central Link Light Rail** (www.soundtransit.org) runs beneath 3rd Avenue from Westlake Station to Sea-Tac airport, making key downtown stops along the way including Pioneer Square and the Chinatown/International District, and north to Capitol Hill (for strolling, shopping and dining on Broadway) and the University of Washington. Adult fares range from $2.50 to $3.25 depending on distance traveled and time of travel; the senior rate is $1, and youth rate is $1.50.

BY MONORAIL The fastest way to get between downtown and Seattle Center is the historic **Seattle Monorail** (www.seattlemonorail.com; ✆ **206/905-2620**), an elevated train built for the 1962 Seattle World's Fair. It leaves every 10 minutes from Westlake Center shopping mall (Fifth Ave. and Pine St.) and covers the 1¼ miles in 2 minutes, dropping you off near the Space

save money: ALL-DAY REGIONAL TRANSIT PASS

If you're planning to travel around Seattle on public transportation, consider getting an **All-Day Regional Transit Pass** for $8. You can use this pass on all of Seattle's public transportation services except for the monorail and on Washington State Ferries. The downside is that you have to buy an ORCA card (a reusable transit card that costs $5 and can be refilled) in order to download the $8 all-day pass from a vending machine. Seniors can get the all-day pass for $4, and the ORCA card for $3.50.

Needle. The monorail operates daily from 9am to 11pm (in winter, Sun–Thurs 8am–8pm; Fri and Sat 9am–11pm). Departures are every 10 minutes. A one-way fare is $2.25 for adults, $1 for seniors, and 75¢ for ages 5 to 12.

BY WATER TAXI A water taxi runs between Pier 55 on the downtown Seattle waterfront to Seacrest Park in West Seattle, providing access to West Seattle's popular Alki Beach and adjacent paved path. For schedules, check with Metro (http://metro.kingcounty.gov). The one-way fare is $5.25 for adults and ages 6 to 18, $2.25 for seniors.

BY FERRY **Washington State Ferries** (www.wsdot.wa.gov/ferries; ✆ **800/843-3779** or 888/808-7977 in Washington or 206/464-6400) is the most extensive ferry system in the United States. These big passenger and car ferries, used primarily by commuters, won't help you get around Seattle itself, but they offer great options for scenic trips from downtown Seattle to Bremerton (1-hr. crossing) and Bainbridge Island (35-min. crossing), among other destinations. One-way walk-on (no car) fares between Seattle and Bainbridge Island are $8.20 for adults, $4.10 for seniors and ages 6 to 18. You'll pay more, of course, if you take your car.

BY CAR

Leave those four wheels at home. Seattle's traffic congestion is bad, parking is limited (and expensive), and streets are almost all one-way. If you do drive to the city, you'll avoid frustration by leaving your car in your hotel parking garage. The city center is well served by public transportation. Plus, Seattle is very walkable. The only time you'll need a car is if you want to explore beyond Seattle proper—that is, north of Seattle Center, east of Lake Washington, south of the sports stadiums, or to any of the islands in Puget Sound (Bainbridge, Vashon, Whidbey)—or take day trips farther afield, to Mount Rainier or La Conner and the tulips fields of the Skagit Valley. The best strategy is to rent only for the days you're going on these day trips.

PARKING On-street parking in downtown Seattle is expensive and extremely limited. Most downtown parking lots charge $25 to $35 per day, though many offer early-bird or after-5pm specials. Some lots near the Space Needle charge less, and you can leave your car there, then take the monorail downtown. Some restaurants and Pike Place Market merchants validate parking permits. Expect to pay about $40 a day for valet parking at downtown hotels.

DRIVING RULES & TIPS Washington State law prohibits texting or talking on a telephone while driving; stiff fines will result if you are caught. You can make a right turn at a red light after coming to a full stop. A left turn at a red light is permissible from a one-way street onto another one-way street after coming to a full stop.

If you park your car on a sloping street, be sure to turn your wheels to the curb. When parking on the street, check the time limit on your parking meter. During rush hour, be sure to check whether or not your street parking space is restricted.

BY TAXI

Taxis can be difficult to hail on the street in Seattle, so it's best to call or wait at the taxi stands at major hotels. Two reliable companies are **Yellow Cab** (www.yellowtaxi.net; ✆ **206/622-6500**) or **Farwest Taxi** (www.farwesttaxi.net; ✆ **206/622-1717**). The flag-drop charge is $2.60; after that, it's $2.70 per mile. A maximum of four passengers can share a cab; the third and fourth passengers will each incur a surcharge of 50¢. Of course, you can also use **Uber** (www.uber.com) and **Lyft** (www.lyft.com) car services to get around.

ON FOOT

Seattle is a surprisingly compact city. Following north-south avenues, you can easily walk from Pioneer Square to downtown Seattle, Pike Place Market, the waterfront, and Seattle Center. Walking from west to east is another story. When you head east from the waterfront, you will be climbing some steep hills or stairways.

WHEN TO GO

Let's face it: Seattle's weather has a bad reputation. As they say out here, "The rain in Spain stays mainly in Seattle." I wish I could tell you it isn't so, but I can't. It rains in Seattle—and rains and rains and rains. However, when December 31 rolls around each year, a funny thing happens: They total up the year's precipitation, and Seattle almost always comes out behind such cities as Washington, Boston, New York, and Atlanta. So it isn't the amount of rain here that's the problem—it's the number of rainy or cloudy days, which far outnumber those of any of the rainy East Coast cities.

Most of Seattle's rain falls between October and April, so if you visit in the summer, you might not see a drop the entire time. But just in case, you should bring a rain jacket or at least an umbrella. Also, no matter what time of year you plan to visit Seattle, be sure to pack at least a sweater or light jacket. Summer nights can be quite cool, and daytime temperatures rarely climb above the low 80s Fahrenheit (upper 20s Celsius). Winters are not as cold as they are in the East, but snow does fall in Seattle.

Because of the pronounced seasonality of the weather here, people spend as much time outdoors during the summer as they can, and accordingly summer is when the city stages all its big festivals. Because it stays light until 10pm in the middle of summer, it's difficult to get Seattleites indoors to theater or music performances. But when the weather turns wet, Seattleites head for the theaters and performance halls in droves.

Seattle Calendar of Events

I've included a very limited sampling below of what I consider "visit-worthy" events. As I can make no claims to psychic abilities, I can't include all of the nifty happenings that haven't yet been announced.

FEBRUARY

The Chinatown/International District Lunar New Year Celebration. See www.cidbia.org for full info. Celebrations are held at Hing Hay Park (423 Maynard Ave. S.), celebrating the Chinese New Year with dragon kites, music, and dance. February 5, 2019.

The Northwest Flower & Garden Show. Gardening buffs head to this extensive and well-curated show at the Washington State Convention and Trade Center. For details on dates go to www.gardenshow.com.

APRIL

The Skagit Valley Tulip Festival. Held in and around La Conner, an hour north of Seattle (see "Day Trips from Seattle," p. 129), this event shows off the enormous fields of tulips and daffodils blanketing the valley with a kaleidoscope of color, accompanied by festivities. See www.tulipfestival.org for info on exact dates.

MAY

U District Street Fair. The first big street fair of the season takes place in north Seattle's lively University District. More info at www.udistrictstreetfair.org.

Seattle International Film Festival. This renowned fest is held at area theaters from mid-May through early June. You'll find details at www.siff.net.

Northwest Folklife Festival. Always held Memorial Day Weekend at Seattle Center honors, it the many cultures that come together in the Northwest. Learn more at www.nwfolklife.org.

JUNE

Fremont Fair. The third weekend in June is time for the wacky Fremont Fair (www.fremontfair.com), which welcomes the summer solstice with a parade and bicyclists in the buff.

Seattle Pride. At the end of the month comes Seattle Pride (www.seattlepride.org), the city's biggest annual gay, lesbian, bisexual, and transgender festival.

JULY

Fourth of July. On Independence Day, head for Lake Union (www.familyfourth.org) to watch the spectacular fireworks over the lake.

Seafair. This is the biggest event of the summer and it starts in early June and last for a month. Highlights are the hydroplane boat races, the Navy's Blue Angels show and the Torchlight Parade. Full details at www.seafair.com.

Bite of Seattle. Held in mid-July, crowds head to Seattle Center to hear live bands and sample treats and wine from local restaurants. More at www.biteofseattle.com

SEPTEMBER

Bumbershoot. Wrapping up the summer is this Seattle Music & Arts Festival), held at Seattle Center on Labor Day weekend. It's a little bit crazy and a lot of fun. See www.bumbershoot.org.

DECEMBER

Argosy Cruises Christmas Ships Festival. During this annual event, held at various locations throughout the month, boats decked out with Christmas lights parade past a number of beaches.

See www.argosycruises.com.

New Year's Eve. On Dec. 31, Seattleites ring in the new year than with New Year's at the Needle (www.spaceneedle.com), Seattle Center.

EXPLORING SEATTLE

DOWNTOWN

Pike Place Market ★★★ LANDMARK/ICON/SPECIALTY SHOPPING/FOOD SPECIALTIES Home to 140 or so farmers and fishmongers and hundreds of small specialty shops, Pike Place Market is Seattle's number one tourist destination. Add in more than 150 crafts vendors and artists and buskers who serenade the milling crowds and you have one seriously bustling marketplace. When the shuffling shoppers and sensory overload become too much, you can duck in to one of the dozens of restaurants, including some of the city's best, and take a tasty time out. In 2017 the market added 30,000 feet of new space, which encompassed a new **Producers Hall** (shops and restaurants; Top Chef contestant Zoi Antonitsas opened the restaurant **Little Fish** in the new space) and an expanded open-air plaza for stands in the warm weather months, with jaw-dropping views, on clear days, of Mount Rainier.

Pike Place Market, originally a farmers market, was founded in 1907 when housewives complained that middlemen were raising the price of produce. The market allowed shoppers to buy directly from producers and save on grocery bills. For several decades, the market thrived. However, World War II deprived the market of nearly half its farmers when Japanese-Americans were moved to internment camps. With the postwar flight to the suburbs, the market was never able to recover from the war years, and by the 1960s, it was no longer the popular spot it had been. When it was announced that the site was being eyed for a major redevelopment project, however, a grass-roots movement arose to save the 9-acre market, and eventually, it was declared a National Historic District.

Market highlights include Rachel, a giant bronze piggy bank directly below the main neon market sign, and the adjacent Pike Place Fish, a fishmonger

Save Cash with a Seattle CityPass

A **CityPass** (www.citypass.com) is one of the best deals is town. You can visit five popular Seattle destinations for half the cost of regular admission (if you take them all in). Better yet, you don't have to wait in line—this is especially helpful at the Space Needle. The passes, valid for 9 consecutive days, will get you into the Space Needle (where general admission is $26 for adults), Seattle Aquarium (general admission $22 for adults), Pacific Science Center or Chihuly Garden and Glass, Museum of Pop Culture or Woodland Park Zoo, and an Argosy Cruises harbor tour of Elliott Bay. A CityPass costs $79 for adults and $59 for kids ages 4 to 12. You can buy them at any of the included attractions, or order them from the website.

Downtown Seattle Attractions

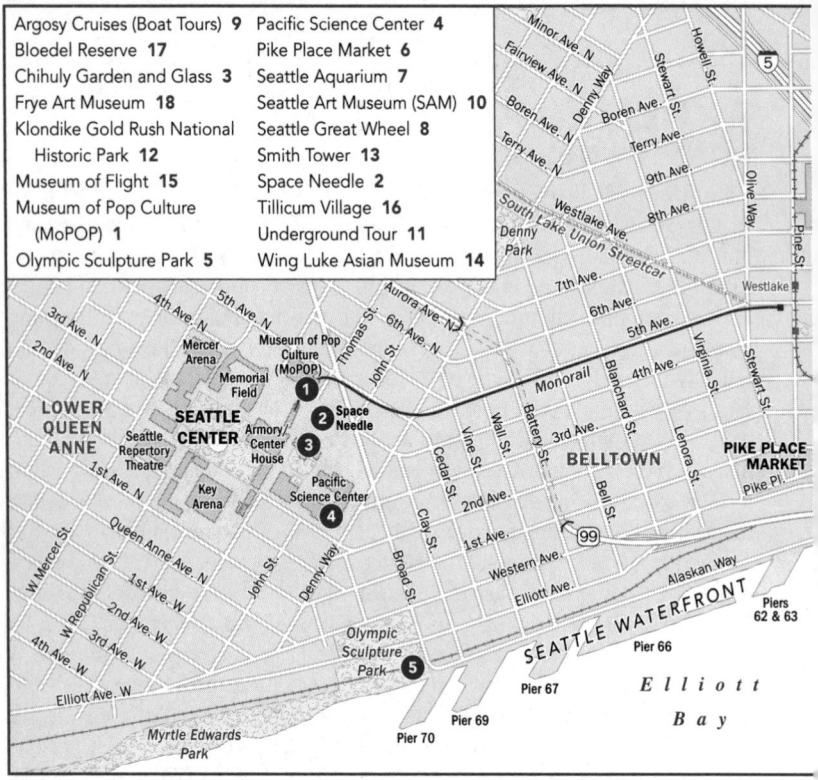

known for its "flying fish." The market's "Gum Wall," in the alley down a flight of stairs from Rachel, is a bit of a sticky subject. No one can agree whether it is art or just a disgusting form of litter. You'll have to decide for yourself.

The market extends along Western Avenue, the street in front, where you'll find still more specialty and ethnic food shops, and if you follow the staircases behind the market (called the Hillclimb), you can get down to the waterfront.

Btw. Pike and Pine sts., at First Ave. www.pikeplacemarket.org. ✆ **206/682-7453.** General business hours daily 10am–6pm; restaurant hours vary. Closed New Year's Day, Thanksgiving, and Christmas.

Seattle Art Museum (SAM) ★★★ ART MUSEUM The postmodern facade by Robert Venturi is clumsy and dated, but the once-cramped gallery spaces have been redesigned and expanded, making a visit to the Seattle Art Museum a real pleasure. Outside, Jonathan Borofsky's giant kinetic sculpture *Hammering Man* pays homage to Seattle's manual-labor workforce. The entrance lobby showcases a big, eye-catching, but rather intellectually shallow installation called *Inopportune: Stage One* by Chinese artist Cai Quo-Qiang

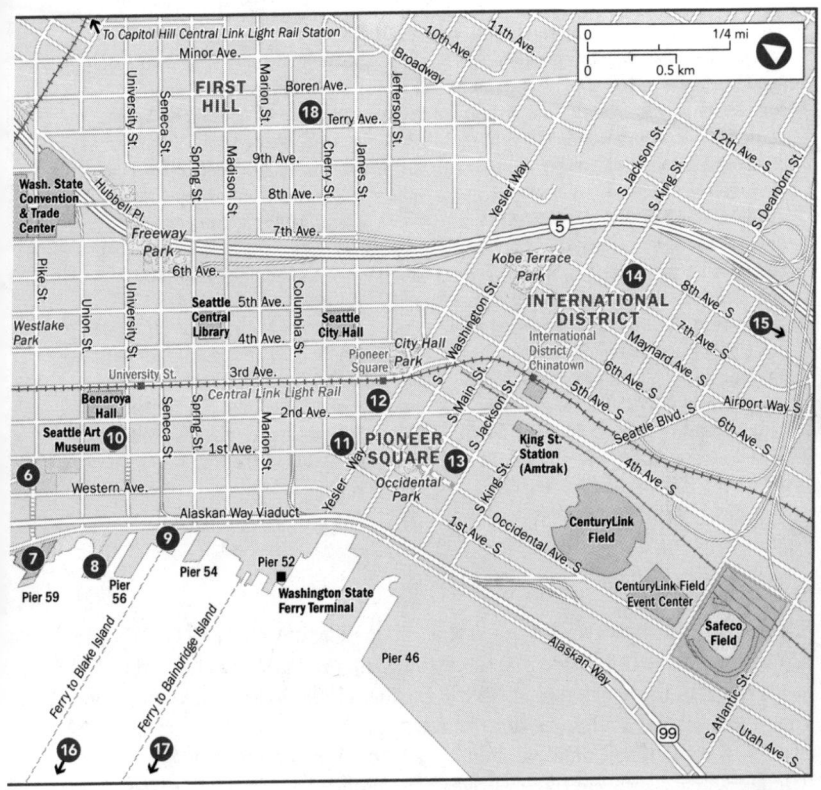

with several full-size cars suspended in a topsy-turvy sequence across the ceiling with colored lights shooting out of their sides. There is usually a first-rate exhibition or traveling show to be seen here, but the permanent collections shouldn't be skipped. One is devoted to painting, furniture, sculpture, and decorative arts from the Pacific Northwest, with historic gems like the mid–19th-century painting *Astoria Harbor,* its ships bathed in golden light, by Cleveland Rockwell. Even more impressive is the sizeable collection of Northwest Coast Native American art, which includes totem poles, masks, wood carvings, and many other treasures. The museum also has noteworthy African Art and Northwest Contemporary Art collections, the latter featuring works by the so-called Big Four (or "mystic") artists (Guy Anderson, Kenneth Callahan, Morris Graves, and Mark Tobey) active in and around Seattle and La Conner, Washington (where there's also a museum dedicated to their work, p. 130) in the 1930s and 1940s.

1300 First Ave. www.seattleartmuseum.org. ✆ **206/854-3100.** $20 adults, $18 seniors, $13 students/teens, free 12 and under; free admission first Thurs–Fri every month. Wed–Sun 10am–5pm (Thurs–Fri until 9pm).

Market Munching

It's impossible to list all the food vendors at Pike Place Market, but here a few favorites that you should keep an eye out for as you cruise through the corridors and different levels. If you're planning a picnic, **DeLaurenti** ★, 1435 First Ave. (www.delaurenti.com; ✆ **800/873-6685** or 206/622-0141), near the market's brass pig, is the perfect spot to get your pâté, sandwiches, and wine. Sausage lovers will like the sandwiches at **Uli's Famous Sausage,** 1511 Pike Place (www.ulisfamoussausage.com; ✆ **206/839-1000**). **Piroshky Piroshky,** 1908 Pike Place (www.piroshkybakery.com; ✆ **206/441-6068**), sells sweet or savory stuffed rolls. At **Beecher's Handmade Cheese,** 1600 Pike Place (www.beecherscheese.com; ✆ **206/956-1964**), you can watch cheese being made and sample some of the products or get some of their fab macaroni and cheese to go. **The Spanish Table,** 1426 Western Ave. (www.spanishtable.com; ✆ **206/682-2827**), a specialty food shop on the lower level, offers Spanish-style sandwiches and swell soups. For something sweet, cold, and creamy, try the rightly-lauded gelato at **Bottega Italiana,** 1425 First Ave. (www.bottegaitaliana.com; ✆ **206/343-0200**), or the conveniently-located **Procopio Gelateria,** 1501 Western Ave. (www.procopiogelateria.com; ✆ **206/622-4280**), which is on the Pike Street Hill Climb that links the waterfront with Pike Place Market.

WATERFRONT

Olympic Sculpture Park ★★★ MUSEUM/PARK/GARDEN/VIEW Covering 9 acres of hillside, the Olympic Sculpture Park stretches from Belltown down to the waterfront at Myrtle Edwards Park. Modern and contemporary monumental sculptures are the focus of the collection, which includes works from regional, national, and international artists, including Alexander Calder, whose sculpture Eagle is one of the highlights of the collection. From just the right perspective, this sculpture perfectly frames the distant Space Needle. What a view! Other noteworthy works include Richard Serra's massive plate-steel Wake, and Split, a life-size stainless steel tree by Roxy Paine. If the sculptures aren't enough to hold your attention, turn your eyes toward the views of Elliott Bay and the distant Olympic Mountains. Down along the water, you'll also find a perfect little beach that was constructed as part of the sculpture park. This diminutive stretch of shoreline feels as wild as any beach on the Olympic Peninsula. An indoor cafe in the PACCAR Pavilion serves soups, panini sandwiches, and a full menu of lattes and desserts.

2901 Western Ave. www.seattleartmuseum.org. ✆ **206/654-3100.** Free admission. Sculpture Park daily sunrise-sunset; PACCAR Pavilion Nov–Feb Sat–Sun 10am–4pm, Mar–Oct Tues–Sun 10am–5pm.

Seattle Aquarium ★★ AQUARIUM/MUSEUM The Seattle Aquarium is a superb introduction to the sea life of the Northwest. You'll get your first glimpse at the giant "Window on Washington Waters" tank, just inside the entrance, where salmon, rockfish, lingcod, and wolf eels swim among gently swaying kelp beds; and sea anemone, sea urchins, sea stars, and corals cling

North Seattle Attractions

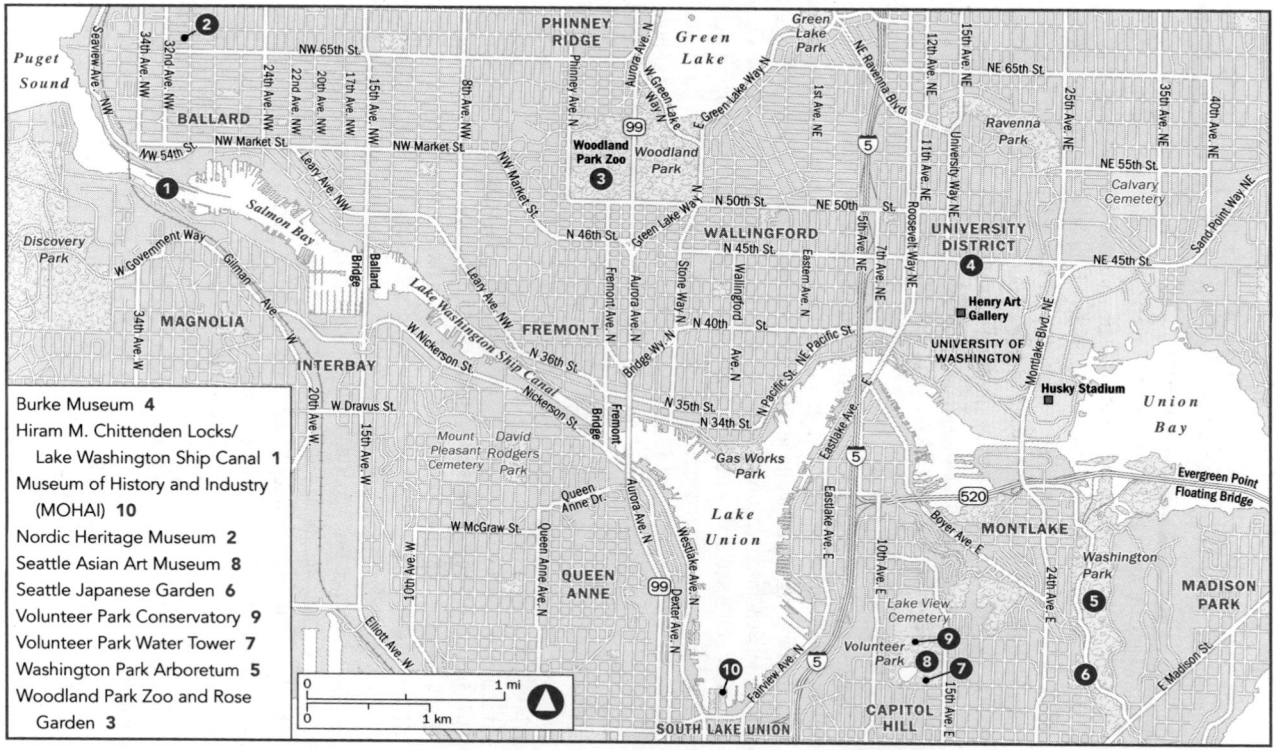

to large rock formations. Three times a day (10am, 11:30am, and 12:15pm) divers wearing special masks enter the tanks and answer questions from the audience. In "Life on the Edge," you can reach in to gently stroke the sea urchins and sea cucumbers that are typically found in Pacific tide pools. The male and female Giant Pacific Octopus are kept in separate tanks with a watery corridor between them until it's time for them to mate, at which point the doors are removed and the two quickly find one another; they are fed at 2 and 4pm daily.

In addition to the many other tanks filled with rare and beautiful fish, the aquarium has outdoor marine mammal pools where adorable (but mean) sea otters float on their backs while eating, and harbor seals dive and bark. You can watch them from the underwater dome or out on the deck. The staff here goes out of its way to answer any questions you or your kids may have.

Pier 59, 1483 Alaskan Way. www.seattleaquarium.org. ✆ **206/386-4300.** Admission $30 adults, $20 children 4–12. Book online to save $2 per ticket. Daily 9:30am–5pm.

Seattle Great Wheel ★★ VIEW/LANDMARK Located on a pier on the Seattle waterfront, the 175-foot-high Seattle Great Wheel is the largest observation wheel on the West Coast. It's a highly enjoyable way of taking in an incomparable view of the city and its surroundings. The observation pods are completely enclosed, seat four, move slowly and silently, and don't sway. On a clear day you'll see across Puget Sound to the Olympic Mountains to the west, and Mount Rainier to the east. On a gray, wet day, you'll have to be content with the Seattle skyline and Elliott Bay. If you want a longer-lasting, high-rise-view experience, opt for a trip up to the top of the Space Needle instead.

1301 Alaskan Way. www.seattlegreatwheel.com. ✆ **206/263-8600.** $14 adults, $12 seniors, $9.50 kids 4–11. Winter Mon–Thurs 11am–10pm, Fri 11am–midnight, Sat 10am–midnight, Sun 10am–10pm; summer Sun–Thurs 10am–11pm, Fri–Sat 10am–midnight.

Tillicum Experience ★★★ TOUR/CRUISE You can only get there by boat, and the entire trip takes about 4 hours, but a journey to Tillicum Village on Blake Island is a unique way to learn more about the Seattle area and the Native American tribes that called this region home for thousands of years. At Tillicum Village, a number of local tribes cooperatively present a traditional salmon bake (the fish is cooked over alderwood fires) in a re-created longhouse followed by a show of traditional dances illustrating stories from the different tribal cultures. And please take my word for it: this is not a hokey experience. The presentation is sophisticated, and the food is quite tasty. It is an entertaining and educational introduction to the pre-European cultural history of Pacific Northwest. Appropriately, the site is forested Blake Island, believed to be an ancient campground of the Duwamish and Suquamish tribes, and the likely birthplace of Chief Seattle. You can enjoy a walk on the beach or a short hike after the performance. The boat trip takes about 45 minutes each way and includes interesting live commentary and history. This is a great family-friendly excursion.

Tillicum Village, Blake Island State Park. Accessible by Argosy Cruises, Pier 55, Seattle Waterfront. www.argosycruises.com. ✆ **206/933-8600.** Price with lunch and cruise: $84 adults, $75 seniors, $32 ages 5–12. Daily May–Labor Day 11:30am departure, Fri–Sat only Mar–Apr and Oct; times vary by month; see website for details.

boat TOURS

To experience something of the maritime character that makes Seattle unique, consider taking one of the family-friendly tours offered daily, year-round, by **Argosy Cruises** (www.argosycruises.com), departing from Pier 55 on the waterfront. Argosy offers a 1-hour narrated harbor cruise that shows off the sights of the Seattle skyline ($27 adults, $22 seniors, $13 kids 4–12); a 2½-hour live-commentary locks tour that takes you through the century-old Chittenden Locks connecting saltwater Puget Sound to freshwater Lake Union ($44 adults, $39 seniors, $20 kids 4–12); and an especially fascinating 4-hour trip with live commentary to Tillicum Village on Blake Island, where you can enjoy a meal of plank-baked salmon and enjoy storytelling and native dances performed by the Coast Salish tribe in a re-created longhouse ($84 adults, $75 seniors, $32 kids 4–12). See above. Check the website for departure times and special Internet discounts for prebooking.

From May through September, **Let's Go Sailing** (www.sailingseattle.com; ✆ **206/624-3931**) at Pier 54 offers daily 90-minute excursions on a 70-foot sailboat ($36 adults, $30 seniors, $22 kids), and 2½-hour sunset cruises ($52 adults, $44 seniors, $33 kids). There is no commentary *per se*, but the captain is right there to answer any questions. This is an open boat, so if it rains you'll get wet.

For another take on maritime Seattle just hop on a commuter ferry operated by **Washington State Ferries** (www.wsdot.wa.gov/ferries) and enjoy a ride, with a scenic skyline view, between downtown and Bainbridge Island. A round-trip passenger-only ferry ticket to the Island costs $16.40 adults, $8.20 for seniors and children 6 to 18.

The cheapest option—and perhaps the best for photo ops of the Seattle skyline—is the King County Water Taxi (www. www.kingcounty.gov/depts/transportation/water-taxi.aspx) which departs hourly from a dock adjacent to the Seattle Ferry Terminal building and makes a 10-minute crossing to Alki Beach in West Seattle for a one-way fare of $5.25 adults and kids, $2.25 seniors. Buy your tickets from the machines at the pier.

SEATTLE CENTER

Chihuly Garden and Glass ★★★ ART MUSEUM Not many living artists are given their own museum, and especially not glass artists. But Dale Chihuly, the Pacific Northwest phenomenon is almost a household name, primarily because of his enormous and enormously intricate glass chandeliers, which hang in museums, casinos, and other public spaces around the world. I used to find Chihuly's work—what I knew of it—a little overwrought and even somewhat vulgar. But a visit to this museum, which opened right below the Space Needle in 2012, changed my mind. Perhaps it was the eye-searing colors of the pieces in contrast to the gray Seattle day, or perhaps it was seeing the almost unbelievable intricacy of the large installations, but Chihuly's artistry is electric when seen in the broader context this museum affords. The museum presents an overview of this Tacoma-born artist's 45-year career, including marvelous early works, such as flattened glass vessels influenced by Native American basketry and pottery. Some works hang from the ceiling, others rise like giant neon-colored underwater seascapes with twisting, nestling, writhing organic shapes that look soft and hard at the same time. Outside, in the museum's garden, Chihuly's vibrant glass pieces rise up like plants and trees among the natural vegetation. Every piece you see in this dynamic museum—which is half funhouse, half shrine—explores, reimagines, and ultimately transcends the traditional boundaries and limitations of glass art. And, by the way, there's an excellent gift shop. Visit before 10am and you will get up to $10 off the regular admission price.

305 Harrison St. (below Space Needle). www.chihulygardenandglass.com. ✆ **206/753-4940.** $29 adults, $22 senior, $18 ages 4–12. Mon–Thurs 8:30am–8:30pm; Fri–Sun 8:30am–9:30pm.

Museum of Pop Culture (MoPOP) ★ MUSEUM I was never a fan of the Experience Music Project, housed in a showy but rather ridiculous and confusing Frank Gehry building next to the Space Needle. It was overpriced and underwhelming. The EMP has now rebranded itself as the Museum of Pop Culture (MoPOP). It's housed in the same ridiculous building and it's still overpriced, but the exhibits are better than they used to be. Now they have big, changing shows (for add-on fees, of course), like a recent one on Jim Henson and the Muppets. And they've reconceived their signature Science Fiction exhibit so that it's quite extensive and intriguing. Also redone is the big, permanent Star Trek exhibit. If you are a Trekkie (I may be the only person in this galaxy who isn't), you won't want to miss it. In 2017 plans were afoot for another revamped former exhibit—this one on Horror—"with walls that bleed," as one employee informed me. There's still a giant screen on the main floor that runs a loop of rock/pop music videos, changing shows on rock icons, and there's still the centerpiece artwork made of electric guitars. So all in all it's better, but is it worth it? In my opinion, not really. You'll save $2 if you order your tickets online; be prepared for a $5 add-on fee for special exhibitions; the tickets are valid for 7 days.

Seattle Center, 325 Fifth Ave. N. www.mopop.org. ✆ **206/770-2700**. Admission $28 adults, $25 seniors, $19 ages 5–17;. Daily summer 10am–7pm, winter 10am–5pm. Closed Thanksgiving and Christmas.

Pacific Science Center ★ MUSEUM If you have kids in tow, this is one museum where everyone will find something to enjoy. Older kids will love the interactive exhibits, such as the new "What is Reality" which explores what tech innovators are up to today, with the chance to try augmented reality glasses and other whizbang new technology. For younger children there's the crawl-and-climb area, with its treehouse and a table-height "stream" for water play. And the Insect Village, is a hit with all ages with its giant robotic insects and live animal displays. A highlight: animatronic dinosaurs, life-size replicas that move their heads and tails and grunt and bellow. My personal favorite here is the Butterfly House, a humid greenhouse where colorful butterflies flit and fly freely. All in all, the museum, housed in a building from the 1962 Seattle World's Fair, is like a giant playhouse dedicated to science and technology. In addition to all the hands-on exhibits, a planetarium hosts evening laser shows and an IMAX theater.

Seattle Center, 200 2nd Ave. N. www.pacificsciencecenter.org. ✆ **800/664-8775** or 206/443-2001, 206/443-4629 for IMAX information, or 206/443-2850 for laser-show information. Admission (including IMAX) $31 adults, $28 seniors, $23 ages 6–15, $19 ages 3–5. Admission price about $10 less without IMAX. Various discounted combination tickets available. Daily 10am–6pm. Closed Thanksgiving and Christmas.

Space Needle ★★★ LANDMARK/VIEW This is one of those iconic structures that architecturally epitomize an era—in this case, the early 1960s—and come to symbolize a city. So you could say that the Space Needle is Seattle's Eiffel Tower. I'm quite fond of the Space Needle and have never forgotten the scary thrill of being taken up to the top of it as a kid. From a distance, it looks like a flying saucer on a tripod, and when it was built for the 1962 World's Fair, the 605-foot-tall Space Needle was meant to suggest "the future" (today it definitely looks retro). Once you finally get into the glass elevator, you'll zoom up 520 feet to an observation deck that provides superb and unobstructed views of the entire city and its surroundings. More than 60 sites are identified on wall panels, and high-powered telescopes let you zoom in on them. The lines in summer and on weekends can be really long, so it's wise to get there early; the admission price allows you to return in the evening to see Seattle at night. (If you purchased a Seattle CityPass described under "Save Cash with a Seattle CityPass," p. 71, you get to skip the long line.) A revolving restaurant, **SkyCity** ★ (reviewed on p. 110), provides a memorable but very pricey spot to dine atop the observation deck (but the price of admission to the Space Needle is included if you dine there). ***Tip:*** You'll pay $6 to $10 less for your admission if you visit during the first 2 hours of opening or the last two hours before closing.

Seattle Center, 400 Broad St. www.spaceneedle.com. ✆ **206/905-2100.** Admission $19–$29 adults, $16–$22 seniors, $13–$18 ages 4–13. Mon–Thurs 10am–9pm, Fri–Sat 9:30am–10:30pm, Sun 9:30am–9:30pm.

PIONEER SQUARE

Bill Speidel's Underground Tour ★★★ TOUR Wonderfully entertaining guides lead visitors into a warren of underground tunnels below Pioneer Square, pointing out businesses that were once at street level until the great fire of 1889 wiped out the city and led to a massive rebuilding and releveling of Seattle. The anecdotes are hilarious and sometimes a bit off-color, but Seattle's history is anything but genteel. You'll learn about exploding toilets, "seamstresses" who never sewed a stitch (and sometimes didn't wear one), city rogues, city fathers and mothers, early businesses, and how the city infrastructure and rebuilding required people to climb ladders to get from one street to the next. Go with a sense of humor and you'll have a great time. There's an intriguing little gift shop at the end of the tour.

Pioneer Building, 610 1st Ave. #200. www.undergroundtour.com. ✆ **206/682-4646.** $22 adults, $20 seniors, $10 ages 7–12. Tours daily throughout the day. Closed Thanksgiving and Christmas Day.

Klondike Gold Rush National Historical Park ★ MUSEUM It's not a park; it's a museum dedicated to a pivotal event in Seattle's history and housed in a historic building in the city's most historic neighborhood (Pioneer Square). In 1897, when word got out that gold had been discovered in Alaska, tens of thousands of wannabe prospectors from around the world, both men and women, descended on Seattle to outfit themselves for the arduous trip north to the Klondike gold fields. A few made their fortunes, but most did not. Seattle had burnt to the ground just a few years earlier, but the gold rush put it on the map and filled the city's coffers. As the closest departure point where prospectors could buy all the provisions and equipment necessary to dig for gold, Seattle had the market cornered. This museum recounts the city's gold-rush rush in an entertaining and informative way, focusing on individuals, their preparations for the journey, and the rough-and-tumble adventures and living conditions they encountered. At 10am and 3pm daily, park rangers give demonstrations of mining techniques; the museum also distributes a darn good "Trails to Treasure" self-guided walking tour map of the historic Pioneer Square neighborhood that dates from the gold rush days.

319 2nd Ave. S. www.nps.gov/klse. ✆ **206/220-4240.** Free admission. Daily 9am–5pm. Closed New Year's Day, Thanksgiving, and Christmas.

Smith Tower Observation Deck ★★★ ARCHITECTURAL LANDMARK/VIEW Buildings twice its size now form the Seattle skyline, but from 1914, when it was completed, until the early 1960s, Smith Tower was not only the tallest building in Seattle, it was the tallest building west of the Mississippi. View junkies and fans of heritage architecture will love zipping up to the 35th floor in one of the last manually operated elevators in the U.S. But before that, there's a short video on the building's history and the (sometimes shady) characters that built it and worked there, and you can do fun things like operate the 1914 switchboard. Beautiful period details abound, including walls and banisters made of solid onyx and gleaming brass elevator cages. The view from the open observation deck is panoramic and unique, taking in all of Seattle. I highly recommended a sunset cocktail or light lunch or dinner in the historic Chinese Room with its ornate teak ceiling.

506 Second Ave. www.smithtower.com. ✆ **206/624-0414.** Admission $19 adults; $15 seniors/kids. Book online to save 10%. Daily 10am–10pm.

CHINATOWN/INTERNATIONAL DISTRICT

Frye Art Museum ★★ ART MUSEUM Located on First Hill, just north of downtown, the Frye was Seattle's first free art museum, thanks to the legacy of Charles and Emma Frye. A child of German immigrants, Charles Frye made his fortune by starting a meatpacking plant during the 1890s gold-rush days (if you take the highly entertaining Underground Tour, described below, you'll see where the meat lockers were). With their wealth, the Fryes began to collect paintings and bequeathed their enormous collection to the city with the stipulation that the works be displayed free to the public in one location. The original collection of portraits, still lifes, and landscapes by late-19th- and

visiting **VOLUNTEER PARK**

Capitol Hill's century-old Volunteer Park, designed by the Olmsted Brothers (see below), is one of the gems of Seattle's park system and has several worthwhile attractions. Chief among them is the **Volunteer Park Conservatory** ★★★ (1402 E. Galer St.; www.volunteerparkconservatory.org; admission by donation; Tues–Sun 10am–4pm), one of only three Victorian-style glasshouse conservatories on the West Coast. You'd never guess from looking at this elegant building that it was shipped as a prefab kit from Brookline, Massachusetts, and assembled on site in 1912. In addition to its many species of palm trees, the central Palm House showcases a collection of tropical orchids, and the Seasonal Display House presents an ever-changing show of color and fragrance (in the spring, it's loaded with blooming bulbs, lilies, cyclamen, azaleas, and hydrangeas). Beyond it is the Cactus House, where the variety of shapes, thorns, and growing habits is remarkable, as are the flowers the cacti produce in the spring. Other rooms showcase ferns and bromeliads.

After visiting the Conservatory, take some time to wander through the rest of Volunteer Park. In the early 1900s, the Olmsted Brothers, America's preeminent landscape design firm (their father, Frederick Law Olmsted, designed New York's Central Park), were hired to draw up a plan that set aside portions of Seattle's uniquely handsome terrain as places for relaxation and recreation. Climb the stairway in the Romanesque-style brick **water tower** (open daily 11am–dusk) located in the southeast corner of the park near the reservoir, where the free **Olmsted Interpretive Exhibit** on the observation deck chronicles the Olmsted legacy in creating Seattle's parks and offers great views of Seattle and Puget Sound. Another highlight of Volunteer Park is the **Seattle Asian Art Museum** ★★ (1400 E. Prospect St.; www.seattleartmuseum.org; ✆ **206/654-3100**), housed in a classic 1933 Art Deco building near the Conservatory. This small museum, the original home of the Seattle Art Museum, usually features rotating exhibits and a permanent collection of ancient and contemporary art treasures from a variety of Asian cultures. But the museum closed in 2017 in preparation for a major expansion and won't be reopening for at least 3 years; check the website for information on other Seattle venues where the museum's programs will be relocated. Across from the museum stands Isamo Noguchi's 1968 outdoor sculpture called *Black Sun*, a circular form created from Brazilian granite; look through the center hole and you'll see the Space Needle.

early-20th-century French, German, and American painters are dramatically exhibited in one enormous room. This layout, which recreates the way the paintings were originally exhibited, changes periodically, so you may see a work by Ernst Lembach, Franz von Stuck or Thomas Hart Benton on one visit, and a canvas by Edward Hopper or an early Picasso on another. In recent years, the museum has added modern and abstract art to the collection and exhibited an impressive array of works by artists active in the Pacific Northwest or with ties to it. Onsite are a lovely little cafe and garden.

704 Terry Ave. (at Cherry St.). www.fryemuseum.org. ✆ **206/622-9250.** Free admission. Tues–Sun 11am–5pm; Thurs 11am–7pm. Closed New Year's Day, July 4th, Thanksgiving, and Christmas. Free tours Tues–Sun 1pm.

Wing Luke Asian Museum ★ MUSEUM Asians and Pacific Islanders have contributed to the growth and culture of Seattle almost from its inception, and this small museum in Chinatown/International District tells their stories. The main exhibit, "Honoring Our Journey," explains how they came to Seattle and why and what they did, in an age of rampant racism, once they were here. One exhibit, called "Camp Harmony D-4-44," focuses on the internment of Japanese-American citizens during World War II, recreating one of the livestock stalls converted into a family holding cell, barbed wire and all; filmed interviews add a human dimension to this episode in U.S. history. The museum is housed in the historic Freeman Hotel, where many early Asian immigrants lived while working in the region's canneries and lumber mills. Tours of the hotel add still more insight into the Asian experience in Seattle, and the museum also offers walking tours of the Chinatown and Japan Town neighborhoods. The museum is named for Wing Luke, the first Asian-American to hold public office in the Northwest.

719 S. King St. www.wingluke.org. ✆ **206/623-5124.** $17 adults, $15 seniors. $12.50 students 13–18, $10 kids 5–12; admission price includes tour of historic hotel. Chinatown walking tour (includes museum admission) $22 adults, $20 seniors, $17.50 students 13–18, $15 kids 5–12. Free admission 1st Thurs of each month. Tues–Sun 10am–5pm (until 8pm 1st Thurs and 3rd Sat of each month). Closed New Year's Day, July 4th, Thanksgiving, Christmas Eve, and Christmas.

SOUTH LAKE UNION

Museum of History and Industry (MOHAI) ★★ MUSEUM It may not have the most exciting name, but there is nothing dull about this museum. It guides visitors through Northwest and Seattle history with fascinating, often hands-on exhibits, historic photos and films, and some wonderful artifacts. Every aspect of Seattle's cultural, scientific, and industrial past is covered, from pre-Great Fire Seattle (in 1889 the city was reduced to ashes), through the Klondike Gold Rush of 1897, the founding of Boeing and the aerospace industry, right up to the arrival of Microsoft and Amazon (where else, but in the Bezos Center for Innovation?). Look up and you'll see one of the first hydroplanes used in the yearly Seafair boat races (these boats can reach speeds of 200mph), look over and you'll encounter one of the earliest computers. It's engaging and engrossing.

820 Terry Ave. N. on the shores of Lake Union www.mohai.org. ✆ **206/324-1126.** $20 adults, $16 seniors, $14 students, free ages 14 and under. Also, free first Thursday of each month. Daily 10am–5pm, Thurs until 8pm.

NORTH SEATTLE INCLUDING BALLAD & UNIVERSITY DISTRICT

Hiram M. Chittenden Locks/Lake Washington Ship Canal ★★ LANDMARK/PARK/GARDEN Created in 1917 by the Army Corps of Engineers, the locks (known locally as the Ballard Locks) link saltwater Puget Sound with freshwater Lake Union and Lake Washington. All day, every day, a passing parade of yachts, barges, fishing trawlers, and other vessels make their way from one body of water to the other. And people line the shore to

THE NEW nordic heritage museum

For years, the **Nordic History Museum** was housed in an old school and its displays were, well, pretty static. But in May 2018 this museum, the only one in the country that celebrates the history, art and traditions of the five Nordic countries (Denmark, Finland, Iceland, Norway, and Sweden) whose immigrants settled in Seattle and the Pacific Northwest, will be moving to brand-new home at 2655 NW Market St. (✆ **206/789-5707;** www.nordicmuseum.org; $8 adults, $7 seniors/students, $6 children; Tues–Sat 10am–4pm, Sun noon–4pm). Alas, the museum wasn't open in time for us to review it for this guide. But, from all reports, it looks like it will be a more dynamic enterprise. You can easily combine a visit to the museum with a visit to the Hiram A. Chittenden Locks (p. 82).

watch, wave, and maybe wish they had a boat of their own. Exhibits in the Visitor Center explain how this engineering feat came about and was executed (water levels in the lakes dropped about 17 feet as a result). If you want to glide through the locks yourself, take the Locks Tour offered daily by Argosy Cruises (see "Boat Tours", p. 77). On the hill above the locks you'll find the **Carl S. English Botanical Garden,** well worth a stroll. Over a 43-year period a botanist named Carl S. English, Jr. transformed the once barren grounds into, in his words, "a garden worthy of serious study." The garden is filled with unusual trees and shrubs; there are more traditional flower gardens down behind the Visitor Center.

3015 N.W. 54th Street (Ballard). www.corpslakes.us/lakewashingtonshipcanal. Visitor Center ✆ **206/783-7059.** Free admission. Locks daily year-round dawn–dusk; Visitor Center May–Sept daily 10am–6pm, Oct–Apr Thurs–Mon 10am–4pm. Free 1-hr. guided tours Mar–Nov (call for tour schedule).

Museum of Flight ★★★ MUSEUM This top-flight museum located at Boeing Field (and sponsored by that giant company) is a paean to every form of flight, flying, and aircraft. The historic Red Barn (Boeing's first manufacturing building), houses exhibits on early aviation, including the mail bag carried by William E. Boeing and Eddie Hubbard on the first international U.S. Air Mail flight from Vancouver, BC to Seattle in 1919. The exhibit ends with the Boeing 707, which ushered in the jet age. The cavernous Great Gallery features dozens of historic aircraft, many of them hanging from the ceiling as though in flight. Visitors can climb into the cockpit of a real Blackbird, the fastest jet ever made. The Personal Courage Wing tells the stories of fighter aviators in World Wars I and II. And at the Airpark, you can walk through legendary aircraft including the Concorde and the first jet Air Force One, used by presidents Kennedy, Johnson, and Reagan. The simulator exhibit lets you try virtual flight and hang-gliding. The museum's Apollo exhibit tells the story of the Cold War space race and displays NASA and Russian spacecraft (and mock-ups) and the rocket engine that launched Apollo to the moon.

For those wondering why this museum is in Seattle: the history of aviation in this city goes back almost as far back as the Wright Brothers. Since it was founded in 1916, Boeing has been the most important player in the United States' aerospace industry and Seattle's economic health and vitality has been closely linked to Boeing's since that time (though high-tech is now just as important).

9404 E. Marginal Way S. www.museumofflight.org. ✆ **206/764-5720.** $23 adults, $19 seniors, $14 ages 5–17; free 5–9pm 1st Thurs of every month. Daily 10am–5pm. Closed Thanksgiving and Christmas. Bus: 124. Take exit 158 off I-5.

Seattle Japanese Garden ★★★ GARDEN/PARK The Japanese influence on Pacific Northwest garden design and plant material has been enormous, and luckily, thanks to the region's cultural ties to Japan, Seattle (and Portland, see p. 160) have the best examples of Japanese gardens outside of Japan. This garden is lovely any time of year, but it is absolutely gorgeous in April and May, when the cherry trees are in bloom, or in the fall, when then bright orange and red tints of the Japanese maples add a burnished luster to the scene. The Seattle Japanese Garden, designed and constructed under the supervision of Japanese garden designer Juki Iida, fits like a jewel into its 3½-acre setting within the University of Washington Arboretum. Opened in 1960, the garden has now had over 60 years to mature and is the oldest formal Japanese garden in the Pacific Northwest. This is a "strolling garden" with several meticulously miniaturized landscapes within it. It is meant to be seen one landscape at a time, like a scroll of painted landscapes that unrolls and reveals new vistas as you follow the winding path around the central lake from one viewpoint to the next. Take your time—that's the point. In addition to a exquisite selection of trees and shrubs, you'll encounter all the elements used in formal Japanese garden design—water, rocks and sand, bridges, stone lanterns, and water basins. Blue herons often fly over from Lake Washington and help keep the *koi* (Japanese carp) population in check. You may see them along the shores and on the rocks in the lake.

Washington Park Arboretum, 1075 Lake Washington Blvd. E. (north of E. Madison St.). www.seattle.gov/parks/parkspaces/japanesegarden.htm. ✆ **206/684-4725.** Admission $6 adults; $4 seniors/students/ages 6–17. Mar Tues–Sun 10am–4pm; Apr Mon noon–7pm, Tues–Sun 10am–7pm; May–July Mon noon–8pm, Tues–Sun 10am–8pm; Aug Mon noon–7pm, Tues–Sun 10am–7pm; Sept Mon noon–6pm, Tues–Sun 10am–6pm; Oct Mon noon–5pm, Tues–Sun 10am–5pm; Nov Tues–Sun 10am–4pm.

Washington Park Arboretum ★★★ PARK/GARDEN Since its official founding in 1935, the arboretum has weathered funding crises, neighborhood controversies, and storms that have toppled trees and frozen shrubs. But it has survived and survived beautifully. Walking trails crisscross the varied terrain of woodland, wetland, and gardens, taking visitors to acclaimed collections of azaleas, rhododendrons, oaks, conifers, camellias, magnolias, Japanese maples, and hollies. The Seattle Japanese Garden (see above) occupies the southwestern portion of arboretum but is separate from it. The arboretum is full of seasonal highlights, and there is always something of special interest to

An Update on the Burke Museum

For decades, the **Burke Museum,** the Washington State Museum of Natural History and Culture, was housed in a cramped, 1960s-era building on the UW campus at 15th Avenue and 45th Street NE. Among its newest treasures is the largest and most intact fossilized T-Rex skull ever discovered. In 2018 the old Burke closed so that the collections can be moved to a brand-new museum, adjacent to the old one, with state-of-the-art galleries and open labs that will allow visitors to watch researchers at work and ask them questions. The opening date for the new Burke was not available at press time, but is scheduled for 2019. Check out the website **www.burkemuseum.org** for updates because this is one new museum you and your kids will definitely not want to miss.

discover (pick up a map in the Graham Visitors Center). But the arboretum's must-see springtime spectacle is, without a doubt, **Azalea Way,** bordered by hundreds of Japanese cherry trees, eastern dogwoods, and an undergrowth of azaleas. It required over 10,000 hours of hand labor by WPA workmen to complete. For a refreshing waterside stroll in any season, walk north along Arboretum Drive East, cross the road, and follow the gravel trail along the shoreline to the large wetlands area that's a favorite spot for birders. But all this only hints at the riches you'll find in this wonderfully explorable urban garden.

2300 Arboretum Drive E. www.arboretumfoundation.org. ✆ **206/325-4510.** Free admission. Arboretum daily dawn–dusk; Graham Visitors Center daily 10am–4pm, closed holidays.

Woodland Park Zoo & Rose Garden ★ ZOO/PARKGARDEN Woodland Park Zoo has won awards for several exhibits, including the primate area with families of gorillas and orangutans, and the African Savanna with giraffes (Lulu, born in 2017, is already a zoo favorite) and zebras. An underwater viewing area gives you a close-up view of frolicking Humboldt penguins from Peru, and there's a popular habitat area for viewing fun-loving meerkats. Other exhibits focus on Alaska, with a terrific brown-bear habitat, and the tropical rainforest. At the Zoomazium, an indoor play area, kids 8 and under can explore nature, listen to stories, and generally burn off energy. The newest exhibits are Molbak's Butterfly Garden, where you can stroll through a lovely garden with 500 butterflies from 15 different North American species flying free around you; and the Microsoft Pollinator Patio, an instructional garden that focuses on ways to create a garden using native plants that attract birds and insects. The zoo also has a historic 1918 carousel.

The 2½-acre **Woodland Park Rose Garden** adjacent to the zoo showcases the genus *Rosa* in all its myriad forms—floribunda, grandiflora, hybrid tea, hybrid musk, miniature, polyantha, rugosa, David Austen, climber, shrub, tree—they're all here. A circular fountain bubbles at the center and a semicircular bas-relief wall fountain burbles at the north end. A rectangular lily pond sits between the two fountains. This elegant and enjoyable rose garden is unique in that it is 100% organic and pesticide-free. Late May through June

bloedel reserve: A NATIVE NORTHWESTERN GARDEN

If you have an interest in gardens and gardening, don't miss an opportunity to visit **Bloedel Reserve** ★★★ on Bainbridge Island (frequent all-day ferry service runs from Seattle to Winslow). This is not the kind of garden with showy flowerbeds, but one in which Northwest native and non-native plants, shrubs, and trees have been skillfully combined to create a series of gardens that are artfully woven into a forested, maritime landscape. In the spring, the woods and meadows are carpeted with naturalized bulbs, and rhododendrons and camellias put on a spectacular show. In the summer and fall, you'll find other plant treasures along the sun-dappled paths.

The garden was created by Prentice Bloedel, son of a timber baron. Bloedel and his wife, Virginia, lived on the property from 1951 to 1986, in a French chateau-style house built by the previous owner in 1931. About 70 acres of the estate were left as undisturbed forest, and the remaining 80 acres were shaped into a remarkably elegant series of gardens and natural areas. Pick up a map at the gatehouse when you arrive because there is no signage along the winding trails, and, if you're able, follow the route that gives you the full tour (you'll need about 1½ hours). At the end of your visit, I can almost guarantee that you'll agree with Prentice Bloedel, who said "The Bloedel Reserve is a place where people find refreshment and tranquility in the presence of natural beauty."

7571 NE Dolphin Dr., 6 miles north of Winslow ferry terminal (turn right on Agate Rd.) www.bloedelreserve.org. ✆ **206/842-7631.** $15 adults, $10 seniors/students, $8 ages 13–18, $5 ages 5–12. Sept–May Tues–Sun 10am–4pm; June–Aug Tues–Wed 10am–4pm, Thurs–Sun 10am–6pm. The #90 bus from the Winslow ferry terminal stops 1 mile from the reserve.

is the best time to see and smell the roses, but some remain in bloom throughout the summer.

750 N. 50th St. www.zoo.org. ✆ **206/684-4800.** Zoo: May–Sept $21 ages 13–64, $19 seniors, $13 ages 3–12; Oct–Apr: $15 ages 13–64, $13 seniors, $10 ages 3–12. May–Sept daily 9:30am–6pm; Oct–Apr daily 9:30am–4pm. Rose Garden: Admission free; daily year-round dawn–dusk.

ORGANIZED TOURS

Within its downtown core, Seattle is an easy walking city—but because of its maritime topography, the layout of the streets doesn't always follow an easily understandable grid. Beyond the downtown it's large and sprawling. To take in more of the Seattle, and to understand it better, you may want to sign up for an organized tour. For boat tours, see the box "Boat Tours" (p. 77) under "Exploring Seattle": the highly entertaining and highly recommended Underground Tour (p. 79) is listed in that section as well.

Walking Tours

Seattle Free Walking Tours (www.seattlefreewalkingtours.com) is a unique pay-what-you-want outfit that offers 4 different themed walking tours (The Market Experience, Seattle 101, Historic Seattle, Seattle True Crime), each led by a knowledgeable and enthusiastic guide and lasting 1 to 1½ hours. At the end of the tour, you tip your guide what you think the tour was worth (I would suggest a minimum of $10 per person). You must reserve a place in advance; tours are offered every day. This is a fun and inexpensive way to wade into Seattle.

See Seattle Walking Tours (www.see-seattle.com; ✆ **425/226-7641**) offers guided walking tours of downtown Seattle with a trained, knowledgeable guide, visiting Pike Place Market, the waterfront, and the Pioneer Square area. With this tour you get to see and learn about Seattle in more depth and at a slower pace. The tours cost $20.

For an insider's glimpse of life in Seattle's Chinatown/International District, hook up with **Chinatown Discovery Tours** (www.seattlechinatowntour.com; ✆ **206/623-5124**). They offer overview tours of the neighborhood and specialized tours based on seasonal foods and cultural icons such as martial-arts movie idol Bruce Lee, who spent time in Seattle. Their "A Touch of Seattle" tour costs $22 adults, $20 seniors, $17.50 students, and $15 kids 5 to 12.

For food-focused tours of Pike Place Market we recommend two companies. **Savor Seattle** (www.savorseattletours.com; ✆ **888/987-2867**) is the first; it charges $72 for a food and drink tour that visits seven downtown and Pike Place Market restaurants; their signature Pike Place Market tour is offered several times a day and costs $44. **Show Me Seattle** (www.showmeseattle.com; ✆ **206/725-4483**), in business since 1994, also charges $44 for a 2½-hour tour of Pike Place Market. Both do an excellent job of curating their tours so that visitors get a taste of a broad range of eateries and stands, without getting overstuffed.

For a fun, informative and family-friendly tour of Seattle's quirkiest neighborhood, take **The Fremont Tour.** It's an interactive experience in which costumed guides use playful street theater to help tell the story of Fremont and it's trove of public art (which includes a giant troll, a statue of Lenin and a rocket). The walk starts at Solstice Plaza (711 N. 34th St.), covers about ½ mile, takes about 90 minutes and costs $20 for adults, $16 for seniors and students, free for kids under 10. This north Seattle neighborhood is full of

Touring Seattle by Duck

World War II amphibious vehicles called Ducks are used for fun and intriguing tours that combine both land and water. **Seattle Duck Tours** ★★★ (516 Broad St.; www.ridetheducksofseattle.com; ✆ **800/817-1116** or 206/441-3825) show off the standard Seattle sights, but then plunge right into Lake Union for a tour of the Portage Bay waterfront, with its many houseboats and great views. The 90-minute tours leave from two locations: across from the Space Needle at 5th and Broad St., and from Westlake Center downtown at 4th Ave. and Pine. Tours cost $37.50 for adults and $17 for kids. There's live narration from a guide as you whiz through the city and into the water; it's informative and sometimes very funny.

Scenic Flights

Seattle is one of the few cities in the United States where floatplanes are a regular sight in the skies and on the lakes. If you want to see what it's like to take off and land on the water, contact **Seattle Seaplanes ★★,** 1325 Fairview Ave. E. (www.seattleseaplanes.com; ✆ **800/637-5553** or 206/329-9638). Their floatplanes take off from Lake Union for 20-minute scenic flights over the city at a cost of $98.

shops, cafes and restaurants where you can enjoy a coffee, a nosh or browse for a handcrafted treasure before or after the tour. Check out dates, tour times, and make reservations at www.thefremonttour.com. The tours usually take place only in the summer.

4 WHERE TO STAY

Seattle offers a wide range of hotel choices. If your time is limited, I'd suggest that you opt for lodgings in downtown or in adjacent Belltown or Pioneer Square areas. From those locations, you can walk or easily access public transportation to all of the major attractions and feel close to the city's urban, bayside heartbeat. I've selected and spread my hotel choices over a wide range of hotel types and prices, the goal being to present you with the best and most interesting options in all price ranges within the central part of the city. Book in advance, and online, and you'll usually pay far less (see our box for web strategies). In the winter, especially, it's sometimes possible to get the price of a luxury hotel down to a more affordable mid-range level. The rates quoted here include taxes (around 16%). If you are driving to Seattle, expect to pay anywhere from $25 to $55 dollars per night for valet parking at your hotel.

And don't forget to check out **Airbnb** (**www.airbnb.com**), **HomeAway** (www.homeaway.com), **VRBO** (www.vrbo.com) and other vacation rental entities. These websites, offering either rooms in private homes or entire apartments, are legal to use in Seattle. A random check on Airbnb showed low-season rooms in Capitol Hill for $77 and $81 per night. HomeAway, for the same period, offered a small, centrally located condo and a cottage for $79 and $125 a night. These prices were approximately $50 to $75 less than you'd pay for a hotel room in central Seattle.

DOWNTOWN

Expensive

Arctic Club Hotel ★★★ There's nothing quite like the Arctic Club in Seattle, and if you're a fan of historic hotels, you'll love this restored relic of the post–gold rush days. Back in 1917, when the Arctic Club was built as an exclusive gentlemen's club for lucky prospectors who struck it rich in the Yukon gold fields, rooms were roomy and forthright, with beamed ceilings, wood baseboards and crown moldings, and beds that were big and solid and covered with woolen blankets. That's how it is today, too, only with updated

TURNING TO THE internet or apps FOR A HOTEL DISCOUNT

Before going online, it's important that you know what "flavor" of discount you're seeking. Currently, there are three types of online reductions:

1. **Extreme discounts on sites where you bid for lodgings without knowing which hotel you'll get.** You'll find these on such sites as **Priceline.com** and **Hotwire.com**, and they can be money-savers, particularly if you're booking within a week of travel (that's when the hotels resort to deep discounts to get beds filled). As these companies use only major chains, you can rest assured that you won't be put up in a dump. For more reassurance, visit the website **BiddingTraveler.com**. On it, actual travelers spill the beans about what they bid on Priceline.com and which hotels they got. I think you'll be pleasantly surprised by the quality of many of the hotels that are offering these "secret" discounts.
2. **Discounts on chain hotel websites.** In 2016, all of the major chains announced they'd be reserving special discounts for travelers who booked directly through the hotels' websites (usually in the portion of the site reserved for loyalty members). They weren't lying: these are always the lowest rates at the hotels in question, though discounts can range widely, from as little as $1 to as much as $50. Our advice: search for a hotel that's in your price range and ideal location (see below for where to do that) and then, if it is a chain property, book directly through the online loyalty portal.
3. **Use the right hotel search engine.** They're not all equal, as we at Frommers.com learned in the spring of 2017 after putting the top 20 sites to the test in 20 cities (including NYC) around the globe. We discovered that **Booking.com** listed the lowest rates for hotels in the city center, and in the under $200 range, 16 out of 20 times—the best record, by far, of all the sites we tested. And Booking.com includes all taxes and fees in its results (not all do, which can make for a frustrating shopping experience). For top-end properties, again in the city center only, both Priceline.com and HotelsCombined.com came up with the best rates, tying at 14 wins each.
4. **Last-minute discounts**. Booking last minute can be a great savings strategy, as prices sometimes drop in the week before travel as hoteliers scramble to fill their rooms. But you won't necessarily find the best savings through companies that claim to specialize in last-minute bookings. Instead, use the sites recommended in point 3 of this list.
5. **Or skip hotels altogether**. See above for our discussion of the savings you can get with online vacation rental sites.

It's a lot of surfing, but in the hothouse world of accommodation pricing, this sort of diligence can pay off.

amenities of all kinds and furniture that evokes the Art Deco era when the club was in its heyday. The exterior of this period gem (on the Seattle Register of Historic Places) is still decorated with the sculpted terra-cotta walrus masks that recalled Alaska to those who had prospected there. The lobby, with its fireplace, ornate Polar Bar, ceiling carvings, and billiard table, instantly

Seattle Hotels

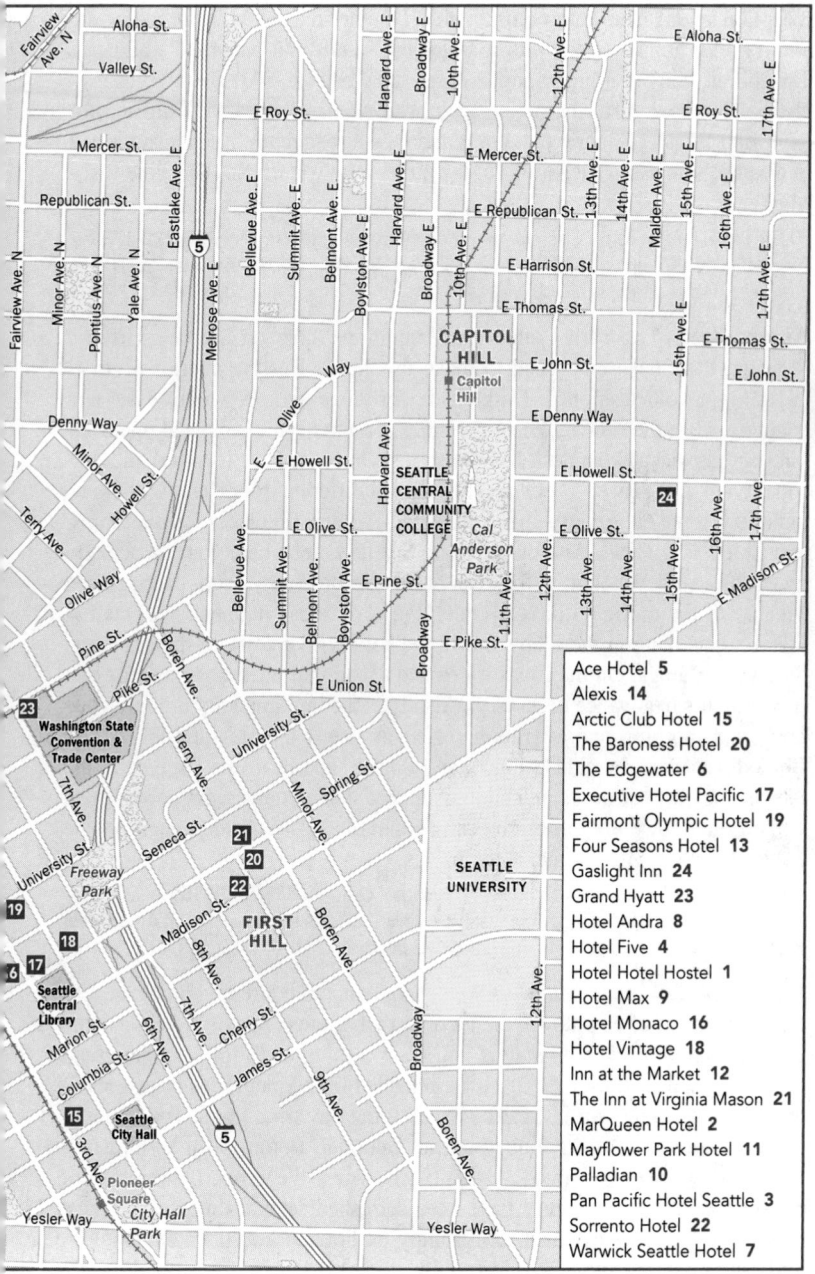
Aloha St.
Valley St.
Fairview Ave. N
E Roy St.
Mercer St.
E Mercer St.
Republican St.
E Republican St.
E Harrison St.
E Thomas St.
E John St.
Denny Way
E Denny Way
E Howell St.
E Olive St.
E Pine St.
E Pike St.
E Union St.
E Madison St.
Olive Way
Pine St.
Pike St.
University St.
Spring St.
Seneca St.
Madison St.
Cherry St.
James St.
Columbia St.
Marion St.
Yesler Way
Fairview Ave. N
Minor Ave. N
Pontius Ave. N
Yale Ave. N
Eastlake Ave. E
Melrose Ave. E
Bellevue Ave. E
Summit Ave. E
Belmont Ave. E
Boylston Ave. E
Harvard Ave. E
Broadway E
10th Ave. E
12th Ave. E
13th Ave. E
14th Ave. E
Malden Ave. E
15th Ave. E
16th Ave. E
17th Ave. E
Minor Ave.
Howell St.
Terry Ave.
Bellevue Ave.
Summit Ave.
Belmont Ave.
Boylston Ave.
Harvard Ave.
Broadway
11th Ave.
12th Ave.
13th Ave.
14th Ave.
15th Ave.
16th Ave.
17th Ave.
Boren Ave.
Terry Ave.
7th Ave.
6th Ave.
8th Ave.
7th Ave.
9th Ave.
3rd Ave.
Boren Ave.
12th Ave.
CAPITOL HILL
Capitol Hill
SEATTLE CENTRAL COMMUNITY COLLEGE
Cal Anderson Park
Washington State Convention & Trade Center
Freeway Park
FIRST HILL
SEATTLE UNIVERSITY
Seattle Central Library
Seattle City Hall
Pioneer Square
City Hall Park
5
24
23
21
20
22
19
18
17
16
15
Ace Hotel 5
Alexis 14
Arctic Club Hotel 15
The Baroness Hotel 20
The Edgewater 6
Executive Hotel Pacific 17
Fairmont Olympic Hotel 19
Four Seasons Hotel 13
Gaslight Inn 24
Grand Hyatt 23
Hotel Andra 8
Hotel Five 4
Hotel Hotel Hostel 1
Hotel Max 9
Hotel Monaco 16
Hotel Vintage 18
Inn at the Market 12
The Inn at Virginia Mason 21
MarQueen Hotel 2
Mayflower Park Hotel 11
Palladian 10
Pan Pacific Hotel Seattle 3
Sorrento Hotel 22
Warwick Seattle Hotel 7

transports you back to earlier decades of travel and adventure. (Photographs of the stern-faced men who funded the all-male club line the walls of the reception area.) The bathrooms in this DoubleTree boutique property are comfortably human-sized, with marble sink stands and patterned wallpaper. The rooms, with their big windows, king-sized beds and Art Deco–style armchairs, also have a sturdy, period look. The Arctic Club is well situated for exploring Pioneer Square, the oldest and most architecturally interesting part of Seattle; you can easily walk to downtown, the waterfront, and Pike Place Market.

700 3rd Ave. (entrance on Cherry). www.thearcticclubseattle.com. ✆ **800/222-8733** or 206/340-0340. 120 units. $175–$319 double. Valet parking $46. **Amenities:** Restaurant; lounge; exercise room; Wi-Fi ($10/day).

Alexis ★★ Two early-20th-century buildings, both on Seattle's Historic Register, have been combined to make this hotel. But the interior decor is anything but old fashioned. Dark shades of taupe and brown are used as a background in the rooms, where paintings, ornate headboards, and one-of-a-kind accessories (like a desk lamp with a sculpted head as its base) add personality to the space. There are dozens of different room configurations, including some enormous suites with wood-burning fireplaces, media rooms, and Elliott Bay views. And this is a rare Seattle hotel where you can actually open the windows, but unfortunately you'll probably keep them closed because of the traffic on First Avenue. Works by local, national, and international artists hang in the lobby and in the gallery-like corridor that connects the two buildings. On the fourth floor is a sauna that guests can use for free (reservations in advance necessary). Also free: a complimentary evening wine hour, and morning and afternoon coffee. A new bar-restaurant called **The Bookstore** serves breakfast, lunch, and dinner. The last time I stayed at the Alexis, the elevator doors in the lobby opened and a young woman wearing a white bridal gown got out of one car, and an older guest with a giant poodle got in the other. That, to me, is the Alexis.

1007 First Ave. (at Madison St.). www.alexishotel.com. ✆ **888/850-1155** or 206/624-4844. 121 units. $215–$285 double. Valet parking $43. Pets accepted (free). **Amenities:** Restaurant; lounge; small exercise room, Aveda day spa; Wi-Fi ($10/day).

Fairmont Olympic Hotel ★★★ Covering an entire city block smack-dab in the heart of downtown, the Fairmont Olympic is Seattle's grande dame of hotels and the place to stay if you want a traditional, full-service, grand hotel experience. Built in 1926, it's embedded in the memories of just about everyone who grew up in Seattle or has spent any time there. The majesty, opulence and scale of its lobby and the Georgian Room is simply unparalleled. Rooms were enlarged in the 1980s, when the property was a Four Seasons, and the furnishings have been refreshed several times since, most recently in 2016, but remain reassuringly traditional. You'll find sumptuous beds and updated but nicely old-fashioned marbled bathrooms with tubs big enough for a soak. The indoor pool opens onto outdoor lounge areas. Step into the vast, chandeliered Georgian Room for breakfast, lunch or afternoon tea and you'll be transported into a world of graceful luxury. **Shuckers** (reviewed p. 103), the hotel's dinner restaurant, is justly famous for its oysters and fresh seafood.

411 University St. www.fairmont.com/seattle/olympic. ✆ **206/621-1700.** 450 units. $199–$303 double; $289–$455 suite. Valet parking $55. **Amenities:** Restaurant; lounge; room service; fitness center; Jacuzzi; year-round indoor pool; full-service spa; free Wi-Fi.

Grand Hyatt ★★ Although its enormous lobby isn't particularly noteworthy, and even seems a bit bare, the rooms at the Grand go beyond the bland, cookie-cutter sterility found in so many large corporate hotels. The doors are solid and heavy, and the comfortable, clean-lined furniture includes a sizeable work desk. But it's the bathrooms that really stand out here and give the Grand a sense of luxury: Wonderfully roomy, with marble floors and countertops, each bathroom has a great soaking tub and a walk-in shower. You can upgrade to a Corner King Suite for only $30 (based on availability), or to one of the 850-square-feet Emerald Suites for an additional $150. The corner suites are palatial in size. Rooms with water views are of course the most popular, but know that you'll be looking looking at the waves through a forest of downtown buildings. The large health Club is well-equipped with cardio and weight machines, as well as free weights. A Ruth's Chris Steak House is accessed from the lobby, and there's also a Starbucks, a NY Deli, and a Blue Sushi for on-site noshes. Step out the front door and you're smack-dab in the center of Pine Street, one of downtown's busiest shopping streets and next to the Seattle Convention Center.

721 Pine St. www.grandseattle.hyatt.com. ✆ **800/233-1234** or 206/774-1234. 425 units. $199–$405 double. Valet parking $55. **Amenities:** Restaurants, health club.

Kimpton Hotel Monaco ★★ You know you're in for something out of the ordinary when you enter the lobby, look up, and see frescoes of leaping dolphins copied from the Palace of Knossos on Crete. Those buoyant mammals are indicative of the sophisticated but playful nature of this Kimpton hotel, created in 1997 from a rather undistinguished office building in downtown Seattle. Patterned wallpapers, lush colors, quirky art, and an unpredictable mix of comfy sofas and chairs add pizzazz to the rooms and suites (former offices); in the suites, curtains rather than doors separate the living and bedroom areas. (Unless you are using the room only to sleep, you might want to steer clear of the smaller rooms that face the grim FBI building next door.) At 5pm, head down to the light, airy, high-ceilinged lobby and curl up next to the fireplace with a glass of complimentary wine. You can also dine at Outlier, the hotel's restaurant. Kids are very welcome at the Monaco, where you can request a pet goldfish for your room or bring your own pet with you. The staff are super-friendly and helpful.

1101 Fourth Ave. www.monaco-seattle.com. ✆ **888/454-8397** or 206/621-1770. 189 units. $199–$475 double. Rates include evening wine tasting. Valet parking $40. Pets accepted (free). **Amenities:** Restaurant; lounge; small exercise room; free Wi-Fi.

Kimpton Hotel Vintage ★★ Occupying a quietly dignified 11-story brick building from the 1920s, the Hotel Vintage is friendly, low-key, and romantic in an under- rather than overstated way. Wine is the theme here, so all the rooms are named for Washington state wineries, and at the complimentary wine hour between 5 and 6pm you can sample excellent West Coast vintages. The newly refurbed rooms are calm and quiet, with patterned carpets, earth-tone walls, and a mix of traditional and contemporary furnishings, including big sofas and sizeable work desks. Bathrooms have nice finishes but are fairly small. Service at this hotel is exceptionally personable, and you can dine on-site at one of Seattle's finest Italian restaurants, **Tulio** (p. 106). The hotel is right across the street from the striking Seattle Public Library designed by Dutch architect Rem Koolhass.

1100 Fifth Ave. www.hotelvintage-seattle.com. ✆ **800/853-3914** or 206/624-8000. 124 units. $139–$325 double. Pets accepted (free). Valet parking $42. **Amenities:** Restaurant; lounge; small exercise room; complimentary wine hour and morning coffee; free Wi-Fi.

Moderate

Hotel Max ★★ Hotel Max is sexy and arty and has a loose-fitting European sensibility geared towards travelers under 40…and the young at heart. There's a complimentary beer tasting every night; and for fans of Seattle's pop/grunge scene, there's the Sub Pop floor, decorated with photos and memorabilia by Charles Peterson, who followed and photographed the bands Nirvana, Pearl Jam, and Soundgarden. The rooms on this floor come with a selection of vintage LPs that you can play on an honest-to-garsh turntable. The rest of the rooms manage the smart trick of being both efficient and sexy, if not quite as cool as the Sup Pop digs, with works by contemporary Pacific Northwest artists on dark gray walls and jolts of bright orange and red accent colors on the beds. The eye-popping red is also used in the bathrooms with their stainless-steel vanities and, in many rooms, separate toilet and tiled shower areas. The only potential drawback in this hotel is that heat and air conditioning come from window-mounted units; on the plus side, this is one of the few hotels where you can open the windows to catch those sweet summertime breezes. Refashioned from a 1927 hotel, it's just a couple of blocks north of all the major downtown action. The hotel's partner restaurant, **Miller's Guild ★★** (p. 103), serves outstanding cocktails and grilled meats.

620 Stewart St. www.hotelmaxseattle.com. ✆ **866/986-8087** or 206/728-6299. 163 units. $147–$242 double. Rate includes complimentary beer hour. Valet parking $40. Pets accepted ($45). **Amenities:** Restaurant; lounge; fitness center; free Wi-Fi.

Mayflower Park Hotel ★★ If you want to stay in a traditional, long-established hotel in the heart of downtown, but don't want to pay the prices charged by the Fairmont Olympic (p. 92), the Mayflower Park is a smart alternative. Built in 1927 and handsomely restored, this heritage beauty welcomes guests with crystal chandeliers, gleaming brass fixtures, and period antiques. The rooms and suites are quiet and comfortable with traditional furnishings; no contemporary surprises here. Bathrooms come with deep tubs and the original tile floors. From the hotel's central downtown location you can easily walk anywhere in central Seattle. The hotel also connects to Westlake Center (with monorail to Seattle Center) and the Seattle light rail to Capital Hill and the University District is right around the corner. A very good restaurant and cocktail bar are on premises. The Mayflower Park is locally owned and the staff here goes out of its way to provide friendly, professional service.

405 Olive Way. www.mayflowerpark.com. ✆ **800/426-5100** or 206/623-8700. 171 units. $149–$369 double. Valet parking $35. **Amenities:** Restaurant; lounge; fitness center; free Wi-Fi.

Inexpensive

Executive Hotel Pacific ★★ I'm giving this downtown hotel two stars not because it's luxurious and stuffed with amenities but because it is relatively small and simple—and has the lowest room rates of any hotel in downtown Seattle. I really like this place. It's in a brick building built in 1928, and it's so unobtrusive that you can walk by and hardly be aware of its presence. The hotel is built on one of Seattle's steep hills, so from the mid-level reception area you walk up to the lounge and elevators or down to the cafe facing Fourth Avenue. The rooms are typical of older hotels in that you can actually open the windows—a feature I always appreciate—and the layout is economical and straightforward. But there's a spark in the decorating, so the beds have high wood headboards and snaps of red on white comforters. There are desks in the king rooms but not in the smaller queen rooms. Bathrooms are small but have been completely retiled and renovated—tubs are too small for bathing, but each one has a rain shower. Head down to the lounge in the evening for the complimentary wine hour—chances are you'll notice that many of the hotel's guests are from Europe, Canada, and Asia, travelers who recognize a good deal.

400 Spring St. www.executivehotels.net. ✆ **888/388-3932** or 206/623-3900. 156 units. $105–$219 double. Valet parking $40. Pets accepted ($25). **Amenities:** Cafe; lounge; complimentary evening wine; small exercise room; free Wi-Fi.

PIKE PLACE MARKET

Expensive

Four Seasons Hotel ★★★ Seattle has plenty of funky and quirky boutique hotels, and lots of corporate cookie-cutter hotels, but if you're seeking calm, refined luxury in the heart of the Pike Place Market area, this hotel can't be beat. The Four Seasons occupies the first 10 floors of a 21-story residential tower overlooking Elliott Bay and the Olympic Mountains. It has a sleek Northwest look, with a long, low lobby fireplace set in a wall of textured basalt, and art from the Seattle Art Museum (located right across the street). The rooms and suites are unusually generous in size and comfort, with a quiet, cocooning quality that invites you to relax and linger. The color scheme here is a soothing white offset by the warm glow of ash wood desks and cabinetry;

the muted palette maximizes the light from floor-to-ceiling windows. Luxurious marble-clad bathrooms feature soaker tubs and walk-in rain showers. This full-service hotel offers a full roster of amenities, including Seattle's only heated, outdoor infinity pool with vistas of the bay and mountains; a truly state-of-the-art fitness center; and, a 6,000-square-foot spa that offers a full menu of skincare treatments and therapies. At **Goldfinch Tavern,** the hotel's casual restaurant, you can sit by a cozy fire and enjoy Northwest-inspired meals. It's a wonderfully inviting spot to sip a cocktail as the sun goes down over Puget Sound.

99 Union St. www.fourseasons.com/seattle. ✆ **206/749-7000.** 147 units. $389–$799 double. Valet parking $50. **Amenities:** Restaurant; lounge; large fitness center; Jacuzzi; year-round outdoor pool; full-service spa; free Wi-Fi.

Inn at the Market ★★★ One of the best small hotels in the Pacific Northwest, the Inn is built on a steeply sloping street between First Avenue and the market, close to the buzz and bustle of Seattle's number one tourist destination (the Pike Place Market) and the busy downtown core. But step into the hotel's quiet inner courtyard and you're in another world. The small lobby, with its cheery fireplace and quietly contemporary decor, is what comfort is all about. There are several different room categories, but basically there are two room types: those with a city view (facing First Avenue) and those with a water view (facing Elliott Bay and the Olympic Mountains). Whatever the view, the rooms are large and uncluttered with a nod to relaxed comfort rather than fussy formality. Colors are muted and calm, furnishings sturdily modern, bathrooms roomy. If your room doesn't have a water view, you can still enjoy one from the roof deck overlooking Elliott Bay and the market, a perfect spot for enjoying a morning coffee or a Seattle sunset. In the rooms, you can open the windows for a breath of fresh air, but be advised that this can be a noisy area, with street life and, in the water-facing rooms, the hum of traffic on the elevated Alaskan Way highway (which will hopefully be gone by 2019). When they're closed, the hotel's double-paned windows and doors block out all the noise. If you want to spring for something really special, book Beecher's Loft, a second-floor open-plan apartment in the building next door. A former architect's studio, it's been completely redone in a Seattle-chic way with a wrap-around balcony that's right above the Pike Place Market.

86 Pine St. www.innatthemarket.com. ✆ **800/446-4484** or 206/443-3600. 70 units. $245–$399 double. Valet parking $39. **Amenities:** Restaurant; lounge; access to nearby health club; free Wi-Fi.

WATERFRONT

Expensive

The Edgewater ★★★ It may seem odd in maritime Seattle, but this is the only hotel that sits on a waterfront pier facing Elliott Bay and Puget Sound. Open the windows of one of the water-view rooms and you'll hear the waves lapping, the gulls crying, and the sounds of harbor craft plying the waters. To be honest, it doesn't make sense to stay here unless you *do* book a waterview room or suite (its on-the-waterfront location is ultimately The Edgewater's biggest selling point). The building is a relic from the 1962 Seattle World's Fair, when it was erected to house workers. Afterwards, it was turned into a hotel with the novel tag line "Fish from every window." Guests could buy bait and tackle at what is now the gift shop and literally drop a line from their rooms—which is what the Beatles were photographed doing when they stayed at The Edgewater during their 1964 world tour (you can book the suite they stayed in). The hotel has been steadily upgrading itself over the decades and is now a swank property with rooms that were completely refurbished recently. Its utilitarian, motel-like facade has been disguised, but something of its quirky, freewheeling spirit still survives in the lobby, where columns mimic tree trunks, and in the rooms, where footstools look like shaggy dogs. Some rooms have gas fireplaces, walk-in showers, and modern claw foot tubs; you can slide open the bathroom wall to enjoy the view and the fireplace while you soak. The Edgewater's **Six-Seven** (as in Pier 67) restaurant (see p. 109) is one of Seattle's best waterfront dining spots. The lively Seattle waterfront begins right outside the hotel's door; the *Victoria Clipper,* a high-speed catamaran that travels daily to Victoria, British Columbia, departs from the adjacent pier; and other cruise-ship and excursion boat tours are all within walking distance. The Olympic Sculpture Park is a 5-minute walk north.

Pier 67, 2411 Alaskan Way. www.edgewaterhotel.com. ✆ **800/624-0670** or 206/728-7000. 223 units. $219–$409 double. Valet parking $43. Pets accepted ($25 in rooms only, no pets in suites). **Amenities:** Restaurant; lounge; exercise room and access to nearby health club; free Wi-Fi.

BELLTOWN

Expensive

Hotel Ändra ★★★ The word ändra in Swedish means "change," and change is what Hotel Ändra is about. The building dates from 1926, but nearly everything in this trendsetting boutique hotel—furniture, fabrics, even bathroom fixtures—comes from Sweden or Scandinavia and reflects a sophisticated and richly textured European aesthetic. The neighborhood where it's located is also undergoing change as Amazon and other corporate giants move their headquarters into the nearby South Lake Union area. The tone is set in the lobby with its distressed plank floors, thick wool carpets, stone-mantled fireplace, and a chic-casual bar on the mezzanine. The rooms have a warm, rich look augmented by soft alpaca-covered headboards, crisp white linens with striped chenille coverlets, patterned drapery, and minimalist wood furniture. All have walk-in closets, vanity areas, and small but well-designed bathrooms with sloping white sinks, lighted mirrors, fluffy Turkish towels, and FACE Stockholm bath products. Downsides? The hotel's fitness center is small and basic, as is the business center. The Ändra's central location makes it an easy walk to all of Seattle's downtown and waterfront attractions and shopping. Within a two-block area, foodies can dine at three of Seattle superchef Tom Douglas's restaurants (**Lola, Serious Pie,** and **Etta's,** reviewed below).

2000 Fourth Ave. www.hotelandra.com. ✆ **877/448-8600** or 206/448-8600. 119 units. $239–$359 double. Valet parking $39. Pets accepted (free). **Amenities:** Restaurant, lounge; small exercise room and access to nearby health club; Wi-Fi ($10/day).

Moderate

Ace Hotel ★ There are now Ace Hotels in several U.S. cities and London, but back in 1999 there was only one, and this was it. The idea and aesthetic behind the brand is an appealing one: Convert old(er) buildings into cool new hotels using reclaimed materials and architectural details; have some of the rooms share bathrooms, European style; and charge a reasonable rate. So this is not a hotel with frills and frou-frou, but it is a hotel that is something of an adventure to stay in. In the century-old building in Belltown, Ace made use of the original brick walls and wood floors but painted them white. Half the rooms share (immaculate) bathrooms, the others have private loos with showers. Each room is unique. Two of them have wall art by famed graffiti artist Shepard Fairey. Others are decorated with nostalgic photos of Washington scenes. The furnishings are simple and minimal—no more than a 1960s-era sculpted plastic chair in some, a vinyl sofa in others. They all have work desks, but the lighting in some rooms could be better. Green plants add a nice living touch to this minimalist urban aesthetic. There are several good restaurants within easy walking distance, the fabulous Macrina Bakery (p. 117) is right across the street, and you can get to Pike Place Market on foot in about 10 minutes. The reception area is up a fairly steep flight of stairs and there's no elevator, so if mobility is an issue, you probably don't want to stay here.

2423 First Ave. www.acehotel.com. ✆ **206/448-4721.** 28 units, 14 with shared bathroom. $129–140 double with shared bathroom; $219–$239 double with private bathroom. Rates include continental breakfast. Parking $39 (secure lot, two blocks away). Pets accepted (free). **Amenities:** Lounge; free Wi-Fi.

Kimpton Palladian Hotel ★★ You can always count on Kimpton to do something unusual at its hotels. This one pays homage to Seattle's hometown heroes, like Bill Gates and Jimi Hendrix. You'll see amusing portraits of them in the lobby, and each room features a "celebrity pillow." The Palladian was created from a 1910 apartment building near the north end of Pike Place Market and close to the new South Lake Union neighborhood. It's a sexy hotel, with many furnishings designed by local talent, which means unusual features like sliding "barn doors" for the bathrooms, and bathrooms that combine showers and claw foot tubs. Each has a dark, Northwest color palette that's enlivened with lovely old rugs and snapping white bedcoverings. And because of the heritage building's configuration, every room is a different shape. The fitness center is small but well-equipped. There's a complimentary wine social every evening, complimentary coffee starting at 5:30am, and a fine on-site restaurant, **Shaker + Spear** (lunch, dinner and weekend brunch). The staff goes out of its way to be helpful. The only downside: no views, thanks to the towers around the hotel.

2000 Second Ave. (at Virginia St.). www.palladianhotel.com. ✆ **858/808-0900** or 206/448-1111. 97 units. $165–$465 double. Valet parking $39. **Amenities:** Restaurant; lounge; fitness center; complimentary wine hour; free Wi-Fi.

Warwick Seattle Hotel ★★ Built in 1981, this French-owned mid-sized hotel in Belltown was ahead of its time in terms of boutique-style amenities, offering an indoor heated pool and floor-to-ceiling angled windows that open up to create an in-room balcony. More recently the rooms were refurbished with an eclectic mix of patterns and furnishings that are both stylish and comfortable. The beechwood work desks are actually big enough to work on and have convenient outlets on the top of the desk. The unique window-balconies let in lots of light and provide a glimpse of Elliott Bay, and, if you're in a higher-floor north-facing room, give you a view of the Space Needle. (But with Amazon and other corporate giants building towers in the nearby South Lake Union area, the urban landscape around here seems to change by the day.) The bathrooms are small but have a nicely luxe feel to them. Additional upscale touches include evening turn-down service, Gilchrist & Soames toiletries, and an on-site restaurant, **Margaux,** which serves French-inspired Northwest cuisine. If you're traveling with kids, they'll love the pool.

401 Lenora St. www.warwickwa.com. ✆ **206/443-4300.** 231 units. $157–$345 double. Valet parking $41. **Amenities:** Restaurant; lounge; heated indoor pool; small exercise room; business center; free Wi-Fi in Executive and Premiere rooms, $11 in other rooms.

Inexpensive

Hotel Five ★ A former Ramada Inn with completely reimagined decor, Hotel Five is a (usually) reasonably priced and conveniently located choice. Although the hotel is not right in the downtown shopping core, you can easily walk there or to Seattle Center within a few minutes, and the cafes and restaurants of Belltown are all around. Now about that room decor: It uses a lot of red (with dark comforters), and it seems to have taken its inspiration from urban graffiti and semi-psychedelic swirl-art paintings. It's not what you'd call serene; however the furnishings are comfortable and the bathrooms are good. Down in the retro-70s-looking lobby, Max's Café serves breakfast and lunch.

2200 Fifth Ave. (at Blanchard St.). www.hotelfiveseattle.com. ✆ **206/441-9785.** 120 units. $140–$230 double. Self-park $37. **Amenities:** Cafe (breakfast/lunch only); free Wi-Fi.

SOUTH LAKE UNION

Expensive

Pan Pacific Hotel Seattle ★★★ The only hotel located right in the South Lake Union neighborhood, the Pan Pacific is ideal for visitors who want to be close to the city's downtown attractions and also explore Seattle's newest neighborhood, home of Amazon's new world headquarters. The lobby, aglow with big windows, travertine floors, a long, low fireplace; and tigerwood accents on the walls, sets the hotel's overall tone of minimalist Northwest and

Japanese fusion style. You'll find the same cool, uncluttered elegance in the rooms and suites, where light-colored stone tile, carpets, and fabric wall coverings serve as calm backdrops for the few well-chosen and well-designed pieces of furniture. (One thing to note is that none of the rooms have twin beds.) The wood-and-stone bathrooms have both a walk-in shower and a deep soaking tub. In-room dining is a special amenity offered to guests staying in the suites. The table is set with flowers and candles, you order from a special menu from **Seastar,** the hotel's well-regarded restaurant, and the meal is served in your room by a waiter. For some added oomph, request a room with a view of the iconic Space Needle. A large gym with state-of-the-art equipment, dry saunas, and a hydropool is located in a separate building across the cobblestoned front plaza. Adjacent to it is a Vida spa offering soothing massages and ayurvedic skincare treatments. A Whole Foods anchors the bottom level of the hotel.

2125 Terry Ave. www.panpacific.com/seattle. ✆ **877/324-4856** or 206/264-8111. 206 units. Double $300–$400. Valet parking $52. Pets allowed ($50 in 3rd floor rooms only). **Amenities:** Restaurant, lounge, fitness room, spa, free Wi-Fi.

FIRST HILL

Moderate

Sorrento Hotel ★★★ This is one of Seattle's three great historic hotels (the other two are the Fairmont Olympic and the Mayflower Park). Like those two, the Sorrento is a hotel full of charming period details and rooms that convey personality rather than conformity, with carved wood moldings, restored vintage furniture, and white marble bathrooms with porcelain pedestal sinks and full-length mirrors. One big difference here is the rich color palette, far more inventive than at the Fairmont or Mayflower Park (and there are unique designer suites, too). The Sorrento beds are remarkably comfortable (Sealy Posturepedic Crown Jewel mattresses and Egyptian cotton sheets). Suites offer more space but even a basic room here is just dandy. You won't be in the thick of downtown Seattle but it's an easy walk to get there, and the Sorrento offers a host of amenities more typically found in luxury hotels that cost twice as much.

900 Madison St. www.hotelsorrento.com. ✆ **800/426-1265** or 206/622-6400. 76 units. $161–$359 double. Pets accepted ($50 per night). Valet parking $39. **Amenities:** Restaurant; lounge; salon; fitness center; free Wi-Fi.

Inexpensive

The Inn at Virginia Mason & The Baroness Hotel ★★★ Three stars for a pair of hotels that are among the least expensive in Seattle? Can it be true? Yes, I'm happy to report that it can be and is. I'm not awarding this coveted three-star rating because these hotels offer luxurious rooms and heated pools. I'm awarding them because of their surprising charm and personality. Both of them are managed as non-profits by Virginia Mason Hospital up on First Hill. That's why they are so inexpensive. Both the Inn and the Baroness are often used by family members of patients in one of the area's three hospitals (this area is called Pill hill for a reason). But there is nothing medicinal about a stay in either property—in fact, I can almost guarantee that you will end up telling your friends about what a great find they are. The guest rooms in both are actually former apartments, and because the Inn dates from 1928 and the Baroness from the 1930 Art Deco era, both of the buildings are loaded with period details that you simply will not find in any other Seattle hotels. At the Baroness, an Art Deco gem, rooms come complete with curving walls and untampered-with period details. A suite here comes with a separate kitchen, a bedroom, and a sitting area—decorated with tasteful traditional furniture and full of original details, like the former phone nook now used as a little library shelf. And, unbelievably, you can order room service at the Inn and get a meal delivered to your door for under $15. You can also dine on-site at the newly opened **Rhododendron Café** or walk downtown (downhill) and find plenty of spots for breakfast in the intriguing First Hill neighborhood. If there's a drawback, it's that some of the west-facing rooms get a white-noise hum from the ventilating system of the hospital next door.

1006 Spring St. www.innatvirginiamason.com. ✆ **800/283-6453** or 206/583-6453. Inn: 79 units; Baroness: 57 units. $119–$229 double. **Amenities:** Restaurant; free Wi-Fi.

CAPITOL HILL

Moderate

Gaslight Inn ★ B&Bs often provide insight into the personality of a neighborhood, thanks to the special architectural style of a once-private residence. At the Gaslight Inn, the style is not Victorian, as the name implies, but Craftsman, a handsome and once-ubiquitous early-20th-century Northwest style characterized by wide porches, overhanging eaves, a low pitched roofline, and handcrafted stone and woodwork. Inside this charming Capitol Hill bungalow, the doors and windows are trimmed with oak and decorated with Stickley furniture and art glass from the same era. There are eight guest bedrooms, some on the first, some of the second floor, some sharing a bathroom, others with private bathrooms, some with decks, some with fireplaces. What they all have in common is a calm, comfortable period ambience and a reasonable price. A heated outdoor pool (summer use only) adds a touch of non-Craftsman luxury.

1727 15th Ave. www.gaslight-inn.com. ✆ **206/325-3654.** 8 units, 3 with shared bathroom. $188 double with shared bathroom; $208 double with private bathroom. Rates include continental breakfast. No children allowed. **Amenities:** Seasonal Jacuzzi; small seasonal heated outdoor pool; free Wi-Fi.

FREMONT

Inexpensive

Hotel Hotel Hostel★★ Clean, safe and friendly—that about sums up Hotel Hotel, located in the artsy, community-minded Fremont neighborhood, about 3 miles north of the Space Needle and near Woodland Park Zoo. It's comfy and basic but nice-looking, with bare brick walls, wood floors and a kind of low-key industrial-chic ambience throughout. A full breakfast is included in your room rate and there's an on-site café with low-cost noshes. As at any hostel, you have various sleeping options: dorm beds, private rooms with shared baths, private rooms with private baths, and family rooms that can accommodate two adults and two kids. Fremont is one of Seattle's most intriguing neighborhoods, and you can get downtown or anywhere else, on public transportation. This is a really good choice for budget travelers.

3515 Fremont Ave. N. www.hotelhotel.com. ✆ **206/257-4543.** 18 units, 3 with private bath. Dorm bed $34 w/breakfast, $114–$140 private room w/bath w/breakfast. **Amenities:** Cafe; communal kitchen; free Wi-Fi.

QUEEN ANNE

Moderate

MarQueen Hotel ★★ The hotel occupies a unique heritage property that was built in the early 1900s as housing to house the chauffeurs and mechanics who worked in a nearby Ford plant. It was turned into a hotel in 1998. Each room is a really small apartment with separate kitchenette (complete with built-in dining nook) and a small living area separated from the sleeping area. The furnishings are comfortable period reproductions; the bathrooms are small but perfectly adequate. The MarQueen is in the Lower Queen Anne neighborhood, completely safe and close to lots of cafes, inexpensive restaurants and easy public transportation, but this is not the swankiest part of town (there's a tattoo parlor across the street). That said, I'd recommend this place for anyone interested in staying in an unusual and reasonably priced hotel with some real character to it.

600 Queen Anne Ave. N. www.marqueenhotel.com. ✆ **206/282-7407.** 59 units, $116–$296 w/continental breakfast. **Amenities:** Lounge; kitchens in rooms; free Wi-Fi.

WHERE TO EAT

Over the last 25 years or so, Seattle's reputation as one of the great restaurant cities in the U.S. has grown steadily. Before that time, there were some good ethnic Asian and Italian restaurants, and always one or two classic French eateries, but eating out in Seattle was mostly about seafood and steak. And the seafood was usually wonderful, because it's hard to ruin a slab of salmon or a fresh Dungeness crab. Creamy clam or oyster chowder, or tomato-based seafood chowders, were on just about every menu.

Then the food scene exploded. Cooking became an esteemed profession and the materials needed to create culinary art were close at hand, where they'd always been, but perhaps not appreciated. The big difference now is that many different styles of cooking and flavoring are used to turn those local ingredients, no matter how humble, into edible adventures. There's also a greater awareness of vegetarian, vegan and gluten-free cooking and many restaurants have options for all three on their menus.

I've covered a wide range of dining choices, some of them old favorites that have lost none of their appeal; some that are special destination restaurants where Seattleites go for good food and fabulous views; and others that showily showcase the "new" style of Pacific Northwest cuisine. Many of Seattle's best downtown restaurants are independent kitchens attached to hotels, others

Happy Hours in Seattle

Nearly every restaurant in Seattle has a Happy Hour, typically between 4pm and 6pm and sometimes late at night. Happy Hour is a great way to sample a restaurant's smaller appetizer plates and enjoy a glass of wine or cocktail at a reasonable price. But here's my real secret for a happy Happy Hour: oysters. Many Seattle seafood restaurants offer freshly shucked oysters for $1 to $2 during their happy hours. Now that is something to make you happy.

are neighborhood spots outside the downtown core. Wherever you choose to eat, I think you will be impressed with the quality of the food and the friendliness of the service.

DOWNTOWN

Expensive

Assaggio ★★★ NORTHERN ITALIAN From the Michelangelo-inspired art (look up!) to the personal welcome by gregarious owner/chef Mauro Golmarvi and his charming wife Connie, to the handmade pastas and melt-in-your-mouth veal dishes, there's no doubt you've entered a world where food is a passion and hospitality is genuine. Everything at this award-winning restaurant, from the simple Margarita pizza and baked lasagna to the sophisticated ossobuco, is memorable. Gluten-free versions of the pastas are available and the wine selection is excellent.

2010 4th Ave. www.assaggioseattle.com. ✆ **206/441-1399.** Main courses $19–$37. Mon–Fri, 11am–2pm, 3–10pm, Sat 5–10pm.

Miller's Guild ★★ PACIFIC NORTHWEST Above all, this is a place for grilled meat and fish. A giant mesquite-burning stove in the open kitchen—the focal point of the sleekly minimalist space—sears steaks, chops and seafood to perfection. Before your main course, whet your appetite with a craft cocktail and maybe some Shigoku oysters. Then, if you're an unabashed carnivore, go for the meat, and especially the juicy chops and steaks from Niman Ranch in California, one of the top purveyors of choice cuts of beef on the West Coast. Sides are extra, but ones like creamy mashed potatoes and crispy Brussels sprouts, are worth it. This is a good happy hour spot (2–5pm and 9–11pm)—you can get a glass of wine for $7, a beer for $5, and smaller, less expensive versions of the lunch and dinner choices.

612 Stewart St. www.millersguild.com. ✆ **206/443-3663.** Main courses $26–$63. Daily 7am–10pm.

Shuckers ★★★ SEAFOOD The world can be your oyster at Shuckers, and I hope it will be, because oysters are what this long-established oyster bar at the Fairmont Olympic Hotel is known for. Shuckers usually has about 8 local varieties on offer and served raw, alongside old-fashioned baked oysters and pan-fried oysters. There is other seafood, too, of course. Every day four or five fresh fish choices are available. Shuckers, located in what was once a

Downtown & Capitol Hill Restaurants

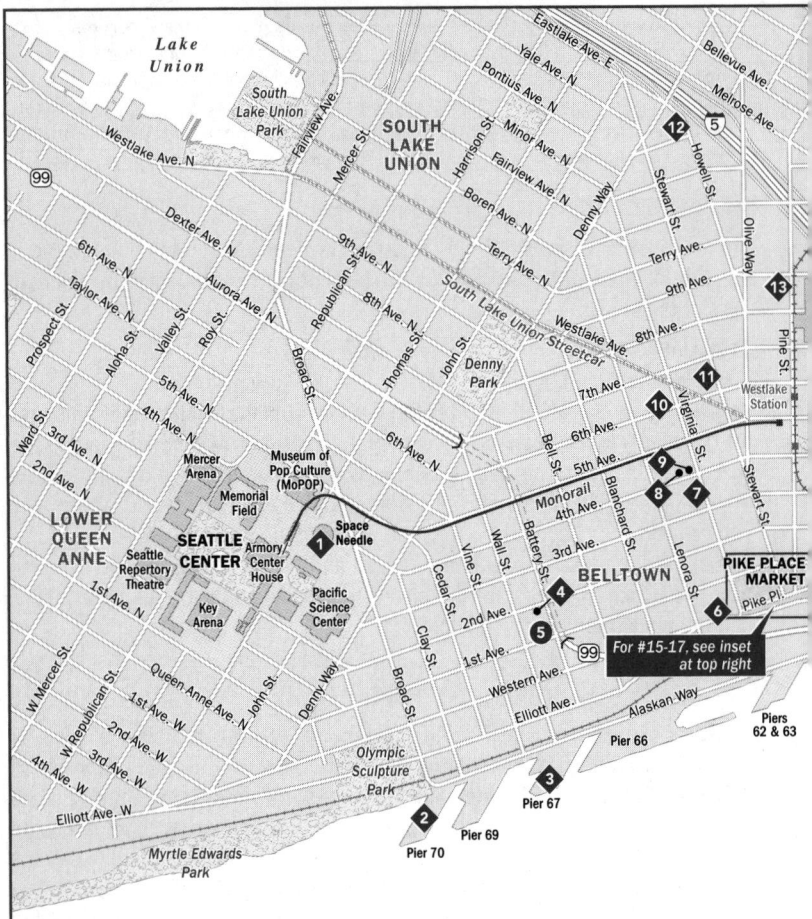

DOWNTOWN RESTAURANTS ◆

Aqua **2**
Assaggio **9**
Café Campagne **16**
Carlile Room **13**
Elliott's Oyster House **23**
Etta's Seafood **6**
Georgetown Liquor Company **28**
Ivar's Fish Bar **24**
Jade Garden **27**
Lola **8**
Mamnoon Street **10**
Marination Ma Kai **30**
Miller's Guild **11**
Niche **34**
Purple Café and Wine Bar **20**
Razzi's Pizzeria **12**
Salty's on Alki Beach **29**
Serious Pie **7**
Shiro's Sushi Restaurant **4**
Shuckers **19**
Six-Seven Restaurant **3**
SkyCity at the Needle **1**
Sound View Café **17**
Tulio **18**
Wild Ginger Restaurant & Satay Bar **21**

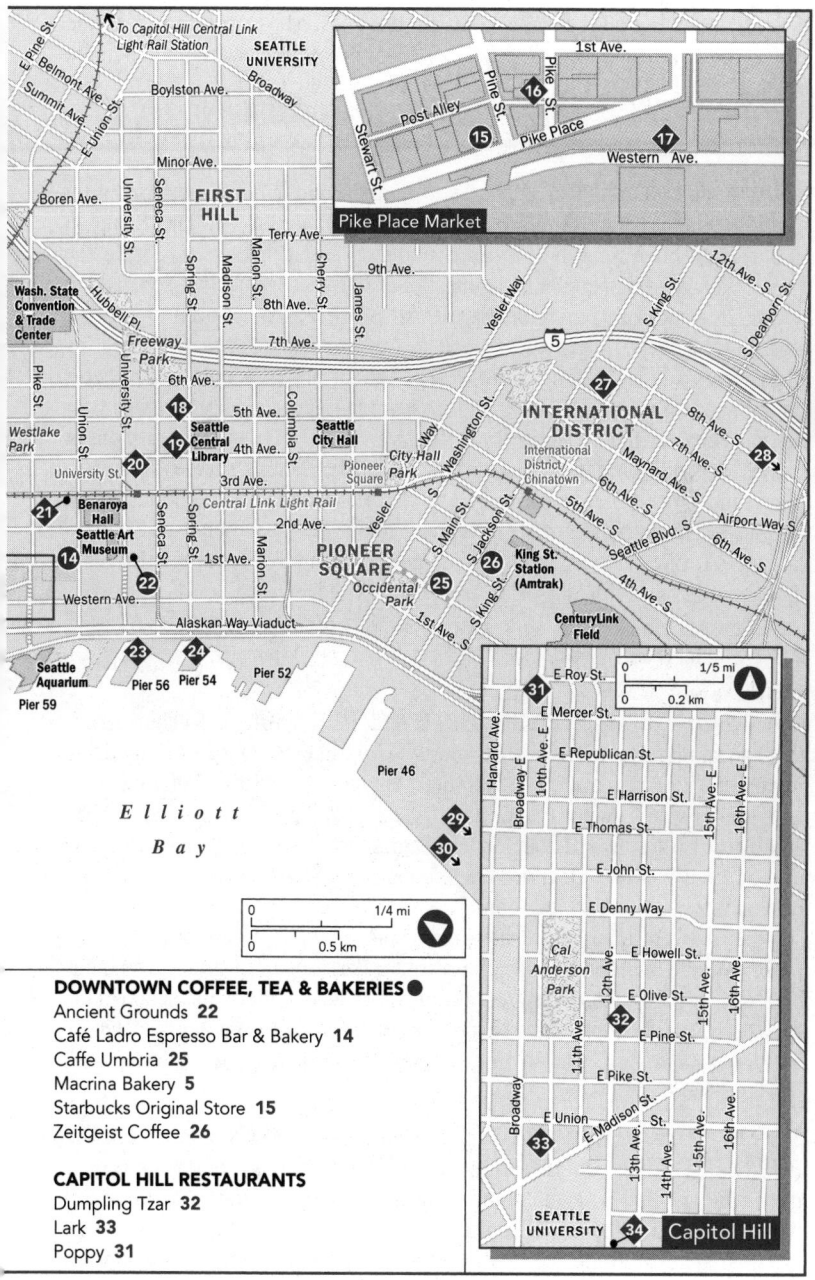

DOWNTOWN COFFEE, TEA & BAKERIES ●

Ancient Grounds **22**
Café Ladro Espresso Bar & Bakery **14**
Caffe Umbria **25**
Macrina Bakery **5**
Starbucks Original Store **15**
Zeitgeist Coffee **26**

CAPITOL HILL RESTAURANTS

Dumpling Tzar **32**
Lark **33**
Poppy **31**

haberdashery shop, has been around for over 35 years and I hope it will be around for 35 more. I'm not that keen on the dark, clubby, "nautical" look of the restaurant, but all is forgiven when those icy-fresh oysters appear on the table. And note that during Happy Hour (3–5pm) oysters on the half-shell are $2 each.

411 University St. (in the Fairmont Olympic Hotel). ✆ **206/621-1700.** Main courses $23–$43. Mon–Sat 11:30am–9pm (Fri–Sat until 10pm), Sun 5-9pm.

Tulio ★★ TUSCAN/ITALIAN Tulio started Tulio about a quarter-century ago, long before the Hotel Vintage appeared on the scene. The Kimpton Group liked his Tuscan-influenced cooking so much that Tulio became the Hotel Vintage's signature restaurant. Today it's run by Tulio's son, and it retains its hands-on, family ambiance. All of the pasta—gnocchi, tortellini, tagliatelle, ravioli, linguine, orecchiette—is handmade every morning by Maria, who's been making it for years. One of her standouts is the sweet potato gnocchi with sage butter and mascarpone; it practically melts in your mouth. For your main course, try the fresh fish of the day—tuna, salmon, or halibut depending on the season. The semolina scallops served on squash puree and topped with pork belly are also noteworthy, as is the succulent braised Kurobuta pork shank served with ricotta whipped potatoes. The restaurant is strong on Italian wines, of course (particularly Barberas and Chiantis), and otherwise limits itself to West Coast vintages.

1100 Fifth Ave. (in Hotel Vintage). www.tulio.com. ✆ **206/624-5500.** Main courses: $18–$35. Mon–Thurs 7am–10pm, Fri 7am–11pm, Sat 8am–11pm, Sun 8am–10pm.

Moderate

Carlile Room ★★ PACIFIC NORTHWEST It's difficult to characterize this appealing restaurant, but that's partly why I like it. The décor is meant to represent a kind of retro late-'60s lounge, but the food is strictly of today with a "plant forward" menu emphasizing the freshest produce available. Most come here for filling and delicious vegetarian meals but there's a small selection of local fish and meat dishes, too. On my last visit I enjoyed delicious heirloom tomatoes with red lentil hummus, beet green chermoula, mint and sesame; and chickpea-fava fritters with almond tahini. That and a perfect peach crumble with buttermilk ice cream for dessert and I was set. The menu here changes daily depending on available produce. Great wine and cocktail selections, too. The restaurant is right across from the Paramount Theater.

820 Pine. www.thecarlile.com. ✆ **206/946-9720.** Main courses $14–$26. Daily 4pm–midnight, Sat–Sun 10am–3pm.

Purple Café and Wine Bar ★★ NORTHWEST/INTERNATIONAL FUSION Diners at Purple are dwarfed by the enormous room, with its huge glass windows and floor-to-ceiling wine storage tower, rising in the middle of the restaurant like fortress of a drink. It's an appropriate centerpiece as wine is a big feature at Purple, with wine flights available and lots of variety in the varietals. Happily, wine pairings are surprisingly inexpensive here compared

North Seattle Restaurants

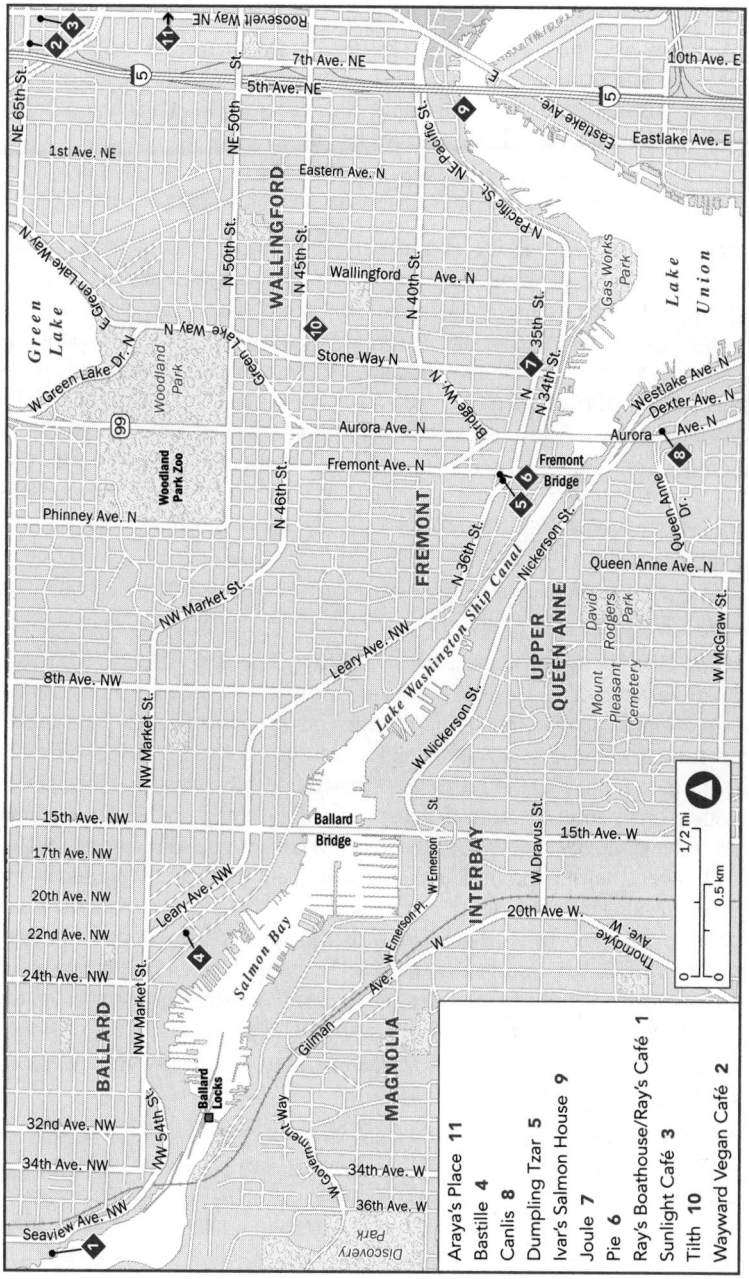

to other Seattle restaurants. As for the food, the menu has creative entrees that make use of on the bounty of the Pacific Northwest (like seafood stew or Dungeness crab and chanterelle mushroom pasta) alongside gastro-pubby fare like crispy-crust pizzas, and burgers made from free-range, Painted Hills beef. The only thing you can't order is quiet—all of the exposed brick and metallic trim in this industrial chic room amplify the clatter of plates and roar of many conversations. Lunch is less expensive but just as noisy.

1225 Fourth Ave. www.purplecafe.com. ✆ **206/829-2280.** Main courses $16–$40. Mon–Thurs 11am–10pm, Fri 11am–midnight, Sat noon–midnight, Sun noon–11pm.

Serious Pie ★★ PIZZA Local star chef Tom Douglas is serious about food, and that includes pizza. His applewood-burning oven turns out artisan-quality pies with crispy, chewy crusts and mouth-wateringly delicious toppings. Two of the best are the Yukon gold potato pizza with rosemary and pecorino, and the sweet fennel sausage pizza with roasted peppers and provolone. These pies are perfectly sized for sharing—don't try to eat one all by yourself, or you'll need to take a nap. The low-ceilinged room is reminiscent of a pub, very informal, always busy. There's beer on tap, a limited wine list, some excellent ciders, and a refreshing array of non-alcoholic concoctions that are as good as any cocktail: try the house-made Seville orange and pink peppercorn on tap.

316 Virginia St. www.seriouspieseattle.com. ✆ **206/838-7388.** Reservations not accepted. Main courses $17–$19. Daily 11am–11pm.

Wild Ginger Asian Restaurant & Satay Bar ★★ ASIAN This Pan-Asian restaurant has long been a Seattle favorite, and because it's across the street from Benaroya Hall, it's perfect for a pre-symphony dinner. I like to pull up a stool at the large satay bar and watch the cooks grill little skewers of everything from chicken to scallops to prawns to lamb. Every skewer is served with a small cube of sticky rice and pickled cucumber; order three or four satay sticks and you have yourself a meal. Of course, you can also sit at a table and have a more traditional dinner. The Panang beef curry (prime rib-eye steak in pungent curry sauce of cardamom, coconut milk, Thai basil, and peanuts) is superb, as is the deliciously pungent duck seasoned with cinnamon and star anise. For pescatarians, the choice should be the black pepper scallops quickly seared in soy sauce and pepper. A surprising number of the dishes are gluten-free; a vegan menu is also available.

1401 Third Ave. www.wildginger.net. ✆ **206/623-4450.** Satays $16–$18; main courses $14–$28. Mon–Sat 11:30am–11pm; Sun 4–9pm.

PIKE PLACE MARKET

Moderate

Café Campagne ★★ COUNTRY FRENCH Tucked away in the secret little courtyard of Inn at the Market, this charming, romantic café-bistro overlooks the crowds and noise of Pike Place Market with a kind of Gallic nonchalance. You're here for the bistro food, not sightseeing, but the sightseeing—or market-watching, anyway—is part of the atmosphere. Try the French onion soup or one of the pâtés as an appetizer, then consider the mussels in wine—so very French, and always on the menu—or the roast chicken. Other dishes change with the seasons, but the cooking here is always reliable and satisfying. That might explain why Café Campagne has been open since 1994. It's a lovely spot for lunch or weekend brunch, too.

1600 Post Alley. www.cafecampagne.com. ✆ **206/728-2233.** Main courses $13–$23 lunch, $17–$25 dinner. Daily 8am–10pm.

Etta's Seafood ★★★ PIKE PLACE MARKET *SEAFOOD* Famous chefs are often associated with a signature dish. In Tom Douglas's case, it's Dungeness crab cakes, which he perfected right here, when the restaurant belonged to someone else and he was an employee rather than the owner. Seattle's most prominent chef-entrepreneur made his name with these crunchy-on-the-outside, creamy-on-the-inside delights, and when you taste one, you'll understand why. But there's more to Etta's than crab cakes. Located in the perpetually busy Pike Place Market neighborhood, with big windows that let you people-watch as you dine (and outside tables in warm weather), Etta's roster of seafood dishes includes seafood chowders, really good fish and chips, razor clams, and less usual offerings, like tuna sashimi salad with green onion pancakes. My last meal at Etta's—fresh oysters followed by their wonderful seafood stew—was truly memorable.

2020 Western Ave. www.tomdouglas.com. ✆ **206/443-6000.** Main courses $16–$38. Mon–Thurs 11:30am–9:30pm; Fri 11:30am–10pm; Sat 9am–3pm and 4–10pm; Sun 9am–3pm and 4–9pm.

WATERFRONT

Expensive

Aqua ★★ SEAFOOD The proper name is Aqua by El Gaucho, but that sounds more like a perfume than a restaurant, so to me it's just plain Aqua. El Gaucho is the name of the famous steakhouse that operates this restaurant. And it puts on quite a trendoid show, with its long serpentine bar and big windows looking out on Elliott Bay (and a great deck for bayside dining when it's warm). I'd stick with the seafood here because that's what Aqua is really about. From a variety of local oysters to seared sashimi-grade ahi tuna, wild Alaskan halibut, and Alaskan king crab legs in truffle aioli, Chef Wesley Hood's seafood is always toothsome. Landlubbers can enjoy one of the 28-day dry aged steaks from Niman Ranch or custom-aged Angus beef prepared on an open-air charcoal grill. Vegetarians can now choose from delicious fresh salads, pastas and curry dishes.

2801 Alaskan Way, Pier 70. www.elgaucho.com. ✆ **206/956-9171.** Main courses $28–$90. Daily 4–11pm.

Six-Seven Restaurant ★★ PACIFIC NORTHWEST The restaurant at The Edgewater hotel (p. 96) on Pier 67 always had a great view—the glass-walled room opens out to a narrow patio overlooking Elliott Bay and the Olympic Mountains—and now it has fine dining as well. The food is locally sourced and usually organic. Menus change with the seasons, but you can never go wrong with the cedar plank king salmon, baked in a traditional Native American way. You can also order unadorned fish and meat selections. The quality is high, and so are the dinner prices (lunch is significantly less expensive; and if you want a good lunch to go, order the Deli Board Bento Box with soup and your choice of sandwich for $18). Six-Seven is a destination restaurant and great for a romantic dining experience.

The Edgewater, Pier 67, 2411 Alaskan Way. www.edgewaterhotel.com. ✆ **206/269-4575.** Main courses lunch $14–$26; dinner $36–$48. Daily 6:30am–9:30pm.

Moderate

Elliott's Oyster House ★★ SEAFOOD It's right on the waterfront, but it's the oysters and seafood that will grab your attention here more than the view (which actually isn't all that great). Elliott's is one of the most trustworthy lunch and dinner dining spots along Seattle's fish-and-chips-oriented waterfront. I love the vast selection of Northwest oysters; sample them the way you might sample wine—each variety has a different size, shape, texture, and taste. If you're an oystermaniac, come during Elliott's oyster happy hour when these briny bivalves cost just $1.50–$2 each. And by the way, the oysters here are not pre-shucked, as they are at most restaurants; they are shucked when you order them. Other Northwest staples like salmon and Dungeness crab are on the menu, but it's really the oysters that shine at Elliott's.

Pier 56, 1201 Alaskan Way. www.elliottsoysterhouse.com. ✆ **206/623-4340.** Main courses $19–$42. Sun–Thurs 11am–10pm; Fri–Sat 11am–11pm.

Inexpensive

Ivar's Fish Bar ★★ SEAFOOD If you're strolling along and get a hankering for a cup of thick, creamy clam chowder, or some good, fresh and not-too-greasy fish and chips (halibut or cod are the best), you can't do better than Ivar. After ordering at the counter, you can sit at benches under the canopy or take your meal with you to one of the nearby piers, where the views are swell and the gulls will be happy to keep your company.

Pier 54, 1001 Alaskan Way. ✆ **206/624-6852.** www.ivars.com. Main courses $8–$15. Daily 10:30am–10pm.

SEATTLE CENTER

Expensive

SkyCity at the Needle ★ NORTHWESTERN Where else in Seattle would you pay $47 for an a la carte pork chop? But, before you bust a gasket and turn away with a disgusted harrumph from the idea of dining at SkyCity, consider that the price of that pricey chop includes admission to the observation deck atop the Space Needle (which now runs from $20 to $29 for adults). That should lessen the pain and make the idea more palatable, and so should the relatively affordable fixed-price brunch and dinner menus. I have fond memories of this restaurant because I was taken here as a child and was thrilled by the view and horrified that frog legs were on the menu ("they taste just like chicken"). The restaurant, which sits atop the observation deck, has been revolving and serving overpriced food since 1962. I'm including it because eating here is a classic Seattle experience and a new chef has considerably upgraded the menus and the cooking.

Space Needle, 400 Broad St. www.spaceneedle.com. ✆ **206/905-2100.** Main courses $42–$69; 3-course daily brunch menu $53; 3-course dinner menu $79. Admission to Observation Deck included with price of meal. Daily 10am–2:45pm, 5–9:45pm.

BELLTOWN

Expensive

Shiro's Sushi Restaurant ★★★ JAPANESE Sushi lovers, whether they're locals or businessmen from Tokyo, flock to Shiro's because, quite simply, it has the best sushi in Seattle. Sushi master and local legend Shiro Kashiba serves only the finest, freshest fish to his customers. For a sumptuous repast, order the chef's selection (aka *omakase*) sushi or sashimi. Tempura and other traditional Japanese favorites are also available. One of Shiro's signature dishes is broiled black cod kasuzuke.

2401 Second Ave. www.shiros.com. ✆ **206/441-9844.** Sushi and sashimi platters $25–$70, main courses $7–$20. Daily 5:30–10:30pm.

Moderate

Lola ★★★ GREEK/MEDITERRANEAN Lamb is Lola's specialty, and it is delectable, whether you order the *manti* (lamb ravioli with yogurt, Aleppo, and pine nuts); the kebabs (with caramelized garlic and red wine); the slow-roasted lamb seasoned with oregano, mint, rosemary, and *jus;* or the lamb burger. This narrow, high-ceilinged, all-booth restaurant was started by Tom and Jackie Douglas over a decade ago and has never waned in popularity. Start with some pita bread and one of the Lola spreads—my favorite is cauliflower and anchovy. Then share a *meze* (small plate)—the traditional Greek salad is excellent; so is the lamb ravioli. If you're not a meat-eater, we recommend the seafood *youvetsi*, a rich soup made with clams, mussels, prawns and squid, for your entree. If you still have room, the Greek yogurt–semolina pudding is light and delish. You won't find better Greek-inspired food in Seattle. Lola also serves a wonderful weekend breakfast and lunch.

2000 Fourth Ave. www.lolaseattle.com. ✆ **206/441-1430.** Main courses $18–$39. Mon–Thurs 6am–midnight, Fri 6am–2am, Sat 7am–2am, Sun 7am–1am.

INTERNATIONAL DISTRICT

Inexpensive

Jade Garden ★ CHINESE In a town blessed with a number of good dim sum spots, this is one of the best for variety and freshness, though the ambience is practical rather than fancy. *Dim sum* is small plates of steamed or fried food that are hustled around the restaurant on carts. When you want something from a particular cart, you motion to the waiter and tell him how many plates of that particular dish you want (dim sum is about sharing). If you're new to dim sum, start with some basics like *humbow* (steamed buns stuffed with sweet barbecued pork), *ha gao* (shrimp dumpling) and sticky rice wrapped in lotus leaves. Don't faint if a cart of steamed chicken feet rolls past: In China they are a delicacy.

424 Seventh Ave. S. ✆ **206/622-8181.** Main courses $6–$14. Daily 9am–midnight.

BALLARD

Expensive

Ray's Boathouse/Ray's Café ★★★ PACIFIC NORTHWEST/SEAFOOD You'll enhance your meal at Ray's if you arrive when it's still light enough to take in the stunning views. Ray's sits right on the water's edge overlooking Shilshole Bay, Bainbridge Island, and the Olympic Mountains. As you might expect from a restaurant that started life as a boathouse, seafood reigns supreme. As a starter, try the rich seafood chowder with razor clams, smoked salmon, fingerling potatoes and fennel layered in a bowl with fresh cream added at the table. For your main course, you can't go wrong with the sumptuous slab of grilled Pacific Northwest king salmon served medium-rare with grilled Manila clams, fregola sarda, and black kale; or with the sablefish (smoked or cooked with sake). The main floor restaurant, open for dinner only, is an elegant, low-ceilinged room with a central bar and giant windows all around. The second floor café, with its high, exposed-beam ceiling, and huge, heated deck is a beloved spot for outdoor, family-friendly dining from spring through fall. Many of the same dishes are served in both dining rooms, but the restaurant is where you'll want to dine if you're in a romantic mood. In the end, I like Ray's because it represents the best of what Seattle seafood restaurants used to be, with fairly straightforward preparation that concentrates on the basic flavors of the fish. In keeping with the times, vegetarian and gluten-free dishes are offered and there's a happy hour between 4 and 6pm.

6049 Seaview Ave. NW. www.rays.com. ✆ **206/789-3770** for Boathouse or 206/782-0094 for Café. Reservations recommended. Main courses $28–$62 at Boathouse, $18–$59 at Café. Boathouse daily 4–10pm, Café daily 11:30am–9pm.

Moderate

Bastille ★ FRENCH The best choices at this fashionable Parisian-style brasserie are the *plats du jour,* such as lamb Bolognese or Dungeness crab salad, but the *plats principaux* won't disappoint, either—they are French classics like cassoulet, roasted chicken, mussels in white wine sauce, and steak frites. This is a lovely place to come for Sunday brunch when the Ballard Farmers Market is in session and you can people-watch from the enclosed patio while enjoying a fluffy omelet.

5307 Ballard Ave. NW. www.bastilleseattle.com. ✆ **206/453-5014.** Main courses $16–$32. Mon–Fri 5–10pm, Sat 5–11pm, Sun brunch 10am–3pm, dinner 5–9pm.

LAKE UNION

Expensive

Ivar's Salmon House ★ SEAFOOD Ivar's is one of Seattle's most iconic restaurants, and made its name with the fish most closely identified with the Pacific Northwest. For centuries, salmon was a mainstay of the Native American tribes in this region, and it was they who developed the alder-smoked cooking method that is the signature salmon style at Ivar's. Although the restaurant keeps up with the times and serves other "upscale" dishes, it's the salmon—grilled or roasted—that defines the place (as does the white clam chowder). Ivar's is meant to resemble a Native American longhouse, only one with great views across Lake Union with Seattle in the distance, and it celebrates Native American heritage with artifacts and photographs. As you dine here you'll be able watch a lot of boat traffic on Lake Union, which adds to the ambience. You can't be in a hurry, though, because the restaurant is large and the service can be slow.

401 NE Northlake Way. www.ivars.net. ✆ **206/632-0767.** Main courses $18–$36. Mon–Thurs 11am–9pm; Fri–Sat 11am–10pm; Sun 9:30am–2pm and 3:30–9pm.

SOUTH LAKE UNION

Inexpensive

Mamnoon Street ★ MIDDLE EASTERN Mamnoon serves dependably tasty Middle Eastern street food with a minimum of fuss and at prices that won't have you rolling your eyes in shock. You'll find all the classics here, many of them vegetarian: hummus, tabbouleh, lamb or chicken shawarma, falafel. The atmosphere here is brisk and friendly. After your meal you might want to stroll around what is now Amazonland (as in Amazon the online retail giant) and have a look at the new, plant-filled biospheres between the giant towers.

2020 6th Ave. (Amazon Building) www.mamnoonstreet.com. ✆ **206/327-9121.** Main courses $7–$11. Daily 11am–9pm (Sun until 8pm).

CAPITOL HILL

Moderate

Lark ★★ PACIFIC NORTHWEST This delightful neighborhood restaurant is the brainchild of Chef Johnathan Sundstrom, who fled the showy downtown food scene to open his own bistro. It's a place that encourages family-style sharing and features only locally produced, seasonal and organic grains, cheese, vegetables, fish, charcuterie, and meats. The fresh fish plates might include local Penn Cove blue mussels with ginger, or wild salmon with nasturtium, baby summer squash and cucumber wasabi emulsion. Vegetables and grains selections, depending on the season, could be farro with foraged chanterelle mushrooms or potato gnocchi with porcini mushrooms. Whatever you do, don't miss the cheeses here. These artisanal delights offer an array of tastes and textures that will wake up your taste buds. By the way: Lark, with its twinkly ceiling lights, fresh flowers and white tablecloths, is a good choice for a romantic night out.

926 12th Ave. www.larkseattle.com. ✆ **206/323-5275.** Main courses $16–$32. Daily 5–11pm, Sunday brunch 10am–2pm.

Poppy ★★★ PACIFIC NORTHWEST If there is one Seattle restaurant that I would recommend to anyone interested in the art of food, it would be Poppy. This bright, assured, and consistently inventive dining mecca, created by chef Jerry Traunfeld (formerly of Herbfarm), presents an American take on the Indian *thali.* That's a compartmentalized platter holding various dishes with many different tastes. On my last trip, my vegetarian thali came with carrot agnolotti with pea sauce and grilled Walla Walla onions. A cluster of side dishes included coconut corn soup with shiso; kohlrabi and cucumber salad with yogurt and dill; minted lentil and goat cheese strudel; glazed radish with cherries and lemon balm; and raspberry, beet and anise hyssop pickle. The medley of textures, herbs, and spices was surprising and delightful. Before you order your thali, though, you must try the eggplant fries with sea salt and honey—there's a reason why they are one of Poppy's signature appetizers and always on the menu. You can dine in Poppy's high-ceilinged dining room or, in summer, out on the sidewalk or in the back herb garden. ***Tip:*** Street parking can be difficult around here; try to fit yourself into the lot behind the restaurant.

622 Broadway E. www.poppyseattle.com. ✆ **206/324-1108.** Thalis $28–$33. Sun–Thurs 5-9:30pm, Fri–Sat 5–10:30pm.

Inexpensive

Pel Meni Dumpling Tzar ★★ RUSSIAN Tzar started life in Fremont as a stand-up indoor food cart. It was so successful, it was able to open this canary-yellow and kitsch-laden Capitol Hill location....for those who prefer to dine while seated. There's only one thing you want at Tzar: the delicious, steamed, bite-size Russian dumplings. They are made with egg noodles wrapped around pork, beef or veggie fillings, and served with your choice of toppings (the best being sour cream and dill). And this wouldn't be a Russian restaurant without vodka. You can get that, or the booze of your choice, at the full bar here. The Fremont stand is at 3516 Fremont Place; prices are the same.

1630 12th Ave. www.dumplingtzar.com. ✆ **206/466-6561.** Main courses $4–$10. Daily 11am–2:30am.

FREMONT

Inexpensive

Pie ★★ AMERICAN/BRITISH The chicken pot pies and lamb pies at this little Fremont storefront shop and café are handcrafted and baked fresh daily. Those are the standard fillings, but there's a savory range of other options, some meat-based, some vegetarian, offered on a rotating basis. Don't expect anything fancy in the way of décor because you won't find it. You order your pie, you get your pie, you sit down outside on Fremont Ave. if the weather is nice, or inside at a counter next to the front window if it's not, and you enjoy your pie. Utensils are plastic. That's it. It's pure and simple Fremont all the way. And oh yes, they have the other kind of pie, too—the one you eat *after* your meal.

3516 Fremont Place. www.savorypie.com. ✆ **206/588-2570.** Main courses $7–$10. Mon–Thurs 9am–9pm, Fri–Sat 9am–10pm, Sun 10am–6pm.

QUEEN ANNE

Expensive

Canlis ★★★ CONTEMPORARY NORTHWEST There aren't many formal restaurants left anymore—I mean the kind where guys must wear ties, and gals can put on their dressiest duds—but this is one of them. By formal,

VEGETARIAN, VEGAN AND GLUTEN-FREE dining in seattle

If you're a vegetarian, a vegan, or on a gluten-free diet, here's a quick list of special restaurants devoted to your dietary restrictions and preferences. They are all good places to eat.

VEGAN

Araya's Place ★★ The first vegan Thai restaurant in the Northwest now has three locations, but this one is the best.

5240 University Way NE. www.arayasplace.com. ✆ **206/524-4332.** Mon–Thurs 11:30am–9:30pm, Fri–Sat 11:30am–10pm, Sun 11:30am–9pm.

Wayward Vegan Cafe ★ This friendly café serves veganized American diner-style food.

801 NE 65th St., Suite C. www.waywardvegancafe.com. ✆ **206/524-0204.** Daily 9am–9pm.

VEGETARIAN

Sunlight Café ★★ This long-established vegetarian restaurant in the Roosevelt neighborhood also serves foods for other dietary restrictions.

6403 Roosevelt Way. www.sunlightcafevegetarian.com. ✆ **206/522-9060.** Mon 8:30am–3pm, Tues–Sun 8:30am–9pm.

Georgetown Liquor Company ★ In addition to the vegetarian menu, there are unique craft drinks, live music and retro video games.

5501 B Airport Way. www.georgetownliquorco.com. ✆ **206/763-6764.** Mon–Fri 11am–2am, Sat–Sun 10am–2am.

GLUTEN FREE

Niche ★ On the menu at this gluten-free café and bakery you'll find sandwiches, waffles, pastries and ice-cream.

808 12th Ave. (at Columbia). www.nicheseattle.com. ✆ **206/999-2801.** Mon 11am–4pm, Tues–Sat 11am–8pm.

Razzi's Pizzeria ★ In addition to traditional pizzas, Razzi's serves vegan, gluten-ree and vegan/gluten-free pies.

1314 Howell St. www.razzispizza.com. ✆ **206/588-2425.** Sun–Thurs 11am–11pm, Fri–Sat 11am–midnight.

however, I don't mean a place that's uncomfortably stiff or stuffy. Canlis's has a special-occasion atmosphere, with live piano music and a quietly stylish dining room, in a two-story bluff-top building. But its impeccable service means that guests are put at ease, whether it's their first time dining here or their 40th. A Seattle fine-dining destination for over 6 decades, this was the first restaurant in Seattle to serve what is now referred to as "contemporary Northwest cuisine." Diners choose dishes from a 4-course tasting menu which offers an array of tempting choices. Steaks from the copper grill, the Canlis salad, and Peter Canlis's prawns (Alaskan spot prawns with vermouth, butter and lime) are perennial favorites that have been on the menu since 1950. There's a comprehensive wine list, including delicious Northwest vintages. Reserve as far in advance as you can, because formality has lost none of its popularity here.

2576 Aurora Ave. N. www.canlis.com. ✆ **206/283-3313.** Reservations essential. 4-course chef's tasting menu $110. Mon–Sat 5:30–9pm; Fri 5–10pm; Sat 5–10pm.

WALLINGFORD

Expensive

Tilth ★★★ NEW AMERICAN Set in a cozy Craftsman bungalow, Tilth showcases the organic and wild bounty of the region. And when I say organic, I mean *organic*: this is one of the few restaurants in the U.S. to receive an organic certification. But that doesn't mean the food isn't fun. Renowned chef and owner Maria Hines—she's a James Beard award winner, and a TV presence from Iron Chef and Top Chef—caters to all comers with food that feels indulgent even when it's the picture of healthfulness. Where else will you find a 5-course vegan *and* a 5-course gluten free tasting menu? Some stellar recent dishes included a zippy chilled pea soup; savory pan-fried Alaskan halibut; red-pepper risotto with eggplant, zucchini and pine nuts; and chocolate ganache cake with cocoa cream and sea salt. Diners can mix and match various dishes, because all the dinner entrees are available as appetizers or main courses. If you've never had a duck burger, this is the place to try one. The desserts are so good that's there's a dessert tasting menu.

1411 N. 45th St. www.tilthrestaurant.com. ✆ **206/633-0801.** Main courses $16–$33, tasting menus $73–$95. Mon–Fri 5–10pm; Sat–Sun 10am–2pm and 5–10pm.

Moderate

Joule ★★★ KOREAN/FRENCH FUSION Though Asian influence is common in the Seattle culinary world, there is nothing common about the cuisine at Joule, a little gem about 15 minutes from downtown Seattle by car. Opened to acclaim in 2007, Joule made its name by using French culinary techniques on typically Asian ingredients. It has retained its French-inspired culinary flair but has now re-invented itself as a Korean steakhouse serving nontraditional cuts of beef with innovative side dishes that blend Asian and American flavors. That means short rib steak with grilled kimchi, or a wagyu hanger steak with smoky pineapple (and by the way, the price for these steaks is fairly low by steakhouse standards, running around $24). If steak is not on your to-eat list, there are rice and noodle dishes (the chilled sesame noodles are first-rate, so is the spicy rice cake with chorizo and pickled mustard greens). The weekend brunch for $19 includes a selection of dishes from a monthly rotating buffet menu and one dish from the kitchen. The only downside: Joule's clean-lined contemporary dining room has side-by-side tables that don't allow for much privacy.

3506 Stone Way N. www.joulerestaurant.com. ✆ **206/632-5685.** Entrees $17–$32. Daily 5pm–10pm, Sat–Sun brunch 10am–2pm.

WEST SEATTLE

Expensive

Salty's on Alki Beach ★ SEAFOOD For a fun Seattle adventure, hop in the water taxi at the Seattle Ferry Terminal on the waterfront, take the 10-minute ride over to Alki Beach in West Seattle, and have lunch, dinner, or weekend brunch at Salty's. A big and perennially popular restaurant, it has one eye-popping view: from the dining room and outdoor decks overlooking

"I HEARD THEY HAVE GOOD coffee IN SEATTLE"

You heard right, my friend. Good bakeries, too. Seattle is full of cafes where you can order your favorite forms of caffeine and sugar. These congenial spots are a way of life in the city where the first Starbucks opened in 1971 and is now visited as a tourist attraction. Here's a brief list of coffees and cafes of special merit.

Ancient Grounds ★ For an unusual Seattle espresso experience, stop in at Ancient Grounds not far from Pike Place Market. It's both a cafe and an intimate art gallery, loaded with intriguing treasures including Native American and Asian masks and netsuke. The espresso is strong, the ambience pure Seattle. Just don't expect smiling or overly friendly service. 1227 1st Ave. ✆ **206/749-0747.** Sun–Fri 7:30am–6pm, Sun noon–4pm.

Caffe Ladro Espresso Bar & Bakery ★★ Serving only organic, fair-trade, shade-grown coffee, Caffe Ladro sells a topnotch latte and a small selection of baked goodies. They have locations elsewhere, but this one is convenient if you're downtown near Pike Place Market or the Seattle Art Museum. 801 Pine St. www.caffeladro.com. ✆ **206/405-1950.** Mon–Fri 6am–6pm.

Caffe Umbria ★★★ The Bizzarri family has been roasting beans since grandfather Ornello opened his first shop in Perugia, Italy. Five blends are available, including fair-trade beans. Enjoy a heavenly extra-foamy cappuccino at their cafe in in Pioneer Square. 320 Occidental Ave. S. www.caffeumbria.com. ✆ **206/624-5847.** Mon–Fri 6am–6pm; Sat 7am–6pm; Sun 8am–5pm.

Macrina Bakery ★★★ This Belltown café is justly famous for its baked goods—their morning bun is the best I've ever had—and for their excellent breakfasts and lunch specials. Get one of their great lattes to go with your nosh and you're set. 2408 1st Ave. www.macrinabakery.com. ✆ **206/448-4032.** Daily 7am–6pm.

Starbucks Seattle's coffee culture began at this little shop at Pike Place Market back in 1971. The very first Starbucks still features the chain's original brand image of the topless mermaid with a double fish tail, an image that was toned down over the years as the Starbucks brand became ubiquitous and they didn't want to offend anyone. 1912 Pike Pl. ✆ **206/448-8762.** Mon–Fri 6am–9pm; Sat–Sun 6:30am–9pm.

Uptown Espresso ★★ I love their velvety smooth lattes and the comfy, hassle-free environments of Uptown Espresso. Established in 1984, they now have 7 locations around Seattle, including this one in Belltown. 2504 4th Ave. (at Wall). www.velvetfoam.com. ✆ **206/441-1084.** Mon–Thurs 5am–10pm; Fri 5am–11pm, Sat 6am–11pm, Sun 6am–10pm.

Zeitgeist Coffee ★★ This spacious European-style coffeehouse in Pioneer Square is an urban oasis and cultural hub that serves up film screenings and rotating exhibits by local artists along with its popular Italian beans, illy Caffe. 171 S. Jackson St. www.zeitgeistcoffee.com. ✆ **206/583-0497.** Mon–Fri

Elliot Bay, you look back and see the downtown towers of The Emerald City gleaming in the sunshine (or peeking through the mist and rain, this being Seattle). Salty's is famous for its weekend brunch buffet, laden with fresh seafood and sweet specialties like gingerbread pancakes and a chocolate fountain that will leave you reeling with a sugar high. The other time-honored tradition here is a sunset dinner—hopefully on a clear summer evening—but for that you'll find the food is overpriced and not very subtle. A better option is to explore Alki Beach and stop in at Salty's Café-Bar afterwards for a happy hour (Mon–Fri 3–6pm, Sat–Sun 4–6pm) glass of wine and a nosh that costs half what it would at dinner.

1936 Harbor Ave. SW. www.saltys.com. ✆ **206/937-1600.** Main courses $14–$25 lunch, $22–$45 dinner, $59 weekend brunch. Mon–Fri 11:15am–3pm and 5–9:30pm; Sat 9:30–1:30pm and 5–10pm; Sun 8:45am–1:30pm and 4:30–9pm.

Inexpensive

Marination Ma Kai ★ KOREAN/HAWAIIAN It's a Seattle tradition to take the water taxi over to West Seattle to dine at Salty's on Alki Beach (see review above). But Salty's can be an expensive proposition, and if you're like me and enjoy street food, or in this case, pier food, you've got a great spot waiting for you right as you get off the water taxi. Marination Ma Kai is the brick-and-mortar location of what began as a food truck. The food is a mouth-watering fusion of Korean and Hawaiian. And the price is right: a miso ginger chicken or spicy beef, pork or tofu taco costs $3 (fish taco $3.50) and comes with a side of tangy slaw. There's also a good kimchi fried rice bowl, pork sliders, and fish and chips with miso or kimchi tartar sauce. This window-service-only dining-spot is frequented by the commuters who use the water taxi—that's why you'll always see a line before or after the boat arrives. But don't worry: the line moves quickly and on a nice day you can eat on their big waterside deck or indoors at the minimally decorated dining room with a view of Elliott Bay.

1660 Harbor Ave. SW. www.marinationmobile.com. ✆ **206/328-8266.** Main courses $3–$14. Daily 8am–8pm.

SHOPPING

The hands-on retail marketplace in downtown Seattle has changed, as it has in virtually every big city in the country, as shoppers turn increasingly to the internet rather than visiting stores. Downtown Seattle is still the home of retail giant **Nordstrom,** which was founded here, but time-honored all-purpose department stores like the Bon Marche are now gone. High-end shops still abound, and you can find every top designer name in a downtown location, but the big retail malls that have long been such a feature of downtown shopping are looking a bit forlorn and undergoing major transformation in an effort to make them more appealing. If you want to find local treasures and unique Seattle specialties, leave downtown and explore the shops in Ballard, Fremont, and other neighborhoods. This is where the fun of shopping for truly unique and often handcrafted items hasn't evaporated—it has actually grown.

Ballard Sunday Farmers Market

Pike Place Market is the best and biggest public market, and open daily, but it is not Seattle's only market. Stretching for two blocks along Ballard Avenue, between NW 20th and NW 22nd avenues in the picturesque heart of the old Ballard neighborhood, the year-round **Sunday Farmers Market** in Ballard is a destination for locals and market-lovers throughout the city. Open from 10am to 3pm, the stalls sell fresh organic produce, cheeses, meats, mushrooms, fish, bread and baked goods, wine, and artisan crafts. There are also ethnic food stalls. Many of Ballard's most delightful shops are open as well, and so are restaurants and places to stop for a coffee and some people-watching.

ART GALLERIES

Davidson Galleries ★ This gallery focuses on both contemporary and antique prints by American and European artists and also features contemporary paintings and sculptures with an emphasis on Northwest artists. 313 Occidental Ave. S. www.davidsongalleries.com. ✆ **206/624-7684.**

Foster/White Gallery ★★★ Forster/White has been one of the premier West Coast art galleries for 50 years and shows the work of top-tier contemporary painters, photographers, and sculptors. 220 Third Ave. S. www.fosterwhite.com. ✆ **206/622-2833.**

Glasshouse Studio ★★ Here, in the oldest glass-blowing studio in the Northwest (it opened in 1971), you can watch glass art being made and check out the works of numerous local glass artists. 311 Occidental Ave. S. www.glasshouse-studio.com. ✆ **206/682-9939.**

Patricia Rovzar Gallery ★ Bold, colorful, often whimsical art can be seen at this gallery adjacent to the Seattle Art Museum. 1225 Second Ave. www.rovzargallery.com. ✆ **206/223-0273.**

Native American Art

Ancient Grounds ★ This eclectic downtown antiques shop and natural-history gallery sells quality Northwest Coast Indian masks and also Japanese masks, rare mineral specimens, and a wide variety of other rare and unusual pieces from all over the world. An espresso bar is on the premises. 1220 First Ave. ✆ **206/749-0747.**

Flury & Company Ltd. ★★ This Pioneer Square gallery specializes in prints by famed Seattle photographer Edward S. Curtis, known for his late-19th- and early-20th-century portraits of Native Americans. The gallery also has an excellent selection of antique Native American art and artifacts. 322 First Ave. S. www.fluryco.com. ✆ **206/587-0260.**

The Legacy Ltd. ★★★ In business since 1933, this is Seattle's oldest and finest gallery of contemporary and historic Northwest Coast Indian and Alaskan art and artifacts. 1003 First Ave. www.thelegacyltd.com. ✆ **800/729-1562** or 206/624-6350.

An Antiques Road Trip

If antiques are your passion, you won't want to miss the opportunity to spend a day browsing the many antiques stores in the historic farm town of **Snohomish,** located roughly 30 miles north of Seattle. The town has over 150 antiques dealers and is, without a doubt, the antiques capital of the Northwest. Frankly, you'll find better deals and (often) higher quality goods here than you will in Seattle proper.

BOOKS

Amazon Books ★★★ BOOKSTORE The online retail giant Amazon opened its first brick-and-mortar bookstore at this University Village location in 2015. It's not as large or comprehensive as Barnes & Noble, but that's the point: the selection is more carefully curated based on all kind of online sales data. This is also a place where you can check out the various Amazon reading devices and take a crash-course on how to live with Alexa. Amazon Prime members receive a discount on purchases. Another Amazon Books opened in 2017 in Bellevue at 575 Bellevue Square. 4601 26th Ave NE. ✆ **206/524-0715.** www.amazon.com.

Barnes & Noble ★★★ BOOKSTORE B&N is the largest bookstore in downtown Seattle, and it remains a great place to browse for new titles and every other title still in print and to attend author signings and events. Another big, browsable B&N is located in Bellevue at 626 106th Ave. NE (✆ 425/451-8463). 600 Pine St. ✆ **206/264-0156.** www.bn.com.

Elliott Bay Book Company ★★★ BOOKSTORE Seattle's best-known independent bookstore carries an excellent selection of titles, including books on Seattle and the Northwest, plus a full roster of author events and book signings. 1521 Tenth Ave. www.elliottbaybook.com. ✆ **800/962-5311** or 206/624-6600.

Metsker Maps of Seattle ★★★ MAPS/BOOKSTORE Before the advent of GPS people relied on "real" maps to find their way around. And real maps are what you'll still find at Metsker, just steps from Pike Place Market. Their selection of maps (both current and antique) is enormous and they also carry travel books to just about every destination you can think of, plus other travel-related gear. Metsker has been in business since the pre-GPS days of 1950. 1151 First Ave. www.metsker.com. ✆ **216/823-8747.**

Peter Miller Books ★★★ BOOKSTORE/DESIGN/LIFESTYLE Anyone interested in architecture and design books and supplies will want to visit this long-established and always-enticing bookstore in downtown Seattle. 2326 Second Ave. www.petermiller.com. ✆ **206/441-4114.**

CRAFTS & HANDMADE GIFTS

The Northwest is a magnet for skilled craftspeople, and shops all around town sell a wide range of high-quality and imaginative pieces. At **Pike Place**

Market (p. 71) and **Ballard Sunday Market** (p. 119), you can see what area craftspeople are creating and meet the artisans themselves.

Curtis Steiner ★★★ ART/JEWELRY/LOCAL CRAFTS Curtis Steiner's decorative arts gallery on Ballard Avenue is worth seeking out for handmade pieces in different media that are of exceptional in quality and unique to Washington. 1549 Ballard Ave. NW. www.curtissteiner.com. ✆ **206/297-7116.**

Fireworks Fine Crafts Gallery ★ LOCAL CRAFTS Playful, bizarre, beautiful—these are just some of the adjectives that can be used to describe the eclectic collection of Northwest crafts sold at this downtown gallery. 210 First Ave. S. www.fireworksgallery.net. ✆ **206/682-9697.**

DEPARTMENT STORES

Eddie Bauer ★★ OUTDOOR APPAREL Eddie Bauer got his start here in Seattle back in 1920, and today the chain that bears his name is one of the country's foremost purveyors of outdoor fashions—although these days, outdoor fashion is looking quite a bit more urban. The flagship downtown store is no more, but there is a still an outlet near the University of Washington. 2690 NE University Village. www.eddiebauer.com. ✆ **206/527-2696.**

Filson ★★ OUTDOOR APPAREL Filson's clothes and accessories are meant to last a lifetime, so if you demand only the best when it comes to outdoor gear, be sure to check out this local institution's flagship store. 2690 1st Ave. S. www.filson.com. ✆ **866/860-8906** or 206/527-2646.

Nordstrom ★★★ DEPARTMENT STORE Known for personal service, Seattle-based Nordstrom ranks among the premier department stores in the United States, and this flagship store features all sorts of boutiques, cafes, live piano music, and other features to make your shopping enjoyable. 500 Pine St. www.nordstrom.com. ✆ **206/628-2111.**

Nordstrom Rack ★★★ DEPARTMENT STORE Nordstrom's discount shop features discontinued lines and one-off clothes and shoes for women, men, and children, all at terrific savings. www.nordstrom.com. 400 Pine St. ✆ **206/448-8522.** Also at 3920 124th St. SE, Bellevue (✆ **425/746-7200**), and 19500 Alderwood Mall Pkwy., Lynnwood (✆ **425/774-6569**).

Northwest Pendleton ★★ SPECIALTY APPAREL/ACCESSORIES For Northwesterners, Pendleton is and always will be the name in classic wool clothing, blankets, and accessories. 1313 Fourth Ave. www.pendleton-usa.com. ✆ **800/593-6773** or 206/682-4430.

REI ★★★ OUTDOOR APPAREL/RECREATIONAL GEAR Recreational Equipment, Inc. (REI) is the nation's largest co-op selling outdoor gear, and the company's impressive flagship is a cross between a high-tech warehouse and a mountain lodge. This massive store sells almost anything you could ever need for pursuing your favorite outdoor sport. It also has a 65-foot climbing pinnacle. With all this under one roof, who needs to go outside? 222 Yale Ave. N. www.rei.com. ✆ **888/873-1938** or 206/223-1944.

FOOD

Fran's Chocolates ★★★ Seattle native Fran Bigelow's salted caramels are so fabulously delicious that even President Obama gave them a plug during a trip to Seattle. Four Seasons Hotel, 1325 First Ave. www.franschocolates.com. ✆ **800/4122-3726.**

Pike Place Fish Market ★ The guys at this Pike Place Market fishmonger are like a carny act, pulling in the crowds with their "flying fish" performance, throwing big silvery salmon back and forth. Choose one of the fresh salmon to take home, and the guys will pack it up for you in dry ice. Pike Place Market, 86 Pike Place. www.pikeplacefish.com. ✆ **800/542-7732** or 206/682-7181.

MALLS/SHOPPING CENTERS

Pacific Place ★★ SHOPPING MALL This downtown mall, adjacent to Nordstrom, contains five levels of upscale shop-o-tainment, including Tiffany & Co., Ann Taylor, Barney's New York, Coach, MaxMara, six restaurants, and a multiplex movie theater. A mall-wide renovation began in 2017 to make it more appealing. 600 Pine St. www.pacificplaceseattle.com. ✆ **877/883-2400** or 206/405-2655.

Westlake Center ★ SHOPPING MALL In the heart of Seattle's main shopping district, this urban shopping mall has specialty stores and an extensive food court. Like Pacific Place, Westlake Center was undergoing renovation at press time and will have a new Saks department store on the top two levels. The mall is also the southern terminus for the monorail to Seattle Center. 400 Pine St. www.westlakecenter.com. ✆ **206/467-1600.**

SOUVENIRS

Made in Washington ★★ REGIONAL PRODUCTS Whether it's salmon, wine, lavender or Northwest crafts, you'll find a varied selection of Washington state products in this shop. www.madeinwashington.com. Pike Place Market, 1530 Post Alley (at Pine St.). ✆ **206/467-0788.** Also at Westlake Center, 400 Pine St. (✆ **206/623-9753**).

Ye Olde Curiosity Shop ★ SOUVENIR SHOP Every inch of this famous tourist trap on the waterfront is covered with souvenirs and crafts, both tacky and tasteful (but mostly tacky). Pier 54, 1001 Alaskan Way. www.yeoldecuriosityshop.com. ✆ **206/682-5844.**

OUTDOOR PURSUITS

It almost goes without saying that this majestically scenic city and region, surrounded by ocean, lakes, and mountains, offers some outstanding recreational opportunities. Get active, the way the Seattleites do, and you'll enjoy the Seattle experience even more.

Biking

With its the steep hills and heavy street traffic, Seattle isn't the easiest place to ride a bike. The first pilot bike-share program failed but as of summer 2017 there were a couple of other new dockless bike-share programs in the city. **Spin** (www.spin.pm) features bright orange bikes in the downtown area with (this being tech-savvy Seattle) on-bike GPS and a cellular modem. **LimeBike** (www.limebike.com) has, yes, lime-green bikes that are mostly in locations around the University of Washington. With both of these programs you download an app to find, unlock, return the bike to a different location, and pay for the ride ($1 for a 30-minute ride). These are not all-day bike rentals; they are basically for short hops around the city. If you are going to ride bikes around Seattle, please wear a helmet—they are not provided with the bikes.

For longer bike rides we recommend **Montlake Bicycle Shop,** 2223 24th Ave. E. (www.montlakebike.com; ✆ **206/329-7333**), rents bikes by the day for $52 to $127. This shop is convenient to the **Burke-Gilman/Sammamish River Trail ★★,** a 27-mile paved and traffic-free pathway created from an old railway bed. The most convenient place to start a ride is at **Gas Works Park,** on the north shore of Lake Union. From here you can ride north and east, by way of the University of Washington, to **Kenmore Log Boom Park,** at the north end of Lake Washington.

The West Seattle bike path along **Alki Beach** is another good place to ride; it offers great views of the sound and the Olympic Mountains. If you'd like to pedal this pathway, you can rent single-speed bikes at **Alki Kayak Tours,** 1660 Harbor Ave. SW (www.kayakalki.com; ✆ **206/953-0237**), which charges $10 per hour. To get there in scenic style, take the water taxi from the downtown waterfront to West Seattle; the dock is right at the Alki Kayak Tours building.

Hiking

Seattleites' favorite spot for a quick dose of nature is **Discovery Park,** 3801 W. Government Way (✆ **206/386-4236**), northwest of downtown, at the western tip of the Magnolia neighborhood. Covering more than 500 acres, this park has many miles of trails and beaches to hike—not to mention gorgeous views, forest paths, and meadows.

Watersports

If you'd like to try your hand at sea kayaking, standup paddleboarding, rowing, or sailing, head to **Moss Bay Rowing, Kayaking and Sailing Center,** 1001 Fairview Ave. N. (www.mossbay.net; ✆ **206/682-2031**), which rents all types of water vehicles at the south end of Lake Union near Chandler's Cove. Rates range from $14 per hour for a single kayak to $20 per hour for a double. From downtown Seattle, this place can be reached on the Seattle Streetcar. The same equipment can be rented at **Alki Kayak Tours** on Alki Beach in West Seattle, described under "Biking," above.

SPECTATOR SPORTS

With professional football, baseball, ice hockey, soccer, and women's basketball teams, as well as the various University of Washington Huskies teams,

Seattle is definitely a city of sports fans. **Ticketmaster** (✆ **800/745-3000** or 206/346-1660; www.ticketmaster.com) sells tickets to almost all sporting events in the Seattle area. You'll find Ticketmaster outlets at area Fred Meyer stores.

Baseball

Seattle's most popular professional sports team is the **Mariners** (www.seattlemariners.com; ✆ **206/346-4000** or 346-4001). They play at **Safeco Field** (1250 1st Ave. S.), a stadium with a retractable roof.

Basketball

The **Seattle Storm** (www.wnba.com/storm; ✆ **877/962-2849** or 206/217-9622), of the Women's National Basketball Association, play in **Key Arena** (305 Harrison St.) at Seattle Center north of downtown. The **University of Washington Huskies** men's and women's basketball teams are also very popular. For information on both the women's and the men's Huskies basketball games, call ✆ **206/543-2200** or go to www.gohuskies.com. Home games are played at **Alaska Airlines Arena at Hec Edmundson Pavilion** (3870 Montlake Blvd. NE) on the UW campus.

Football

Winners of the 2014 Super Bowl, the **Seattle Seahawks** (www.seahawks.com; ✆ **888/635-4295** or 425/203-8000) play at **CenturyLink Field,** 800 Occidental Ave. S. (www.centurylinkfield.com; ✆ **206/381-7500**), which is adjacent to Safeco Field.

The **University of Washington Huskies** (www.gohuskies.com; ✆ **206/543-2200**) play in Husky Stadium on the university campus.

THE PERFORMING ARTS & NIGHTLIFE

Culturally savvy and party-loving Seattle has a world-class symphony, a highly regarded opera company, several award-winning theaters, and lots of bars, lounges, and nightclubs. To find out what's going on, pick up a free copy of ***Seattle Weekly*** (www.seattleweekly.com) or check it out online. On Friday, the ***Seattle Times*** includes a section called "NW Ticket," a guide to the week's arts-and-entertainment offerings.

Bars & Lounges

Alibi Room ★ Tucked away beneath Pike Place Market, this hip bar serves up potent drinks and very good food, and features Friday and Saturday club nights with dance DJs. 85 Pike St. Ste. 410. www.seattlealibi.com. ✆ **206/623-3180.**

Artusi ★★ When you need a hit of Italy, head for this lively aperitivo bar for a grappa or amaro accompanied by excellent *stuzzichini* ("little nibbles"). 1535 14th Ave. www.artusibar.com. ✆ **206/678-2516.**

Bathtub Gin and Co. ★★ All that's missing in this dimly lit, speakeasy atmosphere is the cigarette smoke. Come here for a great cocktail or, on a chilly evening, a signature hot toddy. At the 5–7pm Happy House, wine is $6 a glass and cocktails are $7. 2205 2nd Ave. www.bathtubginseattle.com. ✆ **206/728-6069.**

BOKA Restaurant + Bar ★★ This contemporary bar in the super-upscale Hotel 1000 is a beautiful spot to relax and enjoy gourmet bar food and a seasonal cocktail. 1010 1st Ave. www.bokaseattle.com. ✆ **206/357-9000.**

The Central Saloon ★ The oldest saloon in Seattle is a favorite neighborhood hangout with good food and live rock music. Full plates (all of it comfort food) are half-price during 4–7pm Happy Hour. 207 1st Ave. S. www.centralsaloon.com. ✆ **206/622-0209.**

Cha Cha Lounge ★ Red lighting, kitschy velvet paintings, piñatas hanging from the ceiling, and some incongruous punk and heavy metal set the scene at this popular bar. 1013 E. Pike St. www.chachalounge.com. ✆ **206/322-0703.**

Fireside Room ★★★ This elegant lounge at the time-honored Sorrento Hotel is a romantic spot to stop for a drink, especially on Friday and Saturday nights, when you can hear live music. 900 Madison St. ✆ **206/622-6400.**

Oliver's Lounge ★★★ Unchanged for over 40 years, this relaxing bar at the elegant Mayflower Park Hotel serves award-winning martinis and upscale bar food. During Happy Hour (Mon–Fri 4:30–6pm) appetizers are free when you order a drink. 405 Olive Way. ✆ **206/623-8700.**

Raygun Lounge ★★ It looks kind of unfinished, but that's part of the brainy charm of this spot, which offers dozens of board games you can play while you're eating or drinking (lots of non-alcoholic options). 501 E. Pine St. ✆ **206/852-2521.**

Brewpubs & Wine Bars

Big Time Brewery & Alehouse ★ Seattle's oldest brewpub (established in 1988 close to the University of Washington campus) is done up to look like an old tavern and serves as many as 12 of its own brews at any given time. 4133 University Way NE. www.bigtimebrewery.com. ✆ **206/545-4509.**

Elysian Brewing Company ★★★ Hands-down, Elysian is the best brewpub in Seattle, with especially good stouts and strong ales and a team of creative brewers. 542 First Ave. S. www.elysianbrewing.com. ✆ **206/382-4498.**

The Pike Pub & Brewery ★ In an open, central space inside Pike Place Market, this brewpub makes excellent stout and pale ale, but is best known for its Kilt Lifter Scotch ale. 1415 First Ave. www.pikebrewing.com. ✆ **206/622-6044.**

The Tasting Room ★★ Located in Pike Place Market, this cozy wine bar has the feel of a wine cellar and is cooperatively operated by several small Washington state wineries. You can buy wine by the glass or bottle. 1924 Post Alley. www.winesofwashington.com. ✆ **206/770-9463.**

Downtown & Capitol Hill Performing Arts & Nightlife

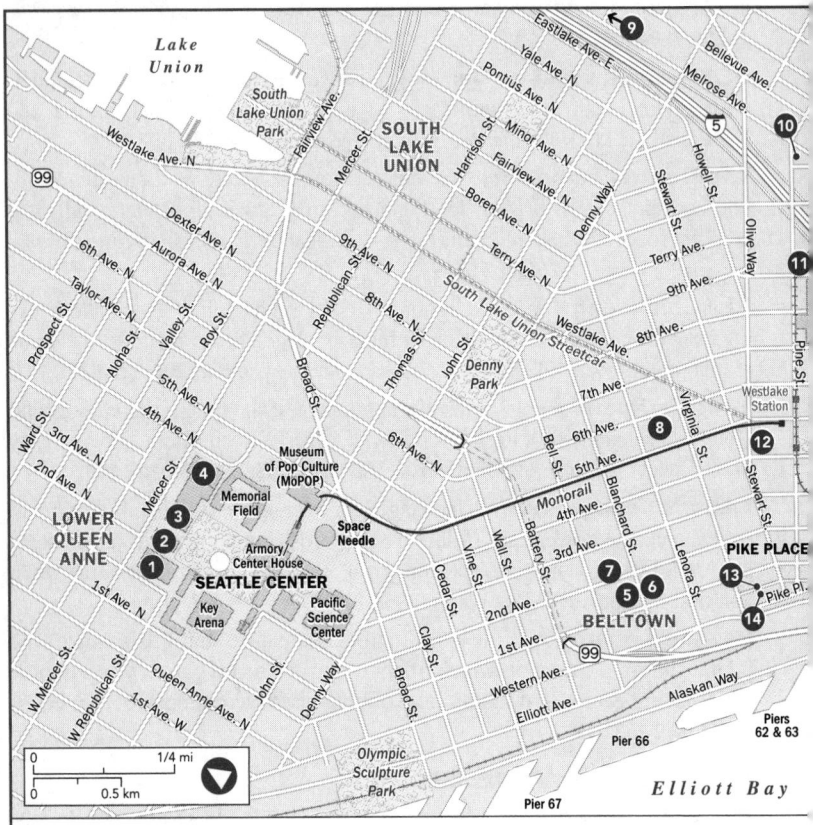

5th Avenue Theatre **19**
ACT (A Contemporary Theater) **20**
Alibi Room **15**
Artusi **29**
Baltic Room **10**
Bathtub Gin & Co. **5**
Benaroya Hall **18**
Big Time Brewery & Alehouse **9**
BOKA Restaurant + Bar **22**
The Central Saloon **23**
Century Ballroom **26**
Cha Cha Lounge **27**
Cornish Playhouse **2**

Dance

Pacific Northwest Ballet ★★★ Seattle's premier dance company presents a wide range of classics, new works, and a yearly *Nutcracker,* with sets and costumes by the late Maurice Sendak, the children's book author. McCaw Hall, 301 Mercer St. www.pnb.org. ✆ **206/441-2424.**

Dance Clubs

Baltic Room ★★★ This swanky, iconic Capitol Hill hangout for the beautiful people stages a wide range of contemporary dance music (mostly

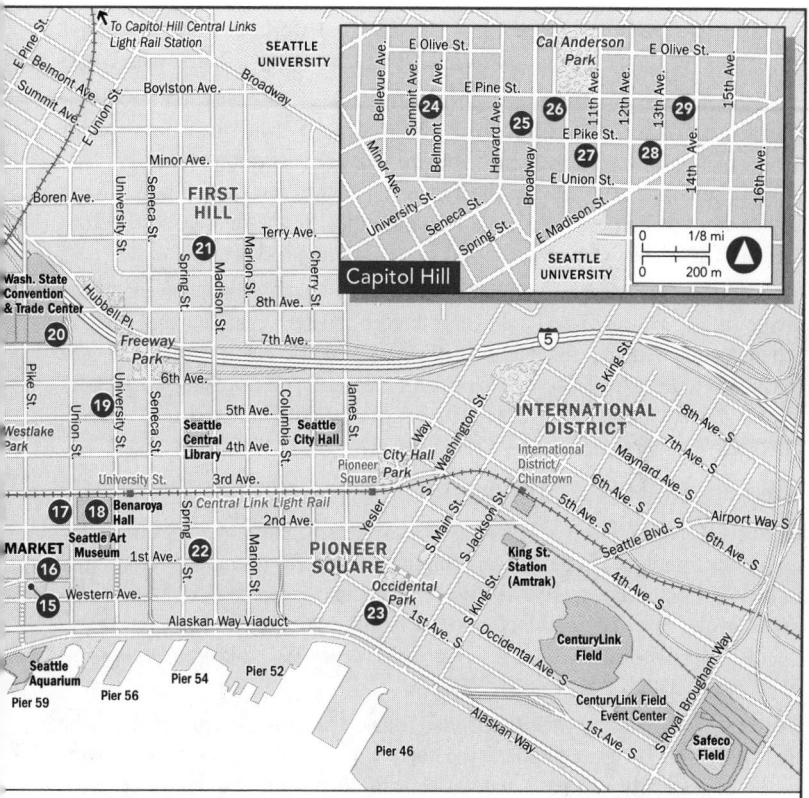

DJs) encompassing everything from electronica to hip-hop and *bhangra* (contemporary Indian disco). 1207 Pine St. www.balticroom.com. ✆ **206/625-4444.**

Century Ballroom ★★★ With a handsome wooden dance floor, this is *the* place in Seattle for a night out if you're into swing, salsa, or tango, complete with lessons early in the evening. 915 E. Pine St. www.centuryballroom.com. ✆ **206/324-7263.**

Neighbours Nightclub ★★ This has been the favorite dance club of Capitol Hill's gay community for years, with different nights of the week featuring different styles of music. 1509 Broadway. www.neighboursnightclub.com. ✆ **206/324-5358.**

Live Music, Cabaret & Jazz Venues

Dimitriou's Jazz Alley ★★★ The lineup of world-class performers at this large, yet somehow intimate, dinner/jazz club never fails to amaze. 2033 Sixth Ave. www.jazzalley.com. ✆ **206/441-9729.**

The Pink Door Cabaret ★★★ There's almost always something out of the ordinary going on here, be it a trapeze artist or accordion player, but Saturday nights are reserved for the fun and naughty burlesque show. Come earlier and you can enjoy a delicious Italian meal in the dining room before the show. 1919 Post Alley. www.thepinkdoor.net. ✆ **206/443-3241.**

The Triple Door ★★★ A sophisticated and enjoyable nightclub and music venue for grown-ups, The Triple Door features an ever-changing and eclectic schedule that features top name performers and the best popular and jazz musicians in Seattle. If you don't come for the music, come to enjoy a cocktail at the Musicquarium Lounge with its enormous aquarium and lively scene. 216 Union St. www.tripledoor.net. ✆ **206/838-4333.**

Opera & Classical Music

Seattle Opera ★★★ Founded in 1963, the Seattle Opera is one of the top opera companies in the U.S., mounting four operas a year at McCaw Hall in Seattle Center. Every 4 years, the company stages Richard Wagner's four-opera cycle, *Ring of the Nibelungen,* a highly anticipated event that draws opera-lovers worldwide. Seattle Center, McCaw Hall, 321 Mercer St. www.seattleopera.org. ✆ **800/426-1619** or 206/389-7676.

Seattle Symphony ★★★ Under Music Director Gerard Schwarz, the Seattle Symphony moved into the top ranks of U.S. orchestras and a new home in the acoustically superb Benaroya Hall in downtown Seattle. Since 2011, French conductor Ludovic Morlot has lead the acclaimed ensemble in a season of classical and pops concerts (2019 will be his final season). Benaroya Hall, 200 University St. www.seattlesymphony.org. ✆ **866/833-4747** or 206/215-4747.

Theater

5th Avenue Theatre ★★★ This elegant playhouse produces some of the liveliest theater in Seattle, including original and Broadway-bound shows and Broadway musicals. 1308 Fifth Ave. www.5thavenue.org. ✆ **206/625-1900.**

ACT (A Contemporary Theatre) ★★ The focus at this energetic venue is on newer plays and playwrights. 700 Union St. www.acttheatre.org. ✆ **206/292-7676.**

Cornish Playhouse (formerly known as Intiman Theatre) ★★★ Serious drama-lovers will love the Tony award–winning Intiman, which has been producing international classics and contemporary plays for over 3 decades. 155 Mercer St. www.intiman.org. ✆ **206/443-2222.**

Paramount Theatre ★★★ From Broadway to rock shows, the Paramount offers superb entertainment in a glamorous, historic setting. 911 Pine St. www.stgpresents.org. ✆ **206/467-5510.**

Seattle Repertory Theatre ★★★ Seattle's top professional theater stages everything from the classics to world premières on its two stages. 155 mercer St. www.seattlerep.org. ✆ **877/900-9285** or 206/443-2222.

DAY TRIPS FROM SEATTLE

La Conner & the Skagit Valley ★★★

70 miles N of Seattle

In a competition for quaintest town in Washington, La Conner would leave the other contenders wallowing in the winter mud. This town, a former fishing village, has a waterfront street lined with restored wooden commercial buildings, back streets of Victorian homes, and the largest tulip and daffodil fields in the U.S. stretching out from the town limits. Add to this three museums, numerous plant nurseries and gardening-related stores, art galleries, luxurious inns, and good restaurants, and you have a town that's perfect for a day trip from Seattle.

La Conner dates from a time when Puget Sound towns were connected by water and not by road, and consequently the town clings to the shore of Swinomish Channel. La Conner reached a commercial peak around 1900 (when steamers made the run to Seattle) and continued as an important grain- and log-shipping port until the Great Depression. It never recovered from the hard times of the 1930s, and when the highways bypassed the town, it became a neglected backwater. The wooden false-fronted buildings built during the town's heyday were spared the wrecking balls of the 1960s, and today these old buildings give the town its inimitable charm.

Beginning in the 1940s, La Conner's picturesque setting attracted several artists and writers, and by the 1970s it had become known as an artists' community. Tourism began to revive the economy, and the town's artistic legacy led to the building here of the Museum of Northwest Art, dedicated to the region's many contemporary artists.

Adding still more color to this vibrant little town are the commercial flower farms of the surrounding Skagit Valley. In the spring, tulips carpet the surrounding farmlands with great swaths of red, yellow, and white. The sight is on a par with anything you would ever see in Holland.

ESSENTIALS

GETTING THERE There is no direct bus or train service to La Conner; daily Greyhound bus and Amtrak service will take you from downtown Seattle to Skagit Station in Mt. Vernon, about 10 miles east of La Conner. So if you go, it will likely be in your own car. From Seattle, drive north on I-5 and take U.S. 20 west toward Anacortes. La Conner is south of U.S. 20 on La Conner–Whitney Road.

VISITOR INFORMATION Contact the **La Conner Chamber of Commerce,** 511 Morris St. (www.laconnerchamber.com; ✆ **888/642-9284** or 360/466-4778). The visitor center is open Mar 15-Sept 10 Mon–Fri 10am–4pm, Sat noon–3pm; Sept 12–Mar 14 Mon–Fri 10am–2pm, Sat 10am–1pm.

> **What's in a Name?**
>
> Although the name sounds like a combination of Spanish and Irish, La Conner is actually named for Louisa A. (LA) Conner, who helped found the town in the 1870s.

FESTIVALS From late March to mid-April, the countryside around La Conner is awash with color as thousands of acres of Skagit Valley tulip and daffodil fields burst into bloom in a floral display that rivals that of the Netherlands. The **Skagit Valley Tulip Festival** (www.tulipfestival.org; ✆ **360/428-5959**), held each year during bloom time, is La Conner's biggest annual festival and includes dozens of events.

WHERE TO DINE

Nell Thorn Restaurant & Pub ★ INTERNATIONAL How could you possibly have a restaurant in La Conner without featuring fresh, local, and mostly organic products? Why would you want to, with such delicious bounty so close at hand? You'll get a good meal here no matter what you order, but seafood is always a standout. The upstairs restaurant is a bit more formal, with a more limited menu. In the pub you can enjoy soups, salads, and sandwiches.

La Conner Country Inn, 205 Washington Ave. www.nellthorn.com. ✆ **360/466-4261.** Main courses $12–$28. Tues–Sun 11:30am–9pm, Mon 3–9pm.

Seeds ★ AMERICAN Skagit County is one of the Northwest's most important farming and gardening regions, and this charming bistro on the edge of downtown is housed in a relic of the area's past—a former seed company. You can get breakfast, lunch, or dinner here, and every meal will feature the freshest of local produce and farm products, from naturally nested eggs and seasonal berries to grass-fed beef and fresh seafood. There's a bit of everything on the menu, including Washington State wines and beers.

623 Morris St. www.seedsbistro.com. ✆ **360/466-3280.** Main courses $10–$28. Daily 11:30am–9pm.

EXPLORING LA CONNER & ITS ENVIRONS

The one must-see museum in La Conner is the **Museum of Northwest Art ★★★,** 121 S. First St. (www.museumofnwart.org; ✆ **360/466-4446**), housed in a large contemporary building downtown. The museum showcases works by Northwest artists, particularly Morris Graves, Mark Tobey, and Guy Anderson, all of whom once worked in La Conner. The museum is open Tuesday through Saturday from 10am to 5pm and Sunday and Monday from noon to 5pm; admission is free.

High atop a hill in the center of town is the **Skagit County Historical Museum ★,** 501 S. Fourth St. (www.skagitcounty.net/museum; ✆ **360/466-3365**), open Tuesday through Sunday from 11am to 5pm; admission is $5 for adults, $4 for seniors and children ages 6 to 12. As the chief repository of Skagit Valley's history, this museum is overflowing with artifacts from daily life over the last century.

Housed in the historic Gerches mansion a few blocks away is the **Pacific Northwest Quilt & Fiber Arts Museum ★★,** 703 S. Second St. (www.qfmuseum.org; ✆ **360/466-4288**). Here, in rooms furnished with local antiques, you'll find a permanent collection of heritage and specially created quilts from around the world along with works by contemporary artists working with all kinds of fibers. The museum is open Tuesday through Sunday from 11am to 5pm (closed Mon–Tues Sept–Mar); admission is $7.

There is excellent **bird-watching** around the Skagit Valley, especially during the winter months when migratory waterfowl, including trumpeter swans, snow geese, and various raptors, including peregrine falcons and bald eagles, flock to the area's marshes, bays, and farm fields. Eight miles north of La Conner at the **Padilla Bay National Estuarine Research Reserve,** 10441 Bayview-Edison Rd. (www.padillabay.gov; ✆ **360/428-1558**), you can bird-watch along 3 miles of trails through fields and along a dike. The reserve is open daily; the interpretive center is open Wednesday through Sunday from 10am to 5pm. Admission is free.

Shopping is the most popular pastime in La Conner, and up and down **First Street** you'll find lots of great galleries, boutiques, and gift shops.

Mount Rainier National Park & Environs ★★★

Paradise: 110 miles SE of Seattle, 70 miles SE of Tacoma, 150 miles NE of Portland

At 14,410 feet, Mount Rainier is the tallest mountain in Washington, and to the sun-starved residents of Seattle and south Puget Sound, this dormant volcano is a giant weather gauge. When the skies clear over Puget Sound, you'll often hear people saying, "The mountain is out!" And when the mountain is out, all eyes turn to admire its snow-covered summit. Thanks to the region's moisture-laden air, Rainier's glaciated slopes remain white throughout the year.

Snow and glaciers notwithstanding, Rainier has a heart of fire. Steam vents at the mountain's summit are evidence that, though this volcanic peak is

Tulip Fields, Gardens & Nurseries

During the Tulip Festival, stop by **Roozengaarde Flowers & Bulbs,** 15867 Beaver Marsh Rd. (www.tulips.com; ✆ **866/488-5477** or 360/424-8531), the largest grower of tulips, daffodils, and spring bulbs in the U.S., and visit their display garden, tulip fields, and gift shop. **At Christianson's Nursery & Greenhouse,** 15806 Best Rd., Mount Vernon (www.christiansonsnursery.com; ✆ **800/585-8200** or 360/466-3821), you'll find hundreds of varieties of roses and lots of other plants as well. Nearby you can tour the beautiful English country gardens of **La Conner Flats,** 15980 Best Rd. (www.laconnerflats.com; ✆ **360/466-3190**), where high tea is served by reservation.

Mount Rainier National Park

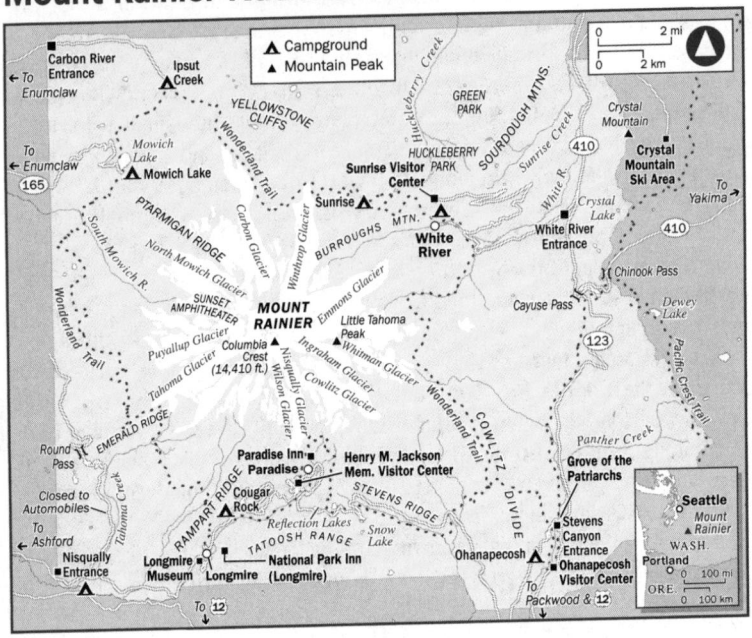

presently dormant, it could erupt again at any time. If scientists are correct in their calculations that Rainier's volcanic activity occurs in 3,000-year cycles, it may be hundreds of years before another big eruption occurs. On the other hand….

Known to Native Americans as Tahoma, Mount Rainier received its current name in 1792 when British explorer Captain George Vancouver named the mountain for a friend (who never even visited the region). The first ascent to the mountain's summit was made in 1870 by General Hazard Stevens (Stevens Pass is named after him) and Philemon Van Trump (no relation to Donald). It was 14 years later that James Longmire built the first hotel on the mountain's flanks. In 1899, Mount Rainier became the country's fifth national park.

ESSENTIALS

GETTING THERE If you're coming from Seattle and your destination is Paradise (the park's most popular area), head for the southwest (Nisqually) park entrance. Take I-5 south to exit 127 and then head east on Wash. 512. Take the Wash. 7 exit and head south toward Elbe. At Elbe, continue east on Wash. 7 At the park entrance, you'll be handed a comprehensive map that includes all trails and facilities. The park entrance fee is $15 per vehicle.

If you don't have a car but still want to visit Mount Rainier National Park, book a tour through **Tours Northwest** (www.toursnorthwest.com; ✆ **888/293-1404** or 206/768-1234), which charges $139 for adults and $109 for children ages 3 to 12 for a 10-hour tour starting in Seattle. These tours operate between late April and early November, and spend most of the day in transit, but you get to see the mountain up close and can do a couple of hours of hiking at Paradise.

VISITOR INFORMATION For park information, contact **Mount Rainier National Park,** 55210 238th Ave. E., (www.nps.gov/mora; ✆ **360/569-2211**). For general information on the area, contact **Visit Rainier** (www.visitrainier.com; ✆ **877/270-7155**).

EXPLORING MOUNT RAINIER NATIONAL PARK

Just past the **main southwest entrance (Nisqually),** is **Longmire,** site of the National Park Inn, the Longmire Museum (with exhibits on the park's natural and human history), a hiker information center, and a ski-touring center that rents cross-country skis and snowshoes in winter.

From here, the road climbs to **Paradise** (elevation 5,400 ft.), a mountainside aerie that affords a breathtaking view. Paradise is the park's most popular destination, so expect crowds. During July and August, the meadows are ablaze with wildflowers, which is why this is such a great place for day hikes. The **Henry M. Jackson Memorial Visitor Center at Paradise** provides panoramic views, and a short walk away is a spot from which you can view Nisqually Glacier. Many miles of other trails lead out from Paradise, looping through meadows and up onto snowfields above the timberline. It's not unusual to find snow at Paradise as late as July.

In summer, you can continue beyond Paradise to the **Ohanapecosh Visitor Center** (✆ **360/569-6046**), open daily from late May through early October. Not far from this visitor center, you can walk through the **Grove of the Patriarchs** (see "Hiking & Backpacking," below). Continue around the mountain to reach the turnoff for Sunrise.

Driving counterclockwise around the mountain, you'll come to **Cayuse Pass.** A short detour from this pass brings you to the picturesque **Chinook Pass** area, where there is a good 4.5-mile day-hike loop trail that begins at Tipsoo Lake and circles Naches Peak.

Continuing around the mountain, you'll come to the turnoff for the park's **White River entrance.** This road leads to **Sunrise,** the highest spot in the park (6,400 feet), and site of some of the park's best day hikes. A beautiful old log lodge serves as the **Sunrise Visitor Center** (✆ **360/663-2425**), open daily from late June through early September. From here you can see not only Mount Rainier, but also Mount Baker and Mount Adams. In July and August, the alpine meadows are full of wildflowers. Some of the park's most scenic trails begin at Sunrise. This area is usually less crowded than Paradise.

OUTDOOR ACTIVITIES IN & NEAR THE NATIONAL PARK

HIKING & BACKPACKING Hikers have more than 240 miles of trails to explore within the park, though the vast majority of park visitors do their hiking at only two places—Paradise and Sunrise. These two alpine areas offer the most scenic day-hiking opportunities, but they can be crowded.

At **Paradise ★★,** the 5-mile **Skyline Trail ★★★** is the highest trail and climbs through beautiful meadows above the tree line. Views of Mount Adams, Mount St. Helens, and the Nisqually Glacier open up along this route. The **Lakes Trail,** of similar length, heads downhill to the Reflection Lakes, with picture-perfect views of the mountain reflected in their waters.

At **Sunrise ★★★** there are also numerous trails of varying lengths. Among these, the 5-mile **Burroughs Mountain Trail** and the 5.5-mile **Mount Fremont Trail** are both very rewarding—the latter even provides a chance to see mountain goats.

The park's single most memorable low-elevation hike is the **Grove of the Patriarchs Trail ★★★.** This 1.5-mile round-trip trail is fairly flat (good for kids) and leads through a forest of huge old trees to a grove of 1,000-year-old red cedars on an island in the Ohanapecosh River. If you've never seen old-growth trees, this is a must. The trail head is near the Stevens Canyon park entrance (southeast entrance).

Another interesting (and easy) low-elevation walk is the **Trail of the Shadows,** a .75-mile loop trail in Longmire. This trail, which circles a wet meadow, leads past bubbling mineral springs.

There are naturalist-led programs and walks throughout the spring, summer, and fall, and on winter weekends, there are guided snowshoe walks. Check the park newspaper for schedules.

WHITEWATER RAFTING The Tieton River, which flows down the eastern slopes of the Cascades, is one of the state's most popular rafting rivers. However, the rafting season lasts for only 10 days during the annual August/September drawdown of water from Rimrock Reservoir. The dates change based on seasonal runoff levels, so you'll need to contact the rafting companies to find out what days they are offering rafting trips. Those companies include **Alpine Adventures** (www.alpineadventures.com; ✆ **800/723-8386**) and **River Riders** (www.riverrider.com; ✆ **800/448-7238** or 206/448-7238). Expect to pay $80 to $100.

WINTER SPORTS There's good cross-country skiing and snow-shoeing at **Paradise**, where 2-hour **guided snowshoe walks,** with snowshoes provided ($4 suggested donation), are offered daily between mid-December and early January and on winter weekends through March. You'll find a ski touring and cross-country ski and snow-shoe rental shop at the **National Park Inn at Longmire** (✆ **360/569-2411**). Snowboarding is popular throughout the year,

A Scenic Train Ride on Mount Rainier

From Memorial Day through October, the **Mount Rainier Scenic Railroad ★** (www.mtrainierrailroad.com; ✆ **888/783-2611** or 360/492-5588) operates vintage steam and diesel locomotives and both enclosed and open passenger cars between the town of Elbe and the southwest entrance to the park. The trips last 1½ to 2 hours and cost $41 to $54 for adults, $21 to $34 for children ages 4 to 12.

though there is no lift to get you up the slope, and it's about a 1½-hour climb to the best snowboarding area.

Just outside the park's northeast corner, off Wash. 410, is **Crystal Mountain** ★★★ (www.skicrystal.com; ✆ **360/663-3050** for general information, or 888/754-6199 for snow conditions), the state's best all-around ski area due to the variety of terrain. You'll pay $74 for an adult all-day adult lift ticket, $50 for seniors.

WHERE TO STAY & DINE

Within the national park, your first choice for meals should be the dining room at the **Paradise Inn**. There's also a dining room in Longmire at the National Park Inn. For quick meals, there are snack bars at the **Jackson Visitor Center**, at **Paradise Inn**, and at **Sunrise Lodge**. In Ashford, the **Copper Creek Restaurant,** 35707 Wash. 706 E., Ashford (www.coppercreekinn.com; ✆ **360/569-2326**), makes good berry pies, and breakfast and espresso are served at **Whittaker's Bunkhouse Café,** 30205 Wash. 706 E. (www.whittakersbunkhouse.com; ✆ **360/569-2439**). In summer, you can get pizza, burgers, and beer at **Rainier Basecamp Bar & Grill,** 30027 Wash. 706 E. (www.basecampgrill.com; ✆ **360/569-2727**), next door to Whittaker's. In Elbe, you can get big, juicy burgers from a little white log cabin called **Scale Burgers,** 54109 Mountain Hwy. E. (✆ **360/569-2247**). If you're heading up to the mountain from Seattle, be sure to stop in Eatonville at **Truly Scrumptious Bakery & Café,** 212 Washington Ave. (www.trulyscrumptiousbakery.com; ✆ **360/832-2233**), where you can get a slice of pie, some bread for a picnic, or a sandwich to go.

National Park Inn ★ Open year-round, this historic alpine lodge on the forested slopes near Longmire dates from 1920 and features a full service dining room and general store, both open to the public (there are also guestrooms). Don't expect anything fussy or fancy here; this is a family-friendly, laid-back dining room with a menu that tries to please everyone, featuring everything from sauteed brook trout and old-fashioned pot roast to mac and cheese. End your meal with warm blackberry cobbler topped with a scoop of vanilla ice cream. You'll enjoy swell views of Mount Rainier from the veranda.

Mount Rainier National Park, Longmire. www.mtrainierguestservices.com. ✆ **360/569-2275.** Main courses $9–$21. Daily 7am–7pm.

Paradise Inn ★★ With its cedar-shake siding, huge exposed beams, cathedral ceilings, gigantic stone fireplace, and spectacular mountain views, Paradise Inn is the quintessential Northwest alpine lodge. If you want to stay overnight in Mount Rainier National Park, try to get a room at this historic lodge dating from 1917. And if you want a special place to dine, check out the inn's dining room, which is open to the public. The cooking here is above average for a park lodge and utilizes local and regional produce and products, including fresh oysters and fish (and good Dungeness crab cakes). You can also order mushroom strudel, a quesadilla, pork roulade, and pastas with fresh toppings. *Note*: the Annex, which has rooms with private baths, will be closed for renovation until 2019, but you can still book a room with shared bathroom in the Lodge.

Mount Rainier National Park, Paradise. www.mtrainierguestservices.com. ✆ **360/569-2275.** 121 units (33 with shared bathroom). $124–$215 double with shared bathroom. Dining room: main courses $15–$31. Dining room daily 7am–8pm. Inn and dining room closed early Oct to late May.

PORTLAND

Oregon's largest metropolis sits at the north end of the Willamette Valley, straddling the Willamette River near its confluence with the Columbia, which acts as a natural dividing line between Oregon and Washington. Like Seattle, 178 miles (286 km) to the north, Portland lies in an area of exceptional and easily accessible natural beauty, and this proximity to so many remarkable and varied landscapes adds to Portland's allure. On a clear day, Mount Hood—the city's alpine mascot—glows on the eastern horizon, about 90 minutes away. The Pacific Ocean is about 70 miles (113 km) to the west, just beyond the Coast Range. A drive through the Columbia River Gorge takes you, in about 1½ hours, through the Cascade Mountains to the high, dry, and much sunnier desert that covers almost two-thirds of the state. And the rolling hills of the fertile Willamette Valley's wine country begin right outside the city limits.

On some days, the air in Portland, cleansed by rain and scented with trees and earth, has a clean, sweet fragrance that goes right to your head. That's because there's green and greenery everywhere—in magnificent Washington Park, along the riverfront, in parks downtown and throughout the city, and in yards and gardens in Portland's many distinctive neighborhoods. The city counts some 200 parks, gardens, and wild spaces within the metropolitan area. Vast Forest Park, covering a huge swath of the city's West Hills, is the largest urban forests in the country.

The creation and protection of green spaces is a long-standing Portland tradition, and that includes farm and forest land outside the city. An urban growth boundary created in 1979 prevents urban sprawl—and has led to rapid development within the metro area. This new residential development, more than anything else, characterizes what's going on in Portland today. For those of us who have lived in or known Portland for a long time, it's frankly unbelievable what has been happening over the past decade, and really, over the past 5 years, since the end of the recession. Portland hasn't seen a building and population boom of this magnitude since World War II, when 100,000 people poured into the area to work in the shipyards. It's exciting for the newcomers, who get to discover a wonderful city, but disorienting (and yes, annoying) for many old-timers, who simply are not accustomed to crowded sidewalks and perennially clogged streets and highways. Portland never wanted to turn into a big city like Seattle; now, it has no choice but to embrace change. As demographics and lifestyles change, Portland is becoming more densely urban than it ever was.

There are newly created neighborhoods like the affluent Pearl District and rediscovered old neighborhoods. One thing that hasn't changed is the Portland notion of living and participating in a neighborhood. The difference is one of self-consciousness; neighborhoods were once just neighborhoods, and now they are becoming "brands" and "districts" and destinations. So today you say, "Let's go over and have dinner on SE Division" or "Let's go hang out on North Mississippi" or "I know a great food cart on SE Hawthorne." This would have been unheard of 15 years ago.

The result is that the city has more vitality as a city than it ever did. The building that's going on everywhere you look is not dictated, as it once was, by "Old Portland" institutions and Old Portland money. For, whether one wants to talk about it in polite society of not, that is one difference between Seattle and Portland—money, and how it's used, and how it's spent. Portland has never been as affluent or "showy" as Seattle, and at times it seems to strive to keep things that way. This is the only city where you will hear people say that something is "too spendy." (At least I've never heard that phrase used anywhere else.) But Portland's old modesty is changing, too, as affluence moves in and upscale "hipness" takes over. Sophisticated new hotels (four opened in 2017 alone) with trendy bars serving "craft cocktails" are springing up all over town.

The so-called "creative class"—a definition given to people who move to Portland not because they have a job, but because they want to live there, and create a job for themselves after they arrive—has transformed the city in many ways. When you visit, you will notice a lot of younger people, and a fashion aesthetic that combines grunge and street fashion with sports paraphernalia.

And to give you an accurate picture of Portland today, I have to mention the homeless situation. Frankly, no one knows what to do about it. Homeless camps, with the problems that go with them, have sprung up and been dismantled and discussed and argued about . . . with no solution. The homeless have become a presence, as they have in San Francisco, and Portland, like San Francisco, simply cannot figure out what to do to help them.

The TV show *Portlandia* embraced and satirized Portland's new and sometimes quirky urban culture. This is a city where people keep chickens in their backyards (at least on the east side), and not because they are into Santeria. They also seem to spend hours in cafes, microbreweries, and hot new restaurants. Talking. Arguing. Theorizing. Yes, it's kind of cerebral. In a way, it's nothing but a new version of the old, pot-smoking, countercultural Portland brought into the 21st century. Only now the pot is legal.

I'm not casting aspersions when I say that Portland lacks Seattle's pulsing, pushing drive. It doesn't have the industries to support that kind of economic va-va-voom. It's never going to be a totally anonymous vertical city because the height of its new buildings cannot exceed 450 feet. But it keeps moving ahead, and so far it hasn't lost its human touch, its human scale or the "old" traditions and charm that gave it character. It's always been a city where people loved to live, and where they often chose to stay even if a better offer came along. For all its newfound urban pizazz, Portland is still a city that likes to go to bed early and wake up to hear birds chirping—or chickens clucking—in the backyard.

FOOD

Everyone and *her* brother now knows that Portland has become a foodie mecca. This is one of the greatest benefits of the "new" Portland, at least for those of us who remember all too vividly when the city had four decent restaurants. The ingredients for great meals were always here—the Pacific Ocean is only 90 minutes away; salmon and steelhead swim up the rivers; just about anything will grow in the fertile Willamette Valley; the vast forests are forageable; and fruits, berries, and nuts have long been staple crops—but it took new chefs with new ideas to turn this local and regional harvest into the kind of exceptional meals that can be had in Portland today. With exceptional Oregon wines to go with them, I might add. Less than an hour away in the wine country, some of the best pinot noirs in the world are being produced. The simple idea of **food carts**—not just one cart selling hot dogs but dozens of carts selling every kind of cuisine imaginable—also got its start here. But don't assume that all the food in Portland is organic, fat-free, gluten-free, low-salt, vegetarian, free-range, or vegan. Sugar still rules—look at the lines in front of Voodoo Doughnut if you don't believe me—and there's plenty of fat in food cart hits like grilled cheese sandwiches and hot, gooey mac-and-cheese.

GARDENS & PARKS

One of the great things about Portland is that it fosters a green thumb. A visitor can't help but marvel at the beauty of home gardens, and the variety of trees, shrubs, and plants that grow in them. This is the City of Roses, after all, with a yearly Rose Festival complete with floral parades and a fun fair. Travelers should make a point of hanging out in some Portland gardens while they're here. The city has three world-class beauties: the **International Rose Test Garden**, the **Portland Japanese Garden**, and **Lan Su Chinese Garden**. Washington Park and Hoyt Arboretum are endlessly explorable, and **Forest Park**, which just happens to be the largest urban forest in the country, is crisscrossed with trails that begin at the end of city streets in Northwest and Southwest Portland. All the greenery, and the rain that supports it, is why the air in Portland sometimes smells so sweet and clean.

NEIGHBORHOODS

To get a feel for the Portland of today, the New Portland, hop on a streetcar or the light rail system and go hang out in some Portland neighborhoods. Once upon a time not so long ago, they were just neighborhoods, some better than others, with a strong community spirit. Today, people flit from one neighborhood to the next because the restaurant/coffeehouse/bakery/microbrewery/

boutique phenomenon has spread all over. There are neighborhoods and streets that have been completely transformed, particularly in **North Portland**, where North Russell Street, North Mississippi, and North Alberta have blossomed in ways unimaginable a few years ago. The **Pearl District**, created in an old warehouse and light industry area, is one of the most successful urban developments in the country. Over in southeast, Division Street and Belmont Street have changed dramatically with new buildings that combine retail, restaurants and residential. And downtown Portland, which remains as attractive and vital as ever, is being upgraded and reinvented everywhere you look. The urban center is not an anonymous warren of designer skyscrapers; it's fairly low-rise (height restrictions prevent tall buildings from usurping the views from the hills) and has a wonderful mixture of architecture and parks to keep it interesting. As you visit residential neighborhoods, don't be surprised if you hear clucking—raising chickens is a new urban pastime in Portland.

So where do people hang out? Portland has more **microbreweries** than any city in the world, and **coffee shops** are big small businesses. People order, sip, start to gab with their friends, and never leave except to go to the bathroom. You also hang out at bars during happy hour, which is huge in Portland. I always thought it was because drinks were cheap, but actually it's because the food is half-price.

The nice thing about hanging out in different parts of Portland is that you don't have to travel for miles to do it. The city is compact and easy to navigate, though you'd be wise to avoid driving during morning, afternoon, and evening rush hours. As you explore, you'll discover what really makes this city so special—its scale, its variety, and its still-charming livability. So goodbye Old Portland. I will miss you. But I have to say, the New Portland, aggravating as it is at times, is a lot more fun and exciting. And there's enough of Old Portland left to "Keep Portland Weird," our other civic motto.

ESSENTIALS

Arriving

BY PLANE

Portland International Airport (PDX; www.flypdx.com; ✆ **877/739-4636** or 503/460-4234) is located 10 miles northeast of downtown Portland, adjacent to the Columbia River. This is one of the easiest airports in the U.S. to navigate, and it's consistently ranked the most user-friendly airport in the U.S. PDX is linked to the city by the easy-to-use MAX light rail system. There's a Travel Oregon **Visitor Information Center** in the baggage claim area where you can pick up maps and brochures.

GETTING INTO THE CITY

BY CAR From the airport, follow signs for downtown. From I-205 you'll exit onto westbound I-84, which crosses the Willamette River via the Morrison Bridge exit and brings you into downtown Portland. The trip takes about 20 minutes if there's no traffic, up to 45 minutes if it's rush hour.

BY LIGHT RAIL The easiest and least expensive way to get into town is to take the Airport MAX (Red Line) light rail line, operated by **TriMet** (www.trimet.org; ✆ **503/238-7433**). MAX operates daily about every 15 to 30 minutes between 5am and midnight. Buy your ticket from the vending machine on the airport station platform. The fare on MAX is $2.50 for adults and $1.25 for seniors (or "Honored Citizens," as they're called in Portland). The trip from the airport to Pioneer Courthouse Square in downtown Portland takes about 40 minutes. (Many downtown hotels lie within 4 or 5 blocks of Pioneer Square; plan on walking from there, or continuing to your hotel via streetcar, bus or another MAX line, because taxis in Portland don't cruise for fares.)

BY TAXI A **taxi** to downtown generally costs between $35 and $45 before gratuity. Taxis are usually available at the lower level Ground Transportation area. It is also legal to use **Uber** or **Lyft**.

BY TRAIN

Amtrak trains stop at historic **Union Station,** 800 NW Sixth Ave. (www.amtrak.com; ✆ **800/872-7245**), about 10 blocks from the heart of downtown Portland. Taxis are usually waiting to meet trains and can take you to your hotel, or you can use Lyft or Uber. If you are renting a car from a downtown car rental office, the agency will usually pick you up at the station. The MAX Yellow and Green lines both run past Union Station and can take you into downtown Portland or across the Willamette River to Portland's east side.

BY BUS

The **Greyhound** bus station is at 550 NW Sixth Ave. (www.greyhound.com; ✆ **800/231-2222** or 503/243-2361), on the north side of downtown near Union Station. You can take MAX from the Greyhound station into downtown. Although you can also easily walk from the station into the heart of downtown, you have to pass through a somewhat rough neighborhood for a few blocks; it's fine during the day, but I wouldn't recommend it after dark or on weekend evenings.

Bolt Bus (www.boltbus.com) is a low-cost bus service to Portland from Vancouver, BC and Seattle to the north, and from Eugene to the south. The Bolt Bus conveniently drops off passengers right downtown on SW Salmon Street between 5th and 6th avenues.

Visitor Information

Travel Portland, 701 SW Sixth Ave. (www.travelportland.com; ✆ **877/678-5263** or 503/275-8355), is in Pioneer Courthouse Square in downtown Portland. Hours are Mon–Fri 8:30am–5:30pm, Sat 10am–4pm, Sun (May–Oct only) 10am–2pm. **Travel Oregon** (www.traveloregon.com; ✆ **503/284-4620**), the state tourism office, has an information desk in the baggage claim area of the Portland Airport; open daily 9am–10pm.

City Layout

Portland is in northwestern Oregon at the confluence of the Columbia and Willamette rivers. (Contrary to what many people think, Portland is *not* on the

Pacific Ocean but about 90 miles east of it.) The **Willamette** (pronounced will-*am*-met) **River,** spanned by eight bridges in the downtown area, cuts through the heart of Portland, dividing it into east and west. **Burnside Street** is the north-south boundary line, dividing the west side into **northwest** and **southwest,** and the east side into **northeast** and **southeast.** The west side rises steadily from the Willamette to about 1,000 ft. in the West Hills, while the residential east side of Portland is relatively flat, though it is punctuated here and there by the hilly remnants of several volcanoes. Just east of the city, the landscape changes to rolling hills that extend about 50 miles to the Cascade Mountains and Mount Hood, the most prominent peak in the Oregon Cascades (11,235 ft.). The Columbia River, to the north, forms the boundary between Oregon and Washington.

The Greater Metro area also includes **Vancouver, Washington**, just across the Columbia River to the north of Portland, although that is an entirely separate city. About 2.35-million people now live in the combined metropolitan areas, and the figure is rising by the day.

MAIN ARTERIES & STREETS

I-84 (**Banfield Fwy.** or **Expwy.**) enters Portland from the east. **I-205,** east of the city, bypasses downtown Portland and runs past the airport. **I-5** runs through the city on a north-south axis. **I-405** circles around the west and south sides of downtown. **U.S. 26 (Sunset Hwy.)** leaves downtown heading west toward Beaverton and the coast. **Ore. 217** runs south from U.S. 26 in Beaverton and connects to I-5.

Neighborhoods in Brief

Everyone who comes to Portland—and even some of us who live here—comments on its many lovely neighborhoods. As the city has grown and diversified, older neighborhoods have been "rediscovered" and their original shopping and retail streets re-invented. The commercial/retail/restaurant areas of several areas, mostly on the east side, are virtually unrecognizable from what they were as recently as the 1990s. Portland has always been community-minded, and the old neighborhoods with their new infill remain the heart and soul of the city.

SOUTHWEST PORTLAND

Downtown Thanks to far-sighted planning efforts, Portland's attractive downtown area has become a model for cities around the country. Compact and pedestrian-friendly, with short 200-square-foot blocks and three historic districts, it's a destination for residents and workers from all over the city. Parks, fountains, public artworks, hotels, restaurants, and a rich texture of building and street materials add to the human-scale appeal. Brick-paved **Transit Malls,** completed in 1978 along SW 5th and 6th Avenues, bisect the main retail and business core.

Starting at the Willamette River, the central downtown area is bounded to the south and north by the curve of I-405. Clustered along the south end are the buildings of **Portland State University** (bounded by I-405, SW Market Street, SW 12th Ave., and SW 5th Ave.). Rising at the north end is the sleek, rhomboid-shaped **U.S. Bancorp Tower** (111 SW 5th Ave.), known locally as "Big Pink." Oregon's tallest building (43 stories), it has a reflective orange-pink facade that plays off the changing light. Downtown extends west to the I-405 Freeway, a monstrosity that cuts right through southwest and northwest Portland at 13th Avenue.

Pioneer Courthouse Square, a brick plaza flanked by the lovely old Pioneer

Courthouse, office buildings from the 1920s covered with white glazed terra-cotta tiles (it's officially the Glazed Terracotta Historic District, but nobody knows that except me, and now you), and a large **Nordstrom** store from the 1980s, is a gathering spot called "Portland's living room." Within downtown's Cultural District (along Broadway and the South Park blocks) are the **Arlene Schnitzer Concert Hall,** home of the Oregon Symphony, the **Portland Center for the Performing Arts,** and **Keller Auditorium**—the city's largest performing-arts venues—as well as the **Portland Art Museum** and the **Oregon Historical Society Museum.** The **South Park Blocks,** a tree-lined park-promenade created on land donated by Portland's early settlers, runs from SW Salmon Street through the campus of Portland State to the I-405. **Tom McCall Waterfront Park,** a wide pedestrian esplanade and park, runs along the Willamette River and is the site of numerous festivals (an amusement park is set up here during the Rose Festival). You'd never guess that this popular riverfront greenway was once a six-lane highway.

The **Yamhill National Historic District,** bounded by SW Naito Parkway, Morrison Street, Taylor Street, and 3rd Avenue, is also considered part of downtown Portland. This compact, six-block area, known for its fine examples of late-19th-century cast-iron architecture, marked the southern end of the city's first, waterfront-based commercial core. In the 1950s, when many buildings in the area were demolished for parking lots and to facilitate construction of the present Morrison Street Bridge, the area became isolated from its contemporaneous extension to the north, the area now known as the Skidmore/Old Town Historic District. Restoration and renovation of the remaining buildings began in the 1970s.

Skidmore/Old Town District Portland's original commercial core is bounded by SW Naito Parkway, SW Oak Street, Third Avenue, and NW Davis Street. Running parallel to the Willamette River, and straddling sections of northwest and southwest Portland, this area, along with the Yamhill Historic District to the south (considered a part of downtown), was part of the 1843 land claim that led to the establishment of Portland. From the mid- to late-19th century it served as the city's main riverfront business and entertainment district. **Skidmore Fountain,** a graceful fountain built in 1888—with caryatids holding aloft a bronze basin in the center of an octagonal granite pool with the inscription, "Good citizens are the riches of a city"—acts as the centerpiece of the district. Cast-iron artifacts from demolished 19th-century Portland buildings are set into an adjacent brick wall and covered arcade that leads to the popular **Portland Saturday Market** (see p. 199). The area began to decline in the 1890s when the logging boom ended and railroads decreased the city's reliance on river trade. **Union Station** (800 NW 6th Ave. near the Broadway Bridge), with its 150-ft. tower proclaiming "Go By Train," was built in 1896 and is a prominent landmark from the railroad era. As the city center shifted west toward higher ground, Old Town gradually became a neglected skid row, and many of the district's brick and cast-iron "commercial palaces" were demolished, leaving gaping holes. Since its designation in 1975 as a National Historic Landmark District, most of the remaining late-19th-century buildings have been restored. Despite the presence of the Portland Saturday Market, the neighborhood has never become a popular shopping district, mostly because some welfare hotels and street people give parts of it a rough edge. With its many clubs and bars, however, it is the city's main nightlife district. The neighborhood is safe during the day, but visitors should exercise caution at night.

Portland Heights Portland Heights, nestled in the hills south of Burnside Street and west of SW Vista, is Portland's oldest and most affluent neighborhood. In gorgeous **Washington Park,** you'll find two of Portland's great gardens (**The International Rose Test Garden** and the **Portland Japanese Garden**) as well as the renowned **Hoyt Arboretum** and the **Oregon Zoo.** This is otherwise primarily a residential neighborhood.

South Waterfront Portland's newest neighborhood is a collection of high-rise offices and condominiums about a mile south of downtown's Tom McCall Waterfront Park.

The Benson Bubblers

Scattered throughout downtown Portland are dozens of cast-bronze four-bubbler drinking fountains installed around 1912 to 1913. They were a gift from Simon Benson, a teetotaling lumber baron who believed a supply of fresh, cool water would help detract from the lure of the saloons. Portland's drinking water comes from Bull Run, a watershed on the northwest slope of Mount Hood, and it is delicious.

The South Waterfront is home to the lower terminal for the Portland Aerial Tram that glides up to Oregon Health Sciences University (OHSU), the huge medical facility that dominates "Pill Hill" above the South Waterfront. There's otherwise not much here to draw visitors.

NORTHWEST PORTLAND

Chinatown Two carved lions stand in front of the colorful **Chinatown Gate** (NW Fourth Ave. and W. Burnside), erected in 1986 to commemorate 135 years of Chinese contributions to the city of Portland and the state of Oregon. The five-tiered gate marks the official entrance to Portland's low-key Chinatown District, bounded by NW Second and Fifth Avenues, West Burnside, and NW Glisan Street. This small area, with its handful of Chinese groceries and restaurants, is wedged between the Pearl District and Old Town. The neighborhood's main attraction is the impressive **Lan Su Chinese Garden.** Because of its proximity to bars on West Burnside Street and the homeless missions and welfare hotels in Old Town, Chinatown is not a good neighborhood to explore late at night.

Pearl District This relatively new (and recycled) neighborhood of galleries, boutiques, restaurants, cafes, brewpubs, parks, and residential and business lofts and condos is bounded by the **North Park Blocks,** Overton Street, I-405, and Burnside Street. It is rather phenomenal how this former warehouse district has grown up and matured into a really pleasant city neighborhood over the last 20 years. It has all the urban amenities a Portlander requires, including **Powell's City of Books, Jamison Park** with its fountain where kids play in the summer, and public transportation provided by the Portland streetcar. Crowds of people come to the Pearl for **First Thursday** (the first Thursday of every month), when galleries premiere new shows and are open late. The Pearl is Portland's well-planned version of new urbanism and one of the city's main upscale neighborhoods for young families, singles, and boomer retirees.

Northwest 23rd & Nob Hill Small in scale and long on charm, **NW 23rd** is the focal point of one of the most attractive neighborhoods in Portland. It's now a hot destination street, known for its shopping, sidewalk cafes, restaurants, and good people-watching. The avenue and its less fashionable twin, **NW 21st,** extend from West Burnside to NW Thurman Street; the blocks between West Burnside and NW Lovejoy streets are the busiest. The upscale commercial aspect of NW 23rd is a fairly recent phenomenon. Two decades ago it was a quiet residential street, a bit shabby around the edges, with little more than a drugstore, a bank, and a couple of stores to serve the needs of the neighborhood. Gradually, the old houses were turned into small shops; existing structures were renovated; and new coffeehouses, boutiques, and restaurants moved in. In the latest phase of development, big "lifestyle" stores like Pottery Barn and Restoration Hardware have grabbed a piece of the commercial action.

The **Nob Hill** neighborhood around NW 23rd Avenue became fashionable in the prosperous 1880s, and there are still many fine Victorian homes to be seen on the streets between NW 17th and NW 25th avenues and NW Everett to NW Thurman streets. These homes are still private residences or have been converted into offices. Farther west, and extending from northwest to southwest, is giant **Forest Park,** one of the largest urban parks and the largest urban forest in the nation. **Pittock Mansion** is literally the high point of Northwest Portland—it sits about 1,000 feet high in Forest Park and overlooks downtown, east Portland and Mt. Hood.

NORTHEAST PORTLAND

Irvington One of Northeast Portland's oldest and most diverse neighborhoods, Irvington is bounded by NE Broadway and NE Fremont between NE 7th and NE 24th. NE Broadway and NE Weidler serve as Irvington's primary commercial streets, with giant **Lloyd Center** mall between them. Like other city neighborhoods, Irvington has undergone an amazing renaissance in the past 2 decades. With its lovely old Victorian and early-20th-century homes on quiet streets shaded by giant trees, it's no wonder that it was "rediscovered" and, after years of being rather run-down, became one of the most expensive residential neighborhoods in Portland.

Alberta Arts District This newly redefined neighborhood, a few miles north of downtown Portland and a mile to the east of I-5, is Portland's most multicultural and creative neighborhood. Now. It used to be pretty run-down and just called Alberta. Because the old houses here are fairly small and used to be relatively inexpensive, it became a popular neighborhood with young, liberal families. Neighborhood shops are full of alternative-lifestyle fashions, on-the-edge (for Portland) art, and lots of the unexpected and the uncategorizable. Cafes, pubs, and restaurants provide plenty of places for making the scene. On the **Last Thursday** of every month, the neighborhood throws a blocks-long, art-oriented street party. Before all this "urban renaissance" happened, Alberta was an area where African-Americans, who came to Portland during World War II to work in the Portland shipyards, lived.

North Mississippi District All these "districts" are new inventions by real estate agents and developers. This area didn't really have a name before it became white, young, and arty. Anchored by the **ReBuilding Center,** a sort of warehouse-sized thrift store full of recycled building materials, the North Mississippi District is 2 miles north of downtown. With plenty of good restaurants, a brewpub, popular music venues, and a couple of great coffeehouses, North Mississippi is a fun neighborhood to explore if you want to get a feel for what it's like to live in the "new" Portland.

SOUTHEAST PORTLAND

Hawthorne This southeast Portland neighborhood, once a countercultural enclave and still "alternative" around its gentrified edges, is full of eclectic boutiques, moderately priced restaurants, a couple of famous old theaters (the **Aladdin** for live music and performance, and the **Clinton Street,** which has been showing *The Rocky Horror Picture Show* every Saturday night since 1978). Just south of Hawthorne Boulevard, beginning at SE 12th Avenue, you'll find the unique **Ladd's Addition** neighborhood, the oldest planned community in Portland, which has five rose gardens and an unusual (and confusing) street layout. **SE Belmont Street,** just north of Hawthorne Boulevard, and **SE Division Street,** to the south, are two of the city's newly rediscovered and revamped neighborhoods, and both areas are well worth exploring.

Laurelhurst The Laurelhurst neighborhood takes its name from lovely Laurelhurst Park, its centerpiece and showplace. Stretching from about SE 30th to SE 39th and from NE Sandy to NE Belmont, Laurelhurst is a sedate, rather low-key, and family-oriented neighborhood. Development started in the first decades of the 20th century, and the area contains a rich mix of residential architecture styles and sizes.

Sellwood Sellwood is the city's antiques district and has many restored Victorian houses. It's a small-scale area with a real neighborhood feel. **Oaks Park**, perched above the Willamette River, is one of the oldest amusement parks in the U.S. and retains a low-key, family-friendly atmosphere. Adjacent Oaks Bottom was Portland's first designated wildlife refuge. Sellwood was once a separate city from Portland, and its quiet residential streets still have a kind of lost-in-time feeling.

Westmoreland & Eastmoreland Just north of Sellwood, surrounding the intersection of SE Milwaukie Avenue and SE Bybee

Boulevard, is the heart of the Westmoreland neighborhood. Westmoreland and adjacent Eastmoreland are primarily residential neighborhoods, mostly laid out and built from the 1920s to 1940s, with a charming mix of bungalows and mansions on curving, tree-lined streets. This area is the home of **Reed College,** a famous liberal bastion. Across from Reed is the beautiful **Crystal Springs Rhododendron Garden.** The Eastmoreland neighborhood is under siege by developers tearing down its old homes and erecting multi-dwelling units; residents are trying to get National Historic Landmark status for Eastmoreland to help preserve its unique characters.

GETTING AROUND

By Public Transportation

Even if you have car, I would encourage you to use public transportation while you're in Portland. Why hassle with the sometimes-awful traffic and search for a scarce parking space, when you can travel around the city via bus, MAX light rail, or the Portland streetcar? They are all operated by **TriMet** (www.trimet.org; ✆ **503/238-7433**). Buy your 2½-hour tickets and day passes on the bus (exact change required), at vending machines at bus and light rail stops, at vending machines on board the streetcar, or at the **TriMet Ticket Office** (701 SW Sixth Ave.), located in Pioneer Courthouse Square behind the waterfall fountain. The office is open Monday through Friday from 8:30am to 5:30pm and Saturdays from 10am to 4pm. Bus and MAX passes and schedules are also available at most Fred Meyer, Safeway, and Albertsons grocery stores throughout the metro area.

The following fares are valid and interchangeable on all forms of TriMet transportation for 2½ hours: adults 18–64 $2.50, seniors ("Honored Citizens") 65+ and youth 7–17 $1.25. There is a lower "streetcar-only" fare described below.

BY BUS TriMet buses operate daily over an extensive network. You can make free transfers between the bus and both the MAX light rail system and the Portland streetcar.

BY LIGHT RAIL The **Metropolitan Area Express (MAX)** is Portland's aboveground light rail system, connecting downtown Portland with the airport (Red Line), the eastern suburb of Gresham (Blue Line), the western suburbs of Beaverton (Red and Blue lines) and Hillsboro (Blue Line), North Portland (Yellow Line), and Clackamas (Green Line). The new Milwaukie extension (Orange Line) runs from Union Station through downtown, crosses the new Tillicum Crossing bridge to Eastmoreland/Westmoreland, and continues on to Milwaukie. Be sure to validate your ticket on the platform before you board MAX. There are

Save Money with TriMet Transportation Passes

A **1-day transportation pass,** which includes all forms of public transportation, costs only $5 for adults, $2 for seniors, and $3.30 for ages 7–17. Use it for only two trips and you've paid for the pass, use it for additional trips during the day and you're saving a lot. You can buy a **7-day pass** for $26 adults, $7 seniors, and $8 ages 7–17.

ticket inspectors who randomly check to make sure passengers have stamped tickets and issue fines to those who don't.

BY STREETCAR **Portland streetcar** (www.portlandstreetcar.org; ✆ **503/238-7433**) runs on three lines, traversing both sides of the Willamette River. The NS Line travels from NW Lovejoy and Northrup, through the Pearl District, downtown, and Portland State University to the South Waterfront District. The A Loop and B Loop run in opposite directions on the same route connecting SW Market (downtown) to the Pearl District, across the Broadway Bridge to the Rose Quarter, Convention Center (Central Eastside), and OMSI (Oregon Museum of Science and Industry). The streetcar lines are a smart way for visitors to get from downtown to the eastside neighborhoods. Streetcar fares are $2 for adults 18-64 and $1 for seniors 65+ and youth 7–17, but that's for the streetcar only; you cannot use a streetcar-only ticket to transfer to buses or MAX.

By Car

CAR RENTALS Portland is a compact city, and public transit will get you to most attractions within its limits. However, if you're planning to explore outside the city—and the Portland area's greatest attractions, such as Mount Hood and the Columbia River Gorge, lie in the countryside within a 1½ hour drive—you'll definitely need a car or a tour company to take you there.

The major car rental companies all have desks at Portland International Airport on the lower level. **Car2go** (www.car2go.com) lets you rent a small two-seater car or larger cars (including Mercedes) from spots all over Portland, drive it as long as you need to, and return it to a convenient drop-off spot—not necessarily where you picked it up—for a standard rate of 35-49¢ per minute. You don't have to pay for gas when you use the car. You do need to become a member before you begin using the service, but after the initial charge there is no annual fee. The same basic rules apply for **ReachNow Car Sharing Portland** (www.reachnow.com/portland), but this service provides various BMW and Mini cars and offers a flat-rate pricing system ($20 for 1 hour, $50 for 3 hours).

PARKING Electronic parking meters take coins, credit cards, and debit cards and issue receipts that must be placed on the **curbside window** of your car. The receipt remains valid elsewhere if you move your car, as long as there is time remaining on it. In most parts of town, you don't have to feed the meters after 7pm, but you do pay for parking on Sundays from 1 to 7pm in some parts of the city. The hourly rate is $2.

The city operates **Smart Park** garages at First Avenue and Jefferson Street, Fourth Avenue and Yamhill Street, 10th Avenue and Yamhill Street, Third Avenue and Alder Street, O'Bryant Square, and Naito Parkway and Davis Street. Many downtown merchants and restaurants validate Smart Park tickets for 2 hours if you spend at least $25.

You can forego credit card and cash payments for parking by using the city's new **Parking Kitty** mobile parking app (**www.portlandoregon.gov/transportation/73554**). Every parking meter has an identifying Zone number posted on the side that you type in along with the amount of time you want to park. Some people find it easy to use, others say that it's neither faster nor more efficient. If you're tech-savvy and app-friendly, you may find it useful, but it also requires all that you sign up with a password to create an account.

SPECIAL DRIVING RULES Oregon state law prohibits texting and talking on a handheld device while driving; stiff fines may result if you are caught doing so. You may turn right on a red light after a full stop and left into the adjacent left lane of a one-way street. If a pedestrian is crossing at a white-striped pedestrian crossing, motorists must come to a complete stop until the pedestrian has reached the sidewalk. There are now green bike-only lanes throughout the city; bicyclists have the right-of-way in the bike lanes.

By Taxi

You won't find cabs cruising the streets—you or your hotel concierge will have to phone for one. **Broadway Cab** (www.broadwaycab.com; ✆ **503/227-1234**) and **Radio Cab** (www.radiocab.net; ✆ **503/227-1212**) charge $2.50 for the first passenger, $1 for each additional passenger, and $2.90 per mile.

By Bike

With traffic a growing problem in Portland, getting around by bike is an increasingly popular mode of transportation—and now it's easier than ever for you to hop on a bike and pedal to your destination. BIKETOWN, launched in 2016, is Portland's bikeshare program, designed for taking quick trips around downtown and the close-in east side. The bright orange bike stations are located in busy areas throughout the Portland core. **BIKETOWN (www.biketownpdx.com)** offers three payment options: a single 30 minute ride for $2.50, a day pass including 180 minutes of ride time for $12, and an annual pass with 90 minutes of ride time per day for $12/month. The plans are available for purchase through the website, mobile app, or at a station kiosk. At the station, you enter the personal identification number (PIN) you received with sign-up or hold your member card above the touch pad, remove the lock, ride the bike, and return it to an open space at any other bike station. It's fun and simple.

Oregon's Cannabis Laws

You've probably heard that since 2015 the recreational use of marijuana has been legal in Portland. That doesn't mean you can stroll down the street puffing on a reefer. You must be **21 years of age** to purchase pot from a licensed retailer (they will check your I.D.). Smoking marijuana in public in Oregon is illegal, even if you're smoking with a vape pen. **You can only consume at home or on private property—but not in your hotel** (because of anti-smoking laws enacted to control the use of tobacco in hotels). This means no bars, community parks, public outdoor smoking areas, on buses and airplanes, or federal land. And don't smoke in your car and then drive when you're stoned: it's dangerous. Getting busted smoking weed in public could result in fines and even jail time.

On Foot

City blocks in Portland are about half the size of most city blocks elsewhere, and the entire downtown area covers only about 13 blocks by 26 blocks. This makes downtown Portland a very easy place to explore on foot. From downtown you can easily walk to the **Pearl District, NW 23rd,** and **Washington Park.** (There are also public transportation options to all those destinations.)

WHEN TO GO

In Portland we like to say that summer begins on July 5th. It's mostly true—or as true as anything can be in an age of rapid climate change. So if want to maximize your chances for sunshine and warm weather, July 5 through September 15 are the best months to visit.

The summers truly are splendid, and life moves outdoors as much as possible. The parks are verdant, the gardens are glorious, there are outdoor festivals galore, and you can sit outside comfortably all evening, until it gets chilly enough for a sweater. That's the beauty of summer Portland—no matter how hot the day, the nights cool down (sometimes by 30 degrees) so that you need a blanket. And when it's hot, it's dry, not humid, because the hot air comes from the deserts east of the Cascades.

Nobody but gardeners believe me when I tell them that Portland and Seattle actually have what is considered a Mediterranean climate. What this means is that it generally rains almost constantly in one form or another from mid-October through June, with plenty of clear days and periods of truly great weather along the way. From November through March, the temperature remains temperate, rarely dipping below freezing and usually hovering in the 40s. By April it starts warming up, though the precipitation persists, and by May and June temperatures rise to the mid-70s with (of late) sudden spikes into the 80s and even low 90s (all temperatures in Fahrenheit). Plants love this climate, and so do gardeners.

As for winter—well, if you're a skier or snowboarder, you know why winter would be a good time to come. The mountain is generally ready to chairlift skiers up its slopes by mid-November—though I hasten to add that in recent years the snow has been arriving later and staying longer.

Portland Calendar of Events

I've included a very limited sampling below of what I consider "visit-worthy" events. As I can make no claims to psychic abilities, I can't include all of the nifty happenings that haven't yet been announced.

FEBRUARY

Portland International Film Festival. This well regarded fest brings films from all over the world to theaters around the city. For a schedule, go to www.nwfilm.org.

Oregon Seafood and Wine Festival. The Oregon Convention Center becomes one huge bistro during this event, which happily coincides with the Dungeness crab season. Learn more at www.pdxseafoodandwinefestival.com.

APRIL

The Spring Beer & Wine Fest. Again at the convention center, this large festival is devoted to craft microbrews, regional wines, spirits, food, crafts, and music. Details at www.springbeerfest.com.

MAY

Cinco de Mayo Fiesta. Celebrates Portland's sister-city status with Guadalajara, Mexico with food, entertainment, and music in Governor Tom McCall Waterfront Park. May 5. More at www.cincodemayo.org.

JUNE

Portland Rose Festival. Stretching out over 3 weeks, the city's oldest (started in 1888) and biggest celebration includes a Grand Floral Parade, a Starlight Parade, the election of the Rose Queen, a waterfront carnival, and dragon boat races on the river. See www.rosefestival.org.

The Portland Pride Festival and Parade. This one happens over a weekend in mid-June, with a parade on Sunday, live entertainment, a drag race (heels, not wheels), and a pet parade. For exact dates, go to www.pridenw.org.

JULY

Waterfront Blues Festival. Over the extended Fourth of July weekend, this fills Governor Tom McCall Waterfront Park with 4 days of national headliners. To learn who will be playing when, go to www.waterfrontbluesfest.com.

Oregon Brewers Festival. The last full weekend in July brings *more* beer to Tom McCall Waterfront Park, this time in the form of a 4-day sudsapalooza, one of the largest and oldest craft-beer festivals in the country. More at www.oregonbrewfest.com.

PDX Pop Now! In late July, indie music fans flock to this free, all-ages festival of local music featuring upwards of 50 artists selected by public vote. Info is at www.pdxpopnow.com.

AUGUST

Bite of Oregon. This mid-August event is a fundraiser for Special Olympics Oregon, and features food and wine samples from local chefs and regional wineries, along with live music, cooking demos, and other entertainment. Details: www.biteoforegon.com.

SEPTEMBER

Musicfest NW. In early September, the 4-day fest fills Waterfront Park and the clubs of Portland with local musicians and national acts. More at www.musicfestnw.com.

The Time-Based Art Festival. Consists of 10 days of modern visual and performance arts sponsored by the Portland Institute for Contemporary Art IPICA. Details: www.pica.org/tba.

NOVEMBER

Northwest Film & Video Festival. In mid-November, this regional festival brings a host of short films, documentaries, and features by independent filmmakers from the Pacific.

DECEMBER

The ZooLights Festival. At the Oregon Zoo, it includes music, kids' activities, and a special holiday train. Details: www.oregonzoo.org.

EXPLORING PORTLAND

Ask a Portlander about the city's must-see attractions, and you'll probably be directed to the **Portland Japanese Garden,** the **International Rose Test Garden,** and the **Lan Su Chinese Garden.** Gardening is a Portland obsession, and thanks to the moist and mild weather here, you'll find some of the finest public gardens in the country. Visiting all the city's noteworthy parks and gardens can easily take up 2 or 3 days. Seattle, and not Portland, is the place where you're more likely to encounter big museums, intriguing exhibitions and splashy traveling art exhibitions. This isn't to say that the Portland Art Museum, which often hosts interesting traveling exhibitions, isn't worth visiting, or that the Oregon Historical Society Museum is not worth your time.

They are, but they tend to have a local rather than an international focus. The city's really not so much about spending hours in museums as it is about exploring neighborhoods, parks and gardens, and nearby nature.

Attractions in & Around Downtown Portland

Any visit to downtown Portland should start on **Pioneer Courthouse Square** ★★★ at the corner of SW Broadway and Yamhill Street. The brick-paved square (restored in 2017) is an outdoor stage for everything from summer outdoor movies to food festivals to flower displays to concerts and protest rallies. A few decades ago it was a parking lot, created in 1951 when the Portland Hotel—a Queen Anne–style chateau and an architectural gem—was demolished. Long before that, Pioneer Square was the site of Portland's first schoolhouse. The octagonal cupola of the Classic Revival **Pioneer Courthouse** (701 SW 6th Ave.) at the east end of the square has been a Portland landmark since it was completed in 1873. The first federal building to be constructed in the Pacific Northwest, the courthouse was designed by Alfred Mullet, who also designed the San Francisco Mint. The two large wings on its west facade were added in 1903.

Today, the square, with its **waterfall fountain** and freestanding columns, is Portland's favorite downtown gathering spot, especially at noon, when the **Weather Machine,** a goofy mechanical sculpture, forecasts the weather for the next 24 hours. Amid a fanfare of music and flashing lights, the Weather Machine sends up clouds of mist followed by a sun (clear weather), a dragon (stormy weather), or a blue heron (clouds and drizzle).

The **Portland Visitor Information Center** and **Tri-Met ticket office** are located behind and beneath the fountains, and a big **Starbucks** with outdoor tables overlooking the square anchors the corner above. Every Monday from June through September a farmers market is held in the square between 10am and 2pm. Check the Pioneer Courthouse Square website (www.thesquarepdx.org) for upcoming events.

Chapman & Lownsdale Squares ★★ PARK Set aside as public parks in 1852, a year after Portland became an incorporated city, these two adjacent blocks planted with elms, pines, cedars, and ginkgo trees form the green heart of Portland's government quarter. They were the scene of anti-Chinese riots in the 1880s and in the 1920s were sexually segregated to protect women from unwanted advances. **Chapman Square** (btw. SW Madison and SW Main), the former women's park, was named for Judge William Chapman, a founder of *The Oregonian* newspaper. Men were confined to **Lownsdale Square** (btw. SW Main and SW Salmon), named for Daniel Lownsdale, a 19th-century Oregon legislator who was also responsible for building the city's first plank road in 1851. Between the two squares, in the center of SW Main Street, is the graceful and iconic **Thompson Elk Fountain** (1900). Roland Perry's life-size bronze statue of an elk—an animal that reputedly grazed here in the early 1850s—stands atop a pedestal with four granite horse troughs at its base.

Bounded by SW Madison St. and SW Salmon St. and SW 3rd Ave. and SW 4th Ave.

Downtown Portland Attractions

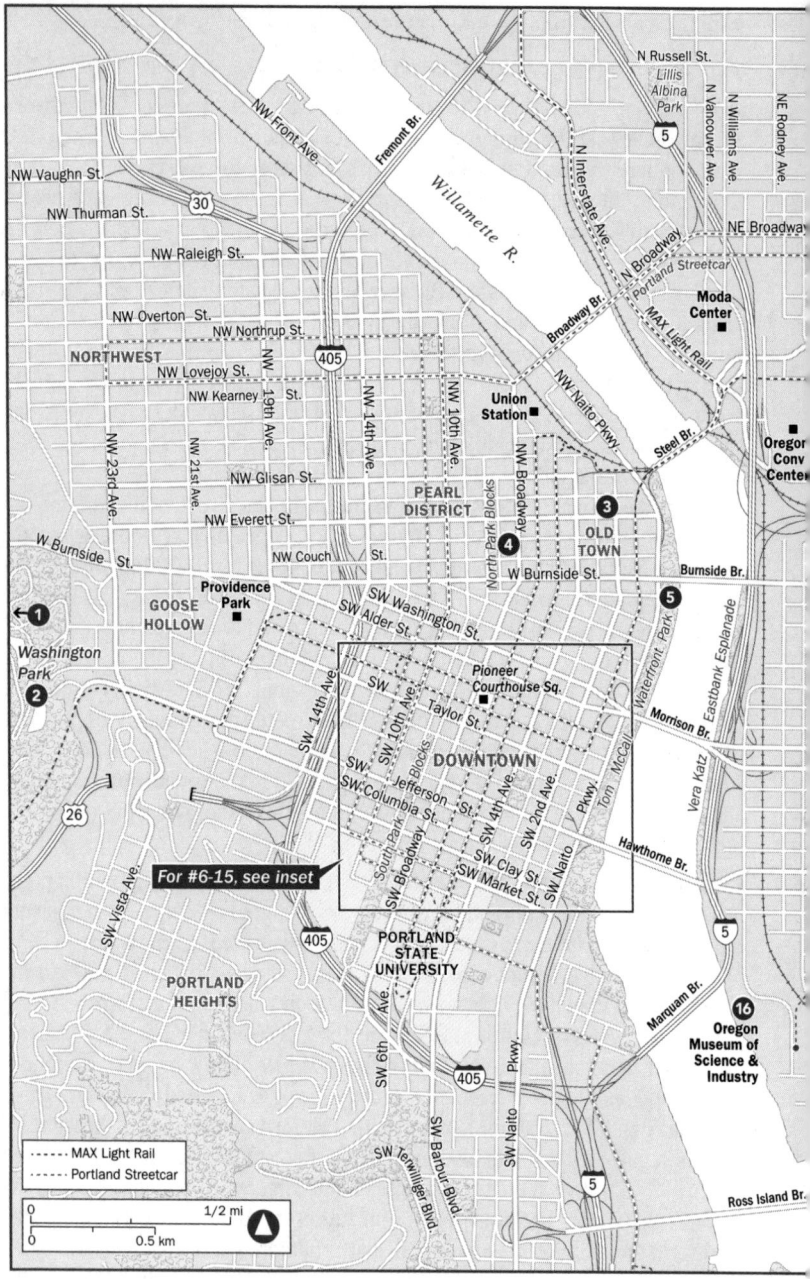

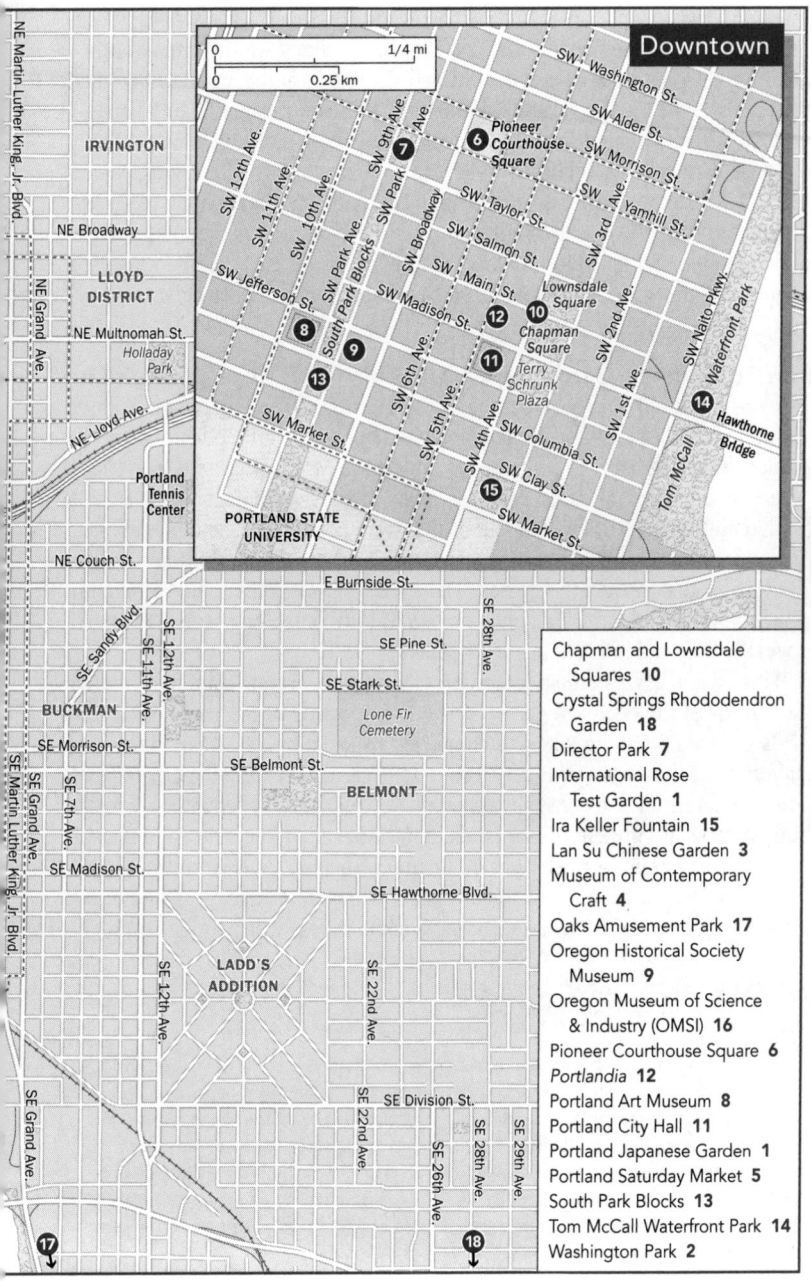
Downtown
0 1/4 mi
0 0.25 km
SW Washington St.
SW Alder St.
SW Morrison St.
SW Yamhill St.
SW Taylor St.
SW Salmon St.
SW Main St.
SW Madison St.
SW Jefferson St.
SW Market St.
SW Columbia St.
SW Clay St.
SW Market St.
SW 12th Ave.
SW 11th Ave.
SW 10th Ave.
SW Park Ave.
SW Broadway
SW 9th Ave.
SW 6th Ave.
SW 5th Ave.
SW 4th Ave.
SW 3rd Ave.
SW 2nd Ave.
SW 1st Ave.
South Park Blocks
Pioneer Courthouse Square
Lownsdale Square
Chapman Square
Terry Schrunk Plaza
SW Naito Pkwy.
Waterfront Park
Hawthorne Bridge
Tom McCall
PORTLAND STATE UNIVERSITY
IRVINGTON
NE Broadway
LLOYD DISTRICT
NE Multnomah St.
Holladay Park
NE Lloyd Ave.
Portland Tennis Center
NE Couch St.
NE Martin Luther King, Jr. Blvd.
NE Grand Ave.
E Burnside St.
SE Pine St.
SE Stark St.
Lone Fir Cemetery
SE Morrison St.
SE Belmont St.
BELMONT
SE Madison St.
SE Hawthorne Blvd.
LADD'S ADDITION
SE Division St.
BUCKMAN
SE Sandy Blvd.
SE 12th Ave.
SE 11th Ave.
SE 7th Ave.
SE Grand Ave.
SE Martin Luther King, Jr. Blvd.
SE 22nd Ave.
SE 26th Ave.
SE 28th Ave.
SE 29th Ave.
1 Chapman and Lownsdale Squares 10
2 Crystal Springs Rhododendron Garden 18
3 Director Park 7
4 International Rose Test Garden 1
5 Ira Keller Fountain 15
6 Lan Su Chinese Garden 3
7 Museum of Contemporary Craft 4
8 Oaks Amusement Park 17
9 Oregon Historical Society Museum 9
10 Oregon Museum of Science & Industry (OMSI) 16
11 Pioneer Courthouse Square 6
12 Portlandia 12
13 Portland Art Museum 8
14 Portland City Hall 11
15 Portland Japanese Garden 1
16 Portland Saturday Market 5
17 South Park Blocks 13
18 Tom McCall Waterfront Park 14
19 Washington Park 2

Ira Keller Fountain ★ PLAZA/FOUNTAIN When it was dedicated in 1971, *The New York Times* architectural critic Ada Louise Huxtable called this fountain "the greatest open space since the Renaissance." It's a rather exaggerated claim, but it goes to show you how hot Portland was in terms of urban planning and public art back in the early 1970s. Inspired by the rivers and waterfalls of the Pacific Northwest (although those don't smell like chlorine—yet), this giant, rugged-looking fountain occupies a full city block directly opposite **Keller Auditorium.** Water flowing down through a grassy park planted with pine trees cascades over a series of multilevel concrete cliffs. Square, irregularly placed platforms over the pool act as stepping stones, allowing visitors to get close to the waterfall and even duck behind it. Angela Danadjieva designed the fountain for Lawrence Halprin & Associates.

SW Third Ave. and SW Clay St.

Lan Su Chinese Garden ★★★ GARDEN Lan Su, in Portland's Chinatown, is not only the best, but the most authentic Chinese garden outside of China. It is a classical Chinese garden, which means that it replicates an urban garden style that came to prominence during the Ming dynasty (1368–1644), when an educated class of scholars, poets, and government officials built walled house-and-garden compounds that were both retreats and private pleasure grounds. In 1999, 65 craftspeople from Suzhou, China (Portland's sister city), came to construct the garden. The intricately detailed architectural components were made in China and shipped to Portland, along with 500 tons of specially chosen rock. The garden opened in 2000.

This is not a Western-style garden where plants reign supreme. Instead, two-thirds of the enclosed garden space is comprised of ornate pavilions and halls grouped around a lake and connected by winding paths and zigzagging galleries. As you wend your way through the garden, visiting the ornate pavilions and admiring the constantly changing views, you'll encounter a wonderfully diverse assortment of plants, including specimen trees, rare and unusual shrubs, and perennials. The chrysanthemum display in November is absolutely spectacular, but there is something of interest here year-round, and concerts and special events, too. To learn about the intricate symbolism in this

Tea in the Chinese Garden

Tea has been a part of Chinese life and culture for over a thousand years. Introduced first as medicine, tea later became associated with Taoist philosophy. Monks used tea to stay awake during long meditation sessions. By the time teahouses became popular, during the Ming dynasty, tea was firmly established as a social beverage, and serving tea had taken on its own elaborate etiquette. At the teahouse, located in the two-story **Tower of Cosmic Reflections** in the **Lan Su Chinese Garden** visitors sample authentic Chinese tea and teacakes while enjoying a view of the garden.

garden, I'd recommend that you take one of the daily tours (usually held between 11am and 2pm, but check the website to confirm).

NW Everett St. and NW Third Ave. www.lansugarden.org. ✆ **503/228-8131.** Admission $10 adults, $9 seniors, $7 students and children 6–18. Apr–Oct daily 10am–6pm; Nov–Mar daily 10am–5pm.

Oregon Historical Society Museum ★★ MUSEUM In the mid-19th century, the Oregon Territory was a land of promise and plenty. Thousands of hardy individuals set out along the Oregon Trail, crossing a vast and rugged country to reach the fertile valleys of this region. Others came by ship around Cape Horn. At this compelling museum, you'll learn about the people who "discovered" Oregon—along with the folks who were here 12,000-or-so years before they arrived. The permanent exhibit "Oregon, My Oregon" offers 50 different displays of artifacts and re-created environments, telling the story of the state from many different perspectives—Native American, settler, 20th-century immigrants, and more. Everything from a 9,000-year-old sandal made out of sagebrush to a lunch counter salvaged from Newberry's downtown department store is on display. Museum docents, with roots stretching back to the days of the Oregon Trail, are often on hand to answer questions. ***Tip:*** The temporary shows are usually too specialized to be of general interest, so concentrate instead on the permanent exhibit and the **Northwest Art Gallery,** which presents an overview of Oregon artists.

1200 SW Park Ave. www.ohs.org. ✆ **503/306-5198.** Admission $11 adults, $9 students and seniors, $5 children 6–18. Mon–Sat 10am–5pm; Sun noon–5pm.

Portlandia ★★ LOCAL LANDMARK/OUTDOOR SCULPTURE They have the same name, but no, I'm not talking about the TV series that satirizes (sort of) life in Portland. This *Portlandia* is a giantess made out of hammered copper, crouching incongruously atop the entrance to the **Portland Building,** clutching a trident in one hand and reaching toward the street with the other—supposedly welcoming people to the hideous building, or maybe trying to flick them away with her finger. The only hammered-copper giantess larger than *Portlandia* is the Statue of Liberty. Because of the weird way she is positioned, most people don't even notice *Portlandia.* Maybe they are averting their eyes from Michael Graves's Portland Building, the first postmodern structure in the United States, and hated by just about everyone because of its dark interiors and graceless exterior. Classically garbed and emotionless, *Portlandia* went up when the building did, in 1985. She was created by Raymond Kaskey, and yes, she does have a cameo in the opening credits of *Portlandia,* the TV show.

Portland Building at 1120 SW Fifth Ave.

Portland Art Museum ★★ ART MUSEUM Located right across from the **Oregon Historical Society Museum,** the Portland Art Museum is the oldest art museum in the Northwest (founded 1892). It used to be one of the most boring art museums in the Northwest, too, but that changed in the 1990s when dynamic new leadership stepped in and gave the museum contemporary

The Bridges of Multnomah County

Six Portland bridges can be seen by strolling the length of Tom McCall Waterfront Park. The three most notable are the buff-colored **Hawthorne Bridge** (1910), the oldest lift-bridge in the country; the **Morrison Bridge,** which opened in 1887 as a wooden toll bridge—the first span across the Willamette—and was replaced in 1905 and 1958; and the **Steel Bridge,** the world's only telescoping double-deck vertical lift bridge. Unfortunately, the draw bridges rarely draw nowadays, as the big cargo ships—remember, Portland is the largest inland port on the West Coast—long ago moved westward towards Swan Island.

relevance and muscle. An expansion scheme in 2000 took over the adjacent Masonic Temple and added thousands of square feet of exhibition space.

The permanent collection begins with European Impressionists and moves right up to the present. However, the best reason to visit is to see the extensive collection of **Native American art and artifacts;** curators have, on occasion, paired the Native art with videos of artists creating the pieces, which help bring the work to life. The contemporary collection in the revamped Masonic Temple is worth a look, too, though I personally find that they have too much work on display, some good, but some mediocre; there are so many pieces hanging in close proximity that it can become a blur. The museum has also had some intriguing traveling shows of late. The small outdoor sculpture court has some very beautiful pieces. Plan to spend at least an hour here.

1219 SW Park Ave. www.portlandartmuseum.org. ✆ **503/226-2811.** Admission $20 adults, $17 seniors and college students, free for children 17 and under. Tues–Wed and Sat–Sun 10am–5pm; Thurs–Fri 10am–8pm.

Tom McCall Waterfront Park ★★★ PARK This grassy, 23-acre park that stretches for about 1½ miles along the Willamette River was once Portland's raucous river port. In 1929, the old downtown wharves were demolished and the first seawall erected; from the 1940s until the 1970s, a major east-west highway plowed through the area. As part of its downtown urban renewal scheme, the city reclaimed the land and named the new park after Tom McCall (1913–1983), an early proponent of land-use planning who served as governor from 1967–1975. (McCall was the Oregon governor who famously said, back in the 1970s, "Come to visit but please don't stay.") The park is frequently used for summertime concerts and festivals, the most famous being the Rose Festival in June, when a Coast Guard ship docks alongside the seawall (an entire fleet used to dock here) and carnival rides are set up. A waterfront esplanade used by strollers, joggers, bicyclists, and Rollerbladers stretches from **RiverPlace** (retail, hotel, and condominium development with a marina at the south end of the park) to the **Japanese-American Historical Plaza** on the north end, planted with cherry trees and commemorating Portland's Japanese-Americans who were sent to internment camps during World War II. **Salmon Street Springs,** a 100-jet fountain with changing water configurations, is a favorite cool-off spot for kids on hot summer days.

Along the Willamette River.

Washington Park Attractions

Portland is justly proud of its green spaces, and foremost among them is **Washington Park** ★★★ (www.washingtonpark.org). The city bought the land in the Southwest hills in 1871. Unlike **Forest Park** (see p. 161), most of Washington Park has been landscaped to serve as a setting for its acclaimed gardens, zoo, and nature-related attractions. Surrounded at its north end by the exclusive Portland Heights neighborhood, the park winds south along the ridge that stretches along the entire west side of the city. This is a great place for hiking, playing tennis, and picnics; in the summer, concerts of all kinds are held in the grassy amphitheater adjacent to the rose garden. SW Kingston Avenue connects the **International Rose Test Garden** (p. 158) and **Portland Japanese Garden** (p. 160) to **Hoyt Arboretum** (see below), the **World Forestry Center Discovery Museum** (p. 161) and the **Oregon Zoo** (p. 158).

You could walk to these attractions, although you'd need most of a day to see them all. MAX, the city's light rail system, includes a stop at Washington Park, providing easy access from downtown to the zoo, the arboretum, and the forestry museum. A **free seasonal shuttle bus** runs from the MAX station to all of the attractions in the park (April/October weekends only 9am–5pm; summer daily 9am–7pm). In the summer a narrow-gauge excursion train runs between the International Rose Test Garden and the zoo. The entrance to the park is at SW Park Place, 2 blocks west of SW Vista. Admission is free. It's open daily from 5am to 10pm.

Hoyt Arboretum ★★ ARBORETUM Over 900 species of trees, some indigenous to the Pacific Northwest and others imported from around the world, are found in the hills and meadows of this 175-acre arboretum at the south end of Washington Park. Trails wind through well-established stands of magnolias, maples, oaks, hawthorns, cherries, and the most extensive conifer collection in the U.S. There are views of Mount Rainier, Mount St. Helens, and Pittock Mansion along the way. The short **Overlook Trail,** just south of the Washington Park light rail station, leads to the **Visitor Center** (you can also drive there), where visitors will find maps and booklets for self-guided tree tours. **Bristlecone Pine Trail** off Fischer Lane is a 1-mile paved trail with disabled access parking.

Washington Park Choo-Choo

Beloved by generations of kids, the little **Washington Park and Zoo Railway** travels between the zoo and the International Rose Test Garden. Tickets for the miniature railway are $5, free for children 2 and under. There's also a shorter route that just loops around the zoo. It's a kid-sized train, just big enough for adults, with open windows, and it winds its way through the forest.

The **Vietnam Veterans of Oregon Memorial** ★★ lies at the southwest corner of the arboretum. From a central, bowl-shaped area, an ascending walkway spirals up to six black granite markers inscribed with the names of those reported as dead or missing from 1959 to 1976. Short texts inscribed above the names provide a "living history" of Oregonians during the war years.

Hoyt Arboretum Visitor Center: 4000 SW Fairview Blvd. www.hoytarboretum.org. ✆ **503/865-8733.** Admission free. Visitor Center Mon–Fri 9am–4pm; Sat–Sun 11am–3pm.

International Rose Test Garden ★★★ GARDEN Established in 1917, the oldest public rose test garden in the U.S. offers a dazzling display of Portland's favorite flower. Some 8,000 roses representing 525 species grow in fragrant, formal terraces overlooking downtown Portland and Mount Hood. The city's fondness for the genus *Rosa* dates back to 1887 and the founding of the Portland Rose Society, the oldest such group in the U.S. In 1907, rose-loving citizens began a campaign to nickname Portland the "City of Roses," which it's been called ever since.

From the parking lot, steps descend to an information kiosk surrounded by elevated beds of miniature roses. Extending east, and covering two broad terraces, is the **American Garden Rose Selections** garden. The roses being tested here are given a code number rather than a name; four plants of each variety are evaluated for 2 years by an official judge using 13 different criteria. The city of Portland annually awards the best-performing roses with a gold or silver medal. Winners are then given fanciful (and sometimes cutesy) names and moved to the **Gold Award Garden,** located on the terraces below the **Beach Memorial Fountain.** The fountain is a walk-through, stainless-steel sculpture designed by Portland artist Lee Kelley and named for Frank E. Beach, who spearheaded efforts to nickname Portland the "City of Roses." **Queens' Walk,** on the lowest promenade, is inset with bronze markers for every Rose Festival queen since 1907. Annual and perennial flowers named in Shakespeare's plays are planted in the **Shakespeare Garden,** in the lower southeast corner. The small **Rose Garden Store,** 850 SW Rose Garden Way (✆ **503/227-7033**), is open in summer and packed with rose-inspired products.

400 SW Kingston Ave. (in Washington Park). www.washingtonpark.org. ✆ **503/823-3636.** Free admission. Daily 7:30am–9pm.

Oregon Zoo ★★★ ZOO The state's top tourist attraction, the Oregon Zoo is best known for its elephants, with the most successful breeding herd in captivity. They reside in the Africa exhibit, which

Portland Rose Festival

The **Portland Rose Festival** (www.rosefestival.org), held every year in June, coincides with the peak blooming time of the roses in the International Rose Test Garden. It is one of the largest floral-themed extravaganzas in the country, with two parades, the crowning of a Rose Queen (a high school competition), and a fun fair set up in **Tom McCall Waterfront Park** (see p. 156). This Portland tradition dates back to 1907.

Washington Park Attractions

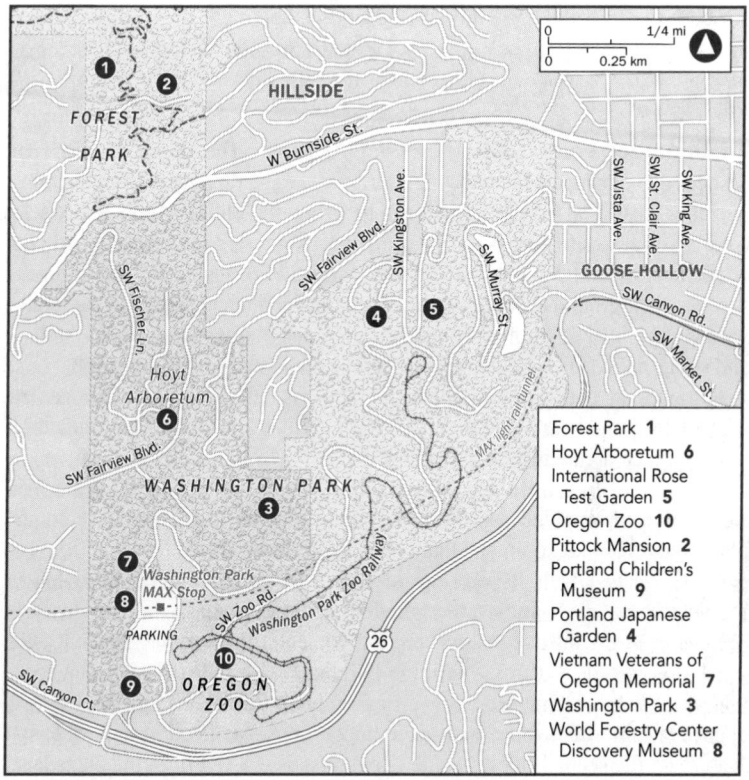

includes a manmade rainforest and a savanna populated by zebras, rhinos, giraffes, and hippos. The Alaskan Tundra has grizzly bears, wolves, and musk oxen, while the Cascade Crest exhibit includes a mountain goat habitat. In Steller Cove, Steller sea lions and sea otters are on display. Other areas of note include an intriguing bat house and the Amazon Flooded Forest. And don't miss the naked mole rats, scurrying around in their glass-walled tunnels. In summer, there are outdoor concerts in the zoo's amphitheater. This is a large zoo and can easily take up 2 or more hours of your time.

4001 SW Canyon Rd. (in Washington Park). www.oregonzoo.org. ✆ **503/226-1561.** Admission (seasonally adjusted) $10–$15 adults, $8–$13 seniors, $5–$10 children 3–11. Late-May to early-Sept daily 9:30am–6pm; early-Sept to May daily 9:30am–4pm; Jan–Feb 10am–4pm.

Portland Children's Museum ★ MUSEUM Located across the parking lot from the Oregon Zoo, this large, modern children's museum has exhibits for toddlers to 13-year-olds. Kids can play in a magical forest, go shopping in a kid-size grocery store, or help build a house. However, it is the Water Works exhibit that is likely to make the biggest splash with your kids. There are also six studios with changing exhibits and opportunities for exploring the visual, literary, and performing arts. Combined with the nearby zoo, this museum makes for an easy all-day, kid-oriented outing.

4015 SW Canyon Rd. www.portlandcm.org. ✆ **503/223-6500.** Admission $10.75 adults and children, $9.75 seniors, free for children under age 1 (free for all on first Fri of each month 4–8pm). Daily 9am–5pm.

Portland Japanese Garden ★★★ GARDEN The most authentic Japanese garden outside of Japan occupies a 5½-acre site directly above the **International Rose Test Garden.** Designed by Professor Takuma Tono, a Japanese landscape master from Tokyo, the garden took 4 years to complete and was opened to the public in 1967 on the site of the old Portland Zoo. The immaculately tended grounds contain superb examples of ancient Japanese gardening styles influenced by Shinto, Buddhist, and Taoist philosophies. Plants, stones, and water are used to create areas of serene and contemplative beauty.

Portland has been buzzing about the fabulous new additions to the garden created by famed Japanese architect Kengo Kuma in 2017. They include a new entrance area with water features and a new introductory pathway up to the lovely **Antique Gate** that served as the garden entrance for 50 years. You can take an open-sided bus from the parking lot up to the garden entrance plaza above, but I recommend that you walk up the graveled footpath from the gate. The path wends its way up through a forest of Douglas fir and now includes new **rock-and-water gardens** below a glass-walled teahouse perched over the hillside. At the very top you enter the dazzling new entrance plaza dominated by Kuma's striking buildings with their living green roofs and glass walls ornamented with vertical bamboo slats. The largest building is a **gallery and bookstore** with an outdoor bonsai collection and waterfall feature on the second floor. The new **teahouse** is entered from the plaza level and provides a floatingly serene forested setting for authentic Japanese tea and refreshments. The third pavilion is used by the gardeners and has an outdoor bonsai gallery to one side. The open plaza between the buildings is used for all kinds of events, from Kabuki performances to concerts.

From the plaza, you pass through another gate to enter the five different gardens that comprise the Portland Japanese Garden. The **Strolling Pond Garden** is the largest garden on the site, with a picturesque Moon Bridge crossing the Upper Pond. Within the **Tea Garden** you'll find a ceremonial teahouse constructed in Japan (using pegs instead of nails), reassembled here in 1968. Farther south, the aptly named Zig-Zag Bridge leads through a waterside area planted with May-blossoming Japanese irises to the **Lower Pond,** where giant koi slowly navigate below a waterfall. The ponds are filled with enormous, brilliantly colored koi.

The **Natural Garden** covers the south hillside, where stone steps wind down past shallow, meandering waterscapes. The abstract, Zen-inspired **Sand and Stone Garden** is at the end, with weathered stones rising from a bed of gravel that's been raked to suggest the sea. Green islands in the **Flat Garden,** to the north, are meant to resemble a sake cup and gourd bottle, symbols of pleasure and happiness. The large wooden pavilion behind the Flat Garden is used for special exhibits and provides a majestic view of Portland and Mount Hood from its eastern terrace.

611 SW Kingston Ave. (in Washington Park). www.japanesegarden.com. ✆ **503/223-1321.** Admission $15 adults, $13 seniors and college students, $10.50 children 6–17. Mar–Sept Mon noon–7pm; Tues–Sun 10am–7pm; Oct–Mar Mon noon–4pm; Tues–Sun 10am–4pm.

World Forestry Center Discovery Museum ★ Trees, beautiful trees. Forests, beautiful forests. We are dependent upon them for our very survival, and we can no longer take them for granted. They are disappearing at an alarming rate and they need all the help and protection they can get. Oregon's economy was founded on logging, and the timber industry, although it no longer has the clout it once did, continues to play an important role in the state. It's also the force behind this museum, which attempts to explain how forests work and how complex they are. Exhibits on the first floor concentrate on the vast forests of the Pacific Northwest, and those on the second floor focus on Russia, China, South Africa, and the Amazon. If you love forests, or want to know more about trees, you will learn something here—but keep in mind that no matter how "sustainable" the practices, the timber industry is about managing forests, not letting them be. There are interesting temporary exhibits staged here throughout the year as well, from photographic exhibits to displays of woodworkers' art.

4033 SW Canyon Rd. www.worldforestry.org. ✆ **503/228-1367.** Admission $7 adults, $6 seniors, $5 children 3–18. Daily 10am–5pm.

Northwest Portland Attractions

You might want to explore urban Northwest Portland by strolling through the **Pearl District,** or down **NW 23rd Avenue** from East Burnside to NW Thurman (see "Neighborhoods in Brief," p. 142). But if you want to enjoy the natural side of Portland, put on some good walking shoes or hiking boots and head up to giant Forest Park.

Forest Park ★★★ PARK On a 1903 visit to Portland, landscape designer John Olmsted (son of Frederick Law Olmsted, who designed New York's Central Park) drew up a city park plan calling for "a succession of ravines and spurs covered with remarkably beautiful woods." His recommendation led to the establishment of 5,000-acre Forest Park in 1948. One of the largest urban parks in North America, this forest is part of a 9,000-acre park system that forms a wildlife corridor to the Coast Range, which divides the Willamette Valley from the Pacific Ocean. The park is home to more than 50 species of mammals—including deer, elk and rarely seen bobcats—and about 150 species of birds. Some 50 miles of interconnected hiking trails wind up and down the slopes of Forest Park, where a canopy of towering Douglas firs rises above an understory of alders, aspens, hemlock, holly, and maidenhair and sword ferns. White trilliums glow along the paths in the spring. The 33-mile-long **Wildwood Trail** connects Forest Park to **Washington Park** (see p. 157) and the **Hoyt Arboretum** (see p. 157) in Southwest Portland. A few old-growth trees can be found behind the **Portland Audubon Society** (5151 NW Cornell Rd.; www.audubonportland.org; ✆ **503/292-6855**).

Forest Park, Portland, OR 97231. www.forestparkconservancy.org. ✆ **503/823-4492.** There are many ways to access the park and its miles of trails; see the website for information and the Forest Park entry for Pittock Mansion, below.

Pittock Mansion ★★ HISTORIC HOUSE/PARK/VIEW The largest and most opulent historic home in Portland is perched on a 1,000-foot-high crest adjoining **Forest Park,** looking east over the city, the river, and the major peaks of the Cascade Mountains. This is one of the great views in Portland and worth a stop even if you don't visit the mansion. Built for Henry Pittock (1835–1919), who came west on the Oregon Trail in 1853 and eventually amassed a fortune as the publisher of *The Oregonian* newspaper, the mansion was designed by San Francisco architect Edward T. Foulkes and completed in 1914. Stylistically, the structure is a French Renaissance Revival chateau with exterior walls of Italian Tenino sandstone. Visitors can wander through on their own, but we recommend the guided tour, which covers the mansion's history and details of its design (which include Portland's earliest vacuum-cleaning system and walk-in refrigerator). The fine period furnishings and rugs are not original to the house but amply convey the luxurious lifestyle of the prominent Portland family that lived here. Nearly one-third of the mansion is taken up by a magnificent marble staircase and hallway constructed of Italian and domestic marbles. The Jacobean-style library, paneled with Honduran mahogany, has a quatrefoil design plaster ceiling and a fireplace of French Caen stone. The elliptical drawing room, with its elaborate plaster moldings and cornices, commands a 180-degree vista of the city and Mount Hood. Superlative plasterwork and marquetry floors are found in the small, circular Turkish smoking room. On the second floor, a four-room master suite used by Pittock and his wife, Georgiana, is flanked by two smaller suites once occupied by the couple's daughters and their husbands. Trailheads into Forest Park are found at the west end of the parking lot and beyond **Gate Lodge,** the former groundskeeper's house.

3229 NW Pittock Dr. www.pittockmansion.org. ✆ **503/823-3623.** Admission $10 adults, $9 seniors, $7 children 6–18. June–Aug daily 10am–5pm; Sept–Dec and Feb–May daily 11am–4pm. Closed Thanksgiving, Dec. 25, Jan 1.

Southeast Portland Attractions

Urban adventurers will enjoy southeast Portland's hopping neighborhoods, including **SE Hawthorne, SE Division, Sellwood,** and **Eastmoreland/Westmoreland** (see "Neighborhoods in Brief," p. 142). There is also a heritage amusement park, a superlative garden, and a popular science and technology museum on the east side by the river.

Crystal Springs Rhododendron Garden ★★ GARDEN After roses, rhododendrons are Portland's favorite flowering shrub. They grow easily in the damp, temperate climate. But forest-loving rhodies are native in Oregon only on a portion of Mount Hood and in the Siskiyou Mountains in southwestern Oregon. Portlanders never saw a rhododendron until some examples arrived from a nursery in England and were exhibited at the Lewis and Clark Exhibition of 1905. Now rhodies are ubiquitous and available in every color and leaf shape imaginable. But all the collecting and hybridizing didn't really begin until 1950, when the first-ever chapter of the American Rhododendron Society was formed in Portland and bought this 7-acre site across from Reed College in Eastmoreland as a garden devoted to rhodies. Lovely year-round, Crystal Springs turns spectacular from April through June, when 600 varieties of rhododendrons and azaleas burst into bloom. From the gatehouse, visitors cross a bridge overlooking a small waterfall and rushing stream and follow paths through the enormous collection of rhodies to **Crystal Springs Lake,** created in 1917 by damming 13 area springs. Congregated near the shoreline and bobbing on the water are coots, widgeons, scaups, wood ducks, mallards, and Canada geese. Paddison Fountain shoots a geyser of water into the lake's South Lagoon.

SE 28th Ave. (1 block north of SE Woodstock Blvd.). www.rhodies.org. ✆ **503/771-8386.** Admission $5 Mar–Sept; free at other times. Daily dawn to dusk.

Oaks Amusement Park ★★ AMUSEMENT PARK In a world filled with head-spinning, gut-spewing, body-slamming amusement parks with astronomical prices, dear old Oaks Amusement Park may seem like a quaintly antiquated anomaly. That's exactly why I like it and am including it here. Oaks is one of the 10 oldest amusement parks in the country, built in 1905 to coincide with the Lewis and Clark Exposition that put Portland on the map. It has a quiet, low-key, old-fashioned charm and a wonderful location right above the Willamette River in Sellwood. The rides? A Tilt-a-Whirl, a Ferris wheel, a roller coaster, go-karts, spinning teacups and a 1917 merry-go-round with a menagerie of hand-carved animals. There are carnival games and a miniature golf course, too. The park is home to a famous roller rink (see website for open rink hours) and a dance hall from 1910. Picnic tables are set up on the bluff and from Oaks Park you can walk down to a rare natural beach on the Willamette River and the nearby **Oaks Bottom Wildlife Refuge.** This is a great excuse to visit the historic Sellwood neighborhood, which was once a separate city.

7805 SE Oaks Park Way. www.oakspark.com. ✆ **800/233-5771**. Summer Rides $3.75; unlimited ride tickets $15.75–$19.95; roller rink $7–$8. Tues–Thurs noon–9pm, Fri–Sat noon–10pm, Sun noon–7pm; open weekends, varying hours the rest of the year (check website); roller rink open year-round.

Oregon Museum of Science and Industry (OMSI) ★★ MUSEUM Located on the east bank of the Willamette River across from the south end of Waterfront Park, this modern science museum has five huge halls, and both kids and adults find the exhibits fun and fascinating. This is a hands-on museum, and everyone is urged to get involved with displays, from a science

WALKING ALONG THE willamette

It's pronounced Will-*am*-ette, not Will-a-*met*, and it flows right through the heart of Portland. This river played an important role in the lives of the Native American Multnomah tribe (Portland is in Multnomah County) and was an essential route for the pioneers who trekked across country on the Oregon Trail and poured into the Willamette Valley in the mid-19th century. Pioneers took boats and rafts down this tributary of the Columbia to Oregon City, which marked the end of the Oregon Trail. It was in Oregon City that land claims could be made. The river was deep enough to allow Portland to become a major inland port—hence all the historic drawbridges that you can see downtown. On the west side, you can stroll along the river downtown at **Tom McCall Waterfront Park** (see p. 156). On the east side, a paved pathway connects **OMSI** to the **Vera Katz Eastbank Esplanade** to the north. The path from OMSI also heads south 3 miles to **Oaks Amusement Park** (described above). Along the pathway beside the museum, several interesting informational plaques tell the history of Portland and its relationship to the Willamette.

playground for young children to physics and chemistry labs for older children. Earth Hall, a multi-dimensional look at the world we live in, includes exhibits on environmental hazards, natural disasters, and climate change. Life Hall deals with the mysteries of human growth and development. The Turbine Hall, devoted to the physical sciences and technology, lets visitors build an aqueduct and program a robot. There are three additional components to the museum, all of which require separate tickets: **The Empirical Theater** (formerly called the OMNIMAX), the **Kendall Planetarium,** which features astronomy and laser-light shows, and my favorite, the **USS *Blueback* submarine** docked in the river right behind the museum. If the last one looks familiar, that's because this is the sub used in the film *Hunt for Red October.*

1945 SE Water Ave. www.omsi.edu. ✆ **800/955-6674** or 503/797-4000. Museum $14 adults, $10.75 seniors, $9.75 children 3–13; Empirical Theater shows $7–$8.50 adults, $5–$6.50 seniors, $6.50 children 3–13; submarine tours $6.75 all ages; planetarium shows $5.75–$7.50; discounted combination tickets available. Mid-June to early-Sept daily 9:30am–7pm; early-Sept to mid-June Tues–Sun 9:30am–5:30pm.

ORGANIZED TOURS

Bike Tours

Pedal Bike Tours at 133 SW Second Ave. (www.pedalbiketours.com; ✆ **503/243-2453**) offers a wide range of outings that focus on Portland history, brewpubs, and food carts. Farther afield, they operate tours of the Columbia Gorge. Prices for in-town tours range from $59 to $69 per person. **Portland Bicycle Tours** at 345 NW Everett St. (www.portlandbicycletours.com; ✆ **503/902-5035**), offers a basic city tour, as well as tours that focus on Portland, the city's food carts and, of course, brewpubs. Tours cost $39 to $59 per person.

Cruises & Sea Kayaking

Portland Spirit (www.portlandspirit.com; ✆ **800/224-3901** or 503/224-3900), a 150-foot yacht, leaves daily year-round from **Tom McCall Waterfront Park** at the foot of SW Salmon Street and cruises west along the Willamette River, offering views of the city skyline and residential areas along the way. It's not terribly exciting terrain, and I have to regretfully report that the meals served on board the lunch and dinner cruises are overpriced and not particularly noteworthy. If you want to see the city by boat, I would recommend taking a basic sightseeing cruise instead ($30 to $40 adults, $20 to $40 kids).

For a more active water-level tour of the Willamette, arrange for a sea kayak tour through the **Portland Kayak Company** ★★ (www.portlandriverkayakcompany.com; ✆ **503/459-4050**); they operate tours (no experience needed) out of the **RiverPlace Marina** at the south end of Tom McCall Waterfront Park. A 2½-hour tour that circles nearby Ross Island costs $49 per person. This company also rents sea kayaks, canoes, and standup paddleboards for $14 to $22 per hour.

Bus Tours

Many visitors use the **Big Pink Sightseeing** trolley bus, which is operated by **Gray Line of Portland** (www.graylineofportland.com; ✆ **503/241-7373**). From its starting point at **Pioneer Courthouse Square,** the trolley bus makes 14 stops around Portland. If you buy an all-day ticket ($34 for adults, $17 children 6–12), you can hop on and off the bus all day. The trolley operates from late May to mid-October.

Do we recommend Big Pink? Not really. The commentary is perfunctory, the price is pretty steep, and because the stops are serviced every 45 to 60 minutes, you'll spend a lot of time waiting around if you choose to hop off and hop on. We think you'll get to know Portland a lot better, and for far less money, if you simply buy a cheap day pass on TriMet (see "Getting Around", above) and take public transportation or walk to the sights that interest you.

Eco Tours of Oregon ★★ (www.ecotours-of-oregon.com; ✆ **888/868-7733** or 503/457-0226) runs bus tours to the Oregon coast, wine country, Mount St. Helens, and up the Columbia River Gorge to Mount Hood. These tours, led by knowledgeable guides, are a good value and let you relax while learning more about the diverse landscapes and ecology of Oregon. Tour prices range from $70 to $109.

With more microbreweries than any other city in the world, Portland has come to be known as Beervana. If you're a lover of craft beers and want to learn more about the local microbrewing scene, book a tour with **Brewvana Portland Brewery Tours** ★ (www.experiencebrewvana.com; ✆ **503/729-6804**), which charges $60 to $99 per person for Friday, Saturday, and Sunday tours that include transportation, tastings, and food. Brewpub tours are also offered on Saturday afternoons by the **Portland BrewBus** (www.brewbus.com; ✆ **503/647-0021**), for $45 per person. Slightly more economical brewery tours that utilize TriMet's light rail line and the Portland streetcar are offered by **Pubs of Portland Tours** (www.pubsofportlandtours.com; ✆ **512/917-2464**). Tours cost $30 and stop at four or more breweries or pubs; you'll also have to purchase a TriMet all-day pass ($5). The quirkiest (and greenest) option? **PDX Pedicabs** ★★ (www.pdxpedicab.com; ✆ **503/828-9888**) offers eco-friendly, pedal-powered brewpub tours for $25 per person.

Walking Tours

Peter's Walking Tours of Portland ★★★ (www.walkportland.com; ✆ **503/704-7900**), led by Peter Chausse, are a swell way to learn more about the city. The downtown visits last 3 hours and take in fountains, parks, historic places, art, and architecture. He also leads walks in the Pearl District, Old Town, and other areas in and around the city. Tours are by reservation and cost $15 for adults and $10 for teens.

OUTDOOR PURSUITS

Biking

Portland is one of America's most bicycle-friendly cities, with miles of paved paths used by bike commuters and recreational bicyclists. Riding a bike around town, you'll definitely feel like a local, exploring out-of-the-way neighborhoods, pedaling along the banks of the Willamette River, and visiting bike-friendly businesses. In 2017, the city installed hundreds of rentable bikes throughout the city, making it easier than ever to pedal around town on your own (see p. 148), but only for half an hour at a time.

An all-day bike rental is something to consider if you want to explore the city and environs over a period of several hours. **Waterfront Bicycles,** 10 SW Ash St., Ste. 100 (www.waterfrontbikes.com; ✆ **503/227-1719**) rents bikes for $9 for 1 hour or $35 per day.

In Tom McCall Waterfront Park, at the foot of SW Salmon Street, and at OMSI (see p. 163), on the east side, you can rent a variety of unusual, family-friendly cycles from **Kerr Bikes** (www.kerrbikes.org; ✆ **503/808-9955**), including three-wheeled and four-wheeled cycles and surreys that carry as many as four adults. Rates range from $15 to $35 per hour. Kerr Bikes is open from March through October; hours vary with the month.

At **Bike Gallery,** 1001 SW Tenth Ave. (www.bikegallery.com; ✆ **503/222-3821**), you can rent a classic commuter bike (with fenders in case of rain) for $35 for 4 hours or $55 for 24 hours.

Hiking

Hiking opportunities abound in the Portland area. For shorter hikes, you don't even have to leave the city; just head to **Forest Park** ★★★ (p. 161), the largest forested city park in the country. Within this urban wilderness, you'll find more than 70 miles of trails. The 30-mile **Wildwood Trail** is the longest trail in the park and will take you all the way up to **Pittock Mansion** ★★ (p. 162) in northwest Portland and **Hoyt Arboretum** ★★ (p. 157) in southwest

Portland. Trail maps are available at the arboretum's **visitor center**, 4000 SW Fairview Blvd. (www.hoytarborteum.org; Mon–Fri 9am–4pm, Sat–Sun 11am–3pm). To get there by car, drive west on West Burnside Street from downtown Portland and follow signs to the arboretum; the MAX stop is Washington Park. Forest Park PDX is a downloadable app that covers all the trails in Forest Park.

WHERE TO STAY

The hotel scene, like every other scene in Portland, has changed dramatically in the last quarter-century. For one thing, Portland now has one. The city used to be plain Jane when it came to lodging, but now there is a raft of stylish, comfortable hotels of all levels of sophistication, including three brand-new hotels and two dramatic makeovers (Hotel Vintage and the Dossier, both downtown) in 2017, with more scheduled to open in 2018. The large, classic hotels are all downtown, but so are a wide range of mid-size and smaller boutique hotels. Most of the downtown hotels have well-known and popular restaurants and lounges attached to them, and from downtown it's easy to get everywhere by public transportation. I've included a couple of excellent B&Bs that give a good perspective on different Portland neighborhoods, and a great hostel in northwest. The prices listed are for a double room in low season (winter) and high season (July–Aug). For our strategy on savings through online bookings, go to p. 89.

Travel Portland, 701 SW Sixth Ave., Portland, OR 97205 (www.travelportland.com; ✆ **877/678-5263** or 503/275-9293) provides a hotel reservation service for the Portland metro area. For information on **B&Bs** in the Portland area, contact the **Oregon Bed & Breakfast Guild** (www.obbg.org; ✆ **800/944-6196**). And, of course, there are many rental options in private homes to be found on **Airbnb** (www.airbnb.com). **HomeAway** (www.homeaway.com), and **VRBO** (www.vrbo.com) and other rental sites. These websites, offering rooms in private homes and sometimes entire apartments, are legal to use in Portland. A check of available Airbnb properties for early 2018 showed 18 private rooms ranging in price from $55 to $100. HomeAway listed some 150 apartments (not rooms) throughout the city, including some very desirable neighborhoods, for prices ranging from $65 to $135 a night. These prices are typically at least $25 to $50 less than what you'd pay for a hotel room just about anywhere in Portland.

DOWNTOWN

Expensive

The Benson ★★★ The Benson was built in 1912, the same year the hotel that became the Ace (reviewed p. 173) checked in its first guests. But the two could hardly be more different in scale, scope, and style. The Benson is Portland's premier "old" hotel; it's called "The Residence of the Presidents" because every president from William Taft on has stayed here (George W. being the lone exception). The Benson has some features typical of an older hotel, primarily slightly smaller rooms and bathrooms, but it has also kept up

Portland Hotels

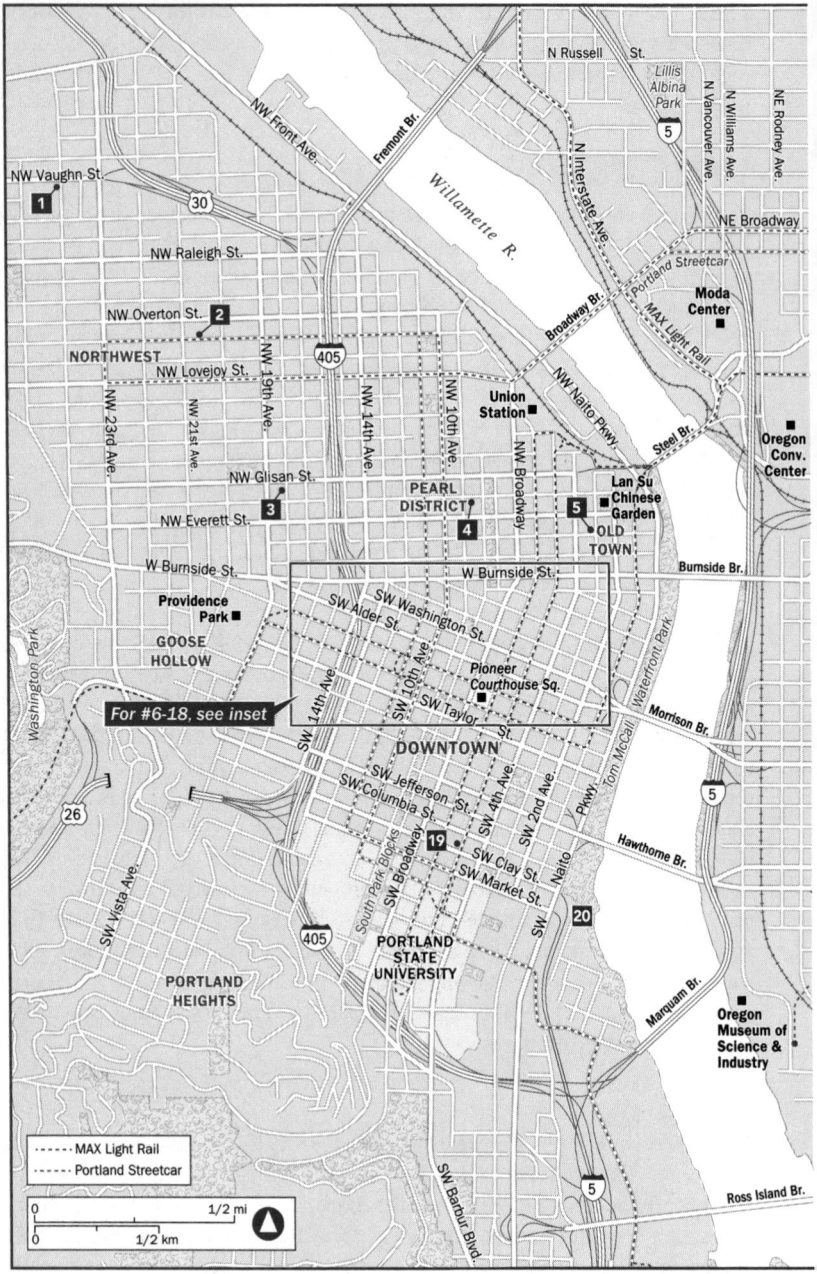

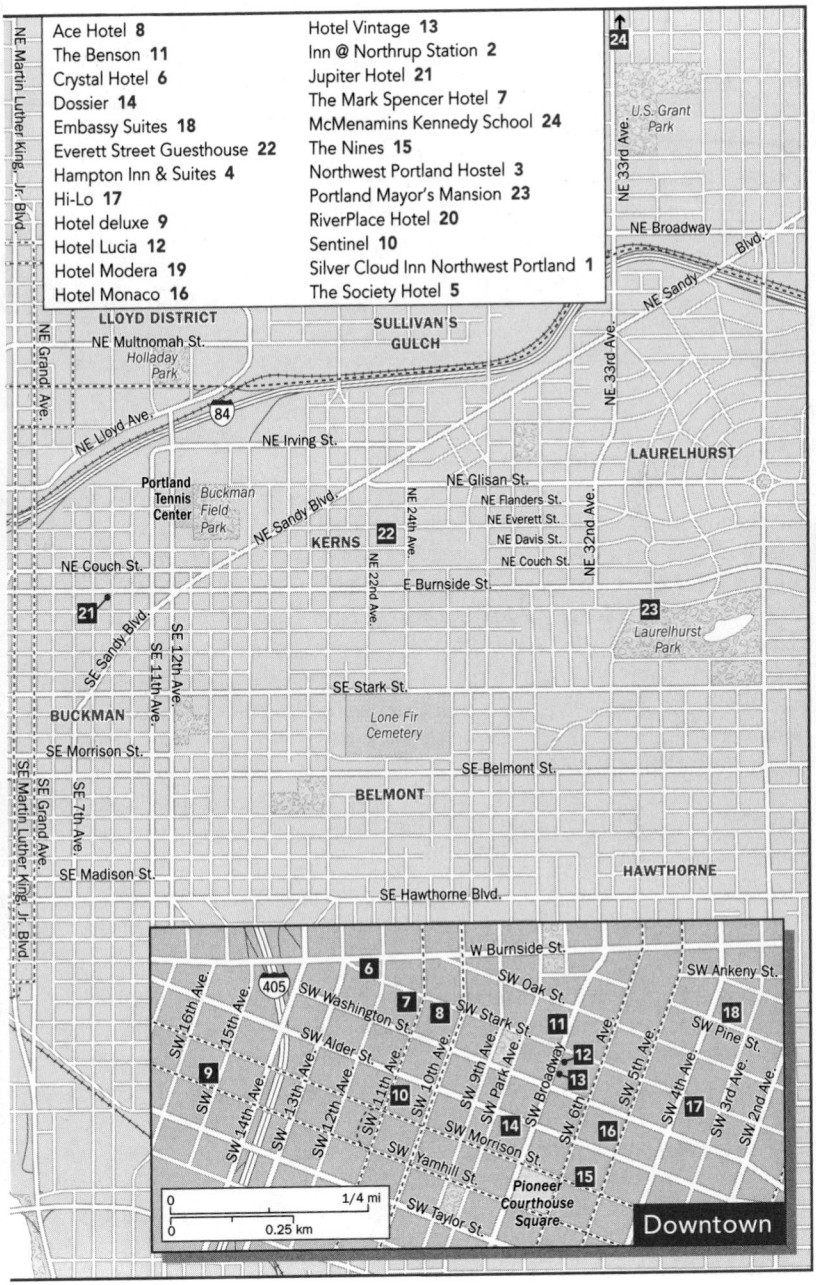
Ace Hotel 8
The Benson 11
Crystal Hotel 6
Dossier 14
Embassy Suites 18
Everett Street Guesthouse 22
Hampton Inn & Suites 4
Hi-Lo 17
Hotel deluxe 9
Hotel Lucia 12
Hotel Modera 19
Hotel Monaco 16
Hotel Vintage 13
Inn @ Northrup Station 2
Jupiter Hotel 21
The Mark Spencer Hotel 7
McMenamins Kennedy School 24
The Nines 15
Northwest Portland Hostel 3
Portland Mayor's Mansion 23
RiverPlace Hotel 20
Sentinel 10
Silver Cloud Inn Northwest Portland 1
The Society Hotel 5
LLOYD DISTRICT
SULLIVAN'S GULCH
LAURELHURST
KERNS
BUCKMAN
BELMONT
HAWTHORNE
NE Multnomah St.
Holladay Park
NE Lloyd Ave.
NE Irving St.
Portland Tennis Center
Buckman Field Park
NE Sandy Blvd.
NE Glisan St.
NE Flanders St.
NE Everett St.
NE Davis St.
NE Couch St.
E Burnside St.
Laurelhurst Park
SE Stark St.
Lone Fir Cemetery
SE Morrison St.
SE Belmont St.
SE Madison St.
SE Hawthorne Blvd.
NE Broadway
NE Sandy Blvd.
U.S. Grant Park
NE Martin Luther King Jr. Blvd.
NE Grand Ave.
NE 33rd Ave.
NE 32nd Ave.
NE 24th Ave.
NE 22nd Ave.
SE Sandy Blvd.
SE 12th Ave.
SE 11th Ave.
SE 7th Ave.
SE Grand Ave.
SE Martin Luther King Jr. Blvd.
W Burnside St.
SW Oak St.
SW Ankeny St.
SW Washington St.
SW Stark St.
SW Pine St.
SW Alder St.
SW Morrison St.
SW Yamhill St.
SW Taylor St.
SW Broadway
SW Park Ave.
SW 16th Ave.
SW 15th Ave.
SW 14th Ave.
SW 13th Ave.
SW 12th Ave.
SW 11th Ave.
SW 10th Ave.
SW 9th Ave.
SW 6th Ave.
SW 5th Ave.
SW 4th Ave.
SW 3rd Ave.
SW 2nd Ave.
Pioneer Courthouse Square
0 1/4 mi
0 0.25 km
Downtown

with the times without sacrificing tradition. The lobby is Portland's loveliest, paneled with (now extinct) Circassian walnut from Siberia, with a cozy fireplace area and a Palm Court that hosts a very popular happy hour. The rooms are quiet, both in terms of noise and decor, which can be a relief after all the busy patterns and furniture types in some of Portland's boutique hotels. The beds have quality TempurPedic mattresses, the service is great, and so is the heart-of-downtown location. **El Gaucho,** the restaurant attached to the Benson, is one of Portland's top steakhouses. (Simon Benson, the timber baron who built the hotel, was the same man who gave Portland the "Benson Bubblers"—those wonderful brass drinking fountains you see all over downtown.)

309 SW Broadway. www.bensonhotel.com. ✆ **800/663-1144** or 503/228-2000. 287 units. $150–$254 double. Valet parking $40. Pets accepted ($25 fee). **Amenities:** 3 restaurants; 2 lounges; bikes; exercise room and access to nearby health club; free Wi-Fi.

Dossier ★★★ Dossier opened in summer 2017 after a complete remake of a rather bland Westin hotel from the 1980s. The new owners have given it a sophisticated elegance without sacrificing comfort. The lobby is surprisingly small and seems somewhat disconnected from the rest of the hotel. But once you're in your roomy room, you probably won't want to leave anyway. Big windows, big city views, natural wood and stone finishes and luxurious fabrics with pops of color add a polished flair to the decor, and so do the two or three photographs by Slim Aarons that hang in every room. (In case you don't know, Slim Aarons was known for his photographs of socialites, jet-setters and celebrities in the 1950s.) The beds can't be beat and the good-sized bathrooms are equipped with big walk-in showers (a few rooms have tubs as well) and high-end, locally produced bath products. It adds up to quality and comfort of a very high order. **Onyx,** the hotel's stylish restaurant-lounge-bar, is right off the lobby, and **Omerta,** the hotel's small, rather romantic restaurant, serves traditional American-Italian food.

750 SW Alder St. www.dossierhotel.com. ✆ **877/628-4408** or 503/294-9000. 205 units. $200–$380 double. Valet parking $33. Pets accepted ($45 fee). **Amenities:** Restaurant; lounge; exercise room; free Wi-Fi.

Hi-Lo ★★★ Opened in summer 2017 in the 1910 Oregon Pioneer Building, the Hi-Lo is a wonderful reuse of a wonderful old Portland building. The lobby is a vast, open space with giant windows, curvy sofas and even swings if you're so inclined. But it's the rooms I love because they take into consideration the history of the building they're in. The Pioneer Building was the first downtown building that used concrete and steel beam construction, and the rooms at the Hi-Lo have one or two concrete walls (they're actually quite handsome), painted steel beams, and concrete floor tiles (with radiant heating). Don't get the idea that you're going to feel like you're in a cell because you're not. The rooms are fairly spacious and decked out with soft pastel-colored furnishings, area rugs, pillows made by Oregon's famous Pendleton woolen mills, immaculate white linens, and original art by Oregon artists. The large bathrooms have big walk-in rain showers (tubs in a few of the rooms) and locally produced MAAK Lab toiletries. The fitness room on the lower level isn't huge but has everything you need for a weight or aerobic workout. Finally, there's a happening bar in one part of the lobby and a restaurant, **Alto Bajo** (see p. 184) that serves creative Mexican cuisine. All in all, it's a memorable place to stay, and you're right across the street from a stand of food carts—what could be more Portland than that?

320 SW Stark St. www.hi-lo-hotel.com. ✆ **971/222-2100**. 120 units. $197–$275 double. Valet parking $39. Pets accepted. **Amenities:** Restaurant; lounge; exercise room; same-day dry-cleaning; free Wi-Fi.

Hotel Vintage ★★★ The Hotel Vintage underwent a rather dramatic makeover in 2016. The long-established Kimpton property was always a wine-themed hotel, and it still is, but the rather staid interior décor was completely re-imagined for a younger Portland demographic. Fittingly, the lobby bar is now called Bacchus and presided over by a wall-sized version of Caravaggio's painting of the god of wine (but with a strategic piercing that is not in the original work). Every night there are complimentary wine tastings hosted by different regional vintners. The new room look is sleek and minimal, with wine-themed accents—maybe a wall piece made of cork or wine labels, or a headboard constructed from oak. Beds are luxuriously sheeted and comfortable, the desks are slabs of butcher block, and some rooms have tables made of petrified wood. The bathrooms have tub-shower combinations. I particularly like the Sky Lofts with their sloping, atelier-like windows, and the Spa Rooms, which feature hot tubs on private balconies. Another draw here is the adjoining restaurant **Pazzo** (reviewed p. 185) with its delicious Northern Italian cuisine. Only from the outside can you tell that the Hotel Vintage occupies one of Portland's oldest downtown buildings, dating from 1894. Inside, it's all about Portland today.

422 SW Broadway. www.hotelvintage-portland.com. ✆ **800/263-2305** or 503/228-1212. 117 units. $166–$336 double. Rates include complimentary evening wine hour. Valet parking $43. Pets accepted. **Amenities:** Restaurant; lounge; exercise room; free Wi-Fi.

The Nines ★★★ The Nines was created on the top nine floors of the old Meier & Frank department store, a Portland retail icon since the 1920s. Clark Gable worked here before he was a star, and the city's first escalator graced the store. The Nines, as in "dressed to . . ." honors the defunct fashion emporium with panache. Throughout the property is fashion-centric artwork; and it's not just the crack staff who greet guests in the reception area—stylishly dressed mannequins are also on hand. The hotel lobby is a soaring, light-filled atrium with limousine-long leather sofas in orchid bright colors—you may feel like you've stepped onto the set of Technicolor movie. The rooms are fairly large and dressed for fun, with fake-jewel shades on swag lamps, bracelet-like drawer handles, cool-blue sofas, and big beds with gleaming white bedspreads. Bathrooms are large and luxurious. Service is a keynote here, with twice-daily maid service, 24-hour room service and a staff that bends over backwards for guests. Once you're inside, the Nines is a world unto itself. **Urban Farmer,** set off to one side of the lobby, is a farm-to-fork steakhouse, while **Departures,** on the top floor, is a cocktail lounge and Asian-inspired restaurant—the most vegetarian-friendly in the city—with an airport lounge look inside and a rooftop terrace for outdoor drinks and dining.

525 SW Morrison St. www.thenines.com. ✆ **877/229-9995.** 331 units. $228–$413 double. Valet parking $47. Pets accepted ($65 fee). **Amenities:** 2 restaurants; 2 lounges; exercise room; free Wi-Fi.

RiverPlace Hotel ★★ Located on the waterfront esplanade at the south end of Tom McCall Waterfront Park, RiverPlace is the only downtown Portland hotel right on the Willamette River. A low-rise building from the 1980s, it enjoys a unique view of the downtown marina (the Portland dragon boat teams launch from just below the hotel). When the weather opens up, so does the hotel—the lobby area flows through to the Willamette-facing side, and you get a real hit of the unique riverfront location. This is a fashionable and friendly Kimpton property, with Kimpton's eclectic style. The decor has nautical hints, but it is really a creature of the postmodern era, meaning it's a pastiche of contemporary styles and patterns. The bed is always what counts most, and these are wonderful. By far the most inviting accommodations here are the suites, with wood-burning fireplaces and views right out over the river. The courtyard-facing rooms are quieter (the Marquam Bridge spans the river just north of the hotel) and some of them open out onto a garden; there are also self-contained condos for longer stays. The bathrooms are nice and large, with enough counter space. Every evening there's a complimentary wine hour featuring Northwest vintages. **Three Degrees,** the hotel's restaurant, serves Pacific Northwest cuisine, and the hotel's outdoor bar area can be a fun mob scene during happy hour on a warm afternoon or evening. It's lovely to stroll along the esplanade out front, or you can borrow one of the hotel's bikes and do a bit of exploring along the riverside bike paths.

1510 SW Harbor Way. www.riverplacehotel.com. ✆ **800/227-1333** or 503/228-3233. 84 units. $174–$403 double. Valet parking $37. Pets accepted (free). **Amenities:** Restaurant; lounge; bikes; access to nearby health club; Jacuzzi; free Wi-Fi.

Sentinel ★★★ The hotel occupies two great historic buildings in downtown Portland: The giant, Renaissance palazzo–style former Elks Club (West Wing)—this must have been the grandest Elks Club in the country—and the lovely former Governor Hotel (East Wing). The decor is the same throughout, but the two buildings offer different room types. Particularly nice are the sixth-floor rooms with private rooftop patios in the East Wing. But I personally like the big windows and original bathroom tile floors in the West Wing. All rooms are fairly spacious, with dark green walls, built-in white cabinets, leather and wool armchairs, and Pendleton blankets accessorizing the beds. The look is traditional and clubby, but enlivened with some interesting artwork that features images of "movers, shakers and visionaries." The grand lobby, with its coffered plaster ceilings, wouldn't look out of place in Rome. Right off that lobby is the **Jackknife Bar,** a **Starbucks,** and **Jake's Famous Crawfish ★★**

(see p. 184)—not the original, which is a few blocks away. The fitness center is the best-equipped of any hotel in Portland. One special touch: As a nod to the age of the building, there's a working Remington typewriter in the lobby area, where you can practice your typing skills as in the days of yore.

614 SW 11th Ave. www.sentinelhotel.com. ✆ **888/246-5631** or 503/224-3400. 100 units. $159–$279 double. Valet parking $43. **Amenities:** Restaurant; lounge; fitness room; free Wi-Fi.

Moderate

Ace Hotel ★★ No other hotel captures Portland's independent spirit better than the Ace. The hotel was always a working-class hotel, started in 1912. It's on the historic register, so much of it couldn't be altered, except for the room decor, which is what really sets the Ace apart. The hotel skips overstuffed luxury and sticks to the basics without sacrificing comfort—although you have to be willing to look on your stay as a bit of an adventure if you're a budgeteer. The lowest-priced rooms have a sink but share a bathroom (another Ace feature). In the rooms with private bathrooms, you can soak in an original claw foot tub. I love that the beds have woolen Pendleton blankets, a true Oregon touch, and that some of the funky furnishings and artworks are refashioned from found objects. All of it works, and adds a touch of creativity that the city's overly decorated boutique hotels miss. There are wall murals in some rooms, turntables with vinyl records in others. For an additional $10, you can enjoy a real breakfast with all kinds of choices.

1022 SW Stark St. www.acehotel.com. ✆ **503/228-2277.** 78 units, 11 with shared bath. $125–$175 double with shared bath, $162–$245 double with private bath. Self-park $34. Pets accepted. **Amenities:** Restaurant; lounge; bikes; access to nearby health club; free Wi-Fi.

Embassy Suites ★★ The rooms don't have all the fashionista frou-frou of downtown's smaller boutique hotels, or the restrained elegance of the Benson (p. 167), but when you enter the lobby of this enormous hotel—with its intricate columns, gilding, and plasterwork—you know you have entered someplace special. Built in 1912 as the Multnomah Hotel, it was one of Portland's grandest of grand hotels. Since 1995 it's been the Embassy Suites, one of only two Embassy Suites properties in the U.S. to occupy a historic building. With its moderate prices, generously sized rooms, indoor pool, and complimentary hot breakfast, this is a top hotel choice for families. And the grown-ups can enjoy a complimentary evening cocktail hour with a full cocktail menu, not just wine—something I haven't encountered in any other local hotel. All of the rooms feature big windows that guests can open, with nice city views that aren't found in other downtown hotels. The downtown location, free Wi-Fi, big exercise room, and historic pizazz of the place are added bonuses.

319 SW Pine St. www.embassyportland.com. ✆ **800/362-2779** or 503/279-9000. 276 units. $160–$270 double w/ full breakfast and complimentary cocktail hour. Valet parking $45; self-parking $35. **Amenities:** Restaurant; lounge; exercise room; Jacuzzi; indoor pool; day spa; free Wi-Fi.

Hotel deLuxe ★★ Years ago this was the Mallory Hotel, which started life pretty grand back in 1912, but by the 1990s was in need of a facelift. (A notable exception being the hotel's famous **Driftwood Room,** a classic and much-cherished time capsule of the 1950s.) The revamped hotel has a Southern California vibe, dressed as it is in pastel yellows and greens. It also takes on a Golden Age of Hollywood theme (color by Deluxe, remember?) by using black and white stills from classic movies to decorate the hallways and rooms—each floor is devoted to a separate director. The least expensive rooms are pretty modest in size, but the double-queen rooms and suites are generously large, some with walk-in closets. Bathrooms are white, gray, and gleaming chrome, with marble floors, tiled walls, and pedestal sinks. You can open the windows—a crack, anyway—and won't be bothered by traffic noise. There's a small fitness room with state-of-the-art Technogym equipment. **Gracie's,** the hotel restaurant, serves unfussy American cuisine. The deLuxe is in a slightly off-center part of downtown, just west of the I-5 freeway. Everything downtown, including destination restaurants like **Tasty n Alder** (see p. 185), is within a short walking distance, and MAX light rail is about a block away, so you can get all over the city with ease.

729 SW 15th Ave. www.hoteldeluxe.com. ✆ **866/895-2094** or 503/219-2094. 130 units. $135–$279 double. Valet parking $33. Pets accepted ($45 fee). **Amenities:** Restaurant; lounge; exercise room; free Wi-Fi.

Hotel Lućia ★★★ It's not every hotel that uses 40 years' worth of photographs by White House photographer David Hume Kennerly to decorate its lounge and corridors. But the Lućia, downtown Portland's most stylish boutique hotel, has the world's largest collection of Kennerly prints, and they are amazing. Get off the elevator at one floor and there's John and Martha Mitchell, he stern, with a pipe, she madcap, grinning behind dark glasses. Fidel Castro, Ansel Adams, Gerald Ford playing pass-the-straw-under-the-nose with a Japanese geisha—you never know who or what you'll encounter. The hotel's million-dollar art collection also includes many portrait paintings by Gregory Grenon, one of Portland's best-known artists. It's all displayed gallery-style. The rooms are comfortable and wonderfully simple in the best sort of way. There's a glass-topped desk, a comfy leather chair with a brightly colored ottoman, and a big comfortable bed; suites have sofas and more legroom. You can open the windows, a feature I always appreciate. The bathrooms are the same size no matter what type of room you get—they're small, but have cool round aluminum sinks, frosted-glass counters, and make efficient use of the space. The Gallery Suite features all original art. Restaurant **Imperial ★★** (see p. 181) serves breakfast, lunch, and dinner; there's also a nice cafe for morning pastry and lunchtime sandwiches, and a special room-service ice cream menu so you can order your favorite homemade treats from **Salt & Straw ★★** (p. 193).

400 SW Broadway. www.hotellucia.com. ✆ **866/986-8086** or 503/225-1717. 127 units. $143–$271 double; $249–$388 suite. Children 18 and under stay free in parent's room. Valet parking $43. Pets accepted ($50 per night). **Amenities:** 2 restaurants; lounge; concierge; exercise room; room service; free Wi-Fi.

Hotel Modera ★★★ Even before you step inside the Hotel Modera, the garden courtyard (with it's "living wall" of vertical plantings), gravel patio, and outdoor fire pits signal this is a sophisticated, yet cozy, place. The Modera was refashioned from a 1950's motel, and today has a bold, contemporary lobby, all glowing orbs and burnished hardwoods. That stylish design flair carries on into the rooms, which have a bit of a modernized Mad Men-vibe. They're small, but touches like anti-fog mirrors, large massage showerheads, and switch-activated "do not disturb" lights outside the door help make them comfortable. The on-site restaurant **Nel Centro** is good, if overpriced. We'd recommend, instead, grabbing a cocktail on the patio next to one of the fire pits—ah! *One drawback*: It's a bit far from the heart of downtown and main dining and nightlife districts like the Pearl.

515 SW Clay St. www.hotelmodera.com. ✆ **877/484-1084** or 503/484-1084. 174 units. $119–$299 double. Valet parking $38. **Amenities:** Restaurant; lounge; access to nearby 24 Hour Fitness; free Wi-Fi.

Hotel Monaco ★★ Whenever I'm in this big, cheerful hotel, I can never quite forget that it was once the Frederick & Nelson department store. It's been the Hotel Monaco since 1996, when it became the first new hotel in downtown Portland to be fashioned from an existing historic building. Stylistically it's hard to pin down, except that it's as far from minimalist as you can get. The big lobby lounge, with its red walls, tufted fainting couches, and high white arches, has a kind of pleasantly flamboyant Regency-Victorian style, and is a fun and lively spot to enjoy the hotel's complimentary wine and cocktail hour with piano accompaniment. Most of the guestrooms are generously sized suites, with sliding doors to separate bedrooms and living areas. The room decor is more "country" than the public spaces, but what country and era, it's impossible to say. Patterns, textures, colors, and furniture styles are layered together in a busy kaleidoscope that keeps your eyes forever hopping. The bathrooms are more soothing, with marble countertops, wallpaper printed with images of Portland's architecture, and tubs big enough for soaking. The service is exemplary. My only complaints? If you're a business traveler, there is no desk—you have to use a table. **Red Star** is a good spot for breakfast, lunch, or dinner. If you just want morning coffee, that's provided in the lobby. The Monaco is only a block from Pioneer Courthouse Square, in the heart of downtown, and within easy walking distance of Powell's Books and the Pearl District.

506 SW Washington St. www.monaco-portland.com. ✆ **888/207-2201** or 503/222-0001. 221 units. $99–$310 double; $158–$361 suite. Rates include complimentary evening wine and morning coffee. Valet parking $42. Pets accepted (free). **Amenities:** Restaurant; lounge; bikes; exercise room; access to nearby health club; free Wi-Fi.

The Mark Spencer Hotel ★ Singers and production crews from the Portland Opera and the casts of touring Broadway shows always stay at the Mark Spencer. Translation: This is a good hotel for extended stays—and for families, as the suites have nice little working kitchens. It's not the most glamorous of downtown hotels, but it's not meant to be. The hotel has been undergoing a gradual refurbishment to freshen up all the rooms and expose some features from the original 1907 structure, like brick walls and beamed ceilings. The one-bedroom suites, with their comfy living rooms and completely separate bedrooms, are the best accommodations here. Is it because of all those performers passing through that the bathroom mirrors are so large and fog-free? Other helpful features for longer-stay guests include a coin-operated laundry, a small but serviceable fitness room, and an expanded continental breakfast and complimentary evening wine hour. The staff here is pleasant and professional, and the location is central to downtown and the Pearl District.

409 SW 11th Ave. www.markspencer.com. ✆ **800/548-3934** or 503/224-3293. 102 units. $169–$249 double with continental breakfast and afternoon wine reception included. Parking $20. Pets accepted ($15 per day). **Amenities:** Exercise room; coin-operated laundry; free Wi-Fi.

Inexpensive

Crystal Hotel ★ Like the Ace (see p. 173), the Crystal epitomizes a certain Portland aesthetic that is down-to-earth. And the rooms with shared bathrooms at the Crystal are the best deals in town. The hotel was created by the McMenamins, the Portland entrepreneur brothers who invented a whole new kind of hotel concept, saving and reinventing historic buildings and turning them into funky, all-in-one environments where you can sleep, eat, drink, and listen to live music. The Crystal Hotel occupies a wedge-shaped building built in 1911. It pays homage to the famous century-old **Crystal Ballroom** (see p. 204) across the street, another McMenamins rescue, where just about every famous performer and band coming through Portland has played. Each of the rooms in the hotel draws some decorative inspiration from a song or performance at the Crystal—it might be lyrics printed on the walls, or posters, or hand-painted murals. The rooms themselves are uniformly dark gray with dark accessories—it's not as gloomy as it sounds, and even the shared-bath rooms have wonderful little touches, like a table for two beside the window. On the ground floor, **Zeus Café** serves down-to-earth Northwest food and beer. In the basement there's a speakeasy, **Al's Den,** where you can hear local bands every night of the week. There's also a heated saltwater soaking pool down there. Here's what you have to know about the Crystal: It is right on busy Burnside Street, and you will get more of a trafficky, urban buzz here than at any other hotel in Portland. The hotel wisely provides earplugs in every room, but if a quiet spot is what you're after, you won't find it here. One big plus is that guests can buy tickets for performances at the Crystal Ballroom, even if a show is officially sold out. The hotel's location may be noisy, but it is central to Portland's downtown urban scene.

303 SW 12th Ave. www.mcmenamins.com. ✆ **855/205-3930** or 503/972-2670. 51 units. $135–$155 double with shared bath; $195–$235 double with private bath. Parking $25 (nearby lot). **Amenities:** 3 restaurants; 4 lounges; soaking pool; free Wi-Fi.

OLD TOWN/CHINATOWN

Inxpensive

The Society Hotel ★★★ This is the best hotel deal in Portland and a place where you can enjoy a memorable stay in the heart of the city for a fraction of what you'd pay at a fancier hotel a few blocks away. Located in still-gritty Old Town/Chinatown, The Society Hotel occupies a late-19th-century building that was originally a hotel for sailors and later used as a Chinese dance hall. Today it is a combined hotel and hostel, but one with well-designed charm. The cheapest option is to rent a bunk bed in the open dorm area. Each bunk has an outlet for recharging your phone, a reading light, a privacy curtain and, best of all, a comfortable mattress. Next up are the small rooms with shared bathrooms. They have windows, a sink, and robes. Then there are the rooms with en-suite bathrooms. On the first floor there's a nice café that serves coffee, food and bar drinks. Best of all, there's a roof terrace with great city views. The Society (as in Sailors' Society, not high society), which opened in 2015, is within easy walking distance of downtown and just 2 blocks from two MAX light rail lines.

203 NW 3rd Ave. www.thesocietyhotel.com. ✆ **503/445-0444.** 38 units, 12 with shared bath, 24 bunks. Dorm bed $35–$55; private room w/bath $129–$169; room with shared bath $69–$109. **Amenities:** Café-bar; free Wi-Fi.

PEARL DISTRICT

Moderate

Hampton Inn & Suites ★★ This large Hilton-brand hotel opened in September 2017 and is the only hotel in the heart of the Pearl District. The location, right on the North Park Blocks, and moderate price makes it a good choice for families with kids. Like other Hampton hotels, this one adheres to a certain stylistic formula that provides quiet and plenty of comfort without finicky, high-end finishes or luxuries. But it gives you a lot for your money, including large rooms with comfortable beds, large bathrooms, and good-sized desks. The inner-facing rooms don't have much of a view, but some of the corner rooms do. There's a large, indoor swimming pool, a rarity in Portland, with water features that children love, and a very nice roof patio with views out over the city. A large and pleasant bar-lounge-restaurant called **Tanner Creek Tavern** is right off the lobby. And another good thing about this hotel: It's close to the streetcar and to everything in the happening Pearl District.

354 NW Ninth Ave. www.portlandpearldistrict.hamptonbyhilton.com. ✆ **800/426-7866** or 503/222-5200. 243 units. $152–$220 double. Valet parking $37. **Amenities:** Restaurant; lounge; fitness room; heated indoor pool; roof patio; free Wi-Fi.

NW 23RD/NOB HILL

Moderate

Inn @ Northrup Station ★★ This boutique hotel right in the heart of the Northwest/Nob Hill/NW 23rd neighborhood is anything but dull. Vivid mix-and-match colors and retro-style furniture enliven the rooms and public areas, almost forcing you to be cheerful. Then again, there's quite a lot to be cheerful about in this hotel, created from a 1970s building. It's great for families, as some of the rooms can sleep up to five people, and all of the rooms have either a small kitchenette with microwave or a full kitchen. The doors open out to little balconies in the less-expensive back units, and larger patios or balconies in the street-facing units. Parking is free, and the Portland streetcar stops right outside—in fact, guests receive a complimentary daily streetcar pass. There's a nice rooftop terrace, too, with patio furniture.

2025 NW Northrup St. www.northrupstation.com. ✆ **800/224-1180** or 503/224-0543. 70 units. $139–$239 double w/continental breakfast. Free parking. **Amenities:** Access to nearby health club; complimentary streetcar pass; free Wi-Fi.

Inexpensive

Northwest Portland Hostel ★★ This Hostel International (HI) complex consists of five adjacent properties—the newest one opened in 2017—clustered around an outdoor courtyard-lounge area that's great for late-night hanging out. There are endless sleeping configurations, including 4-, 6- and 8-bunk dorm rooms (some coed, some of the newer dorm rooms with private bathroom) and private rooms in the three main buildings and the two cottages, all with en-suite bathrooms, shared kitchen and commons area. Sheets and towels are provided. The new building houses the **Hostel Café,** open for breakfast, lunch, and dinner (Mon–Sat until 1am, Sun until midnight). The adjacent commons area and courtyard are open 24 hours a day. And best of all, you can easily walk or bike to just about anything in central Portland.

479 NW 18th Ave. www.nwportlandhostel.com. ✆ **503/241-2783.** 185 units. Dorm bed $31–$40; private room w/bath $94–$114. **Amenities:** Cafe; lounge; free Wi-Fi.

CONCORDIA

Moderate

McMenamins Kennedy School ★★★ This former elementary school (built in 1915) has been brought back to life as possibly the most unusual hotel in town. There's colorful hand-painted art on the walls, a couch-filled movie-theater pub, a brewery, and a saltwater soaking pool outdoors, for starters. Choose from two restaurants, which continue the quirky decorating vibe with paintings and other artwork. Staying here will take you back to your school days: The guest rooms still have original blackboards from when they were used as classrooms, and the water fountains are barely thigh-high. No fewer than three bars are on premises (naughty!)—the two-level Boiler Room, the tiny Honors Bar, and a cigar bar called, of course, the Detention Bar. It's totally unique, the kind of place people tend to love or hate, but if you're among the former (like me), you'll be telling your friends about it for years. ***Note:*** This is a historic building with architectural features that can't be altered, so be aware that some guests complain that these big windows let in too much sun in the summer and don't adequately muffle traffic noise from NE 33rd right outside. Newer and quieter rooms have been created in the English (as in literature) Wing behind the school; this wing, with rooms named after books the McMenamin brothers are particularly fond of, opened in 2012.

5736 NE 33rd Ave. www.mcmenamins.com. ✆ **888/249-3983** or 503/249-3983. 57 units. $195–$235 double. Pets accepted ($15 per day). **Amenities:** 2 restaurants; 4 lounges; soaking pool; free Wi-Fi.

SOUTHEAST PORTLAND

Moderate

Portland Mayor's Mansion ★★★ When you stay at this imposing Colonial Revival red-brick mansion on Laurelhurst Park, you are staying in a piece of Portland history. Mayor H. Russell Albee had it built in 1912 for use as his summer home. Albee's architect was A. E. Doyle, the man who designed every significant building in Portland in that era, including the Portland Public Library. This is a grand mansion, with most of its original features, and it has been beautifully restored and maintained by owner-innkeeper Dick Kroll. The outstanding quality of the original materials and craftsmanship is augmented by interior decor that features a fine-tuned mix of period antiques, contemporary and Asian artwork, and fine (but not overstuffed) furniture. With its white oak and mahogany paneling and staircase, library, solarium, and giant-sized living room, it's definitely an impressive showplace, but it's also comfortable, and guests are encouraged to enjoy its many public rooms. It's also right on Laurelhurst Park, so rooms look out onto giant trees. The guest rooms, all on the second floor, share the sense of sturdy, well-built luxury that characterizes the rest of the house. The three-room master suite is a small apartment unto itself. The other three rooms are smaller and two of them share a bathroom.

3360 SE Ankeny St. www.pdxmayorsmansion.com. ✆ **503/232-3588.** 4 units, 2 w/ private bath. $175–$190 double w/full breakfast included, $280 suite. **Amenities:** free Wi-Fi.

Inexpensive

Everett Street Guesthouse ★★ This 1907 Craftsman-style house is typical of the handsome and well-built family homes constructed in Portland during the early 20th century, when wood was plentiful and craftsmanship levels were high. Innkeeper Terry Rusinow, a former gallery owner, offers a one-bedroom en-suite unit on the lower level of the house and a cottage in back that is perfect for one or two people who want extra privacy. It has its own entrance, kitchenette, washer-dryer, and private patio. This is a good neighborhood to explore: Laurelhurst Park, restaurants, and movie theaters are within walking distance, and you can get downtown in minutes on nearby public transportation.

2306 NE Everett St. www.everettstreetguesthouse.com. ✆ **503/230-0211** or 503/830-0650. 2 units. $88 double (2-night minimum); $118 cottage (3-night minimum). No children. **Amenities:** Bikes; free Wi-Fi.

Jupiter Hotel ★ Created in 2004 from a California-style, mid-century modern motor lodge, the Jupiter is what the hotel business calls an "active property"—meaning it caters primarily to a younger crowd (21–45), has an adjoining bar-lounge-restaurant-concert venue (Doug Fir) with a busy outdoor patio that stays open until 2am, and lets guests have parties as long as they don't get out of hand. It doesn't try to hide any of this, and offers rooms on the Bar-Patio side (noisier), and on the Chill side (quieter), in addition to providing earplugs in the rooms. The rooms themselves are motel-size, but they've been creatively updated in a way that makes them both comfortable and appealing, though the windows do not open and you have to rely on an in-room A/C unit to keep the air moving (and, sometimes, to mask the party noise). Furnishing is sleek and minimalist. The bathrooms have tub-showers and are nicely tiled. On a busy summer's night when the hotel's blue wall lights are on, and the guests' doors are open, and the patio bar is in full swing (and the smell of reefer drifts through the parking lot), this is a world unto itself—not for everyone, but possibly for you. In April 2018 a new expansion called NEXT opened across the street with 67 additional rooms and a new restaurant-bar. The new rooms have city views, expanded amenities and a sleeker, more contemporary look; they're also more tech-savvy for business travelers. I think that may be where you'll want to stay.

800 E. Burnside St. www.jupiterhotel.com. ✆ **877/800-0004** or 503/230-9200. 148 units. $139–$199 double. Parking $15. Pets accepted ($35). **Amenities:** 2 restaurants; 3 lounges; rental bikes; access to nearby health club; free Wi-Fi.

NOB HILL

Moderate

Silver Cloud Inn Northwest Portland ★ This hotel is on the edge of Portland's trendy Nob Hill neighborhood, and though it's also near an industrial area, it's still an attractive and comfortable place. The rooms fronting Vaughn Street get some traffic noise, so if you're a light sleeper request a room on the other side of the building. Reasonable rates are the main draw here, but the rooms are also well designed. The mini-suites have separate seating areas, which makes them good bets for families. To find the hotel, take I-405 to Ore. 30 W. and get off at the Vaughn Street exit.

2426 NW Vaughn St. www.silvercloud.com. ✆ **800/205-6939** or 503/242-2400. 82 units. $129–$199 double w/full breakfast. Free parking. **Amenities:** Exercise room; access to nearby health club; free Wi-Fi.

WHERE TO EAT

The Portland restaurant scene is hot, and it's not just because of all the wood-burning ovens that have been cranking out perfect pizzas for the past few years. The city now has a national reputation for great, small restaurants. Driving this renaissance are lots of creative young chefs and a ready supply of local produce and wines from the Willamette Valley. The bounteous

Many Happy Hours

Happy hour is huge in Portland. And it's not just because the drinks are cheap, although that's certainly part of it. It's actually more about the food. Every good restaurant—I mean *every one*—has a happy hour, with delicious small plates available for about half of their usual price. This is a fab way to save money on eats. I won't go into the details of the arcane rules devised by the Oregon Liquor Commission, but restaurants with bars have to offer food with the booze during happy hour. That's one Oregon law I can live with.

ingredients that can be sourced locally include organic fruits and vegetables; hazelnuts and walnuts; wild mushrooms; and even Oregon truffles. And that's not to mention those local pinot noir, pinot gris, and pinot blanc vintages.

And then, of course, there are the now-famous Portland food carts (see p. 186), which have started something of a national trend. You may have to dine standing up, or at a picnic table, but the grub should be great.

The only catch to the Portland dining scene is that it's spread out, and some of the most talked-about restaurants are neighborhood spots in residential districts away from the city center. Bear in mind that some of these neighborhood gems don't take reservations (always call first), so, unless you arrive before 7pm or after 9pm, you may end up having to wait for a table.

DOWNTOWN (AND SOUTHWEST PORTLAND)

Expensive

Chart House ★ SEAFOOD I don't usually recommend chain restaurants, but I'm making an exception for the Chart House for those who want to dine at a long-standing Portland restaurant while feasting their eyes on a marvelous view—something that's almost impossible to find elsewhere in Portland's urban restaurant scene. Chart House nabbed this primo hillside location decades ago, and the restaurant has been part of Portland's consciousness since "pre-discovery" days, when the city had only a handful of destination tablecloth restaurants. To accompany that special Chart House view of Portland, the Willamette Valley, and Mount Hood, you can enjoy fish from far and near, but I would stick to the Pacific salmon or albacore tuna when it's in season (it'll be freshest). They also do surf-and-turf combinations. The signature dessert is warm lava cake, chocolate outside, chocolate inside, chocolate on top—the sugar rush lasts for hours. If the sun is out, you might want to come here for lunch, or happy hour (daily 4–7pm)—all the better to enjoy that remarkable view.

5700 SW Terwilliger Blvd. www.chart-house.com. ✆ **503/246-6963.** Main courses: lunch $12–$27, dinner $26–$42. Mon–Thurs 11:30am–9:30pm; Fri 11:30am–10pm; Sat 5–10pm; Sun 10am–3pm and 5–9pm.

Imperial ★★ EASTERN EUROPEAN/PACIFIC NORTHWEST Vitaly Paley, the force behind the long-running **Paley's Place** (p. 187) in Northwest Portland, is the chef-owner of this newish downtown hotel restaurant. The name Imperial is a nod to next-door **Hotel Lucia**'s (see p. 174) previous life as the Imperial Hotel and dining room. But imperial may also have something to do with Imperial Russia, since Paley was born in Kiev and likes to make some of the same dishes his grandmother did. They can be very rich, like the duck meatballs with prunes, aromatic spices, and orange gremolata (duck is featured in other dishes, too). But not all is heavy; offerings like the bay scallop crudo with vinaigrette, grapefruit, and cured steelhead caviar are fresh, and satisfying, as is the selection of oysters on the half shell. Because Imperial has a big wood-fired grill, grilled and rotisserie meats are a specialty. Our favorites include the bone-in pork chop with sage and black-pepper honey, the

Portland Restaurants

RESTAURANTS ◆

Alto Bajo **27**
Andina **10**
Ava Gene's **33**
Bamboo Sushi **8, 15, 38, 42**
Bar Avignon **31**
Bijou Café **24**
Caffe Mingo **7**
Chart House **29**
D.C. Vegetarian Food **23**
Escape from New York Pizza **9**
Grassa **3**
Imperial **21**
Jake's Famous Crawfish **14**
Ken's Artisan Pizza **37**
Khao San **11**
Le Pigeon **40**
Luc Lac Vietnamese Kitchen **28**
Pacific Pie **30**
Paley's Place **4**
Pazzo **20**
Petunia's Pies and Pastries **17**
Pok Pok **5, 32**
Rabbit's Café **22**
St. Jack **2**
Sweet Pea **39**
Tasty n Alder **16**
Thrive **41**
Toro Bravo **44**
Vita Café **43**

COFFEE, TEA, BAKERIES & CHOCOLATERIES ●

Caffe Umbria **12**
Moonstruck Chocolate Café **19**
Pearl Bakery **13**
St. Honore Boulangerie **1, 18, 34**
Salt & Straw **6**
Stumptown Coffee **25, 35**
Tao of Tea **36**
Voodoo Doughnuts **26**

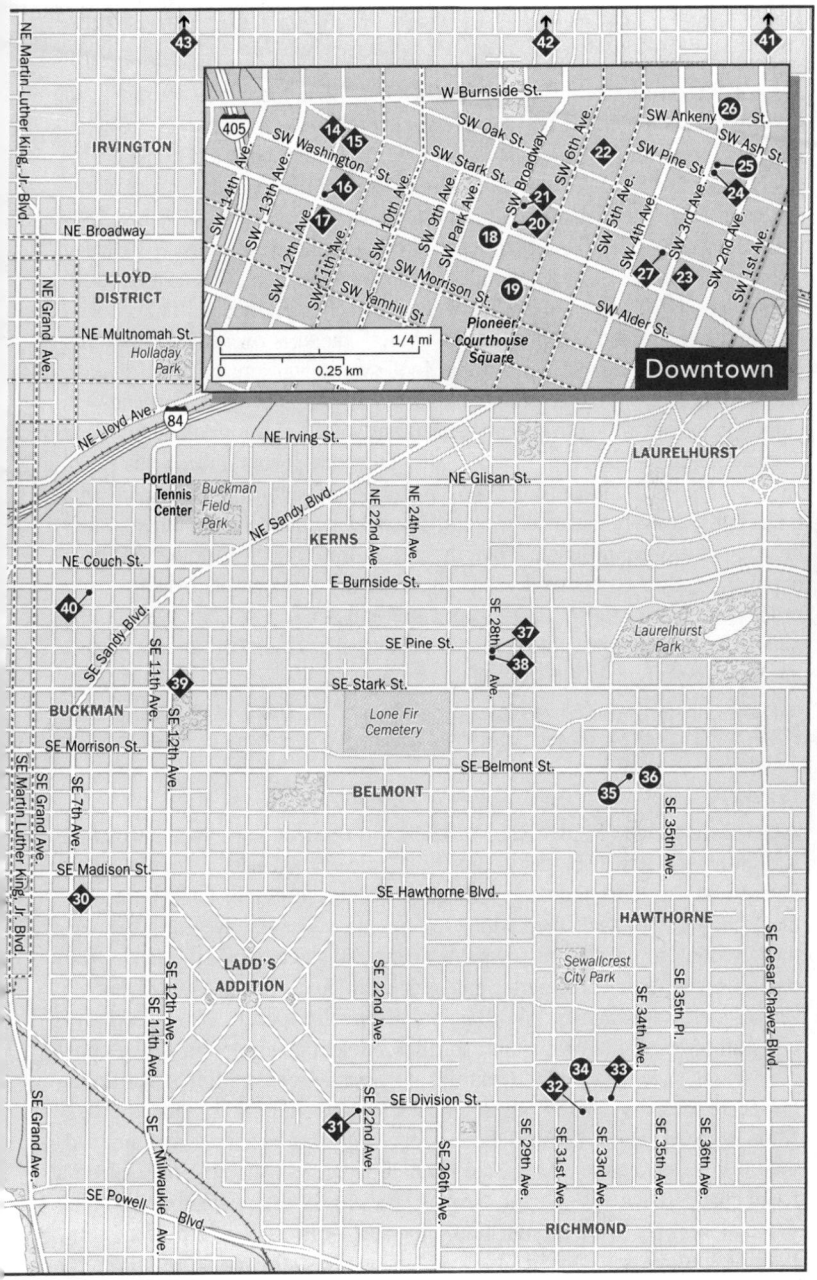
Downtown
W Burnside St.
SW Ankeny St.
SW Ash St.
SW Oak St.
SW Stark St.
SW Pine St.
SW Washington St.
SW Morrison St.
SW Yamhill St.
SW Alder St.
SW 1st Ave.
SW 2nd Ave.
SW 3rd Ave.
SW 4th Ave.
SW 5th Ave.
SW 6th Ave.
SW Broadway
SW Park Ave.
SW 9th Ave.
SW 10th Ave.
SW 11th Ave.
SW 12th Ave.
SW 13th Ave.
SW 14th Ave.
Pioneer Courthouse Square
1/4 mi
0.25 km
IRVINGTON
LLOYD DISTRICT
NE Broadway
NE Multnomah St.
Holladay Park
NE Grand Ave.
NE Martin Luther King, Jr. Blvd.
NE Lloyd Ave.
NE Irving St.
NE Glisan St.
LAURELHURST
Portland Tennis Center
Buckman Field Park
NE Sandy Blvd.
KERNS
NE 22nd Ave.
NE 24th Ave.
NE Couch St.
E Burnside St.
SE Sandy Blvd.
SE 11th Ave.
SE 12th Ave.
SE 28th Ave.
SE Pine St.
Laurelhurst Park
BUCKMAN
SE Stark St.
Lone Fir Cemetery
SE Morrison St.
SE Belmont St.
BELMONT
SE 35th Ave.
SE 7th Ave.
SE Grand Ave.
SE Martin Luther King, Jr. Blvd.
SE Madison St.
SE Hawthorne Blvd.
HAWTHORNE
SE Cesar Chavez Blvd.
LADD'S ADDITION
SE 22nd Ave.
Sewallcrest City Park
SE 34th Ave.
SE 35th Pl.
SE 11th Ave.
SE Division St.
SE 26th Ave.
SE 29th Ave.
SE 31st Ave.
SE 33rd Ave.
SE 35th Ave.
SE 36th Ave.
SE Milwaukie Ave.
SE Powell Blvd.
RICHMOND

roasted half chicken, or a dry-aged rib-eye with horseradish butter. After all that, a house-made gelato or sorbet is a perfect way to end your meal.

410 SW Broadway (adjacent to Hotel Lućia). www.imperialpdx.com. ✆ **503/228-7222.** Main courses $14–$36. Mon–Fri 6:30am–10pm; Sat–Sun 8am–2pm and 5–10pm.

Jake's Famous Crawfish ★ SEAFOOD Some people say "craw" and some people say "cray," but however you pronounce it, crawfish are what Jake's is famous for. And not just any crawfish, but crawfish that come exclusively from Lake Billy Chinook in Oregon's high desert country east of the Cascades. The crawfish season starts there about the end of May and lasts until October. At Jake's, the crawfish are made into a spicy New Orleans/Cajun gumbo-style stew (a good idea, since crawfish aren't the most flavorful of crustaceans). There's a daily list of fresh fish choices, most of them cooked in a fairly unadorned manner. The "Classics" menu is overpriced, but other entrees are good values. Even if the food won't win any culinary awards, Jake's definitely offers a pretty extraordinary ambience for Portland—an authentic turn-of-the-20th-century restaurant with a gleaming mahogany bar shipped around Cape Horn in the 1880s. There are lovely nude ladies posed above, scenic wall murals, and a wonderfully old-fashioned dining room with tablecloths and professional waiters. I would recommend enjoying Jake's unique atmosphere at lunch, when the prices drop by half. Another option is happy hour, always popular at Jake's thanks to the gorgeous bar, when you can order plates for $3 to $7. **Jake's Bar and Grill** at 611 SW 10th Ave. (✆ **503/220-1850**) is under the same management and offers many of the same dishes but lacks the original Jake's inimitable ambience.

401 SW 12th Ave. www.jakesfamouscrawfish.com. ✆ **503/226-1419.** Main courses $12–$19 lunch, $20–$47 dinner. Sun–Thurs 11:30am–10pm; Fri–Sat 11:30am–11pm; Sun 3–10pm.

Moderate

Alto Bajo ★★★ MODERN MEXICAN Yes, you can order guacamole and chips and it will be tasty. But the Mexican food here, whipped up by famed Oaxacan chef Iliana de la Vega and Chicago-import Chip Barnes (of the Windy City's acclaimed Moto restaurant), rewards adventurous diners, those willing to try lesser-known Mexican specialties, like a dip made from pumpkinseed, habanero, garlic and grapefruit juice (sounds weird but it's sensational). The moles at Alto Bajo are also really special. We suggest sampling all three of them with some tortillas: Mole Tamarindo (an earthy chocolate-based sauce made with tamarind and sesame seeds), Mole Amarillo (an Oaxacan specialty made with dry chiles, onions and garlic), and the fiery Mole Rojo (made from onions, chile peppers, ground hazelnuts, sesame seeds and a bit of chocolate). Alto Bajo opened in 2017 in the Hi-Lo Hotel, in a room that's suave enough for business travelers (leather booths, gleaming wood floors) but with enough funky touches—towering potted cacti, straw lighting fixtures, sexy Mexican art—to match the soulful cooking.

310 SW Stark St. (in Hi-Lo hotel). www.altobajopdx.com. ✆ **971/222-2211.** Main courses $12–$30. Daily 6:30am–10pm.

Pazzo ★★ ITALIAN/PACIFIC NORTHWEST One of the true tests of a good restaurant, for me, is the Caesar salad, and Pazzo's passes that test with flying colors; this is maybe the best Caesar in Portland. Pazzo excels with its homemade pastas, too, which are great for sharing. The pappardelle "with grandma's special Sunday meat sauce" (a veal, pork and beef ragu) I had on my last visit was *meraviglioso*, as was an entrée of slow-cooked creamed spring greens. For dessert, the coconut panna cotta is inspired, and the triple chocolate cheesecake (which is not something you'd ever find in Italy) is rich and wonderful. So don't pass this one by. Though it looks like a hundred other Italian joints, the service is tip-top and the food and wine list exemplary.

627 SW Washington St. (in Hotel Vintage Plaza). www.pazzo.com. ✆ **503/228-1515.** Main courses $19–$36. Mon–Thurs 7:30am–9:30pm; Fri–Sat 7:30am–10pm; Sun 8am–9pm.

Tasty n Alder ★★ PACIFIC NORTHWEST This restaurant is now on everyone's short list of places to try. It's a bustling, unpretentious, shared-plates sort of place with good, reasonably priced food and friendly service. The interior is completely unadorned—so Portland—with exposed roof joists and mechanical ducts, and the food is fairly unadorned as well, which is a strong point. For starters, the light and crispy fried oysters are standouts, and the radicchio salad with bacon lardons and a poached egg mixed in is delicious. Although the restaurant is known for its grilled meats, I think the alder plank-smoked salmon is better (certainly far more tender) than the grilled flat iron steak. The entrees are served without sides; you might want to pair your meat or fish with crispy Brussels sprouts or a seasonal root vegetable. End with brûléed banana panna cotta for dessert, and you'll be all set. Tasty's also serves brunch every day until 2pm. It's a good idea to reserve a table.

580 SW 12th Ave. www.tastynalder.com. ✆ **503/621-9251.** Main courses $14–$44. Sun–Thurs 9am–10pm; Fri–Sat 9am–11pm.

Inexpensive

Bamboo Sushi ★★ JAPANESE/SUSHI/SASHIMI I worry about the world's declining fish populations, so a sushi place that only serves sustainably harvested fish from healthy populations is a no-brainer for me. And when the sushi is as fresh and delicious as it is at Bamboo Sushi, I can heartily recommend it to others as well (even though I'm breaking my own rule about not including chain restaurants). The eight-piece rolls here are wonderful for sharing—try "The Local" with albacore tuna, jalapeños, and cucumber topped with East Coast red crab and sesame aioli. The assorted sushi and sashimi plates let you sample the freshest fish of the day. There are also meat dishes, vegetarian options (including vegetarian sushi), and lots of dishes can be made gluten-free. Bamboo Sushi has 3 other Portland locations: **Northwest:** 836 NW 23rd Ave; ✆ **971/221-1925;** daily 5–10pm. **Northeast:** 1409 NE Alberta St.; ✆ **503/232-5335;** daily 4:30–10pm. **Southeast:** 310 SE 28th Ave.; ✆ **503/232-5335;** daily 4:30–10pm.

404 SW 12th Ave. www.bamboosushi.com. ✆ **503/444-7455.** Main courses $11–$35. Daily 11:30am–10pm.

DINING A LA cart

It's such a simple idea, the food cart, and of course it originated in Portland, where hungry residents don't (or didn't) usually have big budgets for dining out but still like good food. Why not join them, and have lunch the Portland way, "a la cart"? The city has become legendary for its hundreds of food carts (trailers, actually) parked in lots all over town. Look for concentrations of them downtown at **SW Stark Street and SW Fifth Avenue; SW Alder Street, and SW Ninth and SW Tenth** avenues; and **SW Third and Ash.** Across the river; on the east side, you'll find carts at **NE 10th and Alberta Street, SE 28th Avenue,** and **SE Hawthorne and 38th Avenue.**

There are many food-cart standouts, and the carts often serve as a springboard (running board?) for new sit-down restaurants. For comfort food from a Culinary Institute of America grad, do **Dinner Bell BBQ** at the SW 9th avenue and Alder St. pod. One block away at 520 SW 10th Ave. you'll find excellent steamed Chinese dumplings at **Bao Bao.** The foods of Ghana are on offer at **Black Star Grill** (SW 4th Avenue at College St.) You'll get fried plantains, meat in a citrusy sauce, and your choice of rice. But these are just a few possibilities for dining inexpensively at spots around town. For other locations and cartloads of information on Portland food carts, go to www.foodcartsportland.com.

At this site you can book a **food-cart tour.** The walking tours are offered Monday through Friday starting around noon at a downtown food cart and last for 60–90 minutes. The $50 tour price includes small bites at four different food carts in different locations. You can roam to different food carts around the city by bike, too. The 3-hour Food Cart Tour offered by **Pedal Bike Tours,** 133 SW Second Ave. (www.pedalbiketours.com; ✆ **503/243-2453**) visits favorite food carts in different neighborhoods for $69 (the price includes samples at all the carts).

Bijou Café ★ PACIFIC NORTHWEST Back before there was a "restaurant scene" in Portland, there was the Bijou Café. It's a good spot for breakfast and lunch (dinner is only served Fridays, but then its accompanied by live jazz). This downtown fixture has remained in business because of its fresh organic food, and because it offers some specialties that you won't find elsewhere else in Portland, like a toothsome oyster hash and a fresh fish sandwich. For breakfast, the French-style omelets are fluffy and delicious. There are also vegetarian choices. It's a nice, non-scenester Portland place to know about.

132 SW Third Ave. www.bijoucafepdx.com. ✆ **503/222-3187.** Breakfast and lunch $7–$15. Mon–Thurs 7am–2pm; Fri 7am–2pm and 6–10pm, Sat–Sun 8am–2pm.

Luc Lac Vietnamese Kitchen ★★ VIETNAMESE This downtown hot spot—a large open room with inverted white umbrellas covering the ceiling—is loud and fun. You line up to place your order, you're given a numbered marker, and then you wait to be called to a table. Drinks will be brought to you but you're responsible for bringing napkins, utensils, and water to your table. The food arrives soon after you're seated. Pho is a favorite dish here: the five-spice beef broth and rice noodles comes with beef, chicken, or tofu and veggies—and sides of cilantro, jalapeños, and lime—for a slurpy, satisfying meal. Also tip-top: the combination vermicelli rice bowl with skewers of pork and chicken. Vegetarians have many choices, including a peanut curry with tofu. On Fridays and Saturdays, Luc Lac stays open until 4am and becomes a kind of club-with-food scene. **Warning:** Luc Lac doesn't accept reservations, so come early or come late but don't come during rush hour (6–8pm) or you may wait up to half an hour for a table. That's the price of popularity. Low prices and good food is the reason for that popularity

835 SW 2nd Ave. (at Taylor St.). www.luclackitchen.com. ✆ **503/222-0047.** Main courses $9–$12. Daily 11am–midnight; Fri–Sat until 4am.

NORTHWEST PORTLAND (INCLUDING NORTHWEST 23RD AND THE PEARL DISTRICT)

Expensive

Andina ★★★ PERUVIAN Peru's cuisine is amazingly diverse and draws from the country's many different food sources: the Pacific, the plains, the mountains, and the jungle. That's why the menu at Andina is a mile long; and surprisingly, you could sample just about everything on it and not find a dud. But since choose you must, we highly recommend the plates of mashed purple potatoes called causa, served layered with fillings like shredded spicy chicken breast and crab-and-tuna salad. There are also plenty of seafood options, including multiple types of ceviche, and a grilled octopus that may be the best in town. This is one of Portland's top destination restaurants, open since 2003. Make a reservation as far in advance as you can, or you won't get in. ***Tip:*** It's easier to get in for lunch, and it's far less of a scene. ***Second tip:*** Andina may be famous for its spicy cocktails, but if you want a delicious, non-alcoholic, and very healthy drink, try a glass of Peruvian *chicha morada,* made from purple corn and loaded with antioxidants.

1314 NW Glisan St. www.andinarestaurant.com. ✆ **503/228-9535.** Main courses, lunch $12–$18; dinner $18–$35. Daily 11:30am–2:30pm, Sun–Thurs 5–9:30pm; Fri–Sat 5–10:30pm.

Paley's Place ★★ NORTHWEST/FRENCH Vitaly Paley, winner of both *Iron Chef America* and a James Beard Award, was one of the first Portland chefs to capitalize on the wealth of fresh ingredients available in the Pacific Northwest. Paley's Place opened in a romantic old Victorian home in Nob Hill in 1995, and the upscale bistro has since embedded itself firmly in Portland's gourmet landscape. The menu relies on locally sourced meat and produce, with dishes such as marinated and grilled quail, and butternut squash and goat cheese ravioli. The crispy sweetbreads could very well make you a convert to offal eating. Other signature dishes include the steak tartare and the Russian panzanella salad with beets, tomatoes, rye, horseradish, and sour cream. Make a reservation if you can—this place is popular—and if the weather cooperates, dine al fresco on the porch, which overlooks bustling NW 21st Avenue.

1204 NW 21st Ave. www.paleysplace.net. ✆ **503/243-2403.** Main courses $17–$36; fixed-price menus $70–$90. Sun–Thurs 5:30–10pm; Fri–Sat 5:30–11pm.

Moderate

Caffe Mingo ★★ ITALIAN You must arrive early or late, or be prepared to wait for a table (reservations are accepted only for parties of six or more). The menu changes weekly, and all the fish, meat, and produce come exclusively from local producers and purveyors. Mingo's menu is delightfully limited to just a few choice selections for each course—fine and fairly simple Italian food is the name of the game here. You might want to start with the roasted artichoke with breadcrumbs and aioli, or one of the fresh salads. I always recommend the *pasta del giorno*, the daily house-made pasta, because over the years they have refined these specials to perfection. I also love the pizzas; there are only two to choose from, but the fennel sausage with cream, spring onions, and Asiago cheese is outrageously good. There's a special menu available if the whole table wants to eat family style. Dessert? Try the chocolate *budino* (a cross between cake and pudding) with berry cream and chocolate cookies. The wine list is as selective as the menu.

807 NW 21st Ave. www.caffemingonw.com. ✆ **503/226-4646.** Main courses $18–$32. Tues–Fri 11am–1pm; Tues–Sun 5–10pm.

St. Jack ★★ FRENCH When this *tres bonne* French bistro and bar moved from its humble southeast location to tonier northwest, it dropped its lunch menu, raised its prices and became dinner only. Fortunately, the wonderful French cooking survived the journey across the river. Many of the dishes here are classics, with tastes that are worth rediscovering. I'm talking about cream of tomato soup baked in puff pastry; seared foie gras on brioche; salad Lyonnaise frisée with bacon lardons, poached egg, and bacon-fat croutons; and a cheese plate with an assortment of fabulous French *fromage*. The *plats principaux* are classics, too, and include mussels meunière, roasted trout, oxtail bourguignon, Lyonnaise onion tart, and that delicious old favorite, duck a l'orange. Enjoy a glass of French wine with your French meal and perhaps finish with Proustian, baked-to-order madeleines. For less expensive sampling, come for happy hour (daily 4–6pm, 10pm–close).

1610 NW 23rd Ave. www.stjackpdx.com. ✆ **503/360-1281.** Main courses $30–$38. Daily 5–11pm.

Inexpensive

Escape from New York Pizza ★★ PIZZA Sometimes, when I want to escape the new Portland of concept restaurants and high-tech babble, I head over for a simple slice at Escape from New York Pizza. This funky hole-in-the-hole in a storefront on NW 23rd is one of the last holdouts of what Portland used to be like: simple, unpretentious, funny and real. (It was founded in 1983 by a guy who fled New York to find just those now-vanishing attributes in Portland.) There are usually two of three pies available by the slice, maybe sausage, maybe pepperoni, maybe veggie, maybe mushroom and olive. The crust is crackling thin, the price is low, and the only other thing they sell is a Caesar salad. You can order a whole pie, too, of course. May it stay around forever.

622 NW 23rd Ave. www.efnypizza.net. ✆ **503/227-5243.** Slice $4–$4.50. Daily 11:30am–11pm.

Grassa ★★ ITALIAN Part of the booming new dining scene that has turned dear old NW 23rd into a kind of Restaurant Row, Grassa is a trattoria known for its made-on-the-premises pasta. The homemade carbs are augmented with seasonally changing sauces made with fresh local ingredients. There are about seven pasta dishes available daily, some of them classics like spaghetti *agli'olio* (with olive oil), and spaghetti *pomodoro* (with tomato sauce), others more adventurous, like spaghetti lemon *chitarra* made with basil and hazelnuts and topped with zucchini and mozzarella crema. Order a salad or a starter plate of fried zucchini fritters to accompany your pasta and you've got a top-notch lunch or dinner for under $20. Grassa has a corner location with big wraparound windows and a pleasant but not particularly memorable interior (although it's fun to watch the pasta being made).

1506 NW 23rd Ave. www.grassapdx.com. ✆ **917/386-2196.** Main courses $11–$15. Daily 11am–10pm.

Khao San ★★ THAI Khao San used to be a food cart but business was so good they moved to a permanent location in the Pearl District. It's very casual and the waitstaff can be a bit stretched at busy times (though always friendly), but the food is consistently tasty. Be aware of your spice-tolerance, however. The first time I ate here and asked for medium spicy, the food practically blew the top of my head off.

1435 NW Flanders. (at 14th Ave.). www.hasosanpdx.com. ✆ **503/227-3700.** Main courses $12–$16. Mon–Fri 11am–10pm; Sat noon–10pm; Sun noon–9pm.

NORTHEAST PORTLAND

Moderate

Toro Bravo ★★★ SPANISH Whether it's Voodoo Doughnuts (see p. 193) or a hot restaurant, Portlanders are willing to wait in long lines to get their food fixes, and the lines become social gatherings. That's usually the case at Toro Bravo, which doesn't take reservations. On weekends, particularly, the line starts to form about half an hour before the doors open. There's a reason why this Spanish tapas place is on everyone's top-five list: The food is remarkably good and reasonably priced, and the service is attitude-free. As you might have guessed, eating here means tapas time—share several plates to enjoy the full array of tastes and textures. Highly recommended: salt cod fritters with aioli, fried Spanish anchovies with fennel and lemon, oxtail croquettes with chili mayonnaise, and grilled asparagus with fried ham. The paella with chorizo, shrimp, clams, and mussels is also distinctive. For $45 a head, your table can enjoy the chef's tasting menu.

120 NE Russell St. www.torobravopdx.com. ✆ **503/281-4464.** Small plates $3–$14; large plates $8–$25. Sun–Thurs 5–10pm; Fri–Sat 5–11pm.

SOUTHEAST PORTLAND (INCLUDING HAWTHORNE DISTRICT AND SOUTHEAST DIVISION)

Expensive

Le Pigeon ★★★ FRENCH Le Pigeon is small and cozy, and dining is at communal tables, which is not to everyone's liking. Since I'm gregarious and

VEGAN, VEGETARIAN & GLUTEN-FREE dining

You'll find that most Portland restaurants offer vegetarian dishes, and more and more of them have gluten-free selections on the menu. But here are a few favorable restaurants for those who don't want to wade through meat-and-wheat-centric menus to find something that suits their tastes or dietary restrictions.

VEGAN

Sweet Pea ★★ The 100% vegan bakery of your dreams with breakfast and lunch items, too.

1205 SE Stark St. www.sweetpeabaking.com. ✆ **503/477-5916.** items. Mon–Sat 8am–6pm, Sun 9am–5pm.

Rabbit's Café ★ Rabbit's is popular with downtowners who come for its breakfasts, vegan bowls, scrambles, and fruit smoothies.

555 SW Oak St. (inside US Bancorp Tower). www.rabbitscafepdx.com. ✆ **503/206-4512.** Mon–Fri 7am–4pm.

VEGETARIAN

DC Vegetarian Food Cart ★★ This downtown breakfast and lunch food cart offers a large variety of fresh vegetarian sandwiches that can also be made vegan.

SW 3rd and Stark. www.dcvegetarian.com. ✆ **503/317-4448.** Mon–Fri 8:30am–3pm.

Vita Cafe ★★ Since 1999, environmentally-oriented and community-minded Vita's has been using only local organic products in its all-vegetarian (with vegan and GF options) dishes.

3023 NE Alberta St. www.vita-cafe.com. ✆ **503/335-8233.** Sun–Thurs 9am–9pm, Fri–Sat 8am–10pm.

GLUTEN FREE

Petunia's Pies and Pastries ★★ Yummy gluten-free baked goods and a new savory menu draw GFers to Petunia's.

610 SW 12th Ave. www.petuniaspiesandpastries.com. ✆ **503/841-5961.** Sun–Wed 9am–7pm, Thurs 8am–9pm, Fri–Sat 9am–10pm.

Thrive ★ Thrive uses free-range and organic proteins and sustainable seafood in its gluten-free offerings.

4641 NE Fremont St. www.thrivesauceandbowls.com. ✆ **971/803-3833.** Tues–Sun 11am–4:30pm.

never averse to jumping into a conversation, the communal table concept works for me. And the food works, too. The menu by James Beard Award-winning chef Gabriel Rucker changes weekly, but leans on daring meat dishes such as beef cheek bourguignon, smoked foie gras, and, yes, pigeon. Even the vegetarian options are worth a visit, like the butter lettuce salad, and stuffed eggplant with sweet potato, pear, walnut, and truffle. Sit at the chef's counter and watch your food being prepared, or grab a seat at one of the communal tables to share a bottle off a wine list worthy of a Parisian bistro. Despite the rave reviews, and the five- and seven-course tasting menus, the atmosphere is less formal than you'd expect—this is Portland, after all, where tasting menus don't rule out jeans and hiking boots.

738 E. Burnside. www.lepigeon.com. ✆ **503/876-8496.** Main courses $17–$39. Daily 5–10pm.

MODERATE

Ava Gene's ★★★ ITALIAN/PACIFIC NORTHWEST Stumptown Coffee kingpin Duane Sorenson and local rock star chef Joshua McFadden combined forces to create one of the hottest eateries in town, on the city's burgeoning foodie street, SE Division. The "Roman-inspired" menu at Ava Gene's delves deep into the bounty of Northwest meats and vegetables, with crusty breads, liquid gold olive oils, and a tripe stew worthy of the Old Country. Try the cauliflower grilled over an open fire with chiles and *tonnato* sauce, or the tagliatelle al carbonara with duck egg and prosciutto. Many of the plates are sized to share, although you probably won't want to. You need to book a table as far in advance as you can; otherwise, you can sit at the chef's counter, which is kept open for walk-ins. Breads and pastries come from Roman Candle Bakery, right next door; you can get a good slab of focaccia there to take home.

3377 SE Division. www.avagenes.com. ✆ **971/229-0571.** Main courses $18–$36. Mon–Thurs 5–10pm, Fri 5–11pm, Sat 4:30–11pm, Sun 4:30–10pm.

Bar Avignon ★★ PACIFIC NORTHWEST/FRENCH The craft cocktails at this neighborhood restaurant are criminally delicious, and the wine list draws kudos, so you could just come here to drink. But better yet, come here to eat *and* drink (maybe during happy hour, Mon–Fri 5–6pm). I have friends who come just for the foraged lettuces salad, house-made charcuterie, and artisan cheeses. I find the lamb and pistachio pate habit forming. So is the seared pork chop with apricot, honeycomb, and rosemary. The menu is short, the food is impeccably fresh, and the touch is light when required and hearty when it needs to be. Share some small plates if you don't want an entree.

2138 SE Division. www.baravignon.com. ✆ **503/517-0808.** Main courses $22–$30. Mon–Thurs 5–10pm; Fri–Sat 5pm–midnight; Sun 5–9pm.

Pok Pok ★★★ THAI Pok Pok is the most authentic Thai restaurant I've eaten at outside of Thailand. Not only are the flavors of the dishes here some of the most vibrant and exotic you'll ever taste, but the whole atmosphere conjures up casual restaurants on the beaches of Thailand. Get the *kai yang* (grilled chicken) and *khao man som tam* (green papaya salad) for an absolute classic straight off the streets of Bangkok. Other specials are the papaya served with salted black crab; and the must-try chicken wings, marinated in fish sauce and sugar and then deep fried. The waitstaff is patient and knowledgeable, and can provide guidance on spice levels (ranging from "not there" to "tongue on fire"). Some people fault this place for serving skimpy portions, but it's the same way in Thailand. Just order another dish; you'll be glad you did. *Tip:* Pok Pok doesn't take reservations, so be prepared to wait for a table (you can call ahead and get your name on the wait list).

While you're waiting for that coveted table to open up, enjoy a cocktail at **Whiskey Soda Lounge,** Pok Pok's bar across the street from the restaurant. Pok Pok has opened new restaurants in Northwest and Northeast Portland. At **Pok Pok NW** (1639 NW Marshall St.; ✆ **971/351-1946;** Mon–Fri 5–10pm, Sat–Sun 11:30am–10pm), you can reserve a table; at **Pok Pok Noi** (1469 NE Prescott; ✆ **503/287-4149;** daily 11:30am–10pm), you can't. They've opened a restaurant in New York, too, but that's for someone else to check out.

3226 SE Division St. www.pokpokpdx.com. ✆ **503/232-1387.** Main courses $9–$14. Daily 11:30am–10pm.

Inexpensive

Ken's Artisan Pizza ★★ PIZZA Here's an idea for a healthy Portland day: Rent a bike (see, p. 148) and pedal over to Ken's. It's on one of the city's busiest bike corridors, about a 15-minute ride from downtown, and offers parking for 24 bikes. Then sit back and enjoy the best pizza in town, cooked to blistered-crust perfection in 2 minutes in a wood-fired, igloo-shaped oven. Ten pizza types are available, all of them topped with the freshest ingredients. You can also order a starter or side salad (I'd recommend the roasted vegetable platter). Local draft beer or a good wine-by-the-glass is on tap to accompany your pizzas. This is a relaxed, family-friendly place with sidewalk seating in the summer and an interior that features huge beams of old-growth Douglas fir salvaged from the famous Jantzen Beach Big Dipper roller coaster, built in 1923.

304 SE 28th Ave. (at Pine St.). www.kensartisan.com. ✆ **503/517-9951.** Main courses $12–$16. Mon–Thurs 5–9:30pm; Fri 5–10pm; Sat 4–10pm; Sun 4–9pm.

Pacific Pie ★★ BRITISH Here you'll find those savory meat pies the Brits invented and the Aussies imported to their shores Down Under (you'll notice a big mural of the Australian outback in the restaurant). Shepherd's pie, lamb pie, steak pie, pork pie, fish pie are all on order—and the chicken pot pie that's more familiar to Americans. This is a nice, unfussy spot to have a hearty and relatively inexpensive lunch. This being Portland, the ingredients used in all the pies are fresh and local. Entrees come with a swell salad or soup. Gluten-free and vegetarian casseroles, wraps, and pies are also available. And oh yes, you can get the *other* kind of pie here, too, and those are just as good. The restaurant is located in an industrial area and caters to the locals who work around there.

1520 SE 7th Ave. www.pacificpie.com. ✆ **503/381-6157.** Main courses $13–$15. Daily 11:30am–9pm.

Coffee, Tea, Bakeries & Chocolatiers

COFFEEHOUSES & CAFES

Coffee is a passion here—we used to say strong coffee helped to speed us up because we were so far behind the East Coast (now that New York comes to Portland for inspiration, the old saying doesn't hold water). In short, you're never far from a good cappuccino or latte in the Rose City. I recommend the following places:

Caffe Umbria ★★★ Started in Seattle by a family from Perugia, this cafe in the Pearl serves, in my opinion, the best lattes in the most sophisticated Italian cafe atmosphere in Portland. There are excellent panini and pastries as well, and wine in the evening. In September 2017 a new Caffee Umbria opened downtown at 710 SW Madison (Mon–Sat 7am–7pm, Sun 7am–5pm).

303 NW 12th Ave. www.caffeumbria.com. ✆ **503/241-5300.** Sun–Wed 7am–7pm, Thurs–Sat 7am–8pm.

Moonstruck Chocolate Café ★★★ At this small, stand-up chocolateria, chocoholics can choose from a variety of hot and cold chocolate drinks and handmade (in Portland) chocolates. There's another (larger) Moonstruck in Northwest at 526 NW 23rd. (✆ **503/542-3400**). 608 SW Alder St. www.moonstruckchocolate.com. ✆ **503/241-0955**. Mon–Fri 8am–8pm, Sat 10am–8pm, Sun noon–6pm.

Stumptown ★★ Many a Portlander swears by the strong, flavorful coffee at this big, bare downtown cafe with an art-school aesthetic. Whether you go for the French press, a latte, or a double shot of espresso, you're sure to get a kick out of this brew. It's so popular, in fact, that it's become a chain, but it all started in Portland. Other local Stumptown locations: Ace Hotel, 1026 SW Stark St. (✆ **503/224-9060**); 4525 SE Division St. (✆ **503/230-7702**); 3356 SE Belmont St. (✆ **503/232-8889**). 128 SW Third Ave. www.stumptowncoffee.com. ✆ **503/295-6144.** Mon–Fri 6am–6pm, Sat–Sun 6am–7pm.

Tao of Tea ★★ Not a coffee drinker? Try this funky teahouse, which specializes in traditional Chinese tea service and feels like it could be in some Kathmandu back alley. 3430 SE Belmont St. www.taooftea.com. ✆ **503/736-0198.** Mon–Sat 11am–10pm, Sun 11am–9pm.

BAKERIES, GELATERIAS & PASTRY SHOPS

Pearl Bakery ★★ One of Portland's first artisan bakeries, Pearl Bakery is famous for its breads and European-style pastries. The *gibassier,* a chewy sweet roll fragrant with anise and orange, is a must-try. The gleaming bakery/cafe is also good for sandwiches, such as a roasted eggplant and tomato pesto on crusty bread. 102 NW Ninth Ave. www.pearlbakery.com. ✆ **503/827-0910. Mon–Fri 6:30am–5:30pm, Sat 7am–5pm, Sun 8am–4pm.**

St. Honoré Boulangerie ★★★ Not only does this place turn out mouth-wateringly authentic French pastries and breads, it makes great coffee and offers a good simple lunch menu, too. They now have branches at 3333 SE Division (✆ **971/279-4433**) and downtown at 501 SW Broadway (✆ **503/954-3049**). 2335 NW Thurman St. www.sainthonorebakery.com. ✆ **503/445-4342.** Daily 6:30am–8pm.

Salt & Straw ★★ We are now in the post–Ben & Jerry's and post-post–Baskin-Robbins world of ice cream, a time when people are willing to stand in line for half an hour and think nothing of plunking down $4 for a scoop of homemade ice cream in a flavor unheard of a few short years ago. Salt & Straw is New Portland's ice cream mecca, serving up flavors like salted caramel cupcake, bacon ale, freckled woodblock chocolate, and honey balsamic vinegar with cracked pepper. The Northwest location is also a bakery; the other two locations are "scoop shops": 3345 SE Division (✆ **503/208-2054**); 2035 NE Alberta St. (✆ **503/208-3867**). 838 NW 23rd Ave. www.saltandstraw.com. ✆ **971/271-8168.** Daily 10am–11pm.

Voodoo Doughnut ★ I'm not a fan of gooey doughnuts, but apparently everyone else in Portland is, because there is always a line here. Voodoo has become a tourist destination where new Portlanders bring their visiting parents and grandparents. Be forewarned that this corner hole-in-the-wall is not in the most savory location, and your wait to get in may be 15 minutes or more; but as I've said elsewhere, standing in line for food is now a Portland thing. Open 24 hours, Voodoo sells voodoo-doll doughnuts (pretzel through the heart, jelly filling), bacon-topped maple bars, vegan doughnuts, and even X-rated doughnuts, packaged in an immediately identifiable pink box. There's a second Voodoo Doughnut across the river at 1501 NE Davis St. (✆ **503/235-2666**). 22 SW Third Ave. www.voodoodoughnut.com. ✆ **503/241-4704.** Open 24 hrs.

SHOPPING

Portland has no sales tax, making it a popular shopping destination for Washingtonians, who cross the Columbia River to avoid paying their state's substantial sales tax.

The Shopping Scene

The retail scene in Portland is changing as fast as it is in the rest of country. Department stores like Macy's (formerly Meier & Frank) that were once downtown anchors, have disappeared or downsized and moved to mall locations. Thankfully, Portland still loves small specialty stores, vintage clothing shops (Portland loves anything vintage or retro), crafts stalls and food markets.

In the blocks around **Pioneer Courthouse Square**, once the heartland of all-purpose shopping in downtown Portland, you'll still find a flagship Nordstrom (and a nearby Nordstrom Rack), Nike, Columbia Sportswear, Apple, Microsoft, Pioneer Place Mall, and numerous upscale boutiques.

The **Pearl District** and **Nob Hill/Northwest,** both in Northwest Portland, are other destination shopping areas. Most of the Pearl District's best shopping is along NW 10th and 11th avenues going north from West Burnside Street. Here you'll find all kinds of trendy boutiques, art galleries, and home-furnishing stores. The best Nob Hill shopping is along NW 23rd Avenue going north from West Burnside Street. Both neighborhoods have block after block of interesting, often one-of-a-kind shops. Along NW 23rd Avenue you'll also find a few national chains like Urban Outfitters, Pottery Barn, and Restoration Hardware.

For shops with a more down-to-earth, funky flair, head southeast to the **Hawthorne District.** Though it's not as antiques-centric as it was a few years ago, SE 13th Avenue in **Sellwood** is still a strollable place to hunt for antiques and collectibles.

Most small stores in Portland are open Monday through Saturday from 9 or 10am to 5 or 6pm. Shopping malls are usually open Monday through Friday from 9 or 10am to 9pm, Saturday from 9 or 10am to between 6 and 9pm, and Sunday from 11am until 6pm. Most art galleries are closed on Monday.

Shopping A to Z

ANTIQUES

Antiques stores are scattered throughout Portland, but the **Sellwood** neighborhood just east of the Sellwood Bridge is the best place for concentrated shopping. One of the first "streetcar suburbs," it has a number of modest Victorian homes—trolley car drivers lived in many of them—and the quiet, unassuming ambience of a small town. **Antique Row,** on SE 13th Avenue between SE Malden and Clatsop streets, has the largest concentration of antiques and collectible stores in the state. Victorian, Mission, and Arts and Crafts wood and wicker furniture, linens, glassware, and paintings are among the items you'll find here. There are two large antiques malls (under the same ownership) on Milwaukie Avenue: **Stars,** 7030 SE Milwaukie Ave. (www.starsantique.com; ✆ **503/239-0346**); and **Stars & Splendid,** 7027 SE Milwaukie Ave. (✆ **503/235-5990**).

ART GALLERIES

On the **first Thursday** of the month, galleries in downtown Portland and the Pearl District schedule coordinated openings in the evening from about 6 to 9pm. In the past few years, this has become quite a scene, and streets are closed off so smaller vendors and craftspeople can also display and sell their wares. On the **last Thursday** of the month, shops and galleries in the **NE Alberta Street** neighborhood (see "Neighborhoods", p. 193) stage a similar event that is just as crowded and maybe a little more fun.

Augen Gallery ★★★ ART GALLERY When it opened over two decades ago, the Augen Gallery focused on internationally recognized artists such as Jim Dine, Andy Warhol, and David Hockney. Today the gallery has expanded its repertoire to regional contemporary painters and printmakers as well. 716 NW Davis St. www.augengallery.com. ✆ **503/546-5056.** Also at 817 SW Second Ave. ✆ 503/224-8182.

Bullseye Gallery ★★★ ART GALLERY Located in the Pearl District, the Bullseye Gallery is Portland's premier art-glass gallery and shows the work of acclaimed glass artists from around the world. This work goes way beyond pretty vases. 300 NW 13th Ave. www.bullseyegallery.com. ✆ **503/227-0222.**

Portland Art Museum Rental Sales Gallery ★★ ART GALLERY This downtown gallery has a wide selection of works by more than 250 Northwest artists. Sales here help support the Portland Art Museum. 1237 SW 10th Ave. www.portlandartmuseum.org. ✆ **503/224-0674.**

Quintana Galleries ★★★ ART GALLERY Quintana is a virtual museum of Native American art, selling everything from Northwest Coast Indian masks to Navajo rugs to contemporary paintings and sculptures by Native American artists. The galleries also carry a smattering of vintage Native American artifacts from both the Northwest and the Southwest, and they now have a Mexican collection as well. The jewelry selection is outstanding. 124 NW Ninth Ave. www.quintanagalleries.com. ✆ **800/321-1729** or 503/223-1729.

Russo Lee Gallery ★★★ ART GALLERY The focus here is on Northwest contemporary artists, showcasing emerging talents as well as the estates of well-known regional artists. This gallery has been in business for more than 25 years and is highly respected. 805 NW 21st Ave. www.laurarusso.com. ✆ **800/925-7152** or 503/226-2754.

BOOKS

Amazon Books ★★ BOOKSTORE Amazon opened its first brick-and-mortar bookstore in Seattle and has now opened a store in Portland at Washington Square Mall in Tigard. Here you'll find a selective inventory of titles based on sales trends and reviews from the retail giant's online division. You can also try out all of Amazon's tablet readers and take crash courses in how to manage Alexa in the Amazon Echo. 9585 SW Washington Square Dr. www.amazon.com. ✆ **503/620-9933.** Daily 10am–9pm.

Barnes & Noble Booksellers ★★★ BOOKSTORE Barnes & Noble has a big, wonderfully browsable bookstore in Lloyd Center with a great selection of current bestsellers and still-in-print titles in all genres. If they don't have it, they'll order it for you. There's another B&N at Clackamas Town Center Mall, 12000 SE 82nd Ave (✆ **503/788-3464**. Both stores host regular author events, booksignings, and book groups. 1317 Lloyd Center. www.bn.com. ✆ **503/249-0800.** Daily 9am–9pm.

Powell's City of Books ★★★ BOOKSTORE Powell's covers three floors on an entire city block. Every booklover in Portland knows about it and has probably shopped there numerous times in the last 40 years. It's a long-standing Portland tourist attraction and remains an all-round fabulous bookstore, with roughly a million books on the shelves. Both new and used are shelved side by side. Pick up a store map to help guide you to the various color-coded rooms. Serious book collectors won't want to miss a visit to the Rare Book Room. City of Books has several satellite stores, including **Powell's Books for Home and Garden,** 3747 SE Hawthorne Blvd.; **Powell's Books on Hawthorne,** 3723 SE Hawthorne Blvd.; and **Powell's Books at PDX,** Portland International Airport, 7000 NE Airport Way, Ste. 2250. 1005 W. Burnside St. www.powells.com. ✆ **800/878-7323** or 503/228-4651. Daily 9am–11pm.

CRAFTS

Hoffman Gallery ★★ ART GALLERY/CRAFTS The Hoffman Gallery is on the campus of the Oregon College of Art and Craft, one of the nation's foremost crafts education centers since its founding in 1907. The gallery hosts installations and group shows by local, national, and international artists. The adjacent gift shop has a good selection of handcrafted items and photography. 8245 SW Barnes Rd. www.ocac.edu. ✆ **503/297-5544.**

The Real Mother Goose ★ ART GALLERY/CRAFTS In business for decades, Mother Goose showcases fine contemporary American crafts, including ceramics, art glass, jewelry, wooden furniture, and sculptural works. Hundreds of craftspeople and artists from all over the U.S. are represented here. 901 SW Yamhill St. www.therealmothergoose.com. ✆ **503/223-9510.** Also at Portland International Airport, Main Terminal (✆ 503/284-9929).

Twist ★★ ART GALLERY/CRAFTS This large store has quite a massive selection of wildly colorful and imaginative furniture, crockery, glassware, and lamps, and also a limited but impressive selection of handmade jewelry by artists from around the United States. 30 NW 23rd Pl. www.twistonline.com. ✆ **503/224-0334.**

DEPARTMENT STORES & FLAGSHIPS

Columbia Sportswear Company ★★ SPORTSWEAR The flagship store for Portland's homegrown and highly regarded Columbia Sportswear features outdoor-oriented fashions and accessories for men, women, and children. 911 SW Broadway. www.columbia.com. ✆ **503/226-6800.**

Columbia Sportswear Company Factory Outlet Store ★★ SPORTSWEAR This outlet store in the Sellwood neighborhood south of downtown and across the river sells remainders and past-season styles from the local sportswear company, which is one of the Northwest's premier outdoor-clothing manufacturers. You'll pay 30 to 50% less here than you will at the downtown flagship store. 1323 SE Tacoma St. www.columbia.com. ✆ **503/238-0118.**

John Helmer Haberdasher ★★ CLOTHING STORE/HATS Whether you're looking for a straw boater, a beret, a wide-brimmed Stetson, a felt fedora, a Panama, or a top hat, you'll find it at this classic haberdashery, which opened in 1921. There are also plenty of men's suits, slacks, and sports jackets. The outlay is very traditional, pretty conservative, and definitely Old Portland. 969 SW Broadway. www.johnhelmer.com. ✆ **866/855-4976** or 503/223-4976.

Nike Factory Company Store ★★ SPORTSWEAR The Nike outlet is one season behind the current season at Nike Portland (see below), selling swoosh-brand running, aerobic, tennis, golf, basketball, kids, and you-name-it shoes, clothing, and accessories, all at discounted prices. 2650 NE Martin Luther King Jr. Blvd. www.nike.com. ✆ **503/281-5901.**

Nike Portland ★★★ SPORTSWEAR The Starbucks of sportswear, Nike is an international super-brand that started right here in the outdoor-loving, sports-oriented Northwest. The Portland flagship store moved to this location in 2013. Like Powell's City of Books, this is a store that doubles as a tourist destination. You'll be greeted upon arrival, and you'll marvel at how little is displayed and how much it all costs. 638 SW Fifth Ave. (at SW Morrison St.). www.nike.com. ✆ **503/221-6453.**

Nordstrom ★★★ DEPARTMENT STORE Directly across the street from Pioneer Courthouse Square, Nordstrom is a top-of-the-line department store that originated in Seattle and takes great pride in its personal service and friendliness. It is devoted almost exclusively to clothing; shoppers can also find top-notch shoes, jewelry, accessories, and cosmetics here. 701 SW Broadway. www.nordstrom.com. ✆ **503/224-6666.** Also at 1001 Lloyd Center. (✆ 503/287-2444) and 9700 SW Washington Square Rd., Tigard (✆ 503/620-0555).

Nordstrom Rack ★★★ DISCOUNT DEPARTMENT STORE They've ratcheted things up and don't have the kind of unbelievable deals that used to lure me here, but you can still find great bargains on high-quality, still-in-fashion looks for men and women. 245 SW Morrison. www.nordstrom.com. ✆ **503/299-1815.**

Portland Outdoor Store ★★★ CLOTHING/ACCESSORIES In business since 1919, this Western-wear store is a Portland institution that feels little changed from decades ago. The big neon sign out front and the old general store atmosphere inside are enough to draw even people who aren't into playing cowboy or cowgirl. Look for Pendleton shirts, leather boots and belts, and Western garb that's meant to be worn in real-life situations. 304 SW Third Ave. ✆ **503/222-1051.**

Pendleton Home Store ★★★ CLOTHING Pendleton wool is as much a part of life in the Northwest as forests and salmon. This company's fine wool fashions for men and women define a casual, comfortable, and warm Northwestern look, and beautiful Pendleton blankets have warmed generations of Northwesterners through long, chilly winters. 220 NW Broadway. www.pendleton-usa.com. ✆ **503/535-5444.**

GIFTS, SOUVENIRS & SPECIALTY STORES

Canoe ★★★ HOUSEWARES/GLASSWARE/HOME DECOR This is the only store in downtown Portland where I actually see people window-shopping. Canoe is simple and sleek and sells only high-quality, well-made items. The emphasis here is on clean, simple, timeless designs. There's a little bit of everything here, although look especially for Finnish and Swedish glassware, furniture, and lighting. 1233 SW 10th Ave. www.canoeonline.net. ✆ **503/889-8545.**

Made in Oregon ★★ LOCAL SPECIALTIES This is your one-stop shop for all manner of made-in-Oregon gifts, food, and clothing. Every product sold is either grown, caught, or made in Oregon. You'll find smoked salmon, filberts, jams and jellies, Pendleton woolens, and Oregon wines. All branches are open daily. 340 SW Morrison St., Ste. 1300 (in Pioneer Place). www.madeinoregon.com. ✆ **866/257-0938** or 503/273-8719. Also at Portland International Airport (✆ 503/282-7827) and Lloyd Center mall (✆ 503/282-7636).

MALLS & SHOPPING CENTERS

Lloyd Center ★★ SHOPPING MALL One of the first covered shopping malls in the country—it opened in 1960—Lloyd Center has kept up with the retail times and remains a popular shopping destination with a Nordstrom, a Macy's, and scores of other small to mid-sized stores, chains, and boutiques. It is also famous for its year-round indoor ice-skating rink. There's a food court and movie theaters, too. My favorite store is **Joe Brown's Caramel Corn** (✆ **503/2872143**), a little slot store beside the skating rink that for over 30 years has been selling absolutely the best caramel corn I have ever found. Between NE Halsey St. and NE Multnomah St., and NE 9th Ave. and NE 15th Ave. ✆ **503/282-2511.**

Pioneer Place ★★ SHOPPING MALL Just a block from Pioneer Courthouse Square in downtown, this is Portland's most upscale shopping center. Pioneer Place is filled with stores selling designer fashions, jewelry, housewares, bath and cosmetic products, children's games, and much more. There's a food court and movie theaters as well. 700 SW Fifth Ave. (between Third and Fifth aves.). www.pioneerplace.com. ✆ **503/228-5800.**

MARKETS

Portland Farmers Market ★★★ OUTDOOR MARKET Everyone lights up when they come to this outdoor market, and I don't mean cigarettes. The finest vegetables, fruits, and produce from local farmers brighten shoppers' days, as do foraged mushrooms, handcrafted cheeses, plants, flowers, fish, eggs, spices, jams, jellies, baked goods, and all manner of artisan goodies. Musicians play; people stroll, talk, and sample; and it's Portland all the way. The market is held on Saturdays from 8:30am to 2:30pm on the campus of Portland State University in downtown Portland; it starts up in mid-March and runs until a week before Christmas. South Park Blocks, SW Park and SW Montgomery St. www.portlandfarmersmarket.org.

Portland Saturday Market ★ LOCAL CRAFTS/MARKET The Portland Saturday Market (held on both Sat and Sun) is a Portland tradition. Every weekend, more than 300 craftspeople sell their wares at this open-air market beside and beneath the Burnside Bridge in Waterfront Park. Some of it is good, some of it is dreck. In addition to the dozens of crafts stalls, you'll find ethnic and unusual foods, and lots of free entertainment. The market is open from the first weekend in March to Christmas Eve, Saturdays 10am to 5pm and Sundays 11am to 4:30pm. Waterfront Park and Ankeny Plaza, SW Naito Pkwy. www.portlandsaturdaymarket.com. ✆ **503/222-6072.**

THE PERFORMING ARTS & NIGHTLIFE

Portland is Oregon's cultural capital, and the city's symphony orchestra, ballet, and opera are all well regarded. A lively theater scene includes a modicum of mainstream and a firestorm of fringe theater companies offering classic and contemporary plays. In summer, festivals move the city's cultural activities outdoors to **Tom McCall Waterfront Park, Washington Park,** and the **Oregon Zoo.**

To find out what's going on during your visit, pick up or call up a copy of *Willamette Week* (**www.wweek.com**), Portland's free weekly arts and entertainment newspaper. *The Oregonian* (**www.oregonlive.com**), the city's daily newspaper, also publishes entertainment-related information in its Friday A&E section and in the Sunday edition of the paper.

Music at the Zoo

When summer hits, Portlanders like to head outdoors to hear music. The city's top outdoor music series is held at the **Oregon Zoo,** 4001 SW Canyon Rd. (www.oregonzoo.org; ✆ **503/226-1561;** see p. 158), which brings in the likes of Pat Benatar, Garrison Keillor, Joan Baez, Indigo Girls, and Ladysmith Black Mambazo. You can picnic on the lawn—and, believe it or not, there aren't any mosquitoes! It's best to arrive early to claim a good spot. The sound system is state-of-the-art. And the crowd is pure Portland—parents with kids, boomers, hipsters, and Gen-Xers, all rolled into one happy summer scene.

Portland Performing Arts & Nightlife

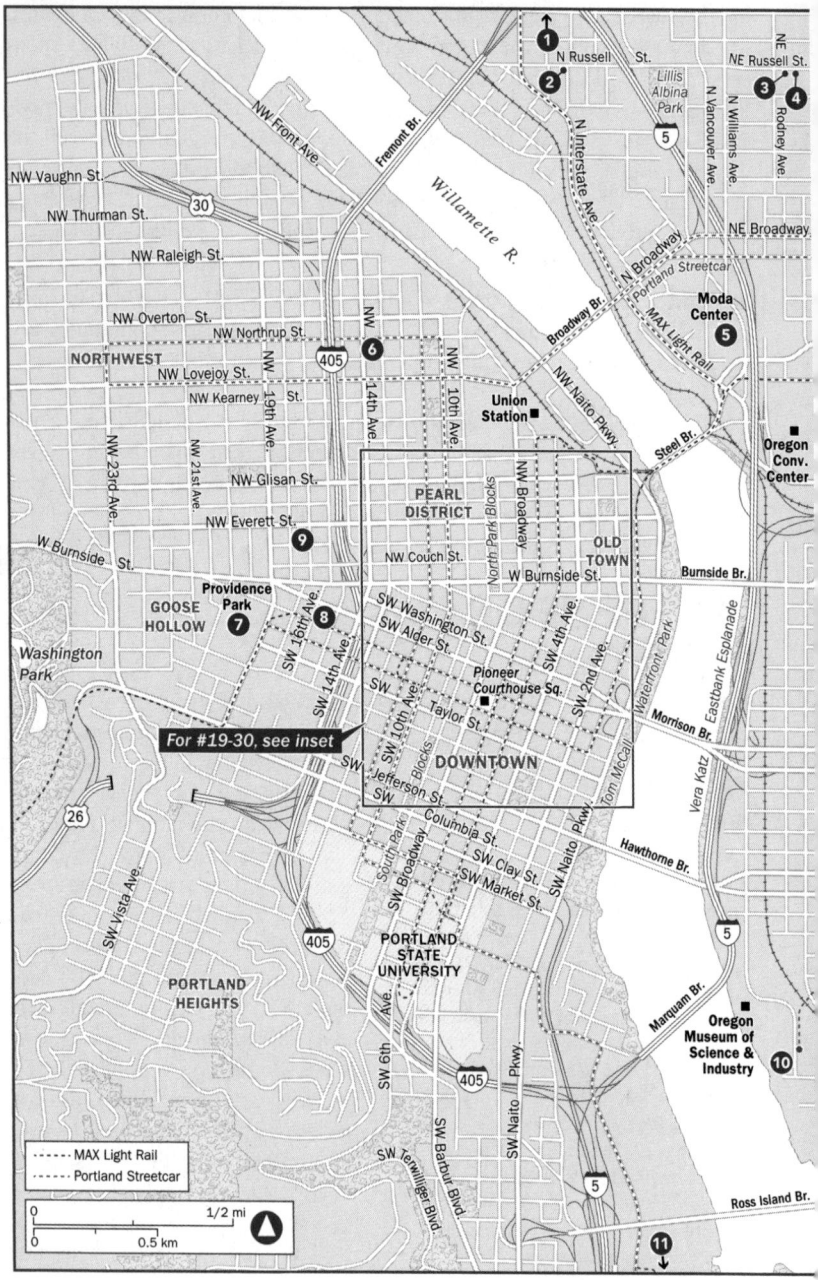

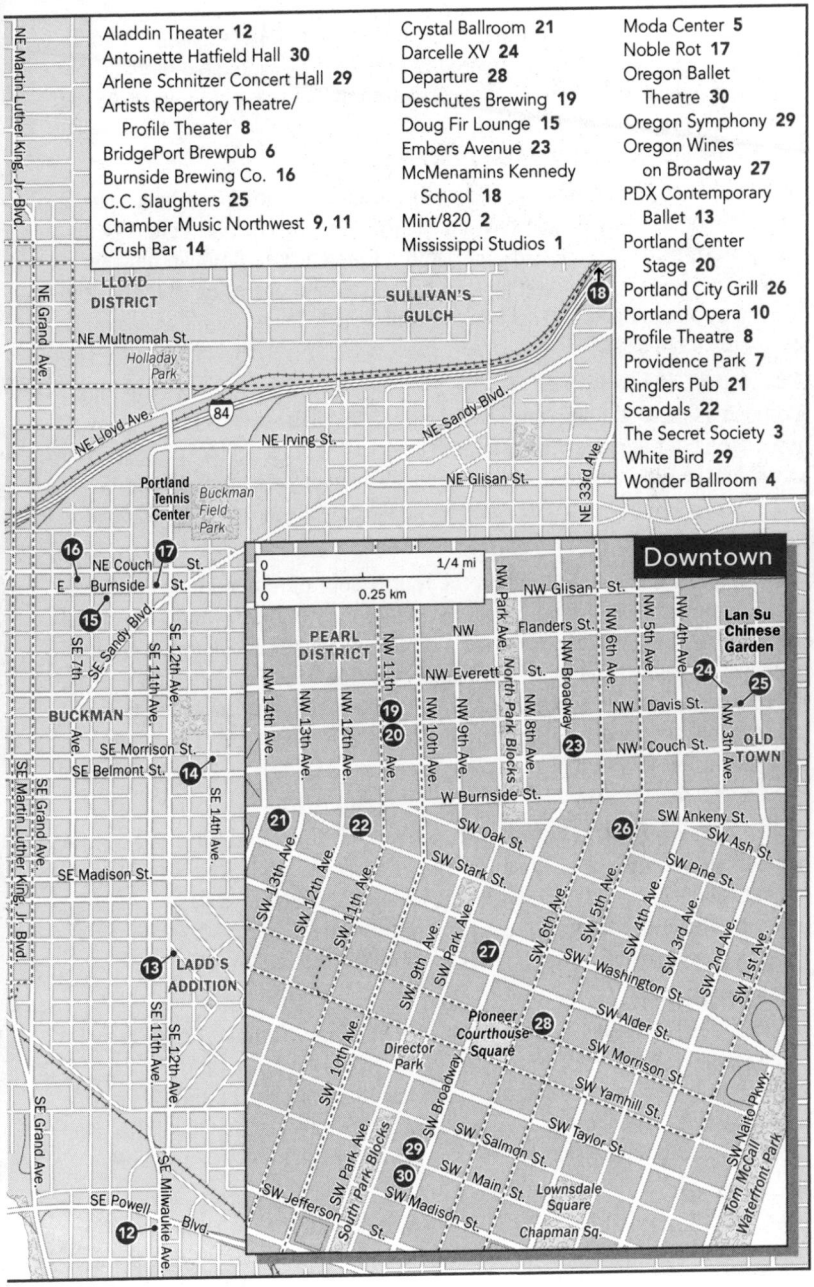
Aladdin Theater 12
Antoinette Hatfield Hall 30
Arlene Schnitzer Concert Hall 29
Artists Repertory Theatre/ Profile Theater 8
BridgePort Brewpub 6
Burnside Brewing Co. 16
C.C. Slaughters 25
Chamber Music Northwest 9, 11
Crush Bar 14
Crystal Ballroom 21
Darcelle XV 24
Departure 28
Deschutes Brewing 19
Doug Fir Lounge 15
Embers Avenue 23
McMenamins Kennedy School 18
Mint/820 2
Mississippi Studios 1
Moda Center 5
Noble Rot 17
Oregon Ballet Theatre 30
Oregon Symphony 29
Oregon Wines on Broadway 27
PDX Contemporary Ballet 13
Portland Center Stage 20
Portland City Grill 26
Portland Opera 10
Profile Theatre 8
Providence Park 7
Ringlers Pub 21
Scandals 22
The Secret Society 3
White Bird 29
Wonder Ballroom 4
Downtown
0 1/4 mi
0 0.25 km
LLOYD DISTRICT
SULLIVAN'S GULCH
NE Multnomah St.
Holladay Park
NE Lloyd Ave.
NE Sandy Blvd.
NE Irving St.
NE Glisan St.
NE 33rd Ave.
NE Martin Luther King, Jr. Blvd.
NE Grand Ave.
Portland Tennis Center
Buckman Field Park
NE Couch St.
E Burnside St.
SE Sandy Blvd.
SE 7th Ave.
SE 11th Ave.
SE 12th Ave.
BUCKMAN
SE Morrison St.
SE Belmont St.
SE 14th Ave.
SE Madison St.
SE Grand Ave.
SE Martin Luther King, Jr. Blvd.
LADD'S ADDITION
SE 11th Ave.
SE 12th Ave.
SE Grand Ave.
SE Milwaukie Ave.
SE Powell Blvd.
PEARL DISTRICT
NW Everett St.
NW Glisan St.
NW Flanders St.
NW Davis St.
NW Couch St.
W Burnside St.
SW Oak St.
SW Stark St.
SW Washington St.
SW Alder St.
SW Morrison St.
SW Yamhill St.
SW Taylor St.
SW Salmon St.
SW Main St.
SW Madison St.
SW Jefferson St.
NW 14th Ave.
NW 13th Ave.
NW 12th Ave.
NW 11th Ave.
NW 10th Ave.
NW 9th Ave.
NW Park Ave.
North Park Blocks
NW Broadway
NW 8th Ave.
NW 6th Ave.
NW 5th Ave.
NW 4th Ave.
NW 3th Ave.
SW 13th Ave.
SW 12th Ave.
SW 11th Ave.
SW 10th Ave.
SW 9th Ave.
SW Park Ave.
SW Broadway
SW 6th Ave.
SW 5th Ave.
SW 4th Ave.
SW 3rd Ave.
SW 2nd Ave.
SW 1st Ave.
SW Park Ave.
South Park Blocks
Director Park
Pioneer Courthouse Square
Lownsdale Square
Chapman Sq.
Lan Su Chinese Garden
OLD TOWN
SW Ankeny St.
SW Ash St.
SW Pine St.
SW Naito Pkwy.
Tom McCall Waterfront Park
12
13
14
15
16
17
18
19
20
21
22
23
24
25
26
27
28
29
30

The Bar & Pub Scene

BARS

Departure ★★ This rooftop bar and restaurant atop **The Nines** hotel in downtown Portland serves good food but also has a remarkable outdoor terrace, very unusual in Portland. People definitely get dressed up to make the scene here, and most of them are under 40—er, make that 30. 525 SW Morrison St. www.departureportland.com. ✆ **503/802-5370.**

Mint/820 ★★★ Mixologist Lucy Brennan, owner of this swanky place, single-handedly turned Portland into a town full of cocktail connoisseurs. Using fresh fruit juices, purées, and unusual ingredients, Brennan reinvented the cocktail and set in motion the city's craft cocktail obsession. Beet-infused martini or creamy avocado cocktail, anyone? 816 N. Russell St. www.mintand820.com. ✆ **503/284-5518.**

Portland City Grill ★★ Located way up on the 30th floor of "Big Pink," Portland's tallest building, this restaurant/bar has the best view in all of downtown. Come for the great happy hour (Mon–Sat 4–7pm and 9pm–close) so you can catch the sunset and a little live piano music with your singles scene. Unico/U.S. Bancorp Tower, 111 SW Fifth Ave. www.portlandcitygrill.com. ✆ **503/450-0030.**

WINE BARS

Noble Rot ★★★ Located on the fourth floor of a modern Lower Burnside building, this stylish wine bar has a killer view of the downtown Portland skyline. You can get various wine flights, and there are plenty of Oregon vintages available. The wine bar also serves excellent food. Signature menu faves include an endive, beet, blue cheese, and hazelnut salad; onion tart; and a super mac and cheese. (For the record, noble rot is a type of grape fungus utilized in the production of sweet dessert wines.) 1111 E. Burnside St. www.noblerotpdx.com. ✆ **503/233-1999.**

Oregon Wines on Broadway ★★★ With just a handful of stools at the bar and a couple of cozy tables, this tiny place is the best spot in Portland to learn about Oregon wines. On any given night there will be 30 Oregon pinot noirs available by the glass, and five white wines as well. 515 SW Broadway. www.oregonwinesonbroadway.com. ✆ **800/943-8858** or 503/228-4655.

BREWPUBS

Portland, or "Beervana," sits at the epicenter of the Northwest craft brewing explosion.

Brewpubs of all shapes and sizes have become central to Portland's identity, and they are great spots to mix with the locals, order some good food, and taste the extraordinary range of handcrafted beers that are now available.

Downtown

Ringlers Pub ★ BREWPUB With mosaic pillars framing the bar, Indonesian antiques, and big old signs all around, this cavernous place is about as

BREWING UP AN empire

With dozens of brewpubs in the metropolitan area, the McMenamins chain is Portland's biggest brewpub empire. The McMenamin brothers didn't exactly start the Portland brewpub phenomenon, but they have expanded its boundaries and put their stamp on the beer culture of Portland by saving, restoring, and converting several historic buildings—including a former poor farm and an elementary school. They also originated a brewpub concept where patrons can sip beer, eat pizza, and watch a movie. Some of the properties (**Crystal Hotel ★** and **Kennedy School ★★★,** for example, see p. 204 and see below, respectively) now serve as funky hotels with restaurants. The McMenamins' commitment to architectural preservation and their strong belief in family-friendly neighborhood pubs have made their properties popular among all age groups. If I had to recommend one McMenamins' property to visit, it would be Kennedy School. McMenamins' beers can hold their own with any brew in Portland, and the food is filling and tasty, but it's not haute cuisine. For a complete list of the brothers' brewpubs, breweries, and historic hotels, visit **www.mcmenamins.com**.

eclectic a brewpub as you'll ever find. A block away are the two associated pubs of **Ringlers Annex,** 1223 SW Stark St. (✆ **503/384-2700**), which occupies a flatiron-shaped building. One of these pubs is below street level with a beer cellar feel, and the other has walls of multi-paned glass. 1332 W. Burnside St. www.mcmenamins.com. ✆ **503/225-0627.**

Northwest Portland

BridgePort Brewpub ★ BREWPUB Large and perennially busy, this brewpub and restaurant in a former warehouse in the Pearl District is one of Portland's oldest. There are eight or more BridgePort beers on tap and a filling menu of pub food. 1313 NW Marshall St. www.bridgeportbrew.com. ✆ **503/241-3612.**

Deschutes Brewing ★★ BREWPUB Located in a converted industrial space, this brewpub has a mountain lodge style similar to that of the famous Timberline Lodge on Mount Hood. There is always a wide range of beers on tap. 210 NW 11th Ave. www.deschutesbrewery.com. ✆ **503/296-4906.**

Southeast

Burnside Brewing Co. ★★★ BREWPUB This gastro-brewpub is a standout because of its creative cooking and industrial-chic decor. Oh yes, the beers are great, too. 701 E. Burnside St. www.burnsidebrewco.com. ✆ **503/946-8151.**

Northeast & North Portland

McMenamins Kennedy School ★★★ BREWPUB The local McMenamins brewpub empire took an old Northeast school and turned it into a brewpub, beer garden, movie-theater pub, and even a hotel (see p. 178). Order up a pint and wander the halls to check out all the cool artwork. 5736 NE 33rd Ave. www.kennedyschool.com. ✆ **503/249-3983.**

The Club & Music Scene

ROCK, BLUES & FOLK

Aladdin Theater ★★★ This former movie theater now serves as one of Portland's main venues for touring performers. The very diverse musical spectrum represented includes blues, rock, ethnic, country, folk, and jazz. 3017 SE Milwaukie Ave. www.aladdin-theater.com. ✆ **503/234-9694.**

Crystal Ballroom ★★★ The Crystal Ballroom first opened in 1914 and has since hosted performers ranging from Rudolf Valentino (who came to dance the tango) and early jazz musicians to James Brown, Marvin Gaye, and the Grateful Dead. The McMenamin Brothers (of local brewing fame) renovated the ballroom in 1997 and refurbished its famous "floating" dance floor, which sits on ball bearings. The venue now hosts a variety of performances and special events nearly every night of the week. **Lola's Room,** a smaller version of the Ballroom, is on the second floor and also has a floating dance floor. **Ringlers Pub** occupies the ground floor. 1332 W. Burnside St. www.crystalballroompdx.com. ✆ **503/225-0047.** Cover $5–$30.

Doug Fir Lounge ★★ Log cabin styling meets Scandinavian modern at this eclectic underground alt-rock club in the lower Burnside neighborhood of southeast Portland. The club is associated with the **Jupiter Hotel** (see p. 179). 830 E. Burnside St. www.dougfirlounge.com. ✆ **503/231-9663.** Cover $10–$20.

Mississippi Studios ★★ This little performance space in north Portland has become one of the city's premier alternative music venues; the calendar here is both eclectic and affordable. 3939 N. Mississippi Ave. www.mississippistudios.com. ✆ **503/288-3895.** Cover $5–20.

Wonder Ballroom ★ Originally opened in 1914 as the hall for the Ancient Order of Hibernians (I didn't know Hibernians could dance) and now on the National Register of Historic Places, the Wonder Ballroom is another of Portland's popular restored ballrooms rededicated to everything from hip-hop to swing to bluegrass. Best of all, **Toro Bravo** (p. 189), one of my favorite Portland restaurants, is on the same block. 128 NE Russell St. www.wonderballroom.com. ✆ **503/284-8686.** Cover $10–$25.

JAZZ

The Secret Society ★★ Gypsy jazz, vintage jazz, Texas swing, big band, jug band, klezmer—you just won't find a more eclectic blend of music than at this second-floor nightclub in north Portland. Not only does this place showcase some of Portland's most distinctive acts, it also does free 6pm shows several nights a week. 116 NE Russell St. www.secretsociety.net. ✆ **503/493-3600.**

CABARET

Darcelle XV Showplace ★★★ In business since 1967 and run by Portland's best-loved drag queen, this cabaret is a campy, comic Portland institution with a female-impersonator show that's been a huge hit for years. There are shows Wednesday through Saturday, catering more to a suburban straight audience than a gay one. Darcelle is the oldest performing drag queen in the U.S. 208 NW Third Ave. www.darcellexv.com. ✆ **503/222-5338.** Cover $20.

The Gay & Lesbian Nightlife Scene

DANCE CLUBS

C.C. Slaughters ★★ Popular with a young crowd, this big Old Town nightclub and martini lounge spins different dance sounds every night. 219 NW Davis St. www.ccslaughterspdx.com. ✆ **503/248-9135.** No cover.

Crush Bar ★★★ This hetero-friendly Southeast bar attracts a diverse crowd and has DJs spinning dance tunes Friday and Saturday nights. 1400 SE Morrison St. www.crushbar.com. ✆ **503/235-8150.** Cover $5–$10 weekends.

The Embers Avenue ★★ Though primarily a gay disco, Embers is also popular with straights. It's a big, sprawling place with lots of flashing lights on the dance floor and sweaty bodies going until the early morning. 110 NW Broadway. ✆ **503/222-3082.** Cover $5–$7 weekends.

Scandals ★★ A gay Portland institution since 1979, this friendly bar and restaurant has karaoke nights, live bands, and daily specials. 1125 SW Stark St. www.scandalspdx.com. ✆ **503/227-5887.** No cover.

Dance

Oregon Ballet Theatre ★★ OBT is best loved for its performances of *The Nutcracker* every December. The rest of the season includes other classics along with contemporary ballets. Keller Auditorium, 222 SW Clay St. www.obt.org. ✆ **888/922-5538** or 503/222-5538.

PDX Contemporary Ballet ★★ This young company synthesizes contemporary and classical ballet movement to create riveting original performances. Their pledge: "If our performances don't challenge a first time viewer's expectations about ballet, we refund their ticket." Every show premieres new choreography, and their dancers hail from all across the U.S.1734 SE 12th Ave. www.pdxcb.com.

White Bird ★★★ Fans of modern dance should check out what's being produced by White Bird—and where, as venues can vary. This organization brings in celebrated companies like Twyla Tharp Dance, the Merce Cunningham Dance Company, the Paul Taylor Dance Company, and the Alvin Ailey American Dance Theater, as well as emerging international dance troupes of all kinds. Arlene Schnitzer Concert Hall, 1037 SW Broadway. www.whitebird.org. ✆ **503/245-1600.**

Opera, Dance & Classical Music

Oregon Symphony ★★★ Founded in 1896, the Oregon Symphony is the oldest symphony orchestra on the West Coast. Each year between September and May, the symphony stages several series, including classical, pops, and children's concerts. Under the leadership of conductor Carlos Kalmar, the Oregon Symphony has become one of the top orchestras in the U.S. Arlene Schnitzer Concert Hall, 1037 SW Broadway. www.orsymphony.org. ✆ **800/228-7343** or 503/228-1353.

Portland Opera ★★ This highly regarded company offers five different productions a year that include grand opera, contemporary opera, chamber opera, and occasionally world premieres. The season runs September through May. Check the website for performance venues because Portland Opera no longer performs exclusively at Keller Auditorium. www.portlandopera.org. ✆ **503/241-1407** or 503/241-1802 for box office.

Chamber Music Northwest ★★★ Summer is the time for Portland's annual, outstanding chamber music binge, a month-long series that starts in late June and attracts the world's finest chamber musicians. Performances are held at Reed College's Kaul Auditorium and St. Mary's Cathedral. www.cmnw.org. ✆ **503/294-6400.**

The Performing Arts

For the most part, the Portland performing arts scene revolves around the **Portland Center for the Performing Arts (PCPA),** 1111 SW Broadway (www.portland5.com; ✆ **503/248-4335**), which comprises five performance spaces in three buildings. The **Arlene Schnitzer Concert Hall ★★,** 1037 SW Broadway, known locally as the Schnitz, is a restored 1920s movie palace that still displays the original Portland theater sign and marquee out front and is home to the Oregon Symphony. This hall also hosts popular music performances, lectures, and many other special events. Directly across Main Street from the Schnitz, at 1111 SW Broadway, is the **Antoinette Hatfield Hall.** This building, constructed in the 1980s, houses the **Newmark** and **Dolores Winningstad theaters** and **Brunish Hall.** The two theaters host productions by local and visiting companies and performers.

A few blocks away from this concentration of venues is the 3,000-seat **Keller Auditorium,** 222 SW Clay St., where groups like **Portland Opera** and the **Oregon Ballet Theatre** perform (they use other venues as well), and which serves as a venue for traveling Broadway shows.

One other downtown performing arts venue worth checking out is the **Old Church ★★,** 1422 SW 11th Ave. (www.oldchurch.org; ✆ **503/222-2031**). Built in 1883, this wooden Carpenter Gothic church is a Portland landmark and serves as a concert venue; every Wednesday at noon it hosts free lunchtime concerts.

Theater

Artists Repertory Theatre ★★ This long-established theater company stages Broadway hits and often includes a world premiere in its season. 1515 SW Morrison St. www.artistsrep.org. ✆ **503/241-1278.**

Portland Center Stage ★★ Portland's largest professional theater company performs in the Gerding Theater at the Armory, a converted armory in the Pearl District. The company stages a combination of classic and contemporary plays and musicals during its September-to-June season. 128 NW 11th Ave. www.pcs.org. ✆ **503/445-3700.**

Profile Theatre ★ Profile stages the works of only one playwright per year (the hits *and* the flops), allowing theatergoers to see the full spectrum of an artist's creative development. They share space with Artists Repertory Theater. 1515 SW Morrison St. www.profiletheatre.org. ✆ **503/242-0080.**

SPECTATOR SPORTS

Moda Center is home court for the **Portland Trail Blazers,** a stage for superstar concerts, and the main focal point of Portland's **Rose Quarter.** In addition to the Moda Center, this sports and entertainment neighborhood includes Veterans Memorial Coliseum (once the Trail Blazers' home, now host to a junior ice hockey team) and several restaurants and bars. Tickets to events are sold through the **Rose Quarter** box office (www.rosequarter.com; ✆ **503/797-9619**). To reach the stadiums, take the Rose Quarter exit off I-5. Parking is expensive, so you might want to consider the easy and inexpensive MAX light rail line from downtown Portland. **Providence Park** (www.providencepark pdx.com; ✆ **503/554-5400**), near downtown, is a much-smaller outdoor sports venue used for soccer (Portland Timbers) and Division I football. It's easily reached by MAX light rail and on foot from downtown.

Basketball

The NBA's **Portland Trail Blazers** (www.nba.com/blazers; ✆ **503/797-9600**) do well enough every year to have earned a very loyal following. Unfortunately, they have a habit of not quite making it all the way to the top. The Blazers pound the boards at the Moda Center (see above). See website for current schedule and ticket information.

Soccer

Major League Soccer's **Portland Timbers** (www.portlandtimbers.com; ✆ **503/553-5550**), play at **Providence Park,** 1844 SW Morrison St., near downtown Portland (see above).

DAY TRIPS FROM PORTLAND

Why do you think everyone loves Portland so much? Of course it's the city itself, but it's also because of what's just outside the city. Some of the most beautifully diverse landscapes in the country (okay, let's say the world) can be visited and enjoyed on day trips from Portland. Below, I've provided a handful of options that range from the dramatic splendor of Mount Hood and the Columbia River Gorge to the rural, rolling hills of the wine country. You could also make a day trip to the Oregon coast. Astoria, Seaside, Cannon Beach, Lincoln City, and the Three Capes Scenic Loop—all described in chapter 6—are excellent day trip possibilities.

THE WINE COUNTRY

Newberg: 25 miles SW of Portland; Dundee: 27 miles SW of Portland; McMinnville: 38 miles SW of Portland

Oregon is famous for its pinot noirs, but these exceptional wines are produced in such small quantities that they usually can't be found outside the region. They are part and parcel of Portland's palate and available at every good restaurant and wine store—even supermarkets. If you want to sample a few of Oregon's exemplary wines and enjoy scenic countryside at the same time, spend an afternoon or weekend visiting the wineries in what Portlanders simply call the "wine country."

Wine is grown in more than one area of Oregon, but the part of the wine country closest to Portland is in the **North Willamette Valley,** which begins in the town of **Newberg** and extends south to **McMinnville** along Ore. 99W. Throughout this region you'll find good restaurants and inns, so you'll never be too far between wining and dining or sipping and sleeping.

Essentials

GETTING THERE You'll find the heart of wine country between Newberg and McMinnville, along Ore. 99W, which heads southwest from Portland.

VISITOR INFORMATION The **Willamette Valley Visitors Association** (www.oregonwinecountry.org; ✆ **866/548-5018**) is a good source of information on this area. For more about the Oregon wine scene, including a calendar of winery events, view the online version of ***Oregon Wine Press*** (www.oregonwinepress.com), a monthly magazine available at area wine shops and wineries. The **Willamette Valley Wineries Association** (www.willamettewines.com; ✆ **503/646-2985**) publishes a free map and guide to the local wineries. You can pick up a copy at almost any area winery.

FESTIVALS The most prestigious festival of the year, and certainly the most expensive ($1,295 for the weekend ticket, $125 to $190 for individual events) is the **International Pinot Noir Celebration,** in McMinnville (www.ipnc.org; ✆ **800/775-4762** or 503/472-8964), held every year on the last weekend in July or first weekend in August. The 3-day event includes tastings, food, music, and seminars. This high-end event is for wine and food connoisseurs and snobs and has to be reserved far in advance. It's better to simply make your own tour of the vineyards.

Touring the Wineries

Forget pretentiousness, grand villas, celebrity wineries, and snobbish waiters—this is not Napa Valley. Oregon wineries for the most part are still small establishments—although, like everything else in and around Portland, some of them are now expanding their vineyards and tasting rooms. Yes, more well-capitalized wineries have been opening with the sole purpose of producing high-priced pinot noir, but most of the region's wineries are still family-owned and -operated and produce moderately priced wines.

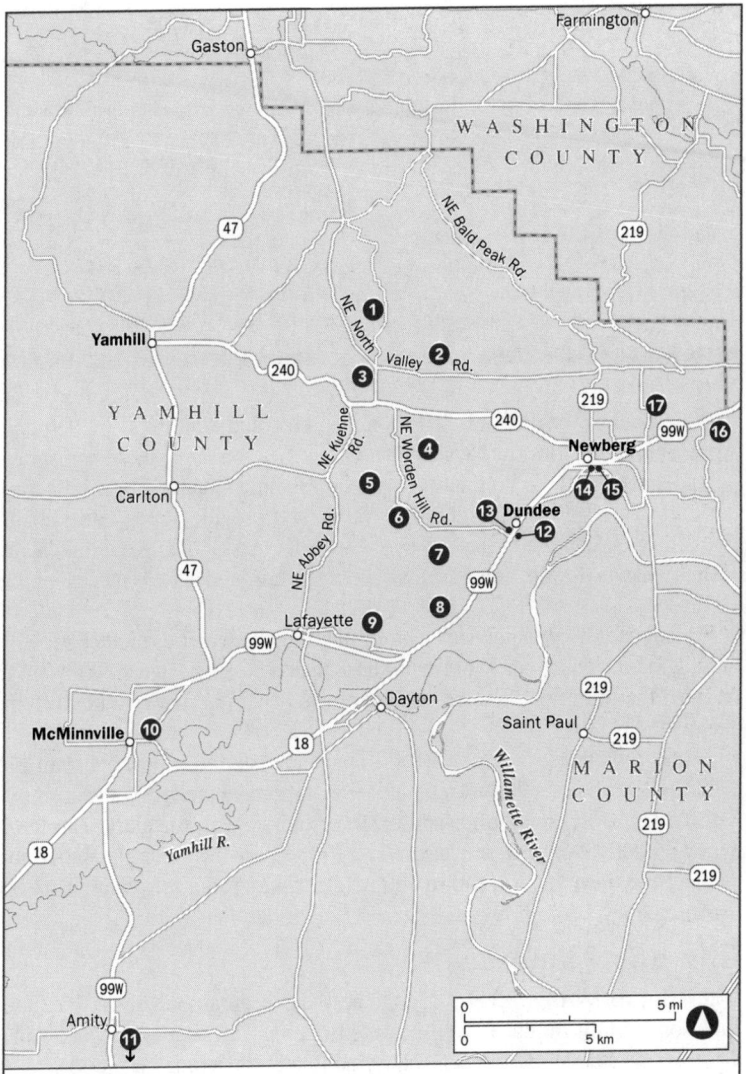

Adelsheim Vineyards **2**
Alexana **4**
The Allison Inn & Spa/ Jory Restaurant **17**
Archery Summit **7**
Argyle Winery **12**
Bethel Heights Vineyard **11**
Chehalem **15**
Domaine Drouhin Oregon **6**
Domaine Serene **5**
Dundee Bistro **13**
The Eyrie Vineyards **10**
The Painted Lady **14**
Penner-Ash Wine Cellars **3**
Rex Hill Vineyards **16**
Sokol Blosser Winery **8**
Stoller Vineyards **9**
Trisaetum Vineyards **1**

STICK TO THE pinots

For the most part, you can forget about cabernet sauvignon, merlot, and zinfandel while you're here. **The Willamette Valley** just isn't hot enough to produce these varietals. With the exception of southern Oregon wineries and a few Willamette Valley wineries that buy their grapes from warmer regions, Oregon wineries have, thankfully, given up on trying to produce cabs and zins. The wines of the Willamette Valley are primarily the cooler-climate varietals traditionally produced in Burgundy, Alsace, and Germany. Pinot noir is the uncontested leader of the pack, with pinot gris running a close second. Gewürztraminer and Riesling are also produced, and with the introduction of early ripening Dijon-clone chardonnay grapes, the region is finally beginning to produce chardonnays that can *almost* compete with those of California. A handful of wineries also make sparkling wines, which are often made from pinot noir and chardonnay grapes.

Wine country begins only a few miles west and southwest of Portland. Approaching the town of Newberg on Ore. 99W, you leave the urban sprawl behind and enter the rolling farm country of Yamhill County. These hills form the northern edge of the Willamette Valley and provide almost ideal conditions for growing wine grapes. The views from these hills take in the Willamette Valley's fertile farmlands as well as the snowcapped peaks of the Cascades.

For anyone simply interested a bit of tippling, the wineries along Ore. 99W are a good introduction. Those with more than a passing interest will want to explore the wineries that are located up in the hills a few miles off the highway.

At most wineries, you'll be asked to pay a tasting fee, anywhere from $15 to $90, depending on the "experience" (i.e., at some wineries, you can simply sample vintages, others offer add-on food and/or vineyard-tour). The fee is typically waived if you purchase wine. In the past few years, as pinot noir prices have risen into the $40 to $60 range, tasting room fees have also been creeping up.

The Best Wineries

Adelsheim Vineyard ★ This winery has been around since the 1970s and consistently produces well-regarded pinots. The single-vineyard wines here are the standouts. You can call ahead to arrange a tour ($25–$50).

16800 NE Calkins Ln, Newberg. www.adelsheim.com. ✆ **503/538-3652.** Tasting fee $15. Daily 11am–4pm.

Alexana ★★ The wines at Alexana are made by Lynn Penner-Ash, one of Oregon's top winemakers (her own winery is just a short drive away), and they are every bit as good as the wines from her own label. Pinot noirs include an estate bottling and a vintage from Shea, considered one of the best vineyards in the state.

12001 NE Worden Hill Rd., Newberg. www.alexanawinery.com. ✆ **503/537-3100.** Tasting fee $25–$50. Daily 11am–5pm.

Archery Summit ★★★ With big wines, a big winery, and a big reputation, Archery Summit is one of Oregon's premier producers of pinot noir. Only pinot noir is produced, and the grapes all come from Archery Summit's own vineyards. Wines are aged almost exclusively in new-oak barrels and spend time in some of the only barrel-aging caves in the state.

18599 NE Archery Summit Rd., Dayton. www.archerysummit.com. ✆ **503/864-4300.** Tasting fee $30–$95. Daily 10am–4pm. West of Dundee on Ore. 99W; turn right on Archery Summit Rd.

Argyle Winery ★★★ Located right on the highway in Dundee, this winery is best known for its sparkling wines and chardonnay, but also produces pinot noir. Due to traffic congestion in Dundee, Argyle is best visited on weekdays or when heading east on Ore. 99W.

691 Ore. 99W, Dundee. www.argylewinery.com. ✆ **888/427-4953** or 503/538-8520. Tasting fee $20. Daily 11am–5pm (summer until 7pm).

Bethel Heights Vineyard ★★★ Set high on a hill and surrounded by more than 50 acres of grapes, Bethel Heights primarily produces chardonnays and fabulous pinot noirs.

6060 Bethel Heights Rd. NW, Salem. www.bethelheights.com. ✆ **503/581-2262.** Tasting fee $15. Feb–Nov Daily 11am–5pm; Dec Sat–Sun 11am–5pm; Jan by appointment. From Ore. 221 in Lincoln, take Zena Rd. west and turn right on Bethel Heights Rd.

Chehalem ★★ At this tasting room, on the eastern edge of downtown Newberg, you can sample the wines of one of Oregon's most respected wineries. Reliable pinot noirs can be found here, as can good chardonnay, pinot gris, and pinot blanc (a less common white wine). You'll also find Riesling and Grüner Veltliner. Tours of the nearby winery are offered Wednesday through Saturday at 11am ($25); reservations are required.

106 S. Center St., Newberg. www.chehalemwines.com. ✆ **503/538-4700.** Tasting fee $20. Daily 11am–5pm (summer Thurs–Sat until 8pm).

Domaine Drouhin Oregon ★★★ Years ago, when France first heard that Oregon wineries were making pinot noir, most French winemakers scoffed. Not Maison Joseph Drouhin of Burgundy; the family bought land in the Red Hills of Dundee and planted vines. Today the Burgundian-style wines of Domaine Drouhin Oregon are superb examples of old-world winemaking—silky, seductive, and well balanced. Tours of the winery ($40) are available by reservation.

6750 Breyman Orchards Rd., Dayton. www.domainedrouhin.com. ✆ **503/864-2700.** Tasting fee $15. Daily 11am–4pm. West of Dundee on Ore. 99W; turn right on McDougall Rd. and right again onto Breyman Orchards Rd.

Domaine Serene ★★★ Located across the road from Domaine Drouhin Oregon, this is another of Oregon's top wineries, with an impressive winemaking facility and the impressive prices to prove it. Great ratings from *Wine Spectator* have made these wines some of the most sought after in the state. Pinot noir, chardonnay, and Syrah are produced here.

6555 NE Hilltop Lane, Dayton. www.domaineserene.com. ✆ **866/864-6555** or 503/864-4600. Tasting fee $20–$40. Daily 11am–5pm. West of Dundee on Ore. 99W; turn right on McDougall Rd. and right again onto Breyman Orchards Rd.

The Eyrie Vineyards ★★ This winery is the oldest producer of pinot noir in Oregon and was responsible for putting Oregon on the international wine map in 1979 and 1980, when its 1975 pinot noir won major competitions in France. Eyrie was also the first vineyard in America to produce pinot gris, which has since become one of Oregon's top white wines.

935 NE 10th Ave., McMinnville. www.eyrievineyards.com. ✆ **888/440-4970** or 503/472-6315. Tasting fee $10–$20. Daily noon–5pm.

Penner-Ash Wine Cellars ★★★ Winemaker Lynn Penner-Ash has been on the Oregon wine scene for years, and her winery between Newberg and Yamhill is one of the more impressive facilities in the area. Set high on a hill with a stupendous view, it would be worth a visit even if Penner-Ash didn't produce such excellent wines. The pinot noirs and Syrahs are out of this world.

15771 NE Ribbon Ridge Rd., Newberg. www.pennerash.com. ✆ **503/554-5545.** Tasting fee $25–$50. Daily 11am–5pm. From Ore. 240 between Newberg and Yamhill, drive north on NE Ribbon Ridge Rd.

Rex Hill Vineyards ★★★ Set amid mature vineyards on the outskirts of Newberg, Rex Hill is a good first stop in wine country. One of the oldest wineries in Oregon, Rex Hill focuses on higher end pinot noir, which can be outstanding. Also look for good and reasonably priced chardonnay and pinot gris.

30835 N. Ore. 99W, Newberg. www.rexhill.com. ✆ **800/739-4455.** Tasting fee $15–$60. Daily 10am–5pm.

Sokol Blosser Winery ★★★ Sokol Blosser sits high on the slopes above the west end of Dundee. Off-dry whites are a strong point here, and the Evolution, a blend of nine different grapes, shouldn't be missed. A walk-through the showcase vineyard provides a unique opportunity to learn about the growing process; tours of the winery ($40) are given Thursday through Saturday at 11pm by reservation.

5000 Sokol Blosser Ln., Dundee. www.sokolblosser.com. ✆ **800/582-6668** or 503/864-2282. Tasting fee $15–$25. Daily 10am–4pm. Southwest of Dundee off Ore. 99W.

Stoller Vineyards ★★ This large, LEED-certified winery produces not only good chardonnay and pinot noir; with an array of photovoltaic panels on the roof, it also produces electricity. The owners are also co-owners of Chehalem winery (see above), one of the most highly respected wineries in the state. Stoller has a cottage and farmhouse available for rent, with a 2-night minimum.

16161 NE McDougall Rd., Dayton. www.stollervineyards.com. ✆ **503/864-3404.** Tasting fee $15. Mon–Thurs 11am–5pm (summer daily until 7pm). Southwest of Dundee off Ore. 99W.

Trisaetum Vineyards ★★★ Few Willamette Valley wineries produce Riesling, but it's one of the specialties at Trisaetum. In any given vintage, the winery will produce several styles, from dry to sweet. Excellent pinot noir is also produced. Try to get a look at the winery's impressive barrel caves.

18401 Ribbon Ridge Rd., Newberg. www.trisaetum.com. ✆ **503/538-9898.** Tasting fee $20. Daily 11am–4pm.

Where to Stay & Eat

NEWBERG

The Allison Inn & Spa ★★★ Every detail in this luxurious boutique resort inn has been carefully designed to enhance your experience of staying in the Oregon wine country. Natural wood, handcrafted furniture, and fine fabrics lend a calm, earthy glow to the large guestrooms. Balconies and terraces look out on Willamette Valley vistas of vineyards, rolling farmland, trees, and mountains. Original art graces the public spaces, the rooms, and the landscaped gardens. Spa-style bathrooms have sliding panels so you can soak and look out at your fireplace and the scenery outside. Of course, there's also a luxurious on-site spa, with an indoor swimming pool. The inn's restaurant, **Jory ★★★,** is highly acclaimed (see below) The Allison is the only resort in the wine country; its high prices reflect the level of comfort and service you'll find here.

2525 Allison Ln., Newberg. www.theallison.com. ✆ **877/294-2525** or 503/554-2525. 85 units. $350–$450 double. Pets accepted ($50 fee). **Amenities:** Restaurant; lounge; fitness center; Jacuzzi; indoor pool; spa; Wi-Fi (free).

Jory Restaurant ★★★ NORTHWEST The Allison Inn's stylish restaurant, under the direction of Chef Sunny Jin (formerly of the French Laundry in Napa), adheres to the same high standards you'll find throughout the resort's property. The windowed walls look south across the Willamette Valley toward the farms and woodlands where much of the food is sourced. Fresh vegetables and herbs are also planted and harvested in the chef's garden on the grounds of the hotel. The menu is seasonal, so you might find starters like a chilled English pea soup, or a freshly picked salad. The preparations are kept fairly simple: If fresh Pacific halibut with asparagus is on the menu, the flavors of both will come through clearly and the fish will be perfectly seared. The wine list here is exemplary and features lots of Oregon pinot noirs, some from the Allison's own vineyards. Reserve in advance here, and request a booth with a view. If you're a real foodie, you might want to sit at the chef's counter and watch the workings of the kitchen.

In The Allison Inn & Spa, 2525 Allison Ln., Newberg. www.theallison.com. ✆ **503/554-2526.** Main courses $24–$45. Mon–Sat 6:30am–9pm; Sun 6:30am–2pm and 5:30–9pm.

The Painted Lady ★★★ FRENCH/NORTHWEST "Painted Lady" is not a hostess, but the name given to brightly colored Victorian houses like the one that houses this award-winning restaurant in downtown Newberg. The menu makes creative use of local and seasonal Willamette Valley meat, vegetables, and fruits, and Pacific Ocean seafood. Halibut might be crusted with valley hazelnuts (long a local crop), gnocchi served with foraged wild mushrooms, locally grown rabbit accompanied by a purée of squash and cauliflower from a nearby farm, and a delicious cheesecake dessert might come with blueberry compote. Wines from local vineyards are featured, of course. Advance reservations are a must.

201 S. College St., Newberg. www.thepaintedladyrestaurant.com. ✆ **503/538-3850.** Prix-fixe menu $110. Wed–Sun 5–10pm.

DUNDEE

The Dundee Bistro ★ NORTHWEST A favorite stop for visitors touring local vineyards near Dundee, this delightful bistro occupies space next to the Ponzi Wine Bar. "Bistronomy"—high-quality food served in a casual, inexpensive fashion—is the philosophy here. All the culinary buzzwords are in play: local, seasonal, sustainable, organic. Garbanzo bean and nettle soup might be your starter, followed by homemade pastas, which are worthy second courses or entrees (the carbonara here is a good one). There's a kid's menu, too.

100-A SW Seventh St., Dundee. www.dundeebistro.com. ✆ **503/554-1650.** Main courses $16–$32. Daily 11:30am–9pm.

MOUNT HOOD ★★★

Government Camp: 56 miles E of Portland; Timberline Lodge: 60 miles E of Portland

Regal, snow-capped Mount Hood is Portland's mascot, or icon, visible from the city on clear days and an integral part of Portlanders' consciousness. At 11,235 feet, this dormant volcano in the Cascade Range is the tallest mountain in Oregon—and also the busiest, since it's a renowned winter ski destination and a year-round outdoor playground within an easy day trip of Portland.

The mountain is just one feature—albeit the most spectacular one—of the 1.1 million-acre **Mount Hood National Forest.** Within the forest are some 95 campgrounds and 50 lakes stocked with rainbow, cutthroat, steelhead, and brown trout. The scenic, free-flowing rivers (the Sandy and the Salmon being the most prominent) are known for their rafting, swimming, and tubing. Both forest and mountain are crisscrossed by an extensive trail system for hikers, cyclists, and horseback riders.

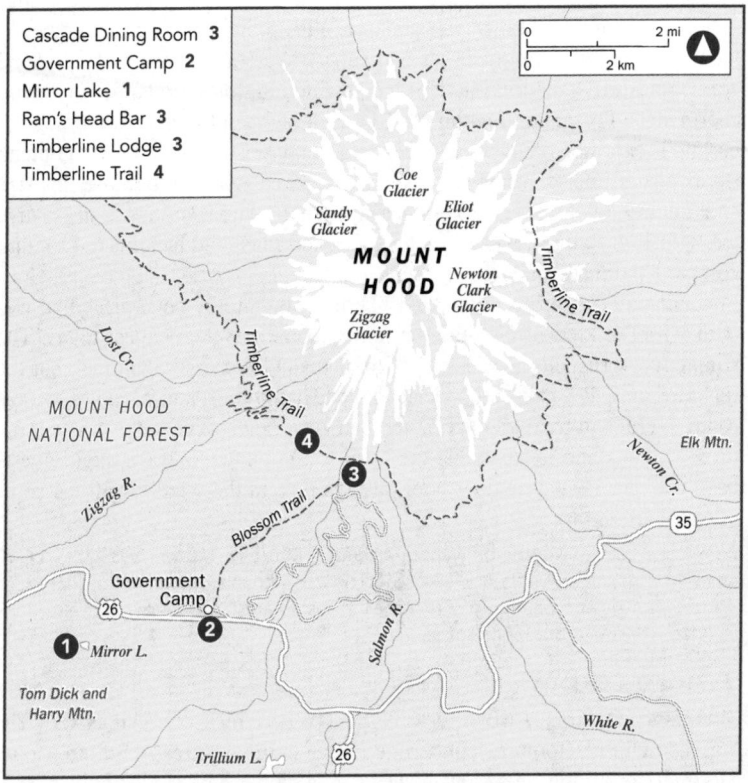

All of this is almost literally in Portland's front yard, about 60 miles east of downtown. A day trip to **Timberline Lodge** serves as a remarkable introduction to the grandeur that is Oregon.

Essentials

GETTING THERE From Portland, drive east on I-84 to exit 16 (Wood Village) and continue east on U.S. 26 to Government Camp; from there, a well-marked road leads to Timberline Lodge.

VISITOR INFORMATION For more information on Mount Hood, contact the **Hood River Ranger Station,** 6780 Ore. 35, Parkdale (www.fs.fed.us/r6/mthood; ✆ **541/352-6002**), which has maps and provides information on permits and road conditions. Online you can also check out www.mthood.info. The commercial site **Mount Hood Territory** (www.mthoodterritory.com) is also packed with useful information, including tips on traveling around the mountain.

Timberline Lodge ★★★

Timberline Lodge is one of the most iconic mountain lodges in the U.S. Constructed during the Great Depression as a WPA project, this classic alpine ski lodge is a paean to the materials and superlative craftsmanship of a bygone era. Both massive and intimate, it has lost nothing of its grandeur or period charm since President Franklin D. Roosevelt came out to inaugurate it. Timberline's enormous stone fireplace, huge exposed beams, and wide-plank floors are as impressive as they ever were—even more so, because this size and quality of wood is no longer available. Woodcarvings, imaginative wrought-iron fixtures, weavings, hand-hooked rugs, and handmade furniture complete the rustic picture.

Staying at Timberline is an atmospheric treat, but it is not a place that was built with the kind of over-the-top luxury some travelers expect today. The simple, cozy rusticity in most of its rooms is not a stylistic gimmick but the real McCoy. The smallest rooms lack private bathrooms, and windows in most rooms were built for durability rather than view-power. The lodge has an array of restaurants and lounges that are open to the public, and overnight guests have use of a heated outdoor pool (always nice in the winter, with the snow piled up around it).

Timberline Lodge. www.timberlinelodge.com. ✆ **800/547-1406** or 503/272-3311. 70 units, 10 with shared bathroom. $145–$155 double with shared bathroom; $160–$365 double with private bathroom. **Amenities:** 4 restaurants; 3 lounges; exercise room; Jacuzzi; year-round outdoor pool; sauna; Wi-Fi (free).

Where to Eat

Cascade Dining Room ★★ NORTHWEST/INTERNATIONAL The Cascade Dining Room in Timberline Lodge is the best restaurant on Mount Hood. It does not have a view, however, and dinner here can be quite expensive (try it at lunch instead). In keeping with the times, the restaurant now tries to be as much "farm to table" as possible, using only locally sourced meats and poultry. The menu is also seasonal. If morel mushrooms are available, definitely try them. Country ham, beef tartare and bison steak are also highly recommended, and there is always fresh fish on the menu. Vegetarian dishes,

Exploring Around Timberline Lodge

Besides having a fabulous view of Mount Hood and the surrounding Cascades, and great skiing (see "Hitting the Slopes" box, p. 217), Timberline Lodge is surrounded by wildflower meadows that burst into bloom in July and August. (Hikers must stay on the trails, because this environment above the timberline is a very fragile ecosystem.)

In summer you can ride the lift up to the Palmer Snowfield behind the lodge, even if you aren't skiing. The **Magic Mile Skyride,** which operates daily from 11am to 2pm (until 3pm Friday through Sunday), costs $18 per passenger (children 7 under 6 free). By the way, don't forget to bring a jacket or sweater, even if it's August.

HITTING THE slopes

There are five downhill ski areas on Mount Hood, though two of these are tiny operations that attract primarily beginners and families. There are also many miles of marked cross-country ski trails. Although opening and closing dates have been readjusted in recent years because of unpredictable weather, the ski season on Mount Hood typically begins around Thanksgiving and runs through March or April. There is also summer snowboarding on the Palmer Snowfield at **Timberline Ski Area.** The single most important thing to know about skiing anywhere in Oregon is that you'll have to have a **Sno-Park permit** ($4/day), which allows you to park in plowed parking areas on the mountain. Permits are available at ski shops and at convenience stores. To visit Mount Hood in the winter, check the website for the **Hood River Ranger Station** (www.fs.usda.gov/mthood) for current weather conditions; you may need snow tires or chains.

Mount Hood Meadows ★★★ (www.skihood.com; ✆ **503/337-2222** or 503/227-7669 for snow report), 12 miles northeast of Government Camp on Ore. 35, is the largest ski resort on Mount Hood, with more than 2,000 skiable acres, 2,777 vertical feet of slopes, five high-speed quad lifts, and a wide variety of terrain. This is the closest Mount Hood comes to having a destination ski resort.

Timberline Ski Area ★★ (www.timberlinelodge.com; ✆ **503/272-3158** or 503/222-2211 for snow report) is the highest ski area on Mount Hood and has one slope that is open throughout the summer, though it can be slushy and is used more by snowboarders than downhill skiers. Mount Hood Meadows is better for general skiing during the winter season, but this is the site of historic **Timberline Lodge.**

If you're interested in cross-country skiing, head to **Mount Hood Meadows Nordic Center ★★,** located at the Hood River Meadows parking lot, 1 mile north of the main entrance to Meadows on Ore. 35. Teacup Lake is maintained by a local ski club (www.teacupnordic.org) and has the best system of groomed trails on the mountain.

like the lentil field roast, are available. Some selections are a bit too complicated, but the overall cooking skill here is quite high.

In Timberline Lodge. www.timberlinelodge.com. ✆ **503/272-3391.** Reservations required for dinner. Main courses $28–$54; lunch buffet $17. Mon–Thurs 11:30am–2pm, Fri–Sun 11:30am–3pm, daily 5:30–8pm.

Ram's Head Bar ★ AMERICAN The restaurant-bar on Timberline's mezzanine level has the big-window mountain view that the Cascade Dining Room lacks, so naturally everyone wants to come here to sit and stare at the snowpack. The experience doesn't suffer when you add signature cheese fondue and a glass of wine, or a pint of microbrew produced at Mt. Hood Brewing just down the road. There are other all-day, anytime choices, too, like delicious clam chowder, charcuterie from Olympic Provisions (a top purveyor in Portland), and artisan cheeses that aren't in a fondue pot. The scene is relaxed and fun and always busy on weekends.

In Timberline Lodge. www.timberlinelodge.com. ✆ **503/272-3391.** Main courses $13–$27. Mon–Thurs 2–11pm; Fri–Sun 11am–11pm.

Columbia Gorge

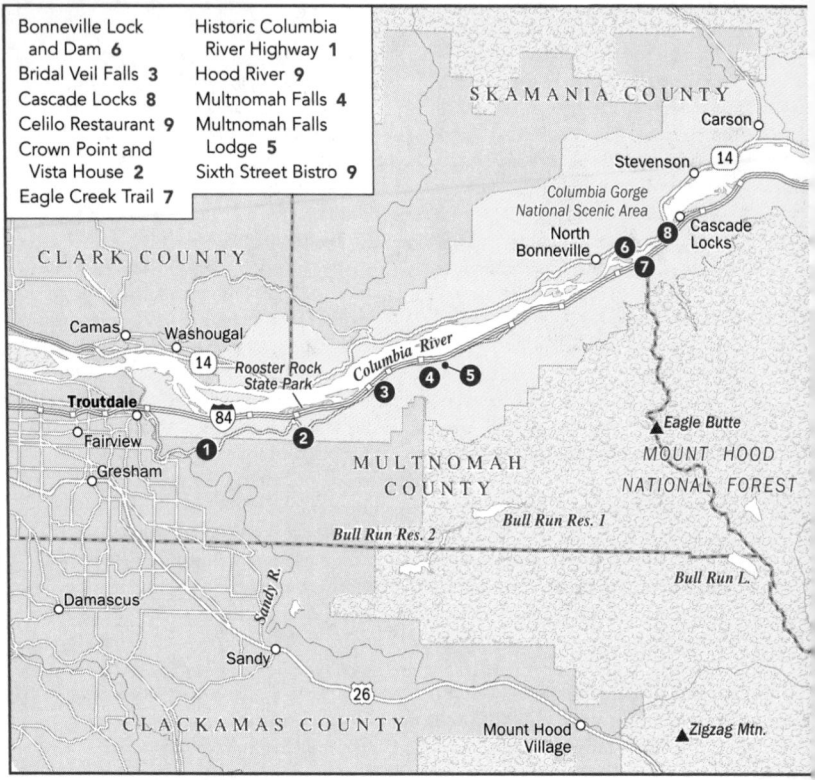

THE COLUMBIA GORGE ★★★

Columbia Gorge National Scenic Area: Begins 18 miles E of Portland

Stretching from the Sandy River in the west to the Deschutes River in the east, the **Columbia Gorge National Scenic Area** ★★★ is one of the most breathtakingly dramatic landscapes in the United States. Carved out over countless eons by enormous glaciers and floods of unimaginable power, this miles-wide canyon with its mile-high basalt cliffs is flanked on its north (Washington) side by **Mount Adams** and on its south (Oregon) side by **Mount Hood,** two Cascade peaks that rise more than 11,000 feet. With a string of dramatic waterfalls, including iconic **Multnomah Falls** ★★★ (Oregon's highest and most famous waterfall), and forests of Douglas fir rising up from the banks of the Columbia River, the Gorge is a year-round recreational area. Hiking trails lead to hidden waterfalls and cliff-top panoramas while windsurfers race across wind-whipped waters at Hood River, the windsurfing capital of the

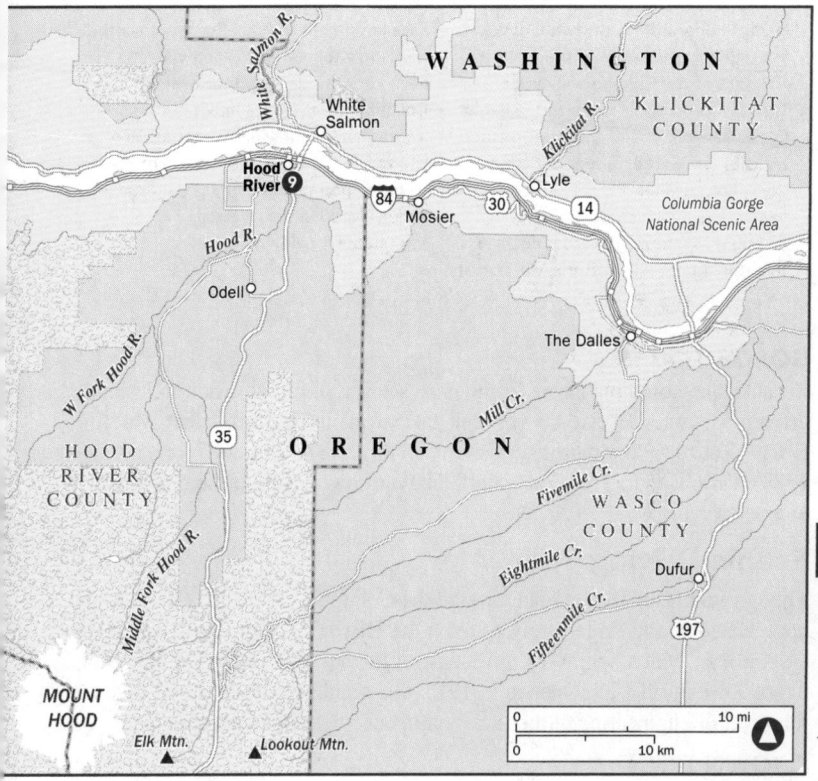

United States. You can explore and enjoy this unforgettable stretch of the Columbia Gorge on an easy day trip from Portland.

Essentials

GETTING THERE I-84 and the Historic Columbia River Highway both pass through the Gorge on the Oregon side of the Columbia River. The most scenic route utilizes both highways and is described in the driving tour below.

VISITOR INFORMATION For information on the Gorge, contact the Columbia River Gorge Visitor's Association (www.crgva.org; ✆ **800/984-6743**), or the **Columbia River Gorge National Scenic Area** (www.fs.usda.gov/crgnsa; ✆ **541/308-1700**). The **Multnomah Falls Lodge Visitor Center** (http://www.multnomahfallslodge.com; ✆ **503/695-2372**) at Multnomah Falls Lodge has maps of hiking trails and is a great source of information on attractions in the Gorge.

Columbia Gorge Wildfire

In September 2017 a devastating wildfire raged through one of the most scenic areas of the Columbia River Gorge. The human-caused fire started in Eagle Creek Canyon, one of the most pristine areas of the Gorge. Tinder-dry conditions, hot weather and winds fanned the flames, which quickly spread over 33,000 acres, forcing evacuations and threatening not only historic Multnomah Falls Lodge but the Bull Run watershed, Portland's source of drinking water. I have kept the day-trip tour of the Columbia River Gorge intact but be aware that you may encounter areas of charred forest along the route. For up-to-date information, contact the organizations listed under "Visitor Information" below.

GORGE TOURS

Because the Columbia River Gorge is so scenic, you might want to leave the driving to someone else so you can take it all in. If so, contact **Martin's Gorge Tours** (www.martinsgorgetours.com; ✆ **877/290-8687** or 503/349-1323). Various tours focus on waterfalls, wildflowers, or wine and cost $49 to $85 per person.

Scenic Driving Tour

Though I-84 is the fastest road through the Columbia Gorge, the Gorge is best appreciated at a more leisurely pace on the **Historic Columbia River Highway ★★★,** which begins 16 miles east of downtown Portland at the second Troutdale exit off I-84. Opened in 1915, this winding, two-lane highway was a marvel of engineering at the time and opened the Gorge to tourism.

CROWN POINT

Your first unforgettable view of the Gorge comes at the **Portland Women's Forum State Scenic Viewpoint ★★★** at **Crown Point,** which provides a 30-mile vista that is nothing short of spectacular. Topping Crown Point is historic **Vista House,** 40700 E. Historic Columbia River Hwy. (www.vistahouse.com; ✆ **503/695-2240**), an octagonal stone structure perched 733-ft. above the river. It was originally built as a way station for travelers along the scenic highway back in 1917. Step into this lovely building to have a look at its architecture and exhibits that tell the story of the construction of the historic highway and the geology of the Gorge. There's also a coffee shop and a gift shop. Vista House is open daily 10am to 6pm from March through October, weather permitting, but Crown Point is open year-round.

WATERFALLS

From Crown Point, the historic highway drops down into the Gorge and passes several beautiful waterfalls. The first of these is 249-foot **Latourell Falls ★,** a diaphanous wisp of water that cascades over basalt cliffs stained lime-green by lichen. A 2.3-mile loop trail leads from this waterfall up to the smaller **Upper Latourell Falls.** Continuing east, you'll come to **Shepherd's**

Dell Falls, Bridal Veil Falls, Mist Falls, and **Wahkeena Falls,** all of which are either right beside the historic highway or a short walk away.

MULTNOMAH FALLS

At 620 feet from the lip to the lower pool, **Multnomah Falls** ★★★ is the tallest waterfall in Oregon and the fourth tallest in the United States. In addition to being the tallest, it's also the most famous waterfall along the historic highway, and the state's most visited natural attraction (in other words, expect crowds). A steep trail leads up to the top of the falls; partway up there's a picturesque arched bridge directly in front of the falls.

The historic **Multnomah Falls Lodge** has a restaurant, snack bar, and gift shop, as well as a **National Forest Visitor Center** with information on the geology, history, and natural history of the Gorge, plus Forest Service trail maps.

BONNEVILLE DAM & EAGLE CREEK

Just after the historic highway merges with I-84 is exit 40, the exit for **Bonneville Lock and Dam** ★ (✆ **541/374-8820**). The visitor center here has exhibits on the history of this dam, built in 1938. One of the most important features here is the fish ladder, which allows adult salmon to return upriver to spawn. Underwater windows let visitors watch the fish as they pass through the ladder (but note that salmon runs have been greatly diminished—because of this dam, which alters the river's seasonal flow and water temperature). To see how trout, salmon, and steelhead are raised before being released into the river, visit the adjacent **Bonneville Fish Hatchery,** 70543 NE Herman Loop (www.dfw.state.or.us; ✆ **541/374-8393**). A **Sturgeon Viewing Center** ★★ allows you to marvel at several immense sturgeons through an underwater window. At this same exit off I-84 (and at Eagle Creek), you'll find access to a section of the **Historic Columbia River Highway State Trail,** a paved multiuse trail that connects the town of Cascade Locks with Bonneville Dam. This trail incorporates abandoned sections of the Historic Columbia River Highway and is open to hikers and bikers. Near the western trailhead, you'll also find the trail to **Wahclella Falls** ★, a little-visited yet very picturesque waterfall tucked back in a side canyon. The trail to the falls is less than a mile long and relatively flat.

Beyond Bonneville Dam is **Eagle Creek,** the single best spot in the Gorge for a hike. The **Eagle Creek Trail** ★★★ leads past several waterfalls; if you have time for only one hike in the Gorge, it should be this one. (Be aware, however, that this is where the 2017 Eagle Creek wildfire began, and the canyon and trail may be closed for part of 2018.)

Not far beyond Eagle Creek is **Bridge of the Gods,** a steel suspension bridge that connects Oregon and Washington at the site where, according to a Native American legend, a natural bridge used by the gods once stood. Geologists now believe that the legend (without the deities) is based in fact; there is evidence that a massive rockslide may have once blocked the river at this point.

CASCADE LOCKS

Just beyond Bridge of the Gods, you'll come to **Cascade Locks.** It was at this site that cascades once turned the Columbia River into a raging torrent that required boats to be portaged a short distance downriver. Built in 1896, the Cascade Locks allowed steamships to pass unhindered and made traveling between The Dalles and Portland much easier. With the construction of the Bonneville Lock and Dam, the cascades were flooded, and the locks became superfluous.

The **Cascade Locks Marine Park** at 355 WaNaPa St. serves as the ticket office for the stern-wheeler ***Columbia Gorge*** ★★ (www.portlandspirit.com; ✆ **800/224-3901** or 503/224-3900), which makes 1- and 2-hour sightseeing cruises and lunch, brunch, and dinner trips on the river from May through October. These cruises provide a great perspective on the Gorge. Fares for the 2-hour scenic cruises are $30 for adults and $20 for children. (I don't recommend the more expensive meal cruises because the food is not particularly good.)

HOOD RIVER

Located 62 miles east of Portland, and easily accessible from I-84, the town of **Hood River** is a good place to end your day trip in the Columbia Gorge before heading back to Portland. Long before windsurfing was invented and Hood River began to bill itself as the "Windsurfing Capital of the World," this small Columbia Gorge town was primarily a lumber town and shipping depot for the apples, peaches, pears, cherries, and plums grown in the vast fruit orchards in **Hood Valley.** You can still drive into Hood Valley and buy sweet Bing and Rainier cherries and other fresh-picked fruit at farm stands along Ore. 35, but it's the windsurfing on the Columbia River that draws recreational enthusiasts from around the globe.

The conditions for windsurfing are ideal at this juncture in the mighty river. Every summer, hot air rising over the desert to the east of the Cascade Range sucks cool air up the Columbia River Gorge from the Pacific, and the winds howl through what is basically a natural wind tunnel. They used to curse these winds in Hood River. Not anymore. Windsurfing and kiteboarding have given the town a new lease on life. Pull into the riverside park and watch the action as riders unfurl their sails and kites, zip up their wetsuits, and launch themselves into the melee of hundreds of other like-minded souls shooting back and forth across a mile of windswept water. Aerial acrobatics like flips and 360-degree turns are common sights.

Many of the town's old Victorian and Craftsman houses have now been restored, giving Hood River a historic atmosphere to complement its lively windsurfing scene.

For more information, contact the **Hood River County Chamber of Commerce,** 720 E. Port Marina Dr., Hood River (www.hoodriver.org; ✆ **800/366-3530** or 541/386-2000), located near the river at exit 63 off I-84.

Hood River sits at the juncture of I-84 and Ore. 35, which leads south to connect with U.S. 26 near the community of Government Camp.

ROOSTER ROCK STATE PARK

If it's a hot summer's day and you're returning to Portland via I-84, you may want to take a dip in the river at **Rooster Rock State Park ★,** with its long sandy beach, and, in a remote section of the park, a clothing-optional stretch. Whether you stop or not, you'll easily spot this riverside monolith, which the explorers Lewis and Clark used as a landmark on their journey down the Columbia to the Pacific Ocean in 1805. Rooster Rock State Park is 13 miles west of Multnomah Falls on I-84.

Where to Eat

Celilo Restaurant ★★ NORTHWESTERN The dinner menu is more interesting, but since you're on a day trip through the Gorge, lunch is probably what you'll have at this upscale Hood River restaurant (but note that lunch is only served weekends, from Friday to Sunday). It's the best place to eat in the Gorge, with a stylish, design-conscious, lots-of-wood interior that evokes a lodge-y Northwest scene. Menus change often, but lunch offerings of locally sourced food typically include a selection of sandwiches: oyster po' boy, pulled pork, barbecued steak, or a Mediterranean vegetarian wrap. There's a good burger, too. Some of the produce is foraged locally, so look for dishes with freshly picked forest mushrooms or greens.

16 Oak St., Hood River. www.celilorestaurant.com. ✆ **541/386-5710.** Main courses lunch $10–$14, dinner $24–$31. Fri–Sun 11:30am–3pm, daily 5–9:30 or 10pm.

Multnomah Falls Lodge ★★ AMERICAN Considering the number of diners served here, this wonderfully scenic old lodge-style restaurant does a pretty good job with its food and service. The building was constructed in 1925 at the base of Multnomah Falls. I'd recommend calling ahead for a reservation and having lunch here on your day trip through the Columbia Gorge. If you're not the designated driver, you might enjoy a huckleberry daiquiri first. The rainbow trout is not wild, but it is from the Northwest, and the grilled salmon is worth trying. There's also mac and cheese, prime rib, a tostada made with Oregon pink shrimp, and a vegetarian choice. For a peek at the thundering falls while you dine, try to get a table in the conservatory room or, in summer, out on the patio.

Historic Columbia River Hwy. (or I-84, exit 31), Corbett. www.multnomahfallslodge.com. ✆ **503/695-2376.** Main courses $13–$25. Daily 8am–9pm.

Sixth Street Bistro ★ AMERICAN/INTERNATIONAL This two-tiered restaurant is all about enjoying good, sturdy food in a laid back environment. On the first floor there's outdoor patio dining, and a lounge with a balcony above. The windsurfing crowd fills this place on summer weekends, sometimes just to enjoy a microbrew. The lunch menu features big club and BLT sandwiches and wraps. Dinner ventures a bit farther afield, with chicken Marsala and baby back ribs joined by pad Thai noodles and a teriyaki stir-fry. Vegetarian and gluten-free items are also available.

509 Cascade Ave., Hood River. www.sixthstreetbistro.com. ✆ **541/386-5737.** Main courses $11–$25. Sun–Thurs 11:30am–9:30pm; Fri–Sat 11:30am–10pm.

THE OREGON COAST

6

I'll never forget the first time I saw, heard, and smelled the Pacific Ocean on the Oregon coast. The pounding roar of the breakers as they rolled in to shore; the driftwood-strewn white-sand beach with its giant, forested headland and offshore monoliths; the sharp, salty breath of the sea—it was all so powerful, a sensory massage that put life in a new perspective that was both enlarging and humbling at the same time.

I thought I had died and gone to heaven. Actually, I'd only gone to Oceanside, a tiny hamlet on the Three Capes Scenic Loop between Tillamook and Pacific City. A friend had an old, lopsided, cedar-shingled beach cottage that had been in the family for decades. It had a delicious damp smell to it—the smell of a house that never entirely dried out—and a wood-burning fireplace, a little kitchen and a couple of tiny bedrooms. Oceanside had one sort-of store, a motel, a tavern, and not much else. That's how much of the coast was before the surging real-estate boom that started in the late 1980s. When you went to "the beach," as Oregonians said, it was to reconnect with nature, walk on shorelines where you were the only person for miles, explore the wind-socked headlands, get soaked by the rain, make love, read books, fix seafood dinners (or go out to one of the very few restaurants), dream by the fire, and let the lullaby of the sea tug you into a deep sleep.

And that's what a trip to the Oregon coast is still about—except that now you don't have to stay in a motel and do your own cooking, unless you want to, because every kind of accommodation is available, from yurts to luxury hotels; every town has at least one or two restaurants; and all the hotels have giant-screen TVs and free Wi-Fi so you can tune out the very nature you came here to enjoy. What hasn't changed, despite all the new building, is that every inch of the Oregon coast remains open to the public. There are no private beaches anywhere along the 363 miles (584 km) of coastline that stretches from Astoria in the north to Brookings in the south. That's why it's sometimes called "the People's Coast."

As for the weather—well, that may be changing, but you still need to bring a fleece, a hoodie, and a windbreaker, no matter what time of year you visit. Maybe a wet suit, too.

I'm kidding. Sort of.

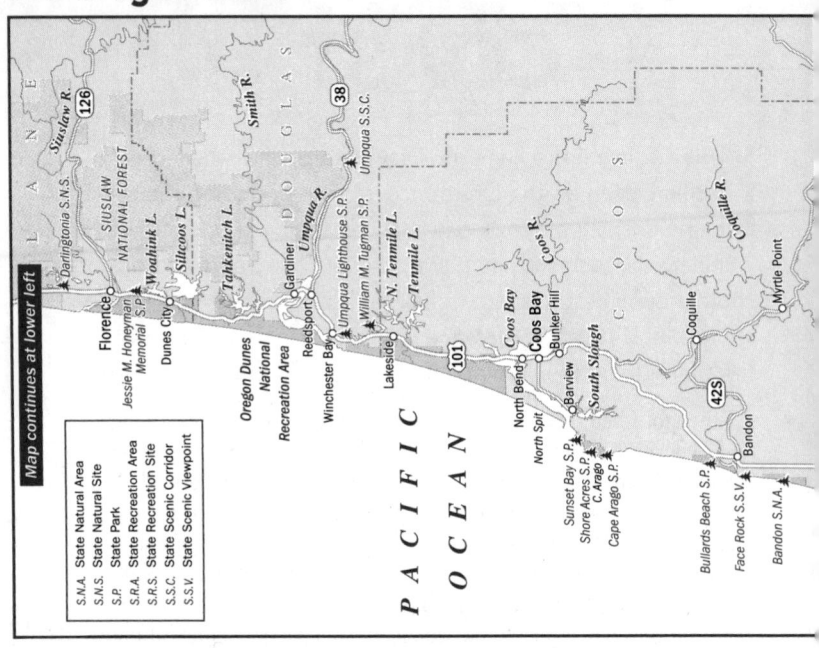
Map continues at lower left
S.N.A. State Natural Area
S.N.S. State Natural Site
S.P. State Park
S.R.A. State Recreation Area
S.R.S. State Recreation Site
S.S.C. State Scenic Corridor
S.S.V. State Scenic Viewpoint
L A N E
Siuslaw R.
126
Darlingtonia S.N.S.
SIUSLAW NATIONAL FOREST
Florence
Jessie M. Honeyman Memorial S.P.
Woahink L.
Siltcoos L.
Dunes City
Tahkenitch L.
Smith R.
Oregon Dunes National Recreation Area
Gardiner
Umpqua R.
D O U G L A S
38
Reedsport
Winchester Bay
Umpqua Lighthouse S.P.
William M. Tugman S.P.
Umpqua S.S.C.
N. Tenmile L.
Tenmile L.
Lakeside
PACIFIC OCEAN
101
Coos Bay
North Bend
Coos Bay
Bunker Hill
Coos R.
North Spit
Barview
South Slough
C O O S
Sunset Bay S.P.
Shore Acres S.P.
C. Arago
Cape Arago S.P.
Coquille
Coquille R.
42S
Bullards Beach S.P.
Bandon
Face Rock S.S.V.
Bandon S.N.A.
Myrtle Point

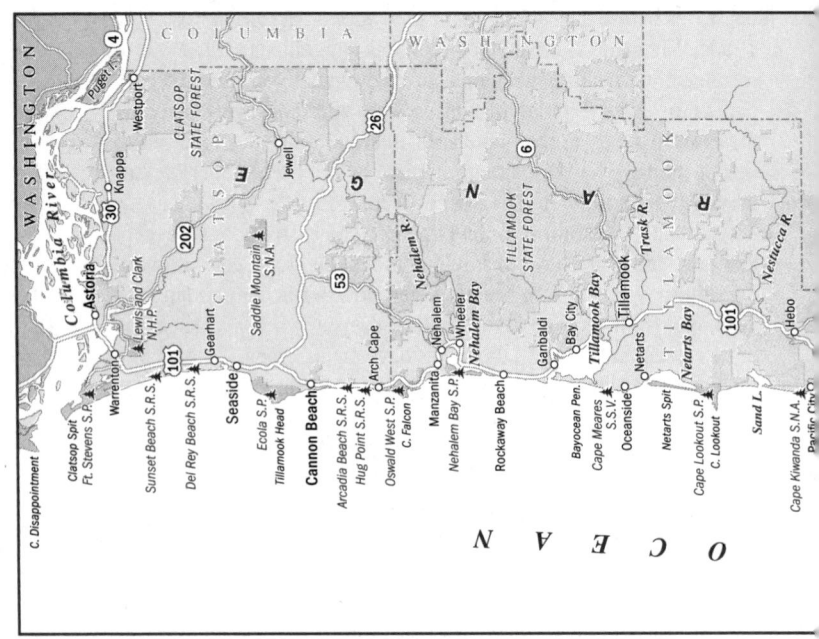
WASHINGTON
Columbia River
Astoria
4
Puget Ch.
30
Knappa
Westport
C O L U M B I A
CLATSOP STATE FOREST
Lewis and Clark N.H.P.
202
Warrenton
Gearhart
Jewell
C L A T S O P
E
Saddle Mountain S.N.A.
101
Seaside
Sunset Beach S.R.S.
Del Rey Beach S.R.S.
Clatsop Spit
Ft. Stevens S.P.
C. Disappointment
Ecola S.P.
Tillamook Head
Cannon Beach
53
G
26
Arcadia Beach S.R.S.
Hug Point S.R.S.
Arch Cape
Oswald West S.P.
C. Falcon
Nehalem R.
Manzanita
Nehalem
Nehalem Bay S.P.
Wheeler
Nehalem Bay
N
W A S H I N G T O N
6
TILLAMOOK STATE FOREST
Rockaway Beach
Garibaldi
Bay City
Tillamook Bay
A
Bayocean Pen.
Cape Meares S.S.V.
Oceanside
Netarts
Tillamook
Trask R.
T I L L A M O O K
R
Netarts Spit
Netarts Bay
Cape Lookout S.P.
C. Lookout
101
Nestucca R.
Hebo
Sand L.
Cape Kiwanda S.N.A.
Pacific City
O C E A N

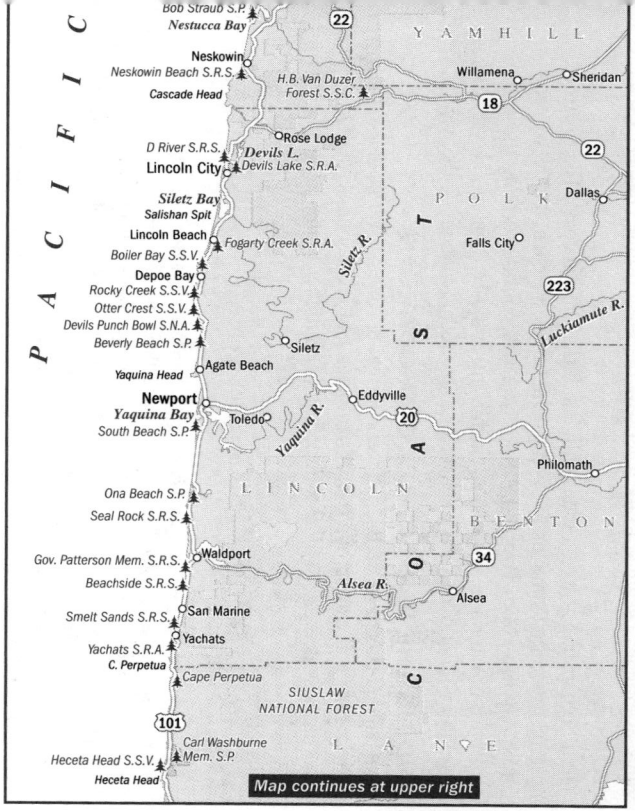
PACIFIC
Bob Straub S.P.
Nestucca Bay
Neskowin
Neskowin Beach S.R.S.
Cascade Head
H.B. Van Duzer Forest S.S.C.
Willamena
Sheridan
YAMHILL
22
18
D River S.R.S.
Devils L.
Lincoln City
Devils Lake S.R.A.
Rose Lodge
Siletz Bay
Salishan Spit
Lincoln Beach
Fogarty Creek S.R.A.
Boiler Bay S.S.V.
Depoe Bay
Rocky Creek S.S.V.
Otter Crest S.S.V.
Devils Punch Bowl S.N.A.
Beverly Beach S.P.
Siletz R.
POLK
Dallas
Falls City
223
Luckiamute R.
Siletz
Agate Beach
Yaquina Head
Newport
Yaquina Bay
South Beach S.P.
Toledo
Yaquina R.
Eddyville
20
Philomath
Ona Beach S.P.
Seal Rock S.R.S.
LINCOLN
BENTON
Gov. Patterson Mem. S.R.S.
Waldport
34
Beachside S.R.S.
Alsea R.
Alsea
Smelt Sands S.R.S.
San Marine
Yachats
Yachats S.R.A.
C. Perpetua
Cape Perpetua
SIUSLAW NATIONAL FOREST
101
Carl Washburne Mem. S.P.
Heceta Head S.S.V.
Heceta Head
LANE
Map continues at upper right

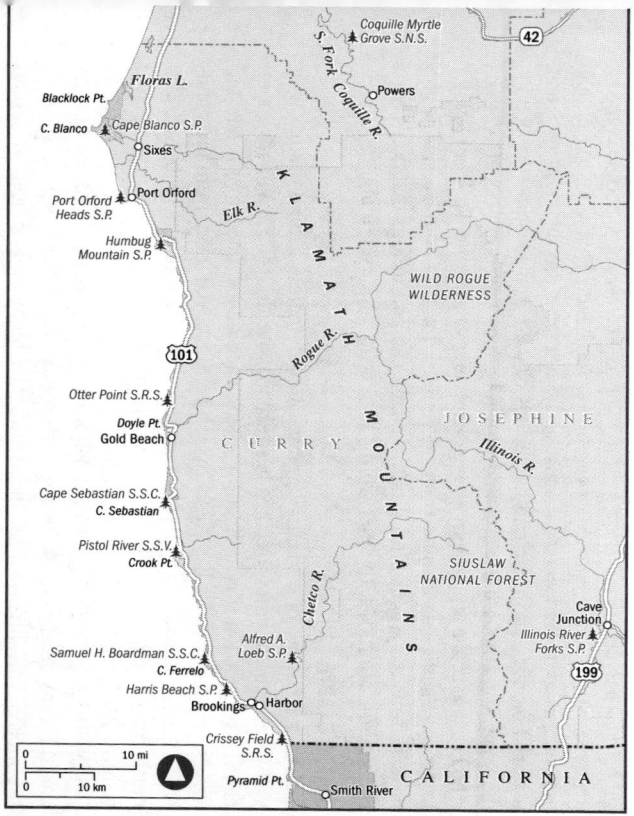
Coquille Myrtle Grove S.N.S.
42
S. Fork Coquille R.
Floras L.
Blacklock Pt.
Powers
C. Blanco
Cape Blanco S.P.
Sixes
Port Orford
Port Orford Heads S.P.
Elk R.
KLAMATH
Humbug Mountain S.P.
WILD ROGUE WILDERNESS
101
Rogue R.
Otter Point S.R.S.
Doyle Pt.
Gold Beach
JOSEPHINE
CURRY
Illinois R.
MOUNTAINS
Cape Sebastian S.S.C.
C. Sebastian
Pistol River S.S.V.
Crook Pt.
Chetco R.
SIUSLAW NATIONAL FOREST
Cave Junction
Illinois River Forks S.P.
199
Alfred A. Loeb S.P.
Samuel H. Boardman S.S.C.
C. Ferrelo
Harris Beach S.P.
Brookings
Harbor
Crissey Field S.R.S.
0 10 mi
0 10 km
Pyramid Pt.
Smith River
CALIFORNIA

WEATHER

This is not a coast where you can swim and it's not a coast where you can sunbathe. The very idea is preposterous. This is a coast where people come to *watch storms,* for heaven's sake. The bigger the better. That's not to say that the weather is never benign. August and September are the "calmest" and warmest months, and there can be periods of calm and sunshine throughout the year. Sometimes it's warm and unwindy, too—but don't count on that. And because of the topography of headlands and valleys, the weather blowing in off the Pacific can change from one mile to the next, one *moment* to the next. In July and August, hot weather inland can pull in fogs that don't burn off until the afternoon. In other words, be prepared for everything.

SHORELINE

This is a coastline of remarkable grandeur and endless natural drama, with vast white-sand beaches stretched between massive, forested headlands, along enormous bays and fifty miles of non-stop sand dunes. The surf pounds and surges against offshore haystacks, which were gnawed away from the mainland over countless eons by winds and the relentless chomping of the sea. The northern and central stretches of forested shoreline are considered temperate rainforest.

U.S. 101, also called the **Coast Highway,** is the backbone of the Oregon coast. It runs parallel to the ocean, with some inland stretches, and is one of the most scenic highways in the world. The highway is graced at several points by bridges designed in the 1930s by the great bridge engineer Conde McCullough.

In this chapter, I give you the highlights of the Oregon coast. The towns of most interest to first-time visitors—**Astoria, Cannon Beach,** and **Newport**—can be day trips from Portland. I hope you will consider driving the entire length, from Astoria to Brookings. Such a trip could be done in 2 days, but I would draw it out over 5 days and savor every scenic mile along the way.

FINDING THE PERFECT ACCOMMODATIONS

From boutique hotels to B&Bs, golf resorts, condos, Rogue River fishing lodges, rustic cabins and campgrounds with tent sites and RV hookups, the Oregon coast has a wide variety of accommodations. Summer (June–September) is

Passes and Passports Along the Coast

State parks, county parks, national-forest recreation areas, outstanding natural areas—along the Oregon coast, numerous state and federal access areas now charge day-use fees. You can either pay these day-use fees as you encounter them ($5 per day) or purchase an **Oregon Pacific Coast Passport** for $10. The Passport is good for 5 days and gets you into all state and federal parks and recreation areas along the coast. Passports are available at Forest Service and Oregon Parks and Recreation offices along the coast. For more information, contact **Oregon State Parks Information Center** (✆ **800/551-6949**) or visit www.oregonstateparks.org.

lighting the way: HISTORIC LIGHTHOUSES ON THE OREGON COAST

Of the nine original lighthouses on the Oregon Coast, seven are open to the public and most are still active. If you time it right, you'll get to go inside, take a tour, maybe go up the stairs to the watch room or even higher to the lantern room. (There are also two privately built lighthouses, but neither is open to the public.) The nine original beacons are wave-and-wind-lashed repositories of Oregon's rich coastal history, and among the more interesting buildings you'll see as you travel along the Oregon coast. I've listed most of them in this chapter, but here's a quick run-down of where they are, from north to south.

- **Tillamook Rock Lighthouse** (p. 252): Built on a rocky island 1.2 miles offshore of Tillamook Head, lit in 1880, decommissioned 1957. The lighthouse can be seen from **Ecola State Park** (p. 252) and from Highway 101 south of Cannon Beach; not open to the public.
- **Cape Meares Lighthouse** (p. 260): The shortest lighthouse on the coast is accessible from **Cape Meares State Scenic Viewpoint** (p. 260), the most northerly cape of the **Three Capes Scenic Loop** (p. 259).
- **Yaquina Head Lighthouse** (p. 274): At 93 feet high, it's the tallest lighthouse on the Oregon coast and part of the **Yaquina Head Outstanding Natural Area** (p. 274).
- **Yaquina Bay Lighthouse** (p. 275): The oldest surviving wooden lighthouse on the Oregon coast was built in 1871 and stands on the southern end of **Newport** (p. 270), just north of the Yaquina Bay Bridge.
- **Heceta Head Lighthouse** (p. 279): The most photographed lighthouse on the Pacific Coast is located off Highway 101 about 12 miles north of **Florence** (p. 283).
- **Umpqua River Lighthouse** (p. 283): Almost identical to Heceta Head (they were built from the same plans), this lighthouse was built on the bluffs overlooking the beach in what is now **Umpqua Lighthouse State Park** (p. 286).
- **Cape Arago Lighthouse:** This lighthouse, built in 1907, is located about 4 miles south of Charleston between **Sunset Bay State Park** (p. 288) and **Shore Acres State Park** (p. 288) on the Cape Arago Highway southwest of Coos Bay.
- **Coquille River Lighthouse** (p. 291): Built on a rocky islet in 1896 and unique, with its cylindrical tower attached to the east side of an elongated, octagonal room, this lighthouse was active until 1939; located in **Bullards Beach State Park** (p. 291) about 2 miles north of **Bandon** (p. 289).
- **Cape Blanco Lighthouse:** Towering above the westernmost point in Oregon, Cape Blanco Lighthouse sits 245 feet above the ocean and is the oldest continuously operating light in Oregon (built in 1870); located in Cape Blanco State Park about 4½ miles north of **Port Orford.**

the high season, when rooms are most expensive and campgrounds are full. From October to May, prices drop and everything along the coast is less busy. In the "Where to Stay" sections below, I describe the best hotels, motels, B&Bs, campgrounds and RV spots in and around the major towns along the Oregon coast.

But there are many other ways to find a place to stay, usually costing far less than commercial properties. **Airbnb** (www.airbnb.com), for example, lists dozens of rooms in private homes and beach cottages, some of them in residential neighborhoods, others in more isolated spots. If you're looking for a place to rent for a week or longer, Airbnb can do that, too, as can **Homeaway** (www.homeaway.com), **VRBO** (www.vrbo.com), and **FlipKey** (www.flipkey.com) among others. Each lists an array of homes, condos and apartmtents, some with beach access, that can sleep up to 10 people. Find the right one and you could spend hundreds less than you would in a hotel room, especially if you're traveling with a large group.

If the great outdoors is your main interest, you might want to stay at a state park or a National Forest Service campground (see below). At the state parks, lodgings options range from pitching a tent to bunking in cabins to renting a yurt. I'm partial to that last type of lodging. These are circular domed tents with electricity, plywood floors, and beds. Yurts make camping in the rain a lot more comfortable and they rent for just $35 to $76 a night. They can be found at 14 coastal parks. For information, contact **Oregon State Parks** (www.oregonstateparks.org; ✆ **800/452-5687**). You can also reserve state parks lodgings of all types through **ReserveAmerica** (www.reserveamerica.com; ✆ **800/452-5687** or 503/731-3411) up to 9 months in advance.

Although National Forest Service campgrounds are generally less developed and less in demand than state-park campgrounds, many campgrounds along the coast do stay full throughout the summer months. For reservations at Forest Service campgrounds, contact the **National Recreation Reservation Service** (www.recreation.gov; ✆ **877/444-6777** or 518/885-3639). These sites can be reserved up to 6 months in advance.

THE NORTH COAST

Starting right at the Columbia River, the border between Oregon and Washington, Oregon's North Coast extends down to Neskowin, close to Lincoln City. This stretch of the coast is backed by the Coast Range, a line of low (but snowy in winter) mountains that you have to pass over to reach the Pacific. Because it can be easily reached from Portland and I-5, the North Coast is the most visited part of the Oregon coast. There is no end of dramatic sea-scenery and long, white-sand beaches here, but there's also history: The explorers Lewis and Clark rafted down the Columbia in 1805 and set up their winter camp at **Fort Clatsop,** near present-day Astoria. And **Astoria** itself is the oldest settlement this side of the Mississippi.

Astoria ★★★

95 miles NW of Portland

History runs deep in Astoria. In fact, you could say that Oregon's Euro-centric history started right here, where the mighty Columbia River spills into the Pacific Ocean. First, in the winter of 1805-06, the explorers Lewis and Clark built Fort Clatsop 5 miles south, establishing an American claim to what

would become the Oregon Country. Five years later, in 1811, fur traders working for John Jacob Astor arrived at the mouth of the Columbia to set up a fur-trading fort that was named Fort Astoria, in Astor's honor, and became the first permanent American settlement west of the Mississippi. Astoria served as an important shipping port for the huge loads of timber cut in Oregon's virgin old-growth forests and shipped around the world. And because no real roads existed along the Oregon coast, Astoria became a port for the passenger and cargo ships sailing from New York around Cape Horn, and for the steamers that worked their way up the Oregon coast from San Francisco. Back then, the river teemed with unimaginable numbers of salmon, and when the salmon-canning boom hit in the 1880s, Astoria became a hustling and bustling little city—the second largest in Oregon—and wealthy merchants, sea captains, timbermen, and fish barons began building the ornate, Victorian-style homes that still dot the steep hillsides. Finnish, German, Swedish, and Norwegian immigrants poured into the burgeoning city to work in the canneries and lumber mills and on fishing boats. World War II saw another maritime boom for Astoria, but when the salmon dwindled because of overfishing, the canneries disappeared. The city's fortunes waned, and by the 1960s Astoria was a pretty sorry-looking place.

It had incredible potential as a tourist destination, but, as the resources that fueled its growth dwindled or dropped away, it lost its economic oomph and couldn't do much more than struggle along. Now that is changing, and people are talking about an Astoria renaissance. More people have discovered or rediscovered Astoria and the scenic splendor of the Columbia River; old homes and derelict buildings have been restored and taken on a new life. The changeover began with the restoration of the Liberty Theater downtown, a venue that now attracts a wide variety of performers; and the revitalization of the old waterfront area, which is now more accessible because of the 5-mile-long Astoria Riverwalk trail. New hotels have been built, old hotels and historic properties have been reimagined, and restaurants, coffee houses, and brewpubs have sprung up. Hopefully, as this transformation takes shape, Astoria will not lose its working-class heritage. There are still buildings here like Suomi Hall, the Finnish community's social center, but other historic places like the old Finnish bathhouse have disappeared.

Because this old city is located just inland from the river's giant, 14-mile-wide mouth, it is more a river port than a beach town. The Coast Guard is a major employer and presence in town, and there's still a big commercial and recreational fishing industry. One new development is that about a dozen cruise ships heading up to Alaska or down to California now dock at Astoria and send their 2,000 or 3,000 passengers into the town for the day or just an afternoon (another reason why new businesses are opening).

For visitors, Astoria's greatest attractions are its restored downtown area, filled with buildings from the 1920s through the 1950s; its hillsides of restored Victorian homes; the scenic views across the Columbia to the hills of southwestern Washington; and the excellent Columbia River Maritime Museum. The combination of historical character, scenic vistas, a lively arts community, and some interesting museums make this one of the most intriguing towns on the Oregon coast.

ESSENTIALS

GETTING THERE From Portland, take U.S. 30 west. From the north or south, take U.S. 101.

GETTING AROUND Astoria has a fairly small downtown core, so you can walk just about everywhere, including to the waterfront. On weekends and in summer (2–6pm) the restored 1913 **Astoria Riverfront Trolley ★★** (✆ **503/325-8790;** fare $1) runs between Pier 39 and the Astoria Red Lion Inn, making several stops along the way; the round trip takes about an hour. The 5-mile Astoria **Riverwalk ★★★,** a flat, paved trail between the Port of Astoria and 40th Street, is a perfect way to explore Astoria's revitalized waterfront on foot, by trolley or by bike.

VISITOR INFORMATION Contact or visit the **Astoria-Warrenton Area Visitor Center,** 111 W. Marine Dr. (www.travelastoria.com; ✆ **800/875-6807** or 503/325-6311), open Monday through Saturday 9am to 5pm (daily summer).

FESTIVALS Astoria has many festivals and events that draw visitors from all over. The annual **Fisher Poets Gathering** (www.fisherpoets.org; ✆ **503/338-2438**), held in late February (usually at Clemente's cafe, see p. 239), celebrates the poetry of commercial fishermen and women; you have to be a fisherperson to read your poetry, but everyone is welcome to attend. In late April, the **Astoria Warrenton Crab, Seafood & Wine Festival** (www.astoriacrabfest.com) draws big crowds to the Clatsop County Fairgrounds. In June, the fairgrounds and the Liberty Theater play host to the fun-and-food-loving **Scandinavian Midsummer Festival** (www.astoriascanfest.com) with performers from Scandinavia and Canada. Also in June, the Liberty Theater serves as the primary venue for the celebrated **Astoria Music Festival** (www.astoriamusicfestival.org; ✆ **503/325-9896**) with a surprisingly sophisticated lineup of classical and pop performances. The **Astoria Regatta** (www.astoriaregatta.org; ✆ **800/535-8767** or 503/861-2288), held every year in mid-August, is the city's biggest festival and includes lots of sailboat races. For a complete listing of all the festivals in the area, visit **www.travelastoria.com**.

EXPLORING ASTORIA

Astoria is the oldest settlement west of the Rockies, and there's more visible history here and in the surrounding vicinity than anywhere else along the Oregon coast. Two worthwhile museums (Columbia River Maritime Museum and the Flavel House) will give you a good introduction to this port and cannery-city's thriving past, and nearby Fort Clatsop, where the explorers Lewis and Clark wintered in 1805-1806, takes you back even further. But look around the downtown core and you'll see the "new" Astoria reclaiming its old buildings for new uses. And if you have time, drive around some of the old neighborhoods where Victorian-era homes are slowly being reclaimed.

In addition to the attractions below, the **Uppertown Firefighters Museum ★,** 2968 Marine Dr. (www.cumtux.org; ✆ **503/325-0920**) can be a worthwhile stop for fans of vintage fires engines. They'll see firefighting equipment from 1875 to the 1960s, including a horse-drawn fire engine. Admission by donation. The hours are erratic so call first to find out if it's open.

Astoria Column ★★ LANDMARK/VIEW Constructed in 1926 atop Coxcomb Hill, the landmark Astoria Column stands 125-feet tall and was patterned after Trajan's Column in Rome. On the exterior wall, a freshly restored mural depicts several major events in the history of the area, including Native American life before the arrival of white Europeans; the discovery of the Columbia River by Captain John Gray in 1792; the arrival of the American explorers Lewis and Clark in 1805; and the arrival of the ship *Tonquin* from New York in 1811sponsored by John Jacob Astor. There are 164 steps up to the top of the column, and on a clear day the view makes the climb well worth the effort: You can see the area's topography better here than anywhere else. Adjacent to the column, the region's rich Native American history, which dates back at least 12,000 years, is commemorated with a memorial to Chief Comcomly, leader of the Chinook Nation at the time of the Lewis and Clark expedition. The memorial is in the shape of a Chinook canoe. On the way to

Watching the Whales

Every spring and winter, gray whales migrate along the Oregon coast, often passing within easy viewing distance. Though whalers nearly harpooned them to extinction, these 50-foot-long, 30-ton leviathans recovered following government protection. Now, approximately 18,000 whales ply the 6,000-mile route between the Bering Sea and Mexico, the longest-known migration of any mammal. Southbound whales pass the Oregon coast from early December to early February, peaking at about 30 whales per hour in the last half of December. Northbound whales are less concentrated, passing from March through June and peaking in late March. Several hundred gray whales live along the Oregon coast year-round. If you want to whale-watch, bring binoculars and try to position yourself on high ground so you can see the "blow," the steamy exhalation whales make when they surface. Whale-watching excursions are available in Depoe Bay (p. 267).

the Astoria Column, stop by **Fort Astoria,** on the corner of 15th and Exchange streets. A log blockhouse and historical marker commemorate the site of the first trading post established by John Jacob Astor's fur traders in 1811.

Coxcomb Hill (drive up 16th St. and follow the signs). www.astoriacolumn.org. ✆ **503/325-2963.** Admission $5 per car. Daily dawn–dusk.

Columbia River Maritime Museum ★★★ MUSEUM Without the Columbia River—the second-largest river in U.S.—there would be no Astoria, and this museum captures the history of the river's exploration, navigation, and commercial uses. Centuries before the Columbia had a name, explorers from different nations had their eye on this mighty waterway, and the museum's collection of rare European maps, dating from the early 1500s to 1792 (when Captain George Vancouver successfully sailed up the river), is something map-lovers will especially enjoy. The problem for most of those explorers, and the problem for vessels today, was that high seas and the Columbia Bar, a shifting sandbar at the river's entrance, made entering the river so treacherous that the area became known as "the graveyard of the Pacific." The museum has a collection of vessels—a Coast Guard rescue ship, a fishing trawler, a sailboat, and the lightship *Columbia*—that illustrate the types of boats found on the Columbia. One vessel on display is a small Japanese fishing boat washed up on a nearby beach after the Japanese tsunami of 2012. Another display features two cannons (or carronades, as they are called) washed ashore after a shipwreck in 1846 and discovered in 2013 after a violent storm uncovered them. There's a section devoted to the enormous salmon canneries in Astoria that began operation in the mid-19th century and lasted until the 1940s. The newest exhibit (it opened in 2017) is called The Science of Weather and contains updated weather tracking and ocean conditions charted by NOAA (National Oceanuc and Atmospheric Administration), a studio that allows visitors to pretend to be a TV weatherperson, and some amazing footage of ships plying stormy seas—I actually got seasick watching and had to stumble away. Give yourself about an hour to see all the river- and sea-related exhibits in this fascinating museum.

1792 Marine Dr. www.crmm.org. ✆ **503/325-2323.** Admission $14 adults, $12 seniors, $5 children 6–17. Daily 9:30am–5pm. Closed Thanksgiving and Christmas.

Flavel House ★★ MUSEUM/HISTORIC HOUSE Many fortunes were made in 19th-century Astoria, and the enterprising Captain George Flavel made his by operating the first pilot service to guide ships across the treacherous Columbia River Bar. In 1885, after making his millions, Captain Flavel (1823–1893) had this imposing Queen Anne–style house built for his wife and three children. (As a side note, Captain Flavel was 30 when he married 14-year-old Mary Christina Boelling, the daughter of a German immigrant who ran a boarding house in Astoria.) Your ticket is a calling card that you present when you step into this enormous and ornate home. It's a self-guided tour with a docent available to answer your questions. How tall are those ceilings anyway? At least 14 feet. The wood used everywhere and for everything, including the commodes, is mostly native Douglas fir. Some of the furniture is original, some of it is typical of the period. This was certainly a far more formal age than our own, though the house, with its giant dining room, sitting room, and library, has a lived-in look. (The last daughter, Nelly, resided here until 1936.) Mrs. Flavel and her two daughters, even though they moved in rather elevated social circles in Astoria and San Francisco, did all the cooking, most of the cleaning, and washed the dishes themselves. The house and its occupants present a fascinating portrait of an upper-middle-class family in the rough-and-tumble Pacific Northwest of the late-19th and early-20th century—do want to watch the 13-minute video in the ticket office (the former carriage house) to learn their background before going in. The nine trees in the Victorian-style garden around the house—a giant sequoia redwood, a camperdown elm, four cork elms, a bay laurel, a pear tree, and a ginkgo—were obtained by Captain Flavel on his voyages and planted after the house was built.

441 Eighth St. www.cumtux.org. ✆ **503/325-2203.** Admission $6 adults, $5 seniors and students, $2 children 6–17. May–Sept daily 10am–5pm; Oct–Apr daily 11am–4pm.

THE goonies IN ASTORIA

It's not *all* about the cult film *The Goonies* at the **Oregon Film Museum,** 732 Duane St. (www.oregonfilmmuseum.org), but there's a lot of talk of that flick, not surprising as it was filmed in Astoria. Housed in the old Clatsop County Jail across from the Flavel House, this ingenious little museum allows visitors to make short films using three different *Goonies*-type sets (the museum then sends a video download of your film). So far, about 30 movies have been filmed in Oregon, and you'll find information and clips of some of them here, plus general information on the movie-making business. (Nowadays, it's TV series like "Portlandia" and "Grimm" that keep Oregon in the cinematic eye.) Half of the building is not a stage set but the real cells used in the Clatsop County Jail—and in *The Goonies* movie.

Heritage Museum ★ MUSEUM If you have a real interest in the history of Astoria and Clatsop County, this local-history museum housed in the former Astoria City Hall might be for you. There's nothing outstanding here, but you'll find browsable collections of Native American and pioneer artifacts as well as archival photographs of the city at various points in its development and the people and personalities who put it on the map.

1618 Exchange St. www.cumtux.org. ✆ **503/325-2203.** Admission $4 adults, $2 children 6–17. May–Sept daily 10am–5pm; Oct–Apr Tues–Sat 11am–4pm.

Pier 39 Heritage Museum ★★ The old cannery on Pier 39, built in 1875, was home to Bumble Bee Seafoods and one of the town's major employers. Today, this cannery is the oldest building on the waterfront—in fact, it's the oldest cannery building in the world—and inside you'll find the fascinating, little-visited and oddly moving Heritage Museum. It's filled with old canning equipment, historic photos, and film clips showing how the cannery operated from the late 19th century until it closed. It's maintained by volunteers and there is absolutely nothing gimmicky or fancy about it; that is what gives it its haunting slice-of-bygone-life quality. At the end of the pier, in the same building, you can have a coffee and pastry at **Coffee Girl** (p. 240). Sea lions often congregate on the breakwater right outside.

100 39th St. www.pier39-astoria.com. ✆ **503/325-2502**. Admission free. Generally open daily 10am–4pm but days and hours may change seasonally.

Waterfront ★★★ HISTORIC NEIGHBORHOOD/PARK The city of Astoria has worked hard to revitalize its historic Columbia River waterfront and to make it accessible to residents and visitors. There are several places in or near downtown where you can enjoy the views and watch the wildlife (seals, bald eagles, herons) and the passing parade of barges and enormous cargo ships. The **Sixth Street Viewing Dock,** a raised viewing platform, provides impressive views of the massive Astoria–Megler Bridge stretching for more than 4 miles across the mouth of the river from Oregon to Washington. On weekends and daily from June through August (noon–7pm), the restored 1913 **Astoria Riverfront Trolley ★★** (✆ **503/325-8790;** fare $1) runs between Pier 39 and the Astoria Red Lion Inn, making several stops along its 4-mile route; the round trip takes about an hour. The 5-mile Astoria **Riverwalk ★★★,** a flat, paved trail between the Port of Astoria and 40th Street, is a perfect way to explore Astoria's revitalized waterfront on foot or by bike.

WHERE TO STAY

For more suggestions, see "Finding the Perfect Accommodations" on p. 228.

Cannery Pier Hotel ★★★ Hands-down, this is Astoria's best hotel. Built atop one of Astoria's old cannery piers right on the Columbia River, it takes advantage of its location by offering wonderful river views from every room. The 1-bedroom corner suites with windows on two sides and a walk-out balcony offer the best outlooks; in one of these you could sit for hours, mesmerized, looking out at the mighty Columbia, the ships and the vast span of the Astoria–Megler Bridge (binoculars are provided to each guestroom).

Every room has a gas fireplace to cozy things up and a clawfoot-style soaking tub, and shutters that open out from the tub area to the living area and the view beyond. The decor uses light woods and natural fabrics to create an upscale but unobtrusive Northwest style. Onsite is a spa with Jacuzzi, Finnish sauna and a small fitness room; you can also book spa treatments. If it's a nice day, you can hop on one of the complimentary bikes and go for a spin along Astoria's 6-mile River Walk; in the evening, the hotel's vintage chauffeured cars will take you to your restaurant and pick you up. A generous continental breakfast is included in the room rate, as is evening wine and appetizers. All in all, this place is just plain great.

10 Basin St. www.cannerypierhotel.com. ✆ **888/325-4996** or 503/325-4996. 46 units. $189–$309 double, $350–$375 suites. Both types include continental breakfast and evening wine and appetizers. **Amenities:** Bikes; exercise room; sauna; spa; free Wi-Fi.

Fort Stevens State Park ★★ RV sites, cabins, yurts, deluxe cabins, tent sites, and several sites accessible for disabled campers are available at this popular, family-friendly campground in a 4,300-acre state park south of Astoria. Recreational opportunities include hiking, swimming in a freshwater lake, 9 miles of bike trails, wildlife viewing, beach walks to a historic shipwreck, and more. Reserve online or call as far in advance as possible.

100 Peter Iredale Rd, Hammond. www.oregonstateparks.org. ✆ **800/452-5687**. $22–$56 campsite, cabin $100.

Hampton Inn & Suites ★★ The views from the river-facing suites in this well-kept, mid-range Hilton franchise property are primo. From your balcony you look out across the broad Columbia and can see seals basking on the rocks below. The hotel is right next to the northernmost stop on the trolley line that runs along the waterfront, and Pier 39 with its heritage museum (it was the Bumblebee salmon canning facility). It's the only hotel in Astoria to have an indoor swimming pool (with heated seawater) and a good-sized exercise room. Rooms and suites are generously proportions and comfortably furnished, although like most franchise properties they have a somewhat corporate look. Breakfast is included in your room rate. It's a particularly family-friendly place to stay, as the studio suites can accommodate up to 6 people.

201 39th St. http://hamptoninn3.hilton.com. ✆ **503/325-1924.** 87 units. $11—$184 double w/continental breakfast included. **Amenities:** Heated indoor pool; large fitness room; free Wi-Fi.

Hotel Elliott ★ The sign painted at the top of this 6-story building, the tallest in downtown Astoria, says simply, "HOTEL ELLIOTT. WONDERFUL BEDS." The building dates from 1924 and it has always been a hotel, though never quite as nice a hotel as it is now, after a complete overhaul. The re-do bridged the gap between the old hotel and the new one by retaining some of the cool vintage features, like Douglas fir doors and detailing, but restyling the room interiors to reflect modern tastes. A muted color palette enhances the sense of calm, and all the windows have been double-paned so the rooms are quiet. Bathrooms have granite counters, tub-shower combinations, and heated floors. Downstairs, to one side of the lobby, there's a pleasant wine bar; in the morning, this is where a continental breakfast is served. On a nice afternoon or evening, head up to the roof garden for a view out over Astoria.

357 12th St. www.hotelelliott.com. ✆ **877/378-1924** or 503/325-2222. 32 units. $119–$229 double w/continental breakfast included. **Amenities:** Lounge; exercise room; free Wi-Fi.

WHERE TO EAT

The "Astoria renaissance" everyone is talking about definitely extends to the city's ever-expanding restaurant scene. Until just 5 years ago, Astoria was a city with a couple of so-so restaurants. Now the area around the restored Liberty Theater at 12th and Commercial has several worthwhile dining spots, and there are also a couple of good places on or near the waterfront. For to-go fare, I'd suggest that you check out the new **food carts** at 13th and Duane streets; there's a pleasant plaza there with picnic tables for outdoor noshing in nice weather.

Baked Alaska ★★ NORTHWEST/PIZZA Built on a pier in downtown Astoria, this restaurant isn't just on the waterfront, it's over the waves. The views are stellar, and the ambiance is calm and woodsy. Baked Alaska started life as a mobile soup trailer in Alaska; when the chef/owner and his wife decided to settle down, they picked Astoria. Begin with the seafood chowder—it's what launched the eatery. For mains try one of the signature Baked Alaska sandwiches, created by the chef when he had only one pizza oven and had to be creative. The sandwiches are made with hand-tossed pizza dough, folded and baked in the oven, and filled with meat and veggies. I would recommend the Cubano with pulled pork, prosciutto and fontina cheese. The handcrafted, brick-oven pizzas here are also worth trying (gluten-free crusts available), and so are the Alaskan cod fish and chips. What's for dessert? You know the answer.

1 12th St. www.bakedak.com. ✆ **503/325-7414.** Main courses $11–$28; 3-course menu $33. Daily 11:30am–9pm (Fri–Sat until 10pm).

BRIDGEwater Bistro ★★★ NORTHWEST A step up in sophistication from Baked Alaska, but still casual (this is the Oregon coast, after all) this large, attractive bistro in a former cannery (near the Cannery Pier Hotel) offers an all-purpose, gluten-free-friendly lunch and dinner menu (90% of the menu can be modified to be gluten-free). Even the fish and chips are gluten-free, although you'd never know it from the taste. If you're coming for dinner, you might want to the try the cioppino, a signature fish soup with Dungeness crab, salmon, crabs, mussels, and scallops. But there are many options here, from small plates to burgers, pan-fried Willapa Bay oysters, fresh fish, a daily seafood cake, and unusual dishes like Dungeness crab mac and cheese. There's also a good wine and beer list and a popular Sunday brunch. The restaurant is right on the river so you'll enjoy outstanding views with your meal.

20 Basin St. www.bridgewaterbistro.com. ✆ **503/325-6777.** Main courses $12–$39. Mon–Sat 11:30am–8 or 9pm; Sun 11am–8 or 9pm.

Carruthers ★★ NEW AMERICAN Astoria's newest restaurant occupies a corner of the 1920s-era Carruthers Building in the "urban renaissance" section of downtown Astoria. It has a crisp, upscale ambiance that makes it a special place to try for dinner. Or, better yet, come here for the popular Happy Hour (4–6pm) and enjoy a well-made cocktail and a couple of the small-plate specials served at the bar. The dinner menu is inventive, sometimes breaking culinary rules, like mixing fish with cheese (the scrumptious scallops atop cheese risotto), and mixing influences—curry carrot ginger lime Greek yogurt soup is a mouthful to order, but what a mouthful! If all this is too creative for you, order the juicy burger—it's so large you may need a hand crank to get your mouth wide enough to eat it.

1198 Commercial St. ✆ **503/741-3443.** Happy hour specials $10–$15; main courses $13–$24. Tues–Thurs 4–10pm, Fri–Sat 4–11pm.

Clemente's Café and Public House ★★★ SEAFOOD/PACIFIC NORTHWEST Owned and operated by a fourth-generation Astorian fishermen, Clemente's is an excellent restaurant for, not surprisingly, fresh seafood. The food here is cooked from scratch and there is nothing gimmicky about it; I personally like places that still serve old-fashioned favorites like shrimp cocktail or crab louis. For a really satisfying lunch, I would recommend the fresh fish sandwiches; the oyster and halibut are served on chewy rustic bread with non-greasy fries and house-made catsup. The fish and chips here are renowned, made from your choice of freshly caught halibut, salmon, cod, or oysters. Clemente's is very much a local institution. It's friendly, unpretentious, and welcomes kids. In nice (windless) weather you can sit out beside the river and watch the ships go by.

175 14th St. ✆ **503/325-1067.** Main courses $10–$28. Tues–Sun 11am–10pm.

T Paul's Supper Club ★★ AMERICAN/PACIFIC NORTHWEST There's a quirky kind of glamour to this eatery, with its light sculptures, whimsical art works, and soaring ceiling. That's enhanced on the nights when live music accompanies the meal (what makes this a "club" we assume). So what if the menu is all over the place, with Caribbean, Mexican, Southern, and Pacific Northwest offerings? Many of the dishes are quite toothsome, like the Cajun halibut tacos and the big-enough-for-two Boom Boom Salad, which is greens, chopped apple, pear, strawberry, red onion, bacon, cheese, and either chicken or shrimp. The burgers and sandwiches are solid and, in keeping with the supper-club shtick, several kinds of steak are available.

360 12th St. www.tpaulssupperclub.com. ✆ **503/325-2545.** Main courses $10–$29. Mon–Thurs 11am–9pm; Fri–Sat 11am–10pm.

ASTORIA AFTER DARK

The major performing-arts venue in Astoria is the **Liberty Theater,** 1203 Commercial St. (www.liberty-theater.org; ✆ **503/325-5922**), a handsomely restored 1920s movie palace that now hosts a surprising array of performers and performances throughout the year. If you're here in the summer, you might enjoy a performance of *Shanghaied in Astoria,* a musical melodrama

COFFEE, BEER, WINE & more

Astoria's all about the food and drink nowadays, so here are a few more tasty options:

Smoked Fish & Deli **Josephson's,** 106 Marine Dr. (www.josephsons.com; ✆ **800/772-3474** or 503/325-2190) is a local seafood-smoking company that opened in 1920 and sells smoked salmon by the quarter-pound. It has a take-out deli counter with clam chowder, salmon burgers, and more.

Coffee For the best latte in town, head down to **Three Cups Coffee House,** 279 West Marine Dr. (✆ **503/325-7487**), the coffee house that shares space with Columbia Coffee Roasters. I love its friendly, funky vibe. In downtown Astoria you can get good espresso at the **Astoria Coffeehouse & Bistro,** 243 11th St. (www.astoriacoffeehouse.com; ✆ **503/325-1787**). Another good caffeine station, is **Coffee Girl,** 100 39th St. (www.thecoffeegirl.com; **503/325-6700**), located at the end of Pier 39 in the world's oldest cannery building. Here you can sit next to the river (inside or out) and enjoy breakfast, lunch, or a delectable pastry with your espresso.

Brewpubs Astoria is big on brewpubs. Downtown on the waterfront, there's the **Wet Dog Café & Brewery,** 144 11th St. (www.wetdogcafe.com; ✆ **503/325-6975**), and at the east end of town, there's the **Rogue Ales Public House,** Pier 39, 100 39th St. (www.rogue.com; ✆ **503/325-5964**), where you can sometimes watch seals just outside the window. Some of the most unusual brews in town are on tap at the **Fort George Brewery & Public House,** 1483 Duane St. (www.fortgeorgebrewery.com; ✆ **503/325-7468**).

Bakery The **Blue Scorcher Bakery Café,** 1493 Duane St. (www.bluescorcher.com; ✆ **503/338-7473**), is Astoria's best bakery, making and selling organic, artisan goods.

Wine The **Cellar on 10th,** 1004 Marine Dr. (www.thecellaron10th.com; ✆ **503/325-6600**), is a well-stocked wine shop that has weekly tastings and occasional winemaker dinners.

that is staged each year by the **Astor Street Opry Company,** 129 W. Bond St. (www.shanghaiedinastoria.com; ✆ **503/325-6104**). Performances are usually held from early July to mid-September.

Fort Clatsop–Lewis & Clark National Historic Park ★★★

5 miles S of Astoria

ESSENTIALS

GETTING THERE From Astoria, head south on U.S. 101 and follow signs.

VISITOR INFORMATION The park's **visitor center** (www.nps.gov/lewi; ✆ **503/861-2471**) is open year-round, mid-June to Labor Day daily 9am to 6pm; Labor Day to mid-June daily 9am to 5pm. Here you'll find interpretive displays, a good bookstore, and park rangers who can provide information on nearby attractions, hiking trails, and other parks.

"Ocian in view! O! The joy!" William Clark wrote in his journal as he stood on a spit of land just south of present-day Astoria in the fall of 1805. He was feeling exultant after the arduous journey he'd undertaken with Meriwether

Lewis and the Corps of Discovery, traveling over 2,500 miles west from St. Louis, across the northern plains, over the Rockies, and down the Columbia River to the Pacific. They had achieved their goal and fulfilled Thomas Jefferson's mandate to find a passageway to the west. But Clark had yet to deal with the weather on the northern Oregon coast. After building Fort Clatsop, where the Corps spent the winter, Clark wrote, "O! How horrible is the day waves brakeing with great violence against the shore . . . all wet and confined to our shelters." Throughout that long winter, there were only 5 days when it didn't rain.

An accurate replica of their shelter, a log stockade which they named Fort Clatsop after the local Clatsop Indians who had befriended them, is what you'll see at this national park. Though archaeologists have never been able to pinpoint the exact location of Fort Clatsop, this replica was built within a few yards of where they believe the original fort stood. The design was based on notes and sketches in William Clark's journal.

It's not a large fort. It was built quickly, and it's very basic, with wooden gates at either end and two rows of small, adjoining cabins facing each other across a central courtyard (which would have been mud instead of the bark chips that are there now), and it provides a glimpse of what life was like for these now-legendary explorers during that endlessly wet winter more than 200 years ago. Sacagawea, the 16-year-old Shoshone woman who made the trek with French-Canadian Toussaint Charbonneau and their infant son, occupied the first cabin to your right upon entering. Lewis and Clark shared the cabin next to them. The Corps slept about eight men to a cabin on the other side. These bare, unfinished cabins had an open firepit at one end with a flue for the smoke, hand-hewn wooden beds, and not much else. (You'll appreciate the luxury of a warm dry bed and a hot shower after a visit here.) From mid-June through Labor Day, park rangers clad in period clothing give demonstrations of some of the daily activities that took place at the fort, including flintlock use, buckskin preparation, and candle making.

A path leads down from the fort to a nearby canoe launch area. The explorers traveled south from Fort Clatsop as far as present-day Seaside—where they boiled seawater to make salt and marveled at a beached whale (Sacagawea insisted on accompanying the men to see it)—and north to Cape

Enjoying Sundays at the Astoria Sunday Market

One of Oregon's largest and liveliest outdoor markets, **Astoria Sunday Market** (www.astoriasundaymarket.com; ✆ **503/325-1010**) is held in downtown Astoria every Sunday from Mother's Day to the second Sunday in October. Some 200 vendors, including farmers, fishermen, foragers, craftspeople and local businesses, spread their fresh produce, artisanal fare and homemade crafts along Commercial St. and 12th St. This city-wide celebration features a food court with a stage where bands from all over Oregon come to play. It's the only market of its kind on the Oregon coast and if you're in Astoria on a Sunday, you won't want to miss it.

Disappointment in Washington State. Both of these sites are part of the Lewis and Clark Historical Park, as is the 6.5-mile **Fort to Sea Trail,** which ends in Seaside. Over on the Washington side of the Columbia, there are two installations by artist Maya Lin that were commissioned as part of the Lewis and Clark bicentennial.

On the short trail from the visitor center to the fort, you'll pass a bronze statue of Sacagawea with her baby on her back. This is a long-overdue tribute to the young Shoshone woman who traveled with the expedition as an unpaid guide and interpreter. She was all of 16 and had given birth just 3 months before the Corps of Discovery set off. Our ideas about "history" and history makers have changed drastically over the last couple of decades. The Native Americans who inhabited the coastal regions of the Northwest had a rich and long-evolved culture of their own that preceded the arrival of Lewis and Clark by thousands of years. But however you view their achievements, Lewis and Clark and the men—and woman—who accompanied them, made an incredible journey through an area previously unknown to colonialists, and their arrival at this spot on the Oregon coast in 1805 marks the beginning of a new era in the settlement of the West.

92343 Fort Clatsop Rd. (off U.S. 101, 5 miles southwest of Astoria). www.nps.gov/lewi. ✆ **503/861-2471.** Admission $3 adults, free for children 15 and under. Mid-June to Labor Day daily 9am–6pm; Labor Day to mid-June daily 9am–5pm.

Seaside ★★

17 miles S of Astoria, 79 miles W of Portland, 7 miles N of Cannon Beach

Seaside, about 2 hours from Portland, is the top family destination on the northern Oregon coast. That means you may want to visit or you may want to avoid it entirely.

The town is one of the oldest beach resorts on the coast. At one time you could get to Seaside by train and a big beachside amusement park was waiting for you when you arrived. But nowadays, if you want to enjoy Seaside's charms, you have to get away from the mall-like hurly-burly of Broadway, its

Paddling on the Lewis and Clark River

At Fort Clatsop—Lewis & Clark National Historic Park you can join a Park Ranger-led **Lewis & Clark River Paddle Tour** ★★★ that lets you paddle in a two-person kayak along the shoreline of the Lewis and Clark River. These 3-hour guided tours, available from late June to early September, are not strenuous and provide a wonderful perspective on the region, its history, and its wildlife. And to make them even more enticing, the kayak tours are free with the price of admission to the park. Kayaks, paddles and life jackets are provided; paddle tours begin at Netul Landing 1 mile south of the Fort Clatsop visitor center. Children must be 10 or older and accompanied by an adult. **Note:** You must make a reservation for these tours in advance, and reservations are on a first-come, first-served basis. For all the specifics, **visit www.nps.gov/lewi.** This is a great experience for the entire family.

the very big mouth OF THE COLUMBIA

The 14-mile-wide mouth of the Columbia River is a sight to behold, and the best place to behold it is from the **South Jetty Overlook** in **Fort Stevens State Park** (www.oregonstateparks.org), about 10 miles south of Astoria. Instead of turning left from Hwy. 101 to reach Fort Clatsop (see above), turn right and follow the signs to Fort Stevens State Park. You want **Parking Lot C,** where you'll find a raised wooden platform that provides a view of the treacherous mouth of America's second-longest river, where it empties into the Pacific. The river's mouth is about a mile away to the north, but this is the closest you'll come to seeing a sight that filled explorers Lewis and Clark with excitement and wonder when they encountered it in the winter of 1805. Shifting and blowing sands have added about a mile to the Pacific shoreline in the 200-plus years since Lewis and Clark arrived. Fort Stevens State Park has some good walking beaches and some excellent campgrounds popular with families; to reserve, go to the park's website.

main drag, because the commercial heart of Seaside is like a Northwest version of Atlantic city; in fact, back in the days of beauty pageants, Seaside is where the Miss Oregon contest was held. Time-share apartment blocks and big, anonymous-looking convention hotels rise up beside the beach and dwarf the smaller, clapboard homes and motels that once characterized Seaside. The town has a touristy tang that makes it popular with 20-somethings who want to drink, smoke pot and party. It's close enough to Portland to make it an easy day trip, so it also draws lots of parents with young kids enjoying a relatively inexpensive day at the beach.

The plusses? First and foremost, that fabulous beach. It extends for miles and is walkable its entire length. There is also a unique promenade from the 1920s lined with well-kept homes and cottages on one side and vast dunes and the ocean on the other. Once you get away from the center, the town is filled with vintage cottages and is really pretty charming. So I'm not saying you can't have a good time here (especially if you have kids), but I am saying that if you're looking for a tranquil, romantic getaway, Seaside is not the place for you.

If you travel just a few minutes north, however, you'll find **Gearhart,** a very different kind of Oregon coast town. This quiet community, which begins on the north end of Seaside, goes out of its way to avoid the kind of hustling tourism that keeps Seaside afloat, has long been a retreat for wealthy Portlanders. It's filled with suburban-size homes on manicured residential streets. Beach access isn't as easy as from Seaside, but that's what helps keep things calm and controlled in Gearhart.

ESSENTIALS

GETTING THERE Seaside is on U.S. 101 just north of the junction with U.S. 26, which connects to Portland. Gearhart is at the north end of Seaside.

VISITOR INFORMATION Contact the Seaside Visitors Bureau,7 N. Roosevelt Dr., Seaside (www.seasideor.com; ✆ **888/306-2386** or 503/738-3097).

FESTIVALS The weekend before Labor Day weekend the town celebrates the **Hood to Coast Run,** a team-marathon even that begins on Mt. Hood ends at Seaside.

EXPLORING SEASIDE & NEIGHBORING GEARHART

Bumper Cars and Tilt-a-Whirl ★ There are a couple of video arcades along busy Broadway but the only arcade I think is worth visiting, and only if you have kids, is this one with old-fashioned bumper cars on one side and an old-fashioned Tilt-a-Whirl on the other. These rides need to be outdoors, on a midway, to be really fun, but since it rains a lot on the Oregon coast, these are in a building that may remind you of a garage. But they're still fun and a nice alternative to the shrieking, glaring, violent video games.

110 Broadway. ✆ **503/738-5540**. Open daily June–Sept 11:30am–9pm; weekends and holidays rest of the year. $3 per ride.

Promenade ★★ Seaside's centerpiece is its 2-mile-long beachfront Promenade (or Prom), built in 1927. At the west end of Broadway, where the Turnaround divides this paved, level walkway into the North Prom and the South Prom, you'll find a bronze statue marking the official end of the trail for the Lewis and Clark expedition of 1805. South of the statue, on Lewis & Clark Way, between the Promenade and Beach drive (8 blocks south of Broadway), stands the **Lewis and Clark Salt Works,** a reconstruction of the fire pit used by members of the expedition to extract salt from seawater. During the winter of 1806, while the Corps was camped at **Fort Clatsop** (see p. 240), near present-day Astoria, Lewis and Clark sent three men southwest 15 miles to make salt from seawater. It took the three men nearly 2 months to produce four bushels of salt for the return trip to St. Louis. Five kettles were used for boiling saltwater on fires that were kept stoked around the clock. There's an interpretive plaque that gives the history of the site and how it was rediscovered.

The Prom is a great place to stroll or bicycle. Every couple of blocks, paths lead through the wide swathes of beachgrass-covered dunes to the beach itself. The homes and cottages along the Prom, both north and south of Broadway, may look fairly modest, but in 2017 one of them on the South Prom was on the market for $2.35 million and a small fixer-upper on the North Prom was tagged at just under a million.

Seaside Aquarium ★ The privately owned Seaside Aquarium is one of the town's most popular family attractions, but it can't hold a candlefish to the superlative Oregon Coast Aquarium in Newport. Still, here you can feed the seals and watch graceful Medusas (jellyfish) and giant Pacific octupuses, tiny pipefish and other creatures of the deep. The 36-foot-long skeleton of a gray whale (the kind that migrates along the Oregon Coast from Alaska to Baja) is visible through one of the windows.

200 N. Promenade. www.seasideaquarium.com. ✆ **503/738-6211.** Admission $8 adults, $6.75 seniors, $3.50 ages 6–13. Daily 9am–5pm.

Seaside Beach ★★★ A lovely white-sand beach begins just south of Seaside at the foot of imposing Tillamook Head and stretches north to the

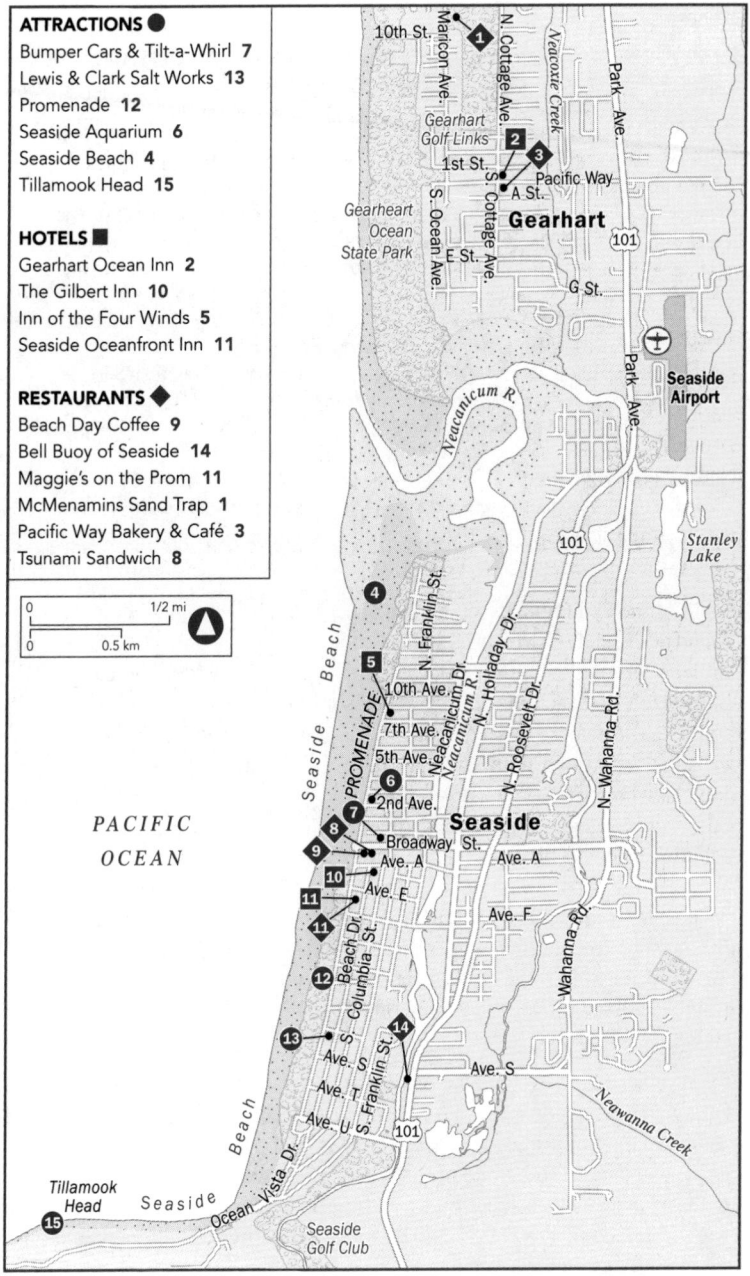
ATTRACTIONS ●
Bumper Cars & Tilt-a-Whirl 7
Lewis & Clark Salt Works 13
Promenade 12
Seaside Aquarium 6
Seaside Beach 4
Tillamook Head 15
HOTELS ■
Gearhart Ocean Inn 2
The Gilbert Inn 10
Inn of the Four Winds 5
Seaside Oceanfront Inn 11
RESTAURANTS ◆
Beach Day Coffee 9
Bell Buoy of Seaside 14
Maggie's on the Prom 11
McMenamins Sand Trap 1
Pacific Way Bakery & Café 3
Tsunami Sandwich 8
0 1/2 mi
0 0.5 km
10th St.
Marion Ave.
N. Cottage Ave.
Neacoxie Creek
Park Ave.
Gearhart Golf Links
1st St.
Pacific Way
A St.
Gearhart
Gearheart Ocean State Park
S. Ocean Ave.
S. Cottage Ave.
E St.
G St.
101
Seaside Airport
Neacanicum R.
Stanley Lake
N. Franklin St.
N. Holladay Dr.
N. Roosevelt Dr.
N. Wahanna Rd.
Seaside Beach
PROMENADE
10th Ave.
7th Ave.
5th Ave.
2nd Ave.
Seaside
Broadway St.
Ave. A
Ave. F
Ave. S
Ave. T
Ave. U
Beach Dr.
S. Columbia St.
S. Franklin St.
Wahanna Rd.
Neawanna Creek
PACIFIC OCEAN
Tillamook Head
Ocean Vista Dr.
Seaside Golf Club

TACKLING tillamook head

The Oregon coast offers hikers a slew of magnificent opportunities and the 6-mile **Tillamook Head Trail** ★★★ from Seaside to Cannon Beach, or vice verse, is one of the best. Tillamook Head is the giant headland that you see jutting into the sea at the south end of Seaside. In the winter of 1806, the explorers Lewis and Clark traversed this 15-million-year-old remnant of a massive basaltic lava flow on an expedition to buy whale blubber from the Indians at Cannon Beach. Clark marveled the view, exclaiming, "I behold the grandest and most pleasing prospect which my eyes ever surveyed." The basic trail is 6 miles long and climbs 1,000 feet through a temperate rainforest of fir and red cedar. There are several signposted hikes of varying distances that you can take from Seaside or from Indian Beach in Ecola State Park in Cannon Beach. You'll enjoy spectacular views of the Pacific Ocean and Tillamook Rock, an offshore island with a lighthouse that operated from 1881 to 1957 (today's it's a privately owned columbarium).

This is a remarkable hike, if you go from one side of Tillamook Head to the other, but it is strenuous and not something you can do in your beach flip-flops and shorts. For more information, visit **www.oregonhiking.com**.

To find the trailhead from Seaside, travel south on Hwy. 101 to the town's southernmost traffic signal, turn west on Avenue U for 2 blocks, and left again at Edgewood, which becomes Sunset, for 1.2 miles to the road's end.

mouth of the Columbia River. You can access the beach right below the Turnaround at the end of Broadway in central Seaside or via one of the many paths that lead through the dunes alongside the Prom. This wide, flat, easily walkable stretch of beach is the biggest reason why Seaside is so popular with families. The water's too cold for swimming, but on warm, sunny days it's perfect for splashing in up to your knees and the surf rolls in with less force than elsewhere on the coast, so kids can play close to the water. Kite flying and beach cycling are popular pastimes. All over town you'll find places that rent four-wheeled bicycles, called surreys, and three-wheeled cycles called funcycles for pedaling on the hard-packed sand when the tide is out. Funcycles cost between $10 and $20 an hour to rent; expect to pay between $20 and $30 an hour for multipassenger surreys. One reliable rental shop is **Wheel Fun Rentals,** Shiloh Inn Waterfront, 30 N. Prom (www.wheelfunrentals.com; ✆ **503/738-8447**). They have three other locations around Seaside.

WHERE TO STAY

If you're heading here with the whole family or plan to stay a while, consider renting a house, a cottage, or an apartment. Offerings range from studio apartments to large luxurious oceanfront houses, and prices span an equally wide range. You can do so on one of the major rental websites (see p. 89 for more on that) or go with a local outfit. **Cannon Beach Property Management** (www.cbpm.com; ✆ **877/386-3402**) is nearby, inspects the properties it rents, and is easily available should anything go wrong.

IN SEASIDE

The Gilbert Inn ★★★ One block from the beach and 1 block south of busy Broadway, in an old residential neighborhood that's now surrounded by bland new hotels and condos, the Gilbert Inn is pretty Queen Anne–style Victorian house with a pretty little yard. It considers itself a "couples retreat"; that means you have to be at least 18 to stay here (or, to put it another, no kids allowed). Built in 1892 by Alexander Gilbert, one of the founding fathers of Seaside, the house retains many of its original interior features, such as walls and ceilings constructed with tongue-and-groove fir planks. The rooms are decorated with comfortable period furnishings but have flat-screen TVs and modern bathrooms. There are 3 rooms on the first floor, in an unobtrusively newer addition; the nicest rooms are the upstairs in the original house, but there is no elevator, so if stairs are an issue, book one of the first-floor rooms. There's a lovely sun room to enjoy, and a fire pit outside.

341 Beach Dr., Seaside. www.gilbertinn.com. ✆ **800/507-2714.** 6 units. $99–$199 double w/continental breakfast. **Amenities:** Free Wi-Fi.

Inn of the Four Winds ★★ You'll find this nice oceanfront motel-ish hotel up at the north end of the Promenade, away from all the activity in the center of town, and that can be considered a real plus. Most of the guest rooms have balconies, expansive ocean views, and gas fireplaces. The units here are large, light, and airy with quietly tasteful contemporary decor. The dunes, with paths down to the beach, are right outside your window.

820 N. Promenade, Seaside. www.innofthefourwinds.com. ✆ **800/818-9524** or 503/738-9524. 13 units. $149–$249 double. **Amenities:** Free Wi-Fi.

Seaside Oceanfront Inn ★★ There's a terrific ocean view from almost every room in this contemporary boutique hotel, and I wish there was a balcony to go with it. Thankfully, you can open a window to hear the surf and smell the salt air, and the windows are big. There are less expensive non-ocean-view rooms, too, but even if you get one of those you should be satisfied. Rooms here invite lounging: They're large, bright, and attractively furnished in a contemporary style that's more design-conscious than most hotels in Seaside. Some units have an upper loft area with a Jacuzzi tub and spa-like bathroom, or an extra bed. **Maggie's on the Prom** (reviewed below), Seaside's one good restaurant, occupies the first floor of this shingled building. It serves breakfast, lunch and dinner, so you could hole up for a romantic weekend and never leave your room—except for a walk on the beach that's right outside your window.

580 Beach Dr., Seaside, OR. www.theseasideinn.com. ✆ **503/738-6403**. 16 units. $119–$189 double. Pets accepted ($25/night in 2nd floor rooms only). **Amenities:** Gas fireplace (some rooms); Jacuzzi (some rooms); free Wi-Fi.

IN GEARHART

Gearhart Ocean Inn ★★★ This 1941 motor-court-style motel has been completely renovated and turned into a collection of cozy, charming, cottage-like studios that offer economical accommodation in a quiet Gearhart neighborhood about 3 blocks from the beach. The two wood-frame buildings, painted white and facing one another across a gravel drive, have trees and pocket gardens in front of each unit, giving them a vintage character. The units, many with bedrooms on the second floor, have been decorated in a mix of country cute and casual contemporary; they have kitchens and Franklin stoves. There's a garden in back where you can barbecue or play badminton.

67 N. Cottage Ave., Gearhart. www.gearhartoceaninn.com. ✆ **800/352-8034** or 503/738-7373. 12 units. $105–$185 double. 2–3 night minimum summer, weekends, and holidays. Dogs accepted ($15 per night). **Amenities:** Bikes; free Wi-Fi.

Where to Eat

IN SEASIDE

If you're looking for a quick meal, some picnic food, or something to take back and cook in your room, drop by the old-timey **Bell Buoy of Seaside ★★,** 1800 S. Roosevelt Dr. (✆ **800/529-2722** or 503/738-6354; www.bellbuoyofseaside.com), which sells cooked Dungeness crabs, award-winning chowder, smoked salmon, fresh seafood, and shrimp or crab melts. Or duck into **Tsunami Sandwich ★**, 11 Broadway (www.tsunamisandwich.com; ✆ **503/738-5427**), just a few yards from the beach. The ingredients used here are high-quality; there are about eight different sandwiches offered daily and you can eat in (on picnic tables) or take out. Tsunami's is open daily at 11am and closes at different times according to the season.

As you may know by now, I am always on the lookout to find the best cup of coffee in every town I visit. In Seaside, it's **Beach Day Coffee ★**, 7 Broadway (ww.beachdaycoffee.com; ✆ **503/338-9619**), just a few steps from the Prom. They use locally roasted coffee and can steam up a foamy latte, squeeze out a zippy espresso and serve a good pastry. The shop is open Monday through Friday from 8am to 4pm, Saturday and Sunday from 7am to 6pm.

Maggie's on the Prom ★★ NEW AMERICAN When Yummy's Wine Bar closed, Maggie's on the Prom became the only fine-dining restaurant left in Seaside. It caters to a food-conscious clientele, including guests at the boutiquey Seaside Oceanfront Inn, where it occupies the first floor and provides room service. The menu here offers many classics (eggs benedict for breakfast, halibut fish and chips for lunch, filet mignon and bouillabaisse for dinner) but it also presents innovative takes on Oregon meats, vegetables, and fruits like their roasted beet and strawberry salad and, for an entrée, heritage pork cooked in Riesling. It's seasonal, local and sustainable, and of course it has gluten-free and vegetarian options (like Oregon chanterelle mushrooms on pasta). The Happy Hour is fun and offers a long list of cocktails. Be aware that Maggie's has a very small dining room; reservations are essential in summer. Maggie, by the way, is not the chef but a cat who used to live in the hotel.

580 Beach Dr. (in Seaside Oceanfront Inn). ✆ **503/738-5403.** www.maggiesontheprom.com. Reservations recommended for dinner. Main courses $12–$34. Daily 8am–9pm.

IN GEARHART

McMenamins Sand Trap ★ AMERICAN This oceanside outpost of the McMenamins brewpub empire overlooks the oldest golf course in Oregon and melds a classic country-club atmosphere with the McMenamins' Deadhead aesthetic. The menu sticks mostly to tried-and-true pub standards—burgers, pizzas, and fish and chips. However, since this is the beach, you can also get steamer clams, crab cakes, and cedar-plank roasted salmon. There are always half a dozen or more McMenamins beers on tap. The building also operates as a McMenamin's hotel with 16 rooms (expanding in 2018 to 36 rooms), most of them overlooking the golf course.

1157 N. Marion Ave. ✆ **503/717-8150.** www.mcmenamins.com. Main courses $8–$23. Mon–Tues 11am–10pm; Wed–Thurs 11am–11pm; Fri 11am–midnight; Sat 8am–midnight; Sun 8am–10pm.

Pacific Way Bakery & Café ★★ SANDWICHES/NORTHWEST This former mom-and-pop grocery store in the center of Gearhart has a classic Cape Cod–style beach feel and is a favorite place to dine in tony, well-heeled Gearhart (if you're staying in Seaside and want a special dinner, come here). The vintage interior harkens back to the 1930s but the food is pretty much of today, a mixture of comfort foods and health-conscious fare. At lunch, there are appetizing sandwiches, soups (clam chowder, of course), fish tacos and crisp, fresh salads. In the evening, you'll find well executed dishes like Oregon Dungeness crab ravioli, halibut piccata, char-broiled pork chops, maple-glazed salmon, and Oregon wild-mushroom macaroni and cheese. There's a good wine list, too. The adjacent bakery, open Thursday through Monday from 7am to 1pm (call for winter hours), is a top place for bread, muffins, and sweet treats.

601 Pacific Way. ✆ **503/738-0245.** www.pacificwaybakery-cafe.com. Main courses $10–$16 lunch, $15–$31 dinner. Thurs–Mon 11am–3:30pm and 5–9pm.

Cannon Beach ★★★

25 miles S of Astoria, 9 miles S of Seaside, 112 miles N of Newport, 79 miles W of Portland

Weathered cedar-shingle cottages, picket fences draped with drifts of nasturtiums, quiet gravel lanes, interesting little art galleries and shops, good restaurants and coffee shops, and a long, flat, gorgeous sand beach presided over by massive monoliths, called sea stacks or hay stacks, rising from the surf—what more could you want from an Oregon beach town? If it weren't for all the other people who also think Cannon Beach is the most wonderful place on the Oregon coast, this would be a misty version of heaven.

Some say that Cannon Beach suffers from chronic quaintness; others complain that it has become too upscale and expensive for its own good. Once it was the Oregon coast's most renowned artists' community, but now Cannon Beach is as much about upscale shopping in tasteful, tucked-away plazas as it is about being in touch with nature. But with so many utilitarian and ticky-tacky towns along the coast, I personally think that well-groomed and always-presentable Cannon Beach is one of the top beach towns on the Oregon coast. Once you get away from the crowds, it still has a village atmosphere, and summer throngs and traffic jams can do nothing to assault the dramatic, in-your-face beauty of Haystack Rock, the famous monolith that rises like a giant plum pudding from the pounding waves of the Pacific.

ESSENTIALS

GETTING THERE Cannon Beach is on U.S. 101 just south of the junction with U.S. 26. From Portland, it takes about 2 hours to get there by car.

VISITOR INFORMATION The **Cannon Beach Visitor Center,** 207 N. Spruce St. (intersection of Sitka and Spruce; www.cannonbeach.org; ✆ **503/436-2623**) is open daily from 10am to 5pm.

GETTING AROUND The town stretches for about 3 miles between the ocean and Highway 101, and is easily walkable. **Hemlock Street,** the main drag in downtown Cannon Beach, is the town's commercial hub, with a concentration of galleries, boutiques, restaurants, and candy and ice cream stores. The **Cannon Beach Shuttle** provides van service up and down the length of town and operates daily with seasonal hours. Look for signed shuttle stops. The fare is $1.

FESTIVALS The **Savor Cannon Beach** (www.savorcannonbeach.com) food and wine festival in early March is a popular event, with food and wine tastings throughout the town. In early June, the **Sandcastle Contest** turns the beach into one vast canvas for sand sculptors from all over the region. This is a well-known Oregon coast event and draws thousands of visitors. In early November, the **Stormy Weather Arts Festival** celebrates the arrival of winter storms with gallery shows and performances. For a current listing of events, visit **www.cannonbeach.org**.

EXPLORING CANNON BEACH

Cannon Beach ★★★ OUTDOOR RECREATION/BEACH Wide, flat, sandy Cannon Beach is a wonderful place to take a long, invigorating beach walk. Haystack Rock adds an undeniably dramatic focal point to the beach, and when the tide is out, you can explore the tide pools at its base. But please don't disturb the sea urchins and starfish, and don't climb up on the monolith—every year, careless climbers have to be plucked off the rock because the tide has come in and stranded them. Besides walking, kite flying and beachcombing are the most popular Cannon Beach pastimes, but you can also enjoy the beach in a variety of other ways. Between Memorial Day and Labor Day, guided horseback rides to Cove Beach and Haystack Rock are offered by **Sea Ranch Stables,** 415 Fir St. (www.searanchrv.com; ✆ **503/436-2815**), at the north entrance to Cannon Beach. Rides cost $80 to $140. These popular excursions are on a first-come, first-served basis, so sign up in person as early as you can.

Cannon Beach History Center & Museum ★ MUSEUM On the surface, Cannon Beach may not look as though it has much history, but from Lewis and Clark's visit to the story of the cannon that gave the town its name,

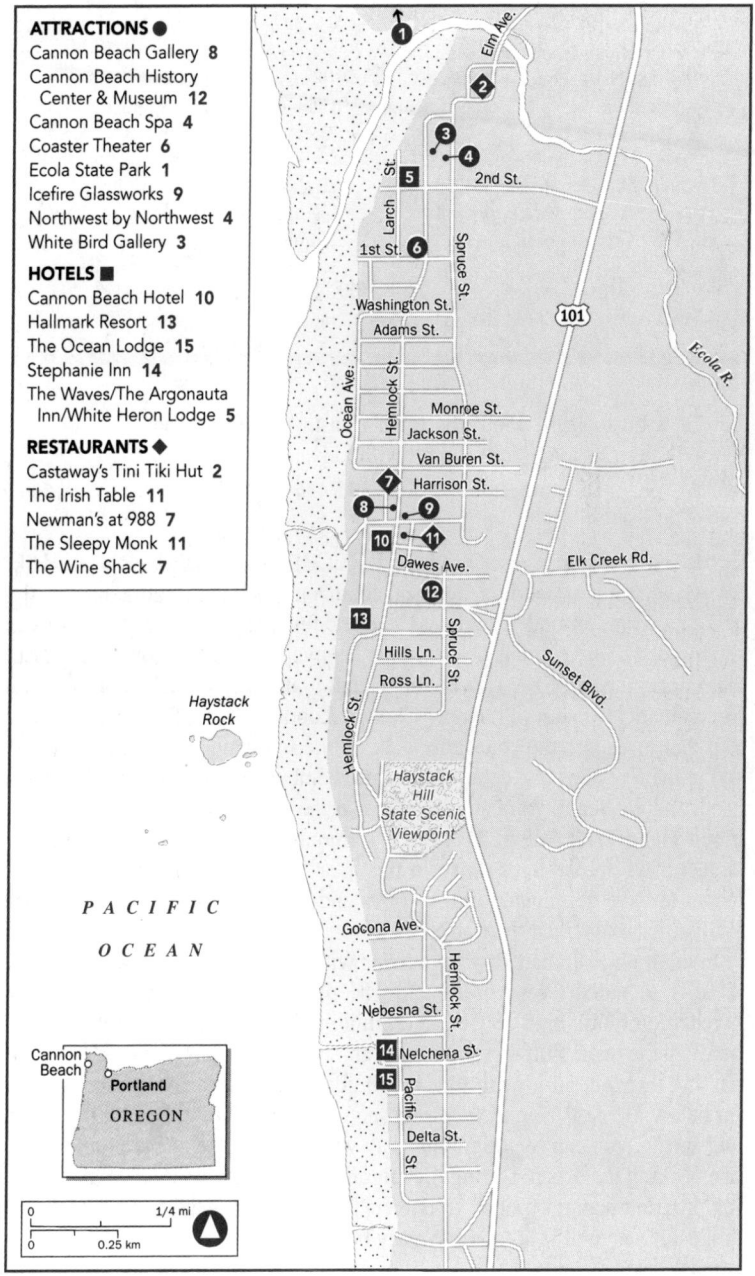
ATTRACTIONS ●
Cannon Beach Gallery 8
Cannon Beach History Center & Museum 12
Cannon Beach Spa 4
Coaster Theater 6
Ecola State Park 1
Icefire Glassworks 9
Northwest by Northwest 4
White Bird Gallery 3
HOTELS ■
Cannon Beach Hotel 10
Hallmark Resort 13
The Ocean Lodge 15
Stephanie Inn 14
The Waves/The Argonauta Inn/White Heron Lodge 5
RESTAURANTS ◆
Castaway's Tini Tiki Hut 2
The Irish Table 11
Newman's at 988 7
The Sleepy Monk 11
The Wine Shack 7
Elm Ave.
2nd St.
Larch St.
1st St.
Spruce St.
Washington St.
Adams St.
101
Ecola R.
Ocean Ave.
Hemlock St.
Monroe St.
Jackson St.
Van Buren St.
Harrison St.
Dawes Ave.
Elk Creek Rd.
Hills Ln.
Ross Ln.
Sunset Blvd.
Haystack Rock
Haystack Hill State Scenic Viewpoint
PACIFIC OCEAN
Gocona Ave.
Nebesna St.
Nelchena St.
Pacific St.
Delta St.
Cannon Beach
Portland
OREGON
0
1/4 mi
0
0.25 km

CANNON BEACH trivia

- **Cannon Beach** was named for a cannon that washed ashore after the U.S. Navy schooner *Shark* wrecked on the coast north of here in 1846.
- Rising 235 feet above the water, Cannon Beach's **Haystack Rock** is the most photographed monolith on the Oregon coast.
- The area's offshore rocks are protected nesting grounds for sea birds. Watch for tufted puffins, something of a Cannon Beach mascot.
- Tillamook Rock is the site of the **Tillamook Rock Lighthouse** (aka "Terrible Tilly"), which was frequently battered by huge storm waves that sent large rocks crashing through the light, 133 feet above sea level. The lighthouse was decommissioned in 1957 and is now used as a columbarium (see "Tackling Tillamook Head", p. 246).

there is a bit to learn about the town's past. A hands-on reproduction of a Native American longhouse is a hit with kids.

1387 S. Spruce St. www.cbhistory.org. ✆ **503/436-9301.** Admission by donation . Wed–Mon 1–5pm.

Ecola State Park ★★★ OUTDOOR RECREATION/STATE PARK Hikers, whale-watchers, surfers, and beachcombers flock to this gorgeous coastal park that wraps around Tillamook Head and features 9 miles of Pacific Ocean shoreline. The hikes include an 8-mile segment of the **Oregon Coast Trail** that is also a part of the **Lewis and Clark National Historic Trail. Indian Beach** marks the start of the new **Clatsop Loop Trail,** a 2.5-mile interpretive trail that gives you the chance to walk on the south side of Tillamook Head, and in the footsteps of Captain Clark and members of the Corps of Discovery. From Indian Beach you can also traverse the entire headland via the **Tillamook Head Trail** (see p. 246) Salal, salmonberry, and some of the region's largest Sitka spruce trees thrive in this area. (One large Sitka spruce is estimated to have germinated in the 1600s and was almost 200 years old when William Clark walked the trail.)

In addition to Indian Beach, popular with surfers and tide-pool explorers, there is secluded **Crescent Beach.** The park also has several picnic areas perched on bluffs high above the crashing waves. The 1-mile stretch of trail between the main bluff-top picnic area and Indian Beach is particularly scenic, passing through old-growth forest with good views of the ocean and beaches far below. Ecola is a good spot to observe coastal wildlife. During the winter and spring, you can see migrating gray whales from one of the promontories overlooking the ocean. During the migration seasons, a popular whale-watching program features trained volunteers to help you spot the grays. In July and August it's a good idea to arrive early because parking can be difficult.

84318 Ecola State Park Rd. (north of Cannon Beach). www.oregon.gov/oprd/parks. ✆ **800/551-6949** or 503/436-2844. Daily dawn–dusk. Day-use fee $5 per vehicle.

More Beaches Near Cannon Beach

Three miles south of town is **Arcadia Beach State Recreation Site ★★,** one of the prettiest little beaches on the north coast. Another mile farther south you'll find **Hug Point State Recreation Site ★★,** which has picnic tables, a sheltered beach, and the remains of an old road that was cut into the rock face of this headland. **Oswald West State Park ★★★,** 10 miles south of Cannon Beach, is one of my favorites of all the parks on the Oregon coast. A short trail leads to a driftwood-strewn cobblestone beach on a small cove. Headlands on either side of the cove can be reached by hiking trails that offer wonderful views. The waves here are popular with surfers (wearing wet suits), and there's a walk-in campground.

WHERE TO STAY

If you're heading here with the whole family or plan to stay a while, consider renting a house, a cottage, or an apartment. Offerings range from studio apartments to large luxurious oceanfront houses, and prices span an equally wide range. Either go with one of the major rental sites (see p. 89) or go with **Cannon Beach Property Management** (www.cbpm.com; ✆ **877/386-3402**) with its knowledgeable staff and hands-on service.

Cannon Beach Hotel ★★ This shingle-sided beaut is one of the oldest hotels on the coast; it celebrated its 100th anniversary in 2014. But there's nothing creaky about it in its present incarnation as a comfortable, well-designed B&B. Appealing touches abound in all the public areas: fresh flowers, a wood fire, big armchairs, and a sense of Zen-like calm. The hotel includes a few century-old cottages with river-rock fireplaces, and a newer Courtyard wing with suites and Jacuzzis; you can choose various room sizes and configurations depending on your needs. You're not on the beach here, or looking out at the beach, but it's minutes away, and the surrounding neighborhood has real charm. In summer, the on-site cafe serves lunch and dinner.

1116 S. Hemlock St. www.cannonbeachhotel.com. ✆ **800/238-4107** or 503/436-1392. 37 units. $99–$279 double w/continental breakfast (for rooms in hotel only). **Amenities:** Restaurant; free Wi-Fi.

Hallmark Resort ★ Hallmark Resort occupies a high bluff looking down on the famous beach of Cannon Beach with Haystack Rock in the distance. The possibilities here run from family-friendly guestrooms that sleep 6 and have full kitchens to oceanfront suites with fireplaces and Jacuzzis. The oceanfront suites with walk-out balconies are the stand-outs. I like the whites and muted tones and light wood colors of the decor because it doesn't detract from the views but seems to enhance them. The resort has a big recreation center with two indoor pools, and it offers spa services. The staff is super friendly and helpful. ***One warning*:** The buildings of this double-decker, tri-sided resort are grouped around a central parking lot that detracts from the views of the less expensive units.

1400 S. Hemlock St. www.hallmarkinns.com. ✆ **888/448-4449** or 503/436-1566. 129 units. $141–$251 double, 2-night minimum in summer. Pets accepted ($20). **Amenities:** Exercise room; 2 Jacuzzis; 2 indoor pools; sauna; spa; free Wi-Fi.

The Ocean Lodge ★★★ What a grand place to stay in Cannon Beach! The wide, sandy beach is right below this gracious inn—you have direct access to it from the ground-floor rooms—and the views are panoramic vistas down to Haystack Rock. The lodge is darn nice, too, its lobby boasting huge rough-cut timber beams and warm wood tones, with a two-story high fireplace. Even if the winds are raging and the rain is pouring, you can comfortably curl up and enjoy the fire or soak in your Jacuzzi. Rooms are sedately elegant, with cream color schemes and the type of furnishings you can sink into and relax. All have kitchenettes, coffee and cookies are always available downstairs, and there's a good (self-serve) continental breakfast in the morning. The staff is terrific. The commercial center of Cannon Beach is about ¾ mile away.

2864 S. Pacific St. www.theoceanlodge.com. ✆ **888/777-4047** or 503/436-2241. 45 units. $249–$279 double w/continental breakfast included. 3-night minimum July–Aug. Pets accepted ($20 per night). **Amenities:** Access to nearby health club; free Wi-Fi.

Stephanie Inn ★★★ The Stephanie Inn is the most classically romantic inn on the Oregon coast—the perfect place for an anniversary or other special weekend away. With flower boxes beneath the windows and neatly manicured gardens by the entry, the inn is reminiscent of New England's country inns, but the beach out the back door is definitely of Pacific Northwest origin. Inside, the lobby feels warm and cozy with its river-rock fireplace, huge wood columns, and beamed ceiling. The guest rooms, all individually decorated, are equally comfy, and most have double whirlpool tubs and gas fireplaces. The beds have fine linens, TempurPedic mattresses, and of course there's evening turn-down service with chocolates. The higher you go in the three-story inn, the better the views and the more spacious the outdoor spaces (patios, balconies, and decks). A bounteous breakfast buffet is served each morning, and complimentary afternoon wine and evening nightcaps are also served. The restaurant (reviewed on p. 256) is a fine-dining haven. And here's something special to consider if you decide to stay at this highest-of-high-end beach hotels: For $69 they will build you your very own bonfire on the beach.

2740 S. Pacific St. www.stephanie-inn.com. ✆ **800/633-3466** or 503/436-2221. 41 units. $359–$519 double w/full breakfast included. No children under 12. **Amenities:** Restaurant; access to nearby health club; free Wi-Fi.

The Waves/The Argonauta Inn/White Heron Lodge ★ Variety is the name of the game in eclectic Cannon Beach, and The Waves plays the game better than any other accommodations in town. This lodge, only a block from the heart of Cannon Beach, consists of more than four dozen rooms, suites, cottages, and beach houses. My favorites are the cottages of The Argonauta Inn, one of them dating from 1906. Surrounded by beautiful flower gardens in the summer, these old cottages (many of which are oceanfront) are the most atmospheric and reminiscent of what Oregon beach cottages used to be like. For sybarites and romantics, there are fireplaces in some rooms and whirlpool spas overlooking the ocean. If you want to get away from the crowds, ask for a suite at the White Heron Lodge. The Waves offers contemporary accommodations, some of which are right on the beach and have great views.

188 W. Second St. www.thewavescannonbeach.com. ✆ **800/822-2468** or 503/436-2205. 55 units. The Waves $109–$175 double; White Heron Lodge $163–$369 suite; Argonauta $97–$289 suite. 3-night minimum July–Aug; 2-night minimum on weekends Sept–June. **Amenities:** Jacuzzi; free Wi-Fi.

Wright's For Camping ★★ You can hear the ocean from the campground, a lovely perk. Wright's has 21 tent and RV sites (but no RV hookups) at this forested, family-run campground just ½ mile from downtown Cannon Beach. You'll find clean restrooms and showers and leashed pets are allowed. If you're traveling in the summer, reserve online as far in advance as you can.

334 Reservoir Rd, Cannon Beach. www.wrightsforcamping.com. ✆ **503/436-2347.** $36–$52 per night.

WHERE TO EAT

On the Oregon coast, seemingly every hotel room has a kitchenette. Which means you could cook your own meals while you watch the waves. For a bottle of wine to take back to your room and enjoy with that meal, stop in at **The Wine Shack,** 124 N. Hemlock St. (www.thewineshack.wine; ✆ **800/787-1765** or 503/436-1100), or **Laurel's Cannon Beach Wine Shop,** 263 N. Hemlock St. (✆ **503/436-1666**). For locally brewed beer, visit **Bill's Tavern & Brewhouse,** 188 N. Hemlock St. (✆ **503/436-2202**).

But this is Cannon Beach, where you'll find more good restaurants than anywhere else along the coast except Newport and Yachats.

Castaways Tini Tiki Hut ★ CARIBBEAN/CAJUN/CREOLE/FUSION In Cannon Beach, land of the year-round fleece and hoodie, this little cottage-restaurant is a local fave, maybe because it does things spicy and tropical. The ingredients may be the ubiquitous crab, shrimp, and seafood of the Oregon coast, but it's cooked up in different ways: the crab turned into fritters, the shrimp curried, and the fish and shellfish in the jambalaya seasoned Cajun style. If seafood doesn't swim with you, try the Haystack Chicken, named after Cannon Beach's most iconic landmark, or the macaroni and cheese with

Savor Cannon Beach

The 4-day **Savor Cannon Beach** festival (www.savorcannonbeach.com) in early March, an annual celebration of Pacific Northwest wine and regional cuisine, includes six wine tasting events and many other related community activities. Approximately 40 Northwest wineries pour tastings at shops, galleries, restaurants and hotels in Cannon Beach during the wine walk on Saturday of the festival.

Andouille sausage. The portions here are large, so you may want to share. And the cocktail menu is fun, too, and rum-based.

316 N. Fir St. ✆ **503/436-8777.** Main courses $16–$23. Wed–Sun 5–9pm.

The Irish Table & The Sleepy Monk ★★ IRISH/COFFEE This little shingle-sided cottage-like building in "midtown" Cannon Beach is a shared-space operation. By day it's The Sleepy Monk coffee house, where you can get a good organic brew and a pastry to go with it. At night, it becomes The Irish Table, one of Cannon Beach's best-loved (and smallest) restaurants. The Irish Table has a petite menu of five starters (a good cheese board, a couple of fresh salads, a couple of seafood appetizers) and as many entrees. The food is more Irish-inspired than typically Irish, but may include vegetarian shepherd's pie with wild mushrooms, lamb chops with a Dijon reduction sauce, a seared flatiron steak, and a fresh fish selection. A few rich desserts are offered, and hot drinks with Irish whiskey. Arrive early or be prepared to wait in line.

1235 S. Hemlock St. ✆ **503/436-0708.** Main courses $20–$29. Sleepy Monk Fri–Tues 8am–4pm; Irish Table Fri–Tues 5:30–10pm.

Newman's at 988 ★★★ FRENCH/ITALIAN The Newman of Newman's 988 is John, the first chef to put Stephanie Inn on the coastal culinary map. He opened his own fine-dining restaurant in a small yellow cottage in "midtown" Cannon Beach. Part of the experience of a meal here is the presentation, which is less fussy than it used to be at Stephanie Inn. The menu is French- and Italian-inspired but relies exclusively on the freshest ingredients of the Pacific Northwest. For appetizers, try the foie gras pasta with Oregon black truffle mushrooms or the crab cakes with parsley, lemon, and shallot aioli. There is a daily ravioli, and lobster ravioli, one of Newman's signature dishes, is always on the menu (keep in mind that lobster is not and never has been harvested in the Pacific Ocean; it comes from the East Coast). Duck breast; marinated lamb rack; and beef medallions with pancetta, onions, and Gorgonzola are typical entree choices. Newman also offers a daily tasting menu and a selection of wines to accompany your meal.

988 S. Hemlock St. www.newmansat988.com. ✆ **503/436-1151.** Main courses $20–$30. Daily 5:30–9pm (closed Mon mid-Oct to July 3). Closed mid-Jan to early Feb.

Stephanie Inn ★★★ PACIFIC NORTHWEST The restaurant at the Stephanie Inn provides the most formal fine-dining experience on the North Coast. It's not for everyone, but if you want a special-occasion restaurant with white linen and attentive service, this is it. (You don't have to be staying at the inn to dine here, nor do you have to dress up, but you should at least be "smart-casual.") The second-floor dining room is all wood and windows, though it does not look out on the Pacific. The menu changes often based on what's seasonal and fresh. If they're available, share the seared scallops as an appetizer: two large scallops with roasted grapes, walnuts, pancetta, aged Gouda fondue, and crispy shallots. On my last visit I had a delicate and delicious creamy asparagus soup with crème fraiche followed by a filet of wild

cannon beach SHOPPING & SPA-ING

For many Cannon Beach visitors, shopping is the town's greatest attraction. In the heart of town, along **Hemlock Street,** you'll find dozens of densely packed small shops and galleries offering original (and not-so) art, fine (and not-so) crafts, souvenirs, gifts, and casual fashions. And because this is a fairly upscale getaway town, relaxing in a spa is also possible.

Galleries **Northwest by Northwest,** 232 N. Spruce St. (www.nwbynwgallery.com; ✆ **800/494-0741** or 503/436-0741) features works by established Northwest artists. **White Bird Gallery,** 251 N. Hemlock St. (www.whitebirdgallery.com; ✆ **503/436-2681**), sells colorful contemporary art and fine crafts. **Icefire Glassworks,** 116 E. Gower St. (http://cbgallerygroup.com/icefire-glassworks; ✆ **888/423-3545** or 503/436-2359) is a glassblowing studio south of downtown. **Cannon Beach Gallery,** 1064 S. Hemlock St. (www.cannonbeacharts.org; ✆ **503/436-0744**) is operated by a local arts organization and mounts shows in a wide variety of styles but which tend to be heavy on beach landscapes.

Spa Book a massage or a skin or hydrotherapy treatment at the **Cannon Beach Spa,** 232 N. Spruce St. (www.cannonbeachspa.com; ✆ **888/577-8772** or 503/436-8772). Prices run between $80 and $105 for an hour-long massage (couples massages are also available). There's a Chocolate Café on the premises.

Alaskan halibut with organic wild rice and grilled asparagus and a citrus/apple/fennel salad. The recommended wine pairing was perfect. There is a nightly four-course, fixed-price dinner that offers a considerable savings over a la carte choices.

2740 S. Pacific St. www.stephanie-inn.com. ✆ **800/633-3466** or 503/436-2221. Main courses $42–$48, fixed-price menu $69. Daily 5:30–8pm (until 8:30pm Sat).

CANNON BEACH NIGHTLIFE

The **Coaster Theater,** 108 N. Hemlock St. (www.coastertheatre.com; ✆ **503/436-1242**), the best-known professional theater on the Oregon coast, presents a season of dramas, comedies, and musicals.

Manzanita ★★

14.5 miles S of Cannon Beach

As the crowds have descended on Cannon Beach, people seeking peace and quiet, less commerce and a slower pace have migrated south to the community of Manzanita. Located south of Neahkanie Mountain, Manzanita enjoys a setting similar to Cannon Beach, but without the many haystack rocks. There isn't much to do except walk on the beach and relax, which is exactly why most people love Manzanita.

The beach at Manzanita stretches for 5 miles, from the base of Neahkanie Mountain to the mouth of the Nehalem River, and is a favorite of both full-body-wetsuit-clad surfers and windsurfers (who also windsurf in the quieter waters of Nehalem Bay just across Nehalem Spit).

TILLAMOOK AND ITS FAMOUS cheese

About 27 miles south of Manzanita, U.S. 101 veers inland about 2 miles from the ocean and comes to the town of **Tillamook.** There's really no reason to stop in Tillamook except to visit the **Tillamook Cheese Factory,** 4175 U.S. 101 N. (www.tillamook.com; ✆ **800/542-7290** or 503/815-1300). It's the most popular tourist attraction in a flat, lush, coastal valley long known as one of Oregon's foremost dairy regions. Tillamook cheese is ubiquitous everywhere in the state—until the recent advent of artisan cheeses, it was the *only* real cheese to be had. At the factory, visitors can observe the cheese-making process (cheddars are the specialty), buy Tillamook ice cream, and browse through a large gift shop where all manner of cheeses and other edible gifts are available. The factory is open daily from 8am to 8pm in the summer, otherwise 8am to 6pm.

Located on the same side of U.S. 101 is the **Blue Heron French Cheese Company,** 2001 Blue Heron Dr. (www.blueheronoregon.com; ✆ **800/275-0639** or 503/842-8281). Created within an old dairy barn, Blue Heron stocks the same sort of comestibles as the Tillamook Cheese Factory, though the emphasis here is on brie (which, however, is not made locally). Blue Heron is open daily from 8am to 8pm in summer and 9am to 6pm in winter.

EXPLORING MANZANITA

It's about the beach and nothing but the beach.

Nehalem Bay State Park ★★ OUTDOOR RECREATION/STATE PARK/BEACH Just south of town, this state park encompasses all of Nehalem Spit and provides access to both Manzanita beach and Nehalem Bay. The park includes a **campground** and has a 1.75-mile paved bike path, a horse camp, and horse trails. At the south end of the spit, large numbers of harbor seals can often be seen basking on the beach. To reach the seal area requires a 5-mile round-trip hike.

9500 Sandpiper Ln., Nehalem. www.oregon.gov/oprd/parks. ✆ **503/368-5154.** Day-use fee $5 per vehicle. Daily 8am–5pm.

WHERE TO STAY

If you want to rent a vacation house in Manzanita, contact **Manzanita Rental Company** (www.manzanitarentals.com; ✆ **800/579-9801** or 503/368-6797), which inspects all of the units it rents and is available should problems arise. That service sometimes translates to higher prices, so if budget is foremost, go with one of the bigger online rental sites (see p. 89).

Coast Cabins ★★★ To call them "cabins" is something of a misnomer—at least if you associate "cabin" with a little rustic cottage from an earlier era. These two-story cedar-shake and glass-fronted cabins are gorgeously sited and outfitted. The decor includes original art, wool area rugs woven in Tibet, clean-lined and unobtrusive Scandinavian-style fixtures and furniture, and private outdoor hot tubs. You're not on the ocean, but close to it, and the wooded setting gives you a real hit of Oregon's history. Like all good things, these cabins have been "discovered" and are hard to book in July and August, so plan ahead, or enjoy them off-season. The newest and most spectacular offering is a luxurious house perched high above Manzanita Beach with ocean views in all directions.

635 Laneda Ave. www.coastcabins.com. ✆ **800/435-1269** or 503/368-7113. 6 units. $163–$475 double. 2- to 7-night minimum on weekends and throughout the summer. Pets accepted ($30 deposit, plus $25 per night). **Amenities:** Access to nearby health club; free Wi-Fi.

The Inn at Manzanita ★★ Nestled among pines and spruce trees within a lovely coastal garden, this contemporary, cedar-sided inn is right in Manzanita but has all the privacy you could want, plus easy access to the beach. There are four different buildings within the complex, and each room is styled differently. There's a different outlook from every room, too, but all of them have fireplaces and balconies, and some have kitchenettes. Gardening on the Oregon coast is not easy, so the park-like grounds and garden here is a special feature.

67 Laneda Ave. www.innatmanzanita.com. ✆ **503/368-6754.** 14 units. $179–$229 double, 2-night minimum on weekends and July to Labor Day; 3-night minimum on some holidays. Pets accepted ($15 per night). **Amenities:** Access to nearby health club; free Wi-Fi.

Nehalem Bay State Park ★★ Located between ocean and bay on a 4-mile sand strip, this state park offers year-round, handicap-accessible campsites, yurts and RV access. Toilets and showers are available.

34600 Gary St, Nehalem, OR 97131. www.oregonstateparks.org. ✆ **800/452-5687.** $22–$56 per campsite.

WHERE TO EAT

For lattes and the latest news, head to **Manzanita News & Espresso,** 500 Laneda Ave. (✆ **503/368-7450**). At the end of the day, wind down at **Vino Manzanita,** 387-D Laneda Ave. (✆ **503/368-8466**), a cozy little wine bar.

Bread and Ocean ★★ NORTHWEST The lunch menu is small—cold sandwiches (fresh tuna, barbecued beef brisket, or a Dagwood on ciabatta); panini with an array of deli specialties; homemade soup—but everything made here is delicious. Maybe that explains why it has been Manzanita's favorite lunch spot since it opened in 2003. That and the baked goods. This is the place to come for a packed picnic-lunch box that you can take to the beach. Dinner is served Friday through Sunday only, and features barbecue.

154 Laneda Ave. ✆ **503/368-5823.** No credit cards. Main courses $$8.50–$24. Wed–Thurs 7:30am–2pm; Fri–Sat 7:30am–2pm and 5–9pm; Sun 8am–2pm and 5–8pm.

Three Capes Scenic Loop ★★★

The Three Capes Scenic Loop, a 35-mile byway off of U.S. 101, begins just west of downtown Tillamook and leads south along the coast past Cape Meares, Cape Lookout, and Cape Kiwanda to end near Pacific City. Together these capes offer some of the most spectacular scenery on the northern Oregon coast. All three are state parks, and all make great whale-watching spots in the spring.

BOB STRAUB STATE PARK: the best beach walk ON THE OREGON COAST

There isn't that much to do in Pacific City—except walk on one of the greatest white-sand beaches along the entire Oregon coast. I'm talking about the miles-long stretch of beach at **Bob Straub State Park ★★★.** To reach it, turn west towards the ocean at the one intersection in Pacific City, cross the Nestucca River, and turn left along a residential road that skirts along between the river and the dunes until you come to the parking lot (no charge). This is my favorite place for a barefoot beach walk (from June through September) in all of Oregon because it's just enough out of the way to keep it relatively undiscovered, and long enough so that even on "busy" summer weekends you may not encounter more than a dozen people and maybe some riders on horseback (I also saw a herd of llamas enjoying the beach on one of my last visits). From the parking lot, you have to climb up and over a dune (any reasonably fit person can do this) to reach the beach with its spectacular views north to Cape Kiwanda and south to Cascade Head. If you walk south along the shoreline for about 2 miles, you'll come to the mouth of the Nestucca River. It's not unusual to see seals sunbathing on the sand spit or hunting fish in the estuary. The winds can be ferocious (bring a hoodie) but I have also enjoyed many warm, sunny days here. If you visit this remarkable beach and fall in love with it, as I did many years ago, promise me you'll tell only your closest friends about it. It's one of those special Oregon coast places that we want to keep secret.

ESSENTIALS

GETTING THERE To start the loop, follow Third Street south out of Tillamook and watch for the right turn for Cape Meares State Scenic Viewpoint. You can also access the loop from the south at Pacific City.

EXPLORING THE THREE CAPES SCENIC LOOP

The road from Tillamook takes you along the shore of **Tillamook Bay** and around the north side of Cape Meares. Just around the tip of the cape, you'll come to **Cape Meares State Scenic Viewpoint ★★★,** the site of the **Cape Meares Lighthouse** (open daily Apr–Oct 11am–4pm). The views from atop this rocky headland are superb.

Continuing south around the cape, you come to the residential community of **Oceanside,** with its white-sand beach and offshore monoliths known as the **Three Arch Rocks.**

Three miles south of Oceanside, is **Netarts Bay,** famous for its excellent clamming and crabbing.

Continuing south, the scenic byway leads to **Cape Lookout State Park ★★** (www.oregonstateparks.org; ✆ **503/842-4981**), where you'll find a campground, picnic areas, beaches, and several miles of hiking trails. The most breathtaking trail leads 2½ miles out to the end of Cape Lookout, several hundred feet above the ocean. There is a $5 day-use fee here.

Cape Kiwanda ★★, just north of Pacific City, is preserved as **Cape Kiwanda State Natural Area.** From the foot of the cape's sandstone cliffs, it's possible to scramble up a huge sand dune to the top of the cape for dramatic views of this rugged piece of shoreline.

The Three Capes Scenic Loop ends at **Pacific City** ★, a small and somewhat helter-skelter fishing town spread out along the Nestucca River. The base of Cape Kiwanda, just to the north of town, is the staging area for Pacific City's dory fleet. These flat-bottomed commercial fishing boats are launched from the beach and plow through crashing breakers to get out to calmer waters beyond. When the day's fishing is done, the dories roar into shore at full throttle and come to a grinding stop as high up on the beach as they can get. This is Oregon's only such fishing fleet, and it's celebrated in Pacific City each year on the third weekend in July with the annual Dory Days Festival, which includes a fish fry. If you'd like to go out in one of the dories and fish for salmon, ling cod, or albacore tuna, contact **Haystack Fishing** (www.haystackfishing.com; ✆ **866/965-7555** or 503/965-7555; $180 per person, two-person minimum). Trips are offered June through September.

WHERE TO STAY

For suggestions on finding alternative accommodations, see p. 230.

In Pacific City

Inn at Cape Kiwanda ★★ Every room has an ocean view—but in many of them, you have to look across a parking lot to see it. That's the one drawback, for me, at this otherwise comfortable and well-run hotel across the street from the busy beach at Cape Kiwanda Natural Area. The pluses are big windows (the corner rooms are best), private balconies, and gas fireplaces. The furnishings here remind me of a suburban home, with a style that leans toward the traditional. The Pelican Pub & Brewery, which runs the inn, is right across the street.

33105 Cape Kiwanda Dr. www.innatcapekiwanda.com. ✆ **888/965-7001** or 503/965-7001. 35 units. $169–$367 double. 2-night minimum on holidays, and on weekends July–Aug. Children 18 and under stay free in parent's room. Pets accepted ($20). **Amenities:** 2 restaurants; lounge; bikes; exercise room; free Wi-Fi.

Cape Lookout State Park ★★ Located on a sand spit between Netarts Bay and the ocean, this Oregon State Park campground has 170 tent sites, 40 RV sites, yurts, cabins, firewood for sale, and accessible bathrooms with showers. Plus, there's easy access to the beach. It's popular year-round, so reserve as far ahead as you can.

13000 Whiskey Creek Rd., Tillamook. www.oregonstateparks.org. ✆ **800/452-5687.** $22–$56 per campsite, cabin $100.

WHERE TO EAT

In Oceanside

Roseanna's Café ★ SEAFOOD/INTERNATIONAL Oceanside was the first coast town I ever stayed in in Oregon, and it didn't have a restaurant—or much of anything except simple cottages and a great beach. When Roseanna's opened in the early 1980s, it became a favorite spot for locals and those driving along the Three Capes Scenic Loop. Unpretentious and with a fabulous view, it was the only eatery for miles around that attempted to do more than greasy fish and chips or burgers. Over the years, this little restaurant in a simple storefront building from the early 1900s hasn't changed much: The food is comfortable and filling if not haute cuisine. Sometimes they add sauces to dishes that would be better without but you can usually get good, unadorned salmon. Roseanna's is famous for its desserts, particularly the fresh huckleberry cobbler. The restaurant doesn't take reservations, so be prepared to wait.

1490 Pacific Ave. www.roseannascafe.com. ✆ **503/842-7351.** Reservations not accepted. Main courses $8–$30. Sun–Thurs daily 9am–8pm; Fri–Sat 9am–9pm.

In Pacific City

The Grateful Bread Bakery ★ This bright, pleasant bakery-bistro, known for its fresh-baked bread and pastries, uses as many unprocessed, organic, and sustainable food as possible and always has vegetarian options. The lunch menu is limited mostly to sandwiches (made with that delicious bread), pizza, salads, daily soups and fish. The fish tacos are terrific; I'm also a fan of their vegetarian chili. If you're jonesing for a latte this is where to get it; organic coffee is just $1 a cup. Service can be slow, but because you're at the coast to unwind, that shouldn't be a problem.

34805 Brooten Rd., Pacific City. www.gratefulbreadbakery.com. ✆ **503/965-7337.** Main courses: $10–$12. Thurs–Mon 8am–3pm.

Pelican Pub & Brewery ★ PUB FOOD When was the last time you sat in a pub with a view of crashing surf, an enormous sand dune, and an offshore monolith? Pelican Brewery offers award-winning brews—Irish Handcuffs, Doryman's Ale, and Kiwanda Cream Ale among them—and a fabulous Cape Kiwanda view. The food here is the hearty kind that goes well with beer and a windblown day at the beach. Like lightly breaded and salted fried calamari, blackened salmon salad, the Tsunami Stout Chili (made with pork and beef and topped with Tillamook cheese), seafood quesadilla, and wild mushroom pie. Pasta and gourmet pizzas are available, too. This is a very laid-back place that welcomes kids. You can sit outside in nice weather.

33180 Cape Kiwanda Dr. www.pelicanbrewery.com. ✆ **503/965-7007.** Main courses $12–$24. Sun–Thurs 8am–10pm; Fri–Sat 8am–11pm.

Stimulus Espresso Cafe ★ COFFEE/LIGHT REFRESHMENTS Noteworthy coffee and maybe a light lunch or a pastry to go with it, are the lures here. Stimulus is airy and congenial, shows the work of local artists, and has live music.

33105 Cape Kiwanda Dr. www.stimuluscafe.com. ✆ **503/965-4551.** Lunch items and pastries $4–$8. Daily 6am–6pm.

THE CENTRAL COAST

Easy access from Portland via I-5 and then Hwy. 18 or Hwy 22 through the Coast Range gives the Central Coast a leg-up in popularity. **Lincoln City** is one of the coast's most-visited and family-friendly destinations, and **Newport,** home the excellent Oregon Coast Aquarium, two lighthouses, and the

heading up CASCADE HEAD

Rising 1,770 feet above sea level, **Cascade Head** is one of the highest headlands on the coast. The headland—with lush coastal rainforest of Sitka spruce and Douglas fir covering its lower flanks and treeless, windswept meadows above—juts out into the sea between the small community of Neskowin (10 miles south of Pacific City on U.S. 101) and the larger town of Lincoln City. On its south side, this rare example of a maritime prairie rises above the Salmon River estuary, and the entire headland is home to native grasses and wildflowers as well as elk, deer, bald eagles, falcons, and great horned owls. The area around Cascade Head is so unique that it has been designated a UNESCO Biosphere Reserve. From a trail head on its south side, the 6-mile **Nature Conservancy Cascade Head Trail** ★★★ climbs up the side and over the top of this magnificent headland all the way to Neskowin. The trail provides spectacular vistas of the Salmon River, the Coast Range, and the Pacific. To reach the trail head, turn west from U.S. 101 onto Three Rocks Road (just north of the Salmon River) and follow it about 2½ miles to Knight County Park at the end. Park there and walk back to Savage Road, where you'll find a half-mile boardwalk trail that takes you to the trail head. There's an initial 1,000-foot elevation gain, after which the trail becomes relatively easy. This is a fragile ecosystem, so stay on the trail. **Note:** No dogs or bikes are allowed. The Nature Conservancy's preserve has been set aside primarily to protect the habitat of the rare Oregon silverspot butterfly. ***Tip:*** The trail has become popular, so arrive early on summer weekends to avoid the crowds.

historic neighborhood of Nye Beach, is the most interesting town along this part of the coast. Whale-watching expeditions leave from the tiny harbor at **Depoe Bay,** and the old town of **Florence,** along the Siuslaw River, has some real historic character. **Yachats,** with its exceptionally beautiful beach, is one of the more affluent communities along the Central Coast.

Lincoln City ★

88 miles SW of Portland, 44 miles S of Tillamook, 25 miles N of Newport

Despite its name, Lincoln City is not a city at all but a collection of five small towns that grew together over the years and now stretch for miles along the coast. The result is that there's no specific town center, and little to distinguish Lincoln City from a commercialized stretch of suburban highway. Motel rates here, though often high for what you get, are generally better than those in coast towns with more charm and better beaches.

Thanks in part to the arrival of a big casino in Lincoln City, the stretch of U.S. 101 between Otis and Depoe Bay, which includes Lincoln City, has become congested sprawl, and a summer weekend in Lincoln City can mean coping with bumper-to-bumper traffic. If at all possible, come during the week or during the off season to avoid the endless traffic and the crowds.

Once you get off U.S. 101, however, Lincoln City has neighborhoods as charming as any on the coast, and at the south end of town, in the Taft District, the city has been working hard to bring back historical character and provide an attractive, pedestrian-friendly area.

Just north of town, in an area known as Road's End, you'll find a long, uncrowded beach with spectacular views to the north.

ESSENTIALS

GETTING THERE Ore. 22 from Salem merges with Ore. 18 before reaching the junction with U.S. 101. From Portland, take U.S. 99W to McMinnville and then head west on Ore. 18. If you're continuing down the coast from Pacific City, continue on Hwy. 101 S.

VISITOR INFORMATION The **Lincoln City Visitor Center,** 540 NE U.S. 101 (www.oregoncoast.org; ✆ **541/994-3302**), is open Wednesday to Monday 10am to 4pm (until 5pm Memorial Day to Labor Day).

FESTIVALS Annual **kite festivals** include the Summer Kite Festival in late June and the Fall Kite Festival in early to mid-October. In addition, Lincoln City has an annual **Sandcastle Building Contest** each year in early August. On the nearby Siletz Indian Reservation, the **Nesika Illahee,** the annual Siletz Pow Wow, takes place on the second weekend in August. For a current listing of events in Lincoln City visit **www.oregoncoast.org**.

EXPLORING LINCOLN CITY

Beach ★★ OUTDOOR RECREATION Lincoln City's 7½-mile-long beach is the town's main attraction. This is not a beach for swimming, but for walking, beachcombing, and, because of the steady winds, the best kite flying on the Oregon coast. Among the better beach-access points are the **D River State Wayside,** on the south side of the D River (the shortest river in Oregon), and the **Road's End State Wayside,** at the north end of Lincoln City. Road's End is also a good place to explore tide pools. You'll find more tide pools on the beach at NW 15th Street. You'll want to bring a hoodie and be prepared for blowing sand; on really windy days it can feel like you're being sandblasted.

Chinook Winds Casino Resort ★ CASINO This massive casino, run by the Confederated Tribes of Siletz Indians, and located right on the beach at the north end of town offers blackjack, poker, slot machines, keno, and bingo, and a video-game room for the kids. Big-name (and not-too-big-name) entertainers, many from the golden-oldy circuit, perform year-round. There's a hotel and restaurants on site but you can't escape the smell of cigarette smoke.

1777 NW 44th St. www.chinookwindscasino.com. ✆ **888/244-6665** or 541/996-582. Admission free. Daily 24 hrs.

Connie Hansen Garden ★★ GARDEN Gardening on the Oregon coast can be a difficult proposition, given the salty air, rocky/sandy soil, and sometimes gale-force winds, so this charming and distinctive coastal cottage garden in a residential section of Lincoln City is both a surprise and a delight for garden lovers. It was created over a 20-year period by its namesake, Connie Hansen, a San Francisco transplant who moved to Lincoln City in 1973. Though small, the garden is planned in such a way that it seems much larger, and surprises are found at every turn of the meandering paths that run through it. Visit in the spring for the primroses, irises, and rhododendrons; in the summer to enjoy a panoply of colorful and unusual perennials; and in the fall to marvel at the burnished colors in the heather berms. Rare trees and shrubs add interest throughout the year. The garden is so unobtrusive from the road that you could pass by and never notice it. To find it, turn off U.S. 101 onto NW 33rd and look for the sign and small parking lot.

1931 NW 33rd St. www.conniehansengarden.com. ✆ **541/994-6338.** Admission by donation. Garden daily dawn–dusk, visitor center Tues, Sat 10am–2pm.

WHERE TO STAY

In addition to the town's many hotels and motels, Lincoln City has plenty of vacation rental houses and apartments offering good deals, especially for families. The best local brokers for these accommodations are **Horizon Rentals** (www.horizonrentals.com; ✆ **800/995-2411** or 541/994-2226) and **Pacific Retreats** (www.pacificretreats.com; ✆ **800/473-4833** or 541/994-4833). Rates generally range from around $1,000 to $7,000 per week for houses that sleep 4 to 12 people. You might be able to do better cost-wise with one of the big online rental sites; see p. 89 for more.

Devil's Lake State Recreation Area ★★ None of the campsites at this Oregon State Park campground have a view of Devil's Lake, but there is a paved walking path that leads right to the lake shore. The park is located just a few minutes from downtown Lincoln City and offers year-round tent campsites, yurts and RV access, plus bathrooms with showers. You can swim and go boating in the freshwater lake. Keep an eye out for wildlife: It's not uncommon to see herons, loons, coots, elk, raccoon, and even bald eagles in the park.

1452 NE 6th Dr., Lincoln City. www.oregonstateparks.org. ✆ **800/452-5687.** $22–$56 per campsite.

Ester Lee Motel ★ This is what a modest, ocean-facing Oregon coast motel used to be like in simpler days, when being at the beach was more about being at the beach than it was about fancy upgraded amenities. I like the Ester Lee for that very reason. Located at the south end of Lincoln City, it's basic, both inside and out, but the rooms have spectacular views (no balconies, however). And the Ester Lee is probably the least expensive oceanview place to stay in Lincoln City. Most units have kitchens and fireplaces (some of them wood-burning, with free firewood). Pay a little more and you can book a cozy cottage that sleeps from two to seven people. There's paved access down to the beach, and grocery stores, restaurants, and the casino are about 4½ miles to the north.

3803 S. U.S. 101. www.esterlee.com. ✆ **888/430-2100** or 541/996-6111. 44 units. Motel $82–$139 double. **Amenities:** Free Wi-Fi.

Looking Glass Inn ★ Located in the historic Taft District and across the street from Siletz Bay, the Looking Glass, with its cedar shingles and white trim, has a classic Cape Cod feel. Only a couple of the rooms here have rather tame partial views of the wild Pacific, seen over parking lots and nearby buildings. But the entrance to the beach on Siletz Bay is only 1 block away. What this all means is that you can get a nice, clean room in this well-maintained and property for less money. That's for digs with whirlpool tubs, balconies, or gas fireplaces. While most hotels that claim to be pet-friendly simply tolerate dogs, this hotel welcomes dogs with open arms. Bring your pooch with you, and your canine companion will get a basket with water and food bowls, sheets, towels, and doggy treats at check in. Speaking of "dining," the famous Mo's chowder house is right across the street from the Looking Glass, and the inn will give you a coupon for a free bowl of Mo's famous clam chowder.

861 SW 51st St. www.lookingglass-inn.com. ✆ **800/843-4940** or 541/996-3996. 36 units. $99–$149 double w/continental breakfast included. Pets accepted ($15/night). **Amenities:** Free Wi-Fi.

Starfish Manor Hotel ★★ From your balcony or whirlpool tub, you'll have a view of miles of beach, and the ceaseless sound of the Pacific will lull you to sleep. If there's a storm, or the weather's chilly, you can turn on your fireplace and feel protected and warm. That's what Starfish Manor is all about. This boutique hotel specializes in romantic getaways, the kind where you can happily hole up in your oceanfront room and reinvigorate your relationship with a loved one, or with yourself and nature. There aren't any kids around, and no barking dogs. The studios and suites are sweet and welcoming, with upscale features like kitchenettes with cherrywood cabinets and granite countertops, and those two-person whirlpool tubs with ocean views. The hotel is at the north end of Lincoln City, away from the day-trippers and casino traffic.

2735 NW Inlet Ave. www.onthebeachfront.com. ✆ **800/972-6155** or 541/996-9300. 17 units. $99–$239 double. No children, no pets. **Amenities:** Free Wi-Fi.

WHERE TO EAT

Bay House ★★★ NORTHWEST The Bay House is one of a rare handful of fine-dining restaurants on the Oregon coast—by which I mean snowy linens on the table, impeccable service, outstanding cuisine, and a worldly selection of fine wines (2,000 bottles!) to pair with your food. It's been around since 1937, with various owners and chefs, and now includes a nice cocktail lounge and wine bar in addition to its glass-fronted dining room with an eye-popping view of Siletz Bay and the Salishan Spit. You might want to start with some smoked-salmon ravioli, or Medjool dates with bleu cheese and citrus-arugula salad. There are typically four entrees on the menu: seafood, beef, duck or game bird, and vegetarian.

5911 SW U.S. 101. www.thebayhouse.org. ✆ **541/996-3222.** Reservations recommended. Main courses $30–$44, tasting menu $79. Wed–Sun 5:30–9pm.

Blackfish Cafe ★ SEAFOOD/AMERICAN Though the food is generally quite good—excellent scallops, a classic clam chowder, flaky fried fish—Blackfish loses some stars for subpar service. Still, you can have a very good meal here if you're willing to ignore the fact that your waiter is ignoring you. We recommend Blackfish for lunch rather than dinner as the prices are more reasonable at lunch, and you'll get a hair more attention from the staff.

2733 NW U.S. 101. www.blackfishcafe.com. ✆ **541/996-1007.** Reservations recommended. Main courses $13–$35. Wed–Mon 11:30am–9pm.

A Secret Spot for an Old-Fashioned Shrimp Cocktail

A shrimp cocktail is not a drink, it's a scoop of sweet, tiny, tender little Oregon bay shrimp slathered with cocktail sauce. You can order these in restaurants, of course, but I always go to **Barnacle Bill's Seafood Market,** 2174 NE Hwy. 101 (✆ **541/994-3022**), an open-fronted seafood store right on the highway. It's been around since 1949, and the fresh fish, Dungeness crabs, and seasonal razor clams have gotten steadily more expensive. But this is where you can still get a shrimp cocktail served in a paper cup with a plastic spoon and a bag of crackers for $5. Barnacle Bill's is open daily 9:30am to 4:30pm. No credit cards.

Kyllo's Seafood & Grill ★★ SEAFOOD It's big, it's loud, it's right on the beach, it's family-friendly, and they don't take reservations so there's always a line for dinner on weekends and during the busy summer months. If you don't want to wait, ask if you can be seated at the bar—the full menu is available, and you can still look out through the giant windows toward the tiny D River (Oregon's shortest) and the beach beyond. I have been eating at Kyllo's for years, and I've never had a bad meal. But I always stick to the basics, like pan-fried Willapa Bay oysters, a halibut sandwich, crab cakes, or fish and chips. The fish and shellfish is always fresh, and your meal comes with various sides that will more than adequately fill you up. This bright, contemporary-looking restaurant is the best casual place to eat in Lincoln City.

1110 NW First Court. www.kyllosseafoodandgrill.com. ✆ **541/994-3179.** No reservations accepted. Main courses $9–$30. Daily 11:30am–9pm.

Otis Cafe ★ AMERICAN For years, the little Otis Cafe has been the spot where locals and in-the-knowers go for a big, old-fashioned breakfast or a filling lunch with a piece of marionberry pie for dessert. It's nothing more than a cheerful roadside diner, 5 miles north of Lincoln City, but it's been "discovered" by Portland beach weekenders, so it's now busier than ever and savvy enough to sell *The New York Times* in addition to the local Lincoln City *News Guard*. But, thankfully, the food remains resolutely old-fashioned: liver and onions (yes, really), pork chops and applesauce, burgers, BLTs, and tuna melts. And let us not forget the gooey cinnamon bun for breakfast.

1259 Salmon River Hwy. (Ore. 18), Otis, OR 97368. www.otiscafe.com. ✆ **541/994-2813.** Main courses $8–$18. Daily 7am–8pm.

Depoe Bay ★★

13 miles S of Lincoln City, 13 miles N of Newport

Unlike other coastal towns in Oregon, Depoe Bay isn't centered around a strollable beach, but around a giant bay and a tiny harbor. In fact, Depoe Bay claims to be the smallest harbor in the world—all of 6 acres. Yet this miniscule and very protected port is home to more than 100 fishing boats and Coast Guard cutters. All of these boats must leave or enter the harbor through a narrow channel that's little more than a crack in the rocky coastline. During stormy seas, it's almost impossible to get in or out of the harbor safely.

Shell mounds and kitchen middens around the bay indicate that Native Americans long ago called this area of the Central Oregon coast home. In 1894, the U.S. government deeded the land surrounding the bay to a Siletz Indian known as Old Charlie Depot. Charlie had taken his name from the army depot where he worked. Old Charlie later changed his name to Depoe, and when a town was founded here in 1927, it took the name Depoe Bay.

Though most of the town is a bit off the highway, you'll find a row of touristy souvenir shops, restaurants, and charter-fishing and whale-watching companies on the inland side of U.S. 101, above the harbor. A sidewalk on the other side of the highway serves as a promenade along this rocky section of the Oregon coast.

ESSENTIALS

GETTING THERE From the north, the most direct route is Ore. 99W/18 to Lincoln City, and then south on U.S. 101. From the south, take U.S. 20 from Corvallis to Newport, and then go north on U.S. 101.

VISITOR INFORMATION Contact the **Depoe Bay Chamber of Commerce,** 223 SW U.S. 101 (www.depoebaychamber.org; ✆ **877/485-8348** or 541/765-2889).

FESTIVALS Memorial Day is the time for the **Fleet of Flowers,** during which local boats carry wreaths out to sea in memory of loved ones. In mid-September the town holds its annual **Salmon Bake,** an opportunity to enjoy traditionally prepared salmon. For info, visit **www.depoebaychamber.org**.

EXPLORING DEPOE BAY

The coastline hereabouts is rocky and unwalkable. Aside from whale-watching and standing on the highway bridge to observe the boat traffic passing in and out of the world's smallest harbor, the most popular activity here, especially when the seas are high, is watching the **spouting horns.** Similar to blowholes, spouting horns can be seen all along the coast, but nowhere are they more spectacular than along the coastline at Depoe Bay, right across from the main tourist strip on U.S. 101. These geyserlike plumes occur in places where water is forced through narrow channels in basalt rock. As the channels become more restricted, the water shoots skyward under great pressure and can spray 60 feet into the air. If the surf is really up, the water can spray a long distance, and more than a few unwary visitors have been doused by a spouting horn.

Whale-Watching ★★★ WILDLIFE TOUR Gray whales *(Eschrichtius robustus)* are migratory mammals that make an annual journey from the Bering Sea to their birthing grounds in Baja California and back again. But there's a resident pod of grey whales that makes its home in the waters of Depoe Bay for 10 months of the year. Small wonder that whale-watching is the top attraction in Depoe Bay. Visitors come from around the world to catch a glimpse of these behemoths. You can whale-watch from many shore observation spots or take one of the whale-watching charters out for a closer look. It's a thrilling and unforgettable sight when you see breeching whales in their natural habitat. Whale-watching trips aboard comfortable cruisers or speedy Zodiacs depart throughout the day from Depoe Bay. Bring your sea legs and your binoculars. **Tradewind Charters,** with a kiosk right on Highway 101 in "downtown" Depoe Bay (www.tradewindscharters.com; ✆ **800/445-8730** or 541/765-2345), offers 1- or 2-hour whale-watching excursions; prices are $20 to $35 adults, $18 to $30 seniors, $10 to $15 ages 5 to 12.

To learn more about gray whales, stop in at Depoe Bay's **Whale Watching Center,** 119 U.S. 101 (www.oregon.gov/oprd/parks; ✆ **541/765-3304**), perched on the cliff above the entrance to the harbor. Rangers and volunteers are on hand to point out gray whales if they are visible, and there are interesting displays about *Eschrichtius robustus.* Memorial Day to Labor Day, the center is open daily from 9am to 5pm; other months open Wednesday through Saturday from 10am to 4pm and Sunday from noon to 4pm.

WHERE TO STAY

Beverly Beach State Park ★★ You're just a few minutes' drive from the Oregon Coast Aquarium and Yaquina Head Natural Area at this forested campground with tent sites, yurts, and RV access. There are accessible bathrooms with showers and there's a playground for kids. You'll have a view of Yaquina Head lighthouse and the headlands of Otter Creek.

198 NE 123rd St., Newport. www.oregonstateparks.org. ✆ **800/452-5687.** $22–$56 per campsite.

Channel House ★★★ Lock me in the Cuckoo's Nest and throw away the key. I won't mind. This extraordinary suite, at the top of the Channel House, is perched right above the ocean—and I mean *right above.* I don't think there's a room anywhere on the Oregon coast that is closer to the water, except the equally fabulous suites on the first and second floors. Lie in bed and the ocean is right there in front of you with no intervening beach, just a bit of rocky shoreline. From these suites, you can watch the boats making their tricky entrances and departures to and from Depoe Bay . . . while sitting in your outdoor whirlpool. It's hard not to love Channel House, because it has everything you could possibly want for a memorable coast experience. The decor is tasteful, upscale, and comfy; there are fireplaces to ward off any chill or induce romance; the kitchens are modern; and the views—well, once you see them, you'll know why I want to be locked in the Cuckoo's Nest.

35 Ellingson St. www.channelhouse.com. ✆ **800/447-2140** or 541/765-2140. 12 units. $199–$330 double w/continental breakfast included. **Amenities:** Free Wi-Fi.

Inn at Arch Rock ★★ Channel House is all contemporary luxury, and the Inn at Arch Rock is more like a wonderfully comfortable beach cottage. Out front is an emerald-green lawn above the cliffs and crashing surf. And some of the rooms here have views that, although not as close to the water, rival Channel House's for sheer eye-popping splendor. The original buildings in this small complex were cottages built in the 1930s; later, a motel-like building was added and, as of 2014, another new wing. The best rooms are on the second floor of the original building—especially #12 with corner windows and a cushioned bench below them that lets you lounge with the ocean just below. There are some nice older features, like wood-burning fireplaces from the 1950s and a little staircase that takes you down to a small, surf-churned beach.

70 NW Sunset St. www.innatarchrock.com. ✆ **800/767-1835** or 541/765-2560. 13 units. $99–$188 double w/continental breakfast. Pets accepted ($10 per night). **Amenities:** Free Wi-Fi.

WHERE TO EAT

If you're in need of a caffeinated pick-me-up while passing through Depoe Bay, stop by the **Pirate Coffee Company,** 10 Vista St. (www.piratecoffeecompany.com; ✆ **541/765-4373**).

Restaurant Beck ★★★ NORTHWEST Restaurant Beck is one of the three upper-echelon fine-dining restaurants along the Oregon coast, the other two being **the Bay House** (p. 266) near Lincoln City and the dining room at the **Stephanie Inn** (p. 256). The presence of an award-winning chef, Justin Wills, and a location in the luxurious Whale Cove Inn (a sister property to the Channel House in Depoe Bay, above), has put Beck on the map. And the cutting-edge cooking, too, of course. Wills is up-to-date with all the current foodie farm-to-table or sea-to-table trends. Foraged wild greens might show up in your salad, your petrale sole might be served with stinging nettle and almond puree, and your halibut prepared with celery root, fiddlehead ferns, and garlic vinaigrette. And how about dried matsutake mushroom ice cream? You just won't find this kind of culinary creativity and experimentation anywhere else on the coast.

At Whale Cove Inn, 2345 S. US. 101. www.restaurantbeck.com. ✆ **541/765-3220.** Main courses $29–$34. Daily 5–9pm.

Tidal Raves ★★ SEAFOOD Tidal Raves, at the south end of Depoe Bay, has been around for years and, because it sticks mostly to classic preparations of fresh seafood with a few creative spin-offs, has had a loyal following since it opened. Part of the appeal here is the incredibly dramatic view that goes along with the professional service. The dining room, with its huge windows and simple wood tables, isn't fussy in any way, shape, or form; the sea and coastal scenery provides all the decoration you could want. Three worthwhile signature dishes are Dungeness crab cakes, fish tacos, and a spinach and oyster bisque. More innovative is the red curry barbecue shrimp.

279 NW U.S. 101. www.tidalraves.com. ✆ **541/765-2995.** Main courses $14–$29. Daily 11am–9pm.

Newport ★★★

12 miles S of Depoe Bay, 24 miles N of Yachats, 58 miles W of Corvallis.

As Oregon coast towns go, Newport has something of a split personality. This lively community of 10,000 on Yaquina Bay is both a working port, with the largest commercial fishing fleet in Oregon, and a tourist destination, home to the Oregon Coast Aquarium, the top attraction on the coast. Along the

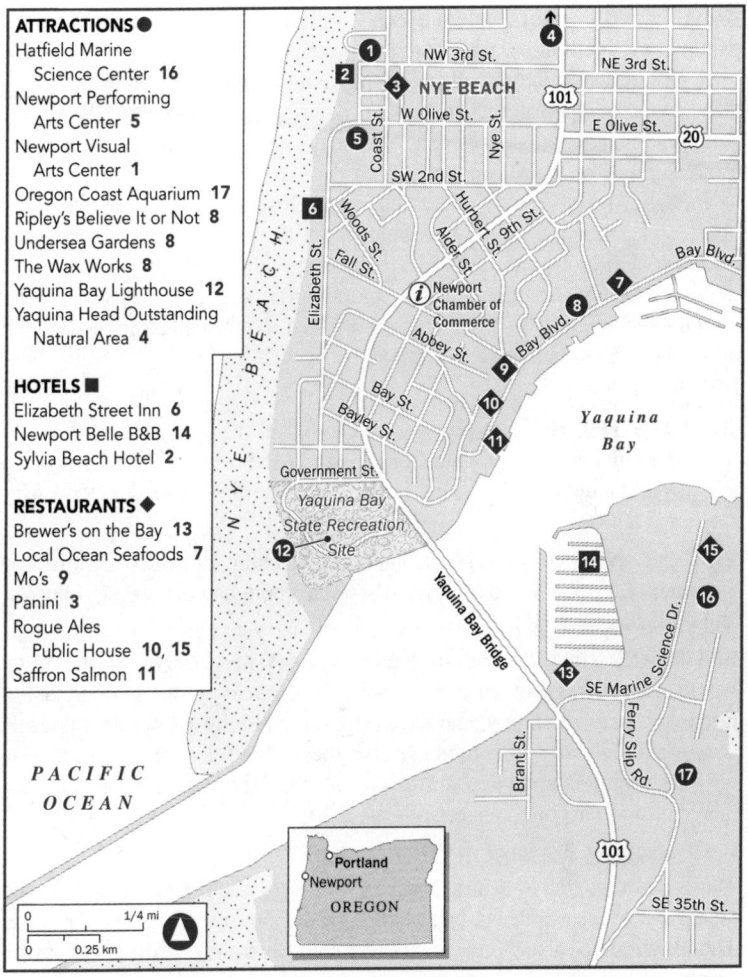

downtown bayfront, dockworkers unloading fresh fish mingle with vacationers licking ice-cream cones as fishing boats, pleasure craft, and Coast Guard cutters ply the waters of the bay. The air smells of fish and shrimp, and free-loading sea lions doze on the docks, waiting for their next meal. Directly across the street, art galleries, souvenir shops, and restaurants crowd together.

The busy bayfront is the center of Newport. The aquarium and Hatfield Marine Science Center are on the south side of Yaquina Bay, reached by the beautiful arched span of the Yaquina Bay Bridge, opened in 1936 and one of seven bridges on the Oregon coast designed by Conde McCullough. At the north end of town is the historic neighborhood of Nye Beach, where many of the charming old cottages and heritage buildings date from the early 1900s, when Newport was developing as one of the coast's first ocean resorts. Nye Beach is home to the Newport Performing Arts Center, a popular year-round venue for performances and art events of all kinds. Newport is also home to two historic lighthouses, which are just 3 miles apart.

In the late 1800s, before all the fishing and the aquarium and the saltwater taffy shops, Newport got its start as an oystering community, and oysters are still important to the local economy. They're raised in oyster beds along Yaquina Bay Road, east of town.

Though in recent years Newport has come close to matching the overdevelopment of Lincoln City, this community on the shore of Yaquina Bay still manages to offer a balance of industry, history, culture, beaches, good restaurants, and family attractions. It's one of the most interesting towns you'll find on the Oregon coast, with a life that's oriented to the sea but not completely dependent on tourism to keep it afloat.

ESSENTIALS

GETTING THERE Newport is on U.S. 101 at the junction with U.S. 20. From Portland, take I-5 south to Corvallis and head west on U.S. 20; the drive to Newport takes about 2½ hours. If you're continuing south from Depoe Bay, stay on U.S. 101.

VISITOR INFORMATION Contact the **Greater Newport Chamber of Commerce,** 555 SW Coast Hwy. (www.newportchamber.org; ✆ **800/262-7844** or 541/265-8801).

FESTIVALS In February, the **Seafood and Wine Festival** is one of the coast's premier events. Artists and craftsmen showcase a variety of art, sculpture, photography, pottery, and jewelry; Pacific Northwest wineries pour the wines; and culinary professionals serve the seafood. For more information, visit www.seafoodandwine.com or contact the Newport Chamber of Commerce (www.newportchamber.org).

EXPLORING NEWPORT

The Bayfront is tourist central for Newport. Here you'll find restaurants, ice-cream parlors, saltwater-taffy shops, chowder houses, and souvenir stores. The Bayfront is also home to commercial fishermen, seafood processing plants, art galleries, and numerous sea lions, who love to lounge on the floating docks adjacent to Undersea Gardens (from the adjacent pier, you can observe them at fairly close range).

The Bayfront is also where you'll find Newport's three tourist traps: **Ripley's Believe It or Not!, The Wax Works,** and **Undersea Gardens,** where a scuba diver feeds fish in a large tank beneath a boat moored on the Bayfront. Geared toward kids, all three of these places share the same address and phone number: **Mariner Square,** 250 SW Bay Blvd. (www.marinersquare.com; ✆ **541/265-2206**). Admission for each is $15 for adults and $8 for children 5 to 12, or $25 for adults and $15 for children to visit all three. Enter at your own risk, and don't come grousing to me if you're disappointed with what you find inside.

Hatfield Marine Science Center Visitor Center ★ AQUARIUM Located near the Oregon Coast Aquarium, this marine research facility of Oregon State University has a few worthwhile exhibits on life in Oregon's coastal waters. It's academic and science-oriented, geared to current topics in environmental and marine research, but the giant Pacific octopuses (yes, octopuses, not octopi, is the plural of octopus) are definitely worth visiting, and there are other marine-related exhibits as well. If your time in Newport is limited, visit the Oregon Coast Aquarium instead.

2030 SE Marine Science Dr. www.hmsc.oregonstate.edu. ✆ **541/867-0226.** Admission by suggested $5 donation. Memorial Day to Labor Day daily 10am–5pm; Labor Day to Memorial Day Thurs–Mon 10am–4pm.

Nye Beach ★★★ NEIGHBORHOOD Newport was one of the earliest beach resort destinations in Oregon, and it was in Nye Beach that the first hotels and vacation cottages were built. Today, this neighborhood, north of the Bayfront along the beach, has been given a new pedestrian-only street and is home to hotels, good restaurants, some interesting shops, and, of course, miles of sandy beach. There's public parking at the turnaround on Beach Drive. The works of local and regional artists are showcased at the **Newport Visual Arts Center,** 777 NW Beach Dr. (www.coastarts.org; ✆ **541/265-6540**). The center is open Tuesday through Sunday from 11am to 6pm. Just a few blocks away, the **Newport Performing Arts Center,** 777 W. Olive St. (www.coastarts.org; ✆ **541/265-2787**), hosts local and nationally recognized ensembles, performers and art exhibits.

Oregon Coast Aquarium ★★★ AQUARIUM He's not here now, but there was an international hoo-haw back in 1996 when Keiko, the orca whale star of *Free Willy,* arrived via UPS at his new home, a huge aquarium built expressly for him at the Oregon Coast Aquarium. For years, Keiko was the superstar of the aquarium, with a cadre of handlers who tried to rehabilitate

behind the scenes **AT THE OREGON COAST AQUARIUM**

I'll never forget my "Octopus Experience" at the Oregon Coast Aquarium, when the long coral-colored tentacle of a Giant Pacific octopus rose gracefully from a tank and gently wrapped itself around my hand and arm. I haven't eaten octopus since because the experience opened my eyes to the consciousness of those remarkable cephalopods. The aquarium isn't currently offering the Octopus Experience (but check to make sure; it depends on whether or not an octopus has been caught in a crab trap and donated to the aquarium until it is released back into Newport Bay). What the aquarium does have is a 45-minute "Behind the Scenes Tour" ($15) during which you're taken around and shown how the aquarium's 15,000 animals are cared for, and a 45-minute "Seal or Sea Lion Kiss" experience ($35). This one includes an animal training session and ends with a fishy kiss from a California sea lion or a harbor seal. Your kids will never forget these eye-opening encounters with the animals.

DON'T MISS YAQUINA HEAD outstanding NATURAL AREA

Yaquina Head Outstanding Natural Area ★★★, is the laborious but apt name for this fascinating piece of coastline, 3 miles north of Newport at 750 NW Lighthouse Dr. (www.blm.gov/or/resources/recreation/yaquina/index.php; ✆ **541/574-3100**). At 93 feet, the still-functioning **Yaquina Head Lighthouse** the area's gleaming white focal point and the tallest lighthouse on the Oregon coast. It's also one of the most easily accessible to visitors. The light began operation in 1874, replacing the earlier Yaquina Bay Lighthouse overlooking Yaquina Bay in Newport (see p. 270). Displays in the adjacent **Yaquina Head Interpretive Center** (open daily 10am–5pm) cover everything from the life of lighthouse keepers and their families to the sea life of tide pools. But this is also a wonderful spot to view seabirds and other sea life. Cormorants and pigeon guillemots roost on the steep slopes, and harbor seals lounge on the offshore rocks, and in early winter and spring you may be able to spot a migrating gray whale. A stairway leads down to a cobblestone beach below the lighthouse, where you can explore tide pools at low tide (there's even a wheelchair-accessible tide-pool trail). Centuries ago, Native Americans lived along this rocky cove, harvesting shellfish and other foods from the sea. Admission is $7 per car (free entry with the Oregon Pacific Coast Passport card). The grounds are open daily from 7am to sunset; tours of the lighthouse are given several times a day but must be reserved in advance online or by calling the number above.

him for life in the wild. This meant trying to restore the natural hunting instincts that had been sucked out of him during his years as a performer in a too-small, too-warm tank in Mexico. Eventually Keiko was released into an underwater pen in an Icelandic fjord, but he never learned how to hunt for his own food and died in 2003 of various complications. His story has always haunted me—for instance, the incredible amount of time and money spent by humans trying to restore the instincts that humans had robbed him of in the first place—and, to me, Keiko still haunts the Oregon Coast Aquarium, where for years he was able to swim in a much larger tank, one filled with seawater instead of chlorine, than he'd ever lived in before. He didn't have to perform, but he was still surrounded by the humans who lined up in droves to watch him through underwater viewing windows.

All of which has nothing to do with the Oregon Coast Aquarium today, which remains one of the top aquariums in the country, and is definitely worth at least a couple hours of your time. Keiko's tank has been reconfigured with a walk-through acrylic tunnel that allows visitors to watch sharks hungrily patrol the waters where Keiko once swam. The aquarium does a superb job of telling about aquatic life in Oregon's cold coastal waters and along its dramatic and varied shoreline. One outdoor exhibit is a walk-through aviary with tufted puffins, a beautiful and endangered shore bird. Another follows the course of a raindrop from mountain stream to sea, illustrating the journey with examples of the fish and animals found along the way. Though it rarely spreads its tentacles the full 20 feet, the giant Pacific octopus is another star attraction. Sandy beaches, rocky shores, salt marshes, kelp forests, and the ocean waters of the Pacific—Oregon's interlinked coastal ecosystems inspire awe, and are full of the creatures you will see or learn about in this riveting aquarium.

2820 SE Ferry Slip Rd. www.aquarium.org. ✆ **541/867-3474.** Admission $23 adults, $20 seniors and ages 13–17, $15 children 3–12. Memorial Day to Labor Day daily 9am–6pm; Labor Day to Memorial Day daily 10am–5pm.

Yaquina Bay State Recreation Site ★★★ LIGHTHOUSE/LANDMARK/HISTORIC SITE The older of Newport's two lighthouses, **Yaquina Bay Lighthouse,** is just north and west of the Yaquina Bay Bridge. This 1871 lighthouse, the oldest building in Newport, is unusual in that the light is in a tower atop a two-story wood-frame house. The building served as both home and lighthouse, and supposedly is haunted—but they say that about just about every lighthouse on the Oregon coast. You can visit the living quarters, furnished in period style, and climb up into the lantern for a look at the light.

846 SW Government St. www.oregon.gov/oprd/parks. ✆ **800/551-6949.** Admission free. June–Sept daily 11am–5pm; winter daily noon–4pm.

WHERE TO STAY

For rental accommodations, see our advice on p. 230.

Elizabeth Street Inn ★★ Even your car has a view at this in-town hotel built. That's because there's a covered parking lot (a boon in car-crowded Newport in the summer) on the lobby level. There are no bad views here; every room looks out on the long, scenic stretch of Nye Beach directly below. The newly renovated decor is tasteful and unobtrusive, with crisp white bed linens, cushy sofas, fireplaces, and kitchenettes. It all adds up to a room you can really relax in. Two other pluses: the full breakfast and the large, indoor, saline pool. Plus, you walk everywhere in Nye Beach from the hotel.

2332 SW Elizabeth St. www.elizabethstreetinn.com. ✆ **877/265-9400** or 541/265-9400. 68 units. $139–$359 double w/full breakfast. Pets accepted ($25 fee). **Amenities:** Exercise room; Jacuzzi; indoor saline pool; free Wi-Fi.

Newport Belle Riverboat Inn ★ For a nautical night on Newport Bay, walk up the gangplank of the Newport Belle, the only stern wheel B&B in North America. This is a unique and charming floating B&B, with 5 rooms, or cabins, all with private bathrooms. The rooms, on two decks, are tiny but have nice touches like beadboard wainscoting, a little table and two chairs, and windows that let in lots of light and give you a sense of being right on the bay (which you are). The decor is quasi-Victorian but kept fairly simple. The public areas on the top deck include a parlor and a sunroom where you can enjoy a complimentary glass of wine in the evening. People with major mobility issues would probably find it difficult to navigate the boat's staircases.

2126 SE OSU Dr., Newport. ✆ **800/348-1922** or 541/867-6290. www.newportbelle.com. 5 units. $150–$175 double w/breakfast included. Pets accepted ($25 per night). No children. Closed Nov to mid-Feb. **Amenities:** Access to nearby health club; free Wi-Fi.

South Beach State Park ★★ This Oregon State Park starts just south of Newport and stretches several miles down the coast. There are tent sites, yurts, accessible bathrooms with showers, and firewood and ice for sale. Paved trails for hikers and bikers and beach access so you can go crabbing, fishing, boating, or beach combing are part of its perks. The park is minutes away from all the attractions in Newport and Yachats. It's a top camping spot if you have kids because guided hikes and interpretive programs are offered in summer.

5580 SW Coast Hwy, Newport. www.oregonstateparks.org. ✆ **800/452-5687**. $22–$56 per campsite.

Sylvia Beach Hotel ★★★ Sylvia's has no TVs, no telephones, and no Wi-Fi, so it's not for everyone. But the funky charm of this century-old hotel, right on Nye Beach, makes it recommendable nonetheless. Usually I'm not that crazy about "theme" rooms, but because the theme at Sylvia Beach is literary, I love it. (Sylvia Beach, in case you don't know, was an American woman with the famous bookstore in Paris, known for championing the likes of James Joyce.) Every room here is dedicated to a different writer: The Colette room is all French elegance, the Mark Twain room abounds with masculine swagger, and the Dr. Seuss room is bright, bold, and funny. As might be expected there's a fabulous library where you can relax by the fire with your favorite book as the waves pummel the beach below. A full breakfast is included, and the hotel's **Tables of Content** restaurant serves a good fixed-price dinner for $28. Oh, and by the way, Shelley, the resident tortoiseshell cat, is very people-friendly.

267 NW Cliff St. www.sylviabeachhotel.com. ✆ **888/795-8422** or 541/265-5428. 20 units. $135–$230 double w/full breakfast. 2-night minimum on weekends. **Amenities:** Restaurant; no TV, phone, or Wi-Fi.

WHERE TO EAT

On a coast not known for its great restaurants, Newport shines like a lighthouse beacon. I hope you like seafood because, as you might expect, there's a lot of it on the menus here.

Local Ocean ★★★ SEAFOOD This glass-fronted restaurant on the Bayfront serves fish and seafood so fresh that you can ask what boat it just came in on. (And it would have come in on a boat, as no farmed fish is served here). The front opens out onto the sidewalk for summer dining, otherwise it's small tables in the colorful, streetside dining room with a showcase of fresh seafood to greet you as you enter. My suggestion is to order three small plates and share them: maybe the fresh mixed-greens salad, an order of panko-crusted pan-fried oysters, and a couple of fish tacos. The fish and seafood is cooked with a minimum of fuss. Local Ocean doesn't take reservations, and at peak times you'll probably have to stand in line. If you have the time, do it.

213 SW Bay Blvd. www.localocean.net. ✆ **541/574-7959.** Main courses $14–$29. Daily 11am–8pm (until 9pm in summer).

Mo's ★ SEAFOOD At Moe's the clam chowder is so thick you can stand a spoon upright in it and it won't fall over. That is what Mo's has always been known for and it's made Mo's an Oregon coast institution. If you have kids in tow it's good to know about, because it's relatively inexpensive compared to neighboring fish joints. There are now Mo's up and down the coast (in Cannon Beach, Lincoln City, and Florence), but this was the first, and it has expanded exponentially over the years and now has an overflow Annex with the same menu and better views. Stick with the basics: seafood sandwiches, fish and chips, or seafood dinners. Be prepared to wait on weekends year-round and every day in summer. Portions are hearty, the quality good, and the cooking unsurprising.

622 SW Bay Blvd. www.moschowder.com. ✆ **541/265-2979.** Main courses $9–$20. Daily 11am–10pm.

Panini ★ COFFEE/PIZZA/BAKERY This funky little spot in Nye Beach makes the best lattes I've found on the Central Oregon coast. They're also dependable on the pizza front, and have a bakery that turns out some delectable rolls (try the one filled with raisins) and pastries. I like this spot because it is so completely unpretentious and friendly—there are a couple of small tables and some room at a counter, but that's it.

232 NW Coast St. ✆ **541/265-5033.** Pizza/snacks $14–$20. Daily 7am–7pm.

Saffron Salmon ★★ NORTHWEST With its walls of glass, bold contemporary styling, and location at the end of a pier on the bayfront, the Saffron Salmon is a swell place to celebrate the ocean's bounty. As you dine on pan-seared salmon with saffron risotto cakes or spicy seafood stew, you'll watch commercial fishermen unloading their catch just outside the window. Keep an eye out for sea lions. Fish just doesn't get any fresher than this. At lunch, go for the saffron salmon sandwich. ***Tip:*** Burgers are available for fish-haters

859 SW Bay Blvd. www.saffronsalmon.com. ✆ **541/265-8921.** Main courses $17–$37 Fri–Sun 11:30am–2:30pm, Thurs–Tues 5–8:30pm. Closed Nov.

NEWPORT PERFORMING ARTS & NIGHTLIFE

The **Newport Performing Arts Center,** 777 W. Olive St. (www.coastarts.org; ✆ **541/265-2787**), hosts a year-round roster of performances and events.

If you're in the mood for a good pint of microbrew ale, visit **Rogue Ales Public House,** 748 SW Bay Blvd. (www.rogue.com; ✆ **541/265-3188**). There's a second Rogue pub, **Brewer's on the Bay** over near the Oregon Coast Aquarium at 2320 OSU Dr. (✆ **541/867-3664**).

Yachats ★★★

24 miles S of Newport, 26 miles N of Florence, 138 miles SE of Portland

Located on the north side of 800-foot-high Cape Perpetua, the village of Yachats (pronounced *yah*-hots) is something of an artists' community that also attracts a goodly number of affluent retirees and what passes these days for "counterculturists." Although there really aren't any non-natural attractions in this village of about 700 people, the natural ones more than suffice.

Yachats is a Chinook word meaning "dark waters at the foot of the mountains," and that sums up perfectly the setting of this small community, one of the few on the Oregon coast that could really be considered a village (it has no major commercial development of any kind). The tiny Yachats River flows into the surf on the south edge of town, where Cape Perpetua, the highest point on the Oregon coast, rears its forested head, and to the east stand the steep, forested mountains of the Coast Range. The shoreline on which the town stands is rocky, with little coves here and there where you can find agates among the pebbles paving the beach. Tide pools offer hours of exploring, and in winter, storm waves create a spectacular show. Uncrowded beaches, comfortable motels, and a couple of good restaurants add up to a top spot for a quiet getaway.

ESSENTIALS

GETTING THERE If you're continuing south from Newport, stay on U.S. 101. From other points north, take Ore. 34 west from Corvallis to Waldport, and then head south on U.S. 101. From the south, take Ore. 126 west from Eugene to Florence, and then head north on U.S. 101.

VISITOR INFORMATION Contact the **Yachats Area Chamber of Commerce,** 241 U.S. 101 (www.yachats.org; ✆ **800/929-0477** or 541/547-3530).

EXPLORING YACHATS

Gray whales come close to shore near Yachats on their annual spring migration, and several take up residence throughout the summer at the mouth of the Yachats River. You can see them in the spring from Cape Perpetua, and south of Cape Perpetua at **Neptune State Scenic Viewpoint,** at the mouth of Cummins Creek, and **Strawberry Hill Wayside.**

Built in 1930 in the shape of a cross, the **Little Log Church & Museum,** 328 W. Third St. (✆ **541/547-3976**), is a repository of local history and still serves as a community gathering point. The museum is generally open from noon to 3pm (closed Thursdays).

Cape Perpetua Scenic Area ★★★ NATURE/OUTDOOR RECREATION/LIGHTHOUSE Looming over tiny Yachats is the impressive bulk of 800-foot-high Cape Perpetua, the highest spot on the Oregon coast. Because of the cape's rugged beauty and diversity of natural habitats, it has been designated a scenic area. The visitor center houses displays on the natural history of the cape and the Native Americans who for thousands of years harvested its seafood. Within the scenic area are 26 miles of hiking trails, tide pools, ancient forests, scenic overlooks, and a campground. Guided hikes are offered (weather permitting) when the visitor center is open. If you're here on a clear day, be sure to drive to the top of the cape for the highest and eye-poppingest vista on the coast. There's good access to the tide pools via a short oceanside trail from the pull-off at the north end of the scenic area. At the **Devil's Churn,** a spouting horn caused by waves crashing into a narrow fissure in the basalt shoreline sends geyserlike plumes of water skyward, and waves boil through a narrow opening in the rocks.

Cape Perpetua Visitor Center, 2400 U.S. 101. www.fs.fed.us/r6/siuslaw. ✆ **541/547-3289.** Admission $5 per vehicle. Summer daily 10am–5:30pm; spring and fall daily 10am–4pm; winter Wed–Sun 10am–4pm.

HECETA HEAD LIGHTHOUSE, SEA LION CAVES & carnivorous plants

On the stretch of U.S. 101 between Yachats and Florence there are three attractions that have long lured travelers along the Oregon coast. Ten miles south of Cape Perpetua, **Heceta Head Lighthouse State Scenic Viewpoint ★★★** is worth a stop to see **Heceta Head Lighthouse,** the most photographed lighthouse on the Oregon coast, and the breathtaking seascape of pounding surf and offshore haystack rocks. Heceta (pronounced "huh-*see*-tuh") Head is a rugged headland named for Spanish explorer Captain Bruno Heceta. The old lighthouse keeper's home is now a bed-and-breakfast (see **Heceta Head Lightstation ★★,** p. 280). Between Memorial Day and Labor Day, free tours are given of the lighthouse keeper's house Thursday through Monday between noon and 5pm. There is a $5 day-use fee to use the park.

One mile south of Heceta Head, **Sea Lion Caves ★★,** 91560 U.S. 101 N. (www.sealioncaves.com; ✆ **541/547-3111**), is the largest sea cave in the United States and has been a popular tourist attraction since 1932. The 300-foot-long cave and a nearby rock ledge are the only year-round mainland homes for Steller sea lions, the larger of the two species of sea lion (bulls can weigh almost a ton). Although you're likely to see quite a few of the sea lions here at any time of year, it is during the fall and winter that the majority of them move into the cave. A combination of stairs, pathways, and an elevator lead down from the bluff-top gift shop to a viewpoint in the cave wall. The best time to visit is late in the afternoon, when the sun shines directly into the cave and the crowds are smaller. Admission is $14 for adults, $13 for seniors, $8 for children 3 to 12. The caves are open daily from 9am to 5pm.

Another 6 miles south is the **Darlingtonia State Natural Site ★,** a small botanical preserve protecting a bog full of rare *Darlingtonia californica* plants, insectivorous pitcher plants also known as cobra lilies. You'll find this fascinating preserve on Mercer Lake Road; there's a turn-off sign from Highway 101. There's no admission or set opening hours.

WHERE TO STAY

In addition to the hotels listed below, plenty of rental homes are available in Yachats. You can find many on such sites as HomeAway and Airbnb.com (see our write-up on p. 230) or go through such local companies as **Ocean Odyssey** (www.ocean-odyssey.com; ✆ **800/800-1915** or 541/547-3637), or **Yachats Village Rentals** (www.97498.com; ✆ **888/288-5077** or 541/547-3501). Rates for most vacation homes range from around $150 to $250 per night but some require a minimum 7-night stay.

Cape Perpetua Campgrounds ★★ You'll have an excellent view of the Pacific and easy access to hiking trails and tide pools at this campground with tent sites, RV access, toilets and water. The location between forest and the beach makes this a popular spot so reserve well in advance.

2200 US-101, Yachats. www.recreation.gov. ✆ **877/444-6777.** $23 per campsite.

The Fireside Motel ★ Located adjacent to Overleaf Lodge, its more upscale sister property, the Fireside is a good choice for families and travelers who don't need on-site spa amenities and other such luxe touches. The real difference between the two properties is that not all of the rooms at the Fireside have views and fireplaces. Also, they do not have the floor-to-ceiling sliding glass doors and private balconies that the Overleaf has, so if you get a balcony room and step outside, you're right next door to your neighbor. That said, the rooms here have many of the same comfortable appointments, many have equally stunning ocean views, and some of them have special features like tongue-in-groove beamed ceilings and kitchenettes. The continental breakfast is not as big and varied as the Overleaf's, and there is a smaller and much less fancy lobby and overall ambience.

1881 U.S. 101 N. www.firesidemotel.com. ✆ **800/336-3573** or 541/547-3636. 43 units. $85–$185 double. w/continental breakfast. Pets accepted ($10 per night). **Amenities:** Access to adjacent spa; free Wi-Fi.

Heceta Head Lightstation ★★ You want picturesque? You want photogenic? You want historic? You want haunted? Stay here, in one of the last remaining lighthouse keeper's houses on the Oregon coast. It's a white Victorian clapboard house with an open front porch, and it sits in an improbably tidy green lawn with a picket fence on a forested cliff not far from the Heceta Head Lighthouse, with views for miles. When houses like this were built, they didn't have "picture windows" or private balconies. If you got through the

MY ENCOUNTER WITH THE ghost AT HECETA HEAD LIGHTSTATION

I had heard it was haunted, of course, but just about every lighthouse or lighthouse-affiliated building on the coast makes that claim. But one clear, moonlit night I was awakened from my slumbers at this historic B&B by the strange sound of something dropping or rolling down the stairs. Chills ran down my spine—until the room became so warm that I had to throw off the blankets. Thump, thump, thump. I didn't get a whole lot of sleep, and the next morning when I walked bleary-eyed into the breakfast room and asked who else had been awakened by all that thumping, everyone looked at me as if I were crazy. Whatever it was that had gone bump in the night apparently didn't bump loud enough to rouse the other guests. But when I did some research on the topic, I discovered that the "manifestations" of the ghost were often the sound of a ball slowly rolling down the stairs and rooms that suddenly became suffocatingly warm. I suppose it *could* have been the furnace snapping on (the manager assured me it wasn't), but I prefer to believe that it was the resident ghost, an older woman dressed all in black and sometimes seen, broom in hand, in the upstairs rooms. I was so taken with the stories I heard (the level-headed local contractor, who climbed a ladder to do some work on the upper floors, saw the lady in black gliding toward him and fled in terror, never to return) that I turned the lady in black into Rue, the ghost that forever sweeps and haunts the Heceta Head B&B in my play *Oregon Ghosts*.

winter without the roof blowing off, you were lucky. What the Lightstation *does* have are handcrafted (but non-fancy) period details, like the wooden staircase to the rooms on the second floor. The rooms all have different outlooks but share a comfortable, period-inspired look. There's a lounge and public kitchen downstairs, and you're served a big breakfast in the morning. ***Two tips*:** The Lightstation fills up quickly so you'll have to make a reservation well in advance of your trip. Once here, you're fairly isolated, so plan accordingly.

92072 U.S. 101 S. www.hecetalighthouse.com. ✆ **866/547-3696** or 541/547-3696. 6 units, 4 with private bathroom. $137–$380 double w/full breakfast included. 2-night minimum on weekends. No children under 10. **Amenities:** Free Wi-Fi.

Ocean Haven ★★ The address of this enviro-friendly retreat is Yachats, but it's really about 8 miles south, perched on a bluff in a Marine Protected and Shorebird Conservation Area. It's meant for guests who really want to commune with nature, so you won't find TVs (though you can still surf with the free Wi-Fi). What you will get is a charming rustic retreat committed to sound environmental practices. Oh, and some pretty spectacular views, too, especially in the North or South View rooms with their walls of glass. For a romantic getaway, book the little cabin with its wood-burning fireplace and ocean-facing deck. Wood-paneled walls give a lovely warmth to all the rooms and cabin; the furniture includes recliners and window-bunks. You can walk to the beach and lots of nearby tidepools.

94770 U.S. 101, Yachats. www.oceanhaven.com. ✆ **541/547-3583.** 5 units. $130–$185 double. **Amenities:** Free Wi-Fi.

Overleaf Lodge ★★ Overlooking the rocky shoreline at the north end of Yachats, this modern hotel offers some of the most luxurious and tastefully decorated rooms on the central coast. Built in a sort of modern interpretation of the traditional Victorian beach cottage, the lodge caters primarily to couples seeking a romantic escape. Guest rooms all have handsome, contemporary renditions of Arts and Crafts style furnishings and ocean views, and most have patios or balconies. (All hear the ocean and at night when the tide is in and the waves are crashing on the rocks below, you'll really feel the power of the Pacific). Many rooms have fireplaces, and the larger ones have two big comfortable armchairs, a fireplace, and a full kitchen; there's a comfy recliner in the smaller rooms. The lodge also rents out attractive cottages that are adjacent to the lodge. The spa area here is quite spiffy, with two heated soaking pools and separate sauna areas for men and women. One of the nicest features in this hotel is the coastal path right behind it, which is easy to walk and takes you along a highly scenic section of the ocean to a long sand beach. And the complimentary breakfast is very generous and filling.

280 Overleaf Lodge Lane. www.overleaflodge.com. ✆ **800/338-0507** or 541/547-4880. 54 units. $175–$325 double w/continental breakfast included. **Amenities:** Spa, exercise room; heated indoor soaking pools; sauna; free Wi-Fi.

WHERE TO EAT

On my never-ending quest for truth, justice, and a decent cup of coffee, I discovered **Green Salmon Coffee and Tea House,** 220 U.S. 101 N. (www.thegreensalmon.com; ✆ **541/547-3077**), where you can get organic, fair-trade coffee, baked goods, and light meals.

Heidi's Italian Dinners ★★ ITALIAN Heidi Travaglia moved to Yachats from New Jersey over 2 decades ago and started her culinary career with a deli and takeout pizza. She now serves dinners only—and they are the best Italian dinners in the area (it's wise to make a reservation here). The restaurant is in a charming little cottage beside the beach in "downtown" Yachats. Try her specialties: *cioppino,* an Italian seafood stew with cod, prawns, scallops, calamari, and shrimp in a spicy tomato base; or Dungeness crab ravioli. Classic spaghetti and meatballs in a marinara sauce is also darn good. There are only about 9 dishes on the menu, and they change every couple of weeks. You can enjoy a good Italian wine with your dinner.

84 Beach. ✆ **541/547-4409.** Main courses $15–$26. Summer Wed–Sun 4:30–8:30pm; winter Fri–Sun 5–8:30pm.

Luna Sea Fish House ★★ SEAFOOD Owner Robert Anthony is a seasonal salmon fisherman, and a Dungeness crabber, who supplies his small, restaurant beside Highway 101 with the freshest of the fresh. In fact, if Anthony hasn't caught it that day, you can be sure someone else has: The restaurant only serves wild caught fish. Once its caught they don't allow the chefs to mess with the taste by adding a lot of frills: The fresh catch is served grilled or fried, typically with a big helping of salad. The salmon fish and chips are wonderful, and they also serve a good slumgullion (clam chowder with white cheeses and bay shrimp). The small restaurant is equally straightforward in décor: blue-and-white-checked oilcloth on the tables, and a heated tent outside to handle larger summer crowds. Luna Sea reminds me of the way the Oregon coast used to be: simple and real. They serve breakfast as well.

153 U.S. 101 N. www.lunaseafishhouse.com. ✆ **541/547-4794.** Main courses $10–$17. Daily 9am–9pm (8pm in winter; 10pm Fri–Sat summer).

Ona ★ SEAFOOD/AMERICAN Ona is the kind of restaurant that makes you want to linger a bit. That may be because you can order a well-made cocktail before dinner, and choose from a good wine list at the meal itself. And the meal will have some twists that you won't find elsewhere on the coast, with dishes like fresh Dover sole wrapped over Dungeness crab and bay shrimp with a pinot gris cream reduction; or "fish and chips" made from panko-crusted rockfish. Ona also makes a tasty three-meat meatloaf using grass-fed beef, lamb, and pork. The window-lined dining room is a pleasant spot; there's an outdoor deck for summer.

131 U.S. 101. www.onarestaurant.com. ✆ **541/547-6627.** Main courses $19–$37. Mon–Fri 11am–9pm; Sat–Sun 11am–3pm (brunch) and 4–8:45pm.

Florence ★★

12 miles S of Heceta Head, 50 miles S of Newport, 60 miles W of Eugene

The sprawl along Highway 101 just north of Florence may make you wonder if you're on the Oregon coast or driving along a mall-laden suburb in Anywhere, USA. But head down from the highway toward downtown Florence, and you'll encounter one of the few communities on the Oregon coast that retains a semblance of historic character. Set on the banks of the Siuslaw River, Florence's Old Town is lined with restored wooden commercial buildings that house restaurants and shops. The **Oregon Dunes National Recreation Area** (see p. 285) starts just south of Florence—hence town's claim to be "Gateway to the Oregon Dunes."

Florence got its start in the 1850s, soon after the California Gold Rush, when premium lumber from Oregon forests was cut and floated down the Siuslaw (sigh-*oo*-slaw) River and shipped south to San Francisco. The town apparently didn't have a name, or couldn't decide on one, until a piece of debris from the shipwrecked *Florence* drifted ashore and spurred someone's imagination.

Although the Florence waterfront has a picturesque charm, I would recommend that you visit Florence for a stroll and lunch, rather than making it an overnight stop.

ESSENTIALS

GETTING THERE Florence is on U.S. 101 at the junction with Ore. 126 from Eugene.

VISITOR INFORMATION For more information on Florence, contact the **Florence Area Chamber of Commerce,** 290 U.S. 101 (www.florencechamber.com; ✆ **541/997-3128**). Their office is open Monday to Friday 9am to 5pm, Saturday 10am to 2pm.

EXPLORING FLORENCE & ENVIRONS

Old Town ★★ NEIGHBORHOOD/HISTORIC DISTRICT Florence's Old Town, on the north bank of the Siuslaw River, is one of the most charming historic districts on the Oregon coast and the town's chief attraction. The restored wood and brick buildings housing shops, galleries, and restaurants capture the flavor of a late-19th/early-20th-century fishing and logging village. There's a promenade along the river, and a tiny park with a view down the riverfront at the site of the old ferry crossing.

Siuslaw Pioneer Museum ★ MUSEUM The pioneer settlers in the Siuslaw River area were primarily loggers and fishermen, and the river was their chief means of transportation (and remained so until the 1930s). Housed in a former church building, this museum tells the story of early life in and around Florence with historic displays that include period rooms and artifacts. There's a small Native American collection, too.

278 Maple St. www.siuslawpioneermuseum.com. ✆ **541/997-7884.** Admission $3. May–Sept daily noon–4pm, closed Mon rest of year. Closed Dec 25–Jan 1.

WHERE TO STAY

Sutton Campground ★ You can reserve tent and RV sites at this campground near Florence, Sutton Lake and the Oregon Dunes. Activities include hiking, fishing, swimming and boating.

4840 Vista Rd., Florence. www.recreation.gov. ✆ **877/444-6777.** $21–26 per campsite.

WHERE TO EAT

Mr. Coffee Finder (that's me) recommends **Siuslaw River Coffee Roasters,** 1240 Bay St. (www.coffeeoregon.com; ✆ **541/997-3443**), for a decent cuppa. **Lovejoy's Restaurant & Tea Room,** 195 Nopal St. (www.lovejoysrestaurant.com; ✆ **541/902-0502**) serves a traditional English tea.

Bridgewater Fish House and Zebra Bar ★ AMERICAN Occupying the most prominent building on Bay Street, a false-fronted general store built in 1901, this restaurant retains the atmosphere of that era. When it's available, and if you want to eat like a real Oregonian (or like Oregonians used to eat), order the whole steamed Dungeness crab, still in its shell, and start cracking. These sweet, delicious crabs are pretty much unavailable outside of the Pacific Northwest. Bridgewater's is good with fish, though not all of it is from local waters, and they also make solidly tasty pastas.

1297 Bay St. www.bridgewaterfishhouse.com. ✆ **541/997-1133.** Main courses $12–$26. Wed–Mon 11am–11pm.

La Pomodori ★★ ITALIAN For the best food in town, head over to 7th and Maple, where La Pomodori cooks up Italian food with a Northwest twist. On the Italian front, there's expert renditions of bruschetta, a caprese salad, sausage gnocchi, and chicken cacciatore. But you can also get Italo-Northwest hybrids like a Reuben on focaccia or Tuscan halibut (served on a bed of spinach with pine nuts and tomatoes). The atmosphere is cozy, and the prices are reasonable for the quality of the food. It's a good idea to make a reservation at least a day in advance.

1415 Seventh St. www.lapomodori.com. ✆ **541/902-2525.** Main courses $12–$26. Tues–Fri 11:30am–2pm and 5–8pm; Sat 5–8pm.

Mari's Kitchen at the Maple Street Grille ★★ ROMANIAN The convoluted name is due to the fact that Chef Mari Lane took over what had been a long-running cottage-turned-restaurant in Old Town. She felt the need to keep part of the old name, and some of the old standards here (like burgers and crusted halibut). But those in the know go for the Eastern Europe choices on the menu, because Mari is from Bucharest, Romania and does her native cuisine proud. Highlights range from a bacon-wrapped meatloaf to veal schnitzel to stuffed cabbage. The apple pie has a crust that's lighter than sea foam (it's extraordinary). If you're strolling in Old Town and want a French-press coffee or a cocktail, this is a nice spot for that, too.

165 Maple St. www.maplestreetgrille.com. ✆ **541/997-9811.** Main courses $10–$25. Thurs–Tues 11:30am–8pm.

THE SOUTH COAST

Oregon's South Coast begins just about where the **Oregon Dunes** do. You could use Florence as the starting point for the South Coast, but more typically Reedsport is considered where this special section of the coast begins, extending all the way down to Brookings on the northern California border. This stretch of coastline isn't exactly remote, but it's away from major inland cities and doesn't have many highways that cut through the coastal mountains and connect it to I-5. Once you get here, trusty U.S. 101 continues down the coast, taking you to Bandon, Gold Beach, Brookings, and into California.

Oregon Dunes National Recreation Area ★★

The Oregon Dunes Recreation Area begins just S of Florence and ends north of Coos Bay

The Oregon Dunes National Recreation Area starts just south of Florence and stretches for almost 50 miles. Recreation is the key word here; the dunes are magnets for all kinds of outdoor activities. Within this vast area of shifting sands—the largest sand dunes on the West Coast—there are numerous lakes, popular sports fishing and water-skiing destinations. There are also places set aside for racing dune buggies, dirt bikes, and other off-road vehicles (ORVs) through the sand dunes.

The Umpqua River divides the national recreation area roughly at its midway point. Along the banks of the river are the little towns of Gardiner, Reedsport, and Winchester Bay. **Gardiner** was founded in 1841 when a Boston merchant's fur-trading ship wrecked near here. An important mill town in the 19th century, Gardiner has several stately Victorian homes. **Reedsport** is the largest of these three communities, and the town of **Winchester Bay** is known for its large fleet of charter-fishing boats. If you want a dunes experience, I would recommend that you explore the dunes on day trips.

ESSENTIALS

GETTING THERE The dunes can be accessed at marked turn-offs all along Highway 101 between Florence and Coos Bay.

VISITOR INFORMATION For more information on the dunes, contact the **Oregon Dunes National Recreation Area Visitor Center,** 855 U.S. 101, Reedsport, OR 97467 (www.fs.fed.us/r6/siuslaw; ✆ **541/271-6000**). From mid-May to mid-September, this visitor center is open daily from 8am to 4:30pm; other months, it is closed on Saturday and Sunday.

There is a $5-per-car day-use fee within the recreation area.

EXPLORING THE DUNES

There are numerous ways to explore and enjoy the dunes and surrounding area. Please see the box below and our info on hiking, also below.

CAMPING & WATER SPORTS **Jessie M. Honeyman Memorial State Park ★★** (www.oregon.gov/oprd/parks; ✆ **541/997-3641**), 3 miles south of Florence, is a unique spot with a beautiful forest-bordered lake and towering

ABOUT THE dunes

The first Oregon dunes were formed between 12 and 26 million years ago by the weathering of inland mountain ranges, but it was not until about 7,000 years ago, after the massive eruption of Mount Mazama (today's Crater Lake), that they reached their current size and shape. That volcanic eruption emptied out the entire molten-rock contents of Mount Mazama, and in the process created the caldera that became Crater Lake, the deepest lake in the U.S.

Due to water currents and winds, the dunes are in constant flux. Currents move the sand particles north each winter and south each summer, while constant winds off the Pacific Ocean blow the sand eastward, piling it up into dunes. Over thousands of years, the advancing dunes have swallowed up whole sections of forests, isolating some groves as remnant tree islands, turning others into parched patches of skeleton forest.

Freshwater trapped behind the dunes formed numerous **freshwater lakes,** many of which are now ringed by campgrounds and vacation homes. These lakes are popular for fishing, swimming, and boating. Lakes within the recreation area include **Cleawox Lake, Carter Lake, Beale Lake,** and **Horsfall Lake.**

European beach grass is changing the natural dynamics of this unusual ecosystem. Introduced to anchor sand dunes and prevent them from inundating roads and river channels, the beach grass has been much more effective than anyone ever imagined. Able to survive even when buried under several feet of sand, the plant has covered many acres of land and formed dunes that effectively block sand from blowing inland off the beach. As Pacific winds blow sand off the dunes into wet, low-lying areas, more vegetation takes hold. The result is that, today, only 20% of the dunes are open sand (the figure was once 80%). It is predicted that within 50 years, the Oregon dunes will be completely covered with vegetation and will no longer be the barren, windswept expanses of sand seen today.

sand dunes. The park offers camping, picnicking, hiking trails, and access to Cleawox and Woahink lakes. On Cleawox Lake, there is a swimming area and a boat-rental facility. The dunes adjacent to Cleawox Lake are used by off-road vehicles.

Umpqua Lighthouse State Park ★★★ (www.oregon.gov/oprd/parks; ✆ **541/271-4118**), near the Umpqua River Lighthouse (see p. 288), is the site of 500-foot-tall sand dunes that are the tallest in the United States. The park, centered around freshwater Lake Marie, offers picnicking, hiking, and camping amid forests and sand dunes.

ELK VIEWING One mile east of Reedsport on Ore. 38, at the **Dean Creek Elk Viewing Area** ★, you can spot 100 or more elk grazing on meadows that have been set aside as a preserve. In summer the elk tend to stay in the forest, where it's cooler.

GOLF The 18-hole **Sandpines Golf Links,** 1201 35th St. (www.sandpines.com; ✆ **800/917-4653**), plays through dunes and pine forest and is one of Oregon's most popular courses. During the summer, you'll pay $59 or $79 for 18 holes. Alternatively, though the course gets mixed ratings, you can try the

18-hole **Ocean Dunes Golf Links,** 3345 Munsel Lake Rd. (www.oceandunesgolf.com; ✆ **800/468-4833** or 541/997-3232), which also plays through the dunes and charges $25 to $42 for 18 holes during the summer.

HIKING There are several places to wander among these sand dunes. If you have time only for a quick walk, head to **Carter Lake Campground,** where you can continue on from the Taylor Dunes viewing platform. The beach is less than a mile beyond the viewing platform, and roughly half this distance is through dunes. From this same campground, you can hike the **Carter Dunes Trail.** The beach is 1½ miles away through dunes, forest, and meadows known as a *deflation plain.* A 3.5-mile loop trail leads from the **Oregon Dunes Overlook** out to the beach by way of Tahkenitch Creek, a meandering stream that flows through the dunes and out to the ocean. Another mile south of the Oregon Dunes Overlook, you'll find the **Tahkenitch Creek Trail Head,** which accesses an 8-mile network of little-used trails that wander through dunes, forest, marshes, and meadows. However, for truly impressive dunes, the best route is the **John Dellenback Dunes Trail ★★,** which has its trail head a half-mile south of **Eel Creek Campground** (11 miles south of Reedsport). This 5.4-mile round-trip trail leads through a 4-mile-long and 2-miles-wide stretch of high, shifting dunes—a quintessential section of the dune landscape.

HORSEBACK RIDING **C&M Stables,** 90241 U.S. 101 N. (www.oregonhorsebackriding.com; ✆ **541/997-7540**), located 8 miles north of Florence, offers rides on the beach and through the dunes. A 1½ hour dune ride costs $80, and a 2-hour ride on the beach costs $95.

OFF-ROAD VEHICLES About 30% of the sand dunes are open to **off-road vehicles (ORVs),** also known as ATVs (all-terrain vehicles), and throngs of people flock to this area to roar up and down the dunes. If you'd like to do a little off-roading, you can rent a miniature dune buggy or ATV from **Sand Dunes Frontier,** 83960 U.S. 101 S. (www.sanddunesfrontier.com; ✆ **541/997-5363**), 4 miles south of Florence. From March through December, guided tours of the dunes in giant dune buggies are offered by **Sandland Adventures,** 85366 U.S. 101 S. (✆ **541/997-8087;** www.sandland.com), 1 mile south of Florence (this company has a little amusement park as well). The tours cost about $16. One-person dune buggies and ATVs rent for about $50 per hour. Down at the southern end of the recreation area, you can rent two- and four-person vehicles from **Spinreel Dune Buggy Rentals,** 67045 Spinreel Rd., North Bend (www.ridetheoregondunes.com; ✆ **541/759-3313**), located just off U.S. 101, about 9 miles south of Reedsport.

SANDBOARDING Sandboarding is basically snowboarding in the sand, and at **Sand Master Park,** 87542 U.S. 101 N., Florence (www.sandmasterpark.com; ✆ **541/997-6006**), you (or your teenage kids) will find 40 acres of sculpted sand dunes designed to mimic a wintertime snowboard park (lots of jumps and rails). June through mid-September, the park is open daily from 9am to 6:30pm; other months, it's open Monday, Tuesday, and Thursday through Saturday from 10am to 5pm, and Sunday noon to 5pm. The park is closed from mid-January through February. Sand boards rent for $10 to $25.

UMPQUA RIVER LIGHTHOUSE The original lighthouse was at the mouth of the Umpqua River and was the first lighthouse on the Oregon coast. It fell into the Umpqua River in 1861 and was replaced in 1894 by the current lighthouse at the entrance to Winchester Bay. Adjacent to the lighthouse is the **Visitors Center & Museum,** 1020 Lighthouse Rd. (✆ **541/271-4631**), a former Coast Guard station with historical exhibits and an information center. At the museum, you can arrange to join a tour of the lighthouse. Tours are offered May through October daily between 10am and 4pm and cost $3 for adults and $2 for children 6 to 16. Across the street from the lighthouse is a **whale-viewing platform;** the best viewing months are November through June.

VIEWPOINTS The easiest place to get an overview of the dunes is at the **Oregon Dunes Overlook,** 10 miles south of Florence. Here you'll find viewing platforms high atop a forested sand dune that overlooks a vast expanse of bare sand. Another easy place from which to view the dunes is the viewing platform on the **Taylor Dunes Trail,** which begins at the **Carter Lake Campground,** 7½ miles south of Florence. It is an easy ½-mile walk to the viewing platform.

Cape Arago Highway ★★★

Coos Bay tries hard, but it simply is not the sort of Oregon coast town that I would recommend to visitors. South of Coos Bay, however, you'll find three state parks and a protected marine estuary that preserve some of the most breathtaking shoreline on the entire south coast.

U.S. 101 begins a 50-mile inland stretch at Coos Bay, not reaching the ocean again until Bandon, so start your exploration of this beautiful stretch of coast by heading southwest from Coos Bay on the Cape Arago Highway.

SUNSET BAY STATE PARK ★

In 12 miles you'll come to **Sunset Bay State Park** (www.oregon.gov/oprd/parks; ✆ **800/551-6949** or 541/888-4902), with one of the few beaches in Oregon where the water actually gets warm enough for swimming (although folks from warm-water regions may not agree). Sunset Bay is almost completely surrounded by sandstone cliffs, and the entrance to the bay is quite narrow, which means the waters here stay fairly calm. Picnicking and camping are available, and there are lots of tidepools to explore.

SHORE ACRES STATE PARK ★★★

Continuing on another 3 miles brings you to **Shore Acres State Park** (www.oregon.gov/oprd/parks; ✆ **800/551-6949** or 541/888-4902), once the estate of local shipping tycoon Louis J. Simpson, who spent years developing his gardens. His ships would bring him unusual plants from all over the world, and eventually the gardens grew to include a formal English garden and a Japanese garden with a lily pond. His enormous mansion was demolished long ago, but the formal gardens and sunken lily pond built atop the cliffs overlooking the Pacific remain, and are a rare and wondrous sight in coastal Oregon.

From the gardens, you can walk down to a tiny cove with rock walls, sculpted by the waves into unusual shapes, rising up from the water. The water off the park is often a striking shade of blue, and **Simpson Beach,** in the little cove, just might be the prettiest beach in Oregon. There is a $5 day-use fee here.

CAPE ARAGO STATE PARK ★★

Cape Arago State Park (www.oregon.gov/oprd/parks; ✆ **800/551-6949**) is the third of this trio of parks. Just offshore from the rugged cape lie the rocks and small islands of Simpson Reef, which provide sunbathing spots for hundreds of seals (including elephant seals) and sea lions. The barking of the sea lions can be heard from hundreds of yards away, and though you can't get very close, with a pair of binoculars you can see the seals and sea lions quite well. The best viewing point is at **Simpson Reef Viewpoint.** On either side of the cape are coves with quiet beaches (the beaches are closed from March to June to protect young seal pups). Tide pools along these beaches offer hours of fascinating exploration during other months.

Bandon ★★★

24 miles S of Coos Bay, 54 miles north of Gold Beach

Once known primarily as the cranberry capital of Oregon (you can see the cranberry bogs south of town along U.S. 101), Bandon is now famed for its world-class Bandon Dunes Golf Resort. It's also set on one of the most beautiful stretches of coastline in the state, where the Coquille River empties into the Pacific. Just south of town, the beach is littered with boulders, monoliths, and haystack rocks that seem to have been strewn by some giant hand. Sunsets are stunning.

During the steamboat age, Bandon was a popular stopping-off point for passengers traveling between San Francisco and Seattle (there was no I-5 or U.S. 101 back then). The town became known as the "Playground of the Pacific." A devastating fire in 1936 put an end to Bandon's playground days. Today, a waterfront boardwalk connects Bandon with the Coquille River and the historic Coquille Lighthouse, one of only a handful of buildings to survive the fire. But even with its post-fire buildings, Bandon exerts a charm all its

south slough NATIONAL ESTUARINE RESEARCH RESERVE

Four miles down Seven Devils Road from Charleston, you'll find the remarkably beautiful **South Slough National Estuarine Research Reserve** ★★★ (www.southsloughestuary.org; ✆ **541/888-5558**). In 1972, the South Slough inlet of the Coos River became the first federally protected estuary in the U.S., and once you see it, you'll understand why these 5,000 acres of tidal flats, vast marshes, and meandering channels are so important to the health of the coastal ecosystem. Stop in at the Interpretive Center for a map and directions to the 1.75-mile trail that takes you through the characteristic estuarine habitats. It's an easy hike, and the pristine coastal scenery is absolutely glorious.

CELEBRATING THE cranberry

It may come as a surprise to learn that Bandon is the cranberry capital of Oregon, but the tart red berries have been farmed on this part of the Oregon coast since 1895. The Bandon cranberry bogs (artificial, not real bogs) produce almost all the cranberries used in Oregon and are added to many products made with cranberries grown on the East Coast. Why? Because they have a deep red color and a higher sugar content. Although most of the cranberry bogs are now owned by huge agri-businesses like Oceanspray, and can't be visited, there are still local cranberry farmers who offer tours of their bogs during the harvest season, from mid-October to early December. Check the website **www.thebandonguide.com** for dates, times and locations. Bandon celebrates all things cranberry during the **Bandon Cranberry Festival**, held the second weekend in September.

own and has the quaint feel of a historic seaside village that attracts artists, craftspeople, backpackers, retirees, and lots and lots of golfers.

ESSENTIALS

GETTING THERE Bandon is on U.S. 101. From the I-5 at Roseburg, head west on Ore. 42 to Coquille, where you take Ore. 42S to Bandon.

VISITOR INFORMATION For more information, contact the **Bandon Chamber of Commerce,** 300 Second St. (www.bandon.com; ✆ **541/347-9616**).

EXPLORING BANDON

The easily strollable **Old Town** area contains a small concentration of shops, crafts galleries, and restaurants. The Bandon area is known for its scenic viewpoints and state parks, its wildlife watching opportunities, and its golf.

Beach Loop Road ★★★ SCENIC DRIVE Head out of Bandon on **Beach Loop Road,** where shoreline monoliths have been sculpted by wind and waves into contorted spires and twisted shapes. All of these rock formations have names, and all of them are part of **Oregon Islands National Wildlife Refuge.**

The first good place to view the rocks and get down to the beach is at **Coquille Point,** at the end of 11th Street. Here you'll find a short, paved interpretive trail atop a bluff overlooking the beach, rock monoliths, and the mouth of the river. A long staircase leads down to the beach. From here you can see **Table Rock** and the **Sisters.**

Face Rock, the area's most famous profile, makes an appearance at **Face Rock State Scenic Viewpoint.** Yes, it does resemble a face gazing skyward, and old Native American legend claimed that the rock is a "she"—a princess turned to stone by an evil sea spirit. Nearby are rocks that resemble a dog, a cat, and kittens (called, no surprise, **Cat and Kittens**). A trail leads down to the beach from the viewpoint, so you can explore some of the rocks at low tide.

South of the rocks, along a flat stretch of beach backed by dunes, are several beach access areas, all of which are within **Bandon State Natural Area.**

Bullards Beach State Park ★★★ STATE PARK/LIGHTHOUSE/SCENIC AREA Across the river from downtown Bandon, **Bullards Beach State Park** (www.oregonstateparks.org; ✆ **541/347-3501**) has beaches, a marsh overlook, hiking and horseback-riding trails, a picnic area, a campground (see "Where to Stay" below), and a boat ramp. Fishing, crabbing, and clamming are all very popular.

Coquille River Lighthouse ★★★ LIGHTHOSE/HISTORIC BUILDING The squat, sturdy and rather charming Coquille River Lighthouse, first lit in 1896, is located on the rocky, windy north bank of the Coquille River in Bullards Beach State Park. This is one of the few lighthouses to be hit by a ship: In 1903 an abandoned schooner plowed right into the tower. Early May through mid-October, tours of the lighthouse are offered daily between 11am and 5pm.

GOLF ★ The premier courses are found at Bandon Dunes Golf Resort (see below), but there are other, less expensive courses in Bandon. **Bandon Crossings Golf Course,** 87530 Dew Valley Lane (www.bandoncrossings.com; ✆ **888/465-3218** or 541/347-3232), is an 18-hole course 5 miles south of town on U.S. 101. Green fees for 18 holes are between $59 and $99 in the summer. The **Bandon Face Rock Golf Course,** 3235 Beach Loop Dr.; ✆ **541/329-1927**), offers a scenic 9 holes not far from famous Face Rock. The green fee is $20 for 9 holes. This course rents 1880s and 1920s vintage golf clubs for golfers who want to play the game the way it used to be. The course was closed in 2017 but expected to reopen in 2018.

West Coast Game Park Safari In the interests of full disclosure, I have to say that I have major issues with places like this. In a world of poachers and disappearing habitats, I understand the need for protection and conservation, but wild animals are wild animals, and when you destroy their natural instincts (to flee humans, for example), you destroy their spirit and ability to survive in the wild. That's what happened with Keiko, the orca whale star *of Free Willy,* who was taken to the Oregon Coast Aquarium (see p. 273) for a well-meant but unsuccessful rehabilitation after being abducted from his pod and forced to spend years as a performer. Here, depending on what young animals they have at the time of your visit, humans are allowed to play with

Insider's Tip: Local Jams and Jellies

Every time I am in this neck of the ocean I make a point to stop at **Misty Meadows,** 48053 U.S. 101 (www.oregonjam.com; ✆ **541/347-2595**), which is not a retirement community but a wonderful store that sells jams and jellies made from locally harvested fruits. And boy, are they good—on toast, an English muffin, a buttered crumpet, ice cream, or as a condiment to meats and fish. I'm talking cranberry, marionberry, blackberry, huckleberry, salal, cherry, and other fruits. Sugar-free varieties are available, and they also have honey, syrups, and barbecue rubs. Misty Meadows is open daily 9am to 5pm. Look for it south of Bandon on the east side of U.S. 101 (after West Coast Game Park Safari).

world-class golf AT BANDON DUNES GOLF RESORT

Golf may be a dying sport, but don't tell that to the passionate linksters who descend on Bandon from all over the world to play world-class golf at **Bandon Dunes Golf Resort ★★★,** 57744 Round Lake Dr. (www.bandondunesgolf.com; ✆ **800/742-0172**). This is not your typical parkland golf course but an ocean-front links course modeled after the legendary courses in Scotland and Ireland, where the game originated. The motto at Bandon Dunes is "Golf as it was meant to be," and what that means is that you walk the course (with or without a caddie) and the course follows the natural contours of the coastal landscape with its dunes, shore pines, gorse, and winds off the Pacific. In all, there are five courses at Bandon Dunes, designed by the likes of David McLay Kidd, Tom Doak, Bill Coore and Ben Crenshaw. They are both scenic and rugged, and playing here is an experience like no other. Since opening in 1999, Bandon Dunes has become one of the top golf destinations in the world, its courses compared to Pebble Beach, Carnoustie, and Pine Valley—and, some would say, better than all of them. Scattered throughout the 9,000-acre resort are lodges and secluded, upscale cottages (see "Where to Stay," p. 293), although you don't have to stay here to play here. There is also a fine-dining restaurant (see "Where to Eat," p. 294). Seasonally adjusted greens fees, per course, range from $75 to $250 for resort guests, and from $100 to $295 for golf-only guests. No golf carts are allowed; caddies are available and charge $80 to $100 per bag. All proceeds from playing the 13-hole, par 3 Bandon Preserve course benefit the Wild Rivers Coast Alliance, and there is also a college-scholarship fund for caddies.

leopard, tiger, or bear cubs. It is a tourist attraction where many families like to stop, and that's all I'll say about it.

46914 U.S. 101 S. (7 miles south of Bandon). www.westcoastgameparksafari.com. ✆ **541/347-3106.** Daily summer 9am–6pm (call for hours in other months). $17.50 adults, $16.50 seniors, $10 ages 7–12, $7 for ages 2–6.

Outdoor Exploring

BIRDWATCHING ★★★ More than 300 species of birds have been spotted in the Bandon vicinity, making this one of the best sites in Oregon for bird-watching. The **Oregon Islands National Wildlife Refuge,** which includes 1,853 rocks, reefs, and islands off the state's coast, includes the famous monoliths of Bandon. Among the birds that nest on these rocks are rhinoceros auklets, storm petrels, gulls, and tufted puffins. The puffins, with their large, colorful beaks, are the most beloved of local birds, and their images show up on all manner of local souvenirs.

The **Bandon Marsh National Wildlife Refuge** (www.fws.gov/oregoncoast/bandonmarsh/index.htm; ✆ **541/347-1470**), at the mouth of the Coquille River, is another good spot for bird-watching. In this area, you can expect to see grebes, mergansers, buffleheads, plovers, and several species of raptors.

WHALE-WATCHING ★★★ At Bandon, as elsewhere on the Oregon coast, **gray whales** migrating between the Arctic and Baja California, Mexico, pass close to the shore and can often be spotted from land. The whales pass Bandon between December and February on their way south and between March and May on their way north. Gray days and early mornings before the wind picks up are the best times to spot whales. Coquille Point (at the end of 11th Street) and the bluffs along **Beach Loop Road** are the best vantage points.

WHERE TO STAY

For rentals—and there are many in this area—go to one of the rental sites. Our advice on p. 230.

Bandon Dunes Golf Resort ★★ You don't have to be a golfer to stay here, but you may feel like a fish out of water if you aren't. That said, Bandon Dunes Golf Resort boasts luxurious accommodations and resort amenities, with secluded duplex and multi-unit cottages nestled around a pond and in quiet forest settings. Rooms and suites are also available at the inn. Unlike most hotels and resorts along the coast, the units here do not have kitchens, but you can get terrific meals at the fine-dining restaurant in the lodge and the casual Pacific Grill in the clubhouse. The decor throughout is upscale Arts and Crafts utilizing natural woods and fabrics, with big Morris-style armchairs. Guests can buy golf packages or receive a discount on individual courses.

57744 Round Lake Dr. www.bandondunesgolf.com. ✆ **888/345-6008.** 186 units. $100–$420 double in lodge or inn. **Amenities:** 5 restaurants; 3 lounges; exercise room; four 18-hole golf courses and one 13-hole par-3 course; Jacuzzi; free Wi-Fi.

Bandon Inn ★ The super-friendly and super-economical Bandon Inn sits on the south bank of the Coquille River overlooking Bandon's Old Town. Rooms in the inn's two buildings are fairly large and decorated in a quasi-country, semi-traditional style that doesn't have much to do with the Oregon coast and better evokes the feeling of an inn on the Eastern Seaboard, with mix-and-match patterns and colors. All the rooms have microwaves and refrigerators, some have balconies, and there are thoughtful amenities like in-room coffeemakers and free local and long-distance U.S./Canada telephone calls. From the inn, a stairway leads down to Old Town with its shops and restaurants.

355 U.S. 101. www.bandoninn.com. ✆ **800/526-0209** or 541/347-4417. 57 units. $84–$185 double; Pets accepted ($15 per night). **Amenities:** Free Wi-Fi.

"Honey, Is That a T-Rex Beside the Highway?"

Yes, dear, it is. The giant T-Rex, frozen in its voracious rampage, stands beside U.S. 101 about 12 miles south of Port Orford, and it will certainly get your attention—or, more likely, that of your kids. The **Prehistoric Gardens & Rainforest,** 36848 U.S. 101 S. (www.prehistoricgardens.com; ✆ **541/332-4463**), is a lost world of life-size dinosaur replicas. Though they aren't as realistic as those in *Jurassic Park,* they'll make the kids squeal with delight (or terror). The gardens are open in the summer daily from 10am to 6pm; other months, call for hours. Admission is $12 for adults, $10 for seniors, and $8 for children 3 to 12. It takes about 20 minutes to walk through the gardens. If you don't want to venture inside, you can get your T-Rex photo op right by the side of the road.

Best Western Inn at Face Rock Resort ★ Get one of the deluxe rooms here with its own little protected patio, and you'll spend hours sitting contentedly, looking out at the glimmering Pacific just across Beach Loop Drive. The Best Western complex sits on 8 acres adjacent to the Old Bandon Golf Links, and it was where golfers often stayed before Bandon Dunes Golf Resort opened in 1999. It's a well-kept and attractive property, dating from 1979, with a big indoor pool open 24 hours. The rooms are comfortable, fairly large, and have full-length tubs in the bathrooms. The decor won't win any awards, but everything is spic-and-span and the prices are very reasonable. From the hotel, there's a path right down to the beach at Face Rock.

3225 Beach Loop Dr. www.innatfacerock.com. ✆ **800/638-3092** or 541/347-9441. 75 units. $99–$130 double w/full breakfast included. Pets accepted ($20 fee). **Amenities:** Restaurant; lounge; bikes; exercise room; Jacuzzi; indoor pool; sauna; free Wi-Fi.

Bullards Beach State Park ★★★ Tent sites, yurts and RV hookups are available at this family-oriented campground. There's a pathway to the beach so you can go crabbing or beachcombing, plus hiking trails and a horse camp. Bandon Lighthouse is nearby, and the town of Bandon has restaurants, shops and galleries to explore.

Bullards Beach State Park, Bandon. www.oregonstateparks.org. ✆ **800/452-5687.** $22–$56 per campsite.

WHERE TO EAT

When it's time for a latte or espresso, stop in at **Bandon Coffee Cafe,** 365 Second St. SE (www.bandoncoffee.com; ✆ **541/347-1144**), in a cottage on the edge of Old Town. For a quick meal of incredibly fresh fish and chips, you can't beat **Bandon Fish Market,** 249 First St. SE (www.bandonfishmarket.com; ✆ **541/347-4282**), which is right on the waterfront and has a few picnic tables. Also here on the waterfront, you can get cooked Dungeness crab at **Tony's Crab Shack,** 155 First St. (www.tonyscrabshack.com; ✆ **541/347-2875**).

Alloro Wine Bar ★★★ ITALIAN Co-owners Jeremy Buck and Lian Schmidt lived, studied, and cooked in Italy before moving to Bandon to open their Oregon coast version of an Italian *enoteca,* a place devoted to wines and the foods that pair well with them. There's no question about it, this little red wood-frame restaurant in Old Town is the most sophisticated spot to dine in town. As you would expect from chefs with their backgrounds, everything they use here is fresh, local, and seasonal—or imported from Italy. Main courses emphasize local seafood (wild salmon, ling cod, albacore tuna, halibut, Dungeness crab, locally caught spot prawns) but rabbit, duck, pork, and steak dishes are also on the menu. I'm a big fan of the *cacciuto*, a Tuscan-stye seafood stew. But their homemade pasta dishes are usually spot on, too—your choices might include pappardelle with oxtail ragu; orecchiette with Italian sausage ragu; or linguine with clams in a white wine sauce. It's best to make a reservation if you want to dine here.

375 Second St. SE. www.allorowinebar.com. ✆ **541/347-1850.** Main courses $26–$36. Summer Thurs–Tues 5–9pm; other months Thurs–Sun 5–8pm. Closed Jan to mid-Feb.

The Gallery ★★★ PACIFIC NORTHWEST/AMERICAN This white tablecloth establishment overlooking the 18th hole at the upscale Bandon Dunes Golf Resort hits a hole in one. You can expect fine service, fine food, and fine wine here, and you don't have to be a golfer or a guest at the resort to enjoy it. Start with some fresh oysters on the half shell or a salad of organic mixed greens with grape tomatoes and cherry vinaigrette. For your main course, try the scallops with pancetta or the Northwest steelhead with orzo and arugula with pine nuts. You can also order a steak; duck breast confit; or roast chicken with fingerling potatoes, zucchini and oyster mushrooms. The food here isn't overly fussy, though it is artfully presented. A sommelier is on hand to help with wine choices. It's best to reserve in advance.

Bandon Dunes Golf Resort, 57744 Round Lake Dr. www.bandondunesgolf.com. ✆ **888/345-6008.** Main courses $24–$60. Daily 7am–10pm.

The Loft Restaurant & Bar ★★ PACIFIC NORTHWEST The Loft is a small, simple space on the second floor of a building on the Bandon riverfront in Old Town, and the food is remarkably good. The first floor serves as a deli (great spot for picnic provisions), wine shop, and bakery. The dinner menu upstairs typically has about seven entrees. I love the smoked salmon goat-cheese tart with beets and walnuts. And being a connoisseur of chicken pot pies, I can honestly say that I've never had one quite as good as the Loft's, made with free-range chicken and wild local mushrooms; try it if it's on the menu. Each dish is created with local, organic produce and locally sourced fish (roasted butterfish is another specialty) and meat. It all adds up to a charmingly tasty meal in a charmingly unpretentious restaurant with a lovely view.

315 First St. SE. www.theloftofbandon.com. ✆ **541/329-0535.** Main courses $16–$28. Restaurant summer Wed–Sun 5–9pm; shorter hours other months; deli summer daily noon–6pm.

Lord Bennett's Restaurant and Lounge ★★ AMERICAN A longtime fave for Sunday brunch or a special-occasion-dinner, Lord Bennett's is housed in a contemporary structure with big windows looking out over the ocean. It's a fairly sedate, dress-up kind of place with good fresh seafood (try the pan-fried oysters from Coos Bay), steaks, chops, chicken, and a handful of pasta dishes, including a vegetarian version. If you come for brunch, enjoy the corned-beef hash, cranberry French toast, and lemon blueberry pancakes.

1695 Beach Loop Dr. (next to the Sunset Motel). www.lordbennetts.com. ✆ **541/347-3663.** Main courses $14–$37. Mon–Thurs 5–9pm; Fri–Sat 11am–2pm and 5–9pm; Sun 10am–2pm and 5–9pm.

Gold Beach ★★★

32 miles S of Port Orford, 54 miles N of Crescent City, CA

Let's look history in the eye before we move on to the golden delights of Gold Beach today. There are a couple of big backstories that have had a major influence on the development of the town and the surrounding region. In 19th-century California, gold prospectors struggled through rugged mountains in search of pay dirt, but when they arrived in Oregon, they discovered they could scoop it up off the beach. The black sands at the mouth of the Rogue River were high in gold, and it was this gold that gave Gold Beach its name. The white, gold-greedy settlers inevitably came in conflict with the local Tututni tribe, whose forbearers had lived in the region for at least 8,500 years. Violence erupted in 1856, but within the year the Rogue River Indian Wars had come to an end, and the Tututnis were removed to a reservation.

When the gold played out, commercial fishermen moved in to take advantage of the river's incredible salmon and steelhead runs (Zane Grey wrote about this period in his novel *Rogue River Feud*). A Scotsman named David Hume became the "Salmon King" of the Rogue, opening canneries that shipped out 16,000 crates of salmon a year. The efficiency of the commercial fishermen's nets and traps quickly decimated the local salmon population, and a hatchery had to be constructed to replenish the runs. Another backstory.

Today, the chief delight is the wild and scenic **Rogue River** that empties into the Pacific at Gold Beach. The Rogue is, to my mind, one of the great rivers of the West, perhaps of the world. You'll see it far below, glittering if the day is bright, darkly mysterious if the weather is foggy or rainy, as you cross the Art Deco Patterson Bridge that spans the north and south banks above the river's wide estuary. There is, of course, a beach at Gold Beach, though it's not really the area's main attraction. That is, and always will be, the Rogue, the most famous fishing and rafting river in the state.

Wildfires and You

Summer wildfires have become a regular occurrence in the Siskiyou Mountains in southwestern Oregon, affecting Rogue River rafting trips and impacting lives and the economy in Curry County. In 2017, the Chetco Bar fire in the Kalmiopsis Wilderness area near Brookings, on the California border, was the country's largest wildfire, burning over 130,000 acres. This is the kind of sad news that no travel writer wants to report, but I want you to be prepared. If you are planning a trip to the southern Oregon coast, or a rafting trip on the Rogue, make sure to check the local weather and fire conditions.

GETTING THERE Gold Beach is on U.S. 101 between Brookings and Port Orford. Coming from the north, the nearest highway connection to I-5 is Ore. 42 from Roseburg to Bandon. Coming from the south, you must either follow U.S. 101 north from California or take U.S. 199 southwest from Grants Pass, Oregon, and then continue north on U.S. 101 to Gold Beach via Brookings.

VISITOR INFORMATION The **Gold Beach Visitor Center,** 94080 Shirley Lane (www.goldbeach.org; ✆ **800/525-2334** or 541/247-7526), in South Beach Park at the south end of town, is open Monday to Saturday 9am to 5pm.

EXPLORING THE GOLD BEACH AREA

As with so many other coastal towns, the attractions of Gold Beach are not in the town itself but in the surrounding area. The Rogue is the focal point here.

Curry Historical Museum ★ MUSEUM This diminutive local history museum has displays of Native American and pioneer artifacts as well as re-created environments such as a miner's cabin that provide an overview of the history of the area.

29419 Ellensburg Ave. www.curryhistory.com. ✆ **541/247-9396.** $2 adults, 50¢ children. Tues–Sat 10am–4pm. Closed Jan.

Hiking There's an abundance of outstanding hiking trails in the area, including the following:

- The trail head for the 6-mile **Rogue River Walk** ★★★ begins 7 miles from the south end of the Patterson Bridge, east on Jerry's Flat Road. The trail provides spectacular views of the Rogue as it weaves through areas with spring wildflowers, myrtlewood groves, and over bridges. There are benches along the way to rest, do some bird watching, and take in the view.
- At the **Frances Schrader Old Growth Trail** ★★★**,** 10 miles up Jerry's Flat Road/South Bank Rogue River Road near the Lobster Creek Campground, you can take a 1-mile loop trail through a stand of majestic, old-growth trees, including a grove of Port Orford cedars; these trees are native to a limited range in southwest Oregon and northwest California.
- Not far from the Old Growth Trail, you'll find the **Myrtle Tree Trail** ★★★ **.** Along this .25-mile trail is the world's largest myrtle tree, 88 feet tall and 42 feet in circumference. From U.S. 101 in Gold Beach, drive east on Jerry's Flat Road (FS Road #33) toward Agness. At approximately 9½ miles, turn left on FS Road #3310, cross the bridge over the river, and turn right on Silver Creek Road (FS Road #3533) and watch for signs. Park at the turn-out on the right side of road; the trail head is on the left side of the road.

For more information on hiking in the Gold Beach area and specific directions to the trail heads, contact the Siskiyou National Forest's **Gold Beach Ranger Station,** 29279 Ellensburg Ave. (www.fs.fed.us/r6/rogue-siskiyou; ✆ **541/247-3600**). The Gold Beach Visitor Center (see p. 296) can also help direct you to the trail heads.

Jerry's Rogue River Museum ★ MUSEUM At the Port of Gold Beach and affiliated with the gift shop for Jerry's Rogue Jets (see below), this is the more modern and informative of the two museums in Gold Beach. It focuses on the geology and cultural and natural history of the Rogue River with small collections of Indian and pioneer artifacts, and it has a menagerie of stuffed animals found on the Rogue.

29880 Harbor Way (Port of Gold Beach). ✆ **541/247-4571.** Admission free. July–Aug daily 9am–9pm; rest of year Mon–Sat 9am–5pm, Sun 10am–5pm.

Jet Boat Rogue River Tour ★★★ BOAT TOUR For most visitors, a jet-boat trip up the Lower Rogue is the easiest way to see a portion of this fabled river. Powerful, shallow-draft hydrojet boats use water jets instead of propellers, allowing them to cross rapids and riffles that are only a few inches deep. **Jerry's Rogue Jets,** 29880 Harbor Way (www.roguejets.com; ✆ **800/451-3645** or 541/247-4571) leaves from the Port of Gold Beach on the south side of the bridge and offers three different trips. The 64-mile **Historic Mail**

Boat Trip follows the route mailboats have taken up the Rogue, delivering mail and cargo, since 1895. The 80-mile **Whitewater Journey** pushes farther up the river to a section of whitewater rapids. On the 104-mile **Wilderness Whitewater** ★★★ trip, you get to enter the wild and scenic section of the Rogue, accessible only to jetboats, rafters, and hikers. Prices range from $50 to $95 for adults, $25 to $50 for children ages 4 to 11. The longer trips include a stop for lunch (additional $8–$10 charge) at one of the fishing lodges on the Rogue (you can make arrangements to stay overnight at the lodge and be picked up by jet boat the next day). Knowledgeable and Coast Guard–certified guides accompany every jetboat trip and provide commentary on the wildlife and geology of the river. You may see deer, black bear, river otters, or bald eagles along the way. This is a safe adventure that everyone will enjoy.

Nesika Beach ★ OCEAN BEACH When you want to get out on the beach, head north of town across the Rogue River to Nesika Beach. To reach the best stretch of this beach, take the North Nesika Beach turnoff and then continue north to the end of the road. Alternatively, continue a little farther north to Old Coast Road, where you'll find a steep trail down to the beach.

WHERE TO STAY

For more suggestions, see our info on rental options on p. 230.

Ireland's Rustic Lodges & Gold Beach Inn ★★★ These charming little cabins were built in 1936, and couldn't be simpler, cuter or more charmingly old school. Each comes with a double bed in an alcove, a couple of easy chairs, a wood-burning fireplace, and a small bathroom with a shower. In the day, stars like Clark Gable would head here to fish and chill. The rustic cabins are now part of a larger, 19-acre oceanfront property that includes the adjacent Gold Beach Inn, with two newer buildings. The cabins with their knotty pine walls have all the charm; the rooms in the other buildings have the

RAFTING THE rogue

A guided **white-water rafting trip** down the wild and scenic Rogue is an unforgettable experience, but it takes some planning, and the rafting season is fairly short. Rafting trips generally start near Agness, about 35 miles up the Rogue from Gold Beach, or Merlin, 130 miles west of Gold Beach near Grants Pass. White-water-rafting companies offer half-day, full-day, or multiday trips that stop at rustic river lodges or campsites along the riverbanks (your guides do most of the work, setting up camp and preparing meals). Area rafting companies include **Rogue Wilderness Adventures** (www.wildrogue.com; ✆ **800/336-1647** or 541/479-9554); **Galice Resort,** 11744 Galice Rd., Merlin (www.galice.com; ✆ **541/476-3818**); **Orange Torpedo Trips,** 210 Merlin Rd., Merlin (www.orangetorpedo.com; ✆ **866/479-5061** or 541/479-5061). Expect to pay around $70 to $80 for a half day and $85 to $95 for a full day. Three-day lodge or camping trips are in the $650 to $1000 range.

views—and great views at that. Those rooms have walls and ceilings of Douglas fir, gas fireplaces, and nondescript but comfy easy chairs. There are also separate houses that are perfect for family reunions or large groups. The grounds here are full of old trees, grassy lawns, and trails down to the beach. There is also a wonderful patio area with three hot tubs (no kids after 10pm) and a solarium. For the price and the view—and the inimitable historic cachet of the little cabins—Ireland's can't be beat.

29346 Ellensburg Ave. (U.S. 101). www.irelandsrusticlodges.com. ✆ **877/447-3526** or 541/247-7718. 40 units. $99–$184 double w/full breakfast included. Pets accepted ($10). **Amenities:** 3 Jacuzzis; free Wi-Fi.

Jot's Resort ★ Good for budgeteers, this motel-style property has acres of asphalt parking lot around it, but once you're in your room you can slide open the glass doors, step out onto a balcony and enjoy views of the mighty Rogue River, its historic bridge, and the fishing and jet boats that make their way up and down the river. Decor is pretty plain, but every room has a comfortable bed, a dining table, and two upholstered chairs. Various room types and configurations are available, from standard rooms to fairly spacious condo units. There's an outdoor and an indoor pool, a reasonably priced restaurant, and the hotel will arrange for jet boat rides and charter fishing boats and guides for you.

94360 Wedderburn Loop. www.jotsresort.com. ✆ **800/367-5687** or 541/247-6676. 140 units. $60–$175 double. Pets accepted ($10–$25 per night). **Amenities:** Restaurant; lounge; indoor and outdoor pools; free Wi-Fi.

Secret Camp RV Park ★ This privately run camp park 3 miles from the Rogue River offers tent sites, full and partial RV hookups, fire pits and bathrooms with showers. There are lots of recreational opportunities nearby (jet boat rides, fishing, hiking).

95614 Jerry's Flat Road, Gold Beach. www.secretcamprvpark.com. ✆ **541/247-2665.** $25 camp site, $35–$42 RV site.

Tu Tu' Tun Lodge ★★★ If we had a four-star rating, you're darn tootin' I'd give it to Tu Tu' Tun. This sublime lodge on the sublimely beautiful Rogue River, 7 miles east of Gold Beach, can't be beat. Open since 1970, Tu Tu' Tun's rooms all have balconies or patios that look out on a wide stretch of one of Oregon's most scenic rivers. Those rooms are luxe, with handcrafted wood detailing, Arts and Crafts–style furnishings, all-natural fabrics, and a romantic ambience that sets it apart from every other hotel in the area. Spring for a fireplace room if you can—these are wood-burning fireplaces—and for added allure, book one of the rooms with an outdoor soaking tub. All kinds of amenities are part of the Tu Tu' Tun experience, including evening wine and hors d'oeuvres and a delicious breakfast. For an additional fee you can enjoy dinner (summer only) at communal tables that seat eight. The lobby/lounge area, with its big fireplace and Arts and Crafts–style furniture, leads out to a patio area overlooking an outdoor pool and lawn that leads down to a stretch of the

Rogue River Lodges

The Rogue is a fabled fishing and rafting river, and over the last century, fishing lodges have been built along the Rogue's south bank in or near the wild and scenic stretch of the river. The lodges are a bit difficult to reach—sometimes accessible only by hiking or jet boat—and their season is limited, but you might want to consider staying at one of these unique and unforgettable spots. The lodges are typically fairly rustic and cater to people who are taking guided rafting trips down the Rogue, or serve as overnight stopovers along the rafting trips. See the "Rafting the Rogue" box, p. 298). Two good lodges to consider are **Cougar Lane Lodge,** 4219 Agness Rd. (www.cougarlane.com; ✆ **541/247-7233**); **Lucas Pioneer Ranch & Fishing Lodge,** 3904 Cougar Lane (www.lucaslodgeoregon.com; ✆ **541/247-7443**).

beach. Jet boats arrive at the lodge's dock in the summer, so guests can take a ride up the river from here. If you're looking for the best, this is it.

96550 N. Bank Rogue River Rd. www.tututun.com. ✆ **800/864-6357** or 541/247-6664. 21 units. $160–$525 double w/full breakfast, evening wine and hors d'oeuvres included. No children under 10 May–Sept. **Amenities:** Restaurant (dining room closed for dinner Nov–Apr); lounge; access to nearby health club; outdoor pool; spa services; free Wi-Fi.

WHERE TO EAT

Coffee alert: The best coffee in Gold Beach is at **Rachel's Coffee House** in the Gold Beach Bookstore at 29707 Ellensburg Ave. (✆ **541/247-7733**).

Anna's by the Sea ★★ NEW AMERICAN Anna's is not like other restaurants along Highway 101 that serve the inevitable "fisherman's platter" or fish and chips. For one thing, it's a block off the highway, and for another thing, it's really small, seating only 14 people. It also serves double duty as Gold Beach's only wine bar and wine store, with a surprisingly large selection of mostly European vintages (which is kind of odd, considering all the good Oregon wines to be had these days). The chef-owner, with a bit of tongue-in-cheek, calls his cooking "nouvelle Canadian prairie cuisine." Whatever you call it, it's usually on the mark taste-wise. The cheeses offered as a starter are all made in-house, and if you order one of the fresh, crisp salads, he might go outside and cut some of the greens. Only four main courses are offered (five in the summer). I would recommend the breast of duck served over mashed potatoes or the wild-caught shrimp with truffle oil. On some weekend nights, a guitar player provides soft music. It can all be a bit eccentric (bone china, heavy cutlery, but if you don't have wine, your water is served in a plastic cup), but you'll get a meal unlike any place else in Gold Beach.

29672 Stewart St. www.annasbythesea.com. ✆ **541/247-2100.** Main course $19–$29. Wed–Sat 5–8pm.

Nor'wester Steak & Seafood ★ SEAFOOD/STEAK Nor'wester has the best view in Gold Beach—it's in the port area with a big, busy dining room that overlooks the mouth of the Rogue and its fleet of fishing boats. There aren't many surprises in this popular steak and seafood place, but the fresh fish of the day is usually good, especially if it's locally caught salmon (spring through summer). Black cod is used for the fish and chips; the oysters (lightly breaded and pan-fried) come from Willapa Bay in Washington. It's fairly expensive for what you get, but remains popular because you can always count on getting a good meal with your view.

10 Harbor Way (in the Port of Gold Beach). www.norwesterseafood.com. ✆ **541/247-2333.** Main courses $24–$36. Daily 5–9pm.

Spinner's ★★ SEAFOOD/AMERICAN Spinner's, like Nor'Wester (reviewed above), has been around for a long time and is where locals often go to celebrate special occasions because it has a nice, dress-up-a-bit atmosphere with art on the walls and white tablecloths in the dining room. It doesn't offer the dramatic views that Nor'wester does, but in terms of quality of the cooking, it's not that much different, except that here there are more time-honored fish dishes on the menu. Steaks and pasta are on offer, too, but I personally would go for the fish, especially the fresh wild salmon roasted on cedar and served with a zinfandel sauce. The pasta with local Dungeness crab is also good.

29430 Ellensburg Ave. www.spinnersrestaurant.com. ✆ **541/247-5160.** Main courses $27–$32. Daily 4:30–9pm.

SHOPPING

The largest bookstore on the Oregon coast, **Gold Beach Books** ★★★, 29707 Ellensburg Rd. (www.oregoncoastbooks.com; ✆ **5431/247-2495**), stocks all the current bestsellers but also has a big selection of new and used books on subjects of local, regional, and state interest, plus a rare-books room. **Rachel's Coffee House** occupies part of this space on Gold Beach's main drag.

If you want to take home some local salmon, albacore or steelhead, **Fishermen Direct Seafood,** 29975 Harbor Way (www.fishermendirect.com; ✆ **888/523-9494** or 541/247-9494), in the Cannery Building at the port, can package it up and freeze it for you.

FAST FACTS

7

SEATTLE, PORTLAND & OREGON COAST

Area Codes In Oregon and Washington, you need to include the area code when dialing local calls. The area codes for Portland are 503 and 971. For the Oregon coast, the area codes are 503 or 541. The area codes for Seattle are 206 or 425.

ATMs The easiest and best way to get cash in the United States is from an ATM (automated teller machine). The **Cirrus** (www.mastercard.com; ✆ **800/424-7787**) and **PLUS** (www.visa.com) networks span the country; you can find them everywhere in Seattle, Portland, and along the coast. You'll find ATMs at banks, gas stations, supermarkets, and convenience stores.

Business Hours Banks are generally open Monday through Friday from 9am to 5pm, and some branches are also open Saturday 9am to 2pm. Stores are open Monday through Saturday from 10am to 6pm (until 9pm at malls), and Sunday from noon to 5pm. Bars are allowed to be open until 2am.

Customs Every visitor 21 years of age or older may bring in, free of duty, the following: (1) 1 liter of alcohol; (2) 200 cigarettes, 100 cigars (but not from Cuba); and (3) $100 worth of gifts. These exemptions are offered to travelers who spend at least 72 hours in the United States and who have not claimed them within the preceding 6 months. It is forbidden to bring into the country almost any meat products (including canned, fresh, and dried meat products, such as bouillon and soup mixes). Generally, condiments including vinegars, oils, pickled goods, spices, coffee, tea, and some cheeses and baked goods are permitted. Avoid rice products, as rice can often harbor insects. Bringing fruits and vegetables is prohibited because they may harbor pests or disease. International visitors may carry in or out up to $10,000 in U.S. or foreign currency with no formalities; larger sums must be declared to U.S. Customs on entering or leaving, which includes filing form FinCEN 105. For details regarding U.S. Customs and Border Protection, consult your nearest U.S. embassy or consulate, or **U.S. Customs and Border Protection** (www.cbp.gov).

Disabled Travelers Thanks to provisions in the Americans with Disabilities Act, most public places are required to comply with disability-friendly regulations—almost all public establishments (including hotels, restaurants, and museums, but not certain National Historic Landmarks) in Portland, all modes of public transportation—bus, light rail, streetcar—provide accessible entrances. In Seattle, newer buses are accessible, as are the light rail and the streetcar from downtown to South Lake Union.

Portland is a particularly wheelchair-friendly city, at least on the relatively flat streets of downtown and the east side; using a wheelchair is much more difficult in the West Hills neighborhoods. Seattle, with its steep downtown streets, is difficult for wheelchairs.

In Seattle, Portland, and along the Oregon coast, many hotels have handicapped accessible rooms. In state parks and national forests, you'll find paved trails designed to accommodate wheelchairs. At **Yaquina Head Outstanding Natural Area** (p. 274) on the Oregon coast outside of Newport, there are even wheelchair-accessible tide pools.

The **America the Beautiful—National Park and Federal Recreational Lands Pass—Access Pass** gives travelers with visual impairments or those with permanent disabilities (regardless of age) free lifetime entrance to federal recreation sites administered by the National Park Service. This includes national parks, monuments, historic sites, recreation areas, and national wildlife refuges. The America the Beautiful Access Pass can be obtained in person at a National Park Service facility that charges an entrance fee, such as Fort Clatsop–Lewis & Clark National Historical Park, or by mail using the form on the website ($10 processing fee). You need to show proof of a medically determined disability. For more information, go to www.nps.gov/fees_passes.htm.

Doctors To find a doctor, check with the front desk or concierge at your hotel.

Cannabis Laws If you are 21 and order (proof of age is required), purchasing small amounts of marijuana for recreational use is legal in Oregon and Washington, but only if purchased from a licensed cannabis retailer. Smoking in any public place, including parks, your hotel room, and on the street, is illegal, and driving while stoned is prohibited. The cannabis laws in Oregon and Washington do not apply outside of the two states.

Drinking Laws The legal age for purchase and consumption of alcoholic beverages is 21; proof of age is required and often requested at bars, nightclubs, and restaurants, so it's always a good idea to bring ID when you go out. Do not carry open containers of alcohol in your car or in any public area that isn't zoned for alcohol consumption. The police can fine you on the spot. Don't even think about driving while intoxicated.

Aside from on-premises sales of cocktails in bars and restaurants, hard liquor can be purchased only in liquor stores. Beer and wine are available in convenience stores and grocery stores. Brewpubs tend to sell only beer and wine, but some also have licenses to sell hard liquor.

Drugstores/Pharmacies Fred Meyer, a major grocery chain in Washington and Oregon, has a pharmacy in many of its stores. Also look for Walgreens (Washington and Oregon) and Bartell (Washington only). Many prescription drugs have different names outside the U.S., so it's important to know what the drug's name is in the U.S.

Electricity Like Canada, the United States uses 110 to 120 volts AC (60 cycles), compared to 220 to 240 volts AC (50 cycles) in most of Europe, Australia, and New Zealand. Downward converters that change 220–240 volts to 110–120 volts are difficult to find in the United States, so bring one with you.

Embassies & Consulates All embassies are in Washington, D.C. If your country isn't listed below, call for directory information in Washington, D.C. (✆ **202/555-1212**), or check **www.embassy.org/embassies**.

The embassy of **Australia** is at 1601 Massachusetts Ave. NW, Washington, D.C. 20036 (www.usa.embassy.gov.au; ✆ **202/797-3000**).

The embassy of **Canada** is at 501 Pennsylvania Ave. NW, Washington, D.C. 20001 (www.canadainternational.gc.ca/washington; ✆ **202/682-1740**). There is a consulate in Seattle.

The embassy of **Ireland** is at 2234 Massachusetts Ave. NW, Washington, D.C. 20008 (www.embassyofireland.org; ✆ **202/462-3939**).

The embassy of **New Zealand** is at 37 Observatory Circle NW, Washington, D.C. 20008 (www.nzembassy.com; ✆ **202/328-4800**). There is a consulate in Seattle.

The embassy of the **United Kingdom** is at 3100 Massachusetts Ave. NW, Washington, D.C. 20008 (http://ukinusa.fco.gov.uk; ✆ **202/588-6500**). There is a consulate in Seattle.

Emergencies Call ✆ **911** to report an emergency, fire, to get the police, or to get an ambulance anywhere in the U.S. This is a toll-free call.

Family Travel For recommendations of kid-friendly attractions and family-friendly activities, see "Seattle, Portland & the Oregon Coast for Families" under "Suggested Itineraries" in chapter 2. Most restaurants in the Pacific northwest can supply a booster seat or high-chair, but special kids' menus are more likely to be found in chain restaurants and neighborhood eateries than in fine-dining establishments. Nearly all attractions offers a reduced rate for children. In general, you will find Seattle, Portland, and the Oregon coast very kid-friendly.

Insurance The websites InsureMyTrip.com and SquareMouth.com serve as good marketplaces for insurance policies, all from reputable companies. In general, you don't need insurance just for a hotel stay or airplane flight. But if you're renting a house, or feel you may need medical insurance, getting travel insurance can be a smart purchase.

Internet & Wi-Fi The Pacific Northwest is very wired. Nearly all hotels and B&Bs in Seattle, Portland, and along the Oregon coast offer free Wi-Fi to guests. Other places to get access to the Internet are cafes and public libraries. Do not expect Wi-Fi or Internet access at campgrounds or in state parks.

LGBT Travelers Gay and lesbian travelers will generally feel very welcome in Seattle, Portland and along the Oregon coast. Both cities offer many venues for LGBT visitors; see "The Bar and Pub Scene" at the end of the Seattle and Portland chapters for a list of LGBT bars and dance clubs. You will find less of a LGBT presence on the Oregon coast.

Mobile Phones If you have a U.S. mobile phone and network, it's a good bet that your phone will work in in Seattle, Portland, and along the Oregon coast, but T-Mobile, Sprint, and Nextel are weak in rural areas and in some places along the coast. If you're visiting from another country, be sure to find out about international calling rates and roaming charges before using your phone in the United States. You could ring up a huge phone bill with just a few calls and texts. Foreign visitors might consider using Skype in lieu of cellphone service (it can be used when you have access to Wi-Fi, which you will at all hotels).

Newspapers & Magazines *The Oregonian* (www.oregonlive.com) is Portland's daily paper. *Portland Monthly* (www.portlandmonthly.com) is a good lifestyle monthly. *Willamette Week* (www.willametteweek.com) is a free weekly news, arts, and entertainment newspaper.

The *Seattle Times* (www.seattletimes.com) and *Seattle Post-Intelligencer* (www.seattlepi.com) are Seattle's daily newspapers. *Seattle Weekly* (www.seattleweekly.com) is the city's free news, arts, and entertainment weekly.

Packing The Pacific Northwest is a very casual place. Seattle has more "dress up" restaurants than Portland does, and the Oregon coast is about staying dry and comfortable in cool, wet weather. The weather can be warm in the summer, but typically cools down considerably at night. In the winter, there is frequent rain, and temperatures tend to hover in the 40s and 50s. When you're packing, think layers. To keep yourself covered, bring a fleece jacket, a hoodie, and a rain jacket.

Passports Every air traveler entering the U.S. is required to show a passport. For more information on passports, see the following:

Australia Australian Passport Information Service (✆ **131-232,** or visit www.passports.gov.au).

Canada Passport Office, Department of Foreign Affairs and International Trade, Ottawa, ON K1A 0G3 (www.ppt.gc.ca; ✆ **800/567-6868**).

Ireland Passport Office, Setanta Centre, Molesworth Street, Dublin 2 (www.foreignaffairs.gov.ie; ✆ **01/671-1633**).

New Zealand Passports Office, Department of Internal Affairs, 47 Boulcott St., Wellington, 6011 (www.passports.govt.nz; ✆ **0800/225-050** in New Zealand or 04/474-8100).

United Kingdom Visit your nearest passport office, major post office, or travel agency, or contact the **Identity and Passport Service (IPS),** 89 Eccleston Square, London, SW1V 1PN (www.ips.gov.uk; ✆ **0300/222-0000**).

Police Call ✆ **911** for emergencies.

Safety Seattle and Portland are generally safe cities, but exercise the usual cautions on the street and while using public transportation. Car break-ins and bike theft are not uncommon, so do not leave items in your car in plain view, and if you're riding a bike, make certain you have a good lock and don't leave the bike unattended for long periods of time. State parks along the coast are generally safe, but again, don't leave anything valuable in your car. This is particularly important to remember at the waterfall parking lots in the Columbia River Gorge area.

Senior Travel Don't be shy about asking for discounts, but always carry some kind of identification, such as a driver's license, that shows your date of birth. Almost all attractions, theaters, and tour companies offer senior discounts.

The U.S. National Park Service offers an **America the Beautiful–National Park and Federal Recreational Lands Pass–Senior Pass,** a lifetime pass that gives seniors 62 years and older entrance to all properties administered by the National Park Service—national parks, monuments, historic sites, recreation areas, and national wildlife refuges—for a one-time fee of $80 plus a $10 handling fee. The pass must be purchased in person at any NPS facility that charges an entrance fee. Besides free entry, the America the Beautiful Senior Pass also offers a 50% discount on some federal-use fees charged for such facilities as camping, swimming, parking, boat launching, and tours. For more information, visit www.nps.gov/fees_passes.htm.

Smoking Smoking is prohibited in restaurants, bars, hotels, public buildings and city and state parks in Washington and Oregon. That prohibition includes marijuana, even though cannabis is legal in the state.

Taxes The United States has no value-added tax (VAT) or other indirect tax at the national level. Every state, county, and city may levy its own local tax on all purchases, including hotel and restaurant checks and airline tickets. These taxes will not appear on price tags. There's no sales tax in Oregon, but there is a 14.5% tax on hotel rooms. You may also have to pay taxes on a rental car in Portland. The sales tax in Washington is currently 6.5%, but because of complex tax laws, it may be as high as 9.5% in some municipalities. The hotel tax in Seattle is 15.6%.

Telephones **Local calls** require 10 digits (so include the area code). **To make calls within the United States and to Canada,** dial the area code and the seven-digit number. **For international calls,** dial 011 followed by the country code, city code, and the number you are calling.

For **directory assistance** ("Information"), dial ✆ 1-800-FREE-411 for local numbers and national numbers in the U.S. and Canada. For **long-distance information,** dial 1, then the appropriate area code plus 555-1212.

Time Washington and Oregon are on Pacific Standard Time, 3 hours earlier than New York.

Daylight saving time (summer time) is in effect from 1am on the second Sunday in March to 1am on the first Sunday in November, and moves the clock 1 hour ahead of standard time.

Tipping In hotels, tip **bellhops** at least $1 per bag ($2–$3 if you have a lot of luggage) and tip the **room-cleaning staff** $2 to $3 per day (more if you've left a big mess for him or her to clean up). Tip the **doorman** or **concierge** only if he or she has provided you with some specific service (for example, calling a cab for you). Tip the **valet-parking attendant** at least $2 every time you get your car.

In restaurants, bars, and nightclubs, tip **service staff** and **bartenders** 15% to 20% of the check; a few restaurants now add an additional 20% service charge to your bill—this takes care of the tipping. Tip **checkroom attendants** $1 per garment, and tip **valet-parking attendants** at least $2 per vehicle.

As for other service personnel, tip **cab drivers** 15% of the fare; tip **skycaps** at airports at least $1 per bag ($2–$3 if you have a lot of luggage); and tip **hairdressers** and **barbers** 15% to 20%.

Toilets You won't find public toilets or restrooms on the streets in Seattle or Portland, so head for cafes, hotel lobbies, bars, restaurants, museums, department stores, railway and bus stations, and gas stations. Large hotels and fast-food restaurants are often the best bet for clean facilities.

Visas Citizens from some countries must have (1) a valid passport that expires at least 6 months later than the scheduled end of their visit to the U.S.; and (2) a tourist visa. For information about U.S. Visas go to **http://travel.state.gov** and click on "Visas." Or go to one of the following websites:

Australian citizens can obtain up-to-date visa information from the **U.S. Embassy Canberra,** Moonah Place, Yarralumla, ACT 2600 (✆ **02/6214-5600**), or by checking the U.S. Diplomatic Mission's website at http://canberra.usembassy.gov/visas.html.

British subjects can obtain up-to-date visa information by calling the **U.S. Embassy Visa Information Line** (✆ **09042-450-100** from within the U.K. at £1.20 per minute; or ✆ **866-382-3589** from within the U.S. at a flat rate of $16, payable by credit card only) or by visiting the "Visas to the U.S." section of the American Embassy London's website at http://london.usembassy.gov/visas.html.

Irish citizens can obtain up-to-date visa information through the **U.S. Embassy Dublin,** 42 Elgin Rd., Ballsbridge, Dublin 4 (http://dublin.usembassy.gov; ✆ **1580-47-VISA** [8472] from within the Republic of Ireland at €2.40 per minute).

Citizens of **New Zealand** can obtain up-to-date visa information by contacting the **U.S. Embassy New Zealand,** 29 Fitzherbert Terrace, Thorndon, Wellington (http://newzealand.usembassy.gov; ✆ **644/462-6000**).

Visitor Information
Contact **Travel Oregon** (www.traveloregon.com; ✆ **800/547-7842**) or **Travel Portland,** 701 SW Sixth Ave., Portland, OR 97205 (www.travelportland.com; ✆ **877/678-5263** or 503/275-9293). Larger towns along the Oregon coast have either a tourist office or a chamber of commerce that provides information; see "Visitor Information" sections in the Oregon Coast chapter for addresses. For information on **camping** in Oregon state parks, contact the **Oregon State Parks Information Center,** 725 Summer St. NE, Ste. C, Salem, OR 97301 (www.oregonstateparks.org; ✆ **800/462-5687**).

For more information about Seattle, contact **Seattle's Convention and Visitors Bureau,** 701 Pike St., Suite 800 (www.visitseattle.org; ✆ **206/461-5800**). This organization operates the **Seattle Visitor Center** inside the Washington State Convention and Trade Center, 7th Avenue and Pike Street (✆ **206/461-5840**); and the **Market Information Center,** Southwest Corner of 1st Avenue and Pike Street in the Pike Place Market (✆ **206/461-5840**). For additional information on other parts of Washington, contact **Washington State Tourism** (www.experiencewa.com; ✆ **800/544-1800**).

Index

See also Accommodations and Restaurant indexes, below.

General Index

5th Avenue Theatre, 128
See also Accommodations and Restaurant Indexes

A

Accommodations,. *See also* Accommodations Index
- Astoria, 236–238
- Cannon Beach, 253–255
- Gearhart, 247–247
- Lincoln City, 265–266
- Newport, 275–276
- Oregon Coast, 228–230
- Portland, 167–180
- Seaside, 246–247
- Seattle, 88–102
- Yachats, 279–281

ACT (A Contemporary Theatre), 128
Adeklsheim Vineyard, 210
Agriculture, 56
Airbnb, 88, 167, 230
Airport MAX, 141
Aladdin Theater, 145, 204
Alaska Airlines Arena at Hec Edmundson Pavilion, 124
Alaskan Way Viaduct, 45, 48
Alberta Arts District, Portland, 145
Alexana, 210–211
Alibi Room, 124
Alien Land Law, 45
Alki Beach, 10, 39, 123
Alki Kayak Tours, 123
Alki Point, 44
All-Day Regional Transit Pass, 68
Allen, Paul, 44–46
Alpine Adventures, 134
Amazon Books, 120, 196
Amazon, 44, 46, 48, 61
Amtrak, 27
Ancient Grounds, 117, 119
Anderson, Guy, 20
Antiques, 120, 194–195
Antoinette Hatfield Hall, 206
Apollo Exhibit, Museum of Flight, vii
Arcadia Beach State Recreation Site, 253
Archery Summit, 211
Area codes, 302
Argosy Cruises Christmas, 70–71
Argosy Cruises, 14–15, 18, 39, 77
Argyle Winery, 211
Arlene Schnitzer Concert Hall, 143, 206
Art galleries, 119, 195
Artists Repertory Theatre, 206
Artusi, 124
Astoria, xiii, 4, 30, 33, 48–49, 230–241
- accommodations, 236–238
- attractions, 233–236
- brewpubs, 240
- dining, 238–239
- festivals, 233
- nightlife, 239–240
- Riverwalk, 232
- Waterfront, 236

Astoria Column, 233–234
Astoria Music Festival, 233
Astoria Regatta, 233
Astoria Riverfront Trolley, 232, 236
Astoria Street Opry Company, 240
Astoria Sunday Market, 241
Astoria Warrenton Crab, Seafood, & Wine Festival, 233
ATMs, 302
Augen Gallery, 195

B

Backpacking, 133
Bainbridge Island, 2, 21, 39
Bakeries, 193–194
Ballard, 66, 82–86
- attractions, 82–86
- dining, 112
- Sunday Farmers Market, 119, 121

Ballards Beach State Park, 291
Baltic Room, 126–127
Bandon, 36–38, 50, 289–295
Bandon Dunes Golf Resort, 38, 50, 291–292
Barnacle Bill's Seafood Market, 267
Barnes & Noble, 120, 196
Bars
- Portland, 202
- Seattle, 124–125

Baseball, 124
Basketball, 124, 207
Bathtub Gin and Co., 125
Bayfront, Newport, 5, 31, 35, 42
Beach Loop Road, 290
Beaches, 16, 49–50
Beavers, 55
Beecher's Handmade Cheese, 74
Belltown, 65, 97–99
Benaroya Hall, 61
Benson, Simon, 144
Bertha (machine), 45
Bethel Heights Vineyard, 211
BiddingTraveler.com, 89
Big Pink Sightseeing, 165
Big Time Brewery & Alehouse, 125
Bike Gallery, 166
BIKETOWN, 148
Biking
- Portland, 148, 164, 166
- Seattle, 122–123

Bill Spiedel's Underground Tour, vi, 21, 79
Bird-watching, 131, 292
Bite of Oregon, 150
Bite of Seattle, 70
Black Oystercatcher, xiv
Bloedel Reserve, 21, 86
Blue Heron French Cheese Company, 258
Boat tours, Seattle, 77
Bob Straub State Park, 260
Boeing 707, 46
Boeing Airplane Co., 44–46, 57
Boeing, William, 57
BOKA Restaurant + Bar, 125
Bolt Bus, 27, 67, 141
Bonneville Dam, 221
Booking.com
Books, 120, 196
Borofsky, Jonathan, 20
Bottega Italiana, 74
Bourgeois, Louise, 19
Bremerton, 2
Breweries, viii
Brewpubs, 3, 125, 202–203, 240
Brewvana Portland Brewery Tours, 165
Bridal Veil Falls, 221
BridgePort Brewpub, 203
Bridges, Multnomah County, 156
Bristlecone Pine Trail, 157
Broadway Cab, 148
Brookings, 38–39
Bullards Beach State Park, 38
Bullseye Gallery, 26, 195
Bumbershoot, 70
Bumper Cars and Tilt-a-Whirl, Seaside, 244
Burke Museum of Natural History and Culture, 62, 85
Burke-Gilman/Sammamish River Trail, 123
Burnside Brewing Co., 203
Burnside Bridge, 58
Burroughs Mountain Trail, 134
Business hours, 302
Bus tours, Portland, 165
Buskers, x

C

Cafes, Portland, 192–193
Caffe Ladro Espresso Bar & Bakery, 117
Caffe Umbria, 3, 117
Calder sculpture, vi
Calder, Alexander, 19
Callahan, Kenneth, 20
Cannabis, 43, 148, 303
Cannon Beach, 4, 30, 33, 41–42, 249–257
- accommodations, 253–255
- attractions, 250–253
- dining, 255–257
- galleries, 257
- nightlife, 257
- shopping, 257
- spa, 257

Cannon Beach Gallery, 257
Cannon Beach History Center & Museum, 250–252
Cannon Beach Property Management, 246
Cannon Beach Spa, 257
Canoe, 198
Cape Arago, 52
Cape Arago Highway, 36–38, 288–289

Cape Arago Lighthouse, 229
Cape Arago State Park, 37, 289
Cape Blanco Lighthouse, 229
Cape Blanco, 52
Cape Kiwanda, 260
Cape Meares Lighthouse, 229, 260
Cape Perpetua, 36, 52
Cape Perpetua Scenic Area, 36, 278
Capitol Hill, Seattle, 20, 46, 66
accommodations, 101
dining, 113–114
Car2go, 147
Carl S. English Botanical Garden, 83
C.C. Slaughters, 205
Cascade Head, 263
Cascade Locks, 222
Cascade Range, 1
Casinos, 49
Cast-iron buildings, 52
Cayuse Pass, 133
Celilo Falls, 51
Cellar on 10th, 240
Cellphones, 47
Central Link Light Rail, 67
The Central Saloon, 125
Century Ballroom, 127
CenturyLink Field, 124
Cha Cha Lounge, 125
Chamber Music Northwest, 206
Chapman Square, 29, 151
Chehalem, 211
Chihuly, Dale, 62
Chihuly Garden and Glass Museum, vii, 12, 20, 61, 77–78
Chinatown
Portland, 144, 176–177
Seattle, 21, 66, 80–82
Chinatown Discovery Tours, 87
Chinatown Gate, 144
Chinatown/International District Lunar New Year Celebration, 70
Chinese immigrants, 44
Chinese Room, Seattle, 3
Chinook Pass, 133
Chinook Winds Casino Resort, 264
Chinookan Indian tribes, 49
Christianson's Nursery & Greenhouse, 131
Cinco de Mayo Fiesta, 150
CityPass, 71
Clackamas Indian tribe, 49
Clark, William, 52
Clinton Street theater, 145
Clubs, Portland, 204–205
Coaster Theater, 257
Cobra Lily, 37
Coffee, 117
Coffee bars, xii
Coffee Girl, 240
Coffee shops, 140
Coffeehouses, 192–193
Columbia Gorge, 218–224
Bonneville Dam, 221
Cascade Locks, 222
Crown Point, 220
dining, 223–224
Eagle Creek, 221
Hood River, 222–223
Rooster Rock State Park, 223
tours, 220
waterfalls, 220–221
wildfire, 220
Columbia Gorge Historic Highway, 27, 40
Columbia Gorge National Scenic Area, 40, 218
Columbia River Gorge, 1, 11, 26, 28
Columbia River Maritime Museum, xiv, 13, 30, 234–235
Columbia River, 11, 49, 51–52
Columbia Slough, 49
Columbia Sportswear Company, 197
Concordia, 178
Conner Louisa A., 130
Connie Hansen Garden, 264–265
Consulates, 303–304
Coos Bay, 48–49
Coquille River Lighthouse, 38, 229, 291
Cornish Playhouse, 128
Crafts, 120–121, 196–197
Cranberries, 290
Crown Point, 27, 40, 220
Cruises, 165
Crush Bar, 205
Crystal Ballroom, 204
Crystal Mountain, 135
Crystal Springs Rhododendron Garden, 146, 162–163
Curry Historical Museum, 296–297
Curtis Steiner, 121
Customs, 302

D

Dalles Dam, 51
Dance
Portland, 205
Seattle, 126–128
Darcelle XV Showplace, 204–205
***Darlingtonia californica*, 37, 279**
Darlingtonia State Natural Site, 36, 279
Dateline
Portland, 49–58
Seattle, 44–48
Davidson Galleries, 119
Dean Creek Elk Viewing Area, 286
Death with Dignity Act, 57
de Heceta, Bruno, 51
DeLaurenti, 74
Denny party, 44
Denver Broncos, 48
Department stores
Portland, 197–198
Seattle, 121
Departure, 202
Depoe Bay, 4, 30–31, 34–35, 42, 267–270
Deschutes Brewing, 203
Dimitriou's Jazz Alley, 128
Dining, *see also* Restaurants Index
Disabled travelers, 302–302
Discovery Park, 123
"Doc" Maynard, 44
Doctors, 303
Domaine Drouhin Oregon, 211
Domaine Serene, 212
Donation Land Act, 50
"Don't Californicate Oregon," 46
Doug Fir Lounge, 204
Downtown, Portland, 3, 142–143
accommodations, 167–176
attractions, 151–157
dining, 181–187
Downtown, Seattle, v, 65, 71–74
accommodations, 88–95
attractions, 71–74
dining, 103–108
Drake, Francis, 51
Drinking fountains, Portland, 144
Drinking laws, 303
Drugstores, 303
Duck tours, 87
Dunes, xiii, 286
Duwanish tribe, 44

E

Eagle Creek, 221
Eastbank Esplanade, ix
Eastmoreland, 145–146, 162
Eastside, Seattle, 66–67
Eco Tours of Oregon, 165
Ecola State Park, xv, 30, 33, 42, 229, 252
Eddie Bauer, 45, 121
Electricity, 303
Elliott Bay Book Company, 120
Elliott Bay, iv, 11, 19, 44
Elysian Brewing Company, 125
Embassies, 303–304
The Embers Avenue, 205
Emerald City, 62
Emergencies, 304
The Empirical Theater, 164
Euthanasia, 57
Events calendar
Portland, 149–150
Seattle, 70–71
The Eyrie Vineyards, 212

F

Family attractions, best, 14–16
Oregon Coast, 15–16, 41–42
Portland, 40–41
Seattle, 14–15, 39–40
Family travel, 304
Farming, 56
Farwest Taxi, 69
Ferries, v, 1–2, 46, 68
Ferris wheel, vii, 2
Filson, 121
Fires, Portland, 51–52, 58
Fireside Room, 125
Fireworks Fine Crafts Gallery, 121
First Hill, 66
First Thursday, 144
Fisher Poets Gathering, 233
Fishermen Direct Seafood, 301
Flagships, 197–198
Flavel House, Astoria, 13, 30, 235
FlipKey, 230
Floating bridge, 45
Floods, Portland, 55, 57
Florence, 36–38, 283–284

Flury & Company Ltd., 119
Food carts, 23, 139, 186
Food, shopping, 122, 139
Football, 124
Forest Park, x, 3, 139, 145, 157, 161–162, 166
Fort Astoria, 234
Fort Clatstop— Lewis & Clark National Historic Park, xv, 13, 30, 33, 240–242
Fort Stevens State Park, 243
Fort Vancouver, 49, 53
Foster/White Gallery, 119
Fourth of July, 70
Frances Schrader Old Growth Trail, 39
Francisco de la Bodega y Quadra, Juan, 51
Fran's Chocolates, 122
Fremont, 3, 66
accommodations, 101–102
dining, 114
Fremont Fair, 70
The Fremont Tour, 87
French-Canadian fur traders, 49
Frye Art Museum, 80–81
Fur traders, 49, 52

G

Gardens, 14, 131, 139
Gas Works Park, 123
Gates, Bill, 44, 46, 57
Gay and lesbian scene, 205
The Gazette, 44
Gearhart, 244–248
accommodations, 247–247
dining, 249
Gelaterias, 193
Gemini space suite gloves, vii
Giant Forest Park, 3–4
Glasshouse Studio, 119
Gluten-free dining, 115, 190
Gold Beach, 12, 38–39, 295–301
Gold Beach Books, 301
Gold rush, 44–45, 55
Golfing, 286–287, 291
The Goonies, 235
Graves, Morris, 20
Gray, Robert, 52
Gray Line of Portland, 165
Great fire, vi, 3, 44
Great Wheel, Seattle, vii, 18, 39, 45, 76
Gregoire, Christine, 47
Greyhound, 64, 141
Grove of the Patriarchs, 133–134
Grunge rock, iv

H

Hammering Man, 20
Handmade gifts, 120–121
Happy Hour, 103, 180
Hatfield Marine Science Center Visitor Center, 273
Hawthorne, 145, 162, 189–192, 194
Hawthorne Bridge, 156
Haystack Rock, 252
Heceta Head, 36, 52, 279
Heceta Head Lighthouse State Scenic Viewpoint, 36, 229, 279
Heceta Head Lightstation, 36
Hendrix, Jimi, 46
Henry M. Jackson Memorial Visitor Center, 133
Heritage Museum, 236
Hiking, 123, 166–167, 287 297
Hiram M. Chittenden Locks, 45, 82–83
Historic Columbia River Highway, 220
Historic sites, best, 12–13
History, Pacific Northwest, 50–58
Age of Exploration, 51–53
Industrialization, 54–58
Settlement, 53–54
Hoffman Gallery, 196
HomeAway, 88, 167, 230
Hood to Coast Run, 244
Hood River, 222–223
Hood River Ranger Station, 215, 217
Horseback riding, 287
Hotels; *see also* Accommodations Index
discounts, 89
Oregan Coast, best, 7–8
Portland, best, 6–7
Seattle, best, 5–6
Hotwire.com, 89
Hoyt Arboretum, 143, 157–158, 166
Hudson Bay Company (HBC), 49, 53
Hug Point State Recreation Site, 253
Huskies, 124

I

Icefire Glassworks, 257
Immigrants, 51
Indian Beach, xv
Insurance, 304
International District, Seattle, 21, 66, 80–82
attractions, 80–82
dining, 111
International Pinot Noir Celebration, 208
International Rose Test Garden, xi, 4, 14, 23, 29, 40, 139, 143,150, 157–158
Internet, 304
Intiman Theatre, 128
Ira Keller Fountain, 23, 154
Irvington, Portland, 53, 145

J

Jade Garden, Seattle, 21
Jamison Park, 144
Jams, 291
Jantzen, 58
Japanese Americans, 46, 54
Japanese-American Historical Plaza, 156
Japanese Garden, Seattle, xii, 4, 14, 84
Jefferson, Thomas, 52
Jerry's Rogue Jets, 38
Jerry's Rogue River Museum, 297
Jessie M. Honeyman Memorial State Park, 285–286
Jet Boat Rogue River Tour, 297–298
John Helmer Haberdasher, 197

K

Kaiser Steel, 57
Kayaking, ix, xiii, 165
Keller Auditorium, 143, 154, 206
Kendall Planetarium, 164
Kenmore Log Boom Park, 123
Kerr Bikes, 166
Key Arena, 124
King County Metro Transit, 62
King Street Station, 64
Klondike Gold Rush National Historical Park, 80

L

La Conner, 20, 28, 129–131
La Conner Flats, 131
Ladd's Addition, Portland, 53, 145
Lake Union, 112–113
Lake Washington, 11
Lake Washington Floating Bridge, 45
Lake Washington Ship Canal, 45, 82–83
Lakes Trail, 134
Lan Su Chinese Garden, 14, 139, 144, 150, 154–155
Last Thursday, 145
Latourell Falls, 220
Laurelhurst, 145
The Legacy Ltd., 119
Let's Go Sailing, 77
Lewis and Clark, xv, 49, 52–53
Lewis and Clark Exposition, 53
Lewis & Clark River Paddling Tour, 242
Lewis and Clark Salt Works, 244
Lewis, Merriweather, 52
LGBT travelers, 304
Liberty Theater, 49, 239
Lighthouses, 229
Light rail, 67, 141, 146–147
LimeBike, 123
Lincoln City, 30, 49, 263–267
accommodations, 265–266
attractions, 264–265
dining, 266–267
Link Light Rail, 46–47, 62
Little Log Church & Museum, 278
Livability, 43
Lloyd Center mall, 145, 198
Longmire, 134
Lovejoy, Asa, 49–50
Lownsdale Square, 29, 151
Lyft, 69, 141

M

Macrina Bakery, 117
Made in Oregon, 198
Made in Washington, 122
Magazines, 304

Magic Mile Skyride, 216
Malls, Seattle, 122
Manzanita, 257–259
Marijuana, 43, 47, 58, 148
Mariners, 124
Market Information Center, 65
Marriage, same-sex, 47, 57–58
Martin's Gorge Tours, 220
MAX, 4, 22–23, 146
Maynard, "Doc," 44
McMenamins, 203
McMenamins Kennedy School, viii, 203
Measure 91, 58
Metro, 67
Metropolitan Area Express (MAX), 4, 22–23, 146
Metsker Maps of Seattle, 120
Microbreweries, 140
Microsoft, 44, 46, 57
Mint/820, 202
Missionaries, 53
Mississippi Studios, 204
Mist Falls, 221
Misty Meadows, 38, 291
Mobile phones, 304
Moda Center, 207
Monorail, Seattle, 40, 67–68
Montlake Bicycle Shop, 123
Morrison Bridge, 156
Morrison Street, Portland, 52
Moss Bay Rowing, Kayaking and Sailing Center, 123
Mount Adams, 218
Mount Fremont Trail, 134
Mount Hood, 11, 27, 41, 214–217
Mount Hood Meadows, 217
Mount Hood National Forest, 214
Mount Rainier, 61–62
Mount Rainier National Park, 11, 21, 131–136
Mount Rainier Scenic Railroad, 134
Mt. St. Helens, 56
Mudslides, 48
Multnomah County, 156
Multnomah Falls, xii, 26, 41, 218, 221
Multnomah Indian tribe, 49
Murray, Ed, 48
Museums, best, 12–13
Museum of Flight, vii, 12, 15, 83–84
Museum of History and Industry (MOHAI), 12, 82
Museum of Northwest Art, 130
Museum of Pop Culture (MoPOP), 40, 78
Music, 128, 204–205
Musicfest NW, 150

N

National Park Inn, Longmire, 134
National Recreation Reservation Service, 230
Native Americans, 45, 50–51, 61
Native American Art, xi, 119, 156
Natural wonders, 10–12
Nature Conservancy Cascade Head Trail, 263
NBA, 46
Nehalem Bay State Park, 258
Neighbours Nightclub, 127–128
Nesika Beach, 298
Newport, xvi, 5, 30–32, 35, 42, 270–277
  accommodations, 275–276
  attractions, 272–275
  dining, 276–277
  nightlife, 277
Newspapers, 304
New Year's Eve, 71
Nightlife
  Astoria, 239–240
  Cannon Beach, 257
  Newport, 277
  Portland, 199–207
  Seattle, 124–129
Nike, 56, 197
Nisqually Earthquake, 47
Nob Hill, Portland, 144–145, 177–178, 180, 194
Noble Rot, 202
Nordic Heritage Center, 62
Nordic History Museum, 83
Nordstrom, 118, 121, 143, 197
Nordstrom Rack, 121, 197
North by Northwest, 257
North Mississippi District, Portland, 145
North Park Blocks, 144
North Portland, 4, 140
Northeast Portland, 145, 189
Northern Pacific Railroad, 55
Northwest 21st, Portland, 144
Northwest 23rd, Portland, 144–145, 149, 161
  accommodations, 177–178
  dining, 187–189
Northwest Film & Video Festival, 150
Northwest Flower & Garden Show, 70
Northwest Folklife Festival, 70
Northwest Pendleton, 121
Northwest Portland, 144, 161–162, 194
Northwest School, 61
Nurseries, 131
Nye Beach, 31, 35, 273

O

Oaks Amusement Park, 40, 163
Oaks Bottom Wildlife Refuge, 163
Oaks Park, 145
Ocean Dunes Golf Links, 287
Oceanside, 261–262
Off-road vehicles, 287
Ohanapecosh Visitor Center, 133
Old Church, 206
Old Town, Florence, 283
Old Town, Portland, 52, 143, 176–177
Oliver's Lounge, 125
Olmsted Interpretive Exhibit, 81
Olmsted, Frederick Law, 53
Olmsted, John, 53
Olympic Mountains, 2, 19, 61
Olympic Sculpture Park, vi, 12–13, 19, 62, 74
Opera, 128, 205–206
Oregon Ballet Theatre, 205
Oregon Bed & Breakfast Guild, 167
Oregon Brewers Festival, 150
Oregon Citizens Alliance (OCA), 56
Oregon City, 50, 54
Oregon Coast, 225–230
  accommodations, 228–230
  Astoria, 230–240
  Bandon, 289–295
  best experiences, 4–5
  Cannon Beach, 249–257
  Cape Arago Highway, 288–289
  Depoe Bay, 267–270
  family attractions, best, 15–16, 41–42
  Florence, 283–284
  Fort Clatsop–Lewis & Clark National Historic Park, 240–242
  gardens, best, 14
  Gearhart, 244–248
  Gold Beach, 295–301
  historic sites, 13
  hotels, best, 7–8
  itineraries, suggested, 28–42
  lighthouses, 229
  Lincoln City, 263–267
  Manzanita, 257–259
  modern times, 48–50
  museums, best, 13
  natural wonders, best, 11–12
  Newport, 270–277
  Oregon Dunes National Recreation Area, 285–288
  restaurants, best, 9–10
  Seaside, 242–248
  shoreline, 228
  Three Capes Scenic Loop, 259–262
  travel timing, 59–60
  weather, 59–60, 228
  Yachats, 277–282
Oregon Coast Aquarium, xvi, 5, 15, 32, 35, 42, 273–275
Oregon Dunes National Recreation Area, xvi, 12, 36–38, 283, 285–288
Oregon Family Fairness Act, 58
Oregon Film Festival, 235
Oregon Historical Society Museum, 23, 29, 143,155
The Oregonian, 199
Oregon Museum of Science and Industry (OMSI), 15, 40, 163–164
Oregon Pacific Coast Passport, 33, 228
Oregon Seafood and Wine Festival, 149
Oregon State Parks, 230
Oregon State Parks Information Center, 228
Oregon Symphony, 48, 205–206
Oregon Trail, 49
Oregon Wine Country, 1, 208–214
Oregon Wines on Broadway, 202
Oregon Zoo, 15, 40, 143, 157–159, 199

Oso, 48
Oswald West State Park, 253
Outdoor activities
Portland, 166–167
Seattle, 122–123
Overlook Trail, 157
Overton, William, 49

P

Pacific City, 5, 11, 261–262
Pacific Northwest Ballet company, viii, 126
Pacific Northwest Quilt & Fiber Arts Museum, 131
Pacific Place, 122
Pacific Science Center, 40, 78–79
Packing, 304
Padilla Bay National Estuarine Research Reserve, 131
Paradise, 133–134
Paramount Theatre, 129
Parking Kitty, 147
Passports, 304–305
Patriarchs Trail, 21
Patricia Rovzar Gallery, 119
PDX Contemporary Ballet, 205
PDX Pedicabs, 166
PDX Pop Now!, 150
Pearl District, Portland, 3, 3, 140, 144, 149, 161, 194
accommodations, 177
dining, 187–189
Pedal Bike Tours, 164, 186
Pendleton Home Store, 198
Penner-Ash Wine Cellars, 212
Perry Ellis International, 58
Peter Miller Books, 120
Peter's Walking Tours of Portland, 166
Pettygrove, Francis W., 49–50
Pharmacies, 303
Pier 39 Heritage Museum, 236
Pier 66, v
Pike Brewing, viii
Pike Place Fish Market, 122
Pike Place Market, v, 1, 17, 20, 45, 71, 74
accommodations, 95–96
dining, 108–109
shopping, 120–121
Pike Pub & Brewery, viii, 125
Pink Door Cabaret, 128
Pioneers, 50
Pioneer Courthouse Square, x, 3, 22, 29, 142, 150, 165, 194
Pioneer Place, 198
Pioneer Square, 65, 79–80
Piroshky Piroshky, 74
Pittock Mansion, ix, 13, 26, 145, 162, 166
Police, 305
Portland
accommodations, 167–180
air travel, 140
Alberta Arts District, 145
antiques, 194–195
art galleries, 195
bakeries, 193–194
bars, 202
basketball, 207
best experiences, 3–4
biking, 148, 164, 166
books, 196
brewpubs, 202–203
bus tours, 165
bus travel, 141, 146
cafes, 192–193
car travel, 140, 147
Chinatown Gate, 144
Chinatown, 144, 176–177
city layout, 141–142
city planning, 55
clubs, 204–205
coffee shops, 140
coffeehouses, 192–193
Concordia, 178
crafts, 196–197
cruises, 165
dance, 205
dateline, 49–58
department stores, 197–198
dining, 180–194
Downtown, 3, 142–143, 151–157, 167–176, 181–187
Eastmoreland, 145–146, 162
event calendar, 149–150
family attractions, best, 15, 40–41
fires, 58
First Thursday, 144
flagships, 197–198
floods, 55
food, 139
food carts, 23, 139, 186
gardens, 14, 139
gay and lesbian scene, 205
gelaterias, 193
gifts, shopping, 198
gluten-free dining, 190
Happy Hour, 180
Hawthorne, 145, 162, 189–192, 194
hiking, 166–167
historic sites, best, 13
hotels, best, 6–7
Irvington, 145
itineraries, suggested, 22–32
Japanese-American Historical Plaza, 156
kayaking, 165
Ladd's Addition, 145
Last Thursday, 145
Laurelhurst, 145
light rail, 141, 146–147
malls, 198
markets, 199
microbreweries, 140
modern times, 46–48
museums, best, 13
music, 204–205
natural wonders, best, 11
neighborhoods, 139–140, 142–146
nightlife, 199–207
Nob Hill, 144–145, 177–178, 180, 194
North Mississippi District, 145
North Portland, 4, 140
Northeast Portland, 145, 189
Northwest 21st, 144
Northwest 23rd, 144–145, 149, 161, 177–178, 187–189
Northwest Portland, 144, 161–162, 194
Oaks Park, 145
Old Town District, 143, 176–177
opera, 205–206
outdoor activities, 166–167
parking, 147–148
parks, 139
Pearl District, 3, 140, 144, 149, 161, 177, 187–189, 194
performing arts, 206–207
Portland Heights, 143
restaurants, best, 9
RiverPlace, 156
Rose Quarter, 207
Salmon Street Springs, 156
SE Belmont Street, 145
SE Division Street, 145, 162
Sellwood, 145, 162, 194
shipyards, 54
shopping centers, 198
shopping, 194–199
Skidmore, 143
soccer, 207
South Waterfront, 143–144
Southeast Portland, 145, 162–164, 179–180, 189–192
souvenirs, 196
spectator sports, 207
streetcars, 147
taxis, 141, 148
theater, 206–207
tours, 164–166
train travel, 141
travel timing, 58–59
Union Station, 141, 143
vegan dining, 190
vegetarian dining, 190
visitor information, 141
walking, 149, 166
Washington Park, 4, 15, 23, 29, 40, 84–85, 143, 149, 157–161, 199
weather, 58–59, 149
Westmoreland, 145–146, 162
wine bars, 202
Portland Aerial Tram, x
Portland Art Museum, xi, 13, 23, 143, 155–156
Portland Art Museum Sales Gallery, 195
Portland Audubon Society, 162
Portland Bicycle Tours, 164
Portland BrewBus, 165
Portland Building, 155
Portland Center for the Performing Arts, 143, 206
Portland Center Stage, 206–207
Portland Children's Museum, 159–160
Portland City Grill, 202
Portland Farmers Market, 199
***Portlandia*, 138, 155**
Portland Heights, 143
Portland International Airport, 27, 140

Portland International Film Festival, 149
Portland Japanese Garden, 14, 23, 29, 139, 143, 150, 157, 160–161
Portland Kayak Company, 165
Portland Opera, 206
Portland Outdoor Store, 198
Portland Pride Festival and Parade, 150
Portland Rose Festival, 150, 158
Portland Saturday Market, 143, 199
***Portland Spirit*, 165**
Portland State University, 142
Portland Streetcar, 4, 26, 147
Portland Timbers, 207
Portland Trail Blazers, 207
Portland Visitor Information Center, 151
Portland Women's Forum State Scenic Viewpoint, 220
Powell's City of Books, xi, 3, 26, 48, 144, 196
Prehistoric Gardens & Rainforest, 293
Priceline.com, 89
Procopio Gelateria, 74
Producer's Hall, 71
Profile Theatre, 207
Promenade, Seaside, 244
Providence Park, 207
Pubs of Portland Tours, 166
Puddletown, 50
Puget Sound, 2, 44, 46, 61

Q

Queen Anne Hill, 66
accommodations, 102
dining, 114–115
Quintana Galleries, 195

R

Radio Cab, 148
Railroads, 52
Raygun Lounge, 125
ReachNow Car Sharing Portland, 147
The Real Mother Goose, 196
ReBuilding Center, 145
Reed College, 146
Regional Transit Pass, 68
REI, 121
ReserveAmerica, 230
Restaurants; see also Restaurants Index
Rex Hill Vineyards, 212
Ringlers Pub, 202–203
RiverPlace, 156
RiverPlace Marina, 165
River Riders, 134
Riverwalk, Astoria, 33, 232
Rocky Mountains, 54
Rogue River, xiii, 12, 51, 296
Rogue River Walk, 39
Rogue Wilderness Adventures, 298
Roosevelt, Franklin D., 46, 54
Rooster Rock State Park, 223
Roozengaarde Flowers & Bulbs, 131
Rose Quarter, 207
Russo Lee Gallery, 195

S

Safeco Field, 124
Safety, 305
Salmon fishing, iv, 56
Salmon Street Springs, 156
Same-sex marriage, 47, 57–58
Sand boarding, xvi, 287–288
Sandpines Golf Links, 286
San Juan Islands, 61
Sandcastle Contest, 250
Savor Cannon Beach, 250, 255
Savor Seattle, 87
Scandals, 205
Scandinavian Midsummer Festival, 233
Scenic flights, Seattle, 88
Scharf, Kenny, xi
Seafair, 70
Seafood and Wine Festival, 272
Sea Lion Caves, xv, 15–16, 36, 279
Sealth, 44
Sea otters, 55
Seaside, 242–248
accommodations, 246–247
attractions, 244–246
dining, 248
Seaside Aquarium, 244
Seaside Beach, 244–246
Sea-Tac International Airport, 27, 46, 62
Seattle
accommodations, 88–102
air travel, 62–64
antiques, 120
art galleries, 119
Ballard, 66, 82–86, 112
bars, 124–125
baseball, 124
basketball, 124
Belltown, 65, 97–99
best experiences, 1–3
biking, 122–123
boat tours, 77
books, 120
brewpubs, 125
bus travel, 64, 67
Capitol Hill, 20, 66, 101, 113–114
car travel, 64, 68
Chinatown, 21, 66, 80–82
CityPass, 71
coffee, 117
crafts, 120–121
dance, 126–12
dateline, 44–48
department stores, 121
dining, 102–118
Downtown, v, 65, 71–74, 88–95, 103–108
driving, 69
duck tours, 87
Eastside, 66–67
events calendar, 70–71
family attractions, best, 14–15, 39–40
ferries, 68
First Hill, 66
food, shopping, 122
football, 124
Fremont, 3, 66, 101–102, 114
gardens, best, 14
gluten-free dining, 115
handmade gifts, 120–121
Happy Hour, 103
hiking, 123
historic sites, 12–13
hotels, best, 5–6
International District, 21, 66, 80–82, 111
itineraries, suggested, 17–22, 27–32
Lake Union, dining, 112–113
light rail, 67
malls, 122
Metro, 67
modern times, 44–46
monorail, 67–68
museums, best, 12–13
music, 128
Native American art, 119
natural wonders, best, 10–11
neighborhoods, 65–67
nightlife, 124–129
opera, 128
outdoor activities, 122–123
parking, 68–69
Pike Place Market, 1, 17, 20, 45, 71, 74, 95–96, 108–109
Pioneer Square, 65, 79–80
Queen Anne Hill, 66, 102, 114–115
restaurants, best, 8
scenic flights, 88
Seattle Center, 15, 19–20, 40, 65, 77–79, 110–111
shopping, 118–122
shopping, 120–121
skyline, vi
South Lake Union, 65–66, 82, 99–101, 113
souvenirs, 122
spectator sports, 123–124
streetcars, 67
taxis, 69
theater, 128–129
tours, 86–88
train travel, 64
travel timing, 58–59
underground tour, 3, 40
University District, 66, 82–86
vegan dining, 115
vegetarian dining, 115
visitor information, 64–65
walking, 69
Wallingford dining, 116
water taxis, 68
Waterfront, 2–3, 18, 39, 48, 65, 74–77, 96–97, 109–110
watersports, 123
weather, 58–59, 69–70
West Seattle, 67, 116–118
wine bars, 125
Seattle Aquarium, 2, 15, 39, 74–76

Seattle Art Museum (SAM), 12, 20, 61, 72–73
Seattle Asian Art Museum, 81
Seattle Center, 15, 19–20, 40, 65
  attractions, 77–79
  dining, 110–111
Seattle's Convention and Visitors Bureau, 64
Seattle Duck Tours, 87
Seattle Free Walking Tours, 87–88
Seattle Great Wheel, vii, 2, 15, 18, 39, 45, 76
Seattle International Film Festival, 70
Seattle Japanese Garden, xii, 4, 14, 84
Seattle Monorail, 67
Seattle Opera, 61, 128
Seattle Post-Intelligencer, 44
Seattle Pride, 70
Seattle Repertory Theatre, 129
Seattle Seahawks, 48, 124
Seattle Seaplanes, 88
Seattle Space Needle, vi–vii, 20, 40, 46, 61, 79
Seattle Storm, 124
Seattle Streetcar, 67
Seattle SuperSonics, 46
Seattle Symphony, 61, 128
Seattle Tacoma International Airport, 46, 62
Seattle Times, 124
Seattle Visitor Center, 64
Seattle Weekly, 124
SE Belmont Street, Portland, 145
The Secret Society, 204
SE Division Street, Portland, 145, 162
See Seattle Walking Tours, 87
Sellwood, Portland, 53, 145, 162, 194
Senior travelers, 305
Shepherd's Dell Falls, 220–221
Shipyards, Portland, 54
Shopping
  Cannon Beach, 257
  Gold Beach, 301
  Portland, 194–199
  Seattle, 118–122
Shore Acres State Park, 14, 37, 288–289
Shoreline, Oregon Coast, 228
Show Me Seattle, 87
Siuslaw Pioneer Museum, 283
Skagit County Historical Museum, 130
Skagit Valley, 28, 129–131
Skagit Valley Tulip Festival, 70, 130
Skidmore Fountain, 143
Skidmore, Portland, 52, 143
Skiing, 217
Skyline Trail, 134
Sleepless in Seattle, 61
Slope soaring, xvi
Smart Park, 147
Smith Tower, 3, 15, 21, 45, 80
Smoking, 305
Snohomish, 120
Sno-Park permits, 217
Snowshoe walks, 134
Soccer, 207
Sokol Blosser Winery, 212
Sound Transit Metro, 62
Southeast Portland, 145, 162–164
  accommodations, 179–180
  dining, 189–192
Southern Pacific Railroad, 55
South Lake Union, Seattle, 45, 48, 57, 61, 65–66, 82
  accommodations, 99–101
  dining, 113
South Park Blocks, Portland, 23, 29, 143
South Slough National Estuarine Research Reserve, 37
South Slough National Estuarine Research Reserve, 289
South Waterfront, 143–144
Souvenirs, 122, 196
Spa, Cannon Beach, 257
Space Needle, Seattle, vii, 20, 40, 46, 61, 79
The Spanish Table, 74
Spectator sports, 123–124, 207
Spin, 123
Spring Beer & Wine Fest, 149–150
Steel Bridge, 156
Statehood, 45
Stoller Vineyards, 212–213
Stormy Weather Arts Festival, 250
Streetcars, 4, 67, 147
Stumptown, 50
Sunrise, 133–134
Sunset Bay State Park, 37, 288
Super Bowl, 48
Starbucks, 17, 46, 117, 151

T

The Tasting Room, 125
Taxes, 305
Taxis, Seattle, 69
Telephones, 305
Territorial Government of Oregon, 50
Territorial University, 44
Texting, 47
Theater
  Portland, 206–207
  Seattle, 128–129
Thompson Elk Fountain, 151
Three Arch Rocks, 260
Three Capes Scenic Loop, 30–31, 34, 42, 229, 259–262
Three Cups Coffee House, 240
Ticketmaster, 124
Tide pools, 5
Tillamook, 4, 11, 260
Tillamook Cheese Factory, 34, 258
Tillamook Head Trail, 246
Tillamook Rock Lighthouse, 229, 252
Tillicum Experience, 76
Timberline Lodge, 27, 41, 215–217
Timberline Ski Area, 217
Time, 305
Time-Based Art Festival, 150
Tipping, 305–306
Tobey, Mark, 20
Toilets, 306
Tom McCall Waterfront Park, 3, 23, 29, 47, 56, 143, 156–157, 165, 199
Tours Northwest, 132
Tours
  Portland, 164–166
  Seattle, 86–88
The Triple Door, 128
Tower of Cosmic Reflections, 154
Trade, 51
Traffic, 46–47
Trail of the Shadows, 134
Train travel, Seattle, 64
Transcontinental Great Northern Railway, 45
Transit Malls, 142
Travel Oregon, 141
Travel Portland, 141, 167
TriMet, 141, 146
Trisaetum Vineyards, 213
Trolleys, 53
Tualatin Valley, 50
Tulip fields, 28
Twist, 196–197

U

Uber, 141
U District Street Fair, 70
Uli's Famous Sausage, 74
Umpqua Lighthouse State Park, 229, 286
Umpqua River Lighthouse, 288
Underground Tour, Seattle, 40
Union Station, Portland, 141, 143
University of Washington, 44, 46, 124
University of Washington Huskies, 124
Upper Latourell Falls, 220
Uppertown Firefighters Museum, 233
Uptown Espresso, 117
Urban Growth Boundary, Portland, 56
U.S. Bancrop Tower, 142
USS *Blueback* submarine, 164

V

Vancouver, George, 44, 52
Vancouver National Historic Reserve, 53
Vancouver, Washington, 142
Vanport, Portland, 55
Vegan dining, 115, 190
Vegetarian dining, 115, 190
Vietnam Veterans of Oregon Memorial, 158
Visas, 306
Visitor information, 306
  Portland, 141
  Seattle, 64–65
Vista House, 220
Volunteer Park, 81
Volunteer Park Conservatory, 81
VRBO, 88, 167, 230
Vulcan company, 45

W

Wahkeena Falls, 221
Walking
  Portland, 149, 166
  Seattle, 69
Wallingford dining, 116
Washington Park, 4, 15, 23, 29, 40, 84–85, 143, 149
  attractions, 157–161
  nightlife, 199
Washington Park Arboretum, 84–85
Washington Park and Zoo Railway, 157
Washington State Ferries, 68, 77
Washington State Tourism, 65
Waterfalls, 220–221
Waterfront Bicycles, 166
Waterfront, Seattle18
Water taxis, 68
Waterfront, Astoria, 236
Waterfront Blues Festival, 150
Waterfront, Seattle, 2–3, 18, 39, 48, 65, 74–77
  accommodations, 96–97
  attractions, 74–77
  dining, 109–110
Watersports, 123
Weather
  Portland, 58–59, 149
  Seattle, 58–59, 69–70
Weather Machine, 151
West Coast Game Park Safari, 291–292
Westlake Center, 122
Westmoreland, 145–146, 162
West Seattle, 67, 116–118
Weyerhaeuser, 55
Whale-watching, 4, 16, 234, 268–269, 292–293
White Bird, 205
White Bird Gallery, 257
White stag sign, x
White-water rafting, 298
Wi-Fi, 304
Wildfire, 220, 296
Wildwood Trail, 26
Willamette Falls, 52
Willamette River, ix, 3, 49, 54, 142, 164
Willamette Valley, xii, 50, 54, 56–57, 208–214
Willamette Valley Visitors Association, 208
Willamette Valley Wineries Association, 208
Willamette Week, 199
Wine bars, 125, 202
Wineries, Portland, xii, 27, 208–213
Wing Luke Asian Museum, 21, 82
Wonder Ballroom, 204
Woodland Park Zoo & Rose Garden, 85–86
World's Fair, 44
World Forestry Center Discovery Museum, 157, 161
World Trade Organization, 47

Y

Yachats, 36, 277–282
  accommodations, 279–281
  dining, 282
Yamhill National Historic District, Portland, 52, 143
Yaquina Bay Lighthouse, xiv, 5, 13, 32, 35, 229
Yaquina Bay State Recreation Site, 32, 35, 275
Yaquina Head Lighthouse, 229, 274–275
Yaquina Head Outstanding Natural Area, 32, 35, 42, 274
Yellow Cab, Seattle, 64, 69
Ye Olde Curiosity Shop, 122
Yesler, Henry, 44
Yukon Gold Rush, 3

Z

Zeitgeist Coffee, 117
ZooLights Festival, 150

Accommodations

Ace Hotel, Portland, 6, 173
Ace Hotel, Seattle, 98
The Allison Inn & Spa, Willamette Valley, 213
Arctic Club Hotel, Seattle, 5, 88–92
Alexis, Seattle, 92
The Argonauta Inn, Cannon Beach, 254
Bandon Dunes Golf Resort, 293
Bandon Inn, 293
Bao Bao, Portland food cart, 186
The Baroness Hotel, Seattle, 6, 100–101
The Benson, Portland, 6, 167–170
Best Western Inn at Face Rock Resort, 294
Beverly Beach State Park, Depoe Bay, 269
Bullards Beach State Park, 294
Cannery Pier Hotel, Astoria, 7, 236–237
Cannon Beach Hotel, 253
Cape Lookout State Park, Pacific City, 261
Cape Perpetua Campgrounds, Yachats, 279
Channel House, Depoe Bay, 7, 269
Coast Cabins, Manzanita, 258–259
Crystal Hotel, Portland, 176, 203
Devil's Lake State Recreation Area, Lincoln City, 265
Dinner Bell BBQ, Portland food cart, 186
Dossier, Portland, 170
Edgewater, Seattle, 5, 96–97
Elizabeth Street Inn, Newport, 275
Embassy Suites, Portland, 6, 173
Ester Lee Motel, Lincoln City, 265
Everett Street Guesthouse, Portland, 179
Executive Hotel Pacific, Seattle, 5, 95
Fairmont Olympic Hotel, Seattle, 92–93
The Fireside Motel, Yachats, 280
Fort Stevens State Park, 237
Four Seasons Hotel, Seattle, 95–96
Gaslight Inn, 101
Gearhart Ocean Inn, 247–248
The Gilbert Inn, Seaside, 247
Grand Hyatt, Seattle, 93
Hallmark Resort, Cannon Beach, 253–254
Hampton Inn & Suites, Astoria, 237
Hampton Inn & Suites, Portland, 177
Heceta Head Lightstation, Yachats, 7, 280–281
Hi-Lo, Portland, 170–171
Hotel Ändra, Seattle, 5, 97–98
Hotel deLuxe, Portland, 6, 174
Hotel Elliott, Astoria, 237–238
Hotel Five, Seattle, 99
Hotel Hotel Hostel, Seattle, 101–102
Hotel Lućia, Portland, 6, 174, 181
Hotel Max, Seattle, 94
Hotel Monaco, Portland, 175
Hotel Modera, Portland, 6, 175
Hotel Vintage, Portland, 7, 171
Inn at Arch Rock, Depoe Bay, 269–270
Inn at Cape Kiwanda, Pacific City, 261
The Inn at Manzanita, 259
Inn at the Market, Seattle, 6, 96
Inn @ Northrup Station, Portland, 6, 177–178
Inn at Virginia Mason, Seattle, 6, 100–101
Inn of the Four Winds, Seaside, 247
Ireland's Rustic Lodges & Gold Beach Inn, 298–299
Jot's Resort, Gold Beach, 299
Jupiter Hotel, Portland, 179–180
Kimpton Hotel Monaco, Seattle, 93
Kimpton Hotel Vintage, Seattle, 94
Kimpton Palladian Hotel, Seattle, 98–99
Looking Glass Inn, Lincoln City, 265–266
The Mark Spencer Hotel, Portland, 175–176
MarQueen Hotel, Seattle, 102
Mayflower Park Hotel, Seattle, 94–95
McMenamins Kennedy School, Portland, 7, 178
Multnomah Falls Lodge, 27, 223
National Park Inn, Mount Rainier, 21, 135
Nehalem Bay State Park, 259
Newport Belle Riverboat Inn, 275
The Nines, Portland, 171–172
Northwest Portland Hostel, 178
Ocean Haven, Yachats, 281
The Ocean Lodge, Cannon Beach, 7, 254
Overleaf Lodge, Yachats, 7–8, 281

The Painted Lady, Willamette Valley, 214
Pan Pacific Hotel Seattle, 99–100
Paradise Inn, Mount Rainier, 21, 135–136
Portland Mayor's Mansion, 7, 179
RiverPlace Hotel, Portland, 172
Rogue River Lodges, 300
Seaside Oceanfront Inn, 247
Secret Camp RV Park, Gold Beach, 299
Sentinel, Portland, 172–173
Silver Cloud Inn Northwest Portland, 180
The Society Hotel, Portland, 176–177
Sorrento Hotel, Seattle, 5–6, 100
South Beach State Park, 276
Starfish Manor Hotel, Lincoln City, 266
Star Grill, Portland food truck, 186
Stephanie Inn, Cannon Beach, 7, 254
Sunrise Lodge, Mount Rainier, 135
Sutton Campground, Florence, 284
Sylvia Beach Hotel, Newport, 7, 276
Timberline Lodge, 27, 41, 215–217
Tu Tu' Tun Lodge, Gold Beach, 8, 299–300
Union Hotel, Astoria, 49
Warwick Seattle Hotel, 99
The Waves, Cannon Beach, 254–255
White Heron Lodge, Cannon Beach, 254–255
Wright's For Camping, Cannon Beach, 255

Restaurants

Alloro Wine Bar, Bandon, 10, 37, 294
Al's Den, Portland, 176
Alto Bajo, Portland, 184
Andina, Portland, 9, 187
Anna's by the Sea, Gold Beach, 38, 300
Aqua, Seattle, 19, 109
Araya's Place, Seattle, 115
Assaggio, Seattle, 103
Astoria Coffeehouse & Bistro, 240
Ava Gene's, Portland, 9, 26, 190–191
Baked Alaska, Astoria, 238
Bamboo Sushi, Portland, 29, 185
Bandon Coffee Cafe, 294
Bandon Fish Market, 294
Bar Avignon, Portland, 191
Bastille, Seattle, 112
Bay House, Lincoln City, 266
Bijou Café, Portland, 186
Blackfish Cafe, Lincoln City, 266
Blue Scorcher Bakery Café, 240
The Bookstore, Seattle, 92
Bread and Ocean, Manzanita, 259
BRIDGEwater Bistro, Astoria, 9, 238
Bridgewater Fish House and Zebra Bar, Florence, 37, 284
Café Campagne, Seattle, 8, 19, 108–109
Caffe Ladro Espresso Bar & Bakery, 19–20
Caffe Mingo, Portland, 29, 188
Caffe Umbria, 20, 26, 192
Canlis, Seattle, 8, 114–115
Carlile Room, Seattle, 106
Carruthers, Astoria, 239
Cascade Dining Room, Mount Hood, 216–217
Castaways Tini Tiki Hut, Cannon Beach, 255–256
Celilo Restaurant, Columbia Gorge, 223
Chart House, Portland, 181
Clemente's Café and Public House, Astoria, 9, 239
Copper Creek Restaurant, Mount Rainier, 135
DC Vegetarian Food Cart, Portland, 190
Departures, Portland, 172
Dundee Bistro, Willamette Valley, 214
El Gaucho, Portland, 170
Elliott's Oyster House, Seattle, 110
Escape from New York Pizza, Portland, 188
Etta's Seafood, Seattle, 20, 109
Fort George Brewery, 240
The Gallery, Bandon Dunes Golf Resort, 10, 38, 295
Georgetown Liquor Company, Seattle, 115
Gracie's, Portland, 174
Grassa, Portland, 189
The Grateful Bread Bakery, Pacific City, 262
Heidi's Italian Dinners, Yachats, 36, 382
Imperial, Portland, 174, 181–184
The Irish Table, Cannon Beach, 9–10, 256
Ivar's Fish Bar, Seattle, 39, 110
Ivar's Salmon House, Seattle, 112–113
Jackknife Bar, Portland, 172
Jade Garden, Seattle, 111
Jake's Bar and Grill, Portland, 184
Jake's Famous Crawfish, Portland, 23, 172, 184
Jory Restaurant, Willamette Valley, 213–214
Josephson's, Astoria, 240
Joule, Seattle, 116
Ken's Artisan Pizza, Portland, 192
Khao San, Portland, 189
Kyllo's Seafood & Grill, Lincoln City, 31, 267
La Pomodori, Florence, 284
Lark, Seattle, 113
Le Pigeon, Portland, 9, 189–190
Little Fish, Seattle, 71
Local Ocean, Newport, 10, 32, 276
The Loft Restaurant & Bar, Bandon, 37, 295
Lola, Seattle, 8, 111
Lord Bennett's Restaurant and Lounge, Bandon, 38, 295
Luc Lac Vietnamese Kitchen, Portland, 186–187
Luna Sea Fish House, Yachats, 36, 282
Maggie's on the Prom, Seaside, 247–248
Mamnoon Street, Seattle, 113
Margaux, Seattle, 99
Marination Ma Kai, Seattle, 118
Mari's Kitchen at the Maple Street Grille, Florence, 284
McMenamins Sand Trap, Gearhart, 249
Miller's Guild, Seattle, 94, 103
Moonstruck Chocolat Café, Portland, 192–193
Mo's, Newport, 32, 276–277
Nell Thorn Restaurant & Pub, 130
Newman's at 988, Cannon Beach, 10, 256
Niche, Seattle, 115
Nor'wester Seafood, Gold Beach, 38, 301
Ona, Yachats, 36, 282
Otis Cafe, Lincoln City, 267
Pacific Pie, Portland, 192
Pacific Way Bakery & Café, Gearhart, 249
Paley's Place, Portland, 181, 187
Panini, Newport, 277
Pazzo, Portland, 171, 185
Pearl Bakery, Portland, 193
Pelican Pub & Brewery, Pacific City, 262
Pel Meni Dumpling Tzar, Seattle, 114
Petunia's Pies and Pastries, Portland, 190
Pie, Seattle, 114
Pok Pok, Portland, 9, 26, 191
Pok Pok Noi, Portland, 191
Pok Pok NW, Portland, 191
Poppy, Seattle, 8, 20, 113–114
Purple Café and Wine Bar, Seattle, 106–108
Rabbit's Café, Portland, 190
Rachel's Coffee House, 300
Rainier Basecamp Bar & Grill, 135
Ram's Head Bar, 217
Ray's Boathouse, Seattle, 112
Rays Café, Seattle, 112
Razzi's Pizzeria, Seattle,115
Red Star, Portland, 175
Restaurant Beck, Depoe Bay, 10, 270
Rhododendron Café, Seattle, 101
Rogue Ales Public House, Newport, 240, 277
Roseanna's Cafe, Oceanside, 9, 34, 261–262
Saffron Salmon, Newport, 32, 277
Salt & Straw, Portland, 174, 193
Salty's on Alki Beach, Seattle, 11, 116–118
Scale Burgers, Mount Rainier, 135
Seeds, 130
Serious Pie, Seattle,108

Shaker + Spear, 98
Shiro's Sushi Restaurant, Seattle, 8, 111
Shuckers, Seattle, 8, 103–106
Six-Seven Restaurant, Seattle, 109–110
Sixth Street Bistro, Hood River, 223–224
SkyCity at the Needle, Seattle, 79, 110–111
The Sleepy Monk, Cannon Beach, 256
Spinner's, Gold Beach, 38, 301
Stephanie Inn, Cannon Beach, 10, 256–257
St. Honoré Boulangerie, Portland, 193
St. Jack, Portland, 9, 29, 188
Stimulus Espresso Cafe, Pacific City, 262
Stumptown, Portland, 193
Sunlight Café, Seattle, 115
Sweet Pea, Portland, 190
Tao of Tea, Portland, 193
Tasty n Alder, Portland, 9, 23, 185
Three Degress, Portland, 172
Thrive, Portland, 190
Tidal Raves, Depoe Bay, 10, 270
Tilth, Seattle, 8
Tony's Crab shack, Bandon, 294
Toro Bravo, Portland, 9, 189
T Paul's Supper Club, Astoria, 239
Truly Scrumptious Bakery & Café, Mount Rainier, 135
Tsunami Sandwich, Seaside, 248
Tulio, Seattle, 106, 116
Urban Farmer, Portland, 172
Vita Cafe, Portland, 190
Voodoo Doughnut, Portland, 193–194
Wayward Vegan Cafe, Seattle, 115
Wet Dog Café & Brewery, 240
Whiskey Soda Lounge, Portland, 191
Whittaker's Bunkhouse Café, Mount Rainier, 135
Wild Ginger Asian Restaurant & Satay Bar, Seattle, 108
Zeus Café, Portland, 176

Map List

Washington & Oregon 2
The Best of Seattle in 3 Days 18
The Best of Seattle in 5 Days 22
The Best of Portland in 3 Days or 5 Days 24
Seattle & Portland in 1 Week 29
Seattle, Portland & the Oregon Coast in 1 Week 31
The Oregon Coast in 1 Week 34
Seattle, Portland & the Oregon Coast for Families 41
Seattle & Environs 63
Downtown Seattle Attractions 72
North Seattle Attractions 75
Seattle Hotels 90
Downtown & Capitol Hill Restaurants 104
North Seattle Restaurants 107
Downtown & Capitol Hill Performing Arts & Nightlife 126
Mount Rainer National Park 132
Downtown Portland Attractions 152
Washington Park Attractions 159
Portland Hotels 168
Portland Restaurants 182
Portland Performing Arts & Nightlife 200
The Wine Country 209
Mount Hood 215
Columbia Gorge 218
Oregon Coast 226
Astoria 231
Seaside & Gearhart 245
Cannon Beach 251
Newport 271

Photo Credits

p i © VanHart; p ii, Courtesy of Visit Seattle / Tim Thompson; p iii © misszin; p iv © Edmund Lowe Photography; p v, top © cdrin / Shutterstock.com; p v, left © Roman Khomlyak; p v, right, Courtesy of Visit Seattle / Alan Alabastro; p vi, top © kerochan / Shutterstock.com; p vi, middle, courtesy of the Underground Tour / Cheryle Easter; p vi, bottom © tusharkoley; p vii, left, Courtesy of Visit Seattle / Howard Frisk Photography; p vii, right, Courtesy of Museum of Flight / Ted Huetter; p vii, bottom, Courtesy of Chihuly Garden and Glass; p viii, top, Courtesy of Pike Brewing Company; p vii, middle, Courtesy of Pacific Northwest Ballet / Angela Sterling; p viii, bottom, Courtesy of McMenamins Kennedy School / Kathleen Nyberg; p ix, top © Josemaria Toscano; p ix, left, Courtesy of Portland Oregon Visitors Association / Jamie Francis-Blue Chalk Media; p ix, right, Courtesy of Portland Oregon Visitors Association / Jamie Francis-Blue Chalk Media; p x, top left, Courtesy of Portland Oregon Visitors Association / www.travelportland.com; p x, top right, Courtesy of Portland Oregon Visitors Association / www.travelportland.com; p x, bottom left, Courtesy of Portland Oregon Visitors Association / Jamie Francis-Blue Chalk Media; p x, bottom right, Courtesy of Portland Oregon Visitors Association / Torsten Kjellstrand; p xi, top, Courtesy of Powell's Books / Denise Dodd; p xi, middle, Courtesy of PAM / Nina Johnson; p xi, bottom, Courtesy of Explore Washington Park; p xii, top left © Bob Pool / Shutterstock.com; p xii, top right, © GagliardiImages / Shutterstock.com; p xii, bottom left, Courtesy of Portland Japanese Garden / Roman Johnston; p xii, bottom right, Courtesy of Portland Oregon Visitors Association / Jamie Francis; p xiii, top © Sherri R. Camp; p xiii, middle © mike krzeszak; p xiii, bottom © Dee Browning; p xiv, top left © Gerald A. DeBoer; p xiv, top right © steve estvanik / Shutterstock.com; p xiv, bottom © Tomas Nevesely; p xv, top © Marisa Estivill / Shutterstock.com; p xv, middle © Pawel Grudysz; p xv, bottom © Nagel Photography; p xvi, top © steve estvanik / Shutterstock.com; p xvi, bottom left © CSNafzger; p xvi, bottom right © Jonathan Lingel.

Frommer's EasyGuide to Seattle, Portland and the Oregon Coast

Published by
FROMMER MEDIA LLC

Copyright © 2018 by Frommer Media LLC. All rights reserved. No part of this publication may be reproduced, stored in a retrieval system, or transmitted in any form or by any means, electronic, mechanical, photocopying, recording, scanning or otherwise, except as permitted under Sections 107 or 108 of the 1976 United States Copyright Act, without the prior written permission of the Publisher. Requests to the Publisher for permission should be addressed to customer_service@FrommerMedia.com.

Frommer's is a registered trademark of Arthur Frommer. Frommer Media LLC is not associated with any product or vendor mentioned in this book.

ISBN 978-1-62887-380-1 (paper), 978-1-62887-381-8 (e-book)

Editorial Director: Pauline Frommer
Editor: Pauline Frommer
Production Editor: Lindsay Conner
Photo Editor: Meghan Lamb
Cartographer: Roberta Stockwell
Cover Design: Howard Grossman

Front cover photo: Seattle Skyline with Space Needle Tower at Dusk © VanHart/Shutterstock

For information on our other products or services, see www.frommers.com.

Frommer Media LLC also publishes its books in a variety of electronic formats. Some content that appears in print may not be available in electronic formats.

Manufactured in the United States of America

5 4 3 2 1

ABOUT THE AUTHOR

Donald Olson is a travel writer, novelist and playwright. His travel stories have appeared in *The New York Times*, *National Geographic*, and many other national publications, and he has written guidebooks for destinations throughout Europe and North America. His Frommer's titles include *Frommer's EasyGuide to Seattle, Portland & the Oregon Coast*; *Frommer's Seattle Day by Day*; and *Frommer's Portland Day by Day*. An avid gardener and photographer, Donald is the author of two best-selling guides published by Timber Press: *Pacific Northwest Garden Tour—The 60 Best Gardens to Visit in Oregon, Washington and British Columbia* (named by *Library Journal* as one of the best reference books of 2014) and *The California Garden Tour—The 50 Best Gardens to Visit in the Golden State*. He is the author of eight novels, some under the name Swan Adamson, and his plays have been produced in New York, London, Amsterdam, Rotterdam and Portland. www.donaldstevenolson.com.

ABOUT THE FROMMER TRAVEL GUIDES

For most of the past 50 years, Frommer's has been the leading series of travel guides in North America, accounting for as many as 24% of all guidebooks sold. I think I know why.

Though we hope our books are entertaining, we nevertheless deal with travel in a serious fashion. Our guidebooks have never looked on such journeys as a mere recreation, but as a far more important human function, a time of learning and introspection, an essential part of a civilized life. We stress the culture, lifestyle, history, and beliefs of the destinations we cover, and urge our readers to seek out people and new ideas as the chief rewards of travel.

We have never shied from controversy. We have, from the beginning, encouraged our authors to be intensely judgmental, critical—both pro and con—in their comments, and wholly independent. Our only clients are our readers, and we have triggered the ire of countless prominent sorts, from a tourist newspaper we called "practically worthless" (it unsuccessfully sued us) to the many rip-offs we've condemned.

And because we believe that travel should be available to everyone regardless of their incomes, we have always been cost-conscious at every level of expenditure. Though we have broadened our recommendations beyond the budget category, we insist that every lodging we include be sensibly priced. We use every form of media to assist our readers, and are particularly proud of our feisty daily website, the award-winning Frommers.com.

I have high hopes for the future of Frommer's. May these guidebooks, in all the years ahead, continue to reflect the joy of travel and the freedom that travel represents. May they always pursue a cost-conscious path, so that people of all incomes can enjoy the rewards of travel. And may they create, for both the traveler and the persons among whom we travel, a community of friends, where all human beings live in harmony and peace.

Arthur Frommer

Before, During, or After your use of a Frommer's guidebook... you'll want to consult

FROMMERS.COM

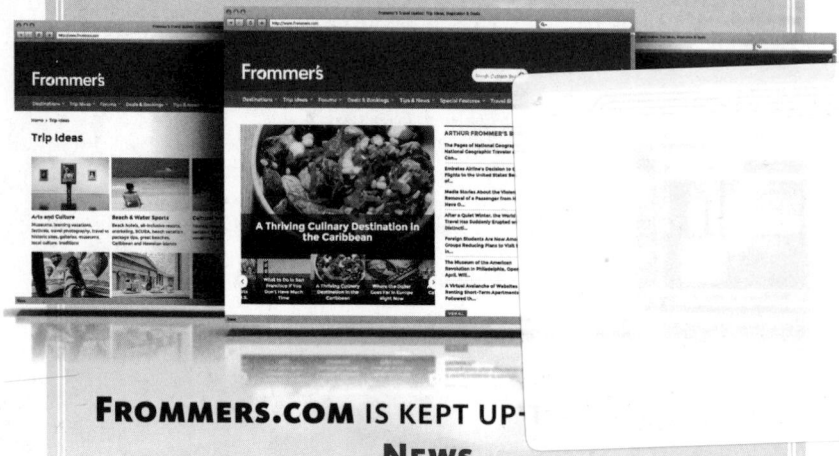

FROMMERS.COM IS KEPT UP-

NEWS
The latest events (and deals) to affect your next vacation

BLOGS
Opinionated comments by our outspoken staff

FORUMS
Post your travel questions, get answers from other readers

SLIDESHOWS
On weekly-changing, practical but inspiring topics of travel

CONTESTS
Enabling you to win free trips

PODCASTS
Of our weekly, nationwide radio show

DESTINATIONS
Hundreds of cities, their hotels, restaurants and sights

TRIP IDEAS
Valuable, offbeat suggestions for your next vacation

***AND MUCH MORE!**

Smart travelers consult ***Frommers.com***